Alien Heart

ALIEN HEART

The Life and Work of Margaret Laurence

Lyall Powers

MICHIGAN STATE UNIVERSITY PRESS

Published in the United States by Michigan State University Press, 2004
1405 South Harrison Road, Suite 25
East Lansing, Michigan 48823
USA

First published in Canada by the University of Manitoba Press, 2003

∞ The paper used in this publication meets the minimum requirements of ANSI/NISO Z39.48—1992 (R 1997) (Permanence of paper).

10 09 08 07 06 05 04 1 2 3 4 5 6 7 8 9 10

Library of Congress Cataloguing in Publication Data

Powers, Lyall H. (Lyall Harris), 1924-
Alien heart : the life and work of Margaret Laurence / Lyall H. Powers.
p. cm.

Includes bibliographical references and index.

1. Laurence, Margaret, 1926-1987. 2. Novelists, Canadian (English)—20th century—Biography.* I. Title.

ISBN 0-87013-714-X (Michigan State University Press edition)

Cover Design: Doowah Design
Text Design: Sharon Caseburg
Dust jacket photo: Margaret Laurence, 1961 (University of Manitoba Archives and Special Collections, Tribune Collection)

Printed and bound in Canada

Financial support for this publication was provided by the Government of Canada through the Book Publishing Industry Development Program (BPIDP); the Canada Council for the Arts; the Manitoba Arts Council; and the Manitoba Department of Culture, Heritage and Tourism. Assistance for the publication of this book has also been provided by the Department of English, University of Michigan, and the Vice-President for Research, University of Michigan.

Visit Michigan State University Press on the World Wide Web at:
www.msupress.msu.edu

For Loretta

and
In Memory of
Jack Cameron Borland
1925-1991

I kept riding into the future forever, practicing a defiant loneliness—that cousin of revolt—blindly groping for the beginning of the lifelong voyage toward myself.... Even early on I noted with my blood, so to speak, that when Moses climbed up the mountain to receive the Law from God, he went alone.

—Arthur Miller, *Timebends: A Life*

Non ignara mali miseris succurrere disco.

—*Aeneid* I:630

Also, thou shalt not oppress a stranger: for ye know the heart of a stranger, seeing ye were strangers in the land of Egypt.

—Exodus 23:9

"I often wonder how much of myself I'm revealing in novels and stories—in fact, I'm revealing the whole thing, but I always fondly hope that this isn't obvious to everyone."

—Margaret Laurence

contents

illustrations

Photos following page 124

Photos following page 268

Credits and Permissions

Photos 1-5, 7 courtesy Catherine Simpson Milne. Photos 8, 19-21, 27 courtesy Jocelyn and David Laurence; photos 8, 27 in York University Archives and Special Collections. Photos 11-13 courtesy Louise Alguire Kubik. Photos 9, 33 courtesy Mona Spratt Meredith. Photos 22, 23 courtesy Margaret Collier. Photos 29, 32 courtesy Zella Clark. Photo 14 courtesy Joyce Friesen. Photo 31 courtesy Anne and Bob Hallstead. Photo 18 courtesy Dalhousie University Archives, Biographical Files. Photos 15-17, 25, 28, 36 courtesy University of Manitoba Archives and Special Collections; photos 15-17, 25, 28 in Tribune Collection. Photo 38 courtesy Lois Wilson. Photo 34 © 1978 National Film Board; all rights reserved. Photos 6, 10, 24, 26, 30, 35, 37, 39, 40 courtesy Lyall Powers.

acknowledgements

I am grateful for financial support from the National Endowment for the Humanities: and from the Department of English, the Office of the Vice President for Research, and the Rackham Foundation of the University of Michigan. I am thankful for a variety of assistance from the family and early friends of Margaret Laurence: Jocelyn and David Laurence, Catherine Simpson Milne, Jack Laurence, Louise Alguire Kubic, Mona Spratt Meredith, Mildred Musgrove, Marguerite Crawford Street, Ruth Faryon, and Wes McAmmond. I benefitted from the conversation and help of Mary Adachi, Madge Hetherington Allen, Sheila and B.W. "Guś" Andrzejewski, Nadine Jones Asante, Don Bailey, A. Gerald Bedford, Jan Bhatti, Jack C. Borland, Hartwell Bowsfield, Robert Chambers, Zella and Sidney Clark, Jean Cole, Nancy Collier, Marie and Gerald Colwell (Elm Cottage), Gordon Elliott, Lincoln Faller, Timothy Findley, the Rev. Charles H. Forsythe, June Friesen, Pansy Goble, John and Angela (Baird) Graham, Anne and Robert N. Hallstead, Joan Johnston, George Lamming, Bernice Lauder Lovell, Mhari Mackintosh, John Marshall, John McClelland, the Rev. Susan McGarry, Mary Turnbull Mindess, Roland Penner, Sid Perlmutter, Michael Peterman, Al and Eurithe Purdy, Malcolm Ross, Enid Delgatty Rutland, the Rev. Tom Saunders, Tamara Stone, Walter and Margaret Swayze, Harold "Nero" Thompson, John

Wadland, Helen Warkentin, Alice Williams, David Williams (University of Manitoba), the Very Rev. Lois Wilson, and Adele Wiseman. For research, my sincere thanks to Eleanor Gignac, Peter James, Danielle Pilon, Shelley Sweeney, the clergy and staff of Neepawa United Church, Dorothy Campbell Henderson and staff of the Margaret Laurence Home (Neepawa), Evelyn A. Vivien and staff of the Beautiful Plains Museum (Neepawa), the staffs of the National Library of Canada, McMaster University Library, Queen's University Library, University of Manitoba Library, University of Toronto Library, University of Winnipeg Library, York University Library, and of the Interlibrary Loan Office in the University of Michigan, and particularly to Arlene (McFarlin) Weismantel of Michigan State University Library and Ken Hernden, Adjunct Archivist in York University Library, for special research assistance. I owe much to the critical readers of all or parts of the manuscript, Walter Swayze, Malcom Ross, Rheinhold Kramer, and especially to Margaret Wigmore and to Patricia Sanders of the University of Manitoba Press, and to Rosemary Goble for assistance in preparing the manuscript; finally, a particular word of thanks to David Carr, Director of the University of Manitoba Press, for general guidance and counsel. I am pleased also to thank my former students for their discussion with me of Margaret Laurence's work, in particular Julie Briscoe, Kent Brothers, Stacey Charlebois, Julie de Ward, Jeanne Elder, Sarah Evens, Lauren Raphael, Lynn Rasmussen, Pam Schmidt, Dave Shand, Rebecca Webb, and Nicole Yohalem.

For general support, encouragement, and advice I am continually grateful to my wife, Loretta Powers.

introduction

I MET MARGARET LAURENCE AT UNITED COLLEGE (NOW THE University of Winnipeg) in the autumn of 1945; she was then Peggy Wemyss. We soon became part of a small group with shared interests in English literature and socialist politics, and in those professors who seemed to be interested in those topics. The friendship persevered past graduation but was tested by her marriage in 1947 and by the departure of a couple of the group to pursue graduate studies in the United States. Mrs. Laurence sustained the friendship by sending us copies of her Canadian novels on publication. I was pleased to take note of her success—an old friend getting published in the US and England!—but I gave the books insufficient attention to recognize on what that success depended. We were all busy with our several pursuits; I was at the University of Michigan teaching courses in the American novel and the modern novel. Then, in the middle seventies, came *The Diviners*. It was a revelation that hit like a ton of bricks.

My own work on two of the best modern novelists, Henry James and William Faulkner, had enabled me to appreciate more fully what Laurence had achieved in her fiction. I recognized her effective manner of expressing notions of good and evil, and her mastery of narrative technique, the ability to convey the perceived truth by means of the realistic facts she chose for her artistic medium. I began to include

The Diviners in my courses. Early on I took a little poll at the end of one of the courses: which of the novels we read would you recommend to an intelligent friend? The result was that one in four ranked the Laurence novel at the top. I reread all her novels and soon enough was offering a seminar (required of senior concentrators in English) on the fiction of Margaret Laurence. That course was a gratifying success—hers, not mine. I would send her a few of the best papers I got each year; she seemed pleased.

Over the ensuing decade it seemed that in spite of all the awards Laurence received, her work was yet undervalued, perhaps because she had ceased producing fiction after *The Diviners*. When I asked her why she had stopped, she said, "Oh, if I were to continue the Manawaka fiction it would be by picking up Pique's story; people would say I was writing about Jocelyn. I couldn't expose my daughter to that." That would prove to be an enormous simplification of what was in fact a complex problem. Then, far too soon, her death. The acute sense of loss prompted me, at her funeral in Lakefield, Ontario, to ask her dear friend and foremost Laurence scholar Clara Thomas if she planned to complete her biography of Margaret. Professor Thomas's quiet "No" determined my choice to pursue that line.

A bold decision, no doubt, but I felt I enjoyed certain advantages for such an endeavour. I came from a background very similar to Laurence's: a city-boy as she was a town-girl, I yet loved the rural farmland of southwestern Manitoba (Holland, Souris, Treherne) as she did the surroundings of Neepawa; there was a strong Scottish element in my immediate ancestry as in hers; baptized a Presbyterian, I was raised in the United Church of Canada as the young Peggy Wemyss was, and in the rich ethnic mix of Winnipeg's North End, with which she early became familiar; I enrolled, inevitably it now seems, in United College and there was Peggy. Beyond that, we shared from early childhood the typically Canadian ambivalence of attitude toward Britain and the United States. The US was physically closer, wealthier, obviously the more materialistic—and enviable; the traditions of Great Britain were stronger (the colonial influence was still present, though hardly onerous, for the likes of us, and World War II had just ended, sadly but proudly, as we met). With all that, however, just precisely where—not to say *who*—were we, and what our affinities? We had a common awareness. In the first half of the twentieth century the question of identity was vexed for Canadians.

In 1956 the novel *The Sacrifice* by Laurence's good friend Adele Wiseman received the Governor General's Award for fiction. It held (and still holds) a particular relevance for Canadians. The first words spoken in *The Sacrifice* constitute the simple question "Where are we?" asked by a Jew who has fled the persecution and pogroms of Ukraine with his wife and remaining son. The tired émigré to Canada asks his question of the conductor on the train, asks it in Ukrainian, then in Yiddish, in Polish, and finally in broken German—all to no avail. The question hangs in the air unanswered as the little family detrains, determined to begin a new life here . . . wherever "here" proves to be. In the same year Northrop Frye addressed that very question, slightly rephrased so that it applied not only to the newly arrived in Canada but to established "citizens" like Peggy Laurence and me as well:

> It seems to me that Canadian sensibility has been profoundly disturbed not so much by our famous problem of identity, important as that is, as by a series of paradoxes in what confronts that identity. It is less perplexed by the question "Who am I?" as by some such riddle as "Where is here?"[1]

The two questions were intimately associated (and perhaps still are). Margaret Laurence addressed them too—at least implicitly—in her Canadian fiction, and nowhere more prominently than in *The Diviners*. There, Morag Gunn decides to return to Canada and so informs her daughter, Pique:

> "Pique, we're going back home."
> "Home?" (What means *home*?)
> "Yes. Home."[2]

Much of Laurence's life may be understood as a sustained attempt to find viable answers to Northrop Frye's associated questions about "who" and "where." This biography will illustrate that attempt.

My title, *Alien Heart*, may simply signal a peculiarly Canadian characteristic of Laurence's generation, but I intend something more specific than that. There is ample evidence, in any case, that the young Peggy Wemyss was distinctly a loner. Although a student leader, popular, and respected in high school, she required and quietly insisted upon her own space and time to herself—as many of the following pages make clear. Consequently, perhaps, she was keenly sympathetic with the underdog, the downtrodden, victims of correctible social and economic ills. Her own feeling and experience of alienation made her more sensitive to the condition of alienation in others. That tendency was directly fed and fostered by the ambience of United College with its emphasis on the social gospel and the distinctly leftist leanings of the faculty—many of whom were also clergymen. That ambience found its complement in the cultural and political features of her neighbourhood in the North End (the Old Left) of Winnipeg—the communist aldermen Joseph Penner, Bill Ross, and Joe Zuken, and the family of her friend Adele Wiseman—and in her career as journalist with two Winnipeg newspapers of the Left, *The Westerner* and *The Winnipeg Citizen*. It seems she had a natural affinity for the Good Samaritan and a quick understanding of the Old Testament admonition to the children of Israel, "And thou shalt not oppress a stranger: for ye know the heart of a stranger, seeing ye were strangers in the land of Egypt" (Exodus 23:9). Indeed, I should have used a piece of that passage for my title—the best available, all round—but Margaret Laurence had already claimed it for her collection of essays *Heart of a Stranger* (1976). *Alien Heart* struck me as next best.

The justification of a biography must be that it illuminates the achievements of its subject. It must answer questions about what features of the life explain and clarify those achievements, what persons and what experiences influenced the subject and in just what ways—and precisely how the influence appears in the achievements. Certain examples of such questions in connection with Laurence's achievements come to mind at once. In her Canadian novels the protagonist is always female: does that feature indicate influence of feminism or is it a result of her own sense of the need for self-reliance imposed by the early death of her mother? A frequent theme in that fiction is the lost father and the quest for a surrogate. Are these two features related to each other and to her frequent depiction of domestic strife? How did her own marriage contribute to that depiction? Just how does the Scottish element in her background find expression in her fiction? Why does Vancouver play so large a role in her stories of Manawaka—in the heart of the prairies? Answers to such questions illuminate her fiction.

There is a reciprocal illumination available as well to the informed biographer. I do not mean the facile reading *into* the fiction of a superficial "confessional" or autobiographical feature. There are, however, situations in which Laurence's account of her own experiences—I mean the actual terms she uses—in letters to friends as well as in published non-fiction is closely matched in the fiction itself; the implicit and unintentional similarity is occasionally revealing. Her interest in Agamemnon and Clytemnestra functions in this way during the period of her attempted reconciliations with her husband in the 1960s; a cluster of short stories together with *The Fire-Dwellers* and augmented by accounts of a visit to Greece in personal letters demonstrably clarifies her handling of her problems.

Another apparent aid to the biographer is Laurence's comments on her own life in letters and her memoir *Dance on the Earth*. It is nevertheless useful to keep in mind Morag Gunn's frank confession to her friend Ella in *The Diviners*: "I like the idea of history and fiction interweaving." The autobiographical sources occasionally do just that. The trick lies not in simply detecting such skewing of historical fact, but in determining the reason for it. For example, Laurence always (there is one vague exception) claimed that "The Drummer of All the

World" (1956) was her first publication as an adult; in fact, "Uncertain Flowering" preceded it by three years. Answering the question of why she should deny the story, set in Somaliland (the only one of hers with that setting), of a young heroine reluctantly bent on asserting her adulthood (the reluctant assertion is the story's oxymoron) casts a helpful bit of light on its author in that moment of her life and career. And there are other such helpful examples of her skewing of historical fact. Furthermore, Rachel and Stacey Cameron (*A Jest of God* and *The Fire-Dwellers*) reflect the domestic situation (as she saw it) in the Laurence household in the middle sixties and, viewed retrospectively, anticipate the resolution of these problems—though not exactly as the two novels resolve them.

As I began my preparation to write this biography, I quickly discovered that there remained at the end of the eighties a number of people who had known the young Peggy Wemyss: her oldest cousin, her three oldest friends of school days in Neepawa, her closest friends at college, and some of her teachers and professors. I wrote to and interviewed a number of them, beginning with the eldest. I was impressed with the vivid recall of many of them and the fact that a substantial number kept letters from and photographs of her.

The willing response of those people whom I have interviewed over the past few years, including the most important members of her literary "tribe," has been heartening and has added to my sense and understanding of the person I knew as a fellow student and friend during the last forty-odd years of her life—from the early years when she was just Peggy Wemyss; through her years as Peggy and then, more properly, as Margaret Laurence; and finally into her quarter century of international fame. I have chosen to refer to her here as "Peggy" through the first thirty-five years of her life, in the hope of enhancing the sense of familiarity and nearness I wanted to achieve and also of my own relationship with her; and then as "Margaret" for the years from 1962 to her death, to reflect her own wishes concerning her personal identification. I did so, further, to emphasize the distinction between the years of childhood and prolonged adolescence, and those of her maturity as she meant to establish it after 1960.

Alien Heart

I.
Peggy (1926-1962)

one

What's in a Name

AT FIRST THEY CALLED HER "PEGGY"—A SMALL MATTER, BUT one that increased in importance to her as the years went by. Shakespeare's Juliet had asked rhetorically, "What's in a name?" There is *much* in a name, as Juliet knew and as the young Peggy would learn. In *The Stone Angel*, Margaret Laurence's novel of 1964, the heroine recalls that her rejected and long-dead husband was the only one to call her by her own name, Hagar. And in *The Diviners*, Laurence's last novel, the first physical intimacy between Morag Gunn and Jules "Skinner" Tonnerre provokes Morag's grateful exclamation, "Oh Skinner":

> "Hey, could you call me by my real name, eh?"
> As though now it was necessary to do this. By right. . . .
> "Okay, I will, Jules." (112)

Then much later, the heroine completes her first novel and, though now married, submits it for publication under her maiden name, Morag Gunn—as though now it was necessary to do this.

The importance of a name in expressing one's identity is paralleled by that of recognizing roots and understanding where one belongs, knowing the meaning of *home*. Establishing identity has always been a matter of concern, especially, perhaps, for those Canadians born in the decade following the Great War. During the twenties (and even the thirties and maybe, occasionally, even later) it came as no surprise to hear "Canadians" singing such lines as "Take me home to Bonnie Scotland / Take me home across the sea. . . ."

Although the British North America Act of 1867 proclaimed the fact of Confederation, it did not establish Canadian national identity for the geographic area involved or for the inhabitants of that area. "Canada" remained what the Act designated her as being—*British* North American, a colony. The Act retained protection of the French language, culture, and religion (Roman Catholicism) guaranteed to the French-speaking inhabitants of Canada East. The contribution of Canadian troops to the successful termination of World War I and of Canadian diplomats to the consequent Treaty of Versailles (1919) instilled a sense of national pride and encouraged a conception of national identity in the inhabitants of Canada. But the returning veterans of that war still marched off the ships onto Canadian soil singing lines like "It's a long, long way to Tipperary, / But my heart's right there." The question of roots was still vexed, and remained so for some time. It was well over half a century before a Canadian writer like Margaret Laurence could claim that while her "long-ago families came from Scotland and Ireland," her "true roots were here"—in Canada.[1]

Her "true roots" were firmly set in Manitoba, Canada. Her world began there on Sunday, 18 July 1926. In the following December, in Neepawa United Church, she was baptized Jean Margaret Wemyss, but almost at once became "Peggy" to family and friends, and remained so for thirty-odd years. The somewhat unusual family name Wemyss (pronounced "weems") is unmistakably Scottish, the nationality the young Peggy was aware of as peculiarly hers—allied with the Anglo-Irish of her maternal grandparents.

The Scottish ran deepest of these roots. In the unpublished typescript "The Wemyss and Simpson Families: Some Facts, Dates, Legends," compiled by Laurence, we read that the Wemysses "were a Lowland Scots family from Fifeshire, a sept of the clan MacDuff."[2] They can trace their ancestry back to the Picts, aborigines of Scotland.

The name "Wemyss" is a corruption of the Gaelic *Uamh*, meaning "cave"; on the Fifeshire coast, beneath the ruins of MacDuff's castle, are caves containing Pictish drawings. From the royal house of the clan Duff came the earls of Fife, finally the dukes of Fife; the clan became the MacDuffs and the direct line of this ancient house is continued in the family of Wemyss. The family name of the earls of Wemyss became Charteris.

The earliest Wemyss document in the possession of Peggy's family concerns the relationship of Robert and Barbara (née Donaldson) Wemyss of Fifeshire; they had two sons of record—and it is striking to follow the focus on pairs of sons in the Wemyss genealogy—John and David. John, a collector of excise taxes in Scotland, married Margaret Morrison in 1817 and became Peggy's great-great-grandfather. Brother David, a mariner in the Royal Navy, had a rather more exotic career that took him to India, where he was wedded—like Joseph Conrad's Lord Jim to his Jewel—to an Eastern bride named Minshoo (a name Peggy clearly remembered). Margaret Laurence tells his story:

> He had two children [with Minshoo], a daughter, Mina, and a son, John. The boy was born in 1839, a year before Captain David died in 1840. . . . Soon after Captain David died, Minshoo went off with another man. . . . The infant John was taken away with his mother. . . . Several years after his death, his brother John is still trying to discover what has happened to the young son and to David's personal effects. . . . the child and Minshoo now cannot be traced. . . . [3]

John and Margaret produced three sons, Robert (born 1824), George, and John (born 1831). In the Wemyss family the names Robert and John recur like items in a litany. Robert became a tea merchant in Edinburgh and married his cousin Catherine Wemyss. He decided at the end of the 1870s to settle in Manitoba—briefly in Winnipeg and then in Raeburn. He is Peggy's great-grandfather. Brother John, later

Sir John Wemyss, baronet, became a lawyer and went to India. There was an interesting connection later between Sir John and his nephew John.

Robert's son John, born in Edinburgh c. 1850, was Peggy's grandfather. He remained in Scotland after his parents emigrated to Canada. He finished his college work at Glasgow University, where he received a classical education with solid training in Latin and Greek languages and literature, and then for several years he articled with a law firm in Glasgow. He intended to go into the Indian Civil Service under the sponsorship of his uncle, Sir John. Uncle John died, however, "at Aligarth, North West provinces of India, 8th March 1878, aged 47."[4] With that avenue closed, nephew John in 1883 followed his parents to Manitoba.

This Wemyss family was part of the large Scottish influx to western Canada. The first settlers in what is now Manitoba were the Scots whom Thomas Douglas, Fifth Earl of Selkirk, sent in 1811 to found a colony, the Red River Settlement, near the junction of the Red and Assiniboine rivers, approximately the site of present-day Winnipeg. The colony's first Protestant clergyman, the Reverend John Black, arrived in 1851. An earlier visitor to the settlement recalls a Presbyterian service in St. Andrew's Church, Kildonan:

> [The] Rev. McTavish was to deliver a discourse in Gaelic. The entire parish had turned out to hear the first sermon preached in the old tongue—blank disappointment spread over the countenances of the congregation as the preacher, ascending the pulpit, delivered his sermon in English.[5]

By 1877 a family of Scots, the Grahams, had already settled in the area of the future town of Neepawa; James Graham built his house on the land that is today Riverside Cemetery, at the northeast corner of the town. That year also saw the arrival of the Reverend James S. Stewart to minister to the Presbyterians of the area, and five years after that the first Knox Church was built near the centre of town, on the corner of First Avenue and Mill Street. By the time Peggy's grandfather John Wemyss arrived in town, the Scots were established and already making their presence felt, and the "auld kirk" flourished.

In Winnipeg, John Wemyss articled with the law firm of Bain, Blanchard, and Mulock. He was called to the bar in 1886. The following year he moved to Neepawa and established a law office on the north side of Hamilton Street, just east of Mountain Avenue and opposite the County Court Building; he was thus in the heart of the town's business section as Neepawa's first resident lawyer. In 1893 John Wemyss married Maggie Harrison, the daughter of Dr. David Howard Harrison and his first wife, Margaret Notman. Dr. Harrison was Neepawa's first banker, retired from a lucrative medical practice in Ontario, and had a prominent political career in Manitoba. He served as premier of the province from 26 December 1887 to 18 January 1888—the shortest tenure of office for any Manitoba premier. The marriage of John and Maggie took place on 13 September.

Not long after settling into marriage in Neepawa and following the death of his father, John Wemyss was informed by lawyers in Scotland that their search for an heir to his Uncle John's baronetcy had led to him and that if he could prove he was indeed nephew to the late Sir John, he could assume his title. When he found that obtaining the necessary proof would cost him money, the canny commoner John Wemyss decided that parading about Neepawa as the new Sir John would bring little advantage and declined the offer.

Even without the knightly title, John Wemyss was clearly a man of quality; he became an adroit and effective civic leader. Persistent legend has it that John Wemyss functioned as solicitor for Neepawa on the occasion of its incorporation in 1883. In fact, however, town records indicate that its first solicitor was one Alexander Stewart; furthermore, John Wemyss did not arrive in Neepawa until April of 1887.[6] His service to the town was nevertheless extensive. He was a member of the school board for twenty-odd years; he served on the board of management of Knox Presbyterian Church, the hospital board, and the parks board. For more than fifteen years he held the positions of secretary to the Beautiful Plains Agricultural Society, of vice-president of the leading sash and door company (Fusee-McFeetors), and of director of the Neepawa Manufacturing Company. A small, dapper man who affected wing collars and carried a walking stick, he was fondly regarded as "wee Johnnie Wemyss"—a real gent with a gentleman's sense of noblesse oblige and known to bear the degree of Master of Arts from a prestigious Scottish university. On a bright and sultry Monday, 16 August 1926, Johnnie Wemyss walked with his briskly decorous step into Neepawa's Canadian Bank of Commerce and dropped dead of a heart attack. He left behind a month-old granddaughter. The granddaughter mourned his passing many years later: "He apparently saw me and held me only once, a sad fact to me, as I have always felt I would have liked to know him. He was the only man in Neepawa at that, or probably any other, time who could read the Greek tragedies and comedies in the original ancient Greek."[7]

Something of the *ton* of the John Wemyss household—at least as perceived by John's widow (a figure poignantly captured in the character Grandmother MacLeod of Margaret Laurence's *A Bird in the House*)—lingers in the lines of a notice published in the *Neepawa Press* for 20 September 1929:

> Mrs. Jno Wemyss, who is leaving Neepawa, is selling the contents of her house on Second Street, on Saturday, September 28 at 2 o'clock. Her home contains some of the most expensive and valuable furnishings. . . . everything will be sold without reserve to the highest bidder.

John and Maggie produced the first three Canadian-born Wemysses of the family, including, once again, a pair of Wemyss brothers: Robert was born in 1894 and John (called "Jack") in 1898; a baby sister, Norma, completed their family in 1902. A third son, born on 31 August 1904, lived exactly one year to the day. The first Canadian Wemyss became

Peggy's father. He got his public-school education in Neepawa and did his last three years of high school at St. Andrew's College in Toronto (it later moved to Aurora, Ontario, its present location). After college, he began articling with a law firm in Winnipeg. Early in 1916 he and his brother enlisted in the 60th Canadian Field Artillery as gunner and driver, respectively. After the war, Robert finished articling in Neepawa with his father, and then became his father's partner in the law firm of Wemyss and Wemyss, Barristers and Solicitors, in the office on Hamilton Street. In 1924 he married Verna Simpson. They became Peggy's parents.

Jack married and moved to Wilkie, Saskatchewan, where he ran a grain elevator for United Grain Growers until he died in 1956. He fathered Peggy's three Wemyss cousins, Norma, John, and Lucy. Norma married another kind of pioneer, Morden Carter, a bush pilot of northern Manitoba. Norma and Morden later settled in Newmarket, Ontario.

The story of the Simpson family begins with Peggy's great-grandparents, Robert Simpson and Anne Hughes of County Tyrone, northern Ireland. They came to Canada in the early 1850s, at the tail end of the "Great Immigration" from the British Isles, and were part of the huge wave of Ulster Protestants who contributed so much to the identity of Upper Canada. Five of their six children were born in Ireland—two daughters and three sons; the youngest, John, was born in Milton, Ontario (some eighty kilometres southwest of Toronto), in 1856—the first Canadian-born member of this Simpson family and Peggy's grandfather.

When his father died, John, about twelve years old, was obliged to quit school and learn a trade to help support the family. He spent a decade as apprentice to a cabinetmaker in Milton. When he reached his majority, he joined the general exodus westward to seek opportunities in Manitoba.

In the spring of 1877 John Simpson set out by train to a Great Lakes port (either St. Catherines or—more likely—Kincardine on

Lake Huron), thence by boat to Duluth, where he took the train again to Fisher's Landing on the Red River, and completed his journey by steamer downriver to Winnipeg. He had financed his trip by plying his trade as cabinetmaker en route. He probably recognized, however, after a few months in the big city, that his services were already fully enough supplied in Winnipeg, so he pushed on.

John Simpson was of tough, determined stock: he *walked* the next 100 kilometres into western Manitoba and stopped in Portage la Prairie, drawn to where a cousin of his was in the men's clothing business there. John joined him in that enterprise.[8] A further security was the young woman from High Bluff (near Portage la Prairie) whom he met and wooed in Portage, Jane Bailey, who had moved west from Amherstburg, Ontario, in 1883 with her family. John and Jane were married in 1886; their first two children—Stuart in 1887 and Ruby in 1888—were born in Portage. At the end of the decade they moved west to the town of Neepawa, where another five children were born to them, the last of whom was daughter Velma. The sixth child (and third daughter), born in 1896, was Verna, who married Robert Wemyss on 25 July 1924, and almost exactly two years later gave birth to Peggy.

The marriage of John Simpson and Jane Bailey united two other British strains, for her ancestors were predominantly southern English, from Sussex. Her grandfather, John Bailey, married Ann Skinner in 1829 and brought her to Canada in 1837 with their first children—they had thirteen in all—and settled in what is now western Ontario. In the early 1850s their oldest, Alfred, married Catherine Brush. These two produced a family of ten between November 1854 and 1877; their third child, a second daughter, was Jane—Peggy's grandmother.[9]

Jane Bailey's maternal line merits a special word. Her maternal grandmother, Elizabeth Lidwell, was born in Ireland and came to Canada in 1809, a child aged twelve. In 1818 she married John C. Brush, who adds yet another strain of ancestral influence peculiarly North American. The first Simpsons came to Canada about 1850, the first Wemysses in the 1870s; John Brush's parents, Stephen and Jemima

(Squires), came to the Canadas as United Empire Loyalists in the early 1780s. So far as Peggy's ancestry in North America is concerned, the line extending back through Grandma Simpson to the Brush family is by far the longest.

Jane Bailey of Amherstburg introduces another ancestral note. There was a persistent rumour in Neepawa from the early years of the twentieth century that a strain of Aboriginal blood ran in the Wemyss family and that it was traceable to Grandmother Simpson. Two of Peggy's friends[10] wrote to me to confirm the rumour when each sent me a clipping from the Winnipeg *Free Press* for 2 January 1988. The article, "A New Look at Peggy Wemyss," by the Reverend Tom Saunders—like Peggy, a graduate of United College—said that in her final novel "she faced up to something that she wanted to acknowledge yet sought to avoid." Her admission that Jules Tonnerre was "the most difficult character" she ever undertook, Saunders saw as a confession "that her maternal grandmother was part native" and that Peggy had finally accepted "the last of her roots." A third friend of school days vouched for the truth behind the rumour: "the only Indian in our young lives was her Grandmother Simpson." Two of Peg's schoolteachers, Wes McAmmond and Mildred Musgrove, quietly supported that claim. Grandmother Simpson had the prominent high cheekbones usually associated with North American Aboriginals. That feature was markedly repeated in Peggy; but it was also repeated from her paternal forebears and is especially marked in photos of her great-grandmother Catherine Wemyss. However, antiquarian Eleanor Gignac of Amherstburg researched Jane Bailey's background and reported finding no Aboriginal association in her background.[11]

Two friends from Peggy's adult years told me, individually, that she had frankly affirmed her Aboriginal ancestry. The late Polish scholar, B.W. Andrzejewski, who helped her with translations from Somali literature, said Peggy informed him of her Canadian-Aboriginal blood in Somaliland early in the 1950s; and Professor David Williams (of St. Paul's College) gave me the same report of her avowal a decade later.[12] Jack Laurence was later surprised at my asking for confirmation of ancestry and firmly denied it.[13] Margaret's own denial came in response to a question from the Ojibwa Alice Williams of the Lakefield area of Ontario: "No. I only wish I were." Canadian writer Don Bailey told me that the same denial came in slightly different form when he introduced Margaret and his half-Cree wife. "I *am* native—because I want to be!" she insisted and added the clarification "I belong to those who don't belong. . . . Only a stranger can help another stranger."[14] On 17 May 1981 Margaret wrote to Adele Wiseman a frank and credible denial: "It isn't that I am uninterested in N. Amer indigenous religions . . I am. But I am not an Indian."[15] The vexed little matter and its resolution casts a helpful light on much of her career and particularly on her late essay on Louis Riel's lieutenant Dumont—"those of us who are not Indian or Métis have not earned the right to call Gabriel Dumont ancestor. But I do so all the same."[16] It is not difficult to see why David Williams believes Margaret's "confession"—if not as fact, then certainly as truth.

John Simpson's career in Neepawa began to blossom in 1895, when he was able to buy John Boyd's furniture store. The following year saw the beginning of his steady progress northward up Mountain Avenue—the principal street in town. In 1896 he built a commercial structure that became known as Oak Hall, and in 1889 he bought land further up Mountain Avenue to build a substantial, two-storey block suitable for two businesses. Completed by September 1901, the Simpson Block housed his furniture and undertaking businesses, and just behind was a one-storey structure that stored materials for the undertaking business. He later added a hardware store.

His success permitted him to buy in 1904 (for $3000) an appropriately imposing brick house, Italian villa style, on the northwest corner of First Avenue and Brydon.[17] He remained a member of the Methodist church in Neepawa and served on the town council. Like most prominent men in town, he belonged to the approved fraternal societies—the Masonic Order, the International Order of Odd Fellows (IOOF), and the Loyal Orange Lodge.

John's second-oldest brother, Joseph, was "a lively bachelor until he passed away at age 94."[18] Little is known about Joseph, but as Grandfather Connor in *A Bird in the House* is patterned on John Simpson, we may assume (given the supporting evidence) that his brother, Dan Connor, a lovable old fraud who never married, is patterned on Joe Simpson. Like the fictional Connor brothers, John and Joe did not get along. Margaret Laurence frequently admitted that *A Bird in the House* is quite heavily autobiographical. Catherine Simpson Milne (Stuart's daughter) confirmed that and added her own testimony as she recalled "Old Uncle Joe, the Irishman" most fondly: "I just adored him. He always came at Christmas; Grandmother always put him into the bath and Grandfather bought him new clothes. Uncle Joe stayed for a month."[19] It is tempting, furthermore, to speculate on the possibility of an "eternal triangle" among John, Jane, and Joe Simpson—as is distinctly implied exists among Timothy, Agnes, and Dan Connor in *A Bird in the House.* In any case, the motif of the pair of brothers with the elder looking after (to some extent) the younger was there in the Simpson family as in the fictional Connor family.

John's eldest son, Stuart, something of a bon vivant, a member of Neepawa's "fast set" along with his brother-in-law Robert Wemyss, was educated at the Methodist Wesley College in Winnipeg. He returned to Neepawa, spent two years in the Merchants Bank of Canada, and married Bertha Frazer in August 1911. They moved into a modest house on the northeast corner of First Avenue and Brydon directly opposite John Simpson's. This became the Simpson Funeral Home, with Stuart a reluctant partner in the undertaking business as he was in his father's furniture business. Stuart finally took over direction of both when he was in his middle twenties. The Simpson enterprises continued to flourish, and in 1929 the funeral home was moved to the northwest corner of First and Vivian, formerly the Presbyterian manse. A simple trade occurred; Stuart's house became the manse. The family lived above the new funeral home; the funeral parlour was on the ground floor.

John Simpson is remembered by old-timers in Neepawa as a shrewd driver of hard bargains, a man of stern moral principles, and a stickler for proper behaviour. The penetrating glare of his steel-blue eyes evidently put the fear of God into those he encountered, and, in the habitual beaver coat he wore in the winters, he must have presented a particularly fierce and feral appearance. A cigar usually clamped in his jaw, he rarely smiled, and when he did, the occasion was memorable. One Neepawa veteran remembers his mother one day announcing, "Someone must have died; I just passed John Simpson on the street, and he was smiling."[20] There must have been a warm and sympathetic human core within the granite exterior he presented to the world. That, at least, is the suggestion offered in a much later memory that Margaret Laurence recorded:

> I saw one day in a museum the Bear Mask of the Haida Indians. . . . The features were ugly and yet powerful. The mouth was turned down in an expression of sullen rage. The eyes were empty caverns, revealing nothing. . . . until I imagined I could see somewhere within that darkness a look which I knew, a lurking bewilderment. I remembered then that in the days before it became a museum piece, the mask had contained a man.[21]

He had no more than five years of formal schooling, yet he had the astute common sense, hard-headedness, and native wit supported by an iron core of courage and determination that made his success possible. A sturdy man, a sojourner and survivor, he lived for almost a century: he was ninety-seven at his death in 1953. Peggy's two grandfathers, different in so many ways, were yet "Pillars of the Nation."

As the Wemyss family heritage was Presbyterian, that of the Anglo-Irish Simpson family was Methodist. The history of Methodism in Manitoba had its beginnings with the arrival of the Reverend George

Young at Winnipeg in July of 1868. Grace Church was established there in 1871. There was some Methodist mission work done in Neepawa in the early 1870s as well, but it was not until 1881 that the first Methodist church was built in town, on the corner of Walker and Ellen. A new church, the Neepawa Methodist, was erected in 1892 on Mountain Avenue south of Ellen Street; it stood and served for a century until a replacement was erected on the same site in 1992.

In Winnipeg, the beginning of an educational institute capable of rivalling the Presbyterian Manitoba College made its appearance in 1873 with the opening of a modest structure, the Wesleyan Institute, at what was to become the heart of downtown Winnipeg. Wesley College proper, erected on a parcel of land on the north side of Portage Avenue between Balmoral and what is now Spence Street, was opened to students in January 1896. It became United College in 1938, and in 1967 the present University of Winnipeg.[22] While the Methodist emphasis on the importance of education was not quite as heavy as the Presbyterian, it was distinct enough. Of equal concern to the church of John Wesley, however, was the preaching and practise of the social gospel. Peggy was to benefit from the united influence of both Presbyterian and Methodist primary interests, as she was from the fused hereditary predilections of the three British strains in her makeup—as well as those of her United Empire Loyalist forebears.

Another aspect of this quality of Peggy's background must be faced—as she faced it as she grew up. The names of the founders of Neepawa in its registers indicate the ethnicity of the town: Graham, Davidson, and Hamilton, and Alexander, Borne, Crawford, Currie, Kilburn, Macrae, McConnell, McFadden, McKay, McKenzie, Murphy, Murray, and Ritchey, as well as Simpson and Wemyss. The names are British and predominantly Scottish. It was strongly WASP and low-church Protestant. The Masonic Order, the Loyal Orange Lodge, and the IOOF flourished in Neepawa society. There was a scattering of eastern Europeans, usually safely contained on their side of the tracks with their spiritual needs tended to in small Roman Catholic housings. And there was even the occasional "Indian" or "Half-Breed";

the proper term "Métis" or "Métisse" was in those days virtually unknown among the proper citizens of Neepawa.

Down on the flats of Neepawa, just east of town, were a couple of Métis families, one by the name of Spence, the other comprised of Pate Chaboyer and his common-law wife, Rosie Neebles. "Pat," as he has been erroneously remembered, was a respected hockey player, and during the Second World War he served with distinction as a sniper in the Canadian army. Although there were few Aboriginal Canadians in Peggy Wemyss's young life, those few made an indelible impression on her "alien heart" and asserted their presence with increasing insistence as her literary career began and flourished. The influence of Pate Chaboyer especially rumbles like a thunderclap through the Manawaka fiction of Margaret Laurence.[23]

"Neepawa" comes from a Cree word meaning "plenty" or "abundance," and was adopted because of the supply of water, fuel, and game that once graced the area. The town is set amid the fertile farmlands of southwestern Manitoba that benefit from its rich black soil. The soil is typical of the lower slopes of Riding Mountain that begin to rise just northwest of the town; the area became a major producer of wheat. In the heydays of Canadian railroading, Neepawa was served by both transcontinental lines, the Canadian Pacific and the Canadian National railways. The cultural traditions of the town are attested to by its Opera House erected in the early years of the twentieth century; when it was destroyed by fire in 1905, the new Roxy Theatre was built to replace it. Among the important speakers heard in Neepawa's Roxy were novelist and feminist Nellie McClung, Prime Minister William Lyon Mackenzie King, and Premier John Bracken. The national opposition of the Conservatives (they became *Progressive* Conservatives under Bracken's leadership), represented by Arthur Meighen and his successor, R.B. Bennett, and the Liberals, represented by Mackenzie King, characterized the political climate of Peggy's early life.

To that opposition must be added the force of a group further to the political left than King's Liberals. The group was led by the Reverend James Shaver Woodsworth, a Methodist minister and son of a Methodist minister. In the federal elections of 1921, he ran for a Winnipeg riding as a member of the Manitoba Independent Labour Party; his success made him the first socialist member of the House of Commons in Ottawa. When, in 1933, the national party, the Cooperative Commonwealth Federation (CCF), was founded, Woodsworth was chosen as party leader. The direct descendant of the CCF is the present New Democratic Party (NDP). Certainly Peggy Wemyss was not much aware of the political climate or the contributions of those political leaders until her young adulthood, but their influence was already in the air and was later of considerable importance to her—especially that of Woodsworth.

Peggy was much more aware of the *natural* climate that moulded life in Neepawa during her early years. With the autumn chill came the flights of the wild geese, high up and ceaselessly honking, headed south in their long, extended V formations but with two or three "leaders" out ahead so that the flying V seemed stretched into a truncated Y, rather like a short-stemmed willow fork. The winters were long and cold; they began in mid- to late October and continued into April. There was usually plenty of snow. It was a great climate for winter sports, skating, hockey, and curling (all on natural ice), or snowshoeing and hiking in soft, light, snug moccasins.

Youngsters in town hustled to school in the morning cold and darkness. School began at 9:00 a.m., lunch was from 12:00 to 1:30, and the afternoon session ended at 4:00. The short winter days were mostly bright and clear under a brilliant sun. Gradually days lengthened and the sun began to make the snowbanks shrink. The Canada geese would come back—gratifyingly—as noisy as ever, clattering up from the south. And suddenly: spring! Birds were in evidence again: the early robins, the wild canaries, the Baltimore orioles, the crows and grackles, and the extravagantly lyrical meadowlarks, with their inimitable song as distinct and unforgettable as the haunting cry of the loons. School released the children in June and the brief, hot summer was upon them. The lucky ones (Peggy was one of them) could count on a week or so on the shores of cold Clear Lake in Riding Mountain National Park, eighty kilometres north of Neepawa. Before they could believe it, the binders were out to begin the harvest and the moon grew big and bright—the harvest moon—and it was time for school to take up again.

Peggy was distinctly a town girl, yet always a *small*-town girl. All the streets of Neepawa led very quickly into the countryside. As an adult, she recalled, "The country, the land is, after all, very close to a small town; it's just beyond the brow of the town hill. So that, although I didn't actually ever live on a farm I lived very close to open country."[24] Human life in tune with nature was an inescapable fact reinforced by readings she heard in church about chores appropriate to phases of the natural cycle—"To every thing there is a season . . . a time to plant and a time to pluck up that which is planted . . . a time to mourn and a time to dance" (Ecclesiastes 3:1-4).

If Peggy always loved to dance on the earth, she also learned early about the time to mourn. Death was a significant feature of her childhood. Before she reached the age of ten, Peggy had lost her paternal grandfather, both parents, her Uncle Stuart, and her maternal grandmother. The severe polio epidemic of 1936 accounted for the death of several children near her own age in Neepawa.

The cluster of deaths touched her closely, yet interwoven with them was a series of complications, disruptions, intrusions that seemed to lend particular emphasis to death and its influence on her impressionable years. The sense of instability prompted by the abrupt losses and the absolute absences was aggravated by the accompanying sense of insecurity fostered by her being moved from one house to another—three such moves within those first ten years. And within these combinations of death and displacement runs the theme of Peggy's irrational sense of guilt—another facet of her "alien heart."

The first death in her young life occurred a mere month after her birth: Grandfather John Wemyss died on 16 August 1926. Grandma Wemyss was left widowed and alone in the sprawling house on Second Avenue. Just over a year later, it was decided that Robert and family should move in with her. Robert was now head of the Wemyss law firm and had a growing family; a large house seemed more suitable than the cottage on Vivian, and they could look after his mother there better. But 1929 brought the Depression, and few families escaped the consequent economic pinch. The Wemysses spent a single Christmas together in 1928 in the house on Second Avenue. By the end of the following summer, the necessary line of action was taken: Grandma Wemyss sold her house and furnishings and moved to Winnipeg to live with her daughter, Norma. The auction sale was set for 28 September 1929. Peggy moved with her parents back into the Vivian Street cottage.

A more deeply traumatic and far more puzzling and emotionally confusing blow fell the following summer. The setting was the Simpson house, Peggy's fourth birthday, mid-July. Aunt Margaret was back home from Calgary, where she was a successful schoolteacher, and Aunt Velma had come out from her nursing position in Winnipeg. Peggy enjoyed the festive gathering. Abruptly, confusion: her mother was stricken there with acute appendicitis and suddenly died of peritonitis, just two days after Peggy's fourth birthday and five days before her own sixth wedding anniversary. That coincidence became a confusion of joy over the prized birthday gift of her first-ever tricycle and puzzled sorrow over the immediate loss of her mother. Before the end of July, she and her father returned to the cottage on Vivian Street, not only without her mother but oddly accompanied by Aunt Marge.

On her sister's death, Margaret Simpson abruptly assumed, at age thirty-nine, the task of caring for her bereft brother-in-law, four years her junior, and for her orphaned niece and namesake, Peggy. She married the widowed Robert a year later and fairly quickly she became "Mum" for Peggy instead of "Aunt Marge."

In 1933 another change occurred with the arrival of Robert Wemyss, Junior. Little Robert was born in May and adopted by her parents soon after. A year and a half later, in January 1935, another blow fell: Peggy's father and her Uncle Stuart had apparently been starting the New Year with celebrations traditional among bon vivants—wassail and high spirits; they were either extending New Year's gaiety or anticipating Twelfth Night festivity. Some careless overexposure to Manitoba's harsh winter weather contributing, both men were seriously stricken with pneumonia. Robert Wemyss died on January 13, Stuart Simpson a week later.

The reduced little family struggled along. Peggy turned nine that summer and entered grade four in September. Before the school year ended, Grandma Simpson died, aged seventy-seven. John Simpson was left alone in his big brick house; he was eighty, and as gruff and intimidating as ever. By the time school began again, Peggy and her brother and mother moved for the third time in Neepawa—into the imposing Big House on First Avenue. That house played an important role in Peggy's life; it was the Neepawa "home" she remembered most vividly. Indeed, Grandfather and his house haunted her maturity, at least until she attempted to "lay the ghost" almost forty years later in *A Bird in the House.*

The baleful atmosphere of Peggy's young life seems to have been sustained by the 1936 outbreak of the terrifying polio epidemic all through southern Manitoba, with its persistent threat of death or permanent injury—"infantile paralysis," it was then called. The horror of the epidemic and its dreadful threats touched Peggy and, in her memory, became associated with her sense of guilt. *Dance on the Earth* records an incident from that time that has significant bearing on that sense. As though to accommodate the demand for a satisfactory interpretation of the incident, Peggy's later recall skews the details in some important ways.

> We didn't stay in the big red-brick [Wemyss] house for long, but we were still there when the polio epidemic happened. . . .
>
> . . . the boys next door seemed very cruel. I didn't attack them or retaliate physically. How could I? I was younger and I was a girl. But I had a kind of burning fury that was sometimes enough to scare the two of them off. Then one of them, Gavin, got infantile paralysis and died.
>
> I remember exactly how I felt. . . . I had scared Gavin away and he had died. It was a great shock. (56-58)

The name "Gavin" carries echoes of romantic literature. There was an older boy named Gavin Lang, but he apparently survived the epidemic.[25] Two other children a couple of years older than Peggy, one a Styles and the other Warren Bradley, died of polio in Neepawa during the fall of 1936. Significantly, the adult memory of Margaret Laurence drew the mortal event more closely in time to the death of her father and associated it spatially with the house on Second Avenue; in addition, the impact of the event is more dramatically focussed through her compressing two boys into one and supplying that one with the romantic name "Gavin."

The childhood trauma as later recalled is persuasive in the way it juxtaposes death and the child's sense of responsibility, of implicit guilt in the matter: a similar association was involved in Peggy's memory of her mother's death and her own satisfaction and joy over the birthday tricycle. Her own birth and her Grandfather Wemyss's death might well have been similarly juxtaposed and so produced the attendant irrational, but effective, sense of guilt. And another feature of the death of "Gavin" demands attention because it is presented in *Dance on the Earth* in terms of a cause-and-effect sequence that produces appropriate punishment. Again, Margaret Laurence's adult and artistically creative memory has adjusted temporal and spatial details to accommodate her unconscious psychological needs:

> Somehow [Gavin's death] is linked in my mind with my mother selling the Wemyss house. It was bought by a local doctor and his family. . . . They had it covered with yellow stucco. It made me very angry. I had no right to be angry. It was no longer our house and in any event, I hadn't really loved that house at all. (58)

The memory is highly significant in its creativity. Peggy's family was no longer living in the Wemyss grandparents' house on Second Avenue at the time indicated for the death of "Gavin" (1935): they had been back in the cottage on Vivian since 1929. The John Wemyss house was indeed sold in 1935, but not by Peggy's mother: that house remained Grandmother Wemyss's and it was she who sold it to the "local doctor," Dr. H.H. Hutchinson. The adjustments made by Margaret Laurence's creative memory thus closely associate the loss of "Gavin," the loss of "home," and the loss of Father, and over all three it casts the pall of personal guilt.[26]

This "creative" skewing of historical fact by Margaret Laurence's recollection is a distinctly different affair from simple misremembering: it actually captures, unconsciously, the essential significance of a cluster of data from her early life—the sense of loss at the death of her father, of uprootedness and consequent threatened identity, and, with that, the nagging and irrational sense of guilt over a failure to know that father before she lost him. That very dilemma is presented as Vanessa's precisely at the centre of *A Bird in the House*. It would seem that in her memoirs Margaret Laurence was, in fact, remembering the life of Vanessa MacLeod as rendered in that fiction rather than her own life in the actual years of the Depression.

The essential significance is sustained by another striking juxtaposition in *Dance on the Earth*. The memoir gives an accurate account of Peggy's final displacement in Neepawa, into the Big House with the bereft, tyrannical, old man, along with her brother and mother:

> So we moved again.
>
> I felt very odd about that move. I had loved that house all my life, but it was for visiting, not for living in. It was my grandfather's stronghold and he ruled it like Agamemnon ruling Mycenae or Jehovah ruling the world . . . it was his domain, not mine. . . . it was there I lived until I left home for college, eight years later. In fact when I think of my childhood home, it is that one more than any other that comes to mind. (63)

The next paragraph of the memoirs begins, tellingly, "Years before, when I was a small child, my father had built me a play-house."

It is easy to believe that the child's attitude to the old man and his domestic domain is accurately captured in the adult's simile describing John Simpson as the awesome dominant figure: "he ruled it like . . . Jehovah ruling the world." Peggy must have seen the Big House as a microcosm of the world at large. There was the jealous god, the punitive paternal figure; but what had she done, she must have wondered, to be in such a position under such dominance? What guilt to merit such punishment? She felt very keenly the loss of her own father—the loving, forgiving, comforting figure who gave her her own playhouse. Except for her grim, ursine Grandpa Simpson, Peggy lived mainly in a world of females, a world of strong, independent-minded women including a talented, intelligent, and fostering mother and two staunch spinster aunts—Ruby and Vem, Mum's remaining sisters; but it was a man's world nevertheless, Grandpa Simpson's world, most immediately. The early pages of *Dance on the Earth* remind us how male-oriented are the rituals of Christianity—the religion of Wemysses and Simpsons—and quote several Christian hymns as partial illustration ("Rise up, O men of God!" "Faith of our fathers!" "Praise, my soul, the King of heaven"); we note the conspicuous omission of the hymn "This is my father's world." After January 1935 the world she knew was certainly not *her* father's. Some aspects of her later life bear evidence of a continuing quest for the missing father.

Despite Verna's early death, her maternal influence was important. She evidently had an enthusiastic and almost childlike devotion to little Peg—talked with her, played with her, and recorded her earliest doings and sayings in a baby-book. On occasion she became so involved in attending to her baby daughter that she lost track of time and forgot to prepare meals. Verna Wemyss was a talented musician, a pianist of considerable promise, and Peggy as an adult proved capable of modest musical composition, some examples of which have been preserved. Peggy also inherited from her mother a sense of humour, a sense of fun, a hint of devil-may-care abandon; and she clearly retained a sense of the conjugal love of Verna and Robert Wemyss.

Robert Wemyss was physically rather a big man; he was a member of the "professional class" of Neepawa and travelled with the local equivalent of "the fast set." It was a Wemyss family legend that the reason young Bob had been sent down east to St. Andrew's College to complete his high school education was that he was "something of a hellion . . . and the local teachers couldn't handle him." Margaret Laurence admits that the story is "perhaps apocryphal," but "I always hoped myself that was the real reason."[27] And perhaps it was. Robert was evidently a competent lawyer, but hardly well-to-do, except comparatively; no one in town was well-to-do in those grim Depression years. But he did drive a car. He was something of a handyman, a respectable amateur carpenter, and the modest little home of the young Wemyss family held many indications of his talent with hammer and saw—various built-in cupboards and cabinets and clothes closets, all gaily painted in bold colours. Most memorable of all, however, was the playhouse he made for Peggy. "It wasn't a tiny little Peter-Pan-and-Wendy effort," she recalled a lifetime later. "This was the real thing. It had a sloped roof and was about the size of a largish woodshed, big enough for an adult to stand up straight in. Dad had even equipped it with windows that opened and window boxes. . . ."[28]

And it was portable enough to accompany Peggy when she moved from the little house on Vivian into Grandfather Simpson's house on

First. She was able to carry with her a private little "home" of her own, and that private dwelling, heavy with memories of her father, served as an important and meaningful refuge.

Margaret Campbell Simpson, second of the strong-willed, independent-minded, and "intellectual" daughters of John and Jane Simpson, was born in March 1890. She graduated from high school in Neepawa with the highest marks in the province of Manitoba. Her father was opposed to "higher education" for his daughters: practical training, he thought, was sufficient preparation for life, and marriage to a reliable and hard-working young man was preferable. The eldest Simpson girl, Ruby, became a nurse, as did the youngest, Velma; Margaret took teacher-training. Only Verna had been indulged for a while in the frivolity—as Grandpa Simpson saw it—of musical education. Margaret did her teaching in Calgary, Alberta, except for an exotic year as exchange teacher in Bermuda (1920-21), and the inspectors were very favourably impressed with her pedagogical ability. Her professional career ended with the death of Verna, but as she stepped into the role of Peggy's "Mum," she continued also in that of an inspirational, encouraging, guiding teacher—only now with a smaller and private audience. She continued also to exert appropriate cultural influence in Neepawa; she was, for example, largely responsible for founding and sustaining Neepawa's public library.

Margaret was careful not to try to "take the place" of Verna, but she did serve as an excellent substitute. She saw to it that her young charge got as much cultural enrichment as she could stand, some of it perhaps intended as compensation for the loss of the musical Verna. She put Peggy into piano lessons and then into violin lessons; Peggy continued the latter pursuit on to the end of her high school years. She even embarked on a series of dancing lessons, both ballroom and tap dancing, that helped foster an essential social grace. Best of all, however, Mum took seriously the girl's interest in literature—in reading, certainly, but also in her youthful attempts at literary creation. She discussed the merits of style in the stories they read together as in the stories from Peggy's own pen. The beginnings of a literary life can most definitely be located in those early colloquies between Mum and daughter. Robert made his own peculiar and apt contribution in the form of a gift to his eight-year-old daughter on the last Christmas they shared (1934): he rescued a small wooden desk from the attic of the Wemyss house on Second Avenue, put it in trim, and painted it a gorgeous turquoise.

After Verna's death, Peggy had another four and a half years with her father, yet her conscious memories of him were not much stronger or more numerous than those of her mother. A good deal of what she "remembered" of him derived from stories that Mum and other members of the family told her, and a good deal also from photographs—as is the case with the young, orphaned Morag in *The Diviners*. Yet the sense of a distinct, paternal figure of love and protection was strong in her; furthermore, her father had left quite tangible mementoes, lasting and useful—the cupboards and cabinets in the Vivian Street house, the Christmas desk, the playhouse, as well as her memories of his study with its cozy fireside. Robert's image is recreated in Ewen MacLeod in *A Bird in the House* (complete with the detail of his cherished collection of *National Geographic* magazines).

Peggy was very much an only child, even after the adoption of her baby brother, Robert Morrison Wemyss. They were as close as any particularly compatible siblings could be, and she always had a protective attitude toward her little brother, who was not a robust child. The seven-year difference in their ages, however, made it difficult—especially during their childhood—for them to be true playmates and to share in various adventures.

Peggy Wemyss's first true playmate was Mona Spratt, a scant two weeks older than she. Similar in temperament from the beginning, they formed a friendship that endured to the end of Peggy's life. In February 1986 Margaret Laurence wrote a tribute to her—

My first my lifelong sister   born
Two weeks before me   same small town
We've known all our lives   left it
But bear it within us   have known
Ourselves as sisters sixty years now
Shared secrets families fears exultances
Needs and rages   news of children
From births to now-adulthoods
We survive   my sister comrade
More or less whole   wholly alive.[29]

two

Small Town Girl

MONA SPRATT WAS PEGGY'S FIRST, DEAREST, AND MOST enduring friend. In the summer of 1932, they turned six, and that fall began formal schooling. During the 1930s another kind of schooling was provided by the Neepawa Nuisance Grounds, a mere block south of the corner of Vivian and Mountain, where Peggy's home was. The Nuisance Grounds offered an educational collection of debris and refuse, the essence of which Margaret Laurence captured in the Homeric catalogue early in *The Diviners*.[1] Peggy and Mona were joined at school by Louise Alguire and Margie Crawford. The friendship among the foursome strengthened as they biked, swam in Clear Lake in summer, skated, snowshoed, and curled in winter.[2] Peg was busily writing even as a schoolgirl; she always had a story or play to work on in her "scribbler," and no friendship, however dear, was allowed to interfere. Her most important reader and critic was her Mum, who took Peggy's work seriously. Their discussion of her writing was, from the beginning, conducted on as adult a level as possible, as were their discussions of published literature.

Peggy's teacher in grade seven, the young Wes McAmmond, used to read stories to the class for fifteen minutes to begin the afternoon. He remembered her clearly, half a century later, as an eager twelve-year-old who would linger in the classroom until all her mates had left to talk tête-à-tête with him. She was somewhat shy and sought adult approval; she told him one afternoon that she was writing a play. And she was "distinctly a loner." The character of the alien heart, the faintly estranged, was already discernible. McAmmond took a lot of photographs of the class during a picnic he arranged, and Peggy was missing from most of them. He shared this evidence with the adult Margaret Laurence and asked, "Where are you?" She readily confessed that "as soon as you started that stuff I headed for the bush." One of the photos, however, catches another aspect of Peggy. The students are all lined up, ready to go on the picnic:

> There she was with her basket. She was the only one with a basket for a picnic basket. I don't know if it was her mother's idea or her idea, but she'd brought along a basket where the other kids would bring a bag with a Coke and a hamburger or a hot dog. . . . But she was properly prepared.[3]

Her Mum saw to it that, as the daughter of the late Robert Wemyss, prominent citizen and social leader, Peggy must look the part of a serious young lady. McAmmond liked Peggy and encouraged her writing, though he gave her only the second-highest marks in the class for composition. Still, one of the stories he introduced her to was *The White Company*—and that was a fruitful kindness.

Conan Doyle's historical romance was an important influence on Peggy. What first would have attracted her attention is the prominence of pairs of brothers, a feature that characterized the Wemyss family history down to her own time. Especially influential, however, is Conan Doyle's use of the Bergersh brothers as the target of his social criticism. They represent the two-pronged oppression of the lower classes by Church and Aristocracy: "They are the twin thieves who live upon our labour," protests one of the lumpen proletariat.[4] Even the hero, Alleyne, is criticized by his beloved Lady Maud for his cloistered upbringing and parochial education: her objection echoes John Milton's "I cannot praise a fugitive and cloistered virtue." The social criticism in *The White Company* helped prepare Peggy for her eager response, in college, to Milton and to William Blake. Specific evidence of the general influence of the novel appears in her story of 1965, "A Bird in the House." There, the young heroine (age twelve), Vanessa MacLeod, sits with her grandmother to await news of her father and pretends to read: "I perched on the edge of the chesterfield and kept my eyes fixed on *The White Company* by Conan Doyle, and from time to time turned a page. I had read it three times before, but likely Grandmother MacLeod did not know that."[5]

As Peggy turned thirteen and entered her last grade before high school, World War II broke out. Other aspects of that year, of course, bulked larger in her view. *Dance on the Earth* recalls the purchase of her first typewriter, "a small second-hand Remington that cost $14. Mum put up half and I paid the other half by earning money babysitting" (74). They knew high school offered courses in typing. A second event, a kind of epiphany, added impetus to that decision:

> I was fourteen and I was walking up the stairs in my grandfather Simpson's house. . . . I can see myself, with my hand on the dark varnished banister. . . . A thought had just come to me . . . : I can't be a nurse; I have to be a writer. I was appalled and frightened. (74)

A couple of lines later: "through highschool and college I thought I would be a journalist."

That summer she had sent a story to the Winnipeg *Free Press* for its annual Summer Story Contest for Young Authors. When the results were announced on the Young Author's Page in the Saturday magazine supplement (page 6) for 28 September 1940, Jean Margaret Wemyss was listed first among the "Specially Good" Honourable Mentions for her story "The Land of Our Fathers." It was not published, and no manuscript survives. But this is likely the story in which Peggy first used the invented Aboriginal name "Manawaka" to refer to Neepawa and the surrounding Manitoba countryside.

Margaret Laurence twice refers to this story subsequently in her adult writing, once in fiction and once in her final memoir, and on both occasions the title of the story is inaccurate. In *A Bird in the House* young Vanessa (the "Peggy" figure in the book) has been working on a story called "The Pillars of the Nation": "my epic on pioneer life. . . . Then came the discovery that Grandfather Connor had been a pioneer, and the story had lost its interest for me."[6] And when Margaret Laurence's memoir refers to her initial successes as a young writer—"in the summer of 1940"—she remembers the title of that first honourable mention story in the Winnipeg *Free Press* as (again) "The Pillars of the Nation" rather than "The Land of Our Fathers."[7] It is certainly arguable that Margaret Laurence could not conceive of Peggy at age fourteen claiming "This Is My Father's World," nor could the adult Margaret allow Peggy to have written about "The Land of Our Fathers"—not even as the fictional Vanessa MacLeod.

During these early years of school, Peggy came to know something of a distant cousin from her Grandmother Simpson's family, the Baileys. A male cousin some ten years her senior, Lorne "Bud" Bailey, came to Neepawa to attend public high school; he was actually a cousin of Peggy's mother and Mum—a nephew of Grandma Simpson. He was apparently a somewhat wistful, dreamy, and idealistic boy, and clearly attractive as a fellow alien to Peggy, who was then fatherless, virtually uncle-less, and with no other male cousins around. Lorne's impression on her was indelible and persistent, and their relationship remained associated in her mind with other attractive males she encountered as she entered her teens.

Lorne Bailey reappeared in Peggy's life in that summer of "The Land of Our Fathers": she visited his family's farm north of Clear Lake, Manitoba, and evidently went through an experience similar to Vanessa's with Chris in "Horses of the Night" (*A Bird in the House*). They camped out during harvest time, near the edge of Swallow Lake. Vanessa is just thirteen, Chris past twenty-one: "We did not wash, and we slept in our clothes. . . . If he wanted me not to be a child—and he did—it was not with the wish that I would be a woman" (148-49).

What Chris wants is an adult conversation with Vanessa. He recalls what her father had meant to him; he talks about religion and about war—all quite seriously. She is honoured but embarrassed by her inability to reply adequately.

Chris functions as a substitute of sorts for Vanessa's lost father. The passages of *Dance on the Earth* devoted to cousin Lorne Bailey, added to Margaret Laurence's presentation of Chris, seem to argue that Lorne filled the same function for Peggy. See "For Lorne (1976)":

> we were far cousins
> we could have loved
> wed
>
> . . .
> One year
> before the war
> one summer before
> I became a woman
> . . .
> I went childcousin with you
> to wildfields weirdfields
> I had known only the wildplaces
> already tamed when I was born . . . (257-59)

High school offered some new challenges and some rewards. Peggy now walked to the north edge of town to Viscount High School (later Neepawa Collegiate Institute). Among her teachers there, Miss Mildred Musgrove played a major role, both as her English teacher and as faculty advisor for *Annals of the Black and Gold*, the student newspaper, on which Peggy worked actively. She made her mark early in the second half of grade nine when a story of hers was published in the Winnipeg *Free Press* on the Young Authors page. "The Case of the Blond Butcher: A Wanted Man" appeared in two parts, on consecutive Saturdays, 18 and 25 January 1941. The story is not a triumph, but it does anticipate in some ways the adult work of Margaret Laurence, and Peggy's preoccupations at age fourteen.

The narrative technique is important: the heroine, Nancy Grayson, is writing in her diary on her sixteenth birthday as the story opens, not just recording the main adventure but holding a dialogue with herself. The first voice carries the narrative while the second voice, critical and censorious, provides commentary on the first—the narrative strategy of all Margaret Laurence's Manawaka fiction. The one difference (apparently) is that the two "voices" in "The Case of the Blond Butcher" seem the reverse of what we find in the Manawaka fiction. (And quite consistent with the adult fiction is the narrator-heroine's clothes consciousness.)

The story is a little moral tale: "good" triumphs. Nancy's friend Dick warns her that the Blond Butcher has escaped from jail and is most likely to show up in their city. Dick's description of the criminal is important: "tall with blond hair, and a moustache, very good looking." A blond stranger bursts in on Nancy and Dick and asks for brief asylum because he is trying to avoid an annoying aunt. When the stranger, Edward Wells, leaves, Dick tells Nancy that that was the Blond Butcher! Nancy rejects the idea: "'Oh rubbish. The Blond Butcher wouldn't have such nice manners,' I said a trifle coldly. (Mr. Wells told me I looked charming. I had on my little brown sports suit, trimmed with green.)" But Dick persists— "he's blond. He could have shaved off the moustache"—and reminds Nancy of the $250 reward for capture of the escaped butcher. She agrees to a plan to trap him, but with grievous visions of Wells being hanged. When Wells comes over to visit Nancy, she phones Dick, who tells her to fly for police help; Nancy does so, learns from the police that the butcher has already been caught fifty miles away, and rushes back home to find Dick there "sitting on Mr. Wells' chest." Explanations clear up everything and Wells forgives the "detective-minded youngsters"; Nancy is hospitalized with an ankle injury incurred while rushing back home. Wells and Dick both send her flowers, but Dick is finally Nancy's choice—

on these terms: "Mr. Wells is a very nice person, but diary, I like Dick lots better. He is more—well, more sort of pleasant to have around. I suppose it's because Mr. Wells thinks us youngsters. (He's nearly 24. I wish he could see me in my new yellow frock.)"

She recognizes she must be kinder to Dick and "get mother to invite him over for dinner some evening. After all, we've been friends practically all our lives." The second-last paragraph of the story takes this wisdom a step further: "Besides, he helps me with my homework." Of course! A happy ending; the good, moral Dick has won Nancy (or vice versa).

Or he has for the moment. The strongly implied tendency of Nancy in quite another direction is merely postponed. Dick is the morally sound "good boy" who alerts Nancy to the approach of evil—and of course anticipates the $250 reward: virtue *pays!* He is wrong, however, in his identification of evil, of Wells as the butcher. Yet Dick is Nancy's proper choice at the end. Wells is not "very good looking," like the Blond Butcher, for he lacks a moustache—the unmistakable sign of maturity and masculinity. (Peggy's father wore a moustache.) But Wells is attractive enough to Nancy as an "older man" of sophisticated good manners. He is "nearly 24," and there is still time for him to grow a moustache. Fortunately he is blond: acceptably WASP. The double entendre in the story's subtitle, "A Wanted Man," is a nice fillip.

Peggy at age fourteen had sketched out a moral dilemma that would become a constant preoccupation of the Manawaka saga. The urge to be conventionally proper, to act in a "politically correct" way, is there regularly confronted by a critical uncovering of the hypocritical, the cosmetic, and thus the fundamentally dishonest quality of the "moralistic" urge; against it is proposed the fundamentally honest and basically natural prompting of our "best self" to be truly moral in the broadest and deepest sense. The Manawaka fiction favours enlightened love and respect of self, the proper self-love that is the basis on which love of neighbour must rest. That attitude is anticipated, just a mite slyly, in "The Case of the Blond Butcher."

Equally noteworthy in the story is the attraction of the "older man" (tall and handsome and adorned, if possible, with a moustache), not only as a figure of fiction but also for Peggy herself in her young life. This anticipates a preoccupation of her adult life and career. We might also note two minor aspects of "The Case of the Blond Butcher" that cast a ray of light on the actual life out of which the story arose: Nancy's dad is mentioned but twice, both times in the phrase "mom and dad," and he has no function whatsoever in the story; and there is a single but poignant reference to Nancy's sibling: "even the kid brother didn't seem so annoying as usual." The now familiar personae in Peggy's personal drama are evident in her initial publication—the young brother, the absent father, the surrogate "older" young man.

Mona Spratt was often fatherless, like Peggy, for Mr. Spratt was a travelling salesman. That was, then, a feeling they could share to some extent. They also shared the friendship of Louise Alguire and Margie Crawford. The foursome trooped off to school clad in the usual uniform—a blue serge tunic with a yoke collar, a white blouse, black cotton stockings, and flat or low-heeled shoes.[8]

Peggy did well in her first year of high school, grade nine: at the close of the year she stood second in her class of thirty-one students. Her performance in the academic courses understandably reflected both her abilities and tastes. Her best marks (percentage grades) came in spelling (96) and music (94), with literature (90), grammar (89), and composition (88) right behind. She was not especially adept in mathematics and science. Since friend Margie Crawford was not particularly adept in literature, she and Peg created a mutual aid society to cover each other's weakness by means of a type of sign language.[9] An exception to the rule for Peggy was physiology, in which she earned a 92. A compensatory surprise, however, was her abysmal performance in French—a 72.

She accumulated a very respectable record. Her program included plenty of "English," with courses in grammar and composition; and, while there was a good sampling of British literature, there was virtually no Canadian—the educational authorities thought there really was no such creature. (Mum filled that lacuna at home.) She studied world history in grade nine, British in ten, and Canadian in eleven.

Extracurricular activities such as debating and dramatics appealed to Peggy. She was a member of the grade nine debating team and, with her partner, defeated the grade ten team in the final of the intermural competition for the school Debating Shield. The decisive topic was "Resolved that Ambition has brought more harm than good to mankind." Peggy and her partner argued for the negative. That year she joined the staff of the student publication *Annals of the Black and Gold*, and, under the guidance of Miss Mildred Musgrove, faculty advisor, Peggy remained on staff through her four years of high school and became increasingly responsible for its production. In grade ten Peggy took the female lead in *Ada Gives Advice* for the school drama festival the following year. And she was a member of the school orchestra. Music was a shared activity among Peggy and her closest friends. She had been exposed to the piano when she was young, and later turned to the violin with somewhat happier results. Louise Alguire was the most accomplished musician in the group: she played piano and was organist in Neepawa's St. James's Anglican Church; Margie Crawford was a clarinetist; Mona Spratt played the guitar. Although Margaret Laurence's censoring memory has it that her career as violinist was brief, Mona, Louise, and Miss Musgrove insist that throughout her four years of high school she played not only in the orchestra at Neepawa Collegiate Institute functions but also at dances and other social gatherings in town. The girls learned ballroom dancing, and there was also a series of tap-dancing lessons (twenty-five cents a time), which only Margie escaped. Peggy was not athletic. Mona recalls, philosophically, that she and Peggy were always the last ones chosen on pick-up teams, and that at school sports events outdoors they cooked the weiners and prepared the buns on the sidelines while Louise and

Margie—the real athletes of the group—carried off ribbons and trophies.

Peggy wanted to try everything. Mildred Musgrove recalled: "Enthusiasm was always a part of Margaret's makeup. When she was editor of the paper, she was very enthusiastic about that, and was racing here and there to get this write-up or that or turn somebody on to do something."[10]

She creates the image of a youngster leaning into the future faster than her feet can carry her. But the school paper captured Peggy's chief enthusiasm. She assumed editorship of the *Annals of the Black and Gold* at the beginning of grade eleven and continued until the end of high school. The quality of her own contributions is not stunningly high—just rather typical schoolgirl journalism; but she covered a broad spectrum of topics and on some occasions wrote most of the items in the publications. Considering that Canadian literature was essentially excluded from the curriculum, it is noteworthy that in one of her stories in the *Annals*, "The Bewitched Shoes" (Easter number, 1942; Peggy in grade ten), the hero bears the name of a famous figure in early Canadian literature—Sam Slick. "The Bewitched Shoes" has little relevance to Thomas Chandler Haliburton's 1835 tales other than the name of the hero; but Peggy's use of the name indicates her Mum's role as supplier of supplementary cultural education. In all respects, Peggy was being raised as a proper young lady—intelligent, well-mannered, and highly respectable. And from grade ten onward, she emerged as a leader of the student body. At the end of grade eleven she was awarded the prestigious Governor General's Medal. The *Annals of the Black and Gold* (via the pen of Mona Spratt) took notice of its editor's achievements:[11]

> The most coveted award in the Neepawa Collegiate was presented at the Graduation Exercises. . . . the Governor General's Medal, . . . won by none other than our busy editor. . . .
>
> In awarding this medal, account is taken not only of academic work but also of athletic, extracurricular activities,

> leadership, initiative, and interest in school activities throughout grades X and XI.
>
> . . . [Peggy] has an average of 81% in her studies. . . . Her most outstanding activity is editing the Annals of the Black and Gold. . . . She has been faithful to the Collegiate Orchestra for three years as an accomplished violinist. Dramatics and debating have also played a part . . . as well as Curling and Basketball in the line of sports. Her initiative, fine leadership, and enthusiasm certainly prove Peggy Wemyss worthy of claiming the honor of such an award. . . .

Other awards from the Governor General's auspices would follow in Peggy's adult life.

Meanwhile, in the spring of 1943, she was anticipating matriculation and then escape with Mona, Louise, and Margie to Clear Lake on the south edge of what is now Riding Mountain National Park—the originals of Diamond Lake and Galloping Mountain in her fiction. The Alguires operated the principal hotel at Clear Lake (as they did in Neepawa), right on the shore. Often the girls gathered at the Spratts' cottage, with Mona's mother a constantly vigilant chaperone, or at the Simpson-Wemyss cottage—in later high school years, unchaperoned! This arrangement was exciting for the teenaged girls.

An inescapable shadow fell across their common path: World War II erupted. A sobering feature was the departure of many young men from Neepawa and the surrounding area—the majority favouring the regiment of the Queen's Own Cameron Highlanders of Canada. Before the fall term of grade eleven began for the sixteen-year-old Peggy and her chums, the Battle of Dieppe struck them closely. Dieppe involved Canadian troops predominantly, especially the Cameron Highlanders, and the Neepawa region anxiously scrutinized the daily report of casualties. The graduating class of Neepawa Collegiate Institute included very few boys. One of them, Don Straith, had been Peggy's first boyfriend for the past two years; he joined the Royal Canadian

Air Force on graduation. Another man lost to Peggy. The next year's class contained no male students at all.

Yet the war had at last broken the stifling grip of the Depression after a decade of imposed scrimping; and while rationing was still in effect, the economic and social climate was generally brighter. Military camps had sprung up around the country. The air force (both the RAF and the RCAF) established stations on the western edge of Neepawa itself and at nearby Carberry, and Manitoba girls met men from abroad. The influx of airmen on leave made the Saturday night dances at Pedlar's ballroom in downtown Neepawa gala affairs. During the summers, a number of RAF men even joined Peg and her friends at Clear Lake and helped keep shipshape the old scow in which she, Mona, Louise, and Margie poked around the lake. There were the traditional beach parties—marshmallows, campfire, romance. It was Peggy who maintained the correct moral tone amid all this: "she was the upright one," Mona and Louise agree. The strong puritanical strain in her United Church upbringing saw to that.

Nevertheless, during the summer in which she turned seventeen, Peggy met an English airman, Derek Armstrong, "smooth-mannered, slight, and soulful"; a moustached "older" man whose British accent made him sound (in Peg's ear) cultured and faintly exotic. To this charmer she lost her heart (although that was apparently all) during his six-week posting in Neepawa. He was unreliable, would fail to keep his "dates" with her. Mona and Louise detested him and were relieved by his subsequent posting to Carberry. He returned to Neepawa to see Peg, but only once or twice. Then nothing. If he survived the war, he returned to England to whatever life awaited him, including, perhaps, a wife and family.[12]

Two other airmen stationed at Carberry, Manitoba, at this time demand a word; one was an Englishman, Frank Collier, and the other a Canadian serving with the RAF, Jack Laurence. They met in 1943 and quickly became friends. Collier gave pre-flight training in a mechanism (the Link Trainer) that simulated actual flying conditions and aircraft responses to controls, to prepare airmen for their next stage—actual flight. Sergeant Jack Laurence was involved in ground-support work and aircraft maintenance. Both were older men, older perhaps even than Derek. Peggy apparently met neither Collier nor Laurence at the Neepawa and Clear Lake revels, yet both men were to play significant roles in her future.[13]

Peggy and her Mum had decided it would be most prudent for her to remain at home and take grade twelve at Neepawa Collegiate Institute and so postpone for a few months the decision about college. The educational system in Manitoba considered grade twelve to be the equivalent of the first year of college, and after the successful completion of grade twelve one was, thus, admitted into the second year of college or university.

If Peggy's short romance with Derek marks a distinction between the fresh, seventeen-year-old girl who had graduated from grade eleven, and the young woman who entered grade twelve in the fall of 1943, a pair of poems she wrote about a year apart draw her last two years of high school closer together. The two poems indeed seem to constitute a pair, for they address a common theme, the problem of religious belief. The earlier poem was evidently written late in 1942, during the fall term of her grade eleven, and the later appeared in the Christmas 1943 issue of *Annals of the Black and Gold.* They bracket the crucial summer, and together give an idea of the kind of serious thought occupying Peggy's mind as she neared the end of her comparatively sheltered life in Neepawa.

The first, "Pagan Point—Wasagaming—Approaching Night," is surprisingly mature; the setting is the shores of Clear Lake. "Pagan Point" is a Wordsworthian pastoral, twenty-seven lines of blank verse augmented by an irregular pattern of rhyme. The poem rehearses the abrupt intrusion of pagan/heathen influence upon a peaceful natural scene, contrasting the pagan past and the Christian present. The loss of the old pagan gods has produced a sense of loneliness in the speaker, but the quiet calm of the present dispensation reconciles her to her situation by mitigating the loneliness with a sense of reverence and peace. The opening scene of calm, cool water and "untroubled sky" is rudely disturbed—

> . . . then the peace is broken by the cry,
> raucous and heathen, of a far-off loon, . . .
> There is unearthly paganism here.
> In this secluded spot, a bird's wild cry,
> Forgotten gods awake and claim anew
> The temple that so long ago they knew.
> In the incessant beating of the waves.
> Old Neptune tells again his scorn of land,
> And in the large moaning of the wind
> Is heard the ancient battle-voice of Thor. (11, 7-18)

The contrast of pagan and Christian is heightened by the juxtaposition of the thunder-born voice of Thor with the voice of the Christian God born in the whirlwind—or in the thunder. The roughness and challenge of the pagan gods is more sharply contrasted with the quiescence and mildness of the Christian by the very fact of their shared feature of thunder. The competing forces vie for the lonely speaker in "this secluded spot."

The poem ends, however, with the apparent resolution of the conflict, with the proposed triumph of Christian reverence.

> Yet now the fierceness of the wind abates. . . .
> The heathen gods are gone—the loneliness
> Has blended with a reverence, a peace. . . .
> The lake is stilled, the marsh birds call no more.
> This is a dim cathedral—full of rest,
> Remote from pain, where Man may find his God.
> This is the oldest chapel in the world.
>
> j m w

The whole poem slopes toward a conclusion that denies the bright light of day, the spur of challenge, vigorous vitality: it presents the triumph of life-denial and baleful comfort. This is the promise of Tennyson's "Lotus-Eaters," whose inner spirit sings "There is no joy but calm!"

> Death is the end of life; ah, why
> Should life all labour be?
>
> . . . is there any peace
> In ever climbing up the climbing wave?

Evidently Peggy's sympathies lay rather with the alternative offered by Tennyson's vigorous Ulysses in the ringing exhortation adopted as school motto by Peggy's Neepawa Collegiate Institute: "To strive, to seek, to find, and not to yield." The resolution of "Pagan Point" is merely apparent; the appealing rhetoric of closure is illusory and conceals the absence of real denouement.

And then there is the voice of the loon: it sounds a sharply alien note and challenges the dominant implication of the poem's proffered resolution at its end—that God's in His heaven and all's right with the world. The loon gives deeper significance to the conflict between the rude pagan and the civilized Christian religious attitudes and also vivifies the natural setting of the poem. The loon and its raucous cry have introduced the pagan/heathen intrusion; the loon is cohort of Neptune and Thor, and its voice utters the same message as theirs. Furthermore, the loon is unmistakably a "real" phenomenon of nature, while Neptune and Thor are comparatively figurative, metaphorical. The apparent triumph at the end of the poem has therefore subdued not only the pagan gods but the *natural* bird as well: "the marsh birds call no more." Nature—vibrant nature—has been more than subdued; it has been overcome.

The important role of the loon emphasizes the almost covert criticism of that kind of Christianity (all too pervasive in young Peggy's experience) that denies true life and urges instead its evasion and the substitution of a quest for peace, quiet, rest, and the descent of night—

and that therefore turns mankind against the claims of nature and so, finally, against itself.

The cry of the loon recurs persistently in the adult writing of Margaret Laurence, urging its natural but alienated claim to freedom from the persecution of civilization's laws and religion's rules, and so playing a significant role in further criticism, not only of those Christian attitudes, but of political and cultural attitudes as well. The deities of "Pagan Point," drawn from Roman and Scandinavian mythology, give way, in Margaret Laurence's African fiction, to the gods of pre-colonial Africa. In that fiction, the conflict is waged between the appeal of old, pagan, African deities and that of the newly introduced Christian deity. In Laurence's subsequent Canadian fiction, the alienated loon is associated not so much with pagan deities as with the First Nations people—often only dubiously tutored in Christianity (and hence like some of her native Africans) and therefore pagan and indeed heathen in the eyes of Canadian WASP colonial eyes. "Pagan Point" is rather a remarkable achievement for a teenager, and it offers important insights into the developing mind and talent of Peggy Wemyss.

The other poem, "Christmas Card" (December 1943), presents a similar dilemma of faith but emphasizes the obverse side of the coin. Rather sophisticated stylistically, it is a series of non-end-stopped iambic pentameter couplets, which gives a sense of headlong pursuit of a satisfactory solution to an urgent problem. The first dozen lines offer a realistic description of the Christmas card—wishing "A Merry Xmas and a glad New Year"—that leads to the gently cynical, rhetorical question, "But how / Could we be happy, singing carols now?" "Now," the moment of composition, was four years into a dreadful war with no clear indication of a possible end, let alone a victory, with many young men, her near contemporaries, already killed in battle. Further, her memory ranges over Christmases "throughout the years—/ Some quick with joy, and others, ours, in tears."

As she ponders the scene, she has a vision of "that first, weary Christmas night," and is led to the poem's first climax.

> I had insisted that my faith was light,
> Yet, as I saw the picture of that night,
> My thoughts were humble and I felt the gleam
> Of beauty in the tale, as in a dream
> The crystal-clear of things unseen one gains,
> And wakened, only emptiness remains. (11, 31-36)

In spite of her claim that her faith was light, she had apprehended the gleam of beauty in the Christmas tale, the beauty that is its truth—the "crystal-clear of things unseen." Wakened, however, she has lost that vision or, at the very least, the ability to give it verbal expression: "These things I could but think, could never say." But as she lists the tangible details of her memories of past Christmases—King George VI's message to the Empire, the Christmas tree itself and the kindred spruce outside, the snow and the sleigh bells, Santa Claus, the Christian church service—she grasps again, via those very things, the essence of Christmas. Furthermore, she briefly anticipates an ecumenical tendency that will develop in her adult work: "The spirit is the same, / I think, throughout the world at this one season. / Although traditions differ without reason." Her vision, dwelling on the data of Christmas, has penetrated to their essence; she does not now waken to find emptiness nor does the means of expression fail her. The poem concludes with a ringing affirmation:

> We must not let this Christmas spirit fade.
> For those brave people, who this night have prayed
> For strength to kill oppression, we must try
> To see that our, and their, faith does not die.
> This vision is of faith that reaches far,
> Of children, gazing at a tinsel star,
> Not knowing that they gaze beyond the skies.
> Nothing must blot that glory from their eyes. (11, 79-86)

It is important to remember that while "Pagan Point" was evidently a rather private performance, "Christmas Card" was a comparatively public one. That is not to say, however, that one is necessarily more personal than the other or more clearly represents Peggy's "real" feelings and ideas. The tension between the attitudes expressed was drawn taut on various occasions during her mature life until it was resolved in her late years.

Grade twelve was demanding, sobering, and maturing. Many educators reckoned that grade twelve was more demanding and rewarding than the first year of college. Certainly the English program was quite substantial and it was accompanied by history, French, mathematics, chemistry, and typing. The grade twelve English course included two novels, Jane Austen's *Pride and Prejudice* and Thomas Hardy's *The Return of the Native*; the drama section, Euripides's *Electra* (in translation), and a Shakespeare, a Shaw, and a Galsworthy; the poetry anthology featured Wordsworth, Tennyson, Browning, and a sampling of Georgians and Edwardians; and always many compositions to write.[14] Four, three-hour, final examinations in June tested students on the work of the entire year in those four areas.

As the end of high school approached, the four girls of Peggy's group grew increasingly restless in their eager desire to escape Neepawa, where everyone seemed to know everyone else's business (or think they did) and the moralistic attitude was prominent. Racial prejudice flourished, hypocrisy was vibrantly alive, cultural and religious bigotry festered; in a word, the establishment WASP mentality was pervasive.

At least that was the Neepawa environment as perceived by Peggy and her closest chums. Escape from such a claustral atmosphere seemed also to offer the opportunity to discover and embrace one's own individual identity. That aspect of the girls' shared restlessness is illustrated by Peggy's way of expressing her exasperation over Neepawa's restraint: "I'm tired of being 'Bob Wemyss' daughter.'" Her father had died when she was eight and a half; her memories of him were warm; but his public persona, as she remembered, representing those features of class, religion, culture, seemed to restrict Peggy herself to a public persona—to prevent her being Peggy Wemyss. Wes McAmmond summed up the situation sympathetically as he looked back to the eighteen-year-old he had known forty years earlier and offered this balanced estimate: "She was tied down. She was at home in a community. Everybody knew who she was. . . . She couldn't take liberties. She could not have fun! I think she was quite glad when she got going to Winnipeg."[15]

The end of grade twelve and the end of summer opened the door to escape to freedom, to The City, where they would pursue higher education—and sophistication. That fall they boarded the train for Winnipeg with some trepidation but great exultation. Margaret Laurence's retrospective view of that escape, thirty years later, was apt: "it's a bloody good thing you got away from this dump. . . . [But] then I found the whole town was inside my head, for as long as I live."[16]

three

Leaning into the Future

IN THE AUTUMN OF 1944, PEGGY WEMYSS FOLLOWED THE PATH her uncle Stuart Simpson had taken when he left Neepawa and went to the city; she enrolled in United College. In the 1940s, Winnipeg, capital of Manitoba, was, and to some extent remains, important as a railway hub and the centre of grain markets in western Canada and for its vital cultural life. When Peggy arrived, the population was nearing half a million, and Winnipeg offered a rich ethnic congeries of mainly European races that tended to keep their languages and cultural traditions alive and intact in the new world. Unlike the United States, Canada has never really fancied itself as a melting pot. The new Canadians typically had their own churches, where services were conducted in their native tongues, and their own native-language newspapers. There was a large Jewish community in the North End and another, somewhat smaller, in the South End. Everywhere, of course, were the establishment WASPs. On the east bank of the Red River was the smaller city of St. Boniface, principally francophone and Roman Catholic, and clinging fiercely to its cultural traditions.

United College on Portage Avenue had originally been Wesley College (after John Wesley), but, following its merger with Presbyterian Manitoba College in 1938—the union of Methodists, Congregationalists, and some Presbyterians in 1925 had founded the

United Church of Canada—it assumed its new name. United College focussed on the liberal arts and Christian evangelism based on Christ's words, "Feed My Sheep," and with special attention to preparation of Protestant clergy. That education and training were informed by the social gospel and a distinctly leftist political orientation, an orientation that had begun half a century earlier.

When Wesley College was founded in 1888, the Reverend J.W. Sparling became principal. He immediately turned to recruitment of faculty, and his first choice was the Reverend Salem Bland to teach New Testament exegesis and church history. The young Bland, comfortably established at Queen's College (now Queen's University), declined the offer but in 1903 did join Sparling's staff. Bland was perhaps the leading exponent of the social gospel in Canada, and soon became a popular lecturer in the college and preacher in the churches of Winnipeg. He believed that the main thrust of Jesus's mission was social reform and social cooperation, and he insisted that such cooperative endeavour for the reformation of society should guide the church into the future.[1]

Bland was soon joined by James S. Woodsworth, a graduate of Wesley College and a medallist in Mental and Moral Philosophy. He offered a course in Living Issues, following his own practical involvement in directing All People's Mission in north Winnipeg. There he confronted the problems of poverty and social neglect among the immigrants from eastern Europe who had poured into Canada.[2] The strong leftist leanings of Bland and Woodsworth led to conflict with the governing board of the college and most of its benefactors. In 1917 Bland was forced to quit his position at Wesley. Woodsworth, by that time pursuing a political career, resigned from that board. He later became leader of the Cooperative Commonwealth Federation (CCF), precursor of the New Democratic Party (NDP).[3]

The traditions of Bland and Woodsworth were carried on by such figures as the Reverend Stanley Knowles, a Wesley graduate of 1933, who was first elected to the House of Commons in 1942—representing

Winnipeg North Centre—as a member of the CCF and subsequently of the NDP. During his forty years in the House of Commons, Knowles became an icon of the Canadian political left. When Peggy entered United College, the intellectual atmosphere was still marked by the legacy of Bland, Woodsworth, and Knowles.

Peggy's major was English literature, but two of the most influential professors under whom she studied were Dr. A.R.M. Lower (history) and the Reverend David Owen (philosophy). In the fall of 1939, Owen and Lower had joined with a member of the CCF, Lloyd Stinson (Wesley graduate), to send a letter to the Canadian prime minister protesting the enactment of the Defense of Canada Regulations of 3 September 1939.[4] The Regulations extended the powers granted a quarter century earlier by the Canadian War Measures Act, which gave the prime minister virtually dictatorial control over the government. Lower expressed the grievance:

> The Canadian War Measures Act was the most complete surrender of parliamentary power made by any English-speaking country (except Newfoundland) since 1540. . . .
>
> The War Measures Act . . . at the opening of the Second World War [reappeared as] an even more stringent and arbitrary set of "Defense of Canada Regulations." It was to do grave injury to the structure of Canadian democracy.[5]

The impact of Lower, Owen, and English professor A.L. Phelps on the students of United College is inestimable; they gave a distinct leftist quality to the intellectual atmosphere of the institution. Some indication of that quality—significant for the development of young minds like Peggy's—occurs in a footnote to Lower's *Colony to Nation*, amplifying his observations on Hitler's Nazism as compared to Western liberalism:

> Protestanism is a "Welt-Bejahung," an affirmation of life; it

> is dynamic and realistic. In its more evangelical forms, it can find liaisons and sympathies with Communism, which possesses its own evangelical social drive. Both Protestantism and Communism look forward to the bettering of man's fate on earth.... Capitalism is simply a pagan attitude towards power and self, and so may shelter with any of these creeds that seem as if they might be of use to it. (556)

Peggy's English program was restricted to writers of the British Isles but was a fairly extensive introduction to that literature from Chaucer to the poets of World War I. Prominent among her professors was Arthur L. Phelps, a bald pixie of a man, not unlike Clement Atlee in appearance, manner, and political persuasion. Phelps wandered around the large Convocation Hall, lecturing on Shakespeare and coyly launching leftist political barbs with appropriate contemporary reference. He was also Faculty Director of the English Club, a group of select Seniors who glanced at recent poetry and discussed Canadian poets—Roberts, Carman, Lampman, Pauline Johnson. Peggy wandered innocently in on the group—a sophomore and co-ed—and was quietly welcomed by Phelps and the club. The event is recalled in *Dance on the Earth* (94-95).

During Peggy's first year in college, returnees from service in the armed forces began to appear in her classes, and the first peacetime autumn in six years, 1945, witnessed a virtual inundation of veterans. Of her old friends, Margie Crawford was at United, but in the science program; Mona Spratt and Louise Alguire were at the University of Manitoba campus in suburban Fort Garry. Madge Hetherington (from Carman, Manitoba) came nearest to replacing Mona as bosom pal; the two decided not to overdo things by becoming roommates, so Peg spent the year with Helen Warkentin in the women's residence. Two young women writers were also important to Peggy: the beautiful and talented Patricia Ann Jenkins, who completed two novels, *A*

Candle to Light the Sun and *From Heaven with a Shout*, under her married name, Blondal, and died in the first bloom of life, shortly after marriage; the other was Mary Turnbull, a year or two older than Peg, independent and sophisticated, who contributed poetry to the university newspaper, *The Manitoban*.

I was regularly in English classes with Peg, including Honours classes—where she was welcome although not officially in the five-year Honours English program. Even in the large lecture classes she was occasionally quite visible—and audible. The usually shy and quiet coed would become spirited and argumentative when the topic roused her and she felt at home on her own turf. She won the Sir James Aikens Scholarship in English ($125) for her third-year work, 1945-1946. The small, intimate Honours classes easily fostered sympathetic camaraderie. My good friend Jack Borland and I quickly became chums (and Borland something more) with Peg. We were also in a psychology class together, taught by an unforgettable clergyman/professor named Cragg. He was capable of illustrating human aesthetic response (as he once did for us) by reference to an easily recognizable young lady in the college: "When she asks me a question and bats those long lashes at me—my shoe-laces become untied!" I remember sitting alone in Tony's coffee shop a day or so later and there overhearing an exchange between Peg and Madge as they bustled out to their next class: "And maybe that's why you and I like hot dogs too much." "Say—that's right!" Sophisticated chuckles.

Peggy's beau in those years was Jack Borland, a young writer, like Mary and Pat. Jack was her first love and came near to being her first lover. They had a good deal in common: both were quite conscious of their Scottish heritage; he had spent his early years in Brandon, just south of Neepawa; and they were writers. Borland became editor of the United College magazine *Vox*, and Peg became his assistant editor. Another student, not then a close friend but destined to become so, was Lois Freeman—a bright, studious, and athletic young woman; she was also the youngest daughter of the Dean of Theology. At the eleventh hour Lois decided against studying physical education and turned to theology. She married fellow student Roy Wilson and both entered the clergy—and with it the tradition of Bland, Woodsworth, and Knowles. In 1980 Lois was elected Moderator of the United Church of Canada—the first woman to serve as head of a mainstream Canadian religious denomination. She was appointed to the Canadian Senate in 1998 and served to 2002.

The influx of veterans in 1945 obliged the college to add faculty. Two attractive additions were Doris Peterson (University of Minnesota) and Robert N. Hallstead (Indiana University). Peggy began a fruitful friendship with Hallstead that lasted until his death in 1967; his lovely wife, Anne, remained her friend for another twenty years. The policy of reciprocal exchange between the university proper and its associated colleges led Peggy to two other significant connections. The first was with Dr. Malcolm Ross, whose challenging course "English Thought in the Seventeenth Century" she took in 1947. He encouraged her in her writing and later, as editor of the *Queen's Quarterly Review*, published one of her earliest adult stories. The second was with a young woman from the Jewish community in Winnipeg's North End, Adele Wiseman. From different campuses and separated by age and class year, they were inevitably drawn together. They dated their friendship from the summer following Peggy's graduation. Shared interest in writing and in political persuasion, as well as their common experience in Ross's seminar, quickly made them fast and permanent friends.[6] Adele would never replace Mona, but she assumed an increasingly important role in Peggy's life, especially as the two began to achieve recognition as writers.

An important part of Peg's extracurricular education came to her in the institution known as "Tony's." It was a combination coffee shop, cafeteria, lunchroom, and general gathering spot, located on the basement floor of the college. There one met friends, engaged in gossip and serious intellectual discussion, or maybe just relaxed over a cup of coffee. It was named after the genial proprietor, Tony Kozyra, who is fondly remembered in *Dance on the Earth*:

> In the days before student counselling, any student with a problem could unburden himself or herself to Tony and be certain of a sympathetic listener. If you were broke, he would let you have a coffee and a doughnut on credit, though it was a point of honour to pay him back as soon as humanly possible. We would sit there for hours after classes or in the evening, talking interminably. Those of us who were writing would show one another our poems and stories. Mostly, however, our two favourite topics of discussion were religion or politics. (97)

Indeed. But a fairly important lacuna lurks between the last two sentences. There was also discussion of literature, especially Canadian literature: Peggy, Mary Turnbull, Borland, and (occasionally) Pat Blondal showed their pieces to each other in the hope that they might one day be part of that literature. A good deal of the discussion centred on the question "What *is* Canadian literature?"

In a brief interview with *Booktalk*, Farley Mowat looked back on the condition of Canadian literature in the years immediately following World War II: "In the early fifties, there was no such thing as a body of Canadian writing. Popular writers were Americans and a few Canadians who'd made it in the States or England. We had to create something from the raw materials right here in this country."[7] It was a dilemma that engaged Peggy and continued to do so persistently and with increasing anguish in subsequent years.

In Tony's she was often in company with the dark-eyed beauty Madge Hetherington, rather more sophisticated, worldly-wise, and self-possessed than Peggy, who was somewhat naïve and innocent, and certainly shy and unsure—until she found herself in a discussion of literature or of the means of achieving social justice or of the purpose and function of religion. Faculty members, some three or four, would be seen in Tony's, but only occasionally; it was a student refuge. Peggy would hurry into Tony's after class or out of Tony's to her next class; she always seemed to be hurrying, eager, her books clutched a bit defensively to her bosom, and she herself always leaning forward from the waist, perhaps determined to break the barricades that confined her to where she was.

There were no creative writing courses in Canadian universities then and certainly not at United College; but there were outlets for good student writers—the all-university newspaper *The Manitoban* and the quarterly put out at United College, *Vox*.

Margaret Laurence recounts that her debut as a student writer was a step taken in fear and trembling:

> Writing by women, in those and the following years, was generally regarded by critics and reviewers in this country with at best an amused tolerance, at worst a dismissive shrug. . . . when I first submitted poems to the University of Manitoba student paper, *The Manitoban*, I sent them in under the name of Steve Lancaster. After the Lancaster bomber, and I had always liked the name Steve.[8]

There is no reason to doubt the veracity of this recollection, unverified though it remains. The stern masculinity of her *nom de plume*, however, failed to win acceptance from the editors. Peggy's hesitancy, in fact, appears to have been somewhat ill-founded. The pages of *The Manitoban* in the fall of 1944 were liberally sprinkled with the names of female authors—Mary Elizabeth Bayer, Marion Ruth Tapper, Lorna Torgerson, Mary Turnbull, Kathleen Watson, among others. Those were not coy pseudonyms chosen by shy male poets. Peggy's own shyness and timidity obliged her to continue masking her sexual identity as published author throughout most of her first year at United College.

Half a dozen of her works (one brief piece of prose fiction and five poems) were published in *The Manitoban* during the first four months of the school year. All but one of those items were signed with only her initials, "J.M.W." The second, her first published poem of college days,[9] was signed "J.M. Wemyss," but, since the fall term was then (13 October 1944) barely a month old, she probably felt her anonymity safe. Her first publication in *Vox* (April 1945) carried her full name, "Jean Margaret Wemyss." Her next two poems in *Vox* (June 1945) relaxed into "Peggy Wemyss."

Between 6 October 1944 and March 1947, Peggy published a total of seventeen poems (eight in *The Manitoban* and nine in *Vox*), three pieces of prose fiction (one in *The Manitoban* and two in *Vox*), and one essay in literary criticism (in *Vox*). The earliest of these (prose) appeared in *The Manitoban* for 6 October 1944, the last in *Vox* for March 1947. Her poetry is markedly superior to her fiction—as was the case with her publications during high school in *Annals of the Black and Gold*. In fact, the fiction—except for the brief initial sketch of 6 October 1944—is singularly uninspired, while some of the poetry is quite engaging. The comment she offers in *Dance on the Earth* on the relationship of these two literary genres as they seemed to her when a student is rather persuasive and constitutes a plausible explanation:

> I was mainly writing poetry, not because my talent particularly lay in that direction but . . . I didn't have enough time to concentrate on prose. Poetry . . . often appeals to young writers as being more in accord with youthfully intense, and usually intensely subjective, feelings. (95-96)

Many of Peggy's poems are in free verse but some are in formal stanza patterns: one is a nearly perfect Petrarchan sonnet, another a lovely little sonnet *manqué*—twelve lines instead of fourteen, and iambic hexameter instead of pentameter—and a beauty in blank verse graced with irregular but gently reverberating rhyme.

Understandably, Peggy's poetry was strongly and most immediately influenced by World War II, which dominated the world while she was a teenager and through her first year of college. A frequent theme in this poetry is alienation from the world and human society and, consequently, loneliness and the desire to escape. The earliest (*The Manitoban*, 13 October 1944) is a lament for the dead—"the sickening torrents of bright blood / Of young men who wished desperately to live"—that opens with an anguished confession of the need to escape, to fly away, "Far away from the terror of brutality, / Away from the strangled cries of women, / The great dry sobs of men whose sons are dead."

And, with that, the desire to escape a world where she is "forced by trivial minds / To mouth trite nothings or explain inanities." The concluding line carries the explanation, "For my heart is sick of a heart-sick world." Her last poem (*Vox*, March 1947), shortly before her graduation—"Bread Hath He"—reiterates the theme of alienation and lovelessness, the failure of human communication. The controlling voice in the majority of her poems is that of the loner, one who has been alienated by the harshness of life and the inadequacies of human response to that prospect, and by the sadness of lost or unattainable love. Furthermore, these poems are without human presence, other than that of the persona who utters her lament. An exception is "Bus Ride at Night" (*The Manitoban*, 20 October 1944); the bus is a kind of corporate womb protecting the riders from the threatening darkness outside. Yet even these riders are unindividuated creatures who share only their loneliness: "Apart we are, with no communication, Alone . . . / Alone . . . / Locked in our own isolated minds."

The loner, the alienated persona, is certainly a reflection of Peggy's temperament during these months, but that is not the whole story. She socialized with fellow students, laughed readily, and enjoyed her special relationship with Borland—who resumed college, as I did, as a veteran in the fall of 1945—and one or two other men. But there was always a facet of her personality that needed its own private space and that asserted itself unmistakably at various times. Jack Borland recalled an impressive instance that occurred during a late-August evening around a bonfire on the shores of Lake Brereton (near the Manitoba-Ontario border); friends Mary Turnbull, Hart Bowsfield, and Nestor Swystun were with them, drawn into quiet conversation. Borland suddenly realized Peggy was no longer with the group; he went to look for her. He soon found her, lying on her back further down the shore and peering up through the darkness. "Are you all right?" he asked. "Oh sure," she said. "I just had to get away and look at the stars." So had she always been, but that need was easily aggravated by the stimuli indicated in Peggy's poems. The persona of the poems must seek solace, alone, as expressed in the opening line of "Thought" (*The Manitoban*, 13 October 1944)—"I have need of wind and hilltops."

None of the poems develops the theme of blessed—indeed, divine—nature more thoroughly than "The Imperishable" (*The Manitoban*, 17 October 1944), fifty-four lines of free verse in praise of the eternally nurturing natural world. It is rich in literary echoes, a mélange of Wordsworth's pantheism, Gray's melancholy flowers "born to blush unseen" ("Elegy Written in a Country Churchyard"—"Some village Hampden, . . . Some mute inglorious Milton, . . . Some Cromwell guiltless of his country's blood"), and Rupert Brooke's slight variation of that in "The Soldier." It begins, "This is earth, the mother," and contrasts her creative and nurturing character with mankind's stupidity and insincerity, and the destructiveness of war—"the twisted dead bodies of young men." And here rise the echoes of Gray and Brooke:

> Perhaps some farmer will turn up a skull with his plough,
> . . .
> Where now he grows his prize wheat.
> Perhaps he will even ponder for a moment,
> Thinking of the boy, and wondering
> If he might have become a great poet or scientist
> Had he not been killed. . . . (11, 23-30)

Peggy's loving description of nature rises finally to a fervent note of praise:

The furrows curve gently toward the green hillside,
And the long sweep of her, the good black soil,
Is outlined clearly against the wide arch of the sky.
Her beauty is in every blade of grass, every tree and flower,
(11, 35-38)

The climax resonates with biblical echoes of Ecclesiastes and Revelation:

She remains,
Because always there will be birth and death, seedtime and
harvest.
This is earth, the mother, the maker and breaker,
The sower and reaper, the beginning and the end.
(11, 51-54)

A more personal and intimate application of the theme appears in the much briefer "This is a land of living things" (*Vox*, June 1945) that affirms

Nothing here is of the dead.
Quietly I walk, wind cloaked,
Hearing the rain's promise
That this land will be my immortality.

This is a corrective to the lurking attraction of permanent escape from mankind's "stupidity and insincerity." Peggy had come closest to that idea of escape in the first poem she published in *Vox* (April 1945), called simply "Song." A correct enough Petrarchan sonnet that anticipates unifying love in a realm beyond time, when

day and night are through. . . .
In the last port
Fearless, eternal, we will realize
One integrated life, the barriers past,
Soul fused in separate soul, no longer lost. (11, 12-14)

There is an alternative to this passive, alienated persona, one ready to confront the threatening forces, less ready to blame "them" than to blame "us": the "Invicta" persona (to adapt the title of Henley's once popular "Invictus"). This persona belongs with the raucous intruders of "Pagan Point"—Neptune, Thor, and the loon. She appears in "Clay-fettered Doors" (*The Manitoban*, 9 November 1945). "I know you. I've seen you before," she begins, addressing someone (clearly herself) who is seeking "a nameless lost thing"—finally identified as "someone who answers to the name of God." She mocks the seeker, who has looked vainly in all the approved places—emporiums of material goods, political arenas, church, and even

> . . . the solid Parliament buildings,
> Stodgy and traditional as plum pudding; practical—
> (Christ, man! Didn't you know that they're busy with
> Affairs
> of State
> there, and even the CCF can't tell you the right
> address?)

The poem ends with the suggestion that the seeker (looking for . . . God) has not looked in the right place—but

> . . . perhaps it wouldn't work after all—
>
> Because it's hard to look people straight in the eye,
> And tear away gently the carefully woven masks.

This implication that divinity resides within the human soul makes a strong connection with "The Imperishable"—that nature too is divine. This theme resurfaced twenty years later in the Manawaka fiction of Margaret Laurence.

One aspect of the satire in "Clay-fettered Doors," the church's failure to satisfy the seeker, is developed in the sonnet *manqué*, "The Departure" (*The Manitoban*, 26 January 1945).

I think there was a woman upon the hill that day,
Young and fair as morning, with loosely-bound hair,
Pure as the pale lilies among the grasses there,
A woman with warm eyes, kneeling as if to pray,
And praying not, but watching the silver morning lake;
A new faint sky with one star not gone;
The hushed forest shining with the light of dawn;
And listening to the low-voiced shore waves break.
"Man with worker's hands, I have watched you walk away.
Strong one, I loved you—will the world so love your life?
Jesus, son of Joseph, I would have been your wife."
I think there was a woman upon the hill that day.

The early voice of Peggy's Christian humanism, the poem anticipates her adult commitment to the social gospel. The "woman upon the hill" is a sister to the Invicta persona: each could have wed this "Man with worker's hands" who has little in common with the "gentle Jesus meek and mild" of some traditions familiar to Peggy.

The Invicta persona speaks again in the last two poems of Peggy's college days, "Song of the Race of Ulysses" and "Bread Hath He," both in the March 1947 *Vox*. The first reviews the opposing forces that sustain the tension in "Pagan Point," the old intrusive heathen gods and the later god of the Christian. The speaker begins, "Yes, I shall tend this gentle hearth, / Because you will it so," but chafes under the yoke of "this your peace." This descendant of Ulysses explains, "there are roads not seen by your calm eyes, / Roads my feet have fiercely trod." Further memories are dark but demanding—"dark altars" and "the heathen gods / That cleft with me the foam-racked oceans, laughing." The dominance of "the loneliness / . . . blended with a reverence, a peace" found in "Pagan Point" is here tenuous. (It is unmistakably Tennyson's Ulysses, the re-domesticated hero, the "idle king," that prompts Peggy's hand: "I cannot rest from travel; I will drink / Life to the lees.") The appeal of the old dispensation has not abated, and if the pagan summons is uttered again through the medium of nature, the speaker will respond positively:

> This alone of vagrant thoughts I surely know—
> That if the pines, harped with black thongs of wind,
> Should mould a harsh exultant symphony of storm,
> I would arise unquestioning and follow.

The speaker desires challenge, not passivity, engagement rather than mere peace.

This speaker resembles some of the personae of Robinson Jeffers, who engaged Peggy's interest at this time, and was the subject of the only critical essay she published during her student days, "The Earlier Fountain: A Study of Robinson Jeffers, his Early Poems and Philosophy." It shares space with her final two poems—the Ulysses "Song" and "Bread"—in the March 1947 *Vox*. Peggy's judgement of Jeffers helps explain the submerging of the passive, accepting, alienated sufferer and the emergence of the active, rebellious, unconquerable alien, especially in "Song of the Race of Ulysses." In her essay she relishes the vigour, toughness, and sinewy muscularity of Jeffers's prosody and the vitality of his characters:

> men and women who move against these strange, wild backgrounds. His people are, as a rule, superactive and violent, tense and turbulent embodiments of the dark potential of the human mind. His most powerful characters, such as Tamar Cauldwell and Orestes, pass through the stage of humanity and succeed in breaking away from it, becoming no longer human beings, but walking alone in the harsh freedom of natural forces.

It seems that Peggy found in Jeffers's characters a realization of her own early idea of the alienated persona. She confesses, however, that "portrayal of an attempt to escape from humanity as being a wholesome reaction . . . seems to me unhealthy." What she finds to condemn in Jeffers's poetry and philosophy is, furthermore, something very like the most salient feature of much of her own poetry of these years: "Jeffers seems to desire to cast away humanity, to escape from the tangled network of human nerves into the freer life of nature. It is obvious that this morbid defeatism serves nothing." The sense of strength and determination that comes from such a pronouncement suggests that Peggy had come to terms with herself and taken a further step into maturity.

She had come to the big city, more than two years earlier, in a surge of relief at her escape from small-town Neepawa and expecting liberation in the city and the college. She could rely on the confidence built upon her successes in Neepawa Collegiate Institute and in her home town, but at United College she found herself grouped with numerous other local success stories. How would she measure up? Furthermore, Peggy's background was emphatically female; Grandpa Simpson was the sole male figure in the family (except for little brother Robert)—and Grandpa was a horror. She had one boyfriend in high school; he left after grade eleven. She was in love with Derek, the English airman, for a few weeks; then he was seen no more. There was the lost Lorne, for the moment forgotten. Now, in the coeducational mix of United College, in the midst of a city full of men, a new problem confronted Peggy: was she pretty enough, nicely enough dressed, "desirable" enough? Her very reluctance to expose her identity in *The Manitoban*—the fruits of that vital, impertinent talent—submitting her first poems under the pseudonym "Steve Lancaster" (if she actually did) and signing her publications with initials alone—indicated her concern about her own femaleness as much as about her prowess as a writer.

Attention she received from Jack Borland bolstered her sense of herself as a desirable woman, a potential sexual partner. Borland's increasingly urgent attentions became, however, a mixed blessing for Peggy, whose sense of sexual propriety had always been strong: though welcome, they had to be arrested at the point propriety demanded. The relationship she had with Borland embraced both her female identity and her identity as a writer: she became both his sweetheart and his assistant in the literary endeavours of *Vox*. All this helps to account for the strength, confidence, and control expressed in her final poems and her literary essay in *Vox* in March 1947.

A complication arose in her final year of college. Frustration engendered by the social relationship of Peggy and Borland finally led to its alteration: at a party late in the fall term of 1946 (perhaps it was a pre-Christmas Ball), we were all more or less together and paired off, but Borland escorted home someone other than Peggy. Precisely why, no one else seems to have known. A terrible blow to Peg's self-esteem, it also caused an upheaval in the domestic setting she shared with Mary Turnbull and Madge Hetherington: Madge left them rather abruptly, breaking off a sturdy friendship. But Peggy's relationship with Borland was unbroken—only altered. Soon enough there was to be compensation for Peggy, balm for a bruised ego, with the appearance of an older, more experienced, and sophisticated man (with a moustache) in her life. And she continued to write.

"Bread Hath He," her last published poem and final piece of writing for student publications, reflects something of her turbulent young life. "Bread" had been anticipated by a pair of lyrics in *The Manitoban* for 13 October 1945, which share the theme of the Solace of Song. The first, "Someday I shall make me a song," is a mélange of the Solace of Nature and the Solace of Song themes: the speaker will make her song of laughter and pain but also of various attractive features of nature (wind, leaves, rain, oceans); she and her song "will tramp the fields" and so escape—"Touching not the frost of their hearts / And listening not to their bitter talk." The second lyric, "When songs are sung," indicates the hoped-for result of the songs, the speaker's ability to release the unresponsive beloved—"and set / The memory of you free. / . . . / And stand at last alone to meet / The phantom winds of night."

"Bread Hath He," however, is more cerebral than emotional: "Because there is no breaking through / Your iron-sheathed spirit," she announces dispassionately—not sadly—she will stoically accept necessity. She offers a brief catalogue of hurts, yet is firmly controlled; and the poem ends where it began—but with an extra step: "Because there is no breaking through /—Let us sing songs against the impending shadows." She both inculpates herself in the diagnosis and includes the failed lover in the solution of the dilemma: "Let us sing. . . ." The principal difference in this utterance of quiet control is that Song becomes an alternate option—neither a companion in escape nor an anodyne.

The only clear reflection of those preoccupations among the prose fiction Peggy published appears in *The Manitoban* for 6 October 1944, a vignette entitled "Fallen King," her college debut. A little boy and his mother visit the zoo; a large polar bear draws their attention. "He had been powerful. He had been a king. His eyes blazed for an instant, then the fires died." The bear is another version of Tennyson's idle king, Ulysses—"How dull it is to pause, to make an end, / To rust unburnished . . . / As though to breathe were life!" The last anthropomorphizing description of the bear concludes, "With his nose buried in the sand, and his old eyes half-closed, he is dreaming—dreaming of the smooth, cool snow-drifts and the flash of Northern Lights in the land of his youth." He is the imprisoned alien, rendered passive and impotent. Peggy succeeds in enlisting our sympathies with the bear and implying that this bear is a mask of humanity's imprisoned nobility—as if the mask had contained a man.

The other two pieces of prose fiction are of interest only because of what they try to do—their largely unrealized ideas—and because they suggest her future work. "Calliope" (*Vox*, Graduation 1945) traces the experiences of a boy lost at an almost idle circus: he has all its exciting features—and some of its Steinbeckian heart-of-gold toughs as guides—all to himself. His mother finally shows up (off stage) to "rescue" him for the real world. But he leaves with regret mixed into the relief. Here is the bittersweet ending. As two of his guides watch, the boy turns to cast a smile back at them:

> It was only a faint glimmer of a smile, but suddenly, with a sharp inexplainable sense of loss, they half guessed what it meant.
>
> . . . They stood in silence for awhile, then Steve shrugged his shoulders.
>
> "C'mon, Joe," he said, "how about tellin' me the one about yer castle on th' Rhine?"

There is a sense of lost innocence and lost wonder, like that in James Joyce's "Araby" in *Dubliners*; there is also the strong implication that we need myths that recover the lost wonder—if not exactly the lost innocence.

The title, "Calliope," of course refers to the universally recognized symbol of circus life and its music. But perhaps it offers a bit more than that. It is not hard to discern that the little myth of this story goes further, reinterprets our human need of "bread and circuses," and offers a redeeming identification of those who can supply the nourishment of circuses—for man does not live by bread only. As one of the nine muses, daughter of Jupiter, perhaps the mother of Orpheus, Calliope is traditionally depicted as crowned with laurel, holding in one hand a trumpet and in the other an epic poem. Calliope inspired and presided over the production of the Homeric epics and other long narratives. That bit of significance hints at a covert tribute on Peggy's part to a muse not satisfied with short, occasional poems.

A year later, in the Graduation number of *Vox* for 1946, Peggy published her longest piece of fiction, entitled "Tal des Wald"—"Sylvan Dell" or "Woodsy Vale," in English. A stranger stops in at a watchmaker's shop to have his watch repaired, and casually asks for information about this part of the country, "the ordinary people who worked and suffered to shape the country to the thing it is." The watchmaker tells him the story of Count Brueckner of Austria, dissolute, a young gambler who wasted his inheritance; he pulled up stakes, gathered his remaining possessions—including his faithful peasants—and decamped to Canada to start afresh in the new land. He prospered materially, married, and fathered a son, but wife and child died; further, his peasants gradually became democratized under the influence of their Canadian neighbours and friends, and petitioned the Count to give them their fair share of the estate's material good. Brueckner acceded to their demands and in fact turned over the whole property to them and left to assume . . . the humble trade of watchmaker. The imported Brueckner Austrians have become part of the Canadian mosaic. Perhaps a bit of chauvinist flag-waving on Peggy's part, but she came by the idea for the story quite honestly: she heard it in childhood. Many years later she wrote to her friend Gabrielle Roy to praise her *Children of the Heart* and especially "the little Ukrainian boy with the lark's voice, and . . . Mederic."

> When I was a child, there was an isolated Ukrainian settlement somewhere near Riding Mountain. . . . The local legend was that the settlement had been started by a Hungarian nobleman who had come to Canada, bringing all the Ukrainian peasants and serfs from his old-country estate (the Ukraine then being part of the Austro-Hungarian empire). He had tried to impose a feudal system on "his" people, until they discovered that they did not need to be serfs of his in the new land. I wrote a story about this, when I was in college, long ago. Mederic's father might have been just such a man.[10]

The increasingly urgent problem of sustaining Canadian traditions and identity, while at the same time faithfully retaining the Canadian mosaic, was already becoming a pressing issue for Peggy, as it would for the mature Margaret Laurence.

A further step toward maturity was her becoming assistant editor of *Vox* at the side of Jack Borland during her final year at United College. The last issue of *Vox* for that academic year (typically issued in September of the next academic year), indicates that the assistant editor is "Peggy Laurence." What's in a name?

During the winter and spring of 1947 Peggy shared rooms with Mary Turnbull in a large house on Roslyn Road—just south of the

Assiniboine River and perhaps a few kilometres from the college. What happened was that Peggy had returned from an informal date with her friend Gren Yeo (whom we all knew) and it continued—innocent but unquiet—onto the fire escape of Sparling Hall. She was enjoying an unusual outburst of confidence in her femininity prompted by appropriate attention from a handsome young man. A brisk exchange with the alerted director of the women's residence ensued, which led to a request that Peg move out. She gratefully acted on Mary's invitation to share her digs in a house on Maryland Street at the corner of Westminster Avenue. They stayed there only one month, and in the following months they changed living quarters some three or four times—at one juncture they shared a three-room apartment with Madge Hetherington on Lipton Street, not very far from the college, and at another found themselves in the North End on Selkirk Avenue, away west of McPhillips Street, very far indeed from the college and a good walk from the end of the streetcar line. Finally, near the end of February 1947, they moved into a commodious room; soon after, Peg became aware that an interesting older man was also living with them in the rooming house, one whose path had almost crossed hers during her last year of high school. Another veteran, another Jack.

four

Citizen Peg

DANCE ON THE EARTH RECORDS THE CRUCIAL ENCOUNTER IN the old rooming house on Roslyn Road where Peggy and Mary Turnbull lived during Peg's last year of college—"an elegant place with old wood paneling and high ceilings," an appropriate setting: "This may sound silly, but one day I came into the house and on the stairs stood a young man. I thought his face not only was handsome but also had qualities of understanding. I said to myself, 'That's the man I'd like to marry'" (102).

A bit romanticized, perhaps, but doubtless true enough. Jack Laurence, a young man thirty years of age, was tall, militarily straight, wiry rather than athletic in build, somewhat sharp-featured with a steady, clear-eyed, and serious demeanour, a strong jaw, a level gaze, and a small and neatly trimmed moustache. He had a thick crop of gently wavy brown hair, and a brow reminiscent of Eustacia Vye's friend Wildeve in *The Return of the Native:*

> . . . a . . . crop of hair impending over the top of his face, lending to his forehead the high-cornered outline of an early Gothic shield; and a neck which was smooth and rounded as a cylinder. The lower half of his figure was of light build.

> Although he was one in whom . . . no woman would have seen anything to dislike. (Book First, Chapter V)

In the eyes of the twenty-year-old Peggy, he was an "older" man and evidently a veteran.[1]

She soon learned that he had a Past full of the exotic, the romantic, the altogether admirable—especially as she understood those qualities. And he had a Scottish background, for his father was from the Shetland Isles, not just a Scot like her Wemyss forebears but a Highland Scot. He had emigrated to Canada shortly before the outbreak of the First World War and settled in British Columbia, where he met another immigrant, Elsie Fry, daughter of an Anglican clergyman in Sussex. They married and the young husband went off to war; a son was born the next August 1916, and named John Fergus Laurence. Some nine years after the end of the war, the Laurences moved to Edson, Alberta.

After young Jack, as he was always called, finished public schooling, he hoarded what he earned in Edson until in 1936 he had boat fare to England. There he joined the Royal Air Force and was trained as a mechanic. In 1938 he was posted to India, and during his four years there earned the nickname of "Driver" Laurence because of his pursuit of excellence and efficiency in his work. Shortly after his arrival in India the Second World War broke out. He was returned to the United Kingdom for 1942-43, then sent, as sergeant-instructor, to the air force base at Carberry, Manitoba. There he began a lasting friendship with the Englishman Frank Collier. At the end of 1944 Jack Laurence transferred from the Royal Air Force to the Royal Canadian Air Force, and three weeks later secured his discharge. In the spring of 1945 he completed an accelerated "refresher" course at United College to prepare for university admission and in the fall term he enrolled in the School of Engineering of the University of Manitoba.[2]

Jack's first residence at 139 Roslyn Road had served as the headquarters for a program called "The Prairie School for Social Advance," directed by a native Scot, Watson Thomson. Thomson emigrated to Canada in 1937, ambitious to foster popular education for participatory democracy. This communitarian socialist founded his School for Social Advance in 1944 after teaching at the University of Manitoba and the University of Alberta. When Tommy Douglas was elected premier of the province of Saskatchewan, the first socialist government in North America, he appointed Watson Thomson to head his Adult Education Division. Thomson described his educational vision in this way:

> To see half a million adults in the province (irrespective of nationality or educational background) becoming active and intelligent participants in the business of running their own public affairs, reshaping their environment and seeing the meaning of their own lives and actions against the background of the great world drama of our age. The educational program will not concern itself with academic credits or with subjects. It will be centered on the actual issues and problems of social living here and now.[3]

By the time Jack moved in, 139 had become a rooming house, but had not lost its recent associations. Another disciple of Thomson and a participant in his education philosophy was John Marshall, with his wife Chris. Furthermore, during the last months of World War II, Frank Collier's interest and curiosity led him to knock on the door of 139 Roslyn Road and find it opened by his recently discharged friend Jack Laurence—to the surprise and delight of both men.

Jack's experience in the United Kingdom and India when he was with the RAF had introduced him to the phenomenon of colonialism and its apparent evil effects for colonizer as well as for colonized. He was more than ripe for induction into programs of social improvement. But he did not remain at 139 Roslyn Road. Halfway through his engineering studies, he moved down the street to number 230, where he encountered Peggy Wemyss.

Peggy's going off to college in "the city" was obviously a version of the Great Escape. Jack Laurence seemed to embody most, if not all, of the features of the ideal escape that Peggy was seeking and, in fact, to push the horizons of her young life even further than she had dreamed possible. With all the palpable attractions of the handsome, sophisticated, dashing, and distinctly male virtues, Jack also offered her the protection and guidance she had lost with the death of her father a dozen years earlier.

Peggy had won the Chancellor's Prize for the academic year 1946-47—with a handy sum of $50. At the end of the year she earned the highest marks in English in the whole of the University of Manitoba. She was graduated that spring with a BA and the award of a prize for poetry. In June she and Mary moved again, to an apartment on Broadway (Devon Court).[4] And she was engaged to marry Jack Laurence that fall in the United Church of Neepawa.

The ceremony took place on 13 September, the anniversary of her grandfather Wemyss's marriage in 1893 to Maggie Harrison. It was a small wedding: Peg's maid of honour was Jean Simpson (no kin, but our classmate and my special friend), her bridesmaid was Margie Crawford (childhood friend from Neepawa doing triple duty for the absent Mona Spratt and Louise Alguire), and Jack's best man was John Marshall. The reception was held in the Vivian Street cottage. Borland and I bused out to Neepawa with our classmate Nestor Swystun (my fellow-North-Ender). We three were disappointed that a single glass of wine (I think it was Mogen David) per participant had to suffice for all the toasts. When Peggy came downstairs to join us, she carefully aimed her bridal bouquet at Jean Simpson and hurled a perfect strike. We all knew the die was cast. An unfortunate highlight of the late evening was a political discussion involving mainly the Laurences versus Margie and her consort; it quickly descended into recriminations against the newlyweds—"Reds," "traitors," "Commies"! The rift was not to be mended. Years later (1988) I wrote to Margie asking for information about Peg's childhood; her reply was pithy: "If you're another Communist we have nothing to say to each other." I wrote back to explain I was simply a Christian. Margie saw no deception there and accepted my rather nice distinction.

The Laurences spent their honeymoon at Clear Lake in the Wemyss-Simpson family cottage. In Winnipeg they took the apartment upstairs in the house of Bill and Ann Ross on Burrows Avenue—just up the street from the family home of Adele Wiseman—in Winnipeg's North End. The Rosses were prominent members of Winnipeg's Left for decades. Ann Ross ran a pioneering inner-city health clinic and Bill led Manitoba's communist party from the late 1940s to the 1970s. Peggy and Adele ran into each other at the Ukrainian Labour Temple in North Winnipeg where common interests had drawn them together.[5] Jack resumed his engineering studies and Peggy became a working wife.

The North End (where I lived from birth to age seventeen) was full of European immigrant and first-generation Canadian families, many of them Jewish, who had escaped from political and social persecution and were thus earnestly prepared to embrace a political philosophy that promised freedom from such oppression and urged the necessity of combating the tyrannies responsible for it. I often walked to school with Ruth and Roland, twin children of our communist alderman, Jacob Penner. Keen awareness of continued social inequality and injustice—an awareness Peg and Jack heartily shared—became a common concern, especially among the lower- and middle-class population of that neighbourhood.[6] The environment and its atmosphere contributed much to Peggy's growth and development.

Part of that growth and development resulted from her new career as journalist—a practical application of her literary talents. Her first job was with a frankly communist weekly newspaper, *The Westerner*. The editorial staff included editor Mitch Sago and John Marshall; Roland Penner (future Attorney General of Manitoba and subsequently head of the University of Manitoba Law School) was a frequent contributor. Peg's first two columns, for 6 and 13 September 1947, appeared under her maiden name since she did not become Peggy Laurence until the latter date.

Dance on the Earth confesses that, "At first I didn't realize that it [*The Westerner*] was a Communist paper (I guess I must have been a naïve kid) and when I discovered its political affiliations, I was surprised but not alarmed" (106). Perhaps the "kid" appeared more naïve in retrospect than she had been in actual fact. In any case, she quickly got in tune with the general editorial line—not unmistakably communist, for that matter, but one of social concern and responsibility, reflecting something quite like the attitudes of the social gospel. Peggy's *Westerner* articles tended to cluster around two or three main features of the news scene.

Her initial piece, on the severe polio epidemic in North America—Winnipeg was then "the center of Canada's most highly infected area" (*Westerner*, 6 September, p. 12)—points out the contributive features of social blight, such as infrequent garbage collection and crowded and inadequate housing, and attacks the government for failing to furnish sufficient funds for research into the causes and treatment of polio. The subsequent articles are devoted to a nasty railway accident near Winnipeg in which thirty-one people lost their lives in the instantaneous conflagration that engulfed the thirteen wooden coaches lighted by acetylene gas lamps of Victorian vintage. The first article charges the Canadian National Railway with culpability in using antiquated equipment and refusing to accept responsibility for the accident—and adds that the Canadian Pacific Railway, the other transcontinental line in the Dominion, is similarly culpable. The second article (the first under her married name), three weeks later, reports on the hearing into the accident and itemizes the railway's failure to confront "the real issue . . . that of railroad responsibility for public safety" (the CNR was government-owned); it also exposes the recklessly inadequate conduct of the hearing. Peggy later published stories on the strike of the United Packinghouse Workers against the big meat-packing companies, Burns, Canada Packers, and Swift Canadian, including a dramatic piece heavily dependent on actual dialogue of the strikers and praising what union action has achieved for them in the past (11 October 1947, p. 7). Her article in praise of the *National Affairs Monthly* for its informative accounts of world affairs, such as the emergence of "Europe's new democracies" (25 October 1947), offers a good example of the political "situation" of Peggy's journalism at this moment of her life:

> the new democracies represent a kind of transition between the free enterprise system and socialism. Reactionary forces, however, are still rampant and have not as yet lost their political influence, especially since they gain aid from abroad. The result is a "sharp, extremely fierce class struggle . . . ," with the state on the side of the common people. (13)

Just beside Peggy's long account (in *The Westerner* for 4 October 1947) of the hearing into the railway accident, there is a modest, unsigned article on the attack made by the acting mayor, Alderman C.E. Simonite, on a Mrs. Margaret Chunn. Mrs. Chunn was elected to a two-year term on the Winnipeg City Council in 1947, joining Joe Zuken, Bill Ross's brother, as one of three communists on City Council. She was currently president of the North Winnipeg Branch of the Manitoba Housewives Consumers' Association, a communist-sponsored group that lobbied for daycare, the maintenance of price controls, and a public housing policy.[7] She had led a small delegation of concerned citizens to the mayor's office to ask Simonite to wire Ottawa at once to demand re-establishment of price controls. "Alderman Simonite refused, accusing the delegation of being the representatives of a single political faction"—i.e., communists. The brief article ends with a reference to that evening's city council meeting, at which Alderman Jacob Penner moved that the council urge the federal government to roll back prices and resume price control—the motion to be considered at the next meeting.

Mrs. Chunn contributed regularly to *The Westerner* a column called "As a Housewife Sees It," but in the October 4 issue Peggy Laurence was her guest columnist and she herself was the subject of Peg's interview. The latter half of the column deals specifically with Simonite's performance before the representatives of the Housewives Consumers' Association. Peggy comments on Simonite, "head of one of Winnipeg's largest real estate firms in the city and his charges of 'politics' and 'communism' against Mrs. Chunn and the women's delegation" (11). Mrs. Chunn's response (admiringly reported) is vigorous and pertinent:

> "Of course prices are politics," . . .
>
> "The cry of 'communist,' on the other hand, is nothing more than the old art of red-baiting. Hitler used it, with horrible results. It has always come easy to the lips of every reactionary, big or small. In our case, it is calculated to weaken the growing opposition to high prices and inflation by alienating public feeling and support."
>
> . . . "The red-baiters forget that more than just communists are affected by rising prices, and that organized opposition comes . . . from more than just the communist ranks." (11)

The culmination of the to-do over Alderman Simonite's McCarthyism appears in the 18 October *Westerner* in its exposé criticism of highly dubious journalism used by the Winnipeg *Free Press*. The *Free Press* had fused into a single story two related but entirely distinct events: Simonite's accusation that an unnamed alderman had accepted a bribe; and Simonite's attack on the communist party. The story was accompanied by photos of Alderman Simonite and Alderman Jacob Penner; and a headline above the fused news stories and the pair of photos reads, "Simonite Charges Alderman Took Bribe." The second paragraph of Peggy's critical article underlines the skullduggery involved in the reporting:

> The body of the story made clear to the careful reader that the two [news events—accusation and attack] were in no way connected, but to the casual reader, the man who merely

> glances at the headlines, the bribe charge and the picture of Penner would seem to be one and the same story. (7)

At the end of the article she gives a short account of Alderman Penner's response to Simonite's anti-communist attack (prompted by Jacob Penner's motion on price control and price rollback): "He did not rave like Mr. Simonite, but he answered, quietly and sanely. The Winnipeg Free Press apparently did not regard this as being of news value for they excluded it from their story entirely."

John Marshall, best man at the Laurences' wedding and associate editor of *The Westerner*, contends that in those days and perhaps through most of her life Peggy was "not political."[8] And if one takes the term in its strictest sense, that contention is perfectly credible. Yet her experience with *The Westerner* and its staff evidently educated her sensibilities and gave impetus to distinct tendencies already developing in her. She found the ambience of *The Westerner* sympathetic, and her departure from that setting was tinged with regret. She did not appear in its columns during the month of November 1947; perhaps she was then contributing unfavourable reviews of Canadian communist poetry[9]—but, in any case, an article of quite a different sort from what she had hitherto been contributing appeared under her name in the issue for 6 December 1947, "Build a Library." It is addressed to country towns and offers advice based on Peggy's knowledge of her Mum's successful efforts in Neepawa a generation earlier. The article ends, "This . . . was a good beginning. The next hundred miles will be told in this column in the 'Westerner' two weeks from now" (10). But there were no sequels: *The Westerner* soon folded and she was without a job.

Peggy offered her journalistic talents to the newly created cooperative newspaper *The Winnipeg Citizen*. Its socio-political tendencies were not markedly different from those of *The Westerner*, and Peggy was as much at home in the new environment of *The Citizen*. A sane and mature summary of her impressions of the *Westerner* and its staff and concerns, offered in *Dance on the Earth*, provides a reliable transition to her sense of the new environment.

> I learned a lot at that paper [*The Westerner*]. I learned that the people whom I knew and worked with . . . were very idealistic. They cared about the sufferings of people everywhere. Those old-time Communists in the forties in Winnipeg were not proposing violent revolution. They were proclaiming a need for social justice in terms of our land, and I discovered that many of their views were close to mine. (107)

Two large-circulation daily newspapers in the city were the *Free Press* and the *Winnipeg Tribune*, both evening papers. During the last year of World War II, the idea arose that the city needed a third newspaper to challenge Winnipeggers and give them another slant on the news. Plans to realize the idea were soon formulated. One group, headed by a Marxist professor of history at United College, Harry Ferns, began in 1946 to organize a cooperative venture supported by loan shares of $50 and simple shares of $5 each; the number of shares purchasable by an individual was strictly limited and the number of shares held gave no shareholder a voting advantage—one vote per shareholder was the rule. The group was encouraged to proceed by the outbreak of a strike against the *Free Press* and the *Tribune* by the International Typographical Union late in 1945. During 1946, Harry Ferns's position as president of the new association was looked at askance by influential forces in United College. Wesley McCurdy, chair of the college's fundraising committee, was publisher of the *Winnipeg Tribune*. Dr. W.C. Graham, principal of United College, cautioned Ferns that the college and its benefactors were opposed to his association with the *Citizen* enterprise and he ought to sever his connections with it.

Professor Ferns's dilemma is reminiscent of Reverend Salem Bland's trouble a generation earlier, when his promulgation of the social gospel in and around Winnipeg prompted the businessmen on the college board to effect his dismissal from Wesley College. Harry Ferns defended his political position to W.J. Parker, chair of the Board of Governors of the University of Manitoba, when the university expressed interest in hiring him after his severance from United, by reference to a speech he had given the preceeding November (1946) to the Institute of Canadian-American Relations in St. Paul, Minnesota. Two paragraphs were especially germane—

> You will recall that at one stage Jesus was asked by one of His followers: 'What shall we do to inherit eternal life?' And Jesus, compelled to give a short and essential answer, replied, 'Love God and love one another.' There is the root of the matter. There is the solution for the problem of inner motivation which is, in my opinion, very practical and valuable in the circumstances of our world.
>
> If we accept this Christian guide as the directing force of our lives, we shall, I think, address ourselves to our complex political problems in a satisfactory way because then we will not frame our politics in terms of what is good for me alone, or my family alone, or my class alone or my country alone. We shall frame our policy in answer to the question, What is good for mankind? What can increase eternal life? What can lead us away from the hell of our own making?[10]

That is the heart of the social gospel, as Salem Bland understood it.

Harry Ferns left the *Citizen* group before the newspaper actually began publication, yet his attitudes coloured its news from its initial appearance on 1 March 1948. His position as president was assumed by George J. Reeve, principal of the high school Ferns had attended in north Winnipeg (St. John's Technical High School) and later head of the bible class of which Harry Ferns had been a member, and finally a professor at St. John's College, the University of Manitoba. The evil star of McCarthyism was evidently already gleaming, and *The Winnipeg Citizen* was, from the outset, victimized by those in the grip of the "Red Scare"—even some members of the CCF worried about signs of communist influence they thought they detected in the newspaper.

The first number of the *Winnipeg Citizen*, published on the first Monday in March 1948, presented on its front page, top and centre, a brief, frank "Statement of Faith—and Purpose." Salient among the items in the statement are these:

> Para. 3. "We believe that cooperation is one of the most important means for the development of democracy and world peace."
>
> Para. 8. "The Winnipeg Citizen is not the agency of any political party, industrial organization or special interest."
>
> Para. 9. "It recognizes the right of labor to organize and will employ union labor on its staff."

It would publish daily, Monday through Saturday. Peggy first appeared, under her own byline, in the second number of the paper, on Tuesday, 2 March. "It's in the Air," her series of daily columns on radio programs, began on page 8. The first gave special attention to the genre of radio drama; subsequent columns also covered music programs, various "specials," soap operas, and comedy shows. Music columns covered Canadian conductor Percy Faith, Toronto composer Healey Willan, the area's perennial favourite Jimmie Gowler and the Farmer Fiddlers, and the whole extent of classical and popular music. Other columns featured the comedy of Wayne and Shuster, and radio dramatists Bernard Braden, Fletcher Markle, and Lister Sinclair.

As Peggy grew more confident with her medium, her critical commentary increased and became more personal, and she wrote with assurance about her own tastes and opinions. She was soon given more space, and her critical authority became prescriptive. Peggy had been out of college for barely a year, and she was still a novice, but the quality of her work for the *Citizen* is distinctly higher than her work for *The Westerner*—more confident and more mature. On Wednesday, 21 July, the day's column announced that "'It's in the Air' would appear once a week." Soon she was writing a much more substantial column every Wednesday for the editorial page; the evening's list of programs continued, daily, somewhere between pages 9 and 19.

Peggy's radio columns convey a developing appreciation of radio drama as an artistic medium and led her to theoretic discussion of narrative and dramatic expression generally and the important distinction between them. She emphasized the dramatic mode—non-discursive, non-explanatory, demonstrative—as her preferred type of expression (Henry James's "*show*, don't *tell*"). A representative statement occurs in her column for Thursday, 11 March:

> Radio drama has, in the last ten years or so, accomplished things that are close to stage plays. For a particular kind of drama, the possibilities are almost unlimited.
>
> The stage has the most convincing setting imaginable, namely, that in the listener's mind. . . .
>
> . . . Staging could not possibly satisfy us all, as radio can do by relying on the listener's own mind. It is as though Shakespearean staging, in all its simplicity, were carried one step further. (9)

Peg's column for Monday, 31 May, page 10, chastises NBC for their adaptation of James's *Washington Square* in their "World's Great Novels" series: "there is far too much subtlety in the James novel." It is not, she claims, a question of subtlety per se but of the kind; the adaptation of *Madame Bovary* was quite manageable but "not the subtlety of the raised eyebrow." She makes her case persuasively and without denigrating either the medium or James's fiction; NBC simply made an ill-advised choice. Peggy has a strong word of praise, in her column for Saturday, 20 March, for the CBC dramatization of E.J. Pratt's epic poem *Brébeuf and His Brethern* (1940)—a long narrative she admired: "The C.B.C. did a judicious job of choosing sections to read, so that a sustained drama not found in Pratt's poem was evidenced in the radio adaptation" (16).

Quite as significant are her grapplings with the question of veracity in expression—realism. Some columns, such as that for Friday, 7

May about William Bendix and his long-running serial "The Life of Riley," address the problem of "phoney" realism. She likes Riley, first, because he is "the only radio personage we know who is a working man. . . . He does not . . . leave each morning in his scrupulously neat tweeds, bound for his equally neat office. Riley, bless his heart, is one of the few radio serial people who sound real"; he is "someone who has to work for his living, someone who isn't appallingly clever, someone whose wife doesn't look like Lana Turner and whose children aren't quiz kids, someone, in fact, who is just a likeable, normally smart and normally stupid creature like the rest of us" (15). Further, Riley is your honest-to-goodness *homme moyen sensuel*, the average guy, whom society tends to victimize and who needs to benefit from the kind of social and political reorganization Peg and Jack were currently talking about in the North End. The average guy is, further, victimized artistically to the extent that his kind is missing from the common dramatic depiction in the popular media—especially radio.

Additional comments on realism came in the discussion of a show called "By the Sea." It depends on sea shanties and so on, but its atmosphere is reinforced with touches of "colour" to heighten its credibility: "'fifteen men on a dead man's chest' type of chit-chat . . . to give a sort of salt-breeze atmosphere to the whole thing. Unfortunately it sounds like a group of announcers playing sailor." The problem of realistic depiction was a topic Peg had discussed in common rooms and in Tony's coffee shop at United College: What is Canadian art? How can we recognize it when we run into it? Will it have Mounties and beavers and maple leaves in it?

Peggy's column for Thursday, 11 May shifts her focus to the Canadian scene, specifically the offerings of two series devoted to the prairie provinces, "Prairie Showcase" and "Winnipeg Drama." Like "By the Sea" with its artificial sea-dog atmosphere, most prairie radio drama sounds phony and, what is worst of all, phony in its Canadianness:

> I do not think a play presented from the prairie region necessarily has to be crammed with Manitoba maples, wheat

> fields and people calling each other "pardner." Too many plays written about the prairies seem to make use of the "wild and woolly west" theme, something which is merely the myth of the prairies, not its real self. (10)

This generalizes theoretically about the basic relation between artistic rendering and photographic reproduction. The column for Tuesday, 13 April ponders the alternatives for "discussion" programs—use of prepared scripts or reliance upon spontaneous and unrehearsed expression; it obliges Peggy to think hard about credibility, realism, and art, and leads her to make suggestions that program directors might look at dubiously but that aspiring young writers ought to take to heart: "Will we have spontaneity, thus sacrificing much material and even coherence, or will we have continuity, achieved through prepared scripts?" (13). She has introduced the problem by referring to a program in the series "These English" that concerned Hyde Park's soapbox orators and depended upon a prepared script; "it sounded more realistic than the actual thing would have done." She soon reaches her precept:

> The function of art is not to present actual life, but to take real happenings and accentuate them dramatically so that they seem real to the reader or listener.
>
> If art is strictly realistic, it is usually dull. If you are going to write about a man who is a bore, you don't do it literally, or the portrait itself would be boring.

Her critical theorizing prompted her to return again and again to consideration of Canadian artists and their problems. She continued her discussion of unfaithful and dishonest depiction of Canadian prairie life (11 May) by offering positive criticism, helpful suggestions for writers who want to write seriously about "this land and its people":

> they must do a great deal more than write reasonable facsimiles of Hollywood westerns or nondescript efforts that drag in the names of Winnipeg or Saskatoon to show they are

> enacted here. They must study the prairies and the factors which mould its people, and they must set down these sincerely and with effort.

To that she appends a warning against a tendency "to idealize the prairies, to talk lyrically about its sunset." Peggy's evident passion for her topic pushes her to a lyricism of her own—

> What of its harshness and bleakness? What of the long snows and the unbearable wind? . . . writers could do worse than admit this is a god-forsaken country, and take it from there. Why, despite its hardness, do people find beauty on the prairies? Why do farmers hate it and yet refuse to leave it? If these things were explored, we might have a "Prairie Showcase" that would really justify its name.

She had some serious justification for that passionate exhortation: W.O. Mitchell's *Who Has Seen the Wind* was published the year before (1947) and its setting recalled to her the works of Martha Ostenso—particularly *Wild Geese* (1925)—and above all the more recent *As For Me and My House* (1941) by Sinclair Ross, which she read just as she began her college years and of which she wrote, twenty years thence, "his extraordinary and moving novel . . . had an enormous impact on me, for it seemed the only completely genuine one I had ever read about my own people, my own place. It pulled no punches about life in the stultifying atmosphere of small and ingrown towns, and yet it was illuminated with compassion."[11]

If these comments were to prove more relevant to her own writing yet to come, she nevertheless refused to restrict her exhortations to the Sinclair Ross type of heroism. The sturdy column of 11 May asserts that Canadian history alone affords plenty of material for heroic treatment: "the story of such men as La Vérendrye or Radisson and Groseilliers could make good plays. The days when fur was king, the treks of the Red River settlers, the building of the C.P.R."

Peggy began developing the "Canadian heroes" theme in her

columns of 17 and 20 March, which discuss E.J. Pratt's epic poem about the martyrdom of Father Brébeuf and his Jesuit colleagues. They had come to the New World to bring the message of Christianity to the Huron and Iroquois peoples. Peggy's comments anticipate her growing interests. The French martyrs are not presented simply as champions of the good in confrontation with the "evil Redman"; their fate is carefully and instructively posed:

> Father Brebeuf brought with him the passionate crusading ecclesiasticism of the Jesuits. . . . these early French priests lived among the Indians, . . . shared their hard lives without possessing the brutality necessary to accept it. For years Father Brebeuf lived with little gentleness in his life outside himself.
>
> . . . it is a phenomenon we have always had with us, and probably always will, the prophet-martyr, the voice crying in the wilderness, the man advanced beyond his environment. . . .
>
> Pratt's poem has . . . captured a good deal of the burning religion of the Jesuits and their indomitable quality. (14)

Peggy praises Pratt's courageous heroes, victimized by the Aboriginal people and the fierce wilderness but who survive to the end through their own peculiar strength of conviction. She knew at first hand, but as yet could allow herself no sympathy with, an example of similar courage and persistent survival—that tough old man (had *he* any gentleness within?) in whose house she had dwelt for eight important years of her life, from ages ten to eighteen, Grandpa Simpson; his "indomitable quality" could also be attributed, in part, to the zeal of his "burning religion." Sympathy for that courageous survivor was slow to achieve recognition in Peggy's bosom. Her young and vigorous anticlericalism is here quiescent. Peggy's brief column for Saturday, 20 May, after she heard the radio drama and reread the epic (and also heard the commentary on Jesuit missions that followed the dramatization, given by "the prominent Canadian historian, A.R.M. Lower," her professor at United College), adds emphasis in a somewhat surprising criticism of Pratt's poem in order to praise the adaptation—his failure "to point up the meaning of the [Jesuit] missions in terms of the growth of this country or of their general significance to humanity as examples of a type of courage that is expressed in different ways throughout history."

Her column of Monday, 22 March addresses directly the matter of Canadian heroic material to writers: "There are few Canadians who gather into themselves the salient features of their times and represent not only their individual story but part of the story of a growing country," but Louis Riel was such a figure and "the drama of his life is indisputable" (14). In Riel, she points out, "was gathered the whole inevitable struggle between red man and white, in a country where the railway to the west was beginning to have great possibilities, commercial and otherwise." With that, another hero.

> There were two strong men in the west at that time. They knew each other well, and both were interested in the fate of the west, above all things. One was knighted by the queen [Victoria] and drove the last spike in the C.P.R. the same year as the other was hanged by the queen's men at Regina. The first was Donald Smith, Lord Strathcona. The other was Louis Riel.[12]

The tragic figure of Louis Riel—"called by historical circumstances to be on the losing side," she notes—continued to haunt Peggy throughout her life: his case came to represent to her that such injustice is always reflexive and ultimately suicidal. The conflict between the Métis Riel, Aboriginal and French, on the one side, and the Scottish prime minister John A. Macdonald and his anti-Métis representative Donald Smith, on the other, was truly emblematic of a Canadian dilemma that is still waiting to be resolved.

Preoccupations were stirring in Peggy's mind as she pointed to fertile moments of Canadian history, "when fur was king, the treks of the Red River settlers, the building of the C.P.R.," and complained in exasperation: "do we get such tales? We do not" (11 May, p. 10). One feels that she herself might like to try her hand at the story of Riel or of Strathcona or the trek from Hudson Bay to the Red River valley.

Peggy's burgeoning Canadianism, her concern with her own folk, their brief past, and their culture and artistic vitality, runs throughout these radio columns. An appropriate summing-up occurs in the column for Wednesday, 11 August, devoted to one of her teachers at United College, the professor of English and faculty mentor of the English Club, Arthur L. Phelps. She recalls fondly his ability to make the literature of the past (particularly Shakespeare's) come alive, but especially his serious concern with Canadian art and culture:

> Phelps was one of the few Canadian men of letters who are aware of this country as an entity; who believe in the potentiality of Canada and its people; and who at the same time maintain a certain balance and objectivity towards things Canadian.
>
> . . . One of his best contributions to Canadian culture in general has been his determinedly honest criticism of it.

Peggy did five more weekly radio columns; that for Wednesday, 22 September 1948 was the last of them. A week later "It's in the Air" appeared under the byline of Cynthia Wilmot, quite without mention of Peggy or her status. The *Winnipeg Citizen* continued for another eight months until the pressure of the other two Winnipeg papers, the *Free Press* and the *Tribune*, took its toll. The *Citizen* was unable to gain access to the major wire services (AP and UPI). The last number appeared on 13 April 1949; its total lifespan was thirteen and a half months.

Largely through the help of Chris Marshall, wife of John, who had been best man at the Laurences' wedding and associate editor of *The Westerner*, Peggy found a position in the office of the Winnipeg YWCA. In a few months, Jack graduated from the University of Manitoba's School of Engineering. They were already making plans for the future that would take them out of Canada and into the Old World.

five

From London to Africa

DURING THE YEARS THAT FOLLOWED HER GRADUATION FROM United College, Peggy was undeniably happy in the domestic scene on Burrows Avenue with the love of her life. She liked being a journalist, and Jack was diligently pursuing his engineering degree. In the summer of 1948 he worked with a surveying team in southern Manitoba. Peg's job and Jack's summer work augmented the monthly allowance he received under Canada's plan for World War II veterans returned to school—something akin to the American GI Bill. They lived modestly and maintained the friendships they had made in Winnipeg.

She had a sense of biding her time, almost holding her breath, until Jack was ready to enter his profession. When that moment arrived in the spring of 1949, Peggy was ready to realize all the romantic potential of her life with Jack. They had made their plans for England, actually going to the Old Country, this earth of majesty—demi-paradise, the Land of Our Fathers—a land her own father had visited when he served with the Canadian army in World War I. Her husband had also been to England with the RAF in World War II, and he had the qualities of sophistication, maturity, and broad experience, qualities her father had displayed. Jack was himself something of an ideal realized, an actualization of the romantic hero she had created in her early story "The Blond Butcher": a figure ten years her senior, an "older man," knowledgeable, unmistakably masculine, and even a bit mysterious—still. This figure would gently guide and protect her as she journeyed forth from her home country and into her past.

The Laurences arrived in England that July without definite plans. To their rescue immediately came the Colliers—Jack's old friend Frank from air force days in Carberry, Manitoba, and his wife, Nancy—who invited them to their home on Shaftesbury Avenue in Kenton, a town near Harrow in Middlesex, and thus not far from London.[1] They stayed three weeks, then moved into London, where Jack had found a position with an engineering firm. Soon afterward, Peg was hired by an employment agency.

The Laurences lived in a small, first-floor, bed-sitting-room flat, #1 Fairfax Mansions, Finchley Road, in Hampstead. Not fashionable, yet another dream come true, for Peggy found herself dealing with the greengrocer, the ironmonger, the wine merchant, and so on; these were terms she knew from the books of her childhood. She was dealing as well with fabulous farthings and florins, shillings and ha'pennies, half-crowns, pennies the size of cartwheels, and the invisible guineas merely alluded to on the price tags in the "best shops." She had magically come to life anew in the "sceptered isle." They did their cooking on a single gas ring; their combined wage was £9 per week (about $36 Canadian). Yet, they were able to manage a healthy diet with salads and fresh fruits regularly. A pound of bacon could be had for less than two shillings (thirty-five cents Canadian), while at home it was ninety cents a pound, and the luxury of half a dozen tangerines was just two shillings and sixpence, or about fifty cents Canadian. An occasional bottle of cider or ale was within their budget, and ten cigarettes their daily allotment. They bought three daily papers and one weekly magazine. Peg wrote to Adele Wiseman (contemplating a move to London) that she and Jack did rather well on £9 a week, while the typical British railwayman had to do it with £9 a *month*.[2] Furthermore, the Laurences went out to concerts and the theatre now and then. "We are, in fact, living in relative luxury and comfort," she assured Adele. The romance of their situation gently covered the more difficult aspects of life, and the "luxury and comfort" did not apply exclusively to the material aspects.

Peggy revelled in the traditional delights of London, to which Jack happily introduced her: Canada House on the west side of Trafalgar Square, the Admiralty Arch, Whitehall and the Horse Guards, the Portrait Gallery and the Tate, the British Museum (now the British Library), Big Ben and the Houses of Parliament, the Embankment, The Strand, Soho with its bookstores and ladies of the night, the Tower Bridge and the Tower itself, and, of course, Hampstead's wonderful Heath.

As though to verify the credibility of her marvellous experiences in London, a figure from Manitoba and her immediate past intruded upon these impressions when they were very nearly at their most pristine. I appeared at their Hampstead flat in early August to announce my imminent marriage, in London, to Peg's recent maid of honour in Neepawa, Jean Simpson. I invited her to return the favour and to bring Jack along too as a sorely needed witness for the ceremony. I was doing post-grad work at the Sorbonne; Jean came over at the end of my first year. The Laurences duly assisted at our wedding that August; the single other guest was another contemporary Winnipegger, Ian Weiss, on holiday from Paris, where he was preparing his doctoral dissertation.

An additional feature of Peg's experience that seemed calculated to test its authenticity was the phenomenon of familiarity she encountered about the city—and not the result of her reading British stories in her earlier years. When she and Jack wandered across Trafalgar Square from Canada House, they found a tall-steepled church at the northeast corner of the square—St. Martin's-in-the Field (as it was then commonly called): there was an Anglican church in the far north end of Winnipeg with that very name. As they strolled away from Trafalgar Square and along The Mall, thoughts of a prominent

Winnipeg street near the Hudson's Bay Company department store and not far from United College came readily to mind. At the end of that stroll, which led them to Buckingham Palace, was the statue of Queen Victoria in her chair just as she sat before the Parliament Building in Winnipeg (though without the "snow upon her snowy hair / And snow upon her feet"). Here, evidently, were the originals, truly the *real thing*, of which the Winnipeg versions seemed pale imitations. And here, thus, one seemed in touch with one's true roots. How exhilarating: like stepping into the pages of a novel by Dickens come to life. This feature of paradoxical and puzzling déjà vu would vex Peggy's perception. For the moment, simple enjoyment of the romantic reality sufficed.

The Laurences' first letters home typify correspondence of this sort: they wrote what they knew the recipients were interested in and would want to hear. The letter of 24 November 1949 to the family of Adele Wiseman contains eight pages from Peggy, three pages from Jack, and two more covered with examples of English advertisements. It affects an attitude of heavy-handed boredom with English structures and scenery; an elaborately blasé tone shrouds its account of castles and cathedrals, palaces and parks—obviously the ironic face of Peggy's enthusiasm. She felt she had to be careful not to seem to be lording it over the folks back home. Keeping in mind her audience of the Wiseman family and their communist friends and neighbours of the Burrows Avenue milieu, she fashioned her accounts especially for the eyes and ears of Ann and Bill Ross and the young couple who had taken over the Laurences' apartment in the Rosses' house, Addie and Roland Penner. And Jack's account is similarly discreet. Peggy comments favourably on the courtesy and the thoughtfulness of the London bus drivers and on the attentive generosity of the employees of the *Daily Worker*, who welcomed the Laurences warmly and took time to explain to them how the presses worked and so on. Peggy was also appropriately caustic in her critical comments on the aristocracy, the several royals, and the inescapable caste system.

A high point in Peg's account of their cultural pursuits in London follows her report on seeing *The Heiress*, an adaptation for the stage of Henry James's novel *Washington Square*. She and Jack also went to the Albert Hall to see Sir Malcolm Sargent conduct the London Philharmonic in a production of Beethoven's *Ninth Symphony*. They were very favourably impressed—and in most appropriate terms. In a letter to Adele of 28 January 1950, Peggy singled out for particular praise the choir's rendition of Schiller's "Ode to Joy" and the importance of its "brotherhood theme":

> Beethoven was really a revolutionary, respectable as his music may be today. My advise [sic] to a progressive rally would be to invest in a really good orchestra, conductor and massed choir; perform Beethoven's Ninth, with the Ode to Joy being sung in English; then take up the collection immediately afterwards! The result would be stupendous!

If England's magic was due to its still being "this royal throne of kings" (George VI was then the British sovereign), Clement Atlee and his Labour government were in fact administering the country's affairs. Peg and Jack found themselves under a government that was markedly a long step further to the left than any Canadian government they had known and hence a full stride closer to a realization of their political ideal. Jack could not avoid, nevertheless, unburdening himself in the early letters home on the topic of the pseudo-socialistic political form actually in place. One feels that he wanted the Burrows Avenue folks to know that he remained a staunch supporter of the true socialist ideals. Yet, in ordinary conversation, he and Peg were pleased at the social advances made under Prime Minister Atlee. Scars of the wounds inflicted upon London by the vicious bombing of World War II still abounded: the whole neighbourhood surrounding St. Paul's Cathedral, for example, was still heavily pockmarked with bomb craters and the debris of former buildings, though the cathedral itself had miraculously survived virtually unscathed. The plans for repair and resurrection of the heart of the Empire were being encouragingly brought to realization. New shops rising out of the detritus also seemed quite in tune with the aims of the new *people's* government. The Laurences admired the prominence in London of enterprises like the Burton Tailors shops, offering good clothing at quite affordable prices "off the peg." The first letter assured the Wisemans: "we haven't got much money, but we've got an awful lot. We've been enjoying London tremendously."

There were the rough moments when unfamiliarity with British ways threatened Peggy's sojourn. Yet Jack manfully squired her safely round the little embarrassments that lurked for the uninitiated. Lining up at the wrong end of a queue at a bus stop was instinctive behaviour for people used to traffic that travelled on the right rather than on the left side of the roadway. When untutored aliens mistakenly lined up at the head of a queue, they were bound to hear barely discreet mutterings of disapproval in which the term "American" or (worse) "Yank" figured largely. Peggy had good reason to hate being thus misidentified. Not so grievous, however, was her early discovery that Londoners tended to react strangely when asked for directions to what she called a "rest room" ("Are you tired, Luv?") or to a "bathroom" ("Do you want the toilet?") But that was all part of the fun of becoming acculturated—"fun" so long as Jack was at her elbow.

The new year 1950 had opened with a flash of good news: the *Canadian Tribune* published one of Peggy's poems in its issue for Monday, 9 January, complete with two photographs appropriate to the subject of the poem. In the letter informing her of the publication and enclosing a tear sheet of the poem, the *Tribune* also acknowledged receipt of another of her poems, this one on the 1949 revolt of the Italian peasants. She sent the news to Adele, exuberantly claiming, "I suppose I should be properly casual about the whole thing, but actually I was, and am, tremendously pleased and encouraged."[3] In addition to that, she and Jack found a stroke of luck, the National Football Pools. One had to guess the results of a large number of football (i.e. soccer) matches each week. Winning the pool brought them the tidy sum of £64, or about $250 Canadian, and that called for a holiday on the continent. They decided on a week or so in Paris where they had friends, my wife and I.

A grand idea! The visit turned out to be a preparatory step into the truly exotic. I found them a modest hotel in the Latin Quarter. On one of their first afternoons in Paris, the four of us were seated at a boulevard café near the Odéon—and not far from a little restaurant that specialized in couscous and related dishes—and Jack suddenly interrupted our conversation, stood up, raised his chin slightly, and sniffed the air. His eyes narrowed somewhat, and he announced, "You can smell the beginning of the East here." Peggy's eyes sparkled, her pupils dilated perceptibly, and she obviously experienced a *frisson* of delight at the hint of shadowy mysteries lurking behind Jack's knowing diagnostic testimony. To share something of the experiences he had had in the exotic Orient would be an added boon. All things considered, perhaps their good luck in winning the football pool was an auspicious omen that augured well for further opportunities, increased liberating encounters.

By this time Jack was becoming restless and dissatisfied with his job in London: he was confined to an office and doing what he felt were mere exercises and repetitions—like chemistry experiments in a high school laboratory—and he wanted the liberty of working in the open air. Early in June 1950 he found an advertisement for a position in the British Protectorate of Somaliland; a civil engineer was sought to take charge, under the Director of Public Works, of the construction of approximately thirty "earth dams" across an area of some 143,000 kilometres, the average capacity of each dam to be forty-five million litres.[4] The plan addressed the severe shortage of water, especially in the areas of the Guban and the virtually waterless Haud. The position sounded like exactly what Jack wanted. It seemed to Peg to be another wonderful opening of doors to wider and richer experience, to be led further from her native Neepawa, beyond the stimulating Winnipeg, even beyond the tireless London, and into the furthest reaches of Empire—into the mysterious East, the exotic Orient, the Dark Continent! She agreed Jack should apply. He did so, at once.

Peggy began reading all she could lay hands on about East Africa, confident of the success of Jack's application. She was also devoting time, inevitably, to her own writing—her poetry and the novel she had begun. The novel tells of a young woman of Scots-Irish background, from a quasi-Neepawa, and in the big city to attend college; there she falls in love with a Ukrainian-Canadian boy. She

> fluctuates between a) unconscious prejudice against his background, expressed at first in a kind of fear of his making love to her, even while she's very attracted to him, and in a desire for him to leave the small-town (and his family) forever, that he can be disassociated from them in her own mind; b) a later realization of the prejudice of those who think they have no prejudices, and the consequent violent reaction . . against her family, to whom Ukrainians are beyond the pale . . and a desire to marry him at once, just because he *is* Ukrainian."

So she described it to Adele (and the two-dot ellipsis is Peg's own) about a year later when she was driving the novel toward its completion: a very personal piece, quite autobiographical, that Peggy was using to deal with problems she herself had had.[5]

This novel remained unpublished, but it contained themes that forced their way into her consciousness again. The theme of the young woman (perhaps a schoolteacher) attracted physically to a "foreigner," an alien, from her own town, one she "ought not" be attracted to, a kind of dirty trick, a joke, on the part of the divine Organizer—that is surely promising. And the strong-minded daughter determined to spite her mean-spirited family and marry the young man beyond the pale, and perhaps face being cast out and ostracized like the sad mother of Ishmael. The source of these themes lay deep in Peggy's earliest experiences and persisted in her memory until its vigorous recall over half a century later. The memory is of Grandfather Wemyss's house in 1934:

> My best friend Mona and I, two small girls [circa eight], used to watch closely while a young man from the north end of town, a Ukrainian, repaired drains and eavestroughs. Mona and I stood beside him, admiring him, his physical strength and his know-how, wanting him to notice us, to admire us. Unfortunately, brainwashed as we had been, not by our parents particularly but by the stratified society in which we had grown up, we tried to get his attention in a horrifying way. "Hunky, hunky, hunky," we chanted to this Ukrainian boy from the other side of the tracks, one of the people whose parents and grandparents had come to Canada at the beginning of the century, as Mona's Irish and my Scots ancestors had. What repulsive little kids. . . . He looked at us very, very straight and said, "Don't you ever say that again." I don't think we ever did.[6]

Adele was much on Peggy's mind in the spring of 1950 as she tried to help her find work in London. Peg wrote to the Director of Education, London County Council, on 11 May, and put Adele in touch with Jewish social work agencies.[7] In July a situation at the Stepney Jewish Girls' School—near the junction of Globe Road and Mile End Road in London's East End—opened up for Adele; she arrived in London in mid-August. She and Peg got together to read and discuss each other's manuscripts.

Jack's application for the position in Somaliland was successful—much rejoicing but their balloon was almost scuttled before it got off the ground. Having signed the contract, Jack was informed by the Colonial Office that there was no provision for an engineer's wife to live in the Protectorate and that Peggy would have to remain behind—for half a year at the very least. "Not bloody likely!" Peg had learned to exclaim by this time. Jack explained that his wife was "a hardy Canadian girl, . . . an accomplished woodswoman, a kind of female Daniel Boone," and could readily live in a tent if necessary. Certainly she was not about to be deprived of her beloved and loving husband for months at a time. He effected a change of attitude, and the Colonial Service decided Mrs. Laurence would be permitted to accompany Mr. Laurence to East Africa.[8]

A most exciting prospect—into the Orient, east of Suez, into the Gulf of Aden, 1001 nights! And Jack knew the East already, having been stationed in India. A marvellous opportunity: veritably exotic, yet, as a British protectorate, safely under the Union Jack.

They both resigned from their London jobs at the beginning of November and began packing for the sojourn in Somaliland. They would have to take all their own household effects—glassware, pots and pans—and clothing appropriate to the climate of East Africa and to the social demands they would face. Jack purchased evening clothes for the first and (he hoped) last time, and Peg a washable evening gown (glazed chintz, she chose), since there would be no dry-cleaning service available in Somaliland, or so they were told.[9] Then they waited. The Colonial Office couldn't tell them until the last minute when travel accommodations would be settled. It was an awkward interval, as they kept repeating farewells.

The Laurences set out in the bleak chill of a grey, sleety December day to cross the English Channel and the North Sea to Rotterdam, where they were to be picked up by a Norwegian passenger-cargo steamer and taken southward into the Mediterranean and on to the Horn of Africa. Their ship, the *Tigre*, was delayed in Antwerp by fog; the Laurences had to spend another five chilly days in the Dutch port, unwilling tourists with little money and increasingly less patience. They visited the Museum Boymans in Rotterdam and spent a day in Delft. But daily living was pricey; they were lodged in an "unfortunately high-class hotel," and affordable eateries were hard to find. They happened on a modest restaurant in a working-class section of Rotterdam and took their noon meal there each day thereafter. They knew no Dutch; the menu was a mystery. Peg pointed mutely to an appetizing pastry—*slagroomwafel. Weiner schnitzel* and *slagroomwafel* saw them through their lunch hours. At night they carried in rolls, cheese, and fruit wrapped in brown paper.[10]

Much of the time, however, they simply kept to their hotel room. Jack had brought with him a copy of Tolstoi's *War and Peace* and busied himself with that. Peg had already finished the shorter *The Brothers Karamazov* she had brought along but then she discovered a Gideon Bible—in English. Methodically she began reading on through the Pentateuch, the account of the children of Israel wandering in the desert, seeking the Promised Land. A prophetic coincidence it proved to be, as the Somalis were also people of the desert. Further, Peggy was particularly taken by the portent of Chapter 23 of Exodus, especially the ninth verse: "Also, thou shalt not oppress a stranger: for ye know the heart of a stranger, seeing ye were strangers in the land of Egypt."

The admonition struck Peggy with signal sharpness. She had already grown severely critical of religion as it had been presented to her back home. She was simply seeking diversion, waiting to be transported the rest of the way from England—where, in spite of similarities in language and cultural traditions, she had been unmistakably a stranger—to British Somaliland, where she was bound inevitably to be even more of a stranger, an alien. That passage of scripture spoke most meaningfully to her; its burden was to remain with her throughout her life. Finally, the *Tigre* arrived.

During the month spent on board the Norwegian vessel, the Laurences found themselves to be the ship's only passengers and comfortably housed in the owner's plush three-room suite. The captain and crew were friendly, and they involved Peg and Jack in their Christmas celebration. There was a festive dinner on Christmas Eve, much drinking of toasts and crying of "*Skol*," and singing of Norwegian carols, with the two Canadians joining in on "Jesus" and "hallelujah."

Peggy also reported to Adele on 27 December that she had just finished the third chapter of her novel set in Canada. The next night the *Tigre* passed through the Strait of Gibraltar, the crew working diligently to make sure they reached Marseilles in time for New Year's Eve. The Mediterranean was cold and windy; life on board ship was warm and friendly.

At the beginning of 1951 they stopped for five days in Genoa—sunny but cold. Strolling through the Staglieno cemetery, Peggy was impressed by the "marble angels [that] loomed like spirits of vengeance among the green-black cypress trees" of the cemetery.[11] Whether those angels reminded her of the white stone angel in the cemetery in Neepawa, they certainly contributed to an image to be dealt with at some future time. Down the west coast of Italy one night, they saw Mount Etna in eruption. Then, southward to Port Said and another day's pause before proceeding through the Red Sea to Aden, there to disembark with all their worldly goods. Farewell to the *Tigre* and to the western world. The Laurences shipped out across the Gulf of Aden in mid-January 1951 to the Somali port of Berbera, their conveyance "a very dirty little tramp steamer," Peg told Adele,[12] that contrasted meanly with their home of the past month and seemed to warn Peg grimly that she was now in another world. Yet she was eager to embrace the romance of this new venture: Somaliland.

On the day following their arrival in Berbera, the Laurences left by truck to drive southwestward, first across the coastal desert called the Guban (meaning "burnt") and then across the inland desert called the Haud (meaning "south"), to report in at the city of Hargeisa—almost on the eastern border of Ethiopia. The girl from Manitoba noted that "the land is empty; the sky is open from one side of the horizon to the other,"[13] realizing that Adele, her friend back home in Manitoba, would grasp the similarity. Hargeisa was the seat of the British government in the Protectorate and the Laurences' anticipated destination. They remained there only a few days, however, and then journeyed back northeastward to the town of Sheikh, upon the range of hills between the Guban and the Haud; it was their home base for the next several months.

Peggy wrote to Adele at the earliest opportunity that Sheikh "is the best place in Somaliland . . . a mountain station, . . . reasonably green all year around, and the weather is absolutely perfect. . . . Our front door is like a picture-frame, and the picture contains the soft line of the hills; and red sand of the valley and the blue green rocks; the green flat-topped trees; a flock of tiny white sheep, grazing a few feet from the house, and tended by a brown-robed Somali woman, with a scarlet head-scarf."[14] It was their first house together that was all their own, and "it's ideal"; but the ambience mattered most: "it is the quiet one notices most about Sheikh. . . . there is a strange air of peace here, almost a Shangri-la atmosphere." The impression persisted, and helps to explain certain subsequent decisions Peggy made concerning her experience in Somaliland and indeed her response to its charm.

It was as if she had been set down in one of the pages of the *National Geographic* magazines her father devoured when she was a girl. No longer her father's world, even at second hand, the scenes were now immediately and directly hers and Jack's to share and cherish. Peg's diary attests to her sense of the marvellous realized:

> At night we went to sleep to the shushing sound of the wind, and in the morning it was the only sound we heard when we wakened. I rose and looked out the window—the whole valley was filled with clouds. . . . We walked out to explore our territory, and found that the early clouds swept so low that we were actually walking through them . . . and I was amazed that such a thing was possible, to walk in the clouds.[15]

It was, in fact, almost too real, for very soon after being settled in—into their "house in the clouds"—Jack was off to work, out on trek, in camp, preparing for construction of the "earth dams," which were rather to be reservoirs—or *ballehs* in the native language. Peggy set down the proposed specifications:

> Each reservoir would be a large rectangular hole dug at the foot of a carefully selected slope. The earth which was removed would be banked up around the sides and lower end, making a huge U with the arms pointing uphill. . . . In order to reach out and gather the water. . . long walls would stretch out from the top of the U. Low banks of earth a thousand feet long or more, these wing-walls would check the water and deflect it very slowly towards the reservoir so that as little silt as possible would be carried with it. Beyond the ends of these walls, ploughed furrows would stretch further out and very slightly up, and would divert and channel the annual bounty on a front of over half a mile.[16]

That achievement depended on preliminary surveying for each site, and the selection, adaptation, and innovative repair of the machinery. Thirty *ballehs* were planned along a twenty-four-kilometre stretch of the Haud, and each *balleh* would provide water for some three months.

Jack was responsible for all the preliminary planning and for the selection and training of staff—a motley crew of various ethnic and tribal backgrounds, religious persuasions, personal experience, and temperament. Peggy remembered especially the oldest of the group, Abdi, a complete Somali—a devout Muslim, a faithful and committed member of his tribe, and a firm traditionalist. He was at heart an old warrior, the best rifle-shot of the whole crew, and Jack's most able driver. Abdi disapproved of most of the young men he had to work with, as being flighty and unsubstantial, as he did of any departure of the Laurences from what he conceived of as the traditional and proper behaviour of sahib and memsahib. Abdi was the model for Yusuf in Peg's short story "Uncertain Flowering." At the other end of the spectrum was Arabetto, a good mechanic with linguistic facility: in addition to his father's Arabic and his mother's Somali, he knew some

Swahili, Italian, and English. He had little affinity with the other workers, who viewed him as a virtual foreigner; he had no tribal connections and seemed to look forward to Somali independence in a world free of past tradition.

A middle position between Abdi and Arabetto was occupied by Mohamed, hired on the Laurences' arrival at Berbera. Just a youth, Mohamed served as houseboy and then cook. He was also their final link with the Protectorate. A Somali with tribal connections, he was yet "modern" enough when he wanted to marry a girl from another tribe to flout the usual requirements. So he found himself somewhat outcast from both his own tribe and that of his wife. Mohamed had lost the sense of belonging, of identity, that his old tribal associations had given him, and yet could not step into the modern world and turn his back on his Somali past. His dearest and most rewarding association (except that with his wife) was what he had with Peggy and Jack: he was theirs and they were his—so long as they remained in Somaliland. He was otherwise almost an alien in his own land.

Then there was the complex, tragicomic Hersi Jama. A devoutly religious Muslim and evidently a *mullah* or lay priest learned in the Koran, he was tolerant of other religions—a quasi-ecumenicist. His uncle, Haji Musa Farah, fought in the Camel Constabulary (formed in 1912 specifically to confront the Dervish forces) and became the highest-ranking Somali in the corps. The leader of the Dervishes was Sayyid Mahammed 'Abdille Hasan—"The Mad Mullah"—whom Peggy knew of as Sultan Mohammed Abdullah Hassan; his followers were fanatically religious and fiercely nationalistic opponents of all foreigners, especially the colonizing British, Ethiopians, and Italians, but above all the British.[17] Hersi was proud of the kinship but he was himself a skinny little fellow with a prominent speech impediment. Most of the other Somalis in camp had little sympathy with Hersi's tribal affiliations. Hersi could read and write Arabic and had some ability in English. As much cut off from the traditional and heroic past as Mohamed, Hersi also looked to the Laurences as representing the way of the future; more balefully than Mohamed, Hersi Jama really belonged nowhere. Peggy could imagine Hersi's dialogue with himself in his dilemma: "I cannot go back," he would lament; "A man must belong somewhere. . . . The new roots may not grow straight, but they have grown too strong to be cut away"; and, more poignantly, more intimately—"I cannot have both gods, and I cannot have neither. A man must belong somewhere."[18]

Ironically, however, with all his unprepossessing stature and his faulty speech, Hersi was a poet and an orator—important qualifications in Somali culture that would also prove valuable to Peggy. It seemed to the Laurences a further irony that Hersi had an absolutely stunning wife, "a queen of a woman," Peg reported to friends in England, describing her in terms she used later to portray the Somali ideal of female beauty: "Tall, with a very lovely and stately figure, and a finely moulded face with copper-coloured skin and rather slanted, dark eyes. She is, also, extremely poised and charming. . . . It is an odd contrast to see them [her and Hersi] together."[19]

Preparations began in February and continued until the first days of July. Peg joined Jack in the Haud for the last week of February and the first of March, her introduction to camp life. Jack took her to visit a reinforcement of an old *balleh*, Abdi driving them in the Land Rover for a round trip of 160 kilometres. The torrential spring rains struck; Abdi took a wrong turn; the Rover became mired in the mud. The trip took them twenty-four hours. While they were stranded, some camel herders spotted them and sent a small rescue team. The rescuers were from a tribe hostile to Abdi's tribe, and a threatening confrontation ensued. The rescuers eyed the rifle resting on the front seat beside Peggy; the alert Abdi assured them that the young wife was a crack shot and had plenty of ammunition. The rescue went ahead and the hostile tribesmen were rewarded.[20]

There were other memorable adventures, in camp and beyond, captured fresh in Peg's immediate reports to Adele Wiseman and in her diaries, and later developed for publication in *The Prophet's Camel*

Bell. Some weeks after the prolonged motor trip, a thief crept into their tent while they slept and took all Jack's equipment and records of the *balleh* project. He was caught and the loot recovered.[21] In August, Peg went with Jack to Djibouti, where he supervised unloading of a shipment of heavy machinery—a task complicated by language barriers; and Jack was driving himself as usual under the hot sun. He came one day to the door of their dwelling to announce, laconically, that he couldn't see. Only heat exhaustion, but a stunning moment for Peggy. That experience prompted them to move into Hargeisa and leave their cherished house in the clouds in Sheikh, at the end of August.[22]

Meanwhile, Peg was writing her novel about the Scottish-Canadian girl in love with a Ukrainian-Canadian youth—set in the fictional area to be called "Manawaka."[23] That April the Laurences met a young couple who spoke their language and were knowledgeable about Somali culture. Mr. and Mrs. Bogumil W. Andrzejewski were in Somaliland doing research. He was a tall, gentle Polish scholar nicknamed Guś ("Goosh"); his wife, Sheila, was a vivacious English girl. They shared with the Laurences a quiet but firm opposition to British colonialism and the roles of sahib and memsahib—Sheila did her own cooking. Their talks together inevitably turned to the topic of Somali language and literature, and prompted Peggy to ask about English translations of Somali poetry. Guś informed her that there were few, if any. Peggy wondered aloud if she might undertake translating some literature—with help, of course. Guś was immediately fascinated by that possibility. "Yes, you might well!" he responded. The question was how much help she would need and where it might come from, and also when she would find time in her busy and exciting life. But the seed had been planted and fertilized by the sympathetic reaction from Guś. By the beginning of May, Peg had sent Adele an example of the Somali short lyric form, translated thus: "In the green Haud there is a tree for poverty to sit under"; "It sounds just like Eliot, doesn't it?"[24]

With literal translations provided by Guś Andrzejewski and his Somali assistant (also a poet) Musa Galaal, Peg worked diligently at the poetry. The prose folk tales occupied some of her attention as well but were less demanding, and she needed less assistance for translating them. A six-week period in camp, from mid-May to the end of June 1951, was highly productive: she finished the eighth of a proposed eleven chapters for her novel, became seriously involved in keeping a diary account of her Somaliland experiences, and pondered several ideas for short stories—in addition to the translations.

Then Peg made an important discovery about her writing. She virtually dropped the nearly completed novel, as the Somali people and their culture demanded much of her attention. Beside Somali poetry and folk tales, the members of Jack's crew fascinated her. She began to try her hand at stories about the native characters in their local setting and also the British colonials she encountered. Early in July she finished one short story and, by the middle of August, two more; and she continued in that genre. But the Andrzejewskis' departure date at the end of August was looming, and Musa Galaal was to leave just before them; she must get as much translating done as possible beforehand. In a letter to Adele she included seven examples of her rendering of the light lyric called *belwo*.[25] One of these illustrates both her poetic talent and her skill as literary editor:

> So perfect are her teeth, one might mistake
> Their whiteness for the palest inner bark
> Cut from a place of Allah's kindly grace
> Where new rains fell and the galol tree flourished,
> And fashioned into a vessel, bound around
> With pearls, pink-glowing, garnered from Zeilah's sea.
>
> (# this poem refers to the light brown or pink line across the teeth, common here, and considered a mark of great beauty.)

Another sign of the nascent professional artist appeared in the same letter to Adele to explain her turning to "local" subjects and justify her new approach to the art of fiction. Concerning the three completed Somaliland short stories, Peg wrote, "Listen, Adele, they're good!" And the necessary confirmation, "Jack thinks so too." Then the theoretical justification:

> [the August stories] written mainly in conversation. . . . are a new way of doing things. . . . sticking to what people actually say, and letting the reactions and feelings and any deeper significance show up between the lines, rather than actually stating it. . . . propaganda in any form is not for me.

Peggy at twenty-five thus developed an idea she had flirted with in her columns for the *Citizen*, the idea of dramatic fiction.

In Peggy's last sojourn in camp with Jack, from the middle of October to beyond the first week of November, she pushed ahead with all her projects—save the abandoned Manitoba novel: "The reason is simple . . it stinks."[26] Guś Andrzejewski and Musa Galaal had left a number of literal translations of Somali poems and some tales before they departed. However, two members of Jack's crew—Arabetto and especially the talented Hersi—were supplying her with their dramatic renditions of Somali tales, in dubious and halting English but with wonderful theatrical accompaniment. She would soon have enough to make a small book—if anyone were interested.

Her own fiction moved apace: by early November she had completed another short story. Peggy summed up her situation in a letter to Guś and Sheila Andrzejewski:

> I have been writing a number of stories, set in "an East African colony" (guess where?). . . . I've done four so far, not counting the first story, which I wrote long ago (the one about the houseboy and the British woman . . . you read it, Sheila) . . . very badly written, . . . I'll leave it for awhile. The other four seem to me to be the best things I've ever written.

> . . . I've sent them to various publications, but I am not being very hopeful about it yet.[27]

A happy coincidence was that the first *balleh* was about to be completed, Balleh Gehli—"Balleh of the Camels." The camp was now a large affair with a crew of some thirty workers and an impressive array of machinery. On moves from one site to another—the *ballehs* were now in various stages of completion—the Laurences had a substantial convoy.

The roads were pretty bad or non-existent, and travel was dusty and stifling and parched; thirst was a constant companion. When the rains came, there was flooding. Peggy found it difficult at first to understand the fatalism of the Somalis in the face of such conditions, summed up in their habitual remark, "*In sha' Allah*"—"if Allah wills it." Before very long she saw the need for such a belief, and for the notorious Somali toughness that accompanied it. There was for her a faint sense of déjà vu in the hard, stiff-necked, sternly religious natives who were thus enabled to survive; although she could not quite identify it yet, here was an equivalent to the tough old man, sternly religious, with whom she had lived during her major school years back in Neepawa, Grandfather Simpson.

Peggy's travelling was soon strictly curtailed. She had found a job, virtually next door to their house in Hargeisa, working for E.P.S. Shirley, Chief Secretary and Commissioner for Native Affairs. At about the middle of November, she became pregnant and her doctor not only forbade travelling but also commanded her to resign from her lovely new job in the Confidential Office: complete rest was required lest she lose the baby. As the *Jilaal* season of harsh drought dragged on into the beginning of 1952, all the stories she had hopefully sent out came sadly home, all but one, "Uncertain Flowering." She had sent it to Whit Burnett of the Story Press, New York, and had evidently forgotten about it. The number of translations of Somali poetry and folk tales that she felt she could manage was now finished, and she turned to creating the substantial Introduction such a collection deserved.

The Laurences had been contemplating a month's leave in Italy at the end of their tour of duty and looking even further ahead to a new posting—perhaps Pakistan but preferably another African location, maybe the Gold Coast. Jack had gained what experience the *balleh* project offered, and additional work there would simply be an exercise in repetition. A good foreman or a fresh, young Native engineer (and a few exemplars of that ilk were then beginning to appear) could easily oversee construction of the additional reservoirs. By early spring Jack had seen two more of them to completion, Balleh Gedid and Balleh Hersi Jama—the latter named to honour the little teller of tales, a member of the crew, who had been injured rather seriously in an accident involving the heavy machinery.[28]

Peggy returned to the Confidential Office at the beginning of April, a position that was made additionally appealing to her because of the interest shown by the Chief Secretary, Philip Shirley, in her personal project of translating Somali oral literature. Shirley knew Somalis well and had a high respect for their culture; he was not at all what Peg had come to feel was the typical, imperialist, colonial administrator. Shirley's sympathetic and intelligent interest in Peg's translations soon involved him in fostering completion of the project and then arranging for its publication by the government of the British Protectorate of Somaliland. The book was titled *A Tree for Poverty* but was not published at once. Another item of suspense was whether Jack's five completed *ballehs* would meet the crucial test. The spring rains could settle that, but would they come before the Laurences had to leave Somaliland?[29]

They had plans to fly from Somaliland to Rome and then on to London at the beginning of June to be settled in England for the birth of their first baby on or about August 10. The spring of 1952 was thus coloured by anticipation concerning the results of their individual and cooperative creativity, a sense chastened by lurking apprehension. With that, the troublesome departure of Abdi contributed further to the tension. The old warrior's aggravated irascibility combined with his unreasonable expectations as faithful retainer to impose an unbearable strain on the whole camp. He luckily fitted into another job elsewhere, and he began "telling everyone what a stinker Jack is, and how he (Jack) never lifted a finger to help him, and indeed cheated him out of his trek allowance [to which, as temporary driver-mechanic, he was not entitled]" and so on. Peg tried to be philosophical about the old man ("at this stage he is a little insane"), but the hurt remained: "One doesn't expect or even want gratitude or anything like that, but it is a bit heartbreaking to find that someone one has liked, admired and respected, has in fact despised one all along."[30]

Relief finally came with the sudden descent of the *Gu* rains. When the downpour abated enough to permit them to venture forth, the Laurences set out with Hersi Jama and Arabetto for their final visit to the Balleh of the Camels:

> And there . . . was the *balleh*. . . . Jack examined it minutely, and nodded, speaking almost brusquely in order not to show how pleased he was.
>
> "Seems satisfactory. . . . It's drained as large an area as I'd hoped, apparently—it's completely filled, anyway. Well, I expected it would be, but it's good to see it. I wonder what the Somalis think of it, now that it's full of water?"[31]

He was satisfied on that point, too, almost at once as Hersi joined him and Peg to express his dismay at the herdsmen watering their camels and the women filling their vessels. He reported hearing the Somalis' rather indignant question, "What is these *Ingrese* doing here, beside our *balleh*?" Peg concludes,

> It was their *balleh* now. They had assimilated it: it belonged here. Jack grinned.
>
> "It's okay. Tell them we're going now, and we won't be coming back."[32]

Peggy and Jack were soon packed and said their farewells all 'round;

the last of them, appropriately, to Mohamed. They left at dawn on Saturday, 7 June 1952, from Nairobi-Aden, and spent a full week in Rome with Adele, who was teaching at the Overseas School of Rome. Then they flew on to London, to the Hampstead flat they had arranged for, not far from the hospital where reliable Nancy Collier had made reservations for Peggy and the Laurence offspring. Beyond that, they knew that an appointment in the Gold Coast awaited them later in the year.

six

Somaliland Creations

"UNCERTAIN FLOWERING," SHE HAD CALLED THE ONE SHORT story that had not come back rejected. Somaliland had been a fertile milieu for Peggy's creativity. She left the Horn of Africa rejoicing in her pregnancy, eager to meet her Mum in London and to give birth to her first child. Peg looked forward as well to publication of her book of Somali translations. There was, furthermore, her evidently forgotten short story—her first, and perhaps only, piece of Somali fiction to achieve publication. It was duly published in *Story: The Magazine of the Short Story in Book Form*;[1] a series of mischances kept Peggy ignorant of its fate until late January 1953—fifteen months after she mailed the manuscript.

"Uncertain Flowering" tells of a couple of weeks one summer in the life of sixteen-year-old Karen Aynsley. She has come back from school in England to spend the long vacation with her parents, Jo and Philip, who are part of the British colonial establishment of Somaliland, which is *home* to Karen. She is on the verge of adulthood; she wants to leave the innocence of childhood and enter the adult world of experience. (The theme is Miltonic, Blakean, Jamesian.) She chafes at being treated as a minor and squirms at being called "kid," "youngster," "child" by her parents and their friends. Karen sees the obvious attempt to prolong her condition of childish innocence as a hypocritical means of covering up the marital infidelity she suspects her parents are guilty of. The climax of the story occurs on the Gymkhana Night Dance at the club.[2]

Her suspicions are strengthened by witnessing the extramarital associations of her mother with Captain Hugh Harrison and of her father with Bess Newton. Karen has been entrusted to the youthful care of Lieutenant Howard Tavershaw at the dance, and Jo Aynsley has asked him to drive her daughter home in Captain Harrison's car. Karen makes a brash attempt to assert her adulthood: she provokes from Tavershaw confirmation of her parents' moral laxity; then she "confesses" to him that she had an affair in England, last winter; arrived home, she quickly draws him into her bed. Slightly drunk, Tavershaw nevertheless soon recognizes that Karen is still a virgin and stops the activity just in time. He apologizes and assures her that her virginity is still intact: "You *do* know you're still . . . all right . . . don't you? You know I didn't actually . . ." (Laurence's ellipses). The story ends quickly with Tavershaw's departure and Karen's bitterly contemplating, alone, his assurance: "'You think I should be glad,' she whispered. 'You really think I should be glad. . . .'"

That is the skeleton storyline, but there is much more. For instance, "Uncertain Flowering" sets up a number of meaningful parallels between Karen's personal situation and the situation of the Native people under the British colonial establishment in Somaliland. Philip and Jo Aynsley and their friends participate fully in the blame for the plight of Karen and of the Somalis alike. As the Aynsleys in particular and their British colonial establishment in general work to arrest Karen's development in the stage of innocence, they also make sure that the Somalis are not recognized as anything other than childish (if not, of course, innocent).

Karen, on the threshold between childhood and adulthood, eagerly grasps the dearest feature of "home" when she revisits the hidden valley of the candelabra trees—the sacred grove of her childhood innocence. The prelapsarian setting is augmented by Karen's resuming the Somali tongue with her old guardian, Yusuf. He is pleased: "You will not wholly forget . . . because I taught you when you were a child" (16). She is actually regressing to the condition of childish dependence and is half aware of that. Embarrassed, she asks, "Am I a child now, Yusuf, or am I . . . ?" He assures her she is no child. At the valley, and now speaking English, she asks Yusuf to confirm her suspicions about her parents' marital infidelity. He spurns her request ("his eyes were angry") and repeats his earlier observation—with a bit more—the wisest response she receives: "'You are no child,' Yusuf said. 'But you are not a woman either'"(19).

Yusuf explains his refusal to answer Karen's request: "I have worked for the 'sirkal' your father for many years"; it indicates his position as a dedicated servant who defends faithfully the wishes and the "honour" of the Aynsleys and the society they represent. He is *theirs* quite as much as Karen is, and while he refuses to relegate her to the state of prolonged childhood, he will not yet contribute to her crossing the threshold into the realm of knowledge of good and evil. Faithful Yusuf remains a Somali servant, and although he is never in the story addressed or referred to by the demeaning term used for other male Somalis—"Boy"—he cannot be separated from them.

"Uncertain Flowering" establishes another parallel between Karen and the Somalis by juxtaposing the term "Boy" to terms applied to Karen—"kid," "child," "youngster"—which she urgently rejects. The terms applied to Karen are scattered throughout the story; the use of "Boy" is concentrated in the setting of the Gymkhana Night Dance. The parallel is strengthened by the associated parallel between the scene at the club and the scene in the valley of the candelabra trees. The scene at the club develops the theme of opposition between the natural and anti-natural:

> They called them, inappropriately, fairy-lights. . . .
>
> There was no real need for the lights outside, for the night was nearly as bright as dawn. But the dancers did not want the light of the sky.

> The moon was alien. . . .
>
> The sand was alien too, and the heat, and the proud impoverished Somalis with enigmatical eyes, who strode across the country herding their camels in all weathers. . . . the deep-throated sullen howl of the hyena was alien, and the mewing of foxes outside the compound at night, and the quavering sadness of the songs the Somalis chanted around their fires.
>
> So the dancers strung up fairy-lights, a little closer than the moon to the skirl of lights in Piccadilly. They clad the camel-herders' sons in white uniforms, and put trays in their hands, and shouted at them, "Bo-oy!" . . . Because so much was alien here, they were sometimes forced to try very hard.
>
> They themselves were not the aliens; that would have meant the end of too much. (22-23)

It is not just that the Somalis are in tune with their environment, but that the sanctity of nature is not to be violated: to do so is to be guilty of serious evil. The sanctity of Karen's valley is emphasized as an appropriate place for prayer (17).

What further connects the two scenes is the parallel between Yusuf and Howard Tavershaw as protective, military consorts for Karen. "Yusuf had been a marksman in the Camel Corps, in the wild days of the later Mullah Campaigns" (16)[3] and Tavershaw is a young subaltern in His Majesty's Armed Service. Yusuf "protects" her from the adult knowledge she seeks and, at the same time, ironically, protects his employers and indeed the whole colonial system that enslaves him. Tavershaw's treatment of Karen is parallel to Yusuf's but mainly in sexual terms: accepting her invitation to bed is admission that she is "no child," and his arresting their sexual intercourse "honorably" recognizes that she is "not a woman, either." Both men nobly support the system, and Tavershaw conforms to colonialist expectations as conspicuously as Yusuf: as the lieutenant has learned to treat the Somali "Boy" in proper colonial fashion at the club, so has he evidently learned how to treat the Somali girl elsewhere. Bess Newton teases the young

Howie about his budding reputation as a real man; when he modestly confesses, "I guess I *am* no great shakes," Bess corrects him—"when they don't speak your language . . . you really excel. Especially if there's a dusky tinge to their skin" (21). This is a familiar theme that depicts miscegenation as synecdoche for slavery, and tacitly argues that evil is self-destructive. In his role as British imperialist "Gentleman," Tavershaw has symbolically robbed the Aynsleys of the innocence (embodied in their Karen) they have laboured to keep intact. The loss is most poignant for Philip, as the story expresses dramatically.

The relationship of Philip Aynsley and his daughter is most significant. The one term Karen does not regret when applied to her is "bairn," her father's term and virtually the only one he uses to address or refer to her. The climax of that relationship in the story occurs during the climactic Gymkhana Night Dance, when the drunken Philip shows up to ask his daughter for a second dance: "'Come on, bairn,' he said, 'dance with me'" (29). Jo has already arranged for Karen to leave with Tavershaw, so Karen must decline her father's invitation. When Jo chides Philip for being tardy with his offer, Karen's defense of him leads to his crucial confession:

> "No," she cried suddenly. "He tried to find me before, didn't you, daddy? That is, I thought I saw you. . . ."
>
> Philip did not answer at once. . . .
>
> "Yes," Philip said unsteadily. "I've been trying to find you . . . all your life." (29) [only the middle ellipsis is mine]

Philip is grieving over his inability really to know his daughter—to "find" her; but he is also expressing his failure to find the innocence Karen symbolically embodies (as implied in the hidden valley scene with Yusuf). That innocence involves the natural, unspoiled goodness still visible, though now seriously tainted, in the colonized Somalis; it is the virtue, neither fugitive nor cloistered, that Milton could praise and the higher innocence that Blake admired.

"Bairn" is a term of special significance in the story. It is Scottish for "child," and Philip is the only one to use it. "Bairn" was naturally not uncommon in the idiom of first-generation Scottish-Canadians—like Laurence's father, Robert Wemyss, and her husband, Jack. As a prominent item in the vocabulary of the father in the story, "bairn" encourages one to associate Philip with Laurence's own father and even to see Laurence "identifying" to some extent with the fictional daughter, Karen—so sympathetically portrayed. Robert Wemyss had died in 1935, when daughter Peggy was just nine years old, yet it is understandable that the loss of her father remained a tender memory for the twenty-five-year-old Laurence and that the unfamiliar milieu of Somaliland and her loneliness there—in spite of Jack's presence much of the time—would reawaken her sense of loss of the protective paternal hand. (The lost father, in fact, bulks large in Laurence's subsequent fiction; he is never completely compensated for.) "Bairn" helps to distinguish between Philip's attitude to Karen and that of all others to her; it thus aids in defining the story's concern with parenthood and colonialism. The relationship of Philip and Karen is quietly echoed in his relationship with Yusuf, which is paternal on Philip's part and filial on Yusuf's.

These parallels between Karen and the Somalis indicate that the story's connection with Africa is not just incidental but integral to the expression of Laurence's concerns with mankind's inhumanity to its own members. Further, these parallels anticipate concerns and narrative strategies that characterize Laurence's subsequent African fiction where she frequently fashions her characters as representatives of their people and place: the individual character becomes a synecdoche for a whole area (as we shall see) without losing individuality—and usually as an alienated individual, an "alien heart."

The much more certain flowering of Peggy's related creative impulse was *A Tree for Poverty*. The title comes from a poem by Ali Hamaal, a passage from which serves as epigraph to the book: "On the plain

Ban-Aul there is a tree / For poverty to shelter under."[4] Her Introduction begins with the common recognition that poetry and stories "are, in general, the most notable part of the Somali cultural field"[5] and then observes: "Always available, the poetry and folk-tales are as free to the impoverished nomad as they are to the Sultan. Somali literature is, in its way, 'a tree for poverty to shelter under'" (2).

But this ideal condition of literature free for all people is accompanied by a fatal flaw: the Somali literary tradition was exclusively oral and depended on reciters of poetry and tellers of tales to be sustained, and was therefore fragile and impermanent—*Verba volant, scripta manent.* When Peggy undertook the task of translation there was no official Somali orthography, although within a decade the newly formed Somali government created a Linguistic Committee under Musa Galaal to address the problem and in 1972 establish an official orthography.[6] Peggy explains that "the purpose of this work is . . . to record poems [and tales] which will otherwise be lost in another fifty years" (2). Her Introduction indicates how she managed to pursue her program. For the poems and for ten of the thirty-six tales published in *A Tree*, she used literal translations provided by Guś and Musa Galaal; obviously the poetry was the more demanding task and required thorough discussion. The system was "a three-way process," she later explained:

> Musa . . . had a wide knowledge of the background and style of Somali poetry, but while his command of English was fluent, he had to discuss the subtler connotations of the words with Guś in Somali. Guś and I then discussed the lines in English, and I took notes on the literal meanings, the implications of the words, the references to Somali traditions or customs. I would then be able to work on this material later, and attempt to put it into some form approximating a poem, while preserving as much as possible of the meaning and spirit of the original.[7]

Peggy worked, thus, to produce an English *equivalent* of the Somali original rather than a strictly literal rendition of it. One might say that the scholarly translator aims at reproducing in another language the *fact* of the original utterance—what it simply *states*; the artistic creator of an equivalent text aims at expressing the complex *truth* of the poetic original—what it *means* with all its intellectual and emotional complexity. Typically, Peggy's *equivalents* are English poems, however modest, in their own right and usually represent faithfully the essence of the Somali originals. Professor Andrzejewski later said of Peggy's talent in this line in general, "What is astonishing is that in spite of the language barrier she developed such empathy with the Somalis that even though her translations are sometimes not very close to the original she conveyed their spirit and atmosphere with a high degree of accuracy."[8] Further, she had been writing poetry of her own, after all, since high school days—or earlier.

Although creating English versions of Somali folk tales did not present the same challenge to her, Peggy did work from literal translations furnished by Andrzejewski and Galaal for ten of the tales included in *A Tree for Poverty*. These are identified simply as "Translated Stories." The remaining twenty-six, divided according to source into "Arabic" (nine tales) and "Somali" (seventeen tales), appear under the rubric "Paraphrased Stories." These were told to Peggy "partly in Somali but mainly in English"; her informants were Musa Galaal, Arabetto, Ahmed Nasir, and especially the talented Hersi Jama.[9] Although she knew other published English versions of a few of these tales, Peggy preferred to use her own sources, as she explained in the Introduction:

> I believe that a good deal of the tone and spirit of the original is contained in these paraphrased stories, as the writing of them was guided both by the general style of the translated stories and by the talented acting of the Somali storytellers. . . . [who] acted them out in a spirited fashion, and from facial expressions alone it was often possible to perceive in a story nuances

The Simpson family at Clear Lake, Manitoba, 1932. Left to right: Margaret "Mum" Wemyss, Bertha (Mrs. Stuart), Grandma Jane Simpson, Velma, Grandpa, William Bailey, Aunt Ett Wemyss, Stuart, Lorne "Bud" Bailey; in front: Catherine and Peggy. Lorne Bailey was the original for Chris in "Horses in the Night," and the topic of the poem "For Lorne" in *Dance on the Earth.*

Peggy at nine months, 1927.

Peggy at four or five years of age with her dolls on Vivian Street.

Peggy in foreground, aged twenty months, in front of Verna, 1928.

One of a pair of armchairs made by Grandpa Simpson, in interior of the Brick House, now Margaret Laurence Home. The chair was donated by Catherine Simpson Milne.

Grandpa Simpson's home, the Brick House, 312 1st Avenue, in Neepawa, Manitoba. Peggy lived there (with "Mum" and brother Bob) from 1936 until she left for college in 1944; her room was in the upper right corner.

Simpson-Wemyss cottage at Clear Lake (built in 1918), c. 1930.

Peggy (aged thirteen) and brother Robert (aged six), 1939.

Margie, Louise, Mona, and Peggy in a scow at the Neepawa dam, 1944.

House of Pate Chaboyer, the source for the Tonnerres' house in Manawaka.

Steps of Spratts' cottage, 1945. Top: Margie and Mona; bottom: Louise and Peggy.

Peggy and friends in Neepawa Collegiate sweatshirts, Clear Lake, 1944. Left to right: Phyllis Ralph, Peggy, Mona, Anne Rowe, Louise, and Margie.

Alguires' front yard, Easter 1945. Left to right: Daphne (Louise's out-of-town friend), Mrs. Alguire, Louise, Mrs. Wemyss ("Mum"), Peggy, Mona, Margie.

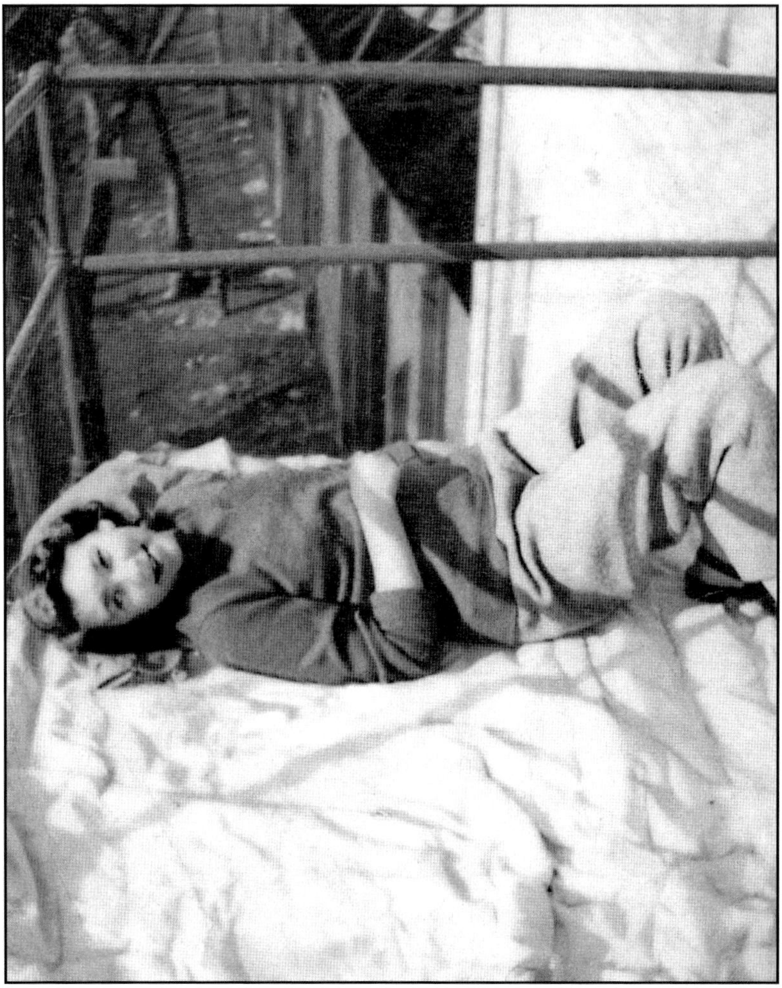

Peggy relaxing on fire escape during United College days, 1945.

Graduation photos of Peggy Wemyss, Lois (Freeman) Wilson, and Jack Borland, 1947.

Malcolm Ross, 1981. Ross taught Peggy English at United College, and published one of her early short stories when she began to write seriously in the 1950s.

Peggy as a bride, September 13, 1947.

Peggy at Sheikh, Somaliland, 1951.

Jack Laurence with tortoise, Somaliland, 1951.

Peggy and baby Jocelyn, London, England, summer 1952.

> which the storyteller's limited English could not adequately express. However, . . . the literary style should not be taken as pure Somali. (17)

The folk tales are thus English *equivalents*, just as are the poems.

The Introduction discusses two prominent poetic genres, the comparatively simple love lyric called *belwo*; and the more complex, demanding, and highly respected *gabei*. The latter was a classic, traditional form; the *belwo* was quite new and expressive of the rapid cultural changes brought with the beginning of World War II. Peggy's account of the origin of these poetic lyrics is tentative:

> They have come into popularity in Somaliland in the last ten years. . . . Some people say that they came, originally, from Egypt or Arabia. Others maintain that a Somali truck-driver invented the form, or that an extremely lovely Somali woman was the first belwo poet. (7)

Subsequent scholarship has established that the *belwo* (or *balwo*) came into existence between 1943 and 1945, that it was indeed the creation of a truck-driver named Cabdi (or Abdi) Deeqsi—not from the bush but a town-dweller; the name *belwo* is a borrowing from the Arabic, meaning "trouble" or "mischief" or "woe is me." One of the earliest writers in this new mode was a good friend of Cabdi, Khadiija Ciija Daraar, who soon became known by her nickname Khadiija Belwo and was evidently quite lovely enough to inspire Cabdi to write the *belwo* for her—"O woman if your beauty were hidden from me, / O Khadiija Belwo, I [would] break [in two]." The popularity of the form was at its height in Hargeisa between 1946 and 1950, and the *belwo* very quickly developed into the longer form called *heello*, which then became the most popular poetic genre in Somalia.[10]

Peggy had hold of essential data, but they were vague and imperfectly developed, and among them was the information that "*belwo*" could best be translated as "a trifle" or "a bauble" (p. 6) rather than as "mischief" (Andrzejewski) or "woe is me" (Johnson). The evident contradiction here is perhaps more apparent than real: given the nature of many love songs—in the western world as well as in the Somali—one might easily substitute for "*belwo*" the American term "blues." Even the best blues songs are "trifles" in comparison with the great operatic arias: the burden of the blues is typically disappointment in love or mistreatment at the hands of others. The second *belwo* in *A Tree* exemplifies this "blues" quality very well.

> I long for you, as one
> Whose dhow in summer winds
> Is blown adrift and lost,
> Longs for land, and finds—
> Again the compass tells—
> A grey and empty sea. (31)

Many of the *belwo* in Peggy's collection are simply brief and brilliant exclamations of praise for the beloved.

The other category discussed in Peggy's Introduction and illustrated in the body of *A Tree* is the more substantial and much admired *gabei* (*gabay* in *Somali Poetry*, edited by Guś and I.M. Lewis). This elaborate form, "considered to be the highest literary form in the culture," is governed by a demanding prosody requiring strict adherence to alliteration. The *gabei* also employs a distinct literary vocabulary; *belwo* does not. Andrzejewski has more recently pointed out the importance of "the rigid criteria of the quantitative patterns" in Somali poetry as a means of distinguishing among various poetic genres.[11] Some, but certainly not all, of Peggy's *equivalents* display effective use of alliteration, though she does not attempt to duplicate that feature as it appears in Somali poetry. A good example is the first *belwo* of *A Tree*; and another is her moving treatment of the *gabei* "Qaraami" ("Passion") by Elmii Bonderii (although the rhythm is Western blank verse). On one occasion Peggy calls attention quite specifically to her use of alliteration; in her note to "Battle Pledge" by an Ogaden chieftain, she admits the impossibility of faithfully reproducing such features of Somali poetry, but confesses, "I have tried to convey something of the effect of Somali alliteration by making the English translation alliterative in 'f'."[12] Peggy did not make the obvious comparison between *gabei* and Anglo-Saxon poetry (*Beowulf*, "The Wanderer," etc.) as it was only later that she became familiar with such poems; they were not included in English courses at United College.[13]

To exemplify the style of the Somali *gabei*, Peggy has relied mainly on extracts, and included only two complete *gabei*—"Battle Pledge" and "Qaraami." But some of those extracts are of considerable interest because of their authors. The most suitable occupations for a Somali man, it was thought, were that of the warrior and the poet (the occupation of sheikh or religious leader is a significant exception); two of the most highly respected Somali poets were also renowned warriors. Both Wiil Waal and Mahammed 'Abdille Hasan (to Peg, Mohammed Abdullah Hassan) are thus represented in *A Tree*. Peggy identified Wiil Waal as a national hero of the sixteenth century who drove the last Galla king from Jigjigga. Her own doubt about the validity of her information is apparent in her note for "The Bond between Kings." Subsequent scholarship discovered that Wiil Waal was Faraax Garaad Xirsi (or Farah Garad Hirsi), a Somali chieftain of the nineteenth century. Andrzejewski characterizes him as "an unusually astute strategist, a ruthless politician, an enlightened social reformer, a patriot and a man of incisive wit who was also known for his spectacular practical jokes."[14] These features are displayed in the five Somali tales that recount his exploits in *A Tree*. The other poet-warrior, represented here by the fragment "To a Friend going on a Journey," was called by the British "The Mad Mullah"; Mahammed 'Abdille Hasan led the Dervishes in their struggle with imperialist colonizers in Somaliland for twenty years at the beginning of the twentieth century. Peggy's note calls him "the best poet in Somaliland for many generations" (37). He was a figure who continued to haunt her imagination, an artist and also a patriot who fought fiercely against intruding colonizers in his native land. In *Heart of a Stranger*, she included an essay devoted to him, "The Poem and the Spear." She was also haunted by the author of "Qaraami," the pathetic young Elmii Bonderii who literally died of unrequited love. She gathered the various tales she had heard about him into "The Epic Love of Elmii Bonderii" for *Holiday*, November 1965; it too was included in *Heart of a Stranger.*

Translations of Somali folk tales make up seventy percent of *A Tree for Poverty*. The Introduction comments on characterization, the predominant categories—moral fables, religious instruction, tales of magic, Somali humour—and the recurrent themes. Some of the headnotes to the tales indicate other English translations that Peggy knew, but always acknowledge that she relied on the version provided by Hersi Jama, Ahmed Nasir, or another of her informants. The tales vary in length from the forty-word Midgan vignette, hardly more than a little joke, to the substantial short story "Ahmed the Woodseller," well over 4000 words. A persistent motif is the underdog, the poor, the misshapen, the alien.

A typical moral tale, "How the Meat Was Divided," tells of the lion ordering Omar the hyena to divide some camel meat among the beasts of prey "into 32 equal parts." Omar gives half to the lion and half to the others. The lion rips an eye out of Omar's head and invites Mother Jackal to try the job: she gives thirty-one shares to the lion and the rest "to all the other animals, for your peaceful division" (53). The lion asks Mother Jackal what taught her to divide meat so wisely; she replies, "the eye of Omar, which I saw hanging from its socket" (54). And in "The Cheating Lesson," a boy asks his uncle to teach him how to cheat in order to earn his "living easily from fools" (57). Uncle agrees, asking only that he be allowed to milk the boy's camel that day. The boy is willing, though he goes without milk for the day. No instruction follows, however, and the boy asks when his uncle will give him the lesson: "I have done so already, he replied" (57).

Peggy's Introduction identifies the "crime *does* pay" type of story, but that type is very close to "The Cheating Lesson": the examples caution against gullibility—warning the underdog to be shrewd and crafty, like Mother Jackal. A number of stories, just a step away from these, resemble the Robin Hood stories of taking from the rich to give to the poor: the five paraphrased Arabic stories featuring the attractive trickster Abana Wys are of this type. Abana and his wife decide in a moment of need to appeal to the Sultan for aid: he reports the death of his wife and asks for money to give her a proper burial. After that succeeds, his wife goes immediately to the Sultana with a matching request. They are unmasked (they have "robbed" the Sultan and they are "the poor") when the benefactors compare notes and go to confront the tricksters, who have jumped into bed to feign death. Sultan and wife debate which of the two was the first to be deceived. Then, "kind-hearted Abana, who could not bear to hear people quarreling," comes to life and confesses the ruse; his wife in turn comes to life to upbrade Abana. Sultan and Sultana burst into laughter; they bid them keep the money and bless them.

More trickery-cum-charity lessons come from five tales about the poet-warrior Wiil Waal, a powerful Sultan who yet champions the underdog, and would foster an egalitarian society—under his benevolent dictatorship. These stories are preceded by a group of Midgan stories, a wise arrangement. Peggy explains that "the Somalis look down on the Midgans as inferior people, and like to laugh at the Midgans' supposed stupidity" (105). In "Wiil Waal and the Midgan's Well," the Sultan announces he will gallop out among his people's wells, blindfolded, on his black stallion; he promises death to the owner of any well the stallion falls into. The people think up various defences, but a certain Midgan says, "If the Sultan wishes to break his own neck . . . let him do so . . ." (122). Wiil Waal reins in his steed and scolds his people: "The Midgan saw this scarf was thin, and he guessed that I could see through it"—and the rest of you are a bunch of fools, he adds. Praise for the alien; chastisement for his "betters."

With the motif of the shrewd underdog and the benevolent trickster-ruler, there are stories that develop the theme of charity as it is found among the poor. That virtue is personified in Nebii Hhudur, a part human and perhaps part divine creature "gifted with eternal life," during which (like Ahasuerus) he must wander the earth in the disguise of a beggar. "Nebii Hhudur and the Dish of Jowari" relates his stopping at the hovel of a very poor couple who have but a single bowl of food left; they share the jowari with the stranger. Next morning the dish is not only full again but continues to replenish itself. The couple sell the surplus jowari, buy camels, "and were never poor again" (78). Nebii Hhudur is not a representative of Fate: he does not oblige the poor couple to be generous but merely gives them the opportunity.

The question of fate, of Islam—*in sha' Allah*, "if Allah wills"—is managed variously, significantly favouring the Western conception of free will (though accepting the Miltonic idea of God's foreknowledge). The admirable free will of the unlikely underdog is prominent in the translated tale "'Igaal Bowkahh." 'Igaal is a "wizened little thing, with one crippled leg, and by no means handsome to look upon" (45). Peggy's Introduction devotes a whole page to him: she notes his essential toughness; far from submitting to the Muslim concept of "Islam," 'Igaal is more like Henley's speaker in "Invictus" ("master of my fate . . . captain of my soul") or like the "Invicta" speaker in several of Peg's poems of college days. Not quite the *mastery* of fate but the determination to move freely and boldly within the perimeters set by fate. The evident irony here Peg noted in *The Prophet's Camel Bell:* "They were not a passive people. They struggled against terrifying odds to get through to the wells. . . . This fatalism did not weaken them. On the contrary, it prevented them from wasting themselves in fury and desperation" (53). A similar attitude appears in her subsequent writing, nowhere more strongly than in *The Fire-Dwellers* (1969).

That Invicta figure emerges impressively in the two stories of Arawailo, "a great black queen" and a cruel tyrant who focusses her villainy on her male subjects. The story of her death is gripping and it—along with "The Story of Deg-Der"—held especial fascination for Peg. She used Hersi Jama's version of "The Death of Arawailo," but the headnote refers to another English version, in R.E. Drake-Brockman's *British Somaliland;* the latter offers something usefully supplemental for our understanding: "Towards the end of her life Arawailo began to show marked favour towards her own sex and great animosity towards her male subjects."[15] Her grandson, aided by a magician, slays Arawailo. The story ends surprisingly:

> Arawailo was given a great funeral by her people. The women, it is said, mourned her death, and put flowers and green branches on her grave. But the men rejoiced, and to show their hatred of the old queen, they threw stones on her grave. . . .
>
> And, until this day, you will still see piles of stones beside a road, shrines to Arawailo, where passing men have thrown a rock onto the heap and passing women have put a green branch there in memory of the queen. (128)

There is obviously more going on here than appears on the surface of the tale, the simple story of how the grandson took fate into his own hands to rid society . . . of what, exactly? Arawailo, to be sure, the cruel tyrant bent on rendering the male population impotent; but what more?

Light on this matter comes from the magical "Story of Deg-Der," who is a female bogey. A good woman at her marriage and a proper homemaker, she bears three daughters. The father is sorry not to have a son. Deg-Der turns cannibal; the husband disappears, she grows hideous. No young men will visit the three girls; they murder their mother. Each girl then marries a handsome and well-to-do swain—the third girl rather reluctantly. This girl bears three daughters and, remembering Mamma, worries. Her husband comes home one day to find the door barred. He offers his wife bribes to let him in—a fat sheep for supper? or a fat camel? a fat . . . boy? a fat . . . girl? Finally,

> "If you want none of these things for your meal," he said, "perhaps the one you hunger for is . . . myself?"

> And then the third daughter of Deg-Der opened the door and met him. (134)

Thus the story ends.

Discussing love poetry in the Introduction, Peggy notes that "after marriage, however, the emotion of love, like the beauty of the woman, becomes rapidly a thing of the past" (9). Women must work hard all day—making the grass houses, "weaving the heavy grass mats, making clothes, preparing the food, looking after the children and the flocks, and a thousand other duties." Furthermore, they are shown little gratitude or even respect. Both tribal and religious traditions place women's status as infinitely inferior to that of men: "A man who treated his wife with unusual thoughtfulness would be laughed at and scorned by the rest of the tribal group" (9). Finally, the Somali practice of clitoridectomy guaranteed that being a woman and especially a wife was inescapably painful.

The end of "The Death of Arawailo" thus carries no surprise in its account of the men's behaviour—given the lot of Somali women—and no surprise in the women's tribute to Arawailo. The queen's decision, as wife and mother, to castrate all the males in her tribe must have touched a sympathetic chord in all her sisters. They would perhaps also sympathize with Deg-Der's cannibalism after marriage and motherhood, and with the repetition in her youngest daughter. There is no concrete evidence that Peggy understood these female characters in just the way I have suggested, although Arawailo and Deg-Der participate in their own way in the typical figure of the alien, with which Peg fully sympathized, but one might suppose that such a sympathy would help to account for the intelligent feminism of Margaret Laurence's fiction—feminism before its time of popularity—and in her personal and public life.

A Tree for Poverty concludes with accounts of three important figures of Somali history—in particular the sheikhs Darod and Ishaak, founding ancestors of the two principal Somali peoples, the Ishaak people mainly in the north—in the British Protectorate of Somaliland.

"The Story of Sheikh Ishaak," which concludes the book, is reminiscent of the "begat" sections of the biblical Old Testament and only slightly less dramatic, but its burden is an important fact of Somali culture. Fiona Sparrow comments most astutely on this final item of the book:

> Laurence . . . gives the founder of the Ishaak people the final word, perhaps, because she lived among his descendants in the Haud of northern Somaliland. . . . So the closing lines of *A Tree for Poverty* are a splendid tribute to the patriarch of the people whose songs and stories she had translated.[16]

Furthermore, the exercise of *A Tree* allowed her to hone her narrative skills—character portrayal, dramatic dialogue, pace, and the challenge of language, but it also let Peg give free rein to her dearest interest in the alienated, both male and female, which dominates her fiction, the product of the alien heart.

seven

The Gold Coast

MEMORIES OF A GOOD VISIT WITH ADELE IN ROME HELPED PEG and Jack to endure the long flight to London in late June 1952. Their nostalgia was mixed with anticipation of the changes that would begin in England. Peggy had finally agreed with Jack that she would feel more at ease delivering their first-born in the comparatively familiar setting of an English hospital—"just like home." They had secured a flat in Hampstead. Nancy Collier had arranged for Peggy to be admitted to the Elizabeth Garrett Anderson Maternity Hospital in Belsize Park.

They were disappointed to discover that the flat they thought was awaiting them was unavailable. In a very few days Jack had found an even better flat at 16 Belsize Lane, Hampstead, not far from where the Laurences had lived when they first came to London. The Maternity Hospital in Belsize Park was on the next street east of Belsize Lane, and a ten-minute walk from the flat.

There was much to be done in the intervening weeks, unpacking all their possessions and arranging furniture in preparation for Peggy's Mum, due to arrive in mid-July, and for the baby, due before mid-August. Peggy was big and feeling clumsy as she moved about "with all the grace of a dinosaur and all the speed of a rheumatic snail," yet she persisted with preparations for giving birth by the "natural" method, according to instruction and assistance provided by the National Health Service. She sang the praises of that service to Adele:

> I get free clinic care . . . , maternity home care . . . , calcium and iron tablets from the clinic (I pay only a shilling for the lot!), free vitamin pills, extra meat and eggs, milk for 1 1/2d per pint instead of 6 1/2d . . . , concentrated orange juice at 5d a bottle . . . , and free dental care.[1]

She concludes with a rousing cheer for the Labour government.

Her Mum arrived in time to help celebrate Peggy's twenty-sixth birthday. Peg took her mother on guided tours around London and its environs. She also found time to talk with her Mum about the creative impulse and her plans to continue writing when the baby arrived. Her Mum understood and admired Peg's commitment to the demanding talent, yet bestowed a cautionary word about the exigent roles of mother and wife. The due date came and went. A week went by, then another, and finally, on Thursday, 26 August, labour began. It lasted thirty-six hours. By the time her daughter was born on the Saturday, Peg was so worn down she hadn't the energy or courage to participate in the "natural" part of the birth. Furthermore, the baby was born sturdy and broad-shouldered, features that complicated matters for both mother and daughter, and resulted in a cracked collarbone for the new arrival. Otherwise she was healthy and handsome and named "Barbara Jocelyn"; Peg wrote Adele that "we will, I think, call her Barbara."[2] Jack had wanted a boy, she reported, but, "I think he is quite pleased with her, and says she is 'really quite good-looking,' which is high praise indeed."

Peggy was kept in hospital until 10 September. Her mother's departure was set for the 11th; she had to return home to take care of her father. After the end of World War II she had sold the Big House on First Avenue, the Simpson house, and moved her father and her son, Robert, into the cottage on Vivian.

The Laurences had to ready themselves—including inoculations against smallpox and yellow fever—for their new venture in the Gold Coast. Their preparations were interrupted in October, when Jocelyn (as she was called from the very beginning) was suddenly smitten with convulsions. They rushed her to Lawn Road Fever Hospital. Her high fever persisted for a week. A spinal tap was done to test for meningitis—and the implications of that decision terrified Peggy: one inevitably *died* from meningitis (or so she believed). Peg was nursing Jocelyn and therefore walked to the hospital, a distance of two miles, every four hours to feed her baby. The convulsions ceased, the temperature dropped, but the baby's problem remained undiagnosed. Another problem then had to be addressed: apparently the baby's smallpox vaccination "didn't take the first time, . . . so she had to be done the day she got out of hospital."[3] Three years later, however, Peggy found out that Jocelyn had been "given her smallpox and yellow fever inoculations too close together and in the wrong order"[4]—and, further, that smaller and less robust babies than Jocelyn had died from such misapplications. At the end of October, just three days after Jocelyn was allowed to leave the hospital, the Laurences set off for their posting in the Gold Coast.

Jack was second in command of a British Public Works project to turn a sleepy little fishing village called Tema into a flourishing port. Tema is twenty kilometres east of the capital city of Accra, and the envisioned port would serve the eastern province of the Gold Coast and link the hinterland of the country with the Accra coastal region; the estimated cost of the project was £9,000,000.[5] Jack was to be stationed first in Accra to direct construction of a road to link the capital and Tema. The Laurences spent most of November 1952 as house guests of Jack's superior and his wife; then they moved into a modern bungalow seven kilometres from the city, one of a row built by the firm Jack was with, Sir William Halcrow and Partners. They also bought a small second-hand car. Peg's description of the bungalow for Adele makes it seem quite "posh":

> hardwood floors in halls and bedrooms; polished tile floors

> in diningroom and livingroom; huge plateglass windows in the livingroom; walls in the diningroom that open up completely, allowing a through current of air; tiled bathroom and kitchen; etc. There is a large livingroom; diningroom; 2 bedrooms; bathroom; lavatory; kitchen; store; and cookhouse outside.[6]

She knew they would soon have to move to Tema but Tema is "a lovely spot right on the sea, with palms all around . . . the sort of place that really suits us better than a city."

As it turned out, they remained in the bungalow just outside Accra for a good sixteen months, until their first leave in April of 1954. Only then, in August that year, did they move out to Tema. By that time they had become acclimatized to West Africa and begun—though not more than that for Peggy—to forget Somaliland. The Gold Coast was quite another kettle of fish from the Horn of Africa; the prominent differences and their impact on Peggy have been well summarized by Fiona Sparrow:

> The unchanging sandy landscape of Somaliland had attracted [her] because it made no compromise with time and because its people had faithfully preserved their own traditions and language. Accra's teeming city streets also fascinated her, but they signalled change, the effects of which had already spread along the forest roads to the villages. . . . Laurence discovered that white culture already had a strong foothold—Christianity as well as the western educational system were well established in the Gold Coast, which had been a British Colony for many years, and she found that the English language had become an important factor in uniting a diversity of ethnic groups.[7]

Peg and Jack were keenly attracted to the exciting young political leader Kwame Nkrumah. Nkrumah was born in the Gold Coast in 1909 of illiterate parents, "a real son of the common people."[8] After a thorough education at home and abroad, and a year lecturing at the London School of Economics, he became Secretary of the United Gold Coast Convention and in December 1947 entered the political arena as a nationalist opponent of British colonialism. He saw that "only a mass based party could carry out the struggle against British colonialism."[9] His opponents were first the Christian missionaries, and then the group of reactionary professional figures who had benefitted from British education and preferment and who wanted that colonial dispensation to continue—men like Dr. J.B. Danquah and Dr. K.A. Busia. In June 1949 Nkrumah helped form the Convention People's Party (CPP), the mass-based party needed to move the Gold Coast toward independence. In the general election of February 1951, the CPP won a landslide victory with Nkrumah himself gaining the largest number of votes. A year later the British government recognized him as prime minister, and he began pursuit of his announced goal of full self-government. When the Laurences arrived in the Gold Coast in 1952, they felt that the country under Kwame Nkrumah resembled England under Clement Atlee: the ideal of government by the people was on the verge of being realized.

The economy of the Gold Coast had to rely on capital from the United Kingdom and the United States. Nkrumah was convinced he could steer a safe course between the risks of foreign influence that accompanied foreign investment and the national benefits that accrued from such international cooperation. He initiated a system of free public education and, by 1952, a program of scholarships to send young scholars to study applied science and skilled trades in colleges and polytechnic institutions in the United Kingdom.[10] Chief among Nkrumah's plans for economic growth was the Volta Project to dam the Volta River and provide hydroelectric power to convert the rich bauxite resources of the country to aluminum. Railroad lines would be built to convey the bauxite to the aluminum works and then the aluminum on to the new port scheduled to be built at Tema.[11] The Laurences were thus involved in Nkrumah's plans for the future of the Gold Coast.

Jack's involvement, directing construction of a road from Accra to Tema, was clear enough; Peggy's was perhaps less obvious. She sympathized fully with Nkrumah's problem with the reactionary opposition that wanted to maintain the status quo, continue the dominance of the tribal chieftaincy, and defend the Anglo-African establishment. In that sympathy she was similar to the American writer Richard Wright, who visited the Gold Coast just a few months after the Laurences had arrived. The impatient Wright concluded his book *Black Power*, an account of his experience in West Africa, with a letter addressed to his host, Dr. Nkrumah, to offer encouragement and a pointed warning: "Have no illusions regarding Western attitudes. . . . If until today Africa was static, it was because Europeans deliberately wanted to keep her that way. . . . The greatest millstone about the neck of Africa for the past three hundred years has been the psychologically crippled white seeking his own perverse personal salvation."[12] Peggy struck the same note in her first letter from Accra to Adele in Winnipeg; although her focus is immediately on religious influence in the Gold Coast, its broader relevance is quite apparent. "The old gods die slowly," she said near the middle of a long letter that touches on many features of the local culture.[13] Indeed, the whole setting of the Nkrumah regime provided her with the basic material for her West African fiction, the constant and fundamental dramatic conflict of those stories and the eloquent metaphor of their surface.

At first she was much occupied by her new role as mother and the demands of setting up house. For a few weeks she had neither time nor energy to write. But a helpful nudge was given by the surprising arrival in January of a letter from Whit Burnett, accepting her short story "Uncertain Flowering" for publication. She had sent him the manuscript at the beginning of November 1951; Burnett's letter of reply is dated July 1952, but it did not reach her until six months later. Peggy explained to Adele that the letter from Burnett had been sent to Somaliland and kept in the main post office until December 1952, "can you imagine!"[14] By the middle of February Peg was managing to work two to three hours daily, initially on a novel set in Somaliland—at Burnett's request—but before long on new translations of Somali poetry as well, and from literal translations supplied as usual by Guś Andrzejewski. She did not yet know just how publication of her book of translations, *A Tree for Poverty*, was to be managed, but it was a relief to be back at work.

Jack, too, was enjoying the new challenge of his work and therefore was also able to enjoy his new daughter. He had stopped referring to Jocelyn as "the baby" before the turn of the year and was calling her "our baby." In February 1953 Peg reported to Adele that Jack is now "fond" of Jocelyn—"thank goodness," she adds. The urban setting of Accra was not without a sense of peril. Her letters recount confrontations with "spitting cobras" whose lethal expectorations are directed at the victim's eyes and with unerring accuracy up to a distance of three metres. There was the constant threat of malaria and also robbers. Peggy now had the baby to think of as well. Yet she and Jocelyn got out into the sunshine daily and spent most weekends at the beach. Even that pleasure carried its threat, however, as Peg discovered that first February, for Jocelyn almost drowned at the beach near Tema when a wave threw the two of them under water and almost tore the baby out of her mother's arms.[15]

The Laurences' social life included the occasional party (although they soon enough discovered that their tolerance of alcohol was very low in West Africa: Peg let it almost completely alone while Jack's modest indulgence left him sober but nauseated)[16] and infrequent visits to the Gold Coast equivalent of the Hargeisa Club of Somaliland. The name of the place was changed from the informative "European Club" to the disarming "Accra Club"; Peggy found the regulars "a dull bunch" and the atmosphere generally "old colonial."[17] The Laurences also noticed that the familiar colonialist terms of address they had objected to in Somaliland—"sahib" and "memsahib"—were not used in Accra; they had been replaced by "master" and "madame," but the social implications were just the same. Peg told Adele that the latter term made her sound "like the proprietress of a low-class brothel."[18]

At mid-year Peg learned that *A Tree for Poverty* would be published by the Eagle Press in Nairobi and that the Somaliland government would defray the expenses. She resumed translating Somali poetry and writing the Somali novel she had promised Whit Burnett. The attraction of Somaliland continued to influence Peggy strongly, and her writing was preoccupied with its exotic appeal for some time. She tried valiantly to force the novel to fruition: three chapters were finished by early June, two more before the end of July. By the end of the summer she had written a "travelogue" script on the Gold Coast that emphasized "the new Africa rather than the old tribal culture."[19] For all that, she remained virtually a "closet" artist: no one but Jack and her good friend Adele was aware she was busily writing in every spare moment. People wondered, Peg supposed, how she put in her time—apart from taking the sun with baby Jocelyn.[20]

A certain uneasiness was plaguing the Laurences during this tour. Peg, of course, was much involved in the demands of motherhood and managing the household, so she scrambled to find time for her writing. Jack was busy professionally, but the novelty of the Gold Coast undertaking was beginning to pall by mid-summer. Plans for their next leave, spring 1954, soon focussed on spending it in Canada. Both sides of the family were eager to see Jocelyn, but equally important was Jack's wish to see at first hand "what the situation for engineering is like at home."[21]

An interesting development resulted from Peg's being unable to type in the evenings lest she awaken Jocelyn: she began writing in longhand, progressed more slowly, and hence pondered such things as word choice, as she did not at her typewriter.[22] A new practice was thus established, which persisted to the end of her career. By mid-September 1953, she had "scrapped" the Somaliland novel—because it was long-drawn-out and had "too much explanation."[23]

As the year moved into its last quarter, the Laurences' uneasiness had deepened into depression. Their future seemed unsure, and Jack especially liked matters properly arranged, settled, and predictable. Although Peg had received a copy of "Uncertain Flowering"—her *first* publication—and completed her "equivalent" English version of a substantial Somali *gabei*, she felt flat and unproductive: the Somali novel (not entirely scrapped, after all) had lain untouched for a couple of months and now looked "stale." Then she was deeply shocked, furthermore, by the startling death of a three-year-old neighbour boy, a victim of cerebral malaria—a very rare disease. He had fallen ill one morning and was dead before noon the same day. The experience touched Peggy and helped develop a central concern of her future fiction:

> It happened so suddenly. . . . One tends to forget, living in clean, safe houses, that death can still come in, for all our care. We've lost something that primitive peoples have . . . the daily awareness of death. We don't like to think of it; we put it from our minds and tell ourselves that our kids are safe. And when it does come, we don't know how to meet it. The little boy's funeral was somehow even more sad here. . . . The flowers, picked that morning, were all dead.[24]

Doubtless, the presence of Jocelyn—now over a year old and already a distinguishable little person in the household—had sharpened Peg's sensitivity both to the unpredictable stroke of death and also to the "civilized" response of people like the bereft parents, and like herself.

Gradually, the Laurences' attitude brightened and they began to look forward to another tour in the Gold Coast after their leave in Canada. Jack had become particularly pleased with his relationship with the chief engineer and in turn enjoyed his respect; he only hoped the company would offer him a suitable salary to return for the new tour. Peggy, too, found herself hoping to come back to the Accra-Tema area: she had "become unexpectedly fond of this place."[25] She had taken up the old Somali novel and begun thorough revision.

Writing now in longhand, she had eighteen pages finished before the end of November; Jack read them and thought he saw improvement—"so that is encouraging," she wrote to Adele. She had also learned that Malcolm Ross, one of her favourite professors at the University of Manitoba, had become editor of *Queen's Quarterly* magazine, at Queen's University in Kingston, Ontario. Adele had given Dr. Ross Peg's address, and he had written to ask for her new translations of Somali poetry or some of her own short stories. She wrote to Guś Andrzejewski to ask permission to send some of the translations they had been working on together. He agreed. With a selection, she also sent along a Somali short story—her earliest, but carefully revised—called "Amiina," "about the Somali girl and the English bloke who shot himself."[26] The story was rejected. Malcolm Ross told her he found the Englishman "pathetic" and the Somali girl "vicious," so Peggy wrote him a long letter, explaining her intention in the story and suggesting he had missed the point. She explained to Adele:

> the Englishman wasn't pathetic, and the native girl was certainly not vicious, in fact, if anything, quite the contrary was true of both; . . . the English boy was not destroyed, as M.R. said, by the native girl—he in fact destroyed himself, symbolically as well as literally, by the naivete of his love—having before hated the Africans, he found his "pet" African, the one who justified all the others, and so began to accept the whole race, but his love, like his hatred, was lacking in true understanding of their motives, attitudes, reactions, etc. In the end, because he accepts Amiina as good, good by his English standards, he is of course disillusioned, and turns once more—from love to hatred. The naivete of Europeans who must think the Africans are either entirely bad or entirely good—always, of course, judging by European standards—that is more or less the theme.[27]

She recognized that if Ross didn't get the point of the story, it was likely the story's fault. Her justification nevertheless alerts us to what will come in her later African fiction.

The Laurences' leave had been set to begin in March 1954, but the New Year's news was that it would be postponed until the end of April. Peg worked steadily at her novel, and Jack kept his eye on her progress. His role as critic can be glimpsed in Peg's breathless letter of 16 January 1954 to Adele. He has in hand episode number four of the new version of the Somaliland novel, and she is "trying not to chew my nails." Her explanation is revealing—and the spaces between the lines are brimming with unconscious revelations:

> Jack is a very good critic, you know. If he says it stinks, then it does in fact stink. The first two times he read this episode, he tore it to bits (it had then been re-written about five times already) so I hope he thinks it stands up better this time. I'm fed up with it. I wish I could disagree with J's criticisms—but they are so damned logical & sound—I always wonder why I didn't see it myself. If I ever write anything with any merit, it will be largely due to him—he's always getting me to rework things until they're at least the best I can do.

The letter ends with a welcome postscript (also in ink): "Jack says Episode #4 is ok now—thank God."

Leave began with the Laurences' departure for London on 28 April 1954. They spent almost a week in Winnipeg as guests of Adele Wiseman's family, on Burrows Avenue, and visited briefly with old friends, then went on to Victoria to divide their time between Jack's family and Peg's Mum, who had moved there to be near her sister Ruby, a nurse. Jocelyn was christened in Victoria with Peg's brother, Robert, as godfather. They could spare just a quick two days in Winnipeg again on their return to the Gold Coast, for their next tour of duty began in August—this time in Tema itself.

Jack assumed the position of third in command of the Tema Harbour Project—a big job and an important step up in his profession, for it meant he would be in administrative work, which he felt was really his cup of tea. That factor contributed much to enhance the atmosphere in the Laurence household, and Peggy was always careful to keep a finger on Jack's professional pulse. On their return to the Gold Coast she learned that *Queen's Quarterly* had accepted her Somaliland story. Ross's letter was dated in May, just a few days after the Laurences had gone on leave. Would the acceptance still hold? An attendant annoyance was Ross's asking whether she had something more recent she could send him. She certainly had—the rough draft of a story set in the Gold Coast that she had shown to Adele in Winnipeg—but it was by no means ready to be sent off. Peg set to work at once to knock the story into shape. She was proud of the result, and Jack thought it the best she had ever done; off it went. Copies of *A Tree for Poverty* arrived at about that time and served to encourage her to continue revision of the Somaliland novel.

Settling into their quarters—"a really nice bungalow," she told Adele—took time and energy away from her writing. Nevertheless, they were already looking ahead to their next leave, about a year away, and once again planning a visit to Italy. Peggy was plagued by a series of illnesses and discomforts: first, a type of "foot rot" and then, almost immediately after that, something called "tumbo fly"—"an insect that lays eggs under the skin, and the larvae burrow merrily along"; one of her arms developed a mass of long blisters that made it look as though it had been burned. Finally, there was a bout of food poisoning that lasted only twenty-four hours but made her feel absolutely wretched.[28] In the midst of all this, so to speak, Peggy became pregnant.

Her condition, misdiagnosed by a young African doctor in Tema, who thought it some kind of neurosis,[29] meant altering their plans for the leave. The bright side was that the baby would not be born in the middle of their leave, as Jocelyn had been, but rather at the end of July 1955. Peg and Jack decided this would be their last child and that the birth would occur in the Gold Coast. Jocelyn was quite thrilled at the prospect of a sibling. As for Jack, "if not as thrilled as Jocelyn and myself," Peggy wrote to Adele, he "is at least philosophical about the whole thing and admits he will probably be crazy about this one, too, when it is actually here."[30] Instead of morning sickness, she suffered from "evening sickness"—as she had with Jocelyn—and it began very early in the pregnancy; she also suffered from afternoon drowsiness and "wasted" (she complained) a couple of hours every day in taking a nap. She was awake enough to play hostess to some forty guests at the Laurences' Christmas morning party.

In spite of all, by the end of the year Peg had finished eleven chapters of the Somali novel. *Queen's Quarterly* returned the Somali story that had been originally accepted and the translations of Somali poetry, but Malcolm Ross kept the Gold Coast story, "The Drummer of All the World"; he hadn't had time to read it yet, he said, but at least he hadn't sent it back to her. Another Gold Coast story, a vague idea, began to engage her imagination as 1954 drew to a close: about an African schoolteacher who had lost the old way of life but not firmly grasped the new. Perhaps promising, it would have to wait its turn. Peg's afternoon drowsiness persisted through the first months of the new year, and she took on a good share of the housework, partly to save money but partly because "I don't think it is a good thing in the tropics for a woman to do very little, physically—that is half the trouble with most [European] women here. . . ."[31]

Word came in June 1955 that "The Drummer of All the World" would appear in the winter issue of *Queen's Quarterly*, and also that Peg's Mum and Aunt Ruby might come to England in September. The Laurences agreed they could manage a visit for Peg and the two children to London in October, and Jack could follow later when his leave officially began; Adele Wiseman also hoped to be in London that autumn. Just before her twenty-ninth birthday, Peg had the first of two "false labours." Later in the month, a second labour suggested the birth was imminent, and Jack again hurried to the garage to get the car. There, awaiting him, was a treacherous, spitting cobra. Several local police responded to his call for help and worked with him to remove the villain—to no avail. They finally enlisted the expertise of an old man from the Northern Territories of the Gold Coast (who was in the area), "a real bushwallah," Peg called him, who "drew the cobra out by some mysterious means, & the whole bunch fell on it with machetes & killed it."[32]

The birth occurred on August 9. Eight hours of labour produced a healthy young brother for Jocelyn in the Ridge Hospital in Accra with the genial aid of a Native midwife—"Robert David Wemyss Laurence." They called him "David." Peggy remained in the hospital for almost a week. (And then, also, she might just name that troubled schoolteacher "Nathanial." She would see.)

The Laurences' plans for their leave had been adjusted so that Jack would accompany Peg and the children to London, departing on October 16 and arriving in England the next day. Mum and Aunt Ruby would live with Peg and Jack until about the end of November, the midpoint of their leave. They all stayed briefly in the expensive flat Mum and Aunt Ruby had let in September, until Jack found something large enough to accommodate them all in Knightsbridge, just a block away from Harrod's department store. Peg scrubbed and scoured it to approximate cleanliness. She could do nothing, however, about the failed central heating, and it was a chilly October and November. David's christening in a nearby Anglican church was a modest affair, but Grandma Wemyss provided a lovely christening cake from Harrod's pastry department. Altogether, grandmother and great-aunt were suitably impressed with Jocelyn and David, and the six-week visit was pronounced a success. At their departure, Peg gave her Mum a long letter she had written and asked that it be left unopened until they were on board ship. Peggy had been moved simply to record how much she loved her—"how much she meant to me, and how much her encouragement of my writing had strengthened me, even though I had had nothing published professionally. I also wanted to tell her that she could not have been more my mother if she had actually borne me."[33]

The remainder of their leave allowed time for Peg and Adele to be together and discuss their dearest concerns—discussions Peg almost desperately needed. At the end of the leave, 8 January 1956, Adele helped with the departure of the four Laurences. They left the London flat at 9:30 in the morning and set off bravely for the airport. Awaiting Peggy in Tema was word that "The Drummer of All the World" would appear in a matter of days, and enclosed was a check for $54.[34] That eased the disappointment she had felt at Ross's rejection of her Somali translations.

The Somaliland Society had been founded in Hargeisa on 5 September 1954, and by the end of that year boasted a membership of eighty-three, including Mrs. Margaret Laurence. The first number of *The Somaliland Journal* (December 1954) contained a flattering if brief review of *A Tree for Poverty* and announced that a signed copy of the volume had been donated to the society by the author. Peggy now sent to *The Somaliland Journal* her complete translation of a Somali *gabei*, excerpts from which she had sent unsuccessfully to *Queen's Quarterly*; it appeared in the third number (December 1956, pp. 138-43): "'To a Faithless Friend,' A *gabei* by Salaan Arrabey translated by Margaret Laurence." She had included nine lines of this 162-line *gabei* in *A Tree for Poverty*, and quoted two lines of the new, completed version in a letter to Adele:

> Behold me! Like a vulture of the Scorched Plains,
> In a deserted place mournful I sit. (53-54)

Shortly after their arrival back in Tema, there returned to her, from more than a year earlier, an idea about a West African schoolteacher caught in a kind of time warp—"he stands . . . 'between today and tomorrow'. . . ."[35] It did not even feel like *her* story; setting it down on paper was more like taking dictation. She explained the phenomenon to Adele:

> It is now over 80 pages and not even half finished . . . and I don't know what to do with the damn thing. It just keeps

> coming. I've got no plan or anything, but somehow it just seems to be there, waiting to be put down, and I can't get it down fast enough. It will be in horribly rough form, but I want to get it down while it is still in the outpouring stage. . . . I've been sitting up about four nights a week until 1 or 2 a.m. and feeling like a million dollars.[36]

This regime of virtual enslavement by the compelling story continued—at an accelerated pace and to an even later hour after midnight—with very little comprehension on Peg's part of what it was all about and certainly with no end in sight. Yet, by the end of May 1956, she knew the story was half done. It had been written from the point of view of the schoolteacher, and the second half would be written from the point of view of a European woman. The mystery of its creation was exhilarating and artistically instructive: "this seems a more desirable way of doing things than too much planning, which I can't help feeling has been my big weakness in the past. Anyway, there is a sense of discovery about it which is very exciting, . . . as long as I don't drop dead from fatigue before I finish it, it may turn out to be something, altho' god knows what."[37]

As discovery continued, Peggy recognized she was relying heavily on the current situation in the Gold Coast, especially the British colonial legacy, but also the movement for independence spearheaded by Nkrumah. She was aware of her own strong bias against the colonialists—the European intruders—but did not characterize that feeling as prejudice: she had seen first and then judged, harshly indeed but not unreasonably, she believed. Her attitude was guided by artistic as well as moral standards. The second half of the novel was proving more difficult to manage than the first: "I tend to be rather fed up at this point with the European community here and that is no attitude to have for writing. I don't want to condemn even them—I only want to understand them." She insisted that "the story isn't a political one, politics are only dealt with indirectly—it isn't in any sense partisan in the political-party sense. But it is in the broad sense."[38]

At that moment Nkrumah and his Convention People's Party were facing a general election. Their opposition from the conservative right and their own drifting away from the original strong basis in the "masses" meant that the election—and with it the evident success of self-government for the Gold Coast—was by no means a foregone conclusion. Nkrumah and the CPP triumphed, however, in the July 1956 elections, and to optimistic liberals like Peggy and Jack Laurence, the future for West Africa looked bright, with full independence in the near future virtually assured. That optimism was reflected in Peggy's novel as it reached its denouement, and she was quite relieved, artistically as well as politically: "the general election here is over," she exclaimed, "and thank god it went the right way, otherwise I'd have had to change the whole novel! . . . The nationalists here represent a return to the past, the CPP (Nkrumah's party) despite their widespread corruption, represent a forward move."[39]

By the end of July Peggy had ended the period of exciting discovery. She knew what the novel was about and was almost sure of how it must end, so that she could offer (in a double airmail letter to Adele Wiseman) a summary, its two main themes, the title, and the names of the two protagonists—one for the first half and one for the second. It was called *This Side Jordan*, from the book of Joshua I:14-15, where Joshua is conveying God's words to the Israelites concerning their passing over the river Jordan—from the land "which Moses gave you on this side Jordan" to the Promised Land—"to possess the land which the Lord your God giveth you to possess it." The emphasis in verse 15, however, focusses on the *preparation* for crossing over Jordan, on the fact that *this* land is theirs, and that the whole undertaking involves their brethren (the Reubenites, the Gadites, and half the tribe of Manasseh) as well as themselves. The implication throughout is that the burden of responsibility is theirs:

> Until the Lord have given your brethren rest, as *he hath given* you, and they have also possessed the land which the Lord your God giveth them; then ye shall return unto the

> land of your possession, and enjoy it, which Moses the Lord's servant gave you on this side Jordan toward the sun-rising.

This verse, with its emphasis on sharing, is somewhat reminiscent of the passage in Exodus about the heart of a stranger that had so impressed Peg in the hotel room in Rotterdam. In fact, this verse 15 might serve as an appropriate epigraph for the novel.

The two characters on whose point of view the form of the novel depends were named by now: *Nathaniel* is the troubled African schoolteacher who tries to escape the last trammels of the Past as preparation for crossing into a brighter future; the European woman, a naïve, liberal-hearted daughter of a Church of England bishop, is *Miranda*. As Peg continued her lengthy resume of the story, she touched on the situation of one of Nathaniel's students, who has been given a token job by Miranda's husband, Johnnie Kestoe; the boy has been only half educated, but he doesn't know that and his optimism is high—"The boy has ideas about the brave new Ghana. . . ."[40] That echo from Shakespeare's *The Tempest* alerts us to the significance of the woman's name. Peggy used *The Tempest* for serious social commentary on the evils of colonialism.

At about the middle of July 1956, Peg visited an African school of which the principal was one Mr. O'Reilly-Wright: "A third-rate African school is featured in my story—that is why I wanted to see if my impressions had been correct. They were. . . . I was delighted to find that I hadn't been wrong—only in my school I hadn't been nearly sordid enough." She has a kind word for O'Reilly-Wright, nevertheless, "a good man in many ways," who was about to visit the USA and most eager, indeed anxious, to get information relevant to the venture. To help prepare him for what he might find there, she referred him to Richard Wright's autobiographical *Black Boy* (1945).[41]

The month of July was a heavy one for Peggy: she had been working relentlessly for six months on the novel and that commitment was taking its toll. She began to suffer from headaches and general queasiness. That condition was aggravated by her sense of guilt—a feeling never very far from the centre of her sensitive psyche—about the amount of time and energy she had stolen from the family in order to write. It was an additional embarrassment that she was virtually a closet artist, that this other commitment remained unavowed except to Adele and Jack. During a moment of depression early in the month, she unburdened herself to Adele—she was discouraged, the strain was beginning to show, and then, "I'm sorry to bore you with all this, but you're the only person I know who will understand."[42] That sentiment was reiterated. Her next letter apologized for involving Adele in her problems, her "doubts and depressions," which are personal as well as professional; and she resumed unburdening:

> I'm sorry I keep chattering on about all this to you. The thing is, I can't talk about it to anyone except Jack, and altho' he is wonderful about it, and has an excellent critical mind, he hasn't actually done this kind of work himself. I often feel I am leading a double life—do you? It seems a kind of irony to me that the thing in life which is most important to me, next to my husband and kids, is something I can never talk about, never let anyone know about, even.[43]

She added, philosophically—and perhaps prophetically—"Anyway, things work towards their conclusion. . . ."

In mid-October a letter from Aunt Ruby in Victoria brought news that Mum had had an operation for cancer and the doctor thought she might not live out another year. The Laurences had already decided to return to Canada when the current tour of duty ended in the spring of 1957, so the idea of going back early was not really upsetting—as news of Mum's condition certainly was. Plans were made for Peg and the two children to leave for Canada early in January 1957, with Jack to follow in April, when his tour would be officially ended. She would have four days in London, mainly with Adele, but the last day, Saturday,

12 January, would be spent with Nancy and Frank Collier and their children.[44] Peg finished the first draft of *This Side Jordan* before she and the children left the Gold Coast ("Jack has read the first few chapters, and likes them"[45]), so she could share her achievement with Adele in London. At the last minute both Jocelyn and David fell ill—food poisoning or worms, she wrote to Adele[46]—but the departure went ahead as planned. Her time in London was memorable: she and Adele had an old-fashioned "all-nighter" as she read reviews of Adele's newly published novel, *The Sacrifice*, and Adele read Peg's *Jordan*.[47] Adele's would win the Governor General's Award; would Peggy's ever see the light of day?

eight

Facing Jordan

AFTER A QUIET FLIGHT ACROSS THE ATLANTIC, PEG AND THE children were met in Montreal by a blast of truly Canadian winter with a -40° temperature. They had a brief visit there, spent a few days with Mona in Vancouver, and finally went on to Aunt Ruby's on Windsor Road in Victoria. The small house accommodated Jocelyn and David in the basement room where Peg's brother slept when he visited. Peggy was allotted the cot in Aunt Ruby's room; returned from hospital after surgery, Mum slept in the other bedroom. At the first opportunity, Peg lugged the cot to the basement, dragged two trunks to the foot and laid an old door across them as a desk, and created "walls" by hanging blankets on a clothesline. She was nearer the children, yet with some privacy. By the end of January they were settled in and Peg had returned to *This Side Jordan*. She had realized Virginia Woolf's ideal of "a room of one's own."[1]

Peg and the children spent one night a week with their Laurence grandparents. Almost at once, Elsie Fry Laurence (Jack's mother), herself a novelist, began to help Peg in typing *Jordan*—eventually she did about thirty percent of the job—and insisted it be submitted to the *Atlantic Monthly* novel contest. Mum spent her days on Ruby's chesterfield in the small living room. There she read and discussed the manuscript of *Jordan* carefully, as she had discussed Peg's writing in the past, pointing out the inequality between her treatment of the Africans and her treatment of the Europeans (which Peg had already noted). At the end of that three-hour session, she gratefully told her mother, "It's dedicated to you."[2]

In mid-March she sent *Jordan* off to the *Atlantic.* On 17 March 1957 she wrote Adele Wiseman a long, rambling letter, loose and disjunctive, as Peg herself felt at the time. Its muddled theme emerges as a lament for the threatened loss of love or life—or of both. She recalled the death of the Gold Coast child, the neighbour smitten with cerebral malaria; she was concerned with the decline of her mother; she was mulling over a possible story about an old woman. Of course, she was thinking of herself and how the demands of her writing made her neglect her family; of loss and alienation, being outcast from life's feast—like what the outcast Ishmael felt in sympathy with his mother, the handmaiden of Abram's wife Sara. Memory of the Gold Coast child whose death amazed family and friends focussed Peg's attention on how people typically respond to death: "that final appointment is something they cannot face, some trying to balance the demands and routine of this life with an increasing need to gather together the threads of the spirit so that when the thing comes they will be ready. . . ."

The conclusion was surprising: "ready—whether it turns out to be a death or only another birth." Another birth brings the obligation to begin again, to resume the tasks of life, while "death is the greatest experience," she added. The story of the old woman will tell of her "moving with tremendous excitement . . . toward a great and inevitable happening." Peg's sympathy was with her, and with the mourners who will be ready to face death rather than "only another birth." The echo here of the conclusion of Eliot's "Journey of the Magi" is quite audible:

> . . . I had seen birth and death,
> But had thought they were different; . . .
> But no longer at ease here, . . .
> I should be glad of another death.

Death of the old gods receives the emphasis; but its importance lies in its opening the way to true Birth. It was an emphasis necessary to Peggy at the moment, although she was not yet fully aware of that fact.

She concluded the letter with a postscript to report that her diet had helped her lose ten pounds. For Jack was to arrive home at the end of April, when the Laurences would move into a place of their own in North Vancouver, 1540 St. Georges Avenue. They had the ground floor of a large house made into three flats, which gave Jocelyn and David (now aged five and two) easy access to an ample yard to play in.[3] Jack joined an engineering consulting firm directed by H.H. Minshall (for twenty years with the Dominion Bridge Company) and was soon advisor on the building of a road up to Squamish, just north of Vancouver, and the construction there of a harbour—a job similar to what he had at Tema in the Gold Coast.

Mrs. Wemyss rallied sufficiently to visit Peggy and family in the late spring, and toward the end of summer they returned the visit. At the beginning of September, Aunt Ruby summoned both Peg and brother Robert (at Nanaimo) to Victoria. Mum had begun a serious decline in which she slipped into irrationality; but one evening toward the end, complete lucidity returned for a moment. As they were about to leave, their mother said to them, "God bless you." Peg observed, "I don't remember her ever saying that before in my life. I think I knew then that I'd never see her again – not her real self. . . ."[4] Mrs. Wemyss died quietly on 25 September 1957.[5] For Peggy it was a most meaningful death.

Her Mum's death was the second in a series of blows that struck the family, as Peg's letter of 1 December 1957 to Adele recounts. First of all was the nearly disastrous purchase of a house shortly after Jack's arrival: the "Contractor-owner was trying to pull a fast one & involve us in a third mortgage which would have ruined us." They escaped with payment of a $20 legal fee. A third blow followed close on Mum's death: Jack fell ill as a result of kidney stones that required surgery;

that was complicated by infection and an abscess. Aunt Ruby came over from Victoria to help care for Jocelyn and David, and to allow Peg to visit Jack in hospital. Asian flu struck the children and Aunt Ruby, and Peg had four invalids to attend to—and she "hit the bottle pretty hard."[6] That was the fourth blow. A fifth fell with the return of the manuscript of *This Side Jordan*. The *Atlantic* had strong criticism of her treatment of the European characters but invited resubmission of a revised version. With Jack incapacitated, Peg was the only family breadwinner; she turned to what she knew best—apart from her own writing. Watson Thomson, Jack's old friend of Winnipeg days, was at the University of British Columbia, and he introduced her to Professor Gordon Elliott,[7] who eagerly offered her a job marking essays. It paid well and Elliott proved a reliable and increasingly helpful friend. This series of "blows" perhaps comprised that kind of "death" that permits rebirths. In any case, she set to work at revision of *This Side Jordan*.

The next five years constituted a crucial time for the Laurences, and especially for Peggy. Jack struggled with the dissatisfaction in his various professional assignments; Peg struggled with her writing, with her vocation itself, with her persistent attraction to Somaliland and particularly with her commitment to her Somaliland novel, acutely with her reliance on Jack's assistance as literary critic and her dependence on him as general mentor and guide, with her confrontation with Canada, and with her need to confront herself. Those struggles were intimately interconnected. Light is shed on Peggy's handling of her problems during those years by a letter she wrote to Adele on 23 July 1956, a typical "unburdening" letter. The burgeoning novel, *Jordan*, provided a focus for that illumination.

The letter opens with an apology for writing the "pretty stupid letter" of 10 July, which explained that for six months she had been writing four nights a week until 2:00 or 3:00 a.m. She justifies unburdening herself to Adele—"you're the only one who understands." The letter of 23 July reiterates that justification, and Peg complains that at age thirty she hasn't done enough, has no novels published. Most telling of all, she is a closet writer; the most important feature of her life, after Jack and children, is something she can't talk about, can never let anyone know about. Especially tantalizing is her comment that, during their recent tour of duty in the Gold Coast, something important happened to her, and Jack is the only one who knows anything about it. The context suggests that "something" had to do with her identity as writer, but especially as the writer of the novel in question, *This Side Jordan*. Letters to Adele from Tema during the preceding four months of 1956 add specific clues, indicating that "something" refers to an identity blessed by an attendant muse or possessed by a daemon—one who is not only compelled to write but obliged to accept special spiritual guidance. The strange "something" continued to assert itself in Peggy's life to the end of her career. She did not always respond as she ought.

The muse sometimes sent unclear signals; the daemon made conflicting demands. The *Atlantic* suggested revisions to the manuscript she had submitted in March of 1957. Peg reinterpreted the signals and demands. She now admitted what she and her mother had both recognized, that all the European characters needed redoing, and particularly that Johnnie Kestoe, rather than Miranda, must be the principal European character and the appropriate foil to Nathaniel Amegbe, the African schoolteacher. She made the adjustments and returned *Jordan* to the *Atlantic*. To prepare for the shift of focus to Johnnie, Peg began reading about Roman Catholicism, as she had read material on the Akan religion to prepare for Nathaniel Amegbe. In a letter to Adele, she affirmed that the Roman Catholic religion "is, & must be, the key to understanding Johnnie"; and then quoted from the order of the mass and observed, "a person raised in that faith could *never* escape it. . . . Like [Graham] Greene's renegade priest, he could never escape the Power and the Glory." She also notes that she is "beginning to feel at home" in Canada; she has not forgotten Africa, "a stinking place, I suppose, but I loved it & I felt at home there as I never did here . . . I'd still go back like a shot. . . . But that is impossible . . . & probably in another year or so I will feel established here."[8]

At the beginning of May the Laurences settled into their new home at 3556 West 21st Avenue in Vancouver. Jack's firm sent him as resident engineer up to Fort St. John to supervise dismantling a collapsed bridge over the Peace River. It suited him just fine. Peg and the children remained in Vancouver but went up to join him for the summer months. Peg had begun revising *Jordan* and benefitting not only from the shift of emphasis to Johnnie Kestoe and working the obvious parallel between him and Nathaniel, but also from her new insight into the Roman Catholic Johnnie. She wrote to Adele from Fort St. John to explain that at last Kestoe returns to the beliefs of his past—as she half anticipated six months earlier; now the directions from muse and daemon came through clearly:

> The European character, Johnnie, goes back to the R.C. Church at the end of the book. I didn't know whether he was going to or not, but he did. . . . a subtle point which I don't really emphasize—the European is the one who returns to the past, in this fashion. The African, for all his weakness, does not.[9]

That matter settled, Peg sent off the manuscript late in the fall and immediately turned to the Somaliland novel once again. She couldn't let it alone. December brought a period of forced idleness as Peggy was laid up with a kidney infection. She took advantage of the forced inactivity to write a typical year-end report to Adele, really a double letter: for 22 December, a newsy-gossipy letter, congratulating Adele on a grant to support her writing, but for 23 December, quite serious in its observations on "home" and herself, which, as usual, reflect on her writing. In the latter half, Peg resumed a topic she had dwelt on briefly in a note added to her August letter to Adele—on the primitive aspects of most religions ("not an entirely bad thing")—and by implication connected that to her concerns about *home*, with a changed attitude: "I really don't care for North America, but if you happen to be born a roman when the empire is falling, where else can you go? Because one *does* care about it, really, I suppose." She clarified the note of reluctance there with an important personal reference:

> Anyway, one can't go on being a stranger in a strange land, as we were in Africa. . . . One cannot identify oneself with another culture, because everyone carries his own culture with him, like his blood-group. I am speaking of the large classifications of culture—a person can move from Europe to America, or vice versa, but the so-called primitive cultures of Africa are something quite different. ⊛

And she appended this revealing note: "⊛They are, to us, Paradise lost."

A comparison of her letters of February 1958 and this of December 1958 to Adele indicates how intimately associated were her life and work, and how she seemed caught between feeling somewhat settled in Canada and not really caring for North America, between the persistent Somaliland novel and the new novel of Ghana (*Jordan*), and, in the latter, between Johnnie Kestoe and Nathaniel Amegbe—particularly Amegbe's conflicted attractions to Past and Future. For Peggy it was not a matter of starting again, of a kind of rebirth, but much more of bidding adieu to what had been, of accepting a death.

The anticipated rejection of her *Jordan* manuscript was soon justified. She began revision at once, but at the same time looked at her material for further Gold Coast short stories, companion pieces to "The Drummer of All the World." She finished four stories by mid-May 1959, just about the time she finished rewriting *Jordan*. At that point, Gordon Elliott generously typed a clean copy and sent it, with a cover letter praising it heartily, to Jack McClelland of the McClelland and Stewart publishing house.

She received some much-needed encouragement in September: the new magazine *Prism International* published her "The Merchant of Heaven" and McClelland and Stewart accepted *This Side Jordan*—conditionally: finding an English and an American publisher would close the deal. Macmillan in England accepted the novel that November, provided she cut it by 10,000 words. "A mere bagatelle," she cooed to Adele.[10] A week's feverish work actually cut 11,000 words; then Peg and family were off to Victoria for Christmas.[11]

Peggy's first letter of 1960 to Adele reported on young David's interest in writers: she and Jack were discussing a male novelist, and David, age four and a half, joined in to ask, "Who ever heard of a book written by a *man*?" Peggy's maternal explanation gives pause: "He had believed that only mothers wrote books, & that writing was in something the same category as cooking or washing dishes—perhaps a necessary work, but not one that would be favoured by any man worthy of the name!"[12] It raises a gloomy question or two, such as "What could have been the source of David's information?"—and what of "any man worthy of the name"? Shortly after that, St. Martin's became the third publisher to accept *Jordan*. She immediately phoned her neighbour Zella Clark to give her the news.[13]

That news helped tide her over a rocky July, when she suffered a gall bladder attack, had surgery, and spent three weeks in hospital. Aunt Ruby came over from Victoria to help her at home. A sense of further relief came with Jack's accepting a job as plant engineer with Wright's Canadian Ropes, what he wanted and maybe the right job at last. He would be away for six weeks of the autumn. Meanwhile, Peg began reviewing books for the *Vancouver Sun* at $10 to $15 a time. *This Side Jordan* came out in November. She took a signed copy across the street to Zella Clark. Zella recalled, "It was then that she asked me if I would please call her Margaret."[14] The request confirmed the recent suggestion from Jan Bhatti, her next-door neighbour—made during a quiet discussion of hairstyling and other details that affect one's sense of self: "You're not 'Peggy'; you're 'Margaret.'"[15] Jack returned to Vancouver early in December. His response to the name change was gaping incredulity; his acquiescence took the form of calling her "M" and the children "J" and "D."[16] She gave the news to Adele in her first letter of that year, explaining the change as something "I've wanted to do for years. I've always detested my name . . . [not] 'Peg,' which I don't mind so much—it was Peggy I hated, so I have killed her off (I hope)."[17]

The historical setting of *This Side Jordan* is a crucial moment in 1956, when the people of the Gold Coast were anticipating independence under their native leader, Kwame Nkrumah—socially and politically a moment of transition. The people were caught between conflicting forces, one attempting to retain the old ways of tribal chieftains and their drummers, the other following Nkrumah's attempt to establish the new way of Ghana's independence and freedom. That Janus-faced middle position was held in place by British colonialism and its Christian missionaries.

The conflict of the opposed forces of Past and Future is dramatized in the dilemma of Nathaniel Amegbe, who has "lost the old life and not yet firmly grasped the new."[18] His commitment to the future is opposed by his own wife and family: Aya, his pregnant wife, nominally Christian and in sympathy with his dedication to the new enlightenment, yet resists going to the hospital in Accra to have her baby, and his uncle persists in offering him the important position of clerk to a chief as an alternative to his teaching job at Futura Academy. In spite of its name, that academy is part of the force that opposes change. Jacob Abraham Mensah is not really devoted to educating the students but concerned, like more prominent Anglo-Africans, with maintaining the status quo, his exalted situation as headmaster. Mensah is thus a subtle antagonist to Amegbe, but Johnnie Kestoe and the other white employees of Allkirk, Moore & Bright are more blatantly opposed to the *apparent* aims of Futura Academy—preparation of Natives to take over those employees' jobs and its whole *raison d'être* in the country.

Peggy put it succinctly in a letter to Adele: Johnnie "despises in Africans what he fears in himself—the newness of their educated position and their inability to cope with it."[19] The novel adds to that his hatred of their relaxed attitude to their physical being and lusty enjoyment of it.

The novel opens as Johnnie is dancing with (and trying to dance like) an inebriated young Ghanaian woman, Charity Donkor, at the nightclub "Weekend in Wyoming." Returning to their table, Johnnie apologizes to his pregnant wife "for dancing with that whore . . ."; she replies, "The only thing I minded was that you—you thought there was something dirty in doing it."[20] Chapter 5 develops this aspect of Johnnie. He has gone into the shop of Syrian Saleh for some cigarettes, and during their idle conversation the proprietor's daughter enters from the rear of the shop. "She was tall and sleek, . . . She smiled at him . . ." (87). Saleh, eyeing Johnnie, comments, "I don't care what a man does, just so he don't pick on Saleh's daughter to do it with" (88). He offers to direct Johnnie to a "proper place" for such doing, but Johnnie declines, "I'm not interested." Saleh replies, "From the way you look at my daughter, I thought maybe you was wondering. . . ."

The motif is enhanced at the opening of chapter 8, which concludes the first half of the book and thus participates directly in the story's climax. Johnnie is involved in an encounter with the "small wife" of the Kestoes' cook, Whiskey. A bush girl of fourteen, she has come upon Johnnie working on his car. They are quite alone. His lust aroused, he touches her breast (134); she turns her eyes away and then looks directly at him. Johnnie responds to the rejection by striking her across the face. "A few minutes later he heard her screams. The blow must have made a betraying welt. Whiskey was beating her. Johnnie grasped the chair-arm and closed his eyes. . . . It was none of his business" (135). This episode follows a brief discussion between Johnnie and his wife about the baleful approach of Africanization, which ends with her hinting at what will blossom into her Plan for

Johnnie's role in the inevitable change—"The Firm can't afford to let everyone go. They need some continuity. But the only Europeans who do stay will be those who show they can work with Africans" (132-33). Then the chapter ends with Johnnie's recognizing the possibilities for him in "the whole treacherous scheme" (140) and offering to play host to the junior partner, Cameron Sheppard, who is coming out from the Home Office, "in connection with the Africanization programme" (144).

Further, Johnnie's visit to Emerald, the virgin prostitute at "Weekend in Wyoming" (end of chapter 12), is precipitated by the sharp confrontation between him and his wife over the realization that the Plan for his role in Africanization is heavy with moral implications. Emerald is mutely fascinated by the strange white man and fearful of displeasing him: "Her uncertainty irritated Johnnie. He wanted her to mock him with herself. Like Victor Edusei's girl [Charity Donkor], the one he had danced with that time. Or like Saleh's serpent-eyed daughter, laughing at his unacknowledged desire" (228). Then it "occurred to Johnnie that he might be her first whiteman. Perhaps, like Whiskey's child-wife, she wondered if whitemen were like black in any way at all, even this way" (229).

Amid the general squalor of the room Johnnie has gone to with Emerald, there is a Gideon Bible and a portrait of Nkrumah, captioned "Freedom" (229)—a meaningful setting. Johnnie, stripped, is about to discover her virginity: "Her slight spasm of fear excited him. She was a continent and he an invader, wanting both to possess and to destroy" (231).

Miranda Kestoe's Plan for her husband to take advantage of Africanization leads to the most direct confrontation of Nathaniel Amegbe and Johnnie Kestoe. Miranda has already imposed her pseudo-liberal attentions on Nathaniel and so persuades him to ask Johnnie to find places with the firm for a couple of the Futura boys. She neglects to tell Johnnie.

Nathaniel chooses two boys who have presented him with gifts in gratitude for the time and care he took to give them this chance—an old custom in Ghanaian culture. Yet, while his main concern was honestly to help his students take a step up into the world of the future and prepare for the new glory of Ghana, the modern Nathaniel must face the fact that he has taken a bribe, has become involved in the practice of barter in human beings. In attempting to advance his laudable purpose, he has allowed himself to be "bought." When Johnnie rejects the two boys, they unintentionally expose Nathaniel's guilt.

That guilt weighs so heavily on Nathaniel that he decides the only option open to him now is to resign from Futura Academy, leave Accra, and accept the position offered to him as clerk to a chief. Miranda's Plan for Johnnie has contributed importantly to Nathaniel's accepting the bribe; the Plan itself is really just another bribe, finally, as Johnnie's willing involvement with Sheppard anticipates the reward of continued employment by the firm, and, finally, the position of manager in Accra. At the centre of this complex arrangement is Miranda. What sort of brave new world are her well-intentioned, pseudo-liberal machinations liable to foster? A revealing parallel to this feature of *Jordon* is the work of another colonial writer, the Barbadian George Lamming (whom Margaret met in Vancouver in the summer of 1962), especially *The Pleasures of Exile*.[21]

Miranda Kestoe is responsible for the Plan—from finding Johnnie a place in the inescapable surge into Africanization (and all the wretched manoeuvring that involves) to the ultimate betrayal and defeat of his colleagues in the firm. Johnnie's anger over Nathaniel's deceiving him (as he believes) with the incompetent candidates for jobs with the firm prompts him to blame Miranda: "You know who had the idea in the first place, for me to start my own Africanization scheme" (216). She, of course, defends herself, and tries to defend Nathaniel as well, confessing she had persuaded him to approach Johnnie, and concludes, "So who's really responsible for what happened? Perhaps we all are" (217). Miranda is yet seeking to absolve herself from blame, for she has been more knowing than she cares to admit. She tells Johnnie she overheard his crucial conversation with Sheppard and also Johnnie's condemnation of his colleagues: "I wakened. . . . I didn't understand, then, why you were doing it, but I know now" (217-18).

> Johnnie did not speak.
>
> "All the things Cameron needed to know," Miranda finished. "All the things he couldn't have found out himself, because people only reveal those things to someone they think they can trust." (218)

Johnnie leaves in a huff.

Johnnie and Nathaniel are similarly manipulated by Miranda. Nathaniel is obviously a Caliban, as defined by Lamming. There is, however, another Caliban figure in the novel, or, rather, there are two characters who represent two distinct phases of the progress of Caliban. The second of these is Victor Edusei.

Victor is the more advanced: "Victor had a degree from the London School of Economics. He had, as well, studied both journalism and accountancy. He had spent six years in U.K." (51). Throughout much of the novel Victor appears to be a figure of wasted ability, certainly in Nathaniel's eyes.[22] He seems without ambition. Yet his criticism of his compatriots, and even of his good friend Nathaniel, is sharp and bitter and cynical: it seems to express more disappointment in the sleepy and passive attitude of his fellow Ghanaians than his apparent lack of ambition would allow. Victor scoffs at Nathaniel's special course, African Civilizations of the Past, claiming there were none worth mentioning (22), and curses Ghanaians as an impractical "race of dreamers" (52). Then, as if anticipating Dominique O. Mannoni's *Prospero and Caliban*,[23] which Margaret would soon read, he declares, "We've been ruled too long by strangers, Nathaniel. We've got the slave mentality"—and, even more cynically, "Slaves aren't humble. . . . They don't want freedom for everybody—all they want is to be the man who holds the whip" (118). Nathaniel accuses Victor of being without sympathy, unable to approve of anything: "What's the matter with you, man? You hate all the old ways, and now you go and hate all the new ones as well. You've got to stand by something" (116-17).

It seems Nathaniel has discovered in Victor a reflection of himself—one who has lost the past and not grasped the future, or even the present. Nathaniel is deceived in this. Victor's response to Nathaniel's attack is puzzling, even though twice iterated and even though he hints broadly enough that his friend is mistaken. "'All right,' Victor said. 'I'll stand by Charity, then.'" Victor launches his attack on Ghanaian dreamers, including Nathaniel, and concludes with a reiteration of his personal option: "You put your faith in Ghana, don't you? The new life. . . . I'm afraid I haven't got your optimism. You can keep Ghana. I'll take Charity." Before Nathaniel has time to savour the rich resonance of the reiteration, Victor's anger has cooled; his face "dissolved, and there was in his eyes an anguish that made Nathaniel turn away, not wanting to see it" (118). Victor laughs, resuming his mask, and ends with a joke: "Charity and I will go fine together. It's like my mother says—it's a pity to spoil two families." For he does "hide from it," as Nathaniel has said.

Yet, dramatic irony is at work. Victor has already been actively promoting Africanization, as we see in his first meeting with Johnnie Kestoe (chapter 3). He then enters with his mask in place, his garb and manner fully that of the somewhat insolent Caliban in front of Johnnie the Prospero-figure, to ask if it is true the firm is considering Africanization. Johnnie rebuffs the query; there follows an abrupt change: "the black man's languor dropped like a snake's sloughed-off skin" (39). The threatening insolence is not boldly apparent—but the deception is at least partially disdained. Victor identifies the girl Johnnie had danced with (the novel's opening scene) as *his* girl: "I watched you, and I didn't like what I saw" (39); then, returning to the rumour of Africanization, he introduces the threat of blackmail—"a story could always be printed . . . as having come from you" (40). Victor's parting shot is the casual "I have many friends in London" (40). This Caliban has won the first round against Prospero.

As the novel moves toward its end, the other Caliban, Nathaniel, seems to decline while Johnnie seems to rise. Miranda's Plan for Johnnie has evidently succeeded; Nathaniel's involvement seems to have obliged him to quit Accra and become clerk to a chief. The two men confront each other at the "Weekend in Wyoming." Highlife Boy Lamptey, his fellow Master at Futura Academy, has taken Nathaniel to the nightclub to cheer him up. Johnnie has come to the nightclub—also alone—bothered by the betrayal that accounts for his own success, and to cheer himself up. Part of Nathaniel's cheer is to be provided by Emerald; he has got drunk and danced and literally run into Johnnie, who, he is sure, is planning to set the police on him, especially since he has just knocked him down. Confirmation comes as Johnnie gets to his feet:

> "No," the whiteman said deliberately. "I've got a better way. This'll clinch the case against you. Assault. It's all I needed. Thanks very much."
>
> "You can't prove anything," Nathaniel heard himself saying. (223)

Lamptey hears Nathaniel's full confession of his involvement with Johnnie, bribe and all, and assures him he can settle everything via a quid pro quo that promises Johnnie "What he's wanted for a long time"—a bush girl, Emerald—in return for forgetting everything he has against Nathaniel. Lamptey adds the persuasive enticement of telling Johnnie that refusing the bargain will lead to Miranda's being informed of "every single thing" (225) about his visit to "Weekend in Wyoming." Johnnie takes Emerald upstairs and, surprisingly, asks her, "What's your name?" (229).

At that moment the agon seems held in stalemate, Johnnie reasserting that "the wheels had been set in motion, and they would keep turning now, whatever he did" (180), and Nathaniel apparently resigned to the clerkship—both yielding to Fate. Yet, chapter 12 ends with Johnnie, the conquering invader, the Prospero, sobbing "as he had not done for nearly twenty years." As chapter 13 ends, Nathaniel has gone with Aya to her church and rehearsed the dilemma of the competing religions he had experienced. In chapter 3 he had realized, "Both gods had fought over him, and both had lost" (32). Now, in chapter 13, he sees himself again as one "over whom both gods had fought and both had lost" (242). Yet, there is reason to hope. At Aya's church Nathaniel is impressed by the sermon of the powerful little preacher and is granted an epiphany in hearing God's message to Joshua—"Don't be afraid. . . . Cross Jordan" (245)—and Joshua's response, "All right, God. I'll try." He joins in the singing, "I'm gonna walk up Jordan shore," and weeps. Then the *old* Caliban in Nathaniel reappears: "He was going back . . . to the Forest and the dark River. . . . What was Jordan to him?" (248). But the epiphany has been vouchsafed.

There is then a birth, and with it a necessary death. Aya gives Nathaniel a son—at the hospital. She is attended by an efficient young nurse, "obviously a 'been-to'" (251), but who speaks to Aya in their common tongue, Twi. Nathaniel exclaims to her, "Our country needs people like you!" (253). It sounds like his commitment to the Future, a farewell to the Past, in spite of what he told Victor. He remembers "he had intended to tell Aya that they were going back to the village," but decides not to—"he did not know why. Perhaps he was waiting for a sign from heaven" (261). Perhaps he was encouraged by Aya's report that Mrs. Kestoe, in the same ward waiting to give birth, had come over to offer kind words, but Aya had repulsed her. In a sense Caliban's consort has stepped up to help him confront the forces of Prospero—and succeeded (the sign from heaven?).

The coincidence of the two births and the meeting of Aya and Miranda on a more equal footing inaugurates the pattern that informs the conclusion of the novel, what looks like a pattern of reconciliation. Not only are those births virtually simultaneous, they create a complementary couple, a male child and a female, as if to suggest a union that might one day produce a new citizen of a brave new world of Free-Dom and the reconciliation of cultural, racial differences. The parallelism is important, rather, to emphasize the reversal involving Nathaniel and Johnnie. It is extended by Nathaniel's passionate outburst at his headmaster's idea of opening an employment bureau to place their boys in firms like Allkirk, Moore & Bright. He urgently points out that the products of Futura Academy are unemployable—beginning with the two sent to Johnnie Kestoe: "The boys were no good. . . . They'd only been given dreams here, only dreams. . . . Don't you know anything?" (269).

He then tells Mensah he is leaving Futura Academy and going back to his village. Mensah, surprisingly, is touched by Nathaniel's harangue and offers him twenty pounds a year more than his clerkship would bring. Nathaniel accepts, recognizing that "he would come back to the school with new authority" (272). "I will stay," he assures Mensah. Nathaniel was at first sceptical of the analogy that he would be—as Mensah put it—the school's soul, its "kra" ("Its guide in a new land, its ferryman across Jordan. . . . when he did not know the way himself?"), and the headmaster its "sunsum" ("Its personality, filled with self, greedy for life, but with an enormous vitality, an enormous will" [273]), but is finally persuaded it "will be all right" (274). He stops at his church on the way home to pray and to declare his intention to stay: "I cannot go back. Never. . . . Let them understand." For himself he adds his strongest affirmation:

> —I cannot have both gods and I cannot have neither. A man must belong somewhere. Mother of men, hear me—
>
> —My God is the God of my own soul, and my own speech is in my mouth, and my home is here, here, here, my home is here at last. (275)

Nathaniel introduced that affirmation by asserting, "The new roots may not grow straight, but they have grown too strong to be cut away. It is the dead who must die. . . ." There is the necessary death.

Second, when Johnnie realizes that his putting Miranda's Plan into action has led to an irrevocable commitment, he is ready, in spite of a small twinge of conscience, to accept the offer Cameron Sheppard extends to him. Sheppard's offer further develops the pattern of reconciliation and Johnnie's acceptance (like Nathaniel's of Mensah's) reinforces the parallel: "'Yes,' he said. 'Certainly I will'" (278). Then Sheppard explains that he has selected a right-hand man for him, "an African. I knew him at the London School of Economics," and shares his vision that "the three of us will work in close co-operation over this Africanization business. You, myself, and Victor" (279). Johnnie recognizes that Victor Edusei has been there from the outset.

This triumvirate to control something of Ghana's future matches the partnership of Nathaniel and Mensah (also dedicated to guide Ghana's future). Nathaniel's brief, sharp attack on Mensah's academy echoes the words of Victor Edusei's last attack on Nathaniel's commitment to education and his headmaster's intentions. Victor thus joins Amegbe and Mensah to form the second triumvirate. "We're a race of dreamers," Victor had said; the passage follows Nathaniel's sense of his pride in Victor—"as a brother would be. . . . He had learned more from Victor than he ever had at school" (51). The novel can complete this second triumvirate tacitly: it has established dramatically that wherever Nathaniel is, so Victor is also—Victor's ideas and Victor's spirit.

There is yet another implicitly completed triad. The two pregnant women in the novel, Aya Amegbe and Miranda Kestoe, are joined by a third—Charity Donkor, who has come to Accra to seek the fertilizing influence of a powerful fetish. That influence comes, however, via the agency of Victor Edusei. He gives Nathaniel the news near the end of chapter 6. Consequently, the two men argue over who would be a suitable mate for Victor, and he declares his choice: "I'll stand by Charity" (117); then, damning the dreamy old Calibans of Ghana, he adds, "You can keep Ghana. I'll take Charity" (118). Victor's love of Charity is in tune with his determination to defeat the misguided

Ghanaians and support those who would work to become responsible citizens of a true democracy.[24] He possesses the virtues necessary to promote such progress, including the chiefest of them—as the novel quietly implies—his Charity.

The novel suggests that love of humankind, without regard for the restrictions of race, tribe, and caste, is what must motivate political and educational improvement. Peggy does not argue that a happy future awaits Ghana, but provides—artistically—a prescriptive account of what is needed to ensure such a future. Enlightened leadership from a Caliban who has mastered Prospero's language and who is possessed of what D.H. Lawrence called "the intelligent heart" must characterize the movement into the democratic future of Ghana and determine who is to be Victor in the struggle for the country's heart and soul. Hence Edusei's position, explicitly and implicitly, in each of the complementary triumvirates; and hence the promise, literally and figuratively, of the third birth—that of the offspring of Victor and his Charity.

That third birth does not occur within the limits of the novel; it will occur "tomorrow," if the necessary conditions are fulfilled. The title of the novel is well chosen to express that idea of conditional success, of a future that *can* be achieved if the work of the present is properly undertaken. *This Side Jordan* follows its source in the first chapter of the Book of Joshua by focussing on the importance of the work done in preparation for crossing the river into the Promised Land. In the long resumé of the nascent novel that she sent to Adele Wiseman, Peggy described Nathaniel's dilemma: "He dreams of the past glories of Ghana, and the glory that will be in the future, but he doesn't know how to achieve it. . . . he stands . . . 'between today and tomorrow.'"[25] At some point between that version and the version ultimately published, Peggy made a slight but significant adjustment to that idea. During the argument with his uncle over the offered clerkship, Nathaniel responds to the observation, "Some day you will know where you belong" (106), with "I belong between yesterday and today." His uncle answers, "But that is nowhere." "'I know,' Nathaniel replied. 'Yes, I know'" (107). That adjustment enables Nathaniel's progress to be fitted most exactly with the implications of the title, *This Side Jordan*; and it also enables the novel to distinguish effectively between the two representatives of Caliban's progress to the position of the new Prospero, man of the future.

The conclusion of the novel is not the neat tucking-in of loose ends it seems. The pair of matching births—the Amegbe male and Kestoe female—is a parallel like the others, not matching equivalents but, rather, mirror images: the Kestoes are a negative inversion of the forward-looking hope the Amegbes represent. The same is true of the matching triads: the educational triumvirate of Amegbe, Mensah, and Edusei has its parallel in the political triumvirate of Kestoe, Sheppard, and—again—Edusei. The latter is suicidal—at least for Kestoe and Sheppard—in its dedication to Africanization, for that is the replacement of Prospero by Caliban.

Yet, the novel is protective of Johnnie, even hinting at his putative redemption through the final chapters. In the episode with Emerald, there are saving touches: he asks the girl her name as though he regarded her as a person; after his vicious deflowering of her "she no longer seemed anonymous to him" (233); the girl reaches out and touches his hand. "He took her hand and held it closely for an instant. Then he stooped and picked up her crumpled green cloth from the floor. Very gently, he drew it across her body. It was all he could do for her, and for himself" (234). The last touch is Johnnie's weeping—a conventional sign of innocence regained, if only momentarily.

In spite of this "protection" of this difficult character, the novel clearly indicates at the close of chapter 15 that the Kestoes are mainly excluded from the major changes that mark the denouement. The triumvirate in which Johnnie participates is not slated for success. Having left their baby with Whiskey's wife, the Kestoes drive out to Sakumono Beach. They walk there—as witnesses only:

> Miranda walked close to the fetish huts. . . .

> . . . She would never know what was inside the huts. . . . They were . . . sealed off as their worshippers were sealed, defying curiosity.
>
> The green ragged leaves of the coconut palms rustled and whispered, ancient untranslatable voices.
>
> But there was another voice on the wind. In the nearby fishing village, a young man was singing a highlife, a new song. (280)

The novel ends, thus, almost on the note on which it began (2), that of the highlife music. And Johnnie is still on the outside looking in.

A fragment of the Kestoe baby's birth scene affirms a theme that helps illuminate the whole matter of apparent reconciliation as seen in the triumvirates, the couples, and the births. Before the actual birth, Johnnie sees the "waters" break: "Johnnie looked at the fluid that gushed from her. . . . this was yellow and thick like pus. How could a living creature issue from that poisonous flood?" (265). Another image with basically the same import rises from Nathaniel's dream of the forest that grows in him, that "spills over with life and death" (104) while he argues with his uncle over his duty to the Past: "The forest floor is carpeted with ferns, and beneath the live green lies the rotting flesh of the plants' last growth, and their death gives new life to the soil. The forest is rank and hot and swelling with its semen. Death and life meet and mate" (105).

Another statement of the theme comes when Nathaniel frets remorsefully over the bribe he has accepted from two of his students: "Could health grow from disease?" (191). One evident result of that disease is that the Kestoe Plan puts Johnnie into the triad with Sheppard and moves Nathaniel to his outburst against Mensah and Futura Academy.

The evil that was British colonialism in the Gold Coast leads to the good that can emerge with the temporary cooperation of Cameron Sheppard, Johnnie Kestoe, and Victor Edusei, and with the educational reform that should result from the new cooperation of Amegbe,

Mensah, and Victor. *This Side Jordan* illustrates the preparation necessary for a successful crossing into the Promised Land: that crossing not only *can* come about, it *must*. "I beg you. Cross Jordan, Joshua." So Nathaniel exhorts his newborn son.

A decade after the appearance of *This Side Jordan*, Margaret Laurence published an essay in which she counted herself lucky that her experience of Africa was responsible for her first published novel.

> I was fortunate in going to Africa when I did—in my early twenties—because for some years I was so fascinated by the African scene that I was in this way prevented from writing an autobiographical first novel. I don't say there is anything wrong in autobiographical novels, but it would not have been the right thing for me—my view of the prairie town from which I had come was still too prejudiced and distorted by closeness.[26]

Clearly, *This Side Jordan* is not autobiographical as we usually understand the term. The surface realism of setting and characters readily deflects our attention from that aspect of the book. The novel developed from an idea for a short story about a Ghanaian schoolteacher. Within a year's time, however, another character, Miranda Kestoe, had entered the picture. Daughter of an Anglican clergyman, she thinks she has "broken away from her class" but really hasn't.[27] The narrative relies about equally on the alternating points of view of the schoolteacher and Miranda, at least through the first draft. As Peggy outlined the novel for Adele Wiseman—within a few months of completing that draft—she presented a strongly reflexive characterization of her heroine: Miranda is prone to "serious but blundering attempts" to make friends with and understand native Africans, and finally realizes that "intellectual tolerance" is insufficient, is, "in fact, only the beginning." Then the first truly revealing remark: "She fails, of course, *as we all do* who try the same thing and with the same naïveté" (my italics). A partial recognition of what she had revealed about herself evidently prompted Peg to add the disclaimer, in ink, as a postscript, "The story is *not* autobiographical."

Peggy had already created a character like Miranda, only male—the English bloke in her story called "Amiina." The Miranda type recurs in later pieces—as Constance in "A Fetish for Love" (1963; with a husband named Brooke who calls her "Con" as Jack Laurence habitually called his young wife "Peg"); and as the narrator of Peggy's first published adult essay, the admittedly autobiographical "The Very Best Intentions" (1964—"I still wore my militant liberalism like a heart on my sleeve. . . . I was anxious to impress upon him [Mensah] not only my sympathy with African independence but also my keen appreciation of African culture").[28] She is also reminiscent of Karen Aynsley of "Uncertain Flowering." She is finally the young Morag who marries Brooke Skelton in *The Diviners* (1974).

By the time of publication, *This Side Jordan* had undergone thorough revision: treatment of the British characters had been softened to "protect" them artistically, and other features had been modified as well. But Miranda persevered and remains very much the character as presented in the letter to Adele—autobiographical.

nine

Taming Tomorrow

IN 1962, MARGARET LAURENCE GATHERED TOGETHER TEN stories set in Ghana at the moment of that country's independence and written over the preceding six years, to form the volume she called *The Tomorrow-Tamer*—a companion volume to *This Side Jordan*. The two books emphasize the evil done by the interference of British colonialism. The tendency of colonial rule was to eradicate the "heathen" traditions of native West Africans and to replace them with "proper" Christian ones. In *The Tomorrow-Tamer* the focus is directed mainly to the native Ghanaians and only secondarily to the British colonialists (predominantly missionaries). The *dramatis personae* is filled out with the native products of British education—"been-to" Ghanaians like Victor Edusei in *Jordan*—and some few sympathetic British characters.

The dilemma of the native Ghanaians might be phrased in such questions as "Whose land is this?" or "To what land do I belong?" It is most directly expressed in the story "The Voices of Adamo," where the orphaned and uprooted Adamo searches for his identity; and that search is focussed in his seeking a *place* to be. He has been away from his plague-ridden village for a year and does not yet know that his family have all died, but he hears his mother's voice one day: "*Adamo—where are you? Adamo—where are we?*"[1] He ends up as a drummer in the army. When he finally gets accustomed to that life, he hears a new voice, "alien but not unknown," that gives him the assurance he has sought—and in the same terms as the old: "*Here, Adamo, you are here*" (218). Adamo's dilemma is, like Nathaniel Amegbe's, expressed with the questions *who*? and *where*? closely associated.

> —I cannot have both gods and I cannot have neither. A man must belong somewhere. Mother of men, hear me—
>
> — . . . my home is here, here, here, my home is here at last. (275)

Amegbe's discovery of the answer to his dilemma is firmly endorsed by Margaret Laurence in the stories of *The Tomorrow-Tamer*, which develop that answer variously.

The predominant themes of this collection inform all her subsequent fiction, and can be grouped under the heading "Compromise." Compromise (or accommodation, adaptation, reconciliation) is the means to settle various conflicts—between Past and Present, and between dedication to tribe or race and the demands of common humanity or general siblinghood.

The earliest of the stories, "The Drummer of All the World," addresses the influence of the Christian missionaries. It is an episodic account of three important moments in the life of Matthew, a British boy born in the Gold Coast. His father is a Protestant missionary dedicated to "saving" the heathen Ghanaians and leading them into the Way of the Cross. Matthew, now in his late twenties, is highly critical of his father's missionary endeavour: "how difficult it was to live down my father's profession. I almost wish I had not tried" (1). He describes his zeal thus: "My father was an idol-breaker of the old school. . . . He forbade the making of wooden figures. I suppose we have to thank men like my father for the sad fact that there are so few carvers of any merit left in West Africa" (4). Matthew refers to the story of Moses and the Golden Calf, a familiar feature of his childhood: "Moses broke the idols of *his own* people" (5; my italics).

Matthew's opposition to his father's zeal was encouraged by his close association with Kwabena, son of Yaa, who is wife of the family cook. Matthew and Kwabena are the same age and were born on the same day of the week; Yaa explains she had suckled Matthew at her breast just as she had suckled Kwabena. The story contrasts Matthew's father's destructive and divisive behaviour against the brotherhood of the two boys, which is *natural* and nourished by Yaa with the milk of human kindness. Peggy gave her the name of the Ghanaian earth goddess, Asaase Yaa.

The budding fraternity of the two boys is strengthened by further Ghanaian influence: Matthew learns native Twi and by the age of six is more fluent in it than in English. Kwabena instructs him in native religious and cultural traditions: "Once for a whole year I called God by the name of Nyame in my silent prayers." And the retrospective narrator's enlightened voice continues, "God of my fathers, I cannot think You minded too much. . . . I think You might have smiled . . . , as Kwaku did, . . . at the boy who thought Africa was his" (10).

That enlightenment begins when Matthew, at age seventeen, returns from England, where he had been sent to school, to find that the Africa he thought was his has changed. Kwabena has lost—or, rather, tried to get rid of—the old ways they had shared. He assures Matthew, "We will not always be slaves to the English. . . . They will have to go." Matthew inevitably replies, "And I with them?" Kwabena carefully answers, "There is a saying—follow your heart, and you perish" (11). Matthew finds a more encouraging change in Kwabena's young cousin Afua, who is blossoming into a beautiful young woman: "She belonged to earth, to her body's love, to toil, to her unborn children" (12). Matthew readily accepts the unaffected implication of her question to him, "Are Englishmen like other men?" He consummates his love of Afua and of all she represents to him: "Possessing her, I possessed all Africa, all earth."[2] The symbolism is somewhat diminished in the revised version of the story for *The Tomorrow-Tamer*—"Possessing her, I possessed all earth" (12).

Matthew returns after a ten-year interval in England to find "nothing was the same." "The country was to have its independence the following year," he recalls, as though that fact obviously accounted for the change.[3] The twenty-seven-year-old Matthew has found that he has lost the right to call "home" the Africa he thought was his. He visits Afua, now married and many times a mother; she approaches, smiling, then recognizes Matthew. The smile disappears; "'I greet you—master,' Afua said. And in her eyes was the hatred, the mockery of all time" (14). He encounters Kwabena, who asks Matthew for his opinion of the country on the brink of independence. He answers, "Independence is the new fetish. . . . I'm not sure that much is gained." Kwabena's response is short: "You would like us to remain forever living in thatch huts, pounding our drums and telling pretty stories about big spiders . . . " (17).

Kwabena thus prompts Matthew's painful recognition that "It was only I who could afford to love the old Africa. Its enchantment had touched me, its suffering—never. . . . I had always been the dreamer who knew he could awaken at will, the tourist who wanted antique quaintness to remain unchanged" (18).

"The Merchant of Heaven"[4] offers a much harsher treatment of the intrusive missionary—this one an American. The merchant in question, Brother Lemon of the Angel of Philadelphia Mission, has come to bring his evangelism to the native Ghanaians "as traders once went to Babylon—for the souls of men" (50). Will Kettridge, the architect scheduled to build a mission-house for brother Lemon ("The name's Le-*mon* . . . accent on the last syllable"), describes his arrival: "He was unusually tall; he walked in a stately and yet brisk fashion, with controlled excitement . . . , the light of future battles already kindling in his eyes, and replete with faith as a fresh-gorged mosquito is with blood" (51).

Brother Lemon wants to replace the native beliefs and practices with Christian—to save their souls. He doesn't particularly like the native creatures. Indeed, he cannot stand to live near them, and the land given for his house is "in the middle of shantytown," which is full of those whose souls he seeks: "It isn't that I mind Africans, Mr. Kettridge. . . . But shantytown—the people live so close together, and it smells so bad, and at night the drums and that lewd dancing they do, and the idolatry. I can't—I don't want to be reminded every minute" (73-74).

His success as proselytizer is predictable: his offering is the latest and gaudiest of attempts provided by various missionary intruders. Amory Lemon's fundamentalism is outdone by that of the simple folk who respond to his evangelism, and their literalist understanding of his gospel—as rendered into their native dialect, Ga—leads to his undoing. A group of old parishioners, blind and lame, rises up to claim that Brother Lemon has failed to fulfill his promises. Their leader rehearses those promises, in pidgin: "Dis man . . . he say . . . he go find we some shade place, he go dash me plenty chop, he mek all t'ing fine too much, he mek we eye come strong . . . " (71). They want action. Lemon denies making such extravagant promises. The mystery is solved when the original text is examined—the last two verses of Chapter Seven of the Book of Revelation of Saint John the Divine: "They shall hunger no more, neither thirst any more. . . ."

A more serious antagonist to Lemon is Kettridge's friend Danso, a native, a "been-to," and an artist interested in decorating Lemon's mission or at least his dwelling. "Are you a Christian, Mr. Danso?" prompts the artist to give his credentials as a Ghanaian Christian: he has been baptized into several varieties of church but asserts that "we had a very fine religion here before ever a whiteman came" (63).[5] The original version of the story has a passage of more than 300 words that recalls the dilemma of Nathaniel Amegbe: "Danso had been brought up a Christian by his parents. But he had grown to know the ancient gods through his grandfather, who still worshipped them" (*Prism*, 62).

Danso proposes a painting on a subject taken from Revelation. Amory Lemon exclaims in disbelief, "You? . . . To paint the throne of heaven?" In the original version (*Prism*, 63), Danso quotes Shylock's famous pleading "Hath not a Jew eyes?"[6] At the story's climax, however, Danso presents Lemon with his painting of the Nazarene: "Danso had not portrayed any emaciated mauve-veined ever sorrowful Jesus. This man had the body of a fisherman or a carpenter. He was well built. He had strong wrists and arms. His eyes were capable of laughter" (75-76).

This Nazarene is a near relative of one whom Peggy Wemyss depicted fifteen years earlier in her sonnet *manqué* "The Departure": "Man with worker's hands, . . . I would have been your wife."[7] An additional touch in Danso's depiction is what truly defeats Brother Lemon: Danso's Christ is black.

"Merchant," like "Drummer," develops the theme of neglect of the Second Great Commandment, denial of reconciliation and compromise. In Matthew's young career we are shown its workings and motivation, and with little discursive commentary. The visible attempt to prune away such commentary in "Merchant of Heaven"—visible in a comparison of the early version in *Prism* with the later in *Tomorrow-Tamer*—produces a more satisfactorily *dramatic* (in Henry James's sense of the term) expression of the theme and an acceptable ambience for the heavily symbolic portrait of the black Christ. And Peggy worked hard at revision of the penultimate section of the story to achieve the necessary dramatic effect. The adaptability and accommodation of Danso and Kettridge contrast with the uncompromising rigour of Amory Lemon, who is not liable ever to learn lessons of common humanity. (The Lemon character reappears in *The Fire-Dwellers*.)

In "The Pure Diamond Man," last in original publication (in *The Tamarack Review*, Winter 1963), Peggy developed her theme by reversing the situation. The "Man" is Philip Hardacre, scion of an English colonialist mining family and himself an amateur anthropologist interested in finding "the true Africa" (187). The Ghanaian "Luck Boy" Tetteh is about to aid Hardacre's quest—for a good fee—with a phony performance of python-god worship ritual. The performance is interrupted by a Christian missionary, but this one, the Reverend Timothy Quarshie, is an African. Quarshie introduces Hardacre to the real fetishist Bonsu—his regular chess opponent and maker of the best bunion cure the suffering Quarshie has found. Hardacre's fee for the legitimate performance will enable the mission to purchase a bell. Quarshie explains to frustrated Tetteh the accommodating—compromise:

> "Yesterday, . . . after all these years, Bonsu finally joined the church. . . . He still believes in the old gods, of course. I cannot ask too much, and maybe it is only a question of names anyway. He will sell herb cures as always, but no more charms or predictions. . . . Bonsu has tonight a special permission [to perform for Hardacre]. Half the money is to go to Saint Sebastian. . . ." (201)

And Bonsu will choose the bell.

Here is the accommodation and constructive compromise absent from "Drummer" and "Merchant": the Christian cleric and the former fetish priest—both Africans—manage a significant reciprocal adaptation.[8] Subsequently, Hardacre has a month of immersion in "the true Africa"—malaria and diarrhoea, guinea-worm and ringworm. He was grateful for Quarshie's prayers and Bonsu's worm cures, though Aspirin proved more effective. Hardacre returned to England, disillusioned. Hardacre has regarded Africans and their cultural practices equally as artifacts. That is an attitude—clinical, objective, unsympathetic, almost impersonal—that he shares with Matthew of "Drummer," Lemon of "Merchant," Connie of "A Fetish for Love," and Miranda Kestoe. It is an attitude that dehumanizes the native people and makes any ameliorative change virtually impossible in the colonized country.

A couple of the *Tomorrow-Tamer* stories focus attention on a complementary type of character who confronts, with some success, the effects of the uncompromising. Those who have themselves experienced exclusion by the unaccommodating seem best able to display such confrontation, as though they can heed God's admonition about not oppressing strangers (Exodus 23:9). They resemble the Good Samaritan (Luke 10:30-37) and are Peggy's "Accommodating Aliens."

"The Perfume Sea," third originally published (*Winter's Tales*, 1960),[9] recounts a critical episode in the life of two accommodating aliens—the barber and hairdresser, Mr. Archipelago, son of an Italian girl and an Armenian sailor, and the manicurist named Doree. They manage to adapt to the new regime and the consequent new market, and so survive. Archipelago and Doree belong neither to the colonial settlement nor to the native. Their dwelling is appropriately "not close either to the white cantonment or to the African houses. It was off by itself, on a jut of land overlooking a small bay" (31). They seem strangers cast up on the shores of the Gold Coast. Their backgrounds are vague; even their names are not truly their own, are, rather, symbolically suggestive.

With the coming of Independence, not only are the worst fears of British colonial officials realized, but the income of Archipelago and Doree is consequently stopped. Their landlord, the Ghanaian merchant K. Tachie, is compassionate, but he must face demands on his own resources, including his daughter Mercy, who wants clothes and cosmetics like any young woman. The accommodating aliens recognize the opportunity and adapt their offerings to suit the new dispensation, beginning with a complete and successful re-do of Mercy Tachie. New customers, Africans, crowd into the new shop of "ARCHIPELAGO & DOREE . . . African Ladies A Speciality" and the hairdresser observes, "By an act of Mercy . . . we are saved" (47).

One other aspect of the lives of Archipelago and Doree, about which the ladies, white and brown, have speculated but never guessed, is the nature of the relationship of the two cosmetologists who share the same isolated house. The passionate apogee of that relationship occurs at the moment when Archipelago, in near despair over their postcolonial poverty, offers Doree his total savings—a solid gold necklace—so she can move into the city where employment possibilities exist. She refuses; doesn't want to leave; asks him, "Don't you think I'd miss you? . . . Don't you know how it would be—for me?"

> They stared at each other, wide-eyed, incredulous. Mr. Archipelago lived through one instant of unreasonable and terrifying hope. Then, abruptly, he became once more aware of himself, oddly swathed in Indian brocade and holding in his fat perspiring hands an ale-glass and a gold necklace. (39)

The short-lived hope is "unreasonable and terrifying" in this moment of *eros*, for it is the asexual *agape* that is principally at issue here. The sensitive Archipelago recognizes and accepts his typically androgynous nature, which is Doree's, as well. Archipelago is really something of an Hermaphroditos with Doree as his spiritual Salmacia: together they represent that general love of humankind, that recognition of siblinghood, in which the erotic element is abstracted or at least subdued. The quality of the love these two accommodating aliens share is gently expressed as they make their exit—"with hands entwined like children who walk through the dark."[10]

The first half of *The Tomorrow-Tamer* ends with "The Rain Child" (seventh published, in *Winter's Tales*, 1962), the classic Laurentian tale of the accommodating alien. It juxtaposes the alienated and detribalized Dr. Quansah, a "been-to" now returned to his native Ghana, and Violet Nedden, the alien British schoolmistress in a Ghanaian girls' school; they are presented as virtually complementary characters, mirror images. Dr. Quansah has brought his daughter, Ruth, to begin school at Eburaso. He explains that this is Ruth's own country, although she was born in England and schooled there, and her only language is English. He now returns, a widower, to be in charge of research at a station nearby. A pathetic victim of detribalization, Ruth cannot fit in at the school, and the native girls cannot abide her. One of them, Kwaale, keeps Miss Nedden informed of Ruth's problems and alienation. Kwaale utters the proverb, "The stranger is like passing water in the drain." Violet counters with, "'Thou shalt not oppress a stranger, for ye know the heart of a stranger, seeing ye were strangers in the land of Egypt'" (114).

Violet Nedden is a mature, liberal-spirited, and un-naïve version of the do-gooders Miranda Kestoe (of *Jordan*) and Connie (of "A Fetish for Love"); she is also a voluntary alien, like Archipelago and Doree (of "Perfume Sea") and similarly possessed of the alien heart. She plays Good Samaritan at the school, which is full of "strangers": first, little Ayesha, of vague identity, who was rescued from child prostitution by Nigerian police; then, sixteen-year-old Yindo, brought down from Dagomba in the north to work on the cocoa farms and now one of the best garden boys at the school; finally, Ruth (and of course Violet herself).

The climax of the story is the Odwira festival. Kwaale and Ruth are near each other in the crowd. Suddenly, a young man shouts at Kwaale, "Fire a gun at me."

> Kwaale threw back her head and laughed. Her hands flicked at her cloth and for an instant she stood there naked except for the white beads around her hips, and her *amoanse*, the red cloth between her legs. Still laughing, she knotted her cloth back on again, and the young man put an arm around her shoulders and drew her close to him. (127)

Miss Nedden thinks, "I could have told [Ruth] it used to be 'Shoot an arrow,' for Mother Nyame created the sun with fire, and arrows of the same fire were shot into the veins of mankind and became life-blood. I could have said that the custom was a reminder that women are the source of life" (128). Ruth, culturally and morally offended—and envious—runs off.

Ruth rushes to the home of David Mackie, son of British colonialists, for solace from her good friend and sympathetic fellow European. To her shocking report, David responds: "I know you're not the ordinary kind of African. You're almost—almost like a—like us" (129). Finding herself stranded amid two kinds of alien corn,

Ruth runs off again. The little Ayesha leads Miss Nedden to Ruth's refuge.

> In the last hut of the row, Yindo sat cross-legged on the packed-earth floor. Beside him on a dirty and torn grass mat Ruth Quansah lay, face down, her head buried in her arms.
>
> Ayesha pointed. (131)

The four principal aliens are thus grouped, all displaying the charitable and educated heart, as well as they are able. Ayesha makes the discovery for Violet when she finds the teacher in tears for the lost Ruth; Yindo explains he tried to be accommodating to the twice-shocked Ruth, who had attempted to discover herself in a fond imitation of Kwaale—shooting her unrequested and unfletched arrow at poor Yindo. The surprised youth "held out his hands then in an appeal both desperate and hopeless. He was a desert man. He expected no mercy here, far from the dwellings of his tribe" (131). Violet Nedden finds "nothing simple enough to say. What words, after all, could possibly have been given to the outcast children?" (132).

Is it a pathetic ending? Dr. Quansah will take Ruth away, as she wants, to a more suitable place. The others have managed what accommodation and adaptation was possible. Violet Nedden, most mature and self-aware of these alien hearts, has accomplished most: "Sitting in my garden and looking at the sun on the prickly pear and the poinsettia, I think of that island of grey rain where I must go as a stranger, when the time comes, while others must remain as strangers here" (133). When Ruth was born, in that island, her mother called her by an African name, which means "child of the rain" (121).

The remaining stories of *Tomorrow-Tamer* are perhaps more specifically hopeful. "Godman's Master" (fourth published, in *Prism*, Spring 1960) tells of another Moses leading an enslaved brother to freedom, if not quite to the liberation he had envisaged. Moses Adu, a "been-to" pharmacist, frees the dwarf Godman Pira (an "oracle" enslaved by his "priest" and kept in a little wooden coffin), descendant of the *pirafo*, once court jesters to the kings of Ashanti.

The grateful Godman wants to dedicate his life to serving Adu and so becomes a burden to the embarrassed pharmacist. The story is a kind of parable to express the evil of colonialism, post-colonial "liberation," and of the vicious mutual dependency and destruction of slavers and enslaved as expressed in Mannoni's *Prospero and Caliban*.[11] At last Moses obliges Godman to leave and truly face life on his own. A year later he sees an ad for a real live oracle, "Hundreds of years old / Smallest man alive," and visits the fair to see Godman and "who owns him this time?" (157).

At the fair, Moses and Godman meet. The dwarf calms Moses's fears that he has simply found himself a new "priest": "These young men who pay to see us—they do not believe, you know, but we make them laugh. . . . One has to be skilled for this work. The *pirafo* used to be fine jesters, and now, perhaps, again" (159). Evidently, Godman owns himself; he is now his own master. In his enslaved state with Faru, he filled a "religious" function for those in that village, but Godman is no longer a false oracle. His explanation carefully points out he has not returned to that situation—and neither have the young men who pay to see him. He has revived the role of his ancestors, of the *pirafo*, with this difference, that he is not now a jester for African kings alone, the Ashantehene, but for the African people. Godman has achieved a reconciliation, modest but real, between the past and the present, between the power of the kings and the power of the people.

Moses's early impression of Godman, "The creature's face was old, as old as Africa, as old as all earth" (143),[12] is echoed as the fair prepares for its next show. "The band began to assemble. . . . The drummer set up the kettle drum and the bass drum, new and shiny, beside the graceful thonged drums and the carved wood drums born of the forest longer ago than anyone could tell" (159-60). Godman's achievement of reconciliation, of necessary compromise, is like Nathaniel Amegbe's in *Jordan*, but even more affirmative.

"The Tomorrow-Tamer" (sixth in initial publication, in *Prism*, Fall

1961), another story of reconciliation, tells of the intrusion of modern technology on the old traditional way of life in the Ghanaian village of Owurasu on the banks of a placid river, sacred to the god Owura. The intruder is a bridge. An obvious symbol for accommodation or reconciliation, it gives employment to the young men of the village. While the new settlement built for the bridgemen (Europeans and strangers) and the old village remain separate and distinct, a number of the bridgemen and the newly employed villagers do meet and mingle quietly at the Chop-Bar run by the merchant Danquah, himself an outsider.

The conflict is focussed in the seventeen-year-old Kofi. He is disturbed by the bridge's sacrilegious intrusion on the sacred grove of the ancestors and its violation of the sacred river itself, and yet he is fascinated by the technological accomplishments of the bridge builders. His fading commitment to the old gods and ritual practices is being steadily replaced by a new commitment—to the bridge, to his role model, the leader of the ironworkers (whom he idolizes), and to the bridgemen's fraternity at Danquah's Chop-Bar. The name of the admired leader of the ironworkers is "Emmanuel"—a name applied to Jesus, meaning "God with us" but also referring to His being born of a virgin; and with that association the name of Danquah's bar gains particular relevance—the "Hail Mary Chop-Bar."[13]

Kofi joins the bridgemen and yet does not so much turn against the elders of the village as urge their acceptance of the bridge as another being comparable to the river it spans, and with some hope of effecting reconciliation between the spirit of the bridge and Owura, the river-god: "he, Kofi, was a man of the bridge. . . . He would tend the bridge as long as he lived. He would be its priest" (100). The final task is painting the bridge. Kofi volunteers for the most dangerous job of all, painting the towers. From on high, Kofi gains a kind of epiphany as he surveys the surrounding countryside and the new road, "a straight red-gold streak pierced like a needle through the forest. . . . he saw that it would emerge soon here and would string both village and bridge as a single bead on its giant thread" (102).

The story reaches its climax, as Kofi, in the grip of *hubris*, becomes the sacrifice that realizes the envisaged reconciliation. "Kofi knew what to do. . . . He was fearless, fearless as Emmanuel. He knew the work of the bridge. . . . The power of it went with him and in him. Exultant, he wanted to shout aloud his own name and his praises. There was nothing he could not do" (102).

He stands atop the bridge and for an instant looks "straight into the sun"—something his admired Emmanuel would never have done. Kofi falls. The view taken by his village is that the bridge had sacrificed its priest (as they still see Kofi) in order to appease the river. Kofi had been wrong about one thing, they decide: "the river had been acknowledged as elder. The queenly bridge had paid its homage and was part of Owurasu at last" (103). "The Tomorrow-Tamer" confronts the problem of necessary accommodation: progress demands bridges, but religious devotion to them by the builders is vain sacrilege, given the true divinity of nature. Reconciliation between the new, technologically expert world and the old, traditional world respectful of nature *is* possible—provided that homage be properly paid.[14]

"The Voices of Adamo" (originally published eighth as "The Spell of the Distant Drum," *The Saturday Evening Post*, 5 May 1962) occupies, appropriately, the penultimate position in the collection. "Appropriately," not only because Margaret Laurence considered this her best story[15] but also because it gathers many of the themes of *The Tomorrow-Tamer* into a climax of tragic pathos and prepares for the gentle conclusion, "A Gourdful of Glory." Adamo is orphaned and uprooted by a plague of smallpox that struck his village when he was a lad of fifteen. Adamo is bereft of the two essential defining features of identity—place and kin—and wanders in search of himself. At the edge of a town he finds something recognizable from his lost past, something of his identity. In a group of soldiers Adamo notices a bandsman cleaning a drum, a drum different from drums he had known but recognizably a drum nevertheless.

> Adamo and the drum found one another. His fingers sensed some way of expressing what his mind and speech could only grope after and fail to grasp. The strange drum uttered to him the voice he now heard only in dreams, the sorrowing of someone once inexpressibly dear to him, someone whose face he could not now visualize however hard he tried. (211)

His natural talent soon qualifies him as a private drummer, signed up "to serve for five years his country, whose name he did not know" (212), and he quickly gains the approval of Captain Fossey, bandmaster. A new voice replaces the voices of his lost kin, who had called, "*Adamo—where are you? Adamo—where are we?*" The new voice assures him, "*You are here*" (218).

A stranger estranged in his own land has come, still a stranger, to a new setting and has managed to adapt to the new ways and the new location—as another accommodating alien—thanks to the one recognizable item, the drum, a means of communication. The drum seems also to assure his future.

The fable develops a complementary feature of reconciliation that confirms his expectations and strengthens his sense of identity. Fossey prepares his bandsmen to play at club dances. The native musicians struggle through the foreign medium of waltzes and slow foxtrots but blossom when they turn to African highlife tunes, their own music; and their star performer is Adamo. "The highlife was their music. For they, too, were modern. They, too, were new. And yet the old rhythms still beat strongly in this highlife. . . ." This passage from the beginning of *This Side Jordan* is an apt commentary on "Voices of Adamo." As the genre of the drum functions to connect Adamo with his past, so his involvement with highlife music connects him with the future. Together they are a statement of reconciliation with special emphasis on the future: highlife music is "their" music as distinct from the Europeans', the colonizers', music. With Adamo as drummer, it is *his* music and therefore *his* connection with the future—the accommodating alien in his action of reconciliation.

With Independence approaching, Bandmaster Fossey plans to leave Adamo in a stable job with the civilian band; failure of communication leads to the murder-suicide that ends the story. Major Appiah has recognized that it "was not death that Adamo feared" (223), but the death-in-life that is the lot of the dispossessed who are unable to answer the questions "Where is here?" and "Who am I?" The way of reconciliation open to Adamo, if things had been different and if clear communication had been possible, offers grounds for hope.

Set in Ghana at the very moment of Independence,[16] "A Gourdful of Glory" (fifth published, in *The Tamarack Review*, Autumn 1960), offers the simple account of a plump, good-natured market woman, Mammii Ama, a petty trader who specializes in clay calabashes, and of her associates at the market—especially of their attitudes to the official advent of Free-Dom.

Mammii Ama has bravely confronted the white woman who teased her that Independence will bring no real change, and declared, "Free-Dom be heah now, dis minute!" Her friend Sabrina is newly pregnant, but Mammii Ama must still pay bus fare, so what is all the to-do about?

Canadian writer Henry Kreisel answered that inevitable question in 1961, with half the *Tomorrow-Tamer* stories still unpublished, ". . . at the end of the story, . . . she has a glimpse of what is really at stake, and she suddenly sees, however hazily, that what is involved in freedom is the dignity of the human person, and she rejoices because she and her people have stood up."[17]

Peggy supplied her own supplemental commentary on the ending of "A Gourdful of Glory" in a passage of "The Perfume Sea"—published at almost the same time—describing life outside the walls around the house of Archipelago and Doree, the life of the simple "loin-clothed fishermen" who expect to continue working hard but display the same kind of confidence as appears in Mammii Ama—"sensing, too, that the land in which they set their . . . feet was new as well as old, and that they, unchanged, were new with it" (35).

These stories of the Gold Coast in the process of becoming Ghana were, with the exception of "The Drummer of All the World," written in Vancouver. They were variously revised for publication together as *The Tomorrow-Tamer*; and the closer the original publication was to the publication of the collection, the less revision was deemed necessary. The revisions most important for an understanding of Peggy's personal development are those that reflect changes in her attitude to the Nkrumah regime in Ghana, mainly changes in the regime itself following Independence, 6 March 1957. The hopes and expectations she had invested in that regime were high, perhaps naïve, and they were thoroughly dashed well before the second of the *Tomorrow-Tamer* stories was published. The changes in Nkrumah and the CPP were manifest early that March, when demonstrations in opposition to the Convention People's Party provoked severe reprisals, including incarceration of the leaders of the Togoland Congress. Ga[18] workers and petty-bourgeois sympathizers demanded better housing, lower food prices, and jobs, leading to the passage of the Avoidance of Discrimination Bill that declared illegal all tribal, religious, and regional political parties. Early in 1958, newly created State of Emergency powers were invoked, various unsympathetic factions were punished by fines and jailing of their leaders; before the end of the year strikes were declared illegal. Thus 1958 became known as the Year of Repression.[19]

The unity of *The Tomorrow-Tamer* derives from its consistent development of the themes discussed and, of course, its constant Ghanaian setting. There is a sense of crescendo achieved in *The Tomorrow-Tamer* by the nature of the final three stories and the order in which they are presented to create a strong, affirmative conclusion. The simple faith of the *free* Mammii Ama, in "A Gourdful of Glory," provides the final note in the book's illustration of spiritual freedom. With that concluding assertion of hope in freedom, tomorrow seems to offer more promise than threat—tomorrow is disarmed, is tamed.

The reception of *This Side Jordan* was generally encouraging, although some of the advance reviews disappointed Peggy by finding the novel gave "a despondent picture" of the situation in Africa. She wrote Adele, "I had felt the book gave quite a hopeful picture. There isn't any easy solution in it, of course."[20] *Jordan* was picked as a Book Society Recommendation for October in England. Further, the *New Statesman and Nation* called the ending "suspiciously sunny" but gave it otherwise a very good review; and Richard Church in the *Bookman* also gave it a favourable review, though he found the conclusion "despairing."[21] However modest, serious critical response to her first novel confirmed the personal adjustment that lay behind her decision to become "Margaret"—even though her announcement to Adele seems heavy-handed in its casual announcement (in a postscript), "did I tell you—I've changed my name to Margaret?"[22]

At first glance, the change seems of little moment: everything she had published as an adult had appeared under "Margaret Laurence." What mattered is what the change meant to herself. The last paragraph of the letter to Adele clarifies that question—and without explicit reference to the Peg-Margaret alteration.

First, she has abandoned the "new" Somaliland novel: she is "sick of Africa" but will complete the Gold Coast stories and feels she doesn't "know enough" about Africa to write a novel. Then—"I think I'd like to come back home. . . . *I don't need* to go away any more, in fact can't go away. . . . I can't run forever to countries (real or imaginary) which I like because they didn't know me when I was young" (my italics). Those few lines intimate what Somaliland has come to mean to her at age thirty-four—a place she *needed* to run away to because she hadn't been known there. And that last remark reflects on her attitude to Canada and also on her attitude to herself:

> I feel the urge to write about the only people I can possibly know about from the inside. . . . I feel I might at last be able to look at people here without blinking. Having hated my own country most of my life, I am now beginning to see why.

> *It's the mirror in which one's own face appears*, and like Queen Elizabeth the First, you smash the mirrors but that doesn't change yourself after all. [my italics]

The paragraph ends with an indication of self-acceptance, of farewell to past interests: she plans to "do something" with the Somaliland diaries "*and then put paid to that phase of my life*. It's over, and I have a strange sense of release and relief" (my italics).[23]

Letting go of the Somaliland connection was not easy for her. The novel she had promised Whit Burnett in 1953 served as a kind of security blanket to which she resorted during the eight years of its existence in five unfinished versions. She picked it up at moments of transition, between one piece of work done and the beginning of another—especially when such moments were stressful. In spring of 1961, she was still pondering resumption of the old comfort job: "I had an odd experience when I was attempting this now-abandoned novel— . . . an entirely different set of characters . . . kept creeping in, as it were, to disturb my thoughts, . . . all people here [Canada]."[24] A month later she reiterates that conflict but with reversed emphasis: "I have tried very hard to get away from writing another novel set in Africa, . . . but unfortunately I can't get away from the characters who have been chatting in my ear for two years. . . ."[25]

Another facet of the "Peggy-Margaret" conflict, or the closely related "Somaliland-Canada," is her decision to disown two publications with distinct Somaliland connections—her story "Uncertain Flowering" and her translation of a major *gabei* "To a Faithless Friend."[26] Her denial of "Uncertain Flowering" is of greater significance. *Story* identified the piece correctly in "Biographical Notes" as "her first story published in the United States" (247). Peg corrected the note for Adele: "it's my first to be published *anywhere* . . . !"[27] Her subsequent periodical publications through autumn 1960 are accompanied by a biographical note acknowledging "Uncertain Flowering" in *Story*. After the name change to "Margaret," there is no further recognition of that piece until the special Laurence tribute in *Canadian*

Author and Bookman for Winter 1966, brief and inaccurate: "Margaret's first short story sale was to Whit Burnett in 1951 [sic] for his annual [sic] anthology 'Story'" (5). No title; vague identification of the magazine. Then nothing, with promotion of "The Drummer of All the World" to first adult publication.[28]

Revision of the copious diaries she had kept during her year in Somaliland was a direct cause of her disowning the short story. It began after a definite boost to her confidence in the spring of 1961. First, *Jordan* won the Beta Sigma Phi first-novel prize of $1000 (chosen by the committee responsible also for selecting recipients of the Governor General's Awards); second, the University of Western Ontario granted her its President's Medal for her story "A Gourdful of Glory." By early fall of 1961 she was hard at work on the diaries; it was a demanding task and offered an engrossing epiphany. She kept Adele abreast: "I have changed so much, and I failed to see so much at the time";[29] then, announcing the task is done, "I found it terribly hard to re-live those years."[30] And it was surely embarrassing to recognize her own youthful qualities in the character of Karen Aynsley. Karen's apparent desire for adulthood, her chafing at her parents' attempts to postpone that status, is contradicted by the girl's basic reluctance to give up the comfortable conditions of her life of innocence and naïveté, dependence and protection. The hidden valley of the candelabra trees is especially useful in expressing the latter aspect of Karen, and with that her relationship with her father, including acceptance of his special term for her, "bairn." The term carries echoes of the Scots idiom of Robert Wemyss, son of a Scottish father—like Jack Laurence as well.

The hidden valley setting, about one third of the way through the story, is very similar to the equivalent setting in the third-last paragraph of Three of *Camel Bell*. That is hardly surprising, as the Laurence scholar Fiona Sparrow points out: the setting derives from "a place she discovered with her husband when they lived at Sheikh. . . . and since it is recalled with the same words and images, it is reasonable to suppose that . . . she drew directly on her diary entry for both. . . ."[31] The two passages are so similar as to emphasize the differences between them—and those differences illuminate the point at issue. The story describes stones scattered about "like the decay of an unknown court. . . . At one side . . . a small brushwood circle, a long-abandoned *zareba*, . . . as though a nomad's little shelter . . . by mistake in the garden of a sultan."[32] The memoir has rock lying about "almost" like "the decayed remains of a temple or court that died out years ago, before any Somali voices came to break the silence once more. . . . the little brushwood *zareba*, as though a nomad's hut . . . by mistake in the garden of a sultan."[33]

The earlier passage emphasizes the unspoiled naturalness of the scene and the absence of human beings; the latter replaces the "little shelter" with a much more civilized "hut," and the "unknown court" of the former is augmented with a "temple," an example of humankind's misguided and intrusive religious institutions—"misguided" because untrammelled nature displays its own quality of divinity. (That distinction was anticipated in Peggy's high school poem "Pagan Point."[34]) The crucial difference between the passages is another such augmentation in *Camel Bell*: "This valley was full of clumps of euphorbia, the candelabra trees, *the milk of which was poisonous*"—my italics distinguish the addition made in the memoir (49) to the otherwise identical passage in the story (18). While "Uncertain Flowering" is concerned with Karen's leaving her Edenic innocence, *Camel Bell* insists that the place was itself tainted from the very beginning.

The whole of Three, "House in the Clouds," is almost an account of the *escape* from innocence. The delightful opening passages prepare for the balancing conclusion at the valley of the poisonous trees. The description of the Laurences' house at Sheikh, that looked "like a child's house of coloured blocks daubed with plasticine," seems appropriate for another Karen Aynsley—a playhouse to play adult in: "in the morning," Peggy and Jack walked out to find "the early clouds swept so low that we were actually walking through them . . . and I was amazed that such a thing was possible, to walk in the clouds" (27). The note of wide-eyed amazement and joyous innocence is again reminiscent of Karen's attitude. The significant difference comes at the end of the chapter of *Camel Bell*, following closely on the revelation about the poisonous trees: "We did not go back again to our house in the clouds. But we carried the memory of its peace with us as a talisman" (50).

> Some natural tears they dropped, but wiped them soon;
> The world was all before them, . . .
> . . . hand in hand, with wandering steps and slow,
> Through *Sheikh* they took their solitary way.[35]

For all her aspirations toward adulthood, Karen refuses to recognize that her Edenic valley is a Paradise already Lost. That attitude Peggy later satirized in the naïve liberalism of Constance in "A Fetish for Love" and more fully in Miranda in *Jordan*. She must have recognized, in late 1960 or early 1961, that her depiction of Karen was close to a portrait of herself in Somaliland, cherishing the safety and solace of the hidden valley near Sheikh, the innocent delight of walking in the clouds, relying on the comfort of an almost paternal companion like Karen's Yusuf—or like another, who might call her "bairn." The shock of such a recognition would account for her disowning "Uncertain Flowering." Another small death. And what may have definitely tipped the scales was Kildare Dobbs's review of *Jordan* in the spring issue of *Canadian Literature*. She told Adele it was "vitriolic"; and the language of her added comment on Dobbs's concurrent "African Poem" is revealing in its similarity to that of her letter of 22-23 December 1958 to Adele—references to "so-called primitive cultures" and "Paradise lost":

> . . . its general outlook was that of the European who finds in so-called primitive cultures the bloody splendour lacking in ours—almost the 'noble savage' outlook. However sad it may be to these seekers after some lost Garden of Eden, the noble

> savages these days are tending to feel they could do with a little less splendour and a little more sanitation.[36]

Adieux to "Uncertain Flowering," and the *gabei* "To a Faithless Friend" comprised yet another small death.

Life for the Laurences continued in 1961 with all the signs of normality. Jack was working up in the Yukon for days at a time; Peggy was busy finishing her dozen Gold Coast short stories; and when they were together in Vancouver they pursued their hobby of making wine, which they had begun in the fall of 1960.[37] She was treated to a little series of tributes to her literary achievement, starting with a cocktail party staged in Vancouver by Jack McClelland, in December 1960, to honour publication of *This Side Jordan*. In the following June she went to Toronto for the Beta Sigma Phi award, and on her way back to the coast she touched base with Anne Hallstead in Winnipeg—Bob was out of town.[38] Another sort of honour was bestowed that summer: she discovered that *The Horn of Africa* by John Buchholzer, a Dane (in its 1959 English translation by Maurice Michael), was a hearty plagiarism of *A Tree for Poverty*.[39] Buchholzer gives no credit whatsoever for the translations of Somali poetry and prose he uses, and he pretends that his sources were the local people he encountered "around the campfire." His translations from the Somali are very close to Margaret's and so are his commentaries. Further, he uses the same spelling as Margaret's for "*gabei.*" Not absolutely peculiar to Margaret, *gabei* was usually spelled *gabay* by Somali scholars—like B.G. Andrzejewski and Musa Galaal. Consider a typical example, Margaret's account compared with Buchholzer's account of the short lyric form *belwo*.

A Tree for Poverty: The literal meaning of the word "belwo" is "a trifle."

> The belwo . . . have come into popularity in Somaliland in the last ten years. . . . The belwo is sung to a distinct tune.

> The various tunes have syncopated rhythms. . . . Belwo verses are strung together . . . to make one long song, but the individual verses are not necessarily related. . . . They are usually linked together by a repetition of the word "heleyoy," which has no meaning in itself, but serves merely as a chorus. (6-7)

The Horn of Africa:

> The latest form . . . popular now for a score of years, is called *belwo*—trifle—and is sung to certain melodies with syncopated rhythms. . . . They are trifles about love linked together by the work *helejoj*, which does not mean anything, but merely serves as a refrain. (94)

All but one of the short lyric pieces and all the Somali tales quoted in *The Horn of Africa* are to be found in *A Tree for Poverty*. Buchholzer's "borrowings" are not absolutely verbatim but roughly camouflaged by slightly different word choice and rearrangement—in the style of a not very bright high-schooler; furthermore, the pieces were apparently first translated into Danish and then retranslated into English by Maurice Michael. There was ample justification for Margaret's indignant outburst to Adele: "he had taken paragraphs and sections directly out of my introduction, and all my ideas and conclusions about Somali literature were presented as his own—and in my words! . . . what he has done is in fact an infringement of the law of copyright."[40]

That August the Laurences went to their retreat at Point Roberts, Washington, where Jack worked at putting cedar shakes on the cottage. What Peg needed most was the comfort and sense of stability that honest work on her own fiction would give. She had made two false starts on novels that summer, and then, as it came to an end, a startling turn of events. Out of the welter of intrusive voices impinging on her imagination—as she had noted six months earlier, voices of Canadian characters—emerged a creature that demanded her attention: a "daft old lady . . . a real tartar. She's crabby, snobbish, difficult, proud as Lucifer for no reason, a trial to her family, etc. She's also—I forgot to mention—dying." Her story had to be told, as the story of *This Side Jordan* had, and Margaret must hear her, willy-nilly. Margaret is not sure what it is all about, but she had already experienced a revelation: "This whole novel is something that goes so far back, with me, and is such a wrenching up of my background, that it is difficult for me to be honest enough."[41]

The superficial signs of stability on the Laurences' domestic scene were bravely sustained as summer gave way to autumn and the new school year. David, now six and beginning grade one, was learning to read; Jocelyn, nine, was not only beginning grade four but was involved in piano lessons, dancing lessons, and Brownies. Peg continued to mark essays, prepared several book reviews per month for the *Vancouver Sun*, and taught Sunday school in a Unitarian church. She and Jack continued their winemaking. Jack "finds his job very interesting still."[42] She was obviously the busy public wife and mother.

Meanwhile, back in the closet, she was vigorously engaged with the daft old lady and taking down her story—"the work of a lunatic, I think. . . . I cannot do it in any other way than the way it comes."[43] A month later, however, she indicated she had taken a bold stride toward self-confidence and self-reliance, and had come to see "that the writer *must* write to please himself first, & then he can only hope that someone will share his viewpoint enough to want to enter his territory." She added, "Maybe I'm hoping to convince myself as well as you."[44] She persevered and had the first draft finished before the end of the year, and then the doubts began again.

As 1962 began, Jack's dissatisfaction with his professional life in Canada worsened, and he was itching to go abroad again. Peg had resumed work on the diaries and was aching to start revision of the "old-lady novel," which she found "terrible."[45] She began to experience disturbing physical symptoms—pounding headaches and weird sensations such as pins and needles in her arms and legs. Her doctor recognized them as signs of "tension." She quit book reviewing, essay marking, and Sunday school teaching.[46] Jack was actually making enquiries about overseas jobs "where basic engineering things needed to be done"; and she hoped it would "work out that way, for his sake. . . . I at least can work anywhere," she told Adele—putting a brave face on it.[47]

But beneath the surface, troubles roiled, and new and more alarming symptoms appeared: Margaret claimed she was in either a manic or a depressive condition all the time, was suffering from both lung cancer and TB, and smoking like a furnace. She knew the cause of these dreadful symptoms, however: she was taking diet pills. That cause, in turn, may itself have been a symptom; but Margaret did not seem to recognize that possibility. She was, in fact, quite pleased about the pills, for she had "shed" fifteen pounds and looked to lose ten pounds more. "It all seemed worth while today when I went downtown and bought a summer dress—sheath style, the first time in several years that I have been able to wear this kind of dress."[48] The testimony of the sheath may have meant for Peg that her "tension" was overcome; yet, a more basic cause of stress was surely the desire to please her husband—a desire not so easy to satisfy. A summer dress just wouldn't do it, as July was crowded with visitors from Jack's family; she finally packed up Jocelyn and David and escaped to Point Roberts. "I decided I *must* get away from everything," she wrote Adele. She interrupted the letter to go to the kitchen and check on the birthday cake she had made for Jack's birthday on the morrow, 6 August, and finished icing: "I, sentimentally, always make him a birthday cake—my reason, ridiculously, is that he never had one as a kid."[49] The birthday cake and the diet pills seem to have had a good deal in common.

August 1962 marked another moment of crisis: she gave in to Jack's request to read her draft of the old-lady novel, called "Hagar." He offered several criticisms; Margaret bristled and "rebelled." Her account of the blow-up is missing. Adele tore it up and "flushed it down the john" as per instructions, she assured her.[50] But Adele's response and Peg's reflective letter of 2 January 1963 provide ample evidence of what provoked the eruption. "You've let this pile up for a long time, Peg,"[51] Adele said, noting that Peg's reaction has come "with the force of a lot of repression released." There were two opposing items: public recognition of her ability as a novelist (the reception of *Jordan*) had built self-confidence; her complex reliance on Jack's "superior" judgement in all matters had become dubious. The conflict between those opposed forces had been growing over the past several months; as her confidence strengthened, her willingness to accept Jack's opinions was turning to resentment. Peg recognized that for a whole year she had been trying "to convince myself that I must be wrong about that novel." Carefully, fairly, Adele acknowledged that "you've always dreaded Jack's disapproval" and then suggested, "Perhaps asking him to pass judgment on your 'creative area' . . . shifts responsibility for your private self on him, too." Peg's letter of 2 January 1963 implies acceptance of the diagnosis—that disagreement about "Hagar" "indicated a lack of communication, on the personal level, which I had long known to be the case, but which I simply could not face except in my solitary late-night sessions with the wine-jug." Within two weeks of the blow-up, Peg and Jack had made their decisions: Jack would accept a job in Pakistan; she would go to England with the children. Painfully enlightened, she confessed to Adele in a letter of 29 August 1962: "I feel free, or reasonably so, from the sense of despair that has been with me for some years now . . . this will be the opportunity to terminate a kind of delayed adolescence, at the advanced age of 36, and it is really now or never." Peg and the children flew out of Vancouver on Friday, 21 October 1962.

They reached London in the third week of October and quickly found a flat in familiar Hampstead. Her landlady, a Mrs. Levene, turned out to be an aunt of Winnipeg's most famous chess master, Abe Yanofsky. She announced her joy: "I feel a tremendous sense of relief being *here* & not *there* (i.e. either Vancouver or Pakistan). . . . I can put away the sleeping pills. . . ."[52] Finally "Hagar" arrived. With that came justification of her rebellion against Jack's criticism: ". . . it is written as I wanted to do it—I had begun on re-writing, following J's criticism, and find now that what I re-wrote is pure unadulterated crap. . . . I . . . will stick to the first draft. . . . The old lady knew what she was doing when she told me her life story. . . ."[53]

Two weeks later she reiterated her conviction about the novel and exuded the self-confidence she had been moving toward since her determination to be "Margaret" rather than "Peggy." The novel now seemed to her to require "far less re-writing than I once thought . . . all the things which I thought were there [are] . . . actually there. When Jack didn't see any of them, I was convinced . . . that I had only deluded myself. . . . but now I feel strongly that they *are* there, and that I wasn't wrong about the book. . . . it says what I wanted it to say. . . ."[54] To a considerable extent, Margaret had come into her own.

At the beginning of 1962 she had told Adele that revising the Somaliland diaries was a chore— "I have changed so much"; the next sentence, expressing dissatisfaction with "Hagar" is, of course, hyperbole: "the novel makes me feel suicidal."[55] Yet, there certainly had been a kind of mortal change in Peggy Laurence—beginning with preparation of *This Side Jordan*—that permitted the emergence of "Margaret." "*Nabad gelyo*," she wrote to conclude *The Prophet's Camel Bell*—her gentle *goodbye to all that*—"May you enter peace."

II.
Margaret (1962-1987)

The Manawaka Years (1962-1974)

ten

Hagar

ACROSS THE ATLANTIC OCEAN SEEMED THE OBVIOUS FLIGHT for, like a good Anglo-Saxon Canadian, Margaret Laurence regarded the British Isles, even in 1962, as her cultural home. There she would feel closer to English writers—both past and present—and there her children would get a proper education. Familiar Hampstead beckoned reassuringly. Furthermore, Margaret could explain her separation from Jack without the appearance of conjugal disruption. Thus she wrote from Vancouver to their friends Nancy and Frank Collier: "Facilities in E. Pakistan appear to be very uncertain, and we do not especially want to take the kids to some place lacking in schools and hospitals, etc. . . . this is the right job for Jack, but . . . quite the wrong move for me. . . ."[1]

Margaret had asked the Colliers for help in getting her settled in London—particularly about council schools in the Hampstead area and "any guest-house type of thing . . . where I could stay while flat-hunting."[2] Before the end of October, Nancy Collier saw Margaret settled in an attractive section of Hampstead, at number 35 Heath Hurst Road, a graceful S-curve street lined with big, Victorian, red-brick houses.[3] Margaret's flat was the top two floors of a tall, three-storey house. On the lower of these was a living room, her bedroom, and the kitchen, and, up a small flight of stairs, an adequate bedroom for each of the children. They shared a bathroom, on the second floor. They were without a phone. The rent was not cheap although about what she had expected, and the lovely high ceilings made the rooms costly to heat. In spite of the drawbacks of #35, its location was almost ideal—five minutes' walk from Hampstead Heath, fifteen from the school, just around the corner from a public library, and a block from a laundrette. She was pleased and relieved to be so lucky.[4]

Settling in helped distract Margaret's thoughts from the truant "Hagar." The only copy, it symbolized her reasons for leaving Jack. How could she have packed up that manuscript in a box of "junk" and sent it off by sea-mail? she wondered, and feared that it would never arrive. Margaret recalled much later, "That parcel took three months to arrive in London."[5] In fact, however, the parcel had been mailed from Winnipeg not earlier than the middle of October; and was in Margaret's hands well before 25 November, when she told Adele of its arrival, for by that date she had had time to read the manuscript and cut out the revisions she had made to please Jack. Transit time for "Hagar" was little more than a month, if that.

She also heard early in November from Alan Maclean, editor at Macmillan, that the British publishing house might accept her collection of short stories, so she devoted a fortnight to typing up anew her Gold Coast stories. She then returned to revision of "Hagar," completed it on the last evening of 1962—a good omen, she felt[6]—and sent it to Maclean.

The new year began with mixed feelings for Margaret—relief at her escape from the claustral life with Jack, and guilt at cutting herself and the children off from him. A sympathetic letter from his mother aggravated the conflict: she told Margaret that in 1918 she had considered leaving with baby Jack, aged two, but thought it would take as much courage to stay as to go, and stayed put. She observed that "it is always easier to do what people expect of you," and then, "Also, as with suicide, one is afraid of failure."[7] Which of her own challenges, Margaret wondered, deserved her courage? Even Maclean's encouraging reception of "Hagar" aggravated her dilemma, though his recognition of what she had done in the novel was very important to her. On Valentine's Day she announced "ALAN MACLEAN . . . LIKES HAGAR!"—

> my faith in life, in myself, in everything, has been miraculously restored to me. . . . this novel meant a lot more than it should have done, to me, as in a way it was (or became) a whole test of my own judgement. . . . one must not be dependent upon anyone else's point of view. . . . my uncertainties about myself were so marked and of such long standing that I cannot help feeling an enormous relief to hear that Alan likes the book. . . .[8]

Yet her attitude to "Hagar" remained mixed, as though she resented it as the cause of her leaving Jack, like a heroine willingly making a necessary sacrifice yet sternly resenting the means by which the sacrifice was made. She recalled mailing the manuscript bundled together with other *junk* that she could just as well do without. In fact, almost two years after the event, she confessed to Adele, "I even tried [maybe] to half get rid of it by packing it off with all the old tennis shoes in that parcel we sent from your place."[9]

The situation was further vexed by the realization that she acutely missed Jack, her sexual partner who had fully awakened her lusty femininity. She insisted to Adele that she was not made for the celibate life. A typical outburst of frustration is her reference to Irving Layton's book of poems *Balls for a One-Armed Juggler*: "in one of his poems he speaks of 'the orgasmless women of Hampstead'—! . . . and for a few moments I considered writing to Irving and saying 'Just you come to Hampstead, baby, & I'll show you who's —' etc."[10] Another serious complication was her worry about financial security, her ability to live by her pen, and, with that, her concern about the fiction she absolutely had to write. That took time and required periods of "creative laziness"; the noun roused her guilt, the adjective salved her sting of consciousness.[11]

Publishers' approval buoyed up Margaret's spirits. By early spring of 1963, Macmillan in England had accepted for publication the two remaining African books—*The Tomorrow-Tamer* and *The Prophet's Camel Bell*—and now "Hagar." In Canada, McClelland and Stewart was expressing interest in the three books, but Jack McClelland wasn't sold on "Hagar" (neither he nor Alan Maclean liked the title) and deemed it madness to think of publishing three of her books in the same year.[12] More encouraging was Ethel Wilson's response to news of Macmillan's accepting "Hagar": it struck exactly the right note.

> I am . . . so glad that the non-African *Hagar* is accepted. . . . Yes—while loving the maple leaf as a Canadian leaf, we both do not feel that "Canadian" (in "the arts" anyway) is the Mapull Leaf Forever, but something different, taking our part in something wider and more human, and what I *do* like so much about you and your writing—you are unselfconscious and un-egoistic—although conscious (deeply so) of your work. You'll never, I'm sure, become the other.[13]

Announcing to Adele (11 February 1963) that "The Sound of the Singing" would appear in *Winter's Tales*, Margaret called it her "first non-African story to be published."[14] The designation "non-African" instead of "Canadian" exactly anticipated Wilson's echo. Margaret's apparent unwillingness to identify these pieces of fiction as "Canadian" is not a matter of caprice but one of serious importance for Canadian artists and especially so at that time. As she abandoned her final attempt to write another novel set in Africa, she had told Adele quite explicitly, "I have no desire to write a 'Canadian' novel in that horrible nationalistic, stilted sense. . . ."[15] This is Margaret's own echo of her objection (in her columns for *The Winnipeg Citizen*) to phony Canadianism in radio drama, and beyond that an echo of the censure I often heard her and her college mates cast (in their discussions in Tony's) on Canadian literature that featured Mounties, beavers, and the "Mapull" leaf.

Margaret developed the distinction further when she spoke at the Canadian Universities Society Literary Supper (among other speakers were writers Blair Fraser and Rumer Godden). She noted that "the strained nationalism of our early writing ultimately gives way to true writing which is concerned only with the creation of individual and unique life on the printed page. . . ."[16] That idea remained a sturdy plank in Margaret Laurence's aesthetic platform.

Her two new pieces of fiction reveal their identity in the terms indicated by Laurence and Wilson. "The Sound of the Singing" begins, "That house in Manawaka is the one which, more than any other, I carry with me." The novel she has been calling "Hagar" begins with a specific reference to an angel, a grave marker, but just a few lines later, still on the opening page, the specific geographical setting of the short story is reaffirmed: "She was not the only angel in the Manawaka cemetery, but she was the first, the largest, and certainly the costliest." Thus Margaret had, almost unwittingly, laid claim to a territory that would in time be recognized as unmistakably hers, her "own little postage stamp of native soil," as she wrote the remaining private and fictional words and set down her title, "Manawaka."

Promise of a virtual saga came with a second short story, evidently a sequel, "To Set Our House in Order" in the *Ladies Home Journal*, March 1964. She referred to these and related stories of the 1960s as something she is "intensely interested in . . . as they are based on childhood persons," that is, persons from her own childhood. The two short stories and "Hagar" deal with characters of Margaret's grandparents' generation—her grandparents themselves and a surrogate Peggy Wemyss, heroine of "The Sound of the Singing" and "To Set Our House in Order."

Her work progressed nicely but Margaret worried constantly about her finances. She told Adele early in the year that if she could sell nine stories to the Canadian Broadcasting Company she would earn enough to live for a year! Then, "But who in hell could write 9 stories in a year, never mind sell them?"[17] She was practical and talented enough to turn her hand to various ancillary jobs without feeling she was prostituting her artistic ability. B.W. Andrzejewski, Guś of Somaliland days, now in England with Sheila, invited her to collaborate with him on a chapter of *An Introduction to Somaliland*—for the government of the Somali republic. Guś also put Margaret in touch with people in the BBC Africa Service, who asked her to do a series of ten radio scripts on worldwide folk tales. She provided two sample scripts. They were accepted at the end of April; she completed the series.

Called "A BATTLE OF WITS: A SERIES OF TEN FOLK TALES FROM VARIOUS PARTS OF THE WORLD, adapted by Margaret Laurence," it began with a general introduction, "to be repeated with each script."[18] The tales are from, in order, Nyasaland, China, Arabia, Germany, Iran, Ghana, Britain, India, Canada, and Russia, each provided with its own brief introduction. The sources are Sir Richard Burton's *Arabian Nights*, the brothers Grimm, the tales of Robin Hood, and the myths of the Tsimshian people (the original inhabitants of northern British Columbia), among others.

There are no Somali tales in the series, but the hand of the creator of *A Tree for Poverty* is perfectly visible: the controlling choice for the "BATTLE OF WITS" recalls Margaret's generous presentation of trickster stories in *A Tree* and her typical sympathy with the downtrodden and the alien. The Indian tale and the Canadian pay their respects to native peoples, the Dravidians and the First Nations of the Canadian west coast. These two tales especially recall the hero of "Wiil Waal and the Midgan's Well" (*A Tree*) and the dwarf Godman Piro of "Godman's Master" (*Tomorrow-Tamer*). The series provided material for ten half-hour broadcasts and brought her between £40 and £50, not the £80 she originally expected, but useful.

In July 1963, Macmillan asked her to serve as a publisher's reader, at five guineas a book, and that led to an invitation to do book reviews for BBC radio. Margaret seemed financially set for the next year or two. McClelland and Stewart were still hesitant about doing her three books; they and Macmillan would breathe much easier if an American publisher accepted a couple of the books as well. Margaret put it bluntly: "all 3 [books] will come out in England and Canada," she informed Adele, "but not in the U.S., which is a tragedy, financially speaking."[19]

She felt secure enough, however, to take a week's holiday in Glasgow. Frances Bolton, daughter of old friends of Jack, was to spend the summer in London and would willingly stay with Jocelyn and David for the last week of June while Margaret went up to see her friend Nadine (née Jones) and her husband, Kwadwo Asante, a Ghanaian medical student at the university. (*The Tomorrow-Tamer* is dedicated to them.) Then, in July, the Camden School for Girls, a first-class grammar school ("one of the best in London," Margaret announced[20]) accepted Jocelyn, who would turn eleven in August and who had passed the "Eleven-plus" exams at age ten-plus. Relief and celebration at the Laurences'! Jocelyn was also preparing to "fly up" from Brownies into the Girl Guides and in August to go to Guides camp. David, age eight in August, occupied himself with reading science books, and building a handsome and useful shelf for his mother's birthday on which she would store her writing materials; and he would try to remember whether she had just turned thirty-seven or seventy-three.[21] A dark cloud—cockroaches—appeared soon after the arrival of Frances's mother. Margaret identified them, with feigned sang-froid, as "beetles" endemic to Hampstead, and, in the imposing Kay Bolton's absence, fiercely attacked the creatures with lethal spray (lavender-scented) and rags. Bolton mamma and daughter were evidently none the wiser.

The high point of the year came in August: Alfred A. Knopf had decided to publish her stories, the memoir, and her Canadian novel simultaneously. When John Cushman, Margaret's agent, phoned from New York to tell her of the decision, he noted, "Listen, honey, this is going to change your life. This is big news."[22]

There remained the titles. Nobody cared for "Hagar" as title for the novel. Margaret proposed a few words from Dylan Thomas; the publishers refused. Having rejected alternatives offered by the publishers, she searched the Psalms and finally looked again into the novel itself. Its opening sentence—"Above the town, on the hill brow, the stone angel used to stand"—gave Margaret the title she needed. "The stone angel," she recognized, "is an image which . . . recurs throughout the book, and it is completely suitable."[23] Yet she retained the closing couplet of Thomas's villanelle as epigraph to the novel: "Do not go gentle into that good night, / Rage, rage against the dying of the light." The title of *The Prophet's Camel Bell* was replaced by *New Wind in a Dry Land* for the US edition of the memoirs.

Her strengthened self-confidence is reflected in her letter telling Adele of Knopf's triple acceptance: she ends the letter "Love, Margaret." She also appends a parenthetical request "(Can you bear to refer to me as Margaret?)," and adds a note in ink in the left margin: "It has nothing much to do with my writing—it's something further back—at least I think so."[24] It marks a further step away from "Peggy," a stronger affirmation of "Margaret." She was now better able to confront two closely related problems: guilt over leaving Jack and the gnawing unease of her consequent celibacy. Reunion with Jack would apparently solve both simultaneously.

She planned to meet with Jack in East Pakistan during his leave at the end of 1963. Her letters to Adele in September and October express her hope to settle with Jack crucial questions about the children's education and what compromise they could make to enable the whole family to be together for at least a part of each year. Margaret feared that difficulties of compromise would be so severe that they would all end up back in the house in Vancouver, "where none of us wants to be, in order to be fair to everybody."[25]

Margaret was beginning to have a social life. Her friends the Barons—novelist Alex and his wife, Dolores—invited her, early in January 1963, to spend a weekend with them at their home near Brighton in August. Horatio ("Rache") Lovat Dickson invited her to the Valentine Ball given by the Canadian Universities Society, of which he was president. She had the week in Glasgow with the Asantes, and in mid-September she entertained Mordecai Richler and his wife, Florence, and Alice Frick. A couple of weeks later she went with Robert Weaver to a party at the Richlers'. But the brightest news of that October was Alan Maclean's asking if she would like to rent his house in the country, down in Buckinghamshire, halfway to Oxford, in the twin towns of Beaconsfield and Penn. "Elm Cottage" was a rambling five-bedroom house on about an acre of land,[26] where Maclean had spent his boyhood summers. A good deal of repair and refurbishing needed to be done, but Elm Cottage and its grounds looked heavenly. Margaret accepted the invitation conditionally: if Jack agreed, she would be glad to rent. She told Adele that the kids were well and "mad keen to find a place of our own where we can be noisy and also have a dog. I agree."[27]

The Elm Cottage possibility closely coincided with news from Jack that his firm would help defray expenses for Margaret's trip to East Pakistan. She would spend the month of November with him, urge the virtue of a substantial home in the countryside, and argue the economic side of the proposition—Maclean's willingness to "rent it to a friend at a fairly low rent."[28] Her professional success now included an interview with the BBC North American Service (which didn't please her but did bring in five guineas) and acceptance by the *Tamarack Review* of "Mask of Beaten Gold" for the autumn number.

She and Jack had a week in Calcutta and then on to the coast. Especially taking was the Black Pagoda of Konarak. Margaret explained it is "supposed to be covered with pornographic carvings—they didn't look pornographic to me; in fact I thought they were charming and full of joy—all the copulating couples bore rather tenderly touching smiles, which was nice."[29] Discussions with Jack went surprisingly well: he agreed to her taking the lease and remaining in England with the children. He would go on working abroad and needed, as she acknowledged to Adele, "a woman who will go with him, no questions asked."[30]

The Laurences agreed that since Margaret was evidently not that woman, she would assume responsibility for two-thirds of her support; Jack would retain visiting rights and would spend his leaves with Jocelyn and David. A productive visit all around: she wrote five short stories during the month.

Returned to Hampstead, Margaret faced the move to Elm Cottage, Beacon Hill, in the village of Penn. New arrangements had to be made for the children's schooling. Jocelyn would go down to a very good grammar school in High Wycombe and David had a mere five-minute walk to the local primary school. And they would have a puppy named Ringo. Basic repairs were made in time for them to move in on Sunday, 29 December; school began a week later. The principal challenge was the heating. Margaret had had no experience with coal fires, but heating also depended on wood, gas, and electricity; she feared that fuel costs alone would bankrupt her. Then the cleaning. But the children felt at home—as she did herself—and both contributed to putting things in order.

Financial stability continued to be a source of worry, but opportunities soon opened up again. She gave a talk on Canadian Literature to the Cambridge Canadian Club in February. *Holiday* magazine invited an essay from her—$500 if accepted. She wrote two and sent them both off. By the end of March she had rented a pair of rooms to newlyweds. *The Stone Angel* was getting a number of good reviews. Most heartening, personally, was the praise from Ethel Wilson and Malcolm Ross for her book of Ghanaian stories and her first Canadian novel. Ross told Margaret that he found *The Tomorrow-Tamer* "the finest collection of stories by a Canadian writer in existence and [they] transcend any 'national' claim to them. They are first-rate by any standard anywhere."[31] Ethel Wilson added to her glowing estimate of the stories a penetrating comment on *The Stone Angel*, which she called "glorious" and "great": "I believe some people could not read it, because it is the very life of life, and they do not know about life. . . . It has splendour. . . . The night in the cannery is terrific."[32]

Perhaps most gratifying was Ross's evaluation of Margaret's achievement in *The Stone Angel*, and its implicit agreement with Ethel Wilson—and Margaret—on its *Canadian* quality:

> My expectations were high—but not high enough. . . . Your technique is so perfectly controlled that it seems effortless . . . and the woman lives through all her dimensions of time, place and *person*. . . . And such a sure handling of idiom with the tang of place in it and yet without the slightest suggestion of a *self-conscious Canadian* accent . . . and I kept hearing echoes of speech from early days and forgotten people.
>
> You have completely avoided sentimentality. . . .
>
> Anyhow, you are well on your way to becoming not only *our* finest novelist but a first-rater by world standards.[33]

> If I had the wings of an angel,
> Or even the wings of a crow,
> I would fly to the top of T. Eaton's
> And spit on the people below.
>
> — *The Stone Angel*

Seeking a suitable title for her novel, Margaret had finally turned to the manuscript itself. The necessary title lay waiting in the opening sentence: "Above the town . . . the stone angel used to stand."[34] "Necessary," because the novel is about Hagar as stone angel: the two are virtually identical. The initial description of the angel emphasizes its blindness, its attitude of superiority and indifference, its association with vanity or overweening pride. Throughout the novel, there are frequent incidental references to these features in Hagar: "She . . . guides me as though I were stone blind" (58); "does she think I've . . . flown away?" (106); son John chides her, "Don't frown like that, angel"

(172); Hagar is angry "at God, perhaps, for giving us eyes but almost never sight" (173); and at John's death Hagar "was transformed to stone" (243); etc.[35] The description is Hagar's and distinctly reflexive: hers is the narrative voice throughout. The opening sentence establishes another important point. Its simple verb, "used to," indicates the dominant mode of the narration: retrospection.

During the two or three weeks of Hagar's ninetieth year, she recalls some eighty-five years of her past. Early on she observes, "Some people will tell you that the old live in the past—that's nonsense" (5). She dwells on the past, not to escape the present but, "rampant with memory," to relive and review it to discover and understand herself, to see how she became who she is in the present, while there is time. Hagar's mind moves over the dual chronological lines of her story, oscillating between past and present as her mind responds to the "triggering" effect of similarities among events, characters, and situations in the two lines. The result is a juxtaposition that creates virtual simultaneity as segments of past and present exist side by side in Hagar's view, for her edification—and for the reader's. Margaret later commented on this aspect of the narrative in *The Stone Angel* that Hagar's "memory sequences [are] triggered by some occurrence in her present";[36] in fact, the triggering works both ways as sometimes a recalled occurrence returns her to a matching occurrence in the present.

Several years after the completion of *The Stone Angel*, Margaret found in her travels in Greece an image that helps illustrate this aspect of her narrative. In 1964, she and Jack (temporarily reunited, took a brief holiday in Greece, from which came the magazine piece "Sayonara, Agamemnon" (1966). In it, she recalls that she and Jack wanted a picture of the archway through which the athletes ran into the arena at Olympia. Just as he was to snap his photo, a "denim-clad American boy stepped into the archway—Today Facing Yesterday." She urged Jack to take the picture anyway. He did. "At that precise moment the boy turned around. Today was facing Today, and they were both holding cameras aimed at each other."[37] Lorraine M. York commented on the importance of "confrontation between today and yesterday" in Margaret's works as represented in this episode.[38] That episode is part of a dominant theme in the essay on Greece: their tour guide was adept at approximating simultaneity in his accounts: "He spoke as though the past and present were one."[39] The scene at Olympia offers an equivalent of the narrative in *Angel*: in both, what might have been Today Facing Yesterday is rather Today Facing Today. As with Marcel Proust, "Yesterday" is *le temps perdu* and that second "Today" is *le temps retrouvé*. Margaret's interest in simultaneity became an ongoing concern.

The opening pages of the novel develop the similarity between Hagar and stone angel to emphasize another important theme in the novel, the conflict between the unspoiled natural and the domestic civilized, the latter an extension of the arrogance that assumes civilization's triumph over the natural cycle of mutability and mortality. Little Hagar, at "about six," fulfills, as does the angel, a decorative and representative function for Jason Currie: "There was I, strutting the board sidewalk like a pint-sized peacock, resplendent, haughty, hoity-toity, Jason Currie's black-haired daughter" (6). She had been trained "to celebrate tidiness" but that notion was already challenged when she was a girl, walking in the cemetery and noticing the contrast between the wild and vigorous cowslips "encroaching upon the dutifully cared-for habitations of the dead." The wild and gaudy flowers belong with "things that grew untended and had grown always, before the portly peonies and the angels with rigid wings, when the prairie bluffs were walked through only by Cree with enigmatic faces and greasy hair" (5).

The persistence of that memory, vivid in Hagar's present moment at age ninety, is justified. Her older brother, Matt, was involved with unsuitable boys of the Métis Tonnerre family in their cock-fighting and had plans to go hunting with Jules Tonnerre—until Jason Currie put his foot down. Such companions were not appropriate for the Curries, whose Scottish past—clan and sept, pipe music and war cry ("*Gainsay Who Dare!*")—has been drilled into Hagar and her brothers.

The Tonnerres are kin to those Cree with greasy hair. The conflicting appeal of the properly civilized and the liberally natural will plague Hagar as she strives for self-recognition.

Hagar's career is punctuated by a series of escapes. First is her escape from Jason Currie and all he has come to mean. After serving a term as the lady at his table and hearth, she renounced the decorative role and married the unkempt Bram Shipley, dirty fingernails, sexual aggressiveness, and all. Her old friend No-name Lottie Dreiser warns her about Bram: "he's been seen with half-breed girls" (47). Hagar had herself already noticed that "he looked like a bearded Indian, so brown and beaked a face. The black hair thrusting from his chin was rough as thistles" (45). Rebellious pride has prompted her marriage to Bram and rendered her an outcast from her family: none of them attends her wedding.

She is shocked by the main event of her wedding night but soon discovers joy in their lovemaking. Yet, she dare not acknowledge it to Bram. She *is*, after all, Jason Currie's daughter. Hagar gives Bram two sons. Nevertheless, Hagar's discomfort with Bram's uncouthness and his with her constant nagging finally drive them apart: "we'd each married for those qualities we later found we couldn't bear, he for my manners and speech, I for his flouting them" (79-80). She was obliged to escape again. She packed up herself and younger son, John, and the trunk that continued to announce her identity, *Miss H. Currie* (140), and fled to the coast. (This is just the first instance of Margaret's use of Vancouver to represent a *deceptive* sanctuary.)

As the journey begins, the narrative makes this second flight parallel to the first: John announces he has lost the Currie plaid pin, which Hagar had bestowed upon him along with the Highland catechism of the Currie heritage. The odyssey of the "lost" pin is significant: John traded it to Lazarus Tonnerre for a knife (which perhaps remains with the Tonnerre family); John later sold the knife to buy cigarettes. "Gone up in smoke," he told his mother, who responded, "*Gainsay Who Dare*" (177). (The knife will be recognizable, if it ever turns up again: its handle is marked ⊣.) But the identity announced by the trunk goes along with her, for, like Milton's Satan, it is her very self she flees.

At this juncture the novel is approaching its midpoint. Hagar plans her third escape, this time from her older son, Marvin, and his wife, Doris. Her freedom is threatened, as they plan to place her in Silverthreads, a "home" for senior citizens. The shape of the narrative and its reliance on two supportive texts begin to assert themselves.

The third escape takes Hagar to the shore and down to the abandoned fish cannery. The descriptive details are eloquent, if comparatively unobtrusive: "The stairway's beginning is almost concealed by fern. . . . I go down cautiously, feeling slightly dizzy. The ferns have overgrown the steps . . ." (151). This is the first half of the familiar pattern of heroic withdrawal and return, or of descent and ascent. Near the bottom she feels like Meg Merrilees and sings her song: "Old Meg she was a gipsy" (151), truly an outdoor girl at home in nature's bosom. She compares Meg's situation with her own—blackberry bushes, not swart enough, and, as for wine, no wildflowers full enough—and realizes she hasn't brought anything to drink. At the shore there is "water everywhere" but, ironically, not to slake her thirst. She naps, thirst returns, and she thinks optimistically, "Perhaps there's a well. Now I'm certain there must be . . . " (153).

These details are soon enough recognizable as introduction to the subtexts—the echo of Keats's poem joins the two—the biblical story of Hagar, handmaiden of Abraham's wife, Sarah, an Egyptian who gives Abraham his first heir, Ishmael, and who is banished for proudly flaunting her fertility before the barren Sarah. In the wilderness God leads her to a well. The loneliness and severe thirst also introduce the text of Coleridge's *The Rime of the Ancient Mariner*. As early as the second chapter, old Hagar has associated herself with Old Meg and with the biblical Hagar. When the Reverend Mr. Troy has come, at Doris's urging, to pay Hagar a visit, she thinks, "Here we sit, the little minister . . . and I the Egyptian . . . sadly altered" (40). She soon makes a specific association between herself and the Ancient Mariner.

What happens during Hagar's three days down at the cannery might be called the *depetrification* of Hagar as stone angel. To accomplish that, she must subdue her overweening pride so as to accept what her memories permit her to discover about herself and her relations with the important men in her life—her husband and her two sons—and to embrace the virtue of Charity instead of being its persecutor. She must learn to give the blessing of love to those who need it, and to recognize that such behaviour is reflexive, reciprocating. Although she has gone down to the shore to escape, it gradually dawns on her that there may be another purpose.

Down there she can acknowledge her love for Bram, understands her waking at night "out of a half sleep and turn to him to find he wasn't beside me, and then I'd be filled with such a bitter emptiness . . . " (160). She recalls returning to Manawaka at John's writing of Bram's severe decline and sympathizing with Marvin's parting words (he too had been summoned by John's news), "I'm sorry, Dad" (182); there Bram had called her name in his sleep and she had gone to him—"that moment I'd willingly have called him back . . . to say even once what Marvin had said . . . " (183). Yet, she confessed, "When we buried Bram . . . it was John who cried, not I" (184).

Hagar's relationship with the maturing John parallels her relationship with Bram and thus illuminates that contrast. The contrast is affirmed in the depiction of John's connection with Arlene Telford. It is most graphically illustrated in the scene in the cemetery when Hagar obliges John to re-establish the toppled Currie stone angel. At first she tries to help but soon stops and explains, pertinently, "I was afraid for my heart"; and she watches John—"I wish he could have looked like Jacob then, wrestling with the angel and besting it, wringing a blessing from it. . . . But no" (179). He does, however, set her up, as she comments, "I never could bear that statue. I'd have been glad enough to leave her." The association of stone angel and Hagar is clear.

But stony Hagar persists, prudishly persecuting the love of her son and Arlene, planning with Arlene's mother to send the girl down east and forbidding John to bring her to the Shipley house. But, Hagar asks herself, "What made me say it? As soon as I'd spoken, I regretted it. But I couldn't humble myself to take back my words" (213). Yet, grounds for hope is provided, dramatically, by the management of Hagar's memory and by the echoes of its idiom. She wanders from the cannery down along the beach and comes upon two children playing house; she finally intrudes to offer some real food from her shopping bag. Startled, they flee, and Hagar reprimands herself. She stumbles and falls, but rights herself and enjoys the triumph: "I've done it. Proud as Napoleon or Lucifer . . ." (191). She rests, ponders, "Perhaps I've come here not to hide but to seek," and, as if in answer, her memory aids—"I remember some other children, once, playing at house . . ." (192). She remembers the love of John and Arlene, her overhearing Arlene's saying, "Let's say this is our house . . . and nobody can come in . . ." and their lovemaking. "His final cry was inarticulate, the voice of the whirlwind" (208), the voice of love appropriately associated with the voice of God.

Chapter Seven has begun with other echoes of that kind, echoes anticipated in connection with Hagar's thirst, and now more specific. Margaret had explained to Adele Wiseman that "Hagar" would not do as the title of the novel: it "makes the biblical parallel too obvious and it is intended only as an echo and no more."[40] But she retained the name for her protagonist, as well as the vanity and the ostracism, the Egyptian identity, her maternity effected by her Bram, etc. The other ancillary text is not more subtly identified at the outset of the chapter, where the newly awakened Hagar becomes aware of her "parched flesh": "*Water water everywhere nor any drop to drink*. That's my predicament. What albatross did I slay, for mercy's sake? Well . . . come on, old mariner, up and out . . ." (186).

This is an obvious enough invocation of Coleridge's modern ballad. The subtlety, however, is in the way Margaret has used that text. She reiterates an association between the two texts barely noticeable at the middle of Five—just after "Old Meg she was a gipsy": "I haven't brought any water" (152) and "Perhaps there's a well. . . . there must be" (153). A few lines after the bold echo of *The Rime of the Ancient Mariner*, a "gang of sparrows" (like a surrogate albatross) aids Hagar by leading her to a bucket of rainwater; "here's my well in the wilderness, plain as you please" (187).

Hagar does not slay the sparrows with a crossbow, but she does shoo them away ungenerously (187). In the next chapter, however, she contributes directly to the death of the seagull that has intruded. Then a stranger comes in. As Margaret has adjusted the biblical story so that Hagar plays a dual role of Egyptian Hagar and Sarah, bearing both sons to Abraham, so does she alter the roles of Mariner and Wedding Guest slightly: *both* have a tale to tell and *both* are obliged to listen—effective reciprocity. Echoes of the Judaeo-Christian tradition have been audible throughout the novel but are inescapable in Eight; the theme of the importance of respecting Nature is also prominent. The stranger is Murray Lees, an audible complement to gipsy Hagar as Merrilees. Furthermore, the stranger's middle name is Ferney—to suit the environment. Lees's tale is about love, organized religion, and a lost son.

His account of his religious connections includes his Anglican mother, who bathed frequently ("in case she smelled," 226) but wouldn't use deodorants in case they left a mark and people saw. The side of Hagar that loved Bram prompts her response: "Fancy spending your life worrying about what people were thinking." His account of Lou, his wife—"she could have prayed the angels themselves right down from heaven, . . . and when she lay down on the moss and spread those great white thighs of hers, there wasn't a sweeter place in this entire world" (227)—moves Hagar to observe he is "rather a coarse man," and she says, "That's a mighty odd combination . . . prayer and *that*." The Currie side of Hagar is also properly at work. The story of their son, Donnie—a "natural child" or a "love child," burned to death while Lees and Lou were at the Tabernacle—touches Hagar closely. "'I had a son,' I say, 'and lost him'" (234).[41]

Hagar recalls that lost son and her contributive role in the loss. She recognizes that her persecution of the love of John and Arlene directly provoked their death. Although that love had caused John to quit his excessive drinking, the threat of Arlene's being sent down east to keep them apart has pushed him off the wagon and into the truck he then drives across the trestle bridge to his and the faithful Arlene's death. That scene involves two of Hagar's abominations—the illicit love of Arlene, who has ridden with him to be of whatever help, and the alien Lazarus Tonnerre, with whom the bet was made. As he is dying, John begs Hagar for her beneficence—a sign of love, of the blessing he seemed to be wrestling for as he righted the stone angel: "You can't, can you?" Significantly, Hagar weeps. Lees's response to this memory, which she has spoken aloud, startles her; he says, "Gee, that's too bad" (244). They sleep.

When Hagar awakens, sick, she thinks Murray Lees is John. She apologizes for opposing his and Arlene's love. Lees gives the reply she needs—from John: "I knew . . . you never meant it." She is content: "I could even beg God's pardon this minute, for thinking ill of Him some time or other" (248). Hagar then sleeps again. Her sojourn has been a success. Lees has summoned Marvin and, on the third day, Hagar is helped to the upper world. She remembers her conversation with Lees and is at first shocked at her failure of fastidiousness. But there was more, "Something else . . . other words . . . as though I'd lost someone only recently" (249). Lees apologizes for his "betrayal" and fixes her with his stare; "He holds my eyes . . . won't let them go . . . waiting for me to pardon him" (252). She does so, pardons or blesses him; she reaches out, touches his wrist, apologizes for being cross, and adds "I'm sorry about your boy." The result is something akin to the contentment she felt by apologizing to John through Murray Lees: "Having spoken so, I feel lightened and eased" (253).

The death of John has been sacrificial, as the death of the albatross was for the mariner; and recognition and acceptance of the sacrifice by the sinner responsible for the sacrificial death makes redemption possible—as though forgiveness is reciprocal, a reflexive love. The mariner wears the albatross like a crucifix—"Instead of the cross the Albatross / About my neck was hung."[42] The love expressed in his appreciation of God's creatures frees the mariner; he is able to pray, and the albatross falls from his neck. Margaret uses a slightly different emphasis: the wounded seagull is clearly reminiscent of Coleridge's albatross, but Hagar herself is intimately associated with her victim. After she tells Lees that she too had a son and lost him, she becomes disoriented: "I dip and dart inside my skull, swooping like a sea gull. . . . I may be swept outward like a gull . . ." (235). Margaret's point is that acts of love and acts of hate are alike reflexive, reciprocal. The implication is that Hagar as stone angel is on her way to *depetrification.*

More remains, however, before she can be fully redeemed; she must confront other demands for her blessing. One such demand is strongly implicit in Marvin's assisting her in ascending the ferny stairway: "He tugs and pulls, sweats and strains, teeters me aloft" (253). His effort is markedly reminiscent of John's wrestling with the Currie angel in the cemetery—like Jacob wrestling with the angel of the Lord—"He sweated and grunted. . . . finally the statue moved, teetered, and was upright . . ." (179). But Marvin's blessing is yet to come.

Implicit apologies to the deceased Bram occur throughout the novel, beginning at least with Hagar's having him buried in the Currie plot in the Manawaka cemetery. In hospital she praises Bram to the friendly Elva Jardine (272); and she is able to give a recognizable blessing to Elva with a gesture that recalls her blessing of Lees (253), and she repeats the praise as she compliments grandson Steven (295); she cries out "Bram" in her sleep, as Elva has called her Tom (275). In the darkness of her semi-private ward, she finds herself walking toward the light in the hallway—"If I reach it, someone will speak. Will the voice be the one I have been listening for?" One word would do—"*Hagar.* He was the only one who ever called me by my name" (284-85).

The Rime of the Ancient Mariner makes a final contribution to the novel in the concluding chapter. The Reverend Mr. Troy pays a last visit, and functions for Hagar as the Hermit of the Wood does for the mariner; to provide the necessary shrift, Troy sings (at her request) "Old Hundredth"—"*Sing to the Lord with joyful voice. . . . Come ye before Him and rejoice*" (291-92). Hagar responds, "I must always . . . have wanted that—simply to rejoice. . . . Every good joy I might have held . . . [was] forced to a standstill by some brake of proper appearances. . . . When did I ever speak the heart's truth?" (292). She concludes her epiphany, "Pride was my wilderness, and the demon that led me there was fear." Hagar proves courageous enough to fetch a bedpan for Sandra Wong when the nurses fail to answer the call. "And now I wonder if I've done it for her or for myself. No matter. I'm here, and carrying what she needs" (301). Of course it matters much. Hagar has demonstrated once again the reflexive quality of Charity. She seems to realize that again in her final scene with Marvin. She confesses, "I'm so frightened," and apologizes to him (as she did to the dead John through the medium of Murray Lees). Marvin holds her hand tightly. "Now it seems to me he is truly Jacob, gripping with all his strength, and bargaining. *I will not let thee go, except thou bless me*. And I see I . . . can only release myself by releasing him" (304). She tells him he has been a better son than John, a fit blessing.

Thus we see the redemption that follows the depetrification of Hagar Shipley, née Currie.

Two questions remain. One has to do with Margaret's use of the biblical account of Hagar and Abraham and the pairs of sons—specifically, the final association of Marvin with Jacob: does her Hagar play the role of Rebekah as well as of Sarah? Perhaps she does, but the focus on the pairs of sons—Ishmael and Isaac, Esau and Jacob, reflected in Marvin and John (and even in Matt and Dan Currie)—matters most. The Shipley boys are not so sharply distinguished as the biblical sons; none of the distinctive features (hairiness vs smoothness, wildness vs domestication, etc.) function with them. The one exception is that Matt Currie and John Shipley have friends among the alien Métis family, the Tonnerres. Margaret evidently wanted to emphasize a basic relatedness between the brothers in each of her pairs; and indeed the adjective applied to the Tonnerres expresses *relatedness—Métis*, like mulatto and mixed. This is the theme of compromise, reconciliation, as it appears in the case of the accommodating aliens of *The Tomorrow-Tamer*. In the biblical account of the descendants of Abraham, reconciliation (or accommodation) figures prominently at last: at Abraham's death, both Ishmael and Isaac are present and together bury their father, and at Jacob's death, the reconciled Esau and Jacob together bury him. In the closing pages of *The Stone Angel* Hagar recalls her last visit to Manawaka, particularly the cemetery with its gravestone marked *Currie* on one side and *Shipley* on the other. John's comment was quite apt: "They're only different sides of the same coin, anyway. . . . They might as well be together there" (184).

After Mr. Troy's last visit, Hagar tells Doris they had nothing to say to each other, and immediately regrets it, is "ashamed," and says, "Oh, I am unchangeable, unregenerate" (293). A minor theme, it is yet perceptible—and significant. At the end of the first chapter of the novel Hagar ponders her age, ninety, and thinks, "when I look in my mirror and beyond the changing shell that houses me, I see the eyes of Hagar Currie, the same dark eyes as when I first began to remember to notice myself" (38). Early in the second chapter, she says, "If I were to . . . approach the mirror softly, . . . I would see there again that Hagar with the shining hair, the dark-maned colt off to the training ring, the young ladies' academy in Toronto" (42). Her black trunk, used to convey her and John to Vancouver, is still marked *Miss H. Currie* (140), and so on. But she has been "altered," like the stone angel in the cemetery. The roughness she had acquired as Hagar Shipley has been smoothed, and the vain arrogance of the Curries has been modified to acceptable pride. Old Hagar can at last apologize to the nurses for speaking sharply, can bless Bram, fetches Sandra's bedpan proudly (but not like Lucifer), and wrests (almost like the Hagar in the mirror—but not quite) "the full glass of water" away from the nurse and takes it into her own hands, "There. There."

Has Hagar learned "too late," as a number of readers believe? Hardly. Like Graham Greene, Margaret Laurence felt it was never "too late" while life lasted.[43]

Is *The Stone Angel* the autobiographical first novel that Margaret was glad to have avoided by writing *This Side Jordan*? Certainly not, in the obvious sense of the term. Yet she did realize that one day she would be obliged to "go back to my own people": "Hagar . . . seemed almost to choose me," she reported. Further, she explained (in 1970), "I recognized that . . . I had to begin approaching my background and my past through my grandparents' generation, the generation of pioneers of Scots Presbyterian origin, who had been among the first to people the town I called Manawaka."[44]

That explanation couples *Angel* with the two Manawaka short stories that preceded it—"The Sound of the Singing" and "To Set Our House in Order"—which Margaret admitted frankly are autobiographical: the former deals with her Simpson grandparents and the latter with her Wemyss grandmother. There is also a slightly veiled reference to the Wemyss background in Hagar's rehearsing for son John the Currie Highland Scots tradition and bestowing on him the Currie silver plaid pin: "Your grandfather got this when his father died. That was your great-grandfather, Sir Daniel Currie. The title died with him—it wasn't a baronetcy" (124). Not an exact equivalent of Wemyss history and legend, but near enough. Sir John Wemyss, Bart (1831-78), knighted for service to the Crown in India, was the brother of the actual great-grandfather; and in his case it *was* a baronetcy. Some fifteen years after his death, Scottish lawyers informed Margaret's grandfather, John Wemyss, that the title was his if he could provide proof of the relationship. Sir John had intended to sponsor his nephew in the Indian Civil Service but died before that could be arranged.

That kind of fraternal thoughtfulness is repeated in other pairs of brothers in the Wemyss family. Sir John's concern for his brother Robert's son repeats their father's (another John's) attempt over a period of years to locate the widow (Minshoo) and son (John, of course) of his brother David in India. That fraternal concern prompted Margaret to recognize a similar concern in her father and uncle Jack, especially during their service in the First World War.[45] The phenomenon undoubtedly encouraged her to find accommodating brotherliness (despite the original biblical example of Cain and Abel) among the pairs in Abraham's dynasty and to approximate it in the Currie and Shipley pairs of *Angel.*

Since Sir Daniel Currie is John Shipley's great-grandfather, the novel equates John with his creator: the actual Sir John Wemyss was the great-grandfather of Margaret Laurence. She, in turn, seems to authenticate that equation in her comments to Adele Wiseman:

> The novel means such a hell of a lot to me, simply because it is me. . . . I don't mean the characters are me, naturally, although some of them are, in some ways. . . . My own dilemma, I see now, is closest to Hagar's son John—in fact, he is the person whom I feel the most for. . . .[46]

Hagar's pair of sons makes her similar to Margaret's Grandmother Wemyss. But the association of Hagar with Margaret herself is easy to see. The eagerness of the young Hagar to escape the stifling atmosphere of the Currie domain is a clear reflection of Peggy Wemyss's desire to escape small-town Neepawa and taste all the delights of the big city; Bram's role in providing a means of escape for Hagar is similar to Jack Laurence's aid to Peggy. Further similarity between Bram and Jack is less obvious.

Another aspect of Hagar's resemblance to Margaret, however, is association with Keats's Meg Merrilees, the gypsy who may be seen to represent escape itself, from the urban, domestic, civilized world, out on "the moors . . . out of doors . . . among the bushes," etc. Her function during Hagar's sojourn down at the cannery—among the ferns—at the shore is obvious. Margaret also assumed, at various moments in her life, the role of Meg readily enough. Her first adult publication was a poem that appeared in the *Canadian Tribune*, 9 January 1950, as she informed Adele: "'Let My Voice Live' by Meg—(A Canadian in England)."[47] Thirty years later, she is still pursuing that identity. In the mid-May "Victoria Days" celebration in Lakefield, Ontario (her last home), she donned "a long print dress . . . on which last year, for the same event, I sewed a bunch of lace I once bought from an English gypsy, plus a long black cape lined with scarlet. . . . Makes me look like Meg Merrilees. . . ."[48]

Perhaps the most revealing similarity between art and life is that between the Hagar-Bram connection and the Margaret-Jack. With Bram, Hagar's sexuality is fully wakened—so fully as to embarrass her into hiding the fact from him; Peggy's was already wakened and eager to accept Jack's legitimate offering. Hagar's almost precipitous rejection of the uncouth Bram, she explains, after the Reverend Mr. Troy's shriving, was due to Pride, to which she was driven by fear. Pride may certainly have driven Margaret to flee from Jack as well, but pride of a different sort: it might be called "pride of pen"—her late-blooming confidence in her talent and in her decision to emerge from the writer's closet. Hagar's acknowledgement that, in spite of all, Bram was the love of her life could well have been Margaret's way of cautioning herself that the same painful discovery might await her. The moving fear in Margaret's case would then have been fear of absolute self-reliance. Nevertheless, *The Stone Angel* remains an unmistakable literary triumph, with a discernible autobiographical cachet.

eleven

Rachel, Rachel

THE YEAR 1964 BEGAN WITH THE SETTLING INTO ELM Cottage. The house was the result of modifications and additions to the modest original structure that dates from the beginning of the eighteenth century. Alan Maclean's father had bought the property (about an acre) as a summer home. Lady Maclean was especially fond of the place and spent the last months of her life there.[1] Alan Maclean lent Margaret a portrait of his mother as a girl, all in white. It hung in the downstairs hall and became the *genius loci*.[2] Margaret could see the portrait from her study and at the end of the day would lean back in her chair and speak to The Lady, who always smiled back (Margaret felt). Indeed, Jocelyn claimed she herself had seen the young lady in white moving about the house; and reports of the existence of the ghost of Elm Cottage persist to the present.[3]

The garden had a pair of beech trees and the majestic elm responsible for the name of the cottage. The untended apple trees yielded enough fruit for Margaret and the children well into the winter months. The mulberry tree, near the front gate, produced an abundance of red-purple fruit. There were daffodils in spring, blackberries in autumn, and an attendant cuckoo.[4] The rose bushes lasted until Christmas, and, while Margaret never had a green thumb, she did plant vegetables among the roses and with some success.[5] The children built tree houses in the garden and Margaret helped them construct a large dollhouse. Ringo's wanderlust led to his removal at Hallowe'en of 1965. He was replaced by two cats, first Calico and then, in the spring of 1967, Topaz.[6] Although Margaret often shared with Adele Wiseman her worry about what she had undertaken in renting the place—she and Jack had agreed she should assume responsibility for two-thirds of her expenses—she also regularly rejoiced in the "kingdom" she had acquired. Elm Cottage gave her time and space to do her work. In good weather she even moved her scribblers into the garden and wrote away with a stubby pencil (as it always seemed to be) at a picnic table under the elm.

Margaret worried about finances and about what she saw as her failure to be the wife Jack needed and to be a good mother to Jocelyn and David. Her mind was somewhat eased by Jack's approval of her renting Elm Cottage, which might become an acceptable site for compromise and even reconciliation of the Laurences. The threat of a return to the house in Vancouver was removed as Jack decided to sell that house and make Elm Cottage his home base.

Ironically, Margaret thankfully turned her back on Canada to write her fiction about it, for the Canadian voices that had demanded her attention in 1961 and produced the wonderful Hagar intruded on her consciousness again. Three voices in particular: one, the voice of a girl, Vanessa MacLeod, two generations younger than Hagar, was intimately familiar. Two stories featuring Vanessa were accepted for publication in 1963—"The Sound of the Singing" for *Winter's Tales* 9 (1963) and "To Set Our House in Order" by *Ladies Home Journal* (1964); other Vanessa stories followed. As she was producing that series—it comprised a virtual *Bildungsroman* when completed—the two other voices, from the generation between Vanessa and Hagar, urgently solicited attention. These were the voices of Stacey and Rachel, daughters of Manawaka's undertaker Niall Cameron, roughly the same age as Margaret. The problem was that each seemed to demand a novel of her own and it was by no means clear which of them ought to be attended to first.[7]

The crucial question was how reunion with Jack would affect her writing: could she be faithful to her duty as wife and also to her function as artist? How would her apparent commitment to writing about Canada accommodate her commitment to living in England? How strong an appeal to Margaret would those insistent Canadian voices exert?

Chances for success of the contemplated reunion—the necessary compromises and the indicated bases of reconciliation—can be predicted in part on the evidence in a couple of short stories (not Vanessa's) Margaret had written during the months preceding her separation from Jack in autumn 1962 and by her report of her visit with him to Greece in the late spring of 1964, which was the beginning of their attempt at reconciliation. The earlier of these stories, "A Queen in Thebes," she called "the only science fiction I've ever done,"[8] clearly an anomaly; but the later, "Mask of Beaten Gold," might well have been included in *The Tomorrow-Tamer* had Margaret not forgotten it was with *The Tamarack Review* when she was putting together the West African volume.[9] It might have replaced the similar "A Fetish for Love."

"Mask of Beaten Gold" tells of the mixed marriage of Candace and Philip Thrane. She is a West African woman trained as a nurse in London, and he is a white British doctor in a Ghanaian hospital; they have a five-year-old son, Jeremy. The marriage is strained: after seven years of marriage the two still don't really *know* each other. The difficulty is obviously Philip, who is arrested by appearances—Candace's (and Jeremy's) brownness and his own whiteness. With terrific suddenness, Jeremy dies of cerebral malaria.[10] Shortly after the funeral Philip tries to recall what the boy looked like. He begs Candace to tell him. She does so but adds, "What did it matter, anyway. . . . It didn't matter, did it?" And the story ends with Margaret's typically gentle and fiercely poignant conclusion: "Candace came to him then, and their mourning was unlocked. They held tightly to one another, concentrating the force of grief on the fact that the child was gone, as though hoping to ward off another grief, worse than a death." "Mask" is a little parable about grievous impediments to human intercourse; it is principally Philip's story.

Brooke and Connie in "A Fetish for Love" and the Thranes of "Mask" are involved in unsatisfactory marriages, and in both cases the husband is to blame. Brooke and Connie have a son. Their Ghanaian servants are childless: old Sunday is sterile and physically abuses Love for failing to give him an heir. Her maternal potential is strongly urged by her capable nurturing of Connie's son. In Connie's case, *love* suffers from Brooke's spiritual sterility, his avuncular condescension. The women are similarly held in a loveless union; both are victims of dire sterility—only the one is physical. The nearly contemporary Philip and Brooke fail because of selfish blindness that impedes satisfactory behaviour. These two may reflect directly on the Laurences' domestic situation. A stronger and more mature Candace and Connie might have confronted Philip and Brooke, leading to a more satisfactory union in each case. Another Brooke, closely resembling Connie's husband, will appear in Margaret's later fiction and reinforce the suggestion that such a character derived in part from her perception of her relationship with Jack.

The "science fiction" story tells of the twenty-year-old heroine left widowed and desolate with her infant son, Rex, at their summer shack in the mountains after the eruption of the feared nuclear holocaust. They are the sole survivors. She and Rex learn self-reliance and courage at the brink of despair. Rex gradually grows into the dominant role of hunter and provider, and, once a severe thunderstorm rekindles the restored forest, the religious leader as well in the worship of fire and of its evident source in the sun. Fire in their cave, of course, becomes essential to their survival and easily assumes symbolic significance in the story. The mother remembers the catastrophe, the collapse of their city: "she saw it like the disintegrating sun, the light like no other light, a dark illumination and not the health that we associate with light."[11]

With that, the nature of the relationship between mother and Rex is inescapable: it threatens, as he grows into young manhood, to blaze forth into something different from the acceptable maternal-filial bond, something perhaps as destructive as the nuclear blast itself; both characters are intuitively aware of the danger as they recognize that their relationship is a combination of reciprocal fear and mutual attraction. That recognition is reminiscent (appropriately) of the paradox identified by Frankenstein's monster concerning his discovery of fire, his "delight at the warmth I experienced from it," his noting that it "gave light as well as heat," and the painful result of his trying to grasp it; then his comment on the irony, "How strange, I thought, that the same cause should produce such opposite effects."[12]

The crisis of the story occurs as Rex discovers his mother's secret relic from the past, a shard of mirror into which she looks to assure herself of her own reality: he calls her "unclean," snatches the mirror away, and hurls it against the rocks, smashing it and whatever sense of identity she has sustained thereby.[13] Yet, as the story ends, she has achieved the compromise by which she can manage to live with the handsome Rex, whom she has moulded into the creature he has become in his maturity—and who will function as a replacement for her lost husband. And as the story ends, she sits at the entrance to the cave, basking in the sun after making sure that supper will be ready when her master, her Rex, returns. She hears again the voice from her past, the fragment of a nursery song her memory has modified slightly as though to fit her present circumstances: "Lavender's blue, dilly dilly, lavender's green, / When *you* are king, dilly dilly, *I* shall be queen" (my italics). The concluding sentence of the story is a tacit reiteration of the life-sustaining force of fire: "Then, inside the cave, one of the children began crying, and she went to give comfort."

"Science fiction," if you like, but with an urgent message about the necessity of compromise if a union is to succeed, if life is to go on. It is a "message" implicit in "A Fetish for Love," in "Mask of Beaten Gold," and in "Uncertain Flowering." "A Queen in Thebes" is inescapably patterned on the Oedipus myth. Yet it seems also to participate in the

Frankenstein myth, as do "A Fetish," "Mask," and even "Uncertain Flowering"—with a reversal of male and female roles. If Rex's mother is clearly a Jocasta, she is also a Frankenstein who recognizes and accepts her responsibility for the creation of this beloved "monster." Margaret has thus fused the stories of Oedipus and Frankenstein. The creator of her monster, the mother, has provided the bride Frankenstein will not risk providing. The revelation of incest, at the conclusion of "A Queen," is a horror, but Margaret has set that horror into a context that confronts the reader with a choice of horrors. Walter Swayze has put the case sagely and persuasively:

> Incest is probably the absolute taboo in most societies. But here, as in *Oedipus Rex* and several other of the greatest tragedies in literature, it is not only frightening, but apparently inevitable. The horror of the ending is what has frightened off most readers. . . . But which is more obscene—an act essential to the continuation of human life in the universe or the bureaucratic annihilation of millions of mothers, fathers and children, many of whom have some chance of experiencing Love in their normal relationship?[14]

These fictions evidently reflect Margaret's view of her situation with Jack. His critical or aesthetic blindness to her work in *The Stone Angel* is present in the personal, conjugal blindness of Philip Thrane in "Mask" and Brooke in "A Fetish," as it is in Rex of "A Queen." Yet there is the strong implication that the woman in each case is culpable as well—for allowing her victimization to proceed, in effect contributing to the immorality of the conjugal situation. "A Queen in Thebes" insists on the absolute necessity of love and of the willingness to make compromises; it is the equivalent of W.H. Auden's assertion that "We must love one another or die." And if one is still unduly horrified at Jocasta's choice, Margaret would offer yet another alternative, a classic choice made in the face of another blind hero—that of Clytemnestra, wife of Agamemnon.

At the beginning of June 1964, Margaret joined Jack in Athens for a twelve-day holiday. They immediately decided to accommodate the different preferences of each other—languishing on the beach near Athens (Margaret's) or taking an educational tour of the islands (Jack's). She wasn't much impressed by the tour until they got to Mycenae, where something caught her imagination: the magical phenomenon of the presentness of the past. Like Thornton Wilder, Margaret had long been fascinated by the work of the archaeologist Heinrich Schliemann and his discovery of the existence of nine cities superimposed on the site of Troy. She was excited to find that in the roadway running under the Lion Gate one could see quite distinctly the grooves made centuries ago by chariot wheels but looking as though they had been made just a month ago. In a letter to Adele Wiseman she reported, ". . . it is not so very difficult to hear Agamemnon returning, in the bitter dust and heat of the day, expecting with a calm and giant egotism to find all well within his fortress and nothing altered from the day he left."[15] It is tempting to see here a tacit juxtaposition of Agamemnon and Jack, who has just returned, expecting to find all well and nothing altered within *his* regained fortress.

The temptation is encouraged by Margaret's recounting in the same letter another exciting confrontation of past and present and the dramatic expression of conflicting appeals. She tells of going up to the ruins of Agamemnon's palace. "It was the only time in the trip when I was *compelled* to break away from the group . . ." (my italics):

> I thought something idiotic such as—thank God, alone at last—when all of a sudden up popped an entire family from behind one of the massive rock walls, and a small boy said in my own speech and accent, "Hi." So I said "Hi," where Agamemnon fell, and didn't know, really, which had the most meaning for me personally, the kid who spoke in a way I could understand, or the King of Men, heroic but *blinder* than Oedipus, and the *compelled* queen.[16]

Beside the association of Jack and Agamemnon there is implicit reiteration of the strained domestic arrangement found in "A Fetish for Love," "Mask of Beaten Gold," "A Queen in Thebes," and "Uncertain Flowering," and with similar emphasis—and also the conflicting appeals of the heroic past and the modest, plebeian present. Yet within that contrast ("which had the most meaning for me personally"?) there is a contradiction: it is not that one or the other held "the most meaning," but that, poised in that particular opposition, they were *equally* meaningful to her. Simultaneously, the kid spoke to her own identity, the product of her own accumulated Canadian experience, and the spot recalling the fiercely blind King of Men spoke to her present moment and identity as the *compelled* consort of her own "King." That counterpoised pair, especially as associated with the domestic problem reflected in these stories, tells us much about the complex of problems Margaret faced at that moment in mid-1964, a complex that did not bode well for the success of any reconciliation between her and Jack. This letter to Adele adds that Jack is to be in British Columbia for two weeks in July to sell the Vancouver house; it thus creates an interesting and paradoxical concatenation of news to ponder.

That summer of 1964, Margaret, Jack, and the children visited Wales, where David was delighted to tromp around a dozen castles. There was also the atmosphere of fierce Welsh warriors and constant echo of the *eisteddfods*—reminiscent for Margaret especially of the stirring oral performances of Somali poets traditionally declaring their *gabeis*, like the Sayyid Mahammed 'Abdille Hasan. Their return took them through Cornwall and Devon. Her account of that holiday for Adele said much about the success of the reconciliation with Jack, such as that she was "back now in the old groove of me trying to split myself three ways [as wife, mother, and writer] . . . and doing a pretty rotten job on all three fronts."[17] She added a comment that recalls the mother in "A Queen in Thebes" secretly stealing a glance at herself in her bit of mirror: "I must *not* begin basically doubting my own reality again, as if I do, I'm really lost." Then followed the little dithyramb about the ripe blackberries and ripening apples—"I have a sense of owning a kingdom" (A Queen in Bucks!). The ambivalent autumn ended with Jack's departure on the second of November for Somaliland. Margaret remained in Elm Cottage, brooding guiltily over her failure to accompany him.[18]

She was also brooding over her struggle with the story or stories of the Cameron sisters: her literary creations insisted on being managed in the proper order, as though they had a mind of their own. Margaret had learned, at the approach of forty, to listen to the wishes of her work. They had allowed her to begin with her grandparents' generation, Hagar's story. The stories demanding her attention throughout 1963 were also about that generation, but as seen through the eyes of Vanessa MacLeod, with dominant focus on her Grandfather Connor, a complement to Hagar Shipley. Margaret had explained to Adele that she was writing these stories as an alternative to the novel, which she "can't contemplate," she said; the stories "are no hell but I am intensely interested in them . . . [and they] are the best thing to do right now."[19] So she continued with them but kept turning back to the Camerons, and by the end of 1964 was working on that material with some confidence.

Two days before Christmas Margaret received a copy of Adele Wiseman's *Old Markets, New World*, a book of reminiscences of the farmers' market in Winnipeg's North End with illustrations. She immediately wrote to compliment Adele: "Your essay reminds me of so many things in my own childhood—not markets, but when you talk of the sleighs with the box-like huts built into them, and the way kids used to hook rides. . . . You hit the right tone—evocation without ever being sentimental."[20] This was one of the Canadian associations that intruded on Margaret's life to awaken her curiosity about Canada and her interest in resuming closer connections with it. The domestic scene at Elm Cottage, however, demanded Margaret's constant attention. At the close of 1964 she had to contend with frozen water pipes and at almost the same time daughter Jocelyn was smitten with tonsillitis.[21]

Then, early in 1965 came the discovery that Elm Cottage was suffering from dry rot. Luckily, that affliction could be quickly cleared up.[22] In the new year Margaret had settled on Rachel Cameron's story rather than the older Stacey's, with whom she had been trying to deal. A problem was that Rachel used not only Margaret's "own speech and accent" (like the boy who said "Hi" where Agamemnon fell) but actually her own *idiom*; and what Margaret wanted—like T.S. Eliot as poet—was "to be released from the sound of my own voice."[23] There is more than aesthetics involved here, however, as she adds, "I suppose I have a very shaky sense of my own reality. . . ."

The sense of her own reality was jarred further by a letter from Jack reporting he had become "deeply involved emotionally although hopelessly" with a twenty-one-year-old American girl in the Peace Corps. Margaret noted the girl was the age she herself had been when she married Jack, and a quick review of the ensuing seventeen and a half years made her recognize that Jack *still* needed a completely dependent wife whom he could protect paternally, and also that Jack, the worshipper of reason and logic, was nevertheless an incurable romantic—"an admirer of the Tristan-and-Isolde thing." Naturally, she observed to Adele, the quality of Jack's emotional involvement would necessarily have been "hopelessly." Margaret finally saw that her situation with Jack had become impossible and that she had known that for at least two years. The holiday in Greece had, despite the retzina and the cheese and olives, opened her eyes to a truth she had not wanted to face. At the beginning of March 1965 Margaret and Jack agreed that separation was an absolute necessity, at least for her. The letter to Adele frankly confesses that five months of Jack's leave (June-October 1964) "were an absolute nightmare in every way, for me. For him, too. . . ." And Margaret felt "more basically hopeful than I have in years. Now I am almost convinced of my own reality."[24]

With that she also felt relieved of some of her guilt regarding her "failure" as wife. The Cameron novel remained a challenge, but she was able to work creatively on other projects. Not long after moving into Elm Cottage, and eager to find supplementary sources of income, Margaret learned that *Holiday* magazine wanted to see some of her non-fiction and would pay $500 for an acceptable article. She turned to her memories of life in Africa, especially in Somaliland, and produced the semi-autobiographical "The Very Best Intentions" (*Holiday*, November 1964). The second, developed from *A Tree for Poverty*, was "The Epic Love of Elmii Bonderii" (*Holiday*, November 1966)—on which she was working when the reconciliation with Jack had begun in June of 1964.[25] Nor is it surprising that Margaret was drawn to the topic of the young man who pined away and died for love of one he had idealized into a dream of perfection, just at the moment she was trying to re-establish her life with Jack, and to ponder the experiences she had shared there with Jack, which both of the *Holiday* pieces reflected. Those memories were quickened by his leaving for Somalia in November, his letters from Mogadishu, and all that followed.

Mid-March 1965 found her working on a substantial essay, "The Poem and the Spear," on the Sayyid Mahammed 'Abdille Hasan, the nationalist leader of his people against British colonial rule. He was a fierce warrior and one of the greatest of Somali poets. Margaret's depiction of the Mad Mullah—as the frustrated British called him—presents a proud victim of oppression fighting for justice. It is easy to recognize her strong sympathy with his struggle against his oppressors and with his using his poetic talent as a weapon—the pen as well as the sword—and to feel that she saw her own situation as in some ways very similar to his. Margaret's article provides two instructive parallels to the Sayyid's predicament that are significantly relevant to her personally: the destruction of the Highland clans by British cannon at Culloden in 1746, and the slaughter of the prairie Métis by the cannon John A. Macdonald sent from Ontario in 1885. The article develops the Canadian parallel by its specific comparison of the Sayyid and Louis Riel:

> both were the leaders of communities of basically tribal and

> nomadic people (the camel herders of Somaliland; the Métis buffalo hunters of the Canadian prairies) faced with imperialist and colonialist powers which possessed only one superior quality, namely superior means of slaughter, and which intended to take over the people's land and administration thereof.[26]

There again is an appeal from the past, from the homeland, and once again mixed with the appeal of African voices.

Her sympathy with the Sayyid and admiration of his courage and talent suggest that Margaret may have felt the stirrings of such qualities in herself. Certainly she had need of them when she shared with Jocelyn and David the decision she and Jack had taken regarding definite separation. They responded as she knew they would: David rushed over to her, climbed on her lap, and bawled openly, but Jocelyn withdrew quietly and with controlled emotions (like her father), and calmly suggested she and her mother manage a shopping trip to London soon, just the two of them. They did that, before the end of March.[27] Courage in hand, Margaret wrote to Adele that she deplored being alone and bearing total responsibility for the two children, but saw that "in fact I have been in that situation for 21/2 years now. . . . Also, I see that I intend to survive, if humanly possible. . . ."[28] The recovered courage also helped her to manage Rachel Cameron, and before the end of June she had finished the first draft of *A Jest of God*.

Margaret continued to be fully occupied with her Manawaka fiction, the two Cameron sisters' novels and the collection of stories about Vanessa MacLeod, through to the end of the sixties. Other familiar themes characterized those years as well, beginning with one immediate result of her breaking with Jack—acute absence of a male partner. After congratulating Adele Wiseman on becoming involved with a sea captain, Margaret confessed, "I feel bloody awful sometimes when I think that my dancing (etc) days are more than likely over."[29] Her "etc" has affiliations with e.e. cummings's poem "my sweet old etcetera" (one of Jack Borland's favourites). She continued to be involved with African matters, particularly West African literature, and this interest persisted in mingling with the strengthening appeal of Canada. New concerns began to assert themselves; the first, a fresh interest in Scotland, the land of her ancestors (she was always taught), which she visited and about which she read seriously—an interest revived by the Cameron sisters. There was, second, a perceptible change in Margaret's view of the exotic, as though she was redefining for herself the relationship between the real and the romantic, both the distinction and the possible interconnection—or perhaps the idea of history and fiction interweaving. The third concern was her anticipation of completing her Manawaka fiction—anticipation, indeed, of the possible end of her writing career.

At the Easter break in 1965, Margaret took Jocelyn and David up into the Highlands of Scotland, to Jemimaville, about forty-five kilometres from Inverness on the Moray Firth, for a week with the Scots writer Jane Duncan. The children played on the beach, went fossil hunting and mountain climbing, and involved their reluctant mother, who returned to Penn "feeling like a new woman."[30] Margaret had visited Nadine and Kwadwo Asante in Glasgow early in the summer of 1963, and reported favourably to Nadine (now back in Vancouver) on the Jemimaville sojourn. She told her that the Cameron novel "is progressing," and "I want to write 4 novels." She had told Adele she wanted "to do two novels, maybe three after this one [Rachel Cameron's novel] and all are more-or-less formed (the bones anyway) in my mind."[31] The package of Manawaka fiction, evidently existing as a whole in Margaret's mind, continued to occupy her, and she fussed over time wasted in brooding over Jack and the marriage: "I could kick myself . . . that I've got so far behind on what I want to do."[32] Grateful for her situation in Penn, she yet looked ahead to David's finishing school ("7 years more") and then a possible return to Canada—or maybe to Africa and the "interesting possibility of living in Africa on my own." That latter suggests less the romantic adventure it was with Jack, and more the experience of the real country of writers like Amos Tutuola, Wole Soyinka, Chinua Achebe, and others whose work she was becoming familiar with and beginning to write about. The letter to Nadine ended with a promise to visit Nadine if she returned to Ghana with her husband, and the almost wistful wish that she could afford to go to Canada on a visit.[33]

Another vivid reminder of the homeland came with Aunt Ruby's visit in June, just as Margaret was completing the first draft of *A Jest of God*. It also awakened memories, as she insisted on calling her niece "Peggy,"[34] and kept alive Margaret's feelings about the new separation from Jack, including being bereft of a male partner. Ruby had written to Margaret, with all the best intentions, offering advice and counsel regarding the domestic difficulties with Jack. Margaret recalled especially (for Adele's delectation) Aunt Ruby's sentence, "Some women in their middle age begin to resent their *marital responsibilities*." The letter of 17 May 1965 explains the phrase she underlined, "meaning of course sex." She could not inform her aunt that for modern wives that was not really the problem, "to say the very least." The letter ends, "if I have to live without a man for the rest of my life, I will go off my rocker."

The end of Aunt Ruby's visit also coincided with word from *Maclean's* that they would publish Margaret's article "In Pursuit of My Past on the Road from the Isles." The article was a result of their visit to Jemimaville.[35] A month later *A Jest* was typed up and dispatched to Alan Maclean at Macmillan's. He liked it. Margaret prepared for another visit to Scotland, 22-28 August—this time alone, as Jocelyn and David were away to see friends down in Sussex.[36] She felt at loose ends and rather depleted, as was usual after completing a major piece of work. That condition was aggravated by news that Jack would be back in England for a year's study of irrigation, leading to a Master's degree, at the University of Southampton. Margaret was soon busy with the second Cameron novel, however, and with preparation of a series of radio scripts on West African literature. The great news of the fall of 1965, though, was acceptance of *A Jest of God* for publication by McClelland and Stewart and by Knopf, although with some reservations about the title.

A problem with Rachel Cameron's novel was that the heroine insisted in speaking in Margaret's own voice, and she wanted to escape that.[37] Furthermore, voice was particularly important in this novel, for voice is a basic medium of communication (even with oneself) and a principal means of "getting in touch" (even with oneself). Communication, its importance and its difficulty, is perhaps the main theme of *A Jest of God*. Rachel's communication with herself is at issue here, for that reflects the way in which she comes to understand herself and so to develop and mature—even at age thirty-four—and to achieve the self-reliance, responsibility, and freedom possible in life.[38] Rachel's interior dialogue expresses a conflict between her social self, the being who must act in accord with the professed values of the Manawaka establishment, and another self who rebels against those stifling guidelines. That conflict is dramatized in Rachel's relationship with her parents and especially with her mother, although her dead father persists as a mystery yet to be solved.

The vexed problem of communication between Rachel and May Cameron develops the familiar Laurentian theme of denial of life, evident in the denial of mutability and mortality. May is representative of her society in this respect: Rachel observes that she doesn't know how old her mother is and dare not ask: "In the world she inhabits, age is still as unmentionable as death."[39] May Cameron chastises Rachel mildly about dropping her attendance at church, not that it is evil but that "I don't think it would look very good" (50). May attends to the appearance, the cosmetic surface, the veneer: she cannot abide the naked truth. When Rachel, at age thirty-four, bounds from the bathtub quite naked to answer the phone, her mother is shocked: "Really, Rachel, that doesn't look very nice" (172). May Cameron is disturbed by every evidence of life's actuality, of real existence: "she's the one who must plump up the chesterfield cushions each night before retiring and empty every ashtray and make the house look as though no frail and mortal creature ever set foot in it" (17). Actual human touch is nasty, in her view. Her husband, Niall the undertaker, was a problem as he carried up from his labours below stairs the aura, if not the aroma, of death; his touch on Mrs. Cameron, scarcely to be thought of, she endured out of her sense of "marital responsibility" (as Aunt Ruby put it to Margaret). Any suggestion of emotion, let alone passion, is to be avoided. May is, of course, supported in all these attitudes by her staid United Church and its minister, of whom Rachel observes, "if the Reverend MacElfrish should suddenly lose his mind and speak of God with anguish or joy, or out of some need should pray with fierce humility as though God had to be there, Mother would be shocked to the core. Luckily it will never happen" (51).

Rachel is annoyed by her mother's attitudes and would oppose them at every turn, albeit tacitly. Part of her dialogue with herself involves Rachel in that very opposition—as she comes to notice. When she meets Nick Kazlik, returned to Manawaka for the summer, she is jarred by what she feels is a sharp retort from him, so she thinks (condescendingly), "The milkman's son" has no justification for his attitude of superiority—"High School or not" (79). Then she catches herself, surprised, "I don't believe that way at all. *It's as though I've thought in Mother's voice*" (my italics).

At the opposite end of the scale from May is Rachel's colleague, teacher of grade five, Calla Mackie, and her supportive religious institution, the Pentecostal Tabernacle of the Risen and Reborn. The contrast between the tabernacle and the Reverend MacElfrish's church is stark, and in that opposition Rachel is involved and her sympathies vexed. She wishes Calla wouldn't talk about the tabernacle in May's hearing because "Mother thinks the whole thing is weird in the extreme." Rachel is embarrassed for Calla in that situation and ashamed of being embarrassed; she wishes Calla would be quiet or she herself could stop worrying about it. When Calla invites her to the tabernacle, perhaps to witness the phenomenon of speaking in tongues, glossalalia, she explains to Rachel—a bit defensively, of course—that "We hold ourselves too tightly these days, that's the trouble. Afraid to let the Spirit speak through us" (33).

At the tabernacle Rachel is inescapably touched and therefore as uncomfortable and intimidated by the physical closeness of the worshippers and their comparatively uninhibited participation as her mother would be. The voice of the preacher "reaches out like arms of strength, to captivate" (41); he talks of the "infilling Spirit," and Rachel wonders if there will be "ecstatic utterances," afraid she will be embarrassed if Calla should speak in tongues. The service becomes increasingly a passionate experience to Rachel, virtually physical, virtually sexual, and, as it rises to its climax, Rachel's response is virtually orgasmic.[40] The man beside her "moans gently, moans and stirs, and moans"; and then "*That voice!*" not Calla's, but her own—"Chattering, crying, ululating, the forbidden transformed cryptically to nonsense, dragged from the crypt, stolen and shouted, the shuddering of it, the fear, the breaking, the release, the grieving—" (45).

Calla takes her home with her through the rain (appropriately), soothes Rachel's embarrassment, kisses her face and "swiftly thereafter" her mouth. The frankness of that carnal communication abruptly awakens Rachel and she flees. She has certainly been touched, and that side of her that rebels against her mother's propriety has, willy-nilly, been meaningfully stirred.

The matter of glossalalia and St. Paul's comments on speaking in tongues (I Corinthians) is important in Margaret's development of the theme of communication in *A Jest*. At the tabernacle the lay preacher's sermon reinforces what Calla has initially told Rachel and its intention is quite evidently the same as Calla's—to allay the fears and possible embarrassment about the phenomenon that may occur. He quotes St. Paul (rather out of context), "God is not the author of confusion but of peace . . ." (I Corinthians 14.33), and emphasizes Paul's recognition that speaking in "divers kinds of tongues" is a sign of the "indwelling Spirit," for "there are diversities of gifts, but the same Spirit" (I Corinthians 12.4-10). While the preacher admits that "Saint Paul advises moderation" and that "the gift of tongues should not replace the more usual forms of worship," he assures the congregation that in "the early Church," in the presence of "ecstatic utterance," the listeners were ecstatic too and that "we can all participate" therefore in the speaker's joy. Shortly before she speaks, Rachel is as critical of the situation in the tabernacle as she is of her mother's minister and congregation:

> All I can visualize are the dimly remembered faithful of Corinth, each crying aloud his own words, no one hearing anyone else, no one able to know what anyone else was saying, unable even to know what they themselves were saying. Are these people mad, or am I? (44)

And she comments on the visualized confusion by quoting to herself, "God is not the author of confusion but of peace."

Much later, after reconciliation, Calla fills in some of the gaps in the service at the tabernacle, for she has reread St. Paul's epistle more attentively and critically. She notices that St. Paul specifically warns against speaking in tongues because it usually results in a failure of communication; she quotes (166), "if I know not the meaning of the voice, I shall be unto him that speaketh a barbarian, and he that speaketh shall be a barbarian unto me" (I Corinthians 14.11). She does not quote the appropriate verses 27 and 28, where St. Paul says that if one speaks "in an unknown tongue," there should be an interpreter present, otherwise "let him keep silent in the church; and let him speak to himself and to God." But she has obviously read those verses: she tells Rachel "I *spoke*, by the way" (167) and adds that it was not in the tabernacle but "When I was alone" (168); she also observes that it was just as well, for "St. Paul says there should be someone there to interpret" (167).

Between those last two passages quoted, Margaret has abruptly inserted Rachel's thoughts: "Perhaps he will phone me tonight. Nick? *Listen*—" (168). But with no interpreter.

St. Paul's point, as Margaret presents it, is that it is all right to *speak* when the Spirit moves you but that it is best to speak privately—lest you sound like a barbarian, or even a fool. Best of all is a combination of Spirit and understanding (I Corinthians 14.15). The urging of the Spirit is a bit like libido—not a bad thing but best kept private: better to utter than burn, but at home. The presentation of St. Paul's—and Calla's—concern with ecstatic utterance illuminates two lines of communication Rachel wants to establish, with the absent Nick and with God, but cannot and thus feels she is playing the fool.

Rachel's experience at the tabernacle, her unwilling awakening and Calla's kiss, prepares her to accept Nick's intrusion into her life and the more intimate and physical communication they establish together.[41] Their sexual encounters enable her to confront, nakedly, the physical and emotional truth about herself she has sought with reluctant eagerness. In addition to his attractive masculinity, Nick has another quality important for Rachel's awakening and liberation: his alien ethnic identity. He is a first-generation Canadian, a Ukrainian, and from the "wrong" side of the tracks in Manawaka. Shortly before their initial sexual intercourse, Rachel confesses to Nick that she always envied him and people like him because of their apparent freedom, being not boxed in but able to speak out:

> I used to get rides in winter on your dad's sleigh, and I remember the great bellowing voice he had, and how emotional he used to get—cursing at the horses, or else almost crooning to them. In my family, you didn't get emotional. It was frowned upon. (108-109)

There is another aspect to Nick's alien quality, his straight black hair (78) and prominent cheekbones (106), which make him a true son of his father, Nestor Kazlik, who has a "bony face, high-cheekboned as a Cree's (230).[42]

Calla Mackie belongs with Nick as alien: her manner of dress, her outspokenness, her religious affiliation, and her lesbianism are her obvious qualifications in the eyes of Manawaka. Their influences on Rachel are similar as they both educate and encourage that side of Rachel that is increasingly critical of the baleful propriety of May Cameron and the society she represents, and also, therefore, work to foster Rachel's liberation from the establishment attitude—to contribute to the disappearance of Rachel's prejudices.[43]

Those liberating influences on Rachel and fostering of her anti-establishment attitudes lead directly to her crucial decision at the climax of the novel. That occurs almost exactly at the physical midpoint of *A Jest of God*. As Rachel is about to prepare the refreshments for her mother's evening of bridge, Nick phones to ask her out and of course she accepts. She informs her mother and the usual fencing match begins, but this time the awakened Rachel prevails.

> *I won't go, then*—I find the words are there already in my throat, and yet I force them back. This newfound ruthlessness exhilarates me. I won't turn back. If I do, I'm done for. Yet I can't look at her, either, or see the sallowness of her face. (123-24)

Things will never be quite the same between them. Rachel has triumphed in the agon with May—and over that side of herself that derives from her mother.

Rachel's important communication with Hector Jonas, her father's successor, and thus with Niall Cameron's memory and mystery, occurs only after she has successfully begun to confront her problems of communication with her mother, Calla, Nick, and with herself. The interview with Hector begins the second half of the novel, but it has been specifically prepared for by some minor details that suggest a critical moment in Rachel's maturing is about to be reached. Following the climactic scene with her mother in Six, Rachel and Nick go to the Kazlik home and will make love indoors for the first time. Nick laughs at their situation, "Waiting until the family is out. Like reverting to adolescence" (125). That comparison recalls Calla's constantly calling Rachel "child," until the experience at the tabernacle; it is easy to see that "reverting to adolescence" is now much more like *achieving* it.[44] Further, as their actual lovemaking begins, Rachel is more relaxed and recognizes, "I can even take off my clothes without feeling very unfamiliar about it. See—I have changed" (126).

Another encouraging sign occurs at the opening of Seven as Rachel prepares to "look after herself" after her lovemaking with Nick. She uses her mother's old douche equipment; it revolts her and she vomits—the equipment looks to her like "a dead fetus" and she vows never to "touch that contraption again" (144). Rachel confirms her commitment to life, and she ponders the miracle of conceiving a child "inside one's structure and have it born alive" (144-45) and firmly rejects assuming the role of "angel-maker." She then decides, at 1:00 a.m., to go down to visit Hector Jonas.

This important visit enhances the depiction of Rachel's progress by bringing into sharp focus the novel's reliance on what Margaret would call a "heroic monomyth."[45] Hector's surname encourages recognition of the myth in question: "Jonas" is obviously a variation of "Jonah" and is thus an echo of the epigraph of *A Jest of God*—a reference to the biblical Jonah, from Carl Sandburg's *Losers*. Hector presides over a setting that sufficiently recalls the belly of the whale, a setting of death that precedes rebirth. Rachel goes down the stairs that lead to the funeral chapel much as Hagar Shipley went down the stairway to her fruitful encounter with Murray Ferney Lees in *The Stone Angel*. Rachel is not on the shore of the Pacific Ocean and in the midst of marine paraphernalia as Hagar is when she talks with Lees—or as Stacey Cameron MacAindra will be when she has her revitalizing encounter with Luke Venturi in *The Fire-Dwellers*. Yet *A Jest of God* compensates for that absence of physical detail by supplying its function via the symbolic use of colour—aided by a realistic detail or two. The colours blue and green dominate the narrative and are frequently enough associated with marine life (literally and figuratively) to encourage identification of them as marine colours.

The colloquy with Hector Jonas is actually a microcosmic expression of the myth of death and rebirth as it informs much of the structure of the whole novel, a pattern of departure (or descent), initiation, and return (or resurrection). Just as Rachel has descended the stairs to Hector's realm, so at the end of the colloquy she ascends the stairs to enter—however slowly—into a new life of liberation, self-reliance, and responsible maturity.

A contributing factor to Rachel's "rise" is her learning some important details about her father that help solve the mystery and lay the ghost. First, the revelation held in her awakened memory of his workroom, "the cluttered paraphernalia and the cosmetics of death" (147), that is, the means of camouflaging the fact of mortality—what Hector scornfully calls "the beautician deal" (149). That is the occupation, and the realm, to which Niall's association with May has relegated him, ironically, because for all his use of the cosmetics of death he yet was obliged to confront and accept the mortal fact itself. (That attitude, refusal to be taken in by the cosmetic surface—like Hector's vaunted "simulated wood" and "Real veneer" [154] in the new chapel—is reinforced by Niall's reply to young Rachel's invitation to him to come and see the parade and the lovely pipe band: "they're playing 'The March of the Cameron Men.'" . . . "Yes, I expect they are, Rachel. It has a fine sound, the lies the pipes tell. You run away now . . ." [70].)

Second, when she asks Hector what he knew of her father, his surprising response is a further revelation: "He had the life he wanted most" (153). Is she, then, her father's daughter and has she the life she wants most? Rachel replies, "If it's true he wanted that life the most, why mourn?" She immediately amends her response, benefitting from the unintended revelation and her consequently sharpened insight, "Why ever cease from mourning?" (153). What Rachel has seen in her father's situation is not the denial of mutability and mortality but a determined withdrawal from that world of denial that smugly sustains itself with the cosmetics of propriety, social "correctness," which is lamentable and pathetic.

Having thus "communicated" with her memory of her father and come to terms with his spirit, Rachel—now "risen and reborn"—leaves Hector to confront the remaining items of her life. She accepts, painfully, the loss of Nick and even his apparent deception with the photograph of himself as a boy; she recognizes the need to be responsible for herself, and maturely determines to accept that condition. She accepts the fact that Calla simply loves her, and with a love that does not need to be qualified with any demeaning adjective but merely regarded as human love. She learns to come to manageable terms with the God she has seen as a cruel jester, as at best uninterested and indifferent so far as our affairs go; or, rather, to reconcile the two views of God held respectively by the two aspects of Rachel we have come to know. The expression of Rachel's "crisis of faith" comes at the conclusion of Nine, introduced by her decision against suicide, her throwing out the barbiturate capsules and her canny refusal to throw out the whiskey—"I'm my father's child, no doubt. Niall Cameron would have dropped dead at anyone who poured out a bottle of whiskey" (209). She finds herself kneeling in prayer—not out of belief but need—"*Help me*" (209):

> We seem to have fought a long time, I and You. . . .
>
> My God, I know how suspect You are. I know how suspect I am.
>
> If You have spoken, I am not aware of having heard. If you have a voice, it is not comprehensible to me. (210)

But she continues to speak to Him, capitalized—another example of glossalalia, perhaps.

The conclusion of the novel has frequently been taken as a bearing out of the apparent promise of the title, *A Jest of God*, with God's jest being the irony of Rachel's desired "pregnancy," that she is pregnant not with a bud of life but with "the growth, the non-life" (221) that is the tumour—even if benign. Benign; another irony.[46] If the jest in Rachel's pregnancy is real, it is that the ironically non-life pregnancy nevertheless is a harbinger of Rachel's ultimate rebirth in the novel. Her apparently ironic announcement while under the anaesthetic—"I am the mother now" (225)—is proven by the final reversal of roles between Rachel and May Cameron: on the bus to Vancouver, Rachel refers to May as "my elderly child" (245). That observation concludes the little argument between them about leaving Manawaka for the coast, with May behaving like a petulant child and Rachel maternally managing her. Indeed, preparation for this denouement began at the opening of Two (one notices in retrospect): "When I first began teaching Mother used to call me every morning, but now I waken before she does."[47] Rachel assumes the role of guide and decision maker at last.

With the fruitful development of that motif and the consequent cancel of the supposed irony of birth, there is also the frequently misunderstood significance of the heroine's name—too readily taken as another piece of irony. On at least two dramatic junctures in the novel, Margaret directly alludes to the biblical story of Rachel, Jacob's wife. "Ironically," again, this biblical source concerns the much desired and successfully wooed and won younger sister of Leah. While Rachel Cameron may have been desired, she certainly was not wed and scarcely wooed. The biblical Rachel is familiar as a symbol of anguished childlessness. Rachel Cameron tells Nick she would like to bear his children and thinks to herself, "Give me my children" (181); and when Dr. Raven makes his surprising diagnosis, Rachel's response sounds to her like "the voice of some woman mourning for her children" (221). Both seem to be echoes of Jacob's childless wife. Again, the apparent irony is double-edged: Margaret trusted her readers to know that Jacob's Rachel, long barren like Abraham's Sarah, was at last granted children, two sons more famous and blessed than all those of her sister Leah—Joseph (of the many-coloured coat) and Benjamin. The implication is that the modern-day Rachel can expect as fertile and satisfying a future as her biblical namesake, "expect," that is, in the same sense that she can expect to get to Vancouver and be reunited with Stacey.

As Rachel Cameron ponders her future at the close of *A Jest*, her thoughts hold a faintly hopeful, comedic tone: "Where I'm going, anything may happen. Nothing may happen. Maybe I will marry . . . have my children . . . maybe. . . ." And then, "I will ask myself if I am going mad. . . ." In that monologue is only sanity and evidently the sound of a single voice, that of the mature Rachel. The double voice and the dual attitude recur, however, in the brief final paragraph: "God's mercy on reluctant jesters. God's grace on fools. God's pity on God." The Pauline adjuration in I Corinthians 3 (which Rachel and Calla have discussed) about wisdom and folly is clearly echoed in those closing lines:

> 18. If any man among you seemeth to be wise in this world,
> let him become a fool, that he may be wise.
>
> 19. For the wisdom of this world is foolishness with God.
> For it is written, He taketh the wise in their own craftiness.
>
> 20. And again. The Lord knoweth the thoughts of the wise,
> that they are vain.[48]

St Paul's adjuration is also strongly present in the last exchange between Rachel and Calla on the topic of her mistaken pregnancy. Rachel says, "you must have thought I was a fool. As, of course, I was." The knowing Calla agrees and answers, "heavens, child, that's the least of your worries." Rachel thinks, "That really is so. It's the least of my worries. What is so terrible about fools? I should be honoured to be of that company" (241). So the three concluding statements of *A Jest of God* may be supplications (i.e., *May* God's mercy *fall* on, etc.), but they may also be constatations—God's mercy *falls* on . . . (etc.) in the natural scheme of things. And in the last of the three we hear the voice of the less sceptical Rachel asking (or indicating) that God's pity fall(s) upon the somewhat bumbling and incommunicative Jester whom the sceptical Rachel spars with and scoffs at throughout the novel.

The story of Rachel Cameron, then, is as open-ended as the biography of any thirty-four-year-old woman with leftover life to live. But *A Jest of God* is as complete a *novel* as, say, *The Stone Angel*: they develop the careers of their respective heroines, Rachel and Hagar, to a definite point of achievement—of maturity, self-reliance, courage, and liberation—and do so with as satisfactory and comedic an ending as any reasonable reader has the right to expect. The story may be "open-ended," but its meaningful shape is quite complete.

A consideration of the reluctance of the Cameron girls' material to yield itself up to Margaret's treatment may throw some light on her own life. From the earliest weeks of 1963 she puzzled over which of the two stories should be handled first, and struggled through a miserable six months regularly complaining that the material was not only recalcitrant but actually terrifying.[49] Finally, in August, she admitted that she had diverted her attention from the Camerons to the short stories about Vanessa's family. Late in March of 1964 she confessed to being "terrified of beginning a novel" and that "last year" she dropped two novels, unfinished, "mainly out of sheer terror or something."[50] The terror derived at least in part from the recognition that in the Cameron sisters' material she was coming face to face with her own most intimate concerns, and that one major attraction of the Vanessa stories was that they allowed her to approach those personal concerns more gradually, from a distance.

At the time of her apparent reconciliation with Jack—the Greece junket at the beginning of June 1964—Margaret seems to have put aside Stacey's story and picked up Rachel's. In letters to both Adele and to Al Purdy, dated 29 June 1967, she tells of burning "hundreds" of pages she had written on Stacey Cameron "3 years ago."[51] Stacey MacAindra née Cameron is a mother of four children, living in Vancouver and married to an "absent" husband, a man from whom she has drifted away, or who has drifted away from her; she feels overwhelmed by the chores of maternity, wifely duties, and the absence of a sustaining love. Stacey's troubled situation is a near equivalent to Margaret's in the fall of 1962 when she decided that leaving Jack and Vancouver was at least an immediate solution to her problems. In mid-1964, Margaret seems to have seen that Stacey's problems began much earlier and that Rachel's story properly confronted those earlier problems and therefore needed to be dealt with first.

Working with Rachel's story, however, brought Margaret into confrontation with another aspect of the terrifying. Rachel's story seemed inescapably Margaret's as well, and it was not just that she spoke with Margaret's voice. On 24 January 1965, Margaret complained to Adele of her difficulties with Rachel: "I kept telling myself the character wasn't me, yet when the circumstances of my life changed, the plot changed, and she *would* persist in speaking in my voice."

Yet she persevered with Rachel's struggle to gain the maturity, courage, and self-reliance necessary for her personal triumph, not knowing until virtually the last moment just what the effective terms of that struggle would be and how the "irony" of God's apparent *jest* would present itself to achieve the denouement and the final shaping of the novel. Her explanation to Adele is virtually an apology: "I can't help the way it turned out. I didn't know it would end like that, but it did. . . . and the ending surprised me."[52] And Margaret must have discovered that ending shortly after the events of March 1965, when the "circumstances of her life" took a distinct change and she agreed with Jack that they must go their separate ways—that the hoped-for fruits of their fresh coming together were not to be reaped. (By early April 1965 she had the novel before her again; she reported progress on it in May; and she had the first draft finished before the middle of June.[53]) And the remarkable relevance of the surprising conclusion of the novel to Margaret's personal situation illuminates her own life and struggle for self-acceptance.

Rachel's "pregnancy," the dearly desired result of her congress with Nick Kazlik, finds its equivalent in the planned outcome of Margaret's attempted reunion with Jack during the time from her sojourn with him in Pakistan in November 1963, through their unbroken reunion beginning with their twelve days together in Greece (June 1964) and Jack's presence at Elm Cottage until his departure for Somalia in November 1964. Ironically, that attempt at fruitful reunion led instead to a more definite separation than ever: its actual result was as distinctly a "non-life" as Rachel's tumour. There is yet a further irony in that the tumour proved "benign," not only medically but morally, since it proved to be the means to Rachel's liberation, her accepting self-reliance and responsibility; so the ironically unfruitful result of the reunion with Jack was liberation for Margaret as it enabled her to recognize that she was in fact quite capable of mature self-reliance and responsibility. In her letter of 8 March 1965, she had confessed to Adele that her nagging "fear about being alone, and responsible for the kids" had prevented her from recognizing her own capability: "but in fact" (the letter continues) "I *have* been in that situation for 21/2 years now. Also, I see now (in quite a cold way) that I could not do anything permanent until I had a house and until I had accumulated a certain amount of money." That letter also indicates that Margaret's progress toward liberation had been hampered by precisely the same moralistic encumbrance as Rachel's—the demands of propriety: "I think the doubts and pendulum-swings of feeling about my writing simply reflected a similar state of mind re: him [Jack]—I fluctuated between feeling I *must* keep the marriage going somehow . . . and feeling I simply could not return to that relationship."

The reciprocal illumination of Rachel's story and Margaret's life assists our recognizing that the *jest* promised by the title of the novel lies not in the irony of the "non-life" growth that usurps the place of the desired bud of vitality, but rather in the fact that one's striven-for goals are sometimes simply unachievable—and, maybe, that one is better off without the achievement sought. Acceptance of that fact of life leads to the liberation that Rachel finally gained, and that Margaret seems to have gained as well—at least for the time being.

twelve

Insistent Voices

ONCE *A JEST OF GOD* WAS INTO HER PUBLISHERS' HANDS, Margaret's project of autumn 1965 was her immersing herself in West African literature in English. Always alert to profitable professional projects that would buy time for her own fiction—especially when it wasn't in process—she had agreed to prepare a series of scripts for the BBC. Thus she began her "do-it-yourself course in contemporary African writing."[1] There were initial difficulties; the program director seemed unsure of what he wanted, and Margaret feared it was something like "the drivelling of an Africa-enchanted Peace-Corps girl" (she told Adele),[2] perhaps like a Peace Corps girl Jack might happen upon. Nevertheless, she had the four scripts ready by the middle of February and began reading before the end of the month. By mid-year she could anticipate conclusion of a book developed from those scripts: *Long Drums and Cannons: Nigerian Dramatists and Novelists 1952-1966.*

Certainly Margaret's modest familiarity with Africa prepared her to respond sympathetically in *Long Drums* to the work of writers like Amos Tutuola, Chinua Achebe, and Wole Soyinka. Yet the impression one gets from her attention to that literature is that she is looking at work very much like her own fiction, not only that of the 1950s—in *The Tomorrow-Tamer* and *This Side Jordan*—but the

Manawaka fiction that followed. She indicates the focus and the basis of her sympathy thus:

> Nigerian writing is concerned with an examination of the psychological damage done during the colonial period, . . . usually portrayed in social, cultural and religious terms, hardly ever in purely racial terms. . . .
>
> . . . the work of [these] writers . . . must surely have done much to restore a true sense of their own past, a knowledge of a tribal society which was neither idyllic, as the views of some nationalists would have had it, nor barbaric, as many missionaries and European administrators wished and needed to believe.[3]

Margaret is careful to indicate that the conflict facing post-colonial Nigeria and its writers is not to be settled by the victory of one set of elements over another; nor do the best Nigerian writers seek such a settlement. Compromise is the ideal: "In terms of social themes, Soyinka seeks to establish a relationship with the past which will neither stifle and dominate man nor sever him from his roots" (44-45). She recognizes the importance of religion and Christian missionaries in the Nigerian dilemma, and notes Achebe's management of that problem in *Things Fall Apart*—observing that he does not blatantly condemn Christianity or even individual missionaries. She takes care of that condemnation herself:

> Naturally Achebe's sympathies are weighted on the side of his ancestors, for it was the Christian missions which came uninvited and which in the end managed to sever two entire generations of Africans from their past and to cause untold psychological harm. . . . What he deplores is their total ignorance of the people to whom they were preaching . . . and their lack of any self-knowledge which might have made them question something of their own motives in desiring to see themselves as bringers of salvation. (106-107)

The missionaries, she argues, simply refused, like the general run of colonizers, to regard the colonized as fellow human beings. She indicates what is everywhere implicit in Achebe's work, that "The greatest tragedy is that of man's lack of comprehension of the reality of others, his lack of comprehension of the validity of differences" (116).

Margaret appreciates the Nigerians' recognition of the importance of individual integrity and their concern over the undue influence of tribalism and of any other external authority, such as colonial government. Her sympathy lies with the importance of the individual's human rights and responsibilities. In her discussion of Soyinka's *A Dance of the Forests* she focusses briefly on the "crucial speech of Forest Head": "This is the supreme deity speaking about man and free will."

> Man has been created with free will, and however much God may break His heart over the acts of His creatures, they must continue to act by themselves, for "to intervene is to be guilty of contradiction." Yet, "to remain altogether unfelt" is to give men cause to believe that they have created God in their own image only out of weakness and fear. Forest Head's view . . . seems to be that the dilemma of gods is that however much they may love or hate mankind, . . . it is men themselves who decide their own fates. . . . (45)

There are, Margaret notes, "strongly Christian undertones" in Forest Head's speech; the position there set forth is indeed very close to that of Milton's God in *Paradise Lost* in explaining God's foreknowledge and the free will of Adam and Eve.[4]

Margaret's appreciation of artistic features of the Nigerians' work reflects on her own and helps define the Laurentian Art of Fiction. She values a particular sort of realism. Literature, she insists, "must be planted firmly in some soil. Even works of non-realism make use of spiritual landscapes which have been at least partially inherited by the writer. . . . the main concern of a writer remains that of somehow creating the individual on the printed page, of catching the tones and accents of human speech, of setting down the conflicts of people who are as real to him as himself" (10).[5] Of course those "people" are just imagined, but imaginary creatures can be more *true* than what we call "the real thing," she implies. In *Arrow of God*, Margaret argues in *Long Drums*, Achebe follows "the course of history with accuracy" but because he embodies that history "within actual persons"—albeit imaginary creations—and focusses that course as "happening to actual persons," his fiction is "a great deal more true than fact" (113). Achebe impresses her as the consummate artist in his depiction of living individual characters. In *Arrow of God*, she writes, Achebe "deals with a large number of characters, and yet none of them fail to come across as individuals, unique and irreplaceable" (111). Furthermore, Achebe "never *makes* his characters speak; he listens to them" (123, my italics).

We have seen Margaret's own confession that she seems not to be the creator of her own fictions, that she writes as though being dictated to. To be faithful to that quasi-divine source of creation, the writer *must* listen, must try not to manipulate his or her characters but let them act as they will and speak as they would be heard. In other words, the imaginary creature—if it is to be *true* and convincing—must be regarded as Margaret approvingly believes the Nigerian writers regard the individual members of actual society, not as ciphers to be manipulated but with respect for their individual integrity and freedom. Consequently, the writer must not *use* his work as a medium for blatant propaganda; he must not preach to or reason with his readers; and he dare not *explain* what he is presenting. Margaret thus affirms, if only implicitly, her affiliation with that line of modern writers whose credo was the preference for the dramatic mode in fiction as in plays upon the stage.

Here is a sample from *Long Drums* of Margaret's approval of that aspect of Achebe's technique:

> he describes rituals . . . by showing the event happening, by allowing the reader to enter. . . . Almost without realising it, we find that we understand at least some things which we did

Margaret Collier, David Laurence, Jocelyn (Queen of the Fairies), Elizabeth Collier, and Peggy, December 1956, at the Colliers' home, England.

Professor B.W. "Guś" and Sheila Andrzejewski, in Senior Common Room, London School of Oriental and African Studies, September 1991.

Margaret Laurence, c. 1963.

The Davidson Memorial statue and Currie gravestone, Riverside Cemetery, Neepawa, looking east. Both the "stone angel" and the Currie gravestone are significantly related to Hagar Currie of *The Stone Angel.*

Margaret Laurence, early 1960s.

Adele Wiseman, 1957.

The Laurences' house in Vancouver at 3556 W 21st Avenue, where they lived from 1958 to 1962.

Heath Hurst Road (the southwest side), Hampstead, where Margaret lived on the second and third floors (with dark green door) with her children from 1962 to 1963.

Margaret and the monument to Louis Riel, St. Boniface Basilica yard, St. Boniface, Manitoba, fall 1966.

David, Margaret, Topaz, and Jocelyn, on the grounds of Elm Cottage, August 1967.

Mona and Margaret, Penn, Bucks., 1973.

Margaret, 1978.

Margaret's home at 8 Regent Street,
Lakefield, Ontario.

Al Purdy, 1975.

Margaret and Lyall Powers, at 8 Regent Street, summer 1983.

The Very Reverend, The Honourable Lois Wilson, O.C.

Thanksgiving, October 1986, at 8 Regent Street. Left to right: Lyall Powers, Margaret Laurence, Jack Borland.

Margaret at Walkerville Station, Windsor, Ontario,
15 October 1984.

> not understand before. We see the old religion not as a set of distant oddities, not as "customs," but as faith, which is a very different thing. (123)

Furthermore, and most important, the shared understanding (Margaret implies) bears witness to the significant *moral* quality of literary art, and thus to the signal importance of the artist. The artist must, however, understand himself first of all (the implication is clear) and be ready to rely on himself—his vision, his sympathy with fellow human beings, above all his faith in his muse—in order to function successfully. The attitude is Emersonian or, indeed, Socratic: the emphasis is upon self-knowledge and self-reliance. Margaret finds these essential qualities in the best of the Nigerian writers, and she observes that they are thus enabled to communicate with readers universally.

> Perhaps the most enduringly interesting aspect of Nigerian literature, . . . as of literature everywhere, is the insight it gives not only into immediate and local dilemmas but, through these, into the human dilemma as a whole. Literature can only do this in very specific and detailed ways. . . . If [the writer] does this well, and as truthfully as he can, his writing may sometimes reach out beyond any national boundary. The best of these Nigerian plays and novels reveal something of ourselves to us, whoever and wherever we are.[6]

These comments help reveal Margaret's keen interest in discovering her own true identity, in coming to understand herself and her compulsion to write. Her response to the character of Demoke the woodcarver in Soyinka's *A Dance of the Forests* is a reflection of her progress in self-knowledge and self-acceptance: "The process of art is seen partly in terms of Demoke's necessity to face within himself the existence of the opposing forces of creation and destruction. . . . He needs to create, but he is also capable of the destruction both of others and of himself" (33). Further, "Demoke has been able to face . . . the never-to-be-understood need to create, . . . the violence and ruthlessness . . . [of] the other side of his nature, the guilt which he bears for the destructive acts he has done. . . . What he cannot face is his own urge towards self-destruction" (44).

This observation is a searing revelation of Margaret's attitude toward herself—the persistent motif of perhaps half her letters to Adele Wiseman during these years: she writes because she is compelled to do so; that compulsion distracts her from her proper duty to husband and children; and she is guilt-ridden by her sense of failed duty. The "urge towards self-destruction" is another motif, much less prominent and seldom apparent to the author of those letters, but is visible at least in the frequent enough implication that the "harm" done by failure of duty to the rest of the family is harm done to herself. Added to that is her sense that her drinking is harmful to her, perhaps an act of self-destruction.

Reading in Nigerian literature and composing the four radio scripts on the topic provided Margaret with a fruitful experience. Apart from the value as cultural and literary criticism (*Long Drums and Cannons* is still consulted by students and scholars in the field), that combined undertaking was obviously helpful to Margaret in her quest for self-knowledge.

Her preoccupation with African affairs often coincides with her preoccupation with Canadian and in fact with Scottish affairs, as though the three were necessarily associated in her mind and similarly related as influences on that quest. In March 1965 she was busy with "The Poem and the Spear" and its comparisons among the Somalis, the Métis, and the Highland Scots as victims of British colonial oppression.

In May Margaret wrote an article based on her visit with Jocelyn and David to Jemimaville, which *Maclean's* magazine accepted in late June 1965. The imposing title reveals the contents accurately: "In Pursuit of My Past on the Road from the Isles." The final preposition is to be noted as heavily significant. In the article Margaret claims total ignorance (a mite disingenuously) of Scottish history, though she was raised in a mist of Scottish traditions: Harry Lauder's songs, strange family heirlooms like the Wemyss sterling plaid pin with its puzzling family crest, and Stevenson's *Kidnapped.* She knew a good deal about the Selkirk settlers, but only after their emigration to the confluence of the Red and Assiniboine rivers in Canada. Her Scots traditions, she early discovered, were really "Mock Scots"; she claims she was "no more Scots than Siamese." So she undertook a reading program to prepare for her visit to the Highlands.

The principal historical focus of the article is the Highland Clearances,[7] the nearly wholesale eviction of the crofters to convert the land to sheep-raising. Margaret ponders the dilemma of those victims betrayed by the very chieftains they had revered and served with eager fealty and who simply sold them out. That "must have been like knowing, really knowing, that one's own father intended, if he could, to murder you."[8] Her reading in Scottish history recalled what she had learned in Somaliland and rediscovered through her immersion in Nigerian literature—that the Highland clans were like "tribal systems anywhere" (26c). And she describes the Highlanders' experience in exactly the same terms she used to describe the Nigerian tribal society's experience of being dispossessed, as "a people bereft, a people who had been psychologically wounded in ways they could not possibly have comprehended" (26c).

Another association, more peculiarly Canadian and a reflection of "The Poem and the Spear," is the similarity between the victims of the Highland Clearances and the victims of the Métis "uprising" in Canada: neither Highland crofters nor Métis had sought confrontation and both lost their homes and perhaps their true identities as well, and suffered alienation from themselves:

> I have the feeling that the Highlander today is in much the same position as the North American Indian. What he really was, in the past, is not comprehended by anyone outside his own tribe, but he has been taken up and glamorized and must act a part now . . . slicked-up, prettified.[9]

A "Canadian" bias emerges as Margaret develops her main theme. She felt "no connection with the actual Scotland" but "half-expected and even hoped to discover some feeling of ancestry there, something that would convey to me a special and personal meaning" (26b). Near Culloden, "something about the land looked familiar to me" (26d). At the end of the journey a young cab driver asks about emigrating to Canada; she encourages him but withholds her reservation—"his children the children of another land, not his, and that this difference would divide them from him forever. . . . It is the fate of immigrants to discover this for themselves" (26g). Her epiphany has begun: "Scotland had become real to me, both in its past and in its present"; but not emotional involvement. The Highland Clearances touched her "as much as the story of the slave trade in Africa, but no more" (26g). Something was stirred, however: "It was the names I could not get away from," names she recognized as Canadian, familiar to anyone who knows Winnipeg and particularly its North End—Bannerman, Kildonan, Matheson, Ross, Selkirk, Sutherland. Suddenly she remembered a summer of her childhood vacationing at Clear Lake with her Great-Aunt Ett, a Wemyss. Ett claimed that the area reminded her of Scotland. Margaret now realized that the land near Culloden had reminded her of "Clear Lake in Manitoba."

The distinction between history derived from reading and that derived from lived experience is facilitated by Margaret's memory of Great-Aunt Ett and Culloden and Clear Lake. The second kind of history, "the kind that has the most power over us," comes to us "in unsuspected ways, the names of tunes or trees that can recall a thousand images, and this almost-family history can be related only to one's first home" (26h).

She wrote the article at Elm Cottage, England, but the point of view, the controlling voice, is unmistakably Canadian. The concluding paragraph reconciles, so to speak, a pair of discoveries intimately related. The features of the fantasy mist of her childhood concerning her Scottish heritage, the "Mock Scots" giftie, have been raised to the status of myth and as such "retain a greater emotional hold on me than the real Scots." ("The myths are my reality," she seems to be saying.) She concludes, "They don't relate to Scotland any more than the transplanted [Canadian] names. . . . I know where they belong." They belong, she might well have declared, in her "first home," her "real country, where I was born." It had been a very meaningful experience to visit the area of Cromarty, virtually just across the firth from Sutherland;[10] and to write of that experience was surely an especial epiphany. I recall vividly frequent visits at Elm Cottage, especially in the summer of 1967, and the conversations between us—she a Canadian domiciled in England and I a Canadian domiciled in the US; the conversations (no matter the topic) were inescapably Canadian in idiom, tone, and attitude.[11]

The crucial epiphany did not disclose itself to Margaret entirely and at once. She wrote to Adele in the spring of 1967 to report, part defensively, on how busy 1966 had been and why—since she and Jack had decided on the need for separation in March of 1965: her absence from Elm Cottage for four months, her involvement with demanding visitors at Elm Cottage for another four months, the distraction of Jack's presence at Elm Cottage for two months. Conclusion: only two months remained for herself and her work; "for the past 12 months I've been going like a bomb."[12] She specified her peregrinations—"41/2 months . . . traveling to Crete, Somalia, Canada and New York, and Egypt."[13] But a number of Margaret's escapades were closely connected with the gradual disclosure of the crucial epiphany.

The year had begun with a spillover from the holidays, as Jack decided to extend his Christmas visit to Twelfth Night. Margaret spent that first week of 1966 at her bed-sitter in Bayswater. She continued work on the Nigerian literature project into February and began the readings in the last week of the month. The children were back in school, but looking forward to a visit to Greece with their mother at the Easter break. It began with two days in Athens, then by ship to Crete for the rest of their two-week vacation. Margaret did not repeat her experience at Mycenae in June of 1964, when the classical setting of Agamemnon's fall was interrupted with "Hi" from a small Canadian boy, but a near equivalent happened as the boat left Piraeus. Tired and hungry (the boat was two hours late), they finally reached the dining room just ahead of an old gentleman. Margaret reports—

> he was a great bear of a man, with spectacles about 2 inches thick, a hearing aid and a small grey goatee. I thought—my God, I know that man. But it was only when I heard him speak in a broad Canadian growl that I really realized. I rose instantly . . . and went over to the table. . . . "You *are* Dr. Lower, aren't you?" And of course it was, A.R.M. Lower himself, who once taught me History at United.[14]

On the following day she and Lower had a long chat ("I was so damn pleased to see him") and he typically announced "the Acropolis should be restored"; and of course he knew just the man for the job—the architect who did Upper Canada Village. Margaret did not comment on this for Adele's benefit, that she didn't know, really, which had the most meaning for her personally, King Minos and his noble rejection of Scylla's offer, or this great bear of a man who growled in a way she could fully understand. She simply reported on Lower's announcement, "I thought this nationalism, for a change, was thoroughly admirable. . . . Saw him again at the Tourist Office in Iraklion . . . and I almost wanted to say to the Creta Tours people . . 'Look after him, eh? He's irreplaceable.'" The holiday, she observed, was "really terrific, as it seemed possible to leave all anxieties behind." After the meeting with Lower, the outstanding features of the holiday were, first, Margaret's renewed delight in Grecian cuisine and, second, the visit (repeated) to the ruins of the Minoan palace at Knossos.

Back to Elm Cottage and down to earth again at the news that Jack's father had died. She suggested to Jack that they share the cost of bringing Jack's mother over to England and invite her to Elm Cottage for a couple of weeks. Agreed. Another visitor was already on the spot, a woman who had long associations with Elm Cottage as she had been the housekeeper and had taken care of Lady Maclean during her last years and sustained her own relationship with the place. The Scottish Ann had agreed to spend some time with the children if Margaret's tentative plans to visit Canada during the autumn of 1966 came to fruition—a tour to promote *A Jest of God*. Ann had been on holiday in North Africa with her common-law husband; they were robbed. She returned alone to wait as her husband sold their caravan and hitchhiked home. Three months later, in the third week of May, he phoned to tell Margaret he had taken up with another woman and had left Ann for good. Margaret had to convey the news to Ann, who immediately succumbed to a catatonic seizure. Doctors were summoned and finally Ann was put into a mental hospital; her son (by an early marriage) was summoned from London. Jack's mother was at Elm Cottage all during that week; Jack did not arrive until the end of the week, the last Friday in May—when the weekly cleaning lady was due. At that point Margaret became "suddenly, SAVAGELY selfish" and escaped to London to keep an appointment with a Sudanese ambassador.[15]

The appointment was not ambassadorial in nature and was doubtless not listed in his official calendar, but it was important for Margaret. She began a report to Adele by saying the past week had been "pure unadulterated Murder," but she corrected that at once with a reference to the appointment for Friday 27 May: "No—I am wrong—one splendid evening (much to my surprise) with the old lion did much to maintain my sanity and morale." When she met "the lion" is unclear, evidently not long before this assignation, for she says, "Thought I might find he was less appealing when I saw him again, but actually is more so," which suggests this was only their second or third "date." Also she tells Adele a couple of days later that she had met the old lion at the same party as she met the Somali Minister of Information—who has just invited her to go to Mogadishu as a guest of his government to participate in the Somali Independence Day celebration of July 1st.[16]

The lion provided a welcome distraction from the frantic scene around the domestic hearth in Elm Cottage. He also provided something for Margaret's normal lusty nature, aggravated and frustrated by her forced celibacy—or near-celibacy. In late April she had exclaimed, "I wish to God I had a lover of whom I was at least fond and vice versa, so at least one could from time to time get away from all these tensions."[17] A month later, thanks for answered prayers: "One is grateful (and my god I really mean this!) for grace received." She explains: "Very nice to meet a man to whom sex isn't a battlefield in which he has to prove himself . . . but rather a matter of very accomplished pleasure."[18] (That is reminiscent of her response to the carved figures on the Black Pagoda of Konarak, which she visited with Jack in 1963: "all the copulating couples bore rather tenderly touching smiles."[19]) Margaret's wistful continuation, "It would be nice to meet a few Canadian men, though," is quite understandable—especially with her confession that she feels "somehow lonely for the sound of her own speech. . . ."[20]

Plans were firming up for Margaret's trip to Canada. Jack would stay with the children at Elm Cottage in September, and a local woman, Mrs. Charlett, agreed to sit with Jocelyn and David during the month of August. She and her husband lived across the road from Elm Cottage, on the grounds of The Beacon, where Mr. Charlett was head gardener; they had known the Maclean family when Alan was a youngster in Elm Cottage.[21] The Canada Council gave a Special Award of $5000 to assist Margaret with her next novel and another $700 for the trip to Canada.[22]

Meanwhile, Margaret had jumped at the invitation to return to Somalia for the Independence fête, hugging herself at the coincidence—the Somali celebration fell on the same day as the Canadian celebration of Dominion Day, July 1st. She left on 27 June and was back in Penn on 4 July, after a "really fabulous time in Somaliland," although she had picked up a tropical bug and was "sick as a dog, with dysentery."[23] Her Canadian tour was to begin in less than three weeks.

The Canadian venture began on a foul note at the luggage pickup in Montreal: her principal piece of luggage, containing her complete wardrobe for Canada, was not there nor did it turn up in Toronto. A representative from McClelland and Stewart escorted her to the apartment on Avenue Road that Jack McClelland had secured for her. Sunday, 31 July, dawned grey and cold: she had plenty of traveller's cheques and a modest deposit at a Canadian bank in Toronto, but no cash. She managed to wheedle a five-dollar loan from the building caretaker. At the beginning of the week the airline had not yet found her luggage but she did reach her old friends Chris and John Marshall. She explained her dilemma, and on Tuesday she and Chris bought Margaret a new wardrobe for $500 (at 1966 prices). The publicity campaign began in earnest with a party at Jack McClelland's.

It wasn't all an unrelieved ordeal. She heard from John Cushman, her agent in New York, that *Holiday* magazine wanted to send her to Egypt to do a couple of articles. She agreed. A few days later Alan Maclean called to ask if she would like to buy Elm Cottage. Pleading temporary penury, she asked could he wait for a definite answer until she got back to Penn. He could.[24]

There was little abatement as the publicity program continued in Montreal, but Adele was there for her spare moments. The month of August sped by, and she still had the prairies and coast to cover. The highlight of her Winnipeg visit was that her alma mater, United College, made her a Fellow of the College—both the youngest and the first woman to be so honoured—at the convocation of 5 October.[25] She visited with her former mentor at United College, Robert Hallstead, and his wife, Anne, and also with Walter Swayze, a young professor of English at the college, and his wife Margaret, who then lived just a block away; they became increasingly dear friends. The Hallsteads drove her out to Neepawa; that experience provided the epiphany for the conclusion of the final piece of *A Bird in the House*—not an experience she had eagerly sought. Walter Swayze recalls:

> she was not easy about encountering her past and all the

> memories that it evoked. Bob and Anne Hallstead almost had to drag her back to Neepawa, and the intensity of her struggle is certainly muted in Vanessa's apparently calm words in [the closing of] "Jericho's Brick Battlements." . . . We saw her the next day, and although she said practically nothing about the visit beyond factual platitudes, we could not miss the trauma in her face and body language.[26]

Margaret was also thoroughly lunched by Adele Wiseman's parents while in Winnipeg.

In Vancouver she saw Gordon Elliott and Nadine Jones Asante. She had dedicated *The Tomorrow-Tamer* to Nadine and her husband, Kwadwo, and was now welcomed as Nadine's houseguest; but media attention became a nuisance. Nadine had a new baby, and the intrusions on her privacy, coupled with disruption of her maternal program, were sorely aggravated by Margaret's apparent blindness to the mayhem her publicity was wreaking on poor Nadine. Exasperated, she demanded that Margaret decamp.[27]

There was, finally, a side trip down to New York to touch base with Margaret's American publisher, Alfred Knopf. While there she made several attempts to reach Adele's friend, the novelist Hannah Green, by telephone, but was unsuccessful. She gave Adele a brief summary of her Canadian sojourn just a week after regaining Elm Cottage: "I did a total of 17 radio interviews, 15 newspaper interviews, 4 TV interviews, and gave 4 talks. How I ever survived is a mystery."[28]

During the week after her return Margaret heard from a literary agent that Joanne Woodward and Paul Newman wanted a movie option on *A Jest of God*. That stroke would make possible purchase of her beloved Elm Cottage. She so informed Alan Maclean and immediately threw herself into consultation with bank managers and solicitors. She also congratulated herself on having accepted the *Holiday* assignment, although she wondered how the Canada Council would view her going to Egypt while holding their generous Special Award grant. (She hoped they wouldn't *view* it at all!) A bonus was that *Holiday* was willing to pay for hotel accommodations in Egypt for Jocelyn and David, so Margaret would not have to be separated from them again so soon (as she felt) after her two and a half months away in Canada.

Jack was still at Elm Cottage finishing his thesis for the MA from Southampton University. Relations between him and Margaret were stable but would become strained, she felt, if the situation were prolonged. He was feeling depressed about the difficulty of finding a job in irrigation. Fortunately, she was busily distracted by plans for the trip to Egypt—background reading and trying to arrange an excursion through the Suez Canal with the Canal Authority Pilot, as no tourist boats were then allowed. She was smitten, at the moment, by the irony that her friend the "old lion" could use his friendship with the Egyptian ambassador to facilitate such an arrangement, but that she could not ask such a favour precisely because of the nature of her relationship with him—"it looks so unethical," she lamented.[29]

They spent a month in Egypt, from the middle of December 1966 to the middle of January 1967. Margaret and the children had a few preparatory days in Cairo, and then went on up the Nile to Luxor, some 100 kilometres south. That was their base for fourteen days, during which they were in the care of Hanafy Bashir, the young Inspector of Guides and second in command at the local State Tourist Office. Margaret was especially impressed (or rather depressed) by the enormity of the monuments the rulers had had erected to themselves, and by the enormity of the egos that prompted such activity—which Shelley captured in his sonnet of 1818 "Ozymandias" (one of the names of King Rameses II). Bashir's favourite among the queens was Nefertari, wife of Rameses II, because she was "intelligent but not *too* intelligent, beautiful but not *too* beautiful, and because she has a gentle face." Margaret astutely observed, "Perhaps Ramesses II believed in his own powers not more than most kings, but considerably less so. Possibly only Nefertari, she of the obligingly reassuring face, ever really knew."[30] Did he remind Margaret of Agamemnon, King of Men?

Guide Bashir also arranged a two-day journey by steamer further up the Nile to the High Dam at Aswan. They returned to Cairo by plane and began specific plans for a visit to the Suez Canal. The Information Department made available one of their cars to take Margaret, Jocelyn, and David to Ismailia, midpoint of the canal and headquarters of the Suez Authority. The completed trip between Suez and Port Said normally took fifteen hours. Margaret decided they could afford half that time; so it was arranged. She and the children boarded a British tanker when the Canal Authority Pilot did, to finish the run to Port Said. David was much impressed by the vessel.

Margaret was again fascinated by the conjunction of Present and Past—rather, the double Past to be perceived, both the vestiges of the ancient Egyptian and the more familiar features of the British Victorian. She recognized the more recent particularly in its legacy of colonial times and practices as she had observed them sixteen years earlier on the way to Somaliland. The Present, however, asserted its demands when they reached the end of their voyage. Margaret pronounced the whole venture "a terrific experience," adding, "I won't regret one minute of it even if *Holiday* refuses the articles." She and the children regained Elm Cottage on a rather lucky Friday the thirteenth, January 1967.[31]

In Penn, Margaret found good news awaiting her. There was a cheque for the movie option on *A Jest of God* taken by Joanne Woodward and Paul Newman. She wrote to Anne and Bob Hallstead that she had got £900, which would enable her to make the down payment of £2000 on Elm Cottage.[32] Plans for purchase moved ahead. Jack had a job as Irrigation Consultant with a branch of the Overseas Development Ministry and would be based in Surrey. He had moved out by now, to Margaret's considerable relief, not just because of his depression at the apparent paucity of jobs open to him but also because of his relocation in Surrey, at least between overseas postings, which meant easy relations with Jocelyn and David. A letter from Robert Weaver announced that Malcolm Ross and Jack McClelland wanted a selection of Sinclair Ross's short stories prepared by Margaret and him—an attractive project. Finally, *Chatelaine* had accepted a revised version of a story she had written two years earlier, another Vanessa MacLeod episode, called "Horses of the Night."[33] To look back over the twelve months that followed the decision Margaret and Jack had taken to go their separate ways is to recognize that she had achieved such success and acclaim as would make a forty-year-old like Margaret Laurence glow with satisfaction—and, in time, with guilt.

The satisfaction would always be mild and temporary; the guilt that plagued the Black Celt would persist. Acceptance of "Horses of the Night" brought to six the number of stories about Vanessa MacLeod and family that she had written and found publishers for since early in 1963. Three of the first four published ("The Sound of the Singing," "To Set Our House in Order," and "The Mask of the Bear") present Vanessa's focus on the generation of her grandparents, the Connors and MacLeods. The fourth (third in composition) focusses on the death of her father; it is called, appropriately, "A Bird in the House"—"means a death in the house"—and lent its title to the book in which all the Vanessa stories were published. That title helps us recognize that the title of the second story is taken from the book of Isaiah, his words to the ailing king Hezekiah: "Thus saith the Lord, set thine house in order; for thou shalt surely die, and not live" (38:1). Also, "Mask of the Bear" tells of the death of Grandmother Connor and the surprising response of Grandfather Connor. The bear in the story, he displays his almost unsuspected humanity by embracing Vanessa and speaking of the deceased in unwonted terms of love and adoration. The end of "Mask" anticipates Vanessa's much later comprehension of that revelation and indirectly anticipates the old man's death: "Many years later . . . I saw . . . the Bear Mask of the Haida Indians. . . . I remembered then that in the days before it became a museum piece, the mask had contained a man." "A Bird in the House," however, ends the first half of the collection with the death of Vanessa's father. The next two stories are poignant recollections of her father and tributes to him by the Métisse Piquette Tonnerre in "The Loons" ("Your dad was the only person in Manawaka that ever done anything good to me") and by Vanessa's cousin Chris in "Horses in the Night" ("He didn't see what I was driving at, mostly, but he'd always listen, you know? You don't find many guys like that").

The Vanessa stories illuminate Margaret's attitudes during the period March 1966 to March 1967. A few days before she left for the Somali Independence fête, Margaret wrote a moving letter to Adele, prompted by the very recent death of Esther, brother Harry Wiseman's wife, but prompted also by her own recent experience with mad, abandoned Ann at Elm Cottage: "Sometimes things hit you in some uncontrollable way, and with me, it is the facts of death . . . and I know I ought to be outgrowing at least some of this, but unfortunately the underlying thing is still there, which is that my father and my two mothers died. So everything in this area is somehow terribly personal."[34] Anticipation of revisiting Somalia and revival of all the fond associations with her first romantic and exotic adventures there with Jack freshened in her mind the sense of the death-like end of her relationship with Jack, a figure who was more than somewhat a substitute for the father she lost so early; and notice the order in which she lists the parents lost to death. Margaret would turn forty in a couple of weeks.

When she went to the United Arab Republic, Margaret was keenly responsive to two features of the setting along the Nile in the Valley of the Kings: first, the enormous monuments of ego and the demand to be remembered; and second, the constant conjunction of past and present. Her comments on Ozymandias/Rameses II are reminiscent of her comments on Agamemnon in her reports of the visit to Mycenae; and they juxtapose past and present in her obvious sympathy with the two wives—Rameses's Nefertari and Agamemnon's Clytemnestra. That conjunction is expressed in explicitly personal terms when she ponders Suez as "the last link with home before the beginning of an exile . . . sometimes forced. . . . more often self-imposed. . . . this final goodbye to England, goodbye to Mama or Mum, goodbye to tea on the lawn or a pint at the pub."[35] That is not only the Victorian past of early colonial days, but the recall of her own initiation, under Jack's protective arm, to the mysterious East as recalled in the opening passages of *The Prophet's Camel Bell*, just sixteen years earlier. Finally the symbols of mankind's constant attempt to evade the inevitable end gripped her imagination.

> Something about the magnificence and the fertility of these structures, something about the tenacity and the ultimate vulnerability of the kings, men who built them in an attempt to defeat the undefeatable, time and death—this will haunt the mind always, as the jackals haunt the temples, for it contains all there is of human paradox.[36]

A discernible echo of Ecclesiastes: "vanity of vanities; all is vanity" (I.i); perhaps an echo that will persist in the mind of the black Celt and provoke the guilt that continued to plague her.

Her one recent disappointment had been her failure to see "the person I most wanted to meet when I was in Canada last summer."[37] On regaining Elm Cottage in January 1967, she found waiting for her a letter from that person—the Canadian poet Al Purdy. Purdy's fifth book of poetry, *The Cariboo Horses*, had won the 1965 Governor General's Award for Poetry. He eventually wrote over forty books and received the Order of Canada in 1982. He had written to Margaret on 10 December to express his disappointment at not meeting her. A lively correspondence began at once. The "chemistry" was there and the relationship quickly became one of the most important in her life. Indeed, a whole new wave of successes was thus begun. She turned almost immediately to preparation of two articles on Egypt, and before the end of February 1967 she had completed one, on Luxor and the Valley of the Kings, and sent it off to *Holiday*; and the other, on the Suez Canal, she had in rough draft. The first was accepted early in March, the second before the end of the month. Margaret was always sensitive to dates (and suspicious of her tendency to be superstitious); thus there was a discernible edge to her announcement to Bob Hallstead that on Good Friday (24 March 1967) she had received news that *A Jest of God* had won the Governor General's Award for Fiction and that news of the acceptance of the Suez article had reached her on the day before that, Maundy Thursday.[38]

Of course the money for the *Holiday* pieces, for the *Chatelaine* story ("Horses of the Night"), and for the movie option on *A Jest*, added to what the Governor General's Award brought, enabled Margaret to buy Elm Cottage. She did so on 12 April 1967. The sense of now having some breathing space and some economic security moved her to resume the story of the other Cameron sister, Stacey. At the beginning of April she told Adele that she was really aching "to get down to a novel . . . the one that has been bugging me for years and which I started so wrongly before" (9 April 1967). Less than a month later she repeated that the urge to get started was "nearly killing me" (2 May 1967). By mid-May she could report to Adele that she had set down the first paragraph.[39]

Before Margaret could devote herself definitely to that novel, however, there were other matters to attend to. She sent the manuscript of *Long Drums and Cannons* to Alan Maclean at the beginning of May.[40] She was making plans for Ottawa less than a month later to receive her Governor General's Award: fly to Montreal on 26 May and stay with Adele Wiseman until 2 June, the day of the ceremonies; then to Ottawa, spend the night at the Beacon Arms Hotel, and return to Montreal for her return flight at 8:00 p.m. on the 3rd.[41] The chance to spend time with Adele and the possibility of meeting Al Purdy in person added to her eager anticipation. Meanwhile, other plans were progressing in Winnipeg for the Manitoba Festival to be held in October 1967. In mid-February Adele urged Margaret to write to the head of the arts council, Professor Christian Jensen (Chair of the French department, University of Manitoba), to ask to be a participant. Margaret agreed but decided she couldn't in effect *request* an invitation, one that would impose on the committee a stiff expense for travel and lodging.[42] Yet Adele could tell Sid Warhaft (Chair of the English department, University of Manitoba) that she was *interested in* the festival. Jensen was given Margaret's address but didn't write to her; Margaret wrote to Warhaft to express her interest, but it was not his place to extend the invitation. All this just before she was to fly to Montreal. She decided not to commit herself to the festival. Adele finally did appear on the panel on 24 October, with writers John Peter and Jack Ludwig, and Harold Rosenberg in Margaret's place; she was quite disgusted with the condescending treatment she and John Peter received from the other two—in spite of Chairman Warhaft's best efforts.[43]

At the beginning of May, Al Purdy invited Margaret to contribute to a collection of essays he was editing under the title *The New Romans: Candid Canadian Opinions of the U.S.*; she would be the "first prospective contributor," he told her.[44] Margaret eagerly accepted and sent him "An Open Letter to the Mother of Joe Bass," which she later included in *Heart of a Stranger*. It is about the victims of violence and the wholesale denial of responsibility, about automation and consequent dehumanization, about the absolute necessity of human communications, with a gentle side glance, therefore, at the necessary role of the literary artist. It is a succinct little gem of a comment from the point of view of the alien, the stranger, who has been a stranger in an alien land.[45] Purdy's response was, "[I] think soberly, logically and particularly, also emotionally, that it is a very fine—article? More like a short story perhaps. It will stand out. . . . Despite its short story aspect, it's an entirely utilitarian piece (which is queer to say about it) that does what I think you want it to do. . . . I have no doubt of its merit whatever, and you shouldn't have."[46] A remunerative complication, self-imposed, was her agreeing to read for Macmillan's at the rate of two manuscripts a month: they paid well. Another complication, non-remunerative, was Jack's Aunt Bea, due to arrive for a visit on the weekend of 19 May; Jack was off in Ethiopia. There was apparently no way this time for Margaret to escape "selfishly, SAVAGELY" to a rendezvous with the old Sudanese lion in London. That relationship seemed to have petered out since their dinner date early in April.[47]

Margaret confidently arranged with Mrs. Charlett to look after Jocelyn and David when she left on the last Friday of May to fly to Montreal. It was a further comfort to learn that the award included a practical $2000 to complement the honour. In Montreal she met Sinclair Ross and they discussed a selection of his short stories for the New Canadian Library.[48] It was gratifying to meet him, another prairie writer, whose austere and poignant novel *As For Me and My House* and short stories had deeply touched her. On Friday, 2 June, she arrived in Ottawa. During the cocktail party between the award ceremony and that evening's banquet, her attention was arrested when (as she reported) "this enormous man shambled in, I thought 'My god, he looks like a cowboy.'" Al Purdy, at last.[49] When she had written to Purdy that her plan was to return to Montreal on the Saturday, she added, encouragingly, "But I do have most of June 3 in Ottawa, as plane does not leave until 8 p.m." (2 May 1967). Their talk that Friday evening cemented the friendship that had begun with their exchange of a baker's dozen of letters in the preceding months, and evidently extended through most of the next day and necessitated a change in plans. She confided breathlessly to Adele, "P.S. almost missed my plane when leaving Ottawa"; and summed up her experience as "a wonderful week, about the best week I've had in a long time."[50] She concluded that she would return to Penn "filled with more affectionate feelings toward Canada than I have harboured in many a long year," and wondered if she could live there again. The answer was unclear.

Unclear, perhaps, for rather intimate reasons, including domestic relationships, which she had discussed with Adele in Montreal and to which she alluded at the opening of the letter. Her attitude to Canada was always coloured by her attitude to Jack, and would continue to be. But it was good to be back in the embrace of Elm Cottage and to make sure her children were all right. And if this was not—or not yet—the time to return to Canada, Canada could at least come to her. The Canadian influx that summer began less than a week after Margaret had settled back into Elm Cottage. Anne and Bob Hallstead had been in England to visit their son Douglas, who was then a student at the University of Bristol, and they came on to Penn to spend the week of 11-17 June with Margaret.[51] My family and I also visited Penn at the end of June.

Margaret went to Oxford on the last day of June to give a talk on Canadian Literature to some Canadian students and others. Jack Ludwig and his wife Leya arrived in London toward the end of July to begin a year's leave, and Margaret met them in town early in August.[52] High tide of the Canadian influx occurred in the first ten days of September. On the 8th, she had a long luncheon with Adele's brother, Harry, and his son, Arnold, in London. Three days later she told Adele she had completed her Introduction to her edition of Sinclair Ross's short stories: "Reading the stories, I felt such a sense of connection with the characters, even though they were in an era slightly before my adulthood. But I know them pretty well. . . . within that era and in that idiom, he has portrayed an entire people, their spiritual goals, their vulnerabilities."

Finally, just before her forty-first birthday, Margaret suffered with David through a truly traumatic experience: one of his friends was killed in an accident. She explained to Anne and Bob Hallstead, "This was D's first experience of death, and it was pretty terrible for him. It has been a godsend for him to have the 2 Powers boys to play with this summer."[53] That bit of good fortune was yet another Canadian conjunction of the summer of '67. Certainly the trauma remained with Margaret until she could lay it to rest in the most appropriate manner available to her—her writing.

Meanwhile, where was Stacey Cameron's story? All the summer of 1967 was, in fact, distracting. Margaret observed that because of all the visitors and the long vacation for the children, she could get nothing done on Stacey's story.[54] Yet the true problem with the story may have been something other than the visitors and the children, or something other than their mere intrusion on her working time.

Perhaps the problem was the very Canadian quality of the visitors and the old dilemma: the appeal of Canada opposed by the appeal of Elm Cottage, and the desire to return to her old home opposed by her sense of duty to Jack and then to Jocelyn and David. All the responsibilities seemed exclusively her own: Square One in three dimensions, the third being responsibility for herself as writer.

One problem with the novel itself was that its heroine, like the heroine of *A Jest of God*, insisted on speaking in Margaret's voice. Now Margaret amended her report to Adele, "in only 1 of my voices, and baby, I've got DOZENS of voices!!"[55] She was also vexed, however, to recognize that the heroine's dilemma was somehow related to her own; yet she insisted, further, "my own dilemma is not utterly different anyway, so perhaps I had to gain this distance to be able to write it." She is referring to the material she had laid aside when she realized the need to write Rachel's story first, and claiming that she can now resume that material with a fresh and healthier attitude. As though to confirm that claim, she took the bold step of destroying all the early manuscript. On 29 June she burned the lot. From that death by fire might come the fresh resurgence of her heroine, like the phoenix. "It is the character who is there. . . . And she is still there."[56]

Catharsis! Within less than a month Margaret had finished the first chapter of the new version of Stacey's story. In August she completed the second chapter, and also culled four pages from the first to send to the *Adam International Review* with the appropriate title "Everything is all right," at the request of the editor, Miron Grindea.[57] Then Stacey balked. Margaret turned away to attend to a story that had been in the back of her mind for a while, a story for children, and its hero is a mole. It was called *Jason's Quest*.

This Jason is not seeking a golden fleece but rather a cure for the malaise that has attacked the folk of his town, Molanium. His society is moribund, caught in the grip of devotion to the past and unwavering fidelity to a transmitted code of manners. The molefolk insist the world is flat. Jason's friend Oliver, the young owl, objects that the world is *not* flat. Jason replies that they all know that but it isn't polite to say so. The two decide to set out together, Oliver questing for wisdom and Jason a cure for the mole malady. They are immediately joined by a pair of cats, Calico and Topaz; the elder wants to commit a noble act to prove that cats are fine, upstanding creatures, and young Topaz (apparently a bit of fluff) wants to see the world and its finery, or, rather, to be seen *by* it while garbed *in* the finery.

Their combined quest exposes them to prejudice, including their own, but principally the most evil extension of it in racial and other discrimination, segregation, and fascism, the result of ignorance and fear. They learn that creatures are a mixture of good and bad. Jason soon begins to question seriously the principles Molanium lives by: *Festina Lente, Be Cautious, Only Idiots Take Risks.* He sees that risks are quite unavoidable if you're going on a quest, so "take reasonable care—then bash on regardless."[58] Jason recognizes, with the help of Perdita, the beautiful mole girl ("Her fur was a pale golden brown"), what the cure must be for the molefolk. She asks, "Doesn't anything ever *change* in Molanium? . . . The way you describe it, nothing ever seems to happen. All this devotion to the past. It's all very well, . . . but surely new things have to happen, too . . . I'd die of boredom" (167).

The faithful four, with Jason as their chosen leader, overcome the obstacles they meet and all fulfill the purpose of their quests. Jason returns with his friends to Molanium, accompanied by his consort, Perdita, and bringing the Boon that will cure the molefolk of their malaise. The pattern of Jason's quest, as Margaret pointed out, is "what the critic Gerald Moore calls the 'heroic monomyth'—Departure—Initiation—Return."[59] It is an engaging fable, full of fun and adventure and fascinating characters. If the story needs a motto, that of Neepawa high school (at least when Peggy Wemyss was a student there) would certainly suffice: "To strive, to seek, to find, and not to yield."

In addition to its development of familiar Laurentian themes, *Jason's Quest* bears Margaret's personal stamp. Jason's two feline friends bear the names of her two cats, Calico and Topaz; crucial moments in the story focus on Hampstead (where she lived with Jack and later with Jocelyn and David) and on Marylebone Station, where one takes the train to travel to Penn/Beaconsfield; Calico gives her address as "Elm Cottage, Penn, Buckinghamshire, England" (48). These signs of peculiarly personal relevance help indicate what gave rise to this "kids' book" that she suddenly "began to write off the top of my head."[60]

Along with all the grief over getting properly started on Stacey's story, Margaret was fretting over her own personal dilemma: whether to remain in Elm Cottage or return to Canada, and what would be best for Jocelyn and David, and for Jack. When she told Al Purdy about burning up the original manuscript of Stacey's story, he suggested that England was not the place for her, a nice cocoon but without nourishing close relationships.[61] She admitted she was living her life as an exile but that a visit, at least, to the homeland would be possible within a year, for Joanne Woodward and Paul Newman had decided to take up their option on *A Jest of God* and the film rights would bring her more than $20,000. Purdy's observation gave impetus to Margaret's thoughts, and at the end of August she shared with him her ideas on where she truly belonged: not in England, for virtually all her friends were Canadian, her income was mainly from Canada and the US, and Canada's educational opportunities far more suitable for Jocelyn and David than they could find in England. A week after that important revelation she had the memorable luncheon with Harry Wiseman and his son. She told Adele about the basic understanding she felt with Harry and how sagely he had, unasked, addressed her dilemma. Margaret had confessed to him "a deep inner need to return to Canada" and her worry over leaving the newly purchased Elm Cottage. Harry's reply—"I used to think I would build a house that would last forever. But nothing lasts forever"—was very close to one of the themes of *Jason's Quest*. Then Harry added, "If I wanted to move, I wouldn't let a house hold me." That was very like Jason's realization to "take reasonable care—and then bash on regardless." Margaret said: "it's as though those were the words I had been, without realizing, waiting to hear. . . . I felt in some odd way that talking to Harry even briefly had clarified all kinds of issues for me. . . ."[62] She then rehearsed for Adele the perceptions she had listed to Purdy as reasons for her to return to Canada; she concluded to Adele, as she had not to Purdy, "The snag seemed to be Jack." She cannot simply say, "Sorry—I'm off to Canada," for that would come close to being as shocking to Jack as her refusal, in 1962, to go with him to Pakistan. "Can't do same again," she finished.

A failure of courage, perhaps, and in spite of the heroic Jason, whose fable of courageous self-reliance and so on seemed to work out her own need for courage to seize the right option in her own dilemma, to prepare herself for such a bold *geste* as Jason's in actual life. It was evidently not to be. Or perhaps the words of Jack's mother returned to her.[63] Margaret continued to oscillate. The urge to go back to Canada was quickened by news received on 21 September that her old friend and mentor at United College, Bob Hallstead, had died. Further, the opportunity to become writer-in-residence at Dalhousie University—the results of efforts by Adele, Malcolm Ross, and the young Dalhousie instructor Don Cameron—presented an acceptable compromise that would postpone taking a definite decision: the Dalhousie job would be merely a visit. Such a compromise was the more attractive as Margaret recognized she was more comfortable, financially, than Jack—certainly a complication.

When the possibility of Elm Cottage had arisen at the end of 1963, Margaret needed Jack's permission; it was granted, and in return Margaret agreed to assume responsibility for two-thirds of her and the children's expenses.[64] After her professional successes of 1966, Jack reduced the allowance he provided for Jocelyn and David.

Furthermore, Margaret came to recognize how touchy Jack was about her making more money than he.[65] Yet Margaret realized, as Jack did not, that her income was not guaranteed and could in fact "stop tomorrow," and with that, she must remember her undeniable duty to herself, to her muse. Happily, she was able to utter, at least to Adele, her own claims for just consideration: "how do I get around the problem of somehow always having for his sake to pretend that all this with my work is some kind of meaningless hobby . . ?" Late in October, Margaret wrote Jack to get his permission to take the children to Canada with her, temporarily, while she spent a term at Dalhousie. (The University of Toronto was looming as another distinct possibility for her as writer-in-residence, but the "Vile Metropolis" still seemed too daunting to merit serious consideration.)

Her letters to Purdy during that month are very nearly as frank as those to Adele. The difference is that while they point to the decision she indicated to Adele, these to Purdy show the other side of her attitude to herself: she tells him that amid all her oscillation she has the "unpleasant feeling" that she has already made her decision and is merely mustering the arguments and evidence now to support it—and with that, "suffering sufficient guilt and pain so that in the end one feels justified in taking the selfish decision one had . . . made some time ago. . . . I think in the end I will act selfishly." Such a perception, however, seemed to promise quite the opposite decision. After a sleepless night, Margaret arose on 24 October to find in the mail a "kind and understanding letter from Jack," and then wrote a denial to both Adele and Purdy—a firm denial of her anticipated decision to return to Canada: she recognized now that she could not return to Canada as long as Jack was working in England. She decided to seek a reconciliation with Jack, "if he'll have me."[66]

Stacey's story had been oscillating as broadly as its author, and once Margaret had definitely decided to remain in England—and, thus, with Jack—the novel began to flow. Stacey's dilemma, Margaret had explained, was somewhat like her own but her own had changed so much she could then manage Stacey's. Indeed, Margaret now professed to look upon all the fussing about a return to Canada as merely an evasion of her proper task of writing Stacey's story,[67] and she was at last determined that there would be no further evasion, no escape—"*there is nowhere to go but here*." At the end of the first week of November 1967, Margaret was through chapter Four and into Five; by the end of the month she had finished Six and expected to have Seven off her hands before Christmas. She would then have just three chapters left to do. She finished the writing in April 1968 and completed the typing-up on Victoria Day—another good omen—and mailed it off to Macmillan's.

thirteen

Nowhere to Go but Here

> "Death destroys a man: the idea of Death saves him."
> E. M. Forster, *Howards End*

THE STORY OF STACEY CAMERON IS A SIMPLE TALE, ALMOST banal—at least superficially. Her dilemma is familiar, yet Margaret's rendering of it engages readers and makes us follow her story eagerly to see if its ending is tragic or happy or maybe just true. Stacey Cameron MacAindra is married to a hard-working but incommunicative husband, Mac, the mother of four children aged two to fourteen, and (a most blatant annoyance) hurtling toward her fortieth birthday. Acute awareness of life's mutability and mortality engages Stacey quite as much as it does Rachel, and *The Fire-Dwellers* makes the point, just as firmly as does *A Jest of God*, that denial of change and death is in fact denial of life. Like her younger sister, Stacey sees escape as an urgent solution.

Stacey seems, however, to have already succeeded in escaping: she has fled the inhibiting clutches of Manawaka and gone to the coast, where she met a man (the equivalent of Agamemnon, King of Men, she felt sure), married him, but is *not* living happily ever after. She has carried all her Manawaka past and its values along with her. Stacey suffers from failure of communication, as Rachel did until her temporary success with Nick Kazlik, and has no one with whom to share her fears or from whom to seek solace and support. The failed escape from Manawaka leads Stacey to try other means of escape—gin and tonic, nostalgic memories of swimming and dancing as a teenager at Diamond Lake, erotic fantasies, and even extramarital affairs. Escape is urgent, for the world is threatening, is on fire.

The Fire-Dwellers opens with the appropriate admonition of a nursery rhyme:

> Ladybird, ladybird
> Fly away home:
> Your house is on fire,
> Your children are gone.[1]

Next, we meet Stacey, fretting about her own aging and all the signs (especially the physical) of her lost youth. She envies neighbour Tess Fogler her svelte and youthful figure, and constantly plans diets she never follows. She indulges in fantasies that feature "*the green beckoning voices of the men still unheld*" (119), and worries about the vulnerability of her four children, and in particular her beautiful Katie, a budding teenager. There is plenty of evidence to justify Stacey's fear of the baleful world. Early in One she wanders through Vancouver's waterfront and, as it seems to Stacey, the scene is a virtual Dance of Death (5). Then, in a rush of guilt, she hurries home, and gets off the bus to the "sound she always dreads to hear"—the screeching brakes of an automobile accident, the young victim the age of her own two boys. Once home, she learns that Ian and Duncan are all right; it turns out that the victim was a friend of Ian's, Peter Challoner, but death has struck too close to home. Lurking in the shadowy borders around the whole scene, like Fortinbras around Hamlet's Elsinore, is the horror of the Vietnam War. The opening chapter ends with Stacey's dream of the burning hillside, the life-threatening fire, and her understandable wish for the ultimate escape, which is followed, however, by the acute and prophetic response to the plausible maxim "not to be born is the best for men": "*Not to be born would be not to have to die. But that would be useless*" (25).

Mac is as intimidated by life as she, and unable to share his fears.

He finds his escape in commitment to his new job with Richalife and its products that foster health and perpetual youth (perhaps), his "rejuvenating" brush-cut hairstyle, his sustained friendship with his wartime buddy Buckle Fennick, and even his little affair with co-worker Delores Appleton. A girl who "can't be more than eighteen or twenty" (131), Delores is reminiscent in this context of the Peace Corps girl of whom Jack wrote to Margaret (in February 1965) that "he had become deeply involved emotionally, although hopelessly." Margaret informed Adele, "She is 21."[2] Virtually Mac's only intercourse with Stacey is the sexual; an exception is their brief but severe disputes about raising children. Mac's devotion to Richalife further weakens the line of communication between him and Stacey. She decides one day to sneak into a company meeting and there sees him seated next to the slim, young Delores Appleton, his "arm around her, not casually but tightly, like a wall against the world" (132). That encounter distinctly focusses Stacey's jealousy. A complement to that is Buckle's jealousy: both feel that Mac has betrayed them—with Delores, for Stacey, and with Thor Thorlakson, for Buckle. Inevitably, the two betrayed come together after Stacey's chance encounter. For Stacey, this is a chance for escape and vengeance together.

Stacey is both attracted and repelled by Buckle. He is stocky and muscular, with "a face like an Iroquois . . . faintly slanted dark eyes . . . hair . . . night black and straight";[3] with that, "His jeans are always too tight and they bulge where his sex is, and it embarrasses me and infuriates me that it does, yet I always look, as he damn well knows and laughs at . . ." (42). He is a trucker: "He drives a diesel dinosaur, a steel monster, . . . roaring full of crazy power. Buckle loves it. It is his portable fortress, his moveable furnace. It is his lover and himself all in one" (44). His favourite pastime on long runs on the Cariboo Highway is to challenge oncoming truckers to a game of "chicken" by moving over to hug or straddle the centre line of the road: if the oncomer accepts it, the test is to see which one will flinch and turn away to his own side first. Buckle is never the one to turn away. Stacey fantasizes driving up north to the Cariboo with him: "*the truck stops. . . . He is poised above her—hard, ready, taut—and she can hardly wait for him to*" (136). She accepts his invitation to his apartment, and there is ready to accept his offer of himself. Buckle, however, keeps himself to himself, onanistically and narcissistically, leaving her as witness "to the agony of his pleasure" (141)—an echo of the description of his diesel, "his lover and himself all in one." So ends the fifth of the novel's ten chapters, the climax of the story. That climactic moment is emphasized by Mac's father as he quotes the opening line of Psalm 69 (the text for the day's sermon), "*Save me, O God, for the waters are come in unto my soul*" (146), and thus introduces another threatening element, water, as a complement to fire.

Buckle informs Mac that Stacey seduced him—complementary vengeance. Mac believes him. The rest of Buckle's story is withheld until after the portrayal of Stacey's next affair, which begins the second half of the novel and in some ways parallels the "affair" with Buckle.

Stacey's attempt to discuss with Mac Buckle's false accusation fails. At Mac's final response, "Can't you just *leave me alone*?" (148), she flees to the shore of the Sound where she can dream of her childhood at Diamond Lake, and particularly of the strange ululating cry of the loons, "witch birds . . . or voices of dead shamans, mourning the departed Indian gods" (153), and of her return at age eighteen to find that the loons have gone, escaped perhaps, "somewhere so far north that people would never penetrate to drive them off again" (154). Finally, Stacey dreams of her own immersion in the fertile medium of Diamond Lake, swimming as far out as she dared, then later dancing, "feeling already the pressure on her lake-covered thighs of the boys" (155). In the midst of this she has also fantasized an escape to an imagined lake, "deep oil blue. . . . somewhere in the Cariboo. The Cariboo country. Up there" (154). Abruptly, Stacey addresses her God: "Okay. I see it, Sir." It is the first of an important series of epiphanies:

> I didn't see it before, but I see it now. . . . That's the place I

> want to get to eh? The Cariboo? Up north? . . . When I imagine it, it always looks like Diamond Lake. Like, I guess I mean, everything will be just fine when I'm eighteen again. Come on, Stacey. Home. (155-56)

She is interrupted by a young man wearing an "Indian sweater in thick wool with Haida or something motifs of outspread eagle wings and bear masks" (157). A kind of careful intimacy is established between them soon after Stacey accepts the invitation into his place. Luke Venturi, like Buckle, promises exciting escape from domestic doldrums. His Indian sweater matches Buckle's Indian appearance (and the lost loons). As Buckle is associated with his truck route up the highway into the Cariboo, so Luke will tell Stacey tales of his experience there. Both invite her to accompany them on excursions up there. She refuses both. Both are possible sexual partners, with Luke as acceptable as she had expected Buckle to be. The similarities, however, effectively differentiate the two men.

First, the water theme, begun with the setting by the Sound, and continued by the interior of Luke's A-frame house: "The [main] room is filled with assorted junk—coarse-webbed fishnets . . . , the big smoke-green thick glass bubbles used as weights on nets. . . . curtains of moss-green sackcloth. . . . a rumpled loose-weave green and grey wool rug . . ." (157-58). Stacey herself sustains that theme: she is suitably dressed in green slacks and sweater (148); with Buckle her slacks were black (133). Luke calls her "merwoman" and tells her, as though it should matter, "I'm Cancer" (169)—his astrological sign is the crab.

The parallel with Buckle seems strengthened by the Cariboo association; and with that begins the series of epiphanies that Buckle first provoked and is continued by Luke's talking about the Cariboo. In both instances, however, "the Cariboo" represents simple escape to Stacey; it was simply that with Buckle and now it is a different matter. Luke tells her about coming upon a little farmhouse in the middle of nowhere and a twelve-year-old who announces that his Mum "*took off, two-three months ago*" (159). Stacey bursts into tears; the surprised

Luke innocently asks her, "Is that where you live?" Does she live there or does she live at Diamond Lake? One answer for both. Luke obliges Stacey to confront herself and recognize what she half perceives already, and provides a gently sympathetic ear to facilitate communication. He functions as a healer, like his namesake "the beloved physician" (Colossians 4:14). The Cariboo is not an escape for Luke but a source for his literary creativity.

On Stacey's return to the Sound four days later, wearing a "cotton dress . . . printed in blue and dark green, like seawater and fir trees" (168), they confess their ages, Luke adding five years to his actual twenty-four and Stacey subtracting four from her thirty-nine. He tells Stacey he is a writer and describes his current project, the story of the *Greyfolk*—a science-fiction account, set in the future, about lost language and racial memories grown dim (178-79). Luke scolds her mildly but firmly about expecting to be criticized and being too ready to respond defensively, and he poses a question that provides another epiphany for her: "What scares you?" Again she must confront herself squarely. She admits to her worries about change and death attacking her children: "Everybody's living dangerously," she declares. "What if they got hurt, killed even?" (172).

This fear, spoken aloud and shared with Luke, becomes another self-confrontation, provoked by his interest and intrusion; it moves her a step closer to full self-recognition. She can talk about her relationship with Mac—originally her Agamemnon, King of Men—who has become, after sixteen years of marriage, "somebody who doesn't talk or who can't or else won't . . . " (176). She and Luke finally make love.[4]

Before their third meeting, three preparatory events intervene that bear directly on the theme of mutability and mortality. The events have less to do with change and death themselves than with the "right" idea of or attitudes to them. Returning home after her second meeting with Luke, Stacey is told of Tess Fogler's obliging Jen to watch the cannibalism of the Fogler goldfish (a reiteration of the theme of "death by water," found in Psalm 69). Jen is unscathed, but the shared confrontation has drawn Stacey and Katie closer: "*We.* They have never before encountered one another as persons. . . . Katie has been unwittingly calling her *Mum* instead of *Mother*" (187).[5] Second, Stacey learns that Ian has nearly met the fate of his friend Peter Challoner by running in front of a car. Stacey muses, "Ian thinks about death—how much? Some people don't know they're ever going to die until it happens to them, but Ian knows he's going to die. . . . and *his* father deals in rejuvenating vitamins" (192). Third, Julian Garvey comes to see Mac about some Richalife pills, to restore his virility or even to prolong his life eternally (194). Significantly, Mac has refused Julian's request.[6] Stacey is ready to visit Luke again.

She is briefly detained by Ian's stomach ache, but gets away to Luke. They make love, and he talks about his *Greyfolk* story and going up north this summer, another epiphany for Stacey.

> There's this place where there's a ferry. . . . this beat-up old raft crawls across the Skeena . . . the river is wild as hell. But the old guy who runs it is calm as anything, probably been there forever. Charon. . . . And there's this village . . . Indian village. . . . lots of people visit the place. . . . The attraction is the totem poles. . . . the totems of the dead. And of the living dead. . . . it's a language which has got lost and now there isn't anything to replace it except silence. . . . (203)

Charon, ancient ferryman to the land of the dead, identifies Buckle's destination up north. Luke invites his merwoman Stacey to accompany him up there; then, coupling the water theme with the fire, he answers her refusal by quoting "Ladybird, ladybird." He provides a fifth epiphany by confessing, "I'm not twenty-nine. I'm twenty-four" (205). Stacey leaves. After a moment for the arithmetic, she recognizes, "I'm old enough to be his mother" (205). They both know the affair is over.

She has benefitted from Luke's sympathetic attention: it has revitalized her and given her some self-confidence. He has obliged her to confront and understand herself and so to feel better about herself. Luke's function as "healer" benefits from his association with the water theme and his "Indian" connection (the Haida sweater and his *Greyfolk* fiction); both contribute to the motif of "unspoiled natural goodness and health," a parallel to Nick Kazlik's role for Rachel in *Jest*. That emphasis gains from the news awaiting Stacey as she hurries home, worried about Ian's stomach ache—Mac's announcement, "Stacey, he's dead" (207).

Not Ian, but Buckle. Margaret has juxtaposed effectively the exits of Luke and Buckle from Stacey's life and also the twin themes of water and fire, respectively, but here in complement, not opposition: death by fire (Buckle's) with death by water (the Fogler fish and Psalm 69). Death by fire beneficently draws Stacey and Mac closer as death by water at the Foglers' drew Stacey and Katie together.

The association of Buckle and death is clarified as Stacey recalls his boast about the game of "chicken"—*I've never yet met a guy who didn't give way*" (136). She comments to herself, "I thought it was pure ego, super confidence, when he said that. But maybe after all it was only disappointment." Then Mac tells her of saving Buckle's life in the Italian campaign of the Second World War. They had taken a shortcut, Buckle driving the truck, and reached a bridge; Mac wanted to get out and search for mines and booby traps. Buckle replied, "*Okay, chickadee, you get out and walk because I'm driving across*" (214). The derogatory "chickadee," suggesting cowardice, echoes "chicken," Buckle's game with his diesel. Then Buckle's reaction to Mac's rescuing him after the bridge blew: "Buckle kept coming to . . . and from the way he looked it wasn't only because he was in pain, it was something else entirely. . . . I couldn't figure it at the time. But later on I thought maybe it was just that I hadn't done him any favour. I hadn't done anything he wanted me to do" (215). But why has Buckle been half in love with easeful death?

Two features of characterization, apparently ironic, help answer that. Buckle's mother is made to participate in the water theme but seems not to belong. On Stacey's visit to Buckle's apartment, his mother is "the undersea giant woman" (141); her return visit, after Buckle's death, reminds her of the "she-whale" (208). Those are reminiscent of the "death by water" theme. Mac identifies Buckle's corpse: "*blood wiped . . . but smears still on the dark skin of his Indian-like face*" (213)—he still looks "like an Iroquois" (42). As "she-whale," the mother specifically recalls the story of Jonah; the language of Psalm 69, quoted by Mac's father, resembles the description of Jonah's plight in the belly of the whale. The Psalmist anticipates a rescue similar to Jonah's: rebirth follows the threatened death by water.[7] The irony of her undersea-whale depiction is the irony of the promise "He that loses his life shall find it." The irony of Buckle-as-Indian is similar.

Buckle seems more and more the opposite of Luke in the Indian theme: he is suicidal, while Luke is anything but. On the other hand, Buckle looks Aboriginal—dark skin, lank black hair. Luke, however, dons his Indian sweater and writes about the Aboriginal village up in the Cariboo. Beyond that is a more bitter irony: Buckle's mother was a prostitute, his father is unidentified, and Buckle is evidently a bastard—a "natural child" or a "love child." With such a beginning, his life could hardly be anything but unfortunate, and society must bear some responsibility for that situation and for his mother's. Like Richard Wright's Bigger Thomas, Buckle has learned what society hates, and, having found it in himself, must hate that self vigorously. What is there to love? He is an alien in his society, a stranger, not to be oppressed by the likes of us, but is.

We know that "Buckle" is a short form of "Arbuckle," but there is something more, something from a poem by one of Margaret's favourite writers, "The Windhover" by Gerard Manley Hopkins. After the octave has described the flight of the falcon, the sestet offers this comment:

> Brute beauty and valour and act, oh, air, pride, plume, here
> Buckle! AND the fire that breaks from thee then, a billion

> Times told lovelier, more dangerous, O my chevalier!
>
> No wonder of it: sheer plod makes plough down sillion
> Shine, and blue-bleak embers, ah my dear,
> Fall, gall themselves, and gash gold-vermilion.

The obvious irony focussed here in "Buckle!" is that when the bird breaks its smooth gliding to plunge and dive (for its prey), all its beauty and valour change to a *fire*, "gash gold-vermilion," and becomes a "billion / Times told lovelier," like the transformed "blue-bleak embers." The poem, subtitled "To Christ Our Lord," is a rehearsal of Christ's sacrifice. Hopkins's depiction resembles Fennick's sacrifice, unwilling and unintentional though it is, for the benefit of Stacey and Mac. The force is his diesel dinosaur; the *fire* in his moveable furnace is willfully spent on his own destruction, but the benefit for Stacey and Mac is clear: Mac is his next of kin and the two are his beneficiaries. Buckle's death is as sacrificial as John Shipley's in *The Stone Angel*—or that of the albatross in *The Rime of the Ancient Mariner*.

Clarification of this facet of Buckle's role begins with Stacey's visit to his empty apartment after his death. There, she thinks, "Buckle—you can't be dead. I can't cry here. . . . But I am. . . . requiem for a truck driver" (235). Immediately on leaving, she hears her name called by a voice from her past. It is a voice connected to the theme of "unspoiled goodness and health," now tragically spoiled, and associated specifically with the Aboriginal motif (its origin in those Cree "with enigmatic faces and greasy hair" who used to walk through the prairie bluffs before displaced by the "civilized" cemetery of Manawaka).[8] It is the voice of the Métisse Valentine Tonnerre—*tonnerre*. The voice out of this Thunder has much to say: she tells of the death of her sister Piquette (Stacey's age) and of her children, by fire: "she was stoned out of her mind, most likely" (237). Valentine (born on 14 February) is another kind of "love child," another stranger, like all the Tonnerres. Stacey's tacit response to her of course embraces Buckle as well, for it is another requiem:

> Even her presence is a reproach to me, for all I've got now and have been given and still manage to bitch on and on about it. And a reproach for the sins of my fathers, maybe. The debts are inherited and how could the damage ever be undone or forgiven? . . . Piquette and her kids, and the snow and fire. (237)

Val tells of her own imminent departure—"Long trip. The last one" (238). Stacey's mention of Mac and Richalife triggers Val's last disclosure, that Thor Thorlakson was little snot-nosed Vernon Winkler back in Manawaka. Stacey sees that Thor's persecution of Mac was really aimed at herself in fear that she might recognize and expose him. Relieved, she thinks to herself as she parts company with the Tonnerre girl, "God of *thunder*. Vernon Winkler" (241; my italics)—a multivalent pun. Margaret drops a corner of the protective "Indian" blanket over Thor/Vernon, another "stranger," alienated from birth, like poor Buckle and all the post-Riel Métis.

Margaret was as reluctant to create an Ebenezer Scrooge character as she was an Iago. Experience causes change in both Mac and Stacey, but they remain quite recognizable as the two we have always known. Stacey has not forgotten Luke Venturi and continues to appeal to him in her imagination as Rachel Cameron appealed to the departed Nick Kazlik in *A Jest of God*; but there is more than frustration and helpless appeal in her tacit utterances, such (especially) as this: "Oh Luke. I want to go home, but I can't, because this is home" (227).[9] The ability to make that important recognition is shared with Mac. As he looks back at Thor's needling and blatant mistreatment (at their final Richalife party), he considers quitting the job but reasons as she did: "I don't see how I can stay and yet I don't see how I can leave, either" (235). Stacey's reverie resonates with special significance: "*The place is a prison, but not totally so. It must be an island . . . where people are free to walk around but nobody can get away. . . . and there is nowhere to go but here*" (235).

As Nine moves to its close, Mac's father stumbles on the stairs and falls. Stacey and Duncan help him up, and she tells "Dad," as she can now call him, that he must come and live with them. Mac reluctantly agrees, "there's nothing else we can do" (259). Ten reveals that Mac's brush cut has completely grown out and that he is to be the new local manager as Thor has been called to the main office in Montreal. At the beach Duncan is almost drowned (Duncan/Jonah threatened with death by water); Ian rescues him and gets unusual praise ("You did fine.") from Mac (268); Duncan later returns to the water. Jen speaks![10] Stacey observes:

> I was wrong to think of the trap as the four walls. It's the world. The truth is that I haven't been Stacey Cameron for one hell of a long time now. Although in some ways I'll always be her, because that's how I started out. But from now on, the dancing goes on only in the head. (275)

At the end we have the necessary reprise of the nursery rhyme "Ladybird, ladybird" with one miniscule but significant adjustment—

> Fly away home;
> Your house is on fire,
> Your children are . . .

At last, not "gone." Stacey then utters the truth about fire with her question, "Will the fires go on, inside and out? Until the moment when they go out for me, the end of the world" (279). Of course.

The element of fire in the novel is an equivalent of the element of water as in the story of Jonah. It is fire as it functions in the myth of the phoenix, not the exclusively destructive force that Stacey saw it as much of the time. In *The Fire-Dwellers*, fire is closer to the phenomenon manifest at Pentecost, when men spoke in tongues and were adorned with the flames of the Holy Ghost, the fire of divinity ("ah my dear"). Or, like the fire in one of Margaret's early African stories, "The Rain Child" (1962), where she refers to the frank recognition of human love: "Shoot an arrow," a young man would call to a pretty girl (or, later, "Fire a gun at me"), and she would briefly display all her beauty unadorned:

> Mother Nyame created the sun with fire, and arrows of the same fire were shot into the veins of mankind and became life-blood. I could have said that the custom was a reminder that women are the source of life. But I did not . . .—why should they care about anything other than the beat of their own blood?[11]

In *The Fire-Dwellers* the element of fire is the *élan vital*, the life force, unless the absence of love (*agape*) perverts it, leaves it unredeemed and only destructive. Clara Thomas, the perceptive Laurence scholar and Margaret's friend, made the point simply:

> Stacey has to recognize once and for all that, dangerous and frightening as the fire-element is, neither she nor the ones she loves can move to or live in any other. Her own weeks of intensified flame [with Luke Venturi] have, however, had a clarifying effect on her.[12]

In answer to a letter from Purdy full of such crusty observations as "you can't run scared all the time, or a large part of it, or you won't get much outa life, which is the only life we have," Margaret wrote a lengthy reply.

> I personally do believe that we are all living dangerously all the time, but whereas this thought once made me exceedingly anxious, it no longer does so. The Fire-Dwellers represents to some degree . . . how I feel now about some things—at least in the latter part of it with some kind of acceptance—no, not acceptance, more like the feeling that the world is a bloody terrifying place and life is terrifying but this is a thought which can be looked at without shattering the individual self.[13]

It is very nearly the idea, or attitude, that saves in Forster's words.

Margaret wrote to Al Purdy when she felt the novel was "moving at last" to complain that "the old narrative methods won't any longer work—too slow and not *immediate* enough" (my italics).[14] There are three features of the narrative technique in *Fire-Dwellers* that account for the novel's ability to involve the readers' sympathetic response. The first is Margaret's reliance on dramatic presentation: the action comes to us, to a considerable extent, immediately, via the dialogue between characters who are simply there before us. Second, there is the contribution of narrative point of view—who tells the story and from what angle of vision. It is a combination of third-person narrative and first person. Clearly, the novel relies heavily on Stacey's idiom and point of view. It opens with the nursery rhyme ("Ladybird, ladybird") and then gives us Stacey's (first-person) comment: "Crazy rhyme. Got it on the brain this morning. . . . Why anybody would want to teach a kid a thing like that, I wouldn't know." And so on. The next paragraph shifts to third person, but it uses the familiar device of the mirror to reflect Stacey's view of things, Stacey's angle of vision: "The full-length mirror is on the bedroom door. Stacey sees images reflected there, distorted by the glass. . . ." The third-person narrative in *The Fire-Dwellers* is typically of this sort, a kind of camouflaged first-person narrative point of view that seems to dominate the narrative although it is third person throughout. It is like having two related versions of Stacey's own story; therefore, sympathy with the narrator/heroine is enhanced: the authority of the "omniscient" third-person narrator is diminished, and the dramatic immediacy of the presentation is strengthened.

The initial first-person narrative of the opening paragraph quoted above ("Crazy rhyme") becomes the kind of "internal dialogue" found in *A Jest of God*: "Maybe it's okay, though. Prepares them for what they can expect. Stacey, you sure are joyful first thing in the morning. First thing hell. It's a quarter to nine, and here's me not dressed yet." This development is a complementary dramatic aspect of the presentation. The reader witnesses, immediately, Stacey's very personal struggles with herself, and the augmented dramatic mode makes possible more intimate sympathy with her. Some important breadth is given to this "internal dialogue" (in which the saner, calmer Stacey corrects and criticizes the more impetuous and frantic Stacey) by the occasional substitution of God for one of the Staceys: the would-be dieter, confronted by Tess Fogler's shortbread, layer cake, and three-inch mocha icing, exclaims (tacitly), "Shut up, God. I feel too lousy not to eat" (78). Later, she ponders death and her lifeless life: "Something should happen before it's too late. Idiot-child, what more could happen? What more do you want? You've got—yeh, I know, God. No need to write me a list. And I'm grateful. . . . Don't let anything terrible happen to the kids" (114). We come to know Stacey as we see her struggling with herself and her problems, and with her God as well as with her better self. She is truly a sister to Rachel with her difficult God.

The third aspect of Margaret's narrative technique in *The Fire-Dwellers* is something she learned in part from lyric poetry, although she employs it in her fiction to satisfy a particular need in the interest of conveying real life. She says again, "The old narrative forms won't work any longer," and she frets about how to write her story "as it really is."[15] On 6 June 1967, she had asked Purdy, rhetorically, "how to get across the multiplicity of everything." She offered him a light-hearted but revealing answer four months later:

> Thought I had discovered a sensational new narrative method the other evening—there was only one thing wrong with it; in practice, it proved to be unreadable. Thought of it in terms of the inner and outer going on simultaneously, side by side on the page—fine if you had a two-foot wide page and a reader with four eyes.[16]

"Simultaneously" is the key word.

The effect of Stacey's numerous nostalgic flashbacks to her life as a girl in Manawaka, to being a youngster and a teenager at Diamond

Lake, to the earliest of her experiences with Mac, all these interrupt the pell-mell flow of the present to give us views of the past at the same time, so to speak. In so doing Margaret creates a fuller sense of Stacey Cameron MacAindra, "all at once." Late in the novel Stacey emphasizes that technique in observing (as Hagar did in *The Stone Angel*) that although she hasn't been "Stacey Cameron" for a long time, "in some ways I'll always be her, because that's how I started out" (272). Repetitions in the texture of the novel are sometimes a means of character development, as when Thor Thorlakson repeats, virtually verbatim, his autobiographical testimonial to the gratifying effects of Richalife products in Five (129) what he uttered in Two (34-35). Stacey comments to herself, "Does he just press his navel and the record switches on?" But such repetitions also reinforce the impression of stasis, of arrested chronological development, simultaneity. Shortly after her recognition that Stacey will in some sense always be Stacey Cameron, she returns to bed and "On the bedroom chair rests a jumble of Stacey's clothes . . . stockings like nylon puddles, roll-on girdle in the shape of a tire . . ." (277). It is a detailed echo of the first third-person paragraph at the opening of the book that completes the whole cycle, just as an effective lyric poem sustains itself through echo and other means of repetition to an ending that carries with it the impact of the whole poem instantaneously—or simultaneously—that has preceded it: "I measure time by how a body sways," "Before the indifferent beak could let her drop," "Death, thou shalt die."

This last aspect of Margaret's technique in *The Fire-Dwellers* complements what it is employed to express, Stacey's complete epiphany about the inescapable wholeness of life. Stacey has learned the importance of "getting the big picture," of seeing life steadily and seeing it whole; and the technique of approximating simultaneity shows us, along with Stacey, what that picture is—held as still but filled as full as can be. There is nowhere to go but here.

Margaret was vehement in her denial of autobiographical influence in *The Fire-Dwellers*. She was, by this time, well enough known to be recognized as similar to Stacey MacAindra, at least superficially—a young, middle-aged Canadian mother and homemaker associated (in spite of her dwelling in England) with Vancouver and having a prairie background. *The Fire-Dwellers* evidently takes place in 1966. As soon as Margaret had Rachel's novel finished and off her hands in August 1965, she turned to Stacey's; and it was her basic concern. That December Margaret wrote to Nadine Jones Asante about the acceptance of *A Jest of God* and added,

> the next one will have to be broader, better, etc. . . . It's the same goddam novel I asked you to light candles for, about 3 years ago [i.e., *Fire-Dwellers*]. Maybe one of these days it will get going. Or maybe I will sink into the swamp of those who are too scared and who therefore drink too much—in the end it amounts to this—if you are too frightened to live, you will die and that is that.[17]

Not only is that a recognizable sketch of Stacey and a brief statement of the theme of her novel, it also serves to establish 1966 as the crucial year of creation of *The Fire-Dwellers*.

In that year Margaret turned forty, and Stacey in the novel is thirty-nine; while Margaret had just two children to Stacey's four, Jocelyn Laurence turned fourteen in 1966, and Katie MacAindra is fourteen; David Laurence was eleven that year and the only son, whereas Ian is ten and Duncan seven—yet Ian suffers the loss by death of his friend Peter Challoner as David lost a friend of his. The relationship between David and his father closely resembles that between the MacAindra boys and Mac. More important is the similarity between the Margaret-Jack relationship and the Stacey-Mac relationship. The name "Mac" echoes "Jack," but is probably just a coincidence (though a noticeable one), as "Stacey" very faintly echoes "Peggy." Margaret's guilt about failing as wife and mother, especially in her unwillingness to accompany Jack wherever his jobs took him, is reflected in Stacey's feelings of guilt throughout the novel, beginning in One, where she wishes she "could only go away and leave him [Mac] alone, take the sword off his neck" (19); Margaret wrote Nadine Jones Asante that Jack "*did* feel I was a millstone, and also the kids, and used to say he could not work where he wanted to, etc. . . ."[18] Ironically, Margaret saw, and enabled Stacey to see, that the role of father was an important one. Still pondering separation from Jack in the fall of 1967, Margaret confronted the question, "Can I cut the kids off from him? . . . Especially David, who (although J[ack] doesn't realize it) needs him much more than Jocelyn does."

> David relies on me for all the day-to-day reassurance and affection, but he needs Jack in other ways that are terribly important—as a kind of confirmation of his own ideas of what a man should be; as someone whose opinions he values very much more than he values mine (he knows I approve of him whatever he's like), but his father's approval is gained with much more difficulty and is therefore much more valued.[19]

Part of Mac's problem is Stacey's disagreement with him on parental discipline. When Ian has been shaken by his near accident and has locked himself in his room, Mac is about to go up and demand proper behaviour. Stacey vigorously restrains him.

> Mac removes her hand from his sleeve. He turns and walks into his study.
>
> Okay. Have it your way, Stacey. Do anything you like with them. Ruin them, for all I care. (193)

Stacey is pleased at Mac's interest in the wooden car Ian has made, but notes it is an exception: "It's good when it's like that. . . . Ian needs it so much. He doesn't give a damn for my approval. He knows he's got it anyway. It's Mac's he needs" (50).

Jack Laurence's initial response to the birth of Jocelyn and then to the birth of David was, as we have seen, a chill indifference; and that indifference apparently recurred; at least, so it seemed to Margaret. She understood his need to reduce the amount he contributed for the support of the children, but there were other chilly demonstrations—and quite the sort we have seen in Mac's performance. When the Laurences were considering a holiday in 1968 and the options were Ireland and Italy, Jack favoured Ireland as the less expensive excursion, but Margaret, Jocelyn, and David wanted the sun of Italy; Margaret footed the bill for the difference in cost. On their return from Italy she reported to Adele:

> you know, this is very hard on him, really. . . . He keeps telling me I've made more than he has in the past several years and alas that is true. By a fluke in my terms, but he doesn't see that. Maybe I just should have gone to Ireland. . . . He has decided, apparently, to opt out re: theories of kid-rearing, and says he leaves it all to me, which makes me feel about 2000% more responsible than I want to feel, although he is doing it with the right feelings, in his terms, as he thinks we disagree so he's given up, and where does this leave me? He is so terribly tolerant. . . .[20]

Margaret's generosity in that letter persists with her further characterization of Jack for Adele (in familiar terms):

> I guess I would find him easier if he made more mistakes, but he generally doesn't. He doesn't ever drink too much or get overtly angry—if he's angry, it is all kept inside. He never wastes money, as I do. He's physically so fit, unlike me . . . fit and hardworking and a really good person . . . —and I am speaking truly seriously—and he makes me feel such a slob. He doesn't mean to—I know that.

Mac MacAindra is recognizable in those lines, reminiscent of such scenes as Duncan's bad dream near the end of One—

> And didn't your mother ever get up in the night when you had a bad dream?
>
> I didn't have any bad dreams that I can think of.
>
> I don't believe you. You've forgotten.
>
> I'm not in the habit of forgetting.
>
> . . . .
>
> Mac—don't be angry.
>
> I'm not angry.
>
> You are.
>
> Stacey, I am not angry. I am merely trying to point out that you are babying that boy. . . . (23)

This is the sort of intercourse that *looks* like "communication" but is in fact a denial, and a denial that chills and frustrates Stacey and makes her feel at times like a non-person.

Silence was something Margaret specifically mentioned to Adele in discussing the possibility of going to the University of Toronto as writer-in-residence: she knew it would be instructive to find out what writers twenty years her junior have to say about the "human dilemma," "what they cannot, however, know, is the unmeasurable—the way the pain feels twenty years after . . . (the silences between people who had vowed communication)."[21] Earlier that fall she had raised the question of accepting such a post at Dalhousie University and confessed to Adele that she lacked the courage to confront her own Agamemnon—the voice of Duty (when he speaks): "to be quite frank with you, I am petrified about a face-to-face encounter with him over this basic problem . . . what is hard to assail is an authority which one subconsciously feels to be unassailable."[22]

A revealing detail of Stacey's relationship with Luke might be overlooked except that Margaret repeats it. At the outset of their first two meetings, she rather abruptly asks, "What do you do?" (160); next, just after her confession about Mac as Agamemnon, she asks, "What's he do, your dad?" Luke then observes, "People always want to know what a guy does. I wonder why is that?" (177). Margaret knew the answer. She had written Adele a little confession about the tendency "to evaluate oneself in relation to work, rather than in relation to oneself as a person, because (at least . . . for me) one is very apprehensive about the latter kind of evaluation. Scared."[23] Stacey's sensitivity resembles Margaret's own.

Peggy had sought and thought she had found in Jack Laurence an authority who would give her his approval, which she worked steadily to win. That is very nearly Stacey's situation. Of course, Jack Laurence was not necessarily just exactly the person portrayed in Mac MacAindra, but much rather the person portrayed most frequently in Margaret's letters—as he appeared to her. Her perception of Jack contributed salient features to her depiction of Mac. As Margaret was "protective" of her fictional characters, she was doubly careful about giving the impression that her fiction depicted her own life and the people in it. Hence, her stern denial of the autobiographical element.

Margaret did acknowledge (particularly to Adele Wiseman and Al Purdy) how close to autobiographical *The Fire-Dwellers* actually was. She wrote to Purdy soon after the novel went to the publishers, "we are living dangerously all the time": "*The Fire-Dwellers* represents to some degree the way I felt when living in Vancouver, . . . constantly threatened by prospects of doom and destruction, . . . it also represents how I feel now about some things. . . ."[24] Two weeks later, the same to Adele: "All I am doing, . . . is reiterating in my personal terms some of the themes which were dealt with better, because more distanced from myself and put into someone else, in my novel . . . (the main character definitely *not* being me, and yet we have a hell of a lot in common). . . ."[25]

Margaret evidently decided to make the best of what was given. She grasped reconciliation with Jack (he would be away much of the time anyway) and got on with Stacey's story. The last months of writing seemed to bring Margaret the reward of her decision. In February of 1968, she told Adele, "I don't need to return to Canada to live—only to visit, sometimes," and further that she is "more settled in mind than for 3-5 years . . . renaissance of feeling between Jack and myself. . . ."[26] A month later, the novel completed, she informed Adele that "Jack left today for British Honduras . . . miraculously we seem closer than in many years, which is like a kind of unexpected gift." In the postscript, another reward: Jocelyn has a boyfriend.[27] She would remain in her beloved Elm Cottage. Her guilt regarding Jack was soothed: she was in her "place" as wife and homemaker for him whenever he was there in Penn. She explained to Adele, "what I've got here isn't ideal but it is real"[28]—or *there is nowhere to go but here.*

Able to work out Stacey's dilemma, Margaret could work out her own. The comedic denouement of Stacey's problems reflects Margaret's sense of resolving her own, not a "happy ever after" answer but a manageable one, *real.*

Is *The Fire-Dwellers*, then, really fiction or is it autobiography? Yes, both at the same time. Margaret provided a more useful answer. Looking back over her work from *This Side Jordan* to *The Fire-Dwellers*, she saw "it has all been an expression of my scene. . . ."

> In other words, what I was trying to get at, in this new novel, was a dilemma which I have personally felt and that's why I wanted to do it, but which I also recognize as one which very many women of my age must experience. I didn't pick it because it would have a wide appeal. . . . I wrote because it was there to be written.[29]

This is a "key" to her ability to treat her subjective, personal material in an objective way. Whatever *The Fire-Dwellers* did for Margaret personally and privately—in its autobiographical mode—it became, once published, a public representation of the human condition that is capable of awakening a wide sympathetic response because of the truth of the depiction.

One aspect of Margaret is missing from Stacey—her being a writer. The missing aspect has been deflected onto Luke Venturi, budding author of the *Greyfolk* fiction. Another specific detail so deflected is Luke's astrological sign: he is a Cancer, as Margaret was. To give those features to Stacey would be to risk giving away the whole autobiographical show and also complicating the development of Stacey, who has quite enough on her plate. The brief love affair that Stacey has with Cancer-author Luke may be a reflection of Margaret's devotion to her Cancer-author personal self. The busy homemaker-mother-wife-*and writer* all in one is a creation that "may be taken up or not, later."

In the meantime, Margaret could ponder her claim that what she had *here* might not be ideal but was real: she might need to define "real" more carefully and "ideal" as well, and decide whether "here" meant exclusively Penn, Bucks. She might face the question of where she could truly feel at home: "Home?" She had written Adele Wiseman, "I'm never likely to be entirely at home anywhere, but I do love this place [Elm Cottage] more than I can remember loving any other place except the house I was born in."[30] Margaret knew, of course, the familiar warning "You can't go home again." She once commented on that, "On the other hand, is it so certain that one can't? Not in the sense of home as you once knew it, but in another sense."[31]

Come on, Stacey. Home.

fourteen

Home

MARGARET'S DECISION TO BE RECONCILED WITH HER HUSBAND at the end of October 1967 evidently released the Stacey Cameron MacAindra novel, as though her own life and Stacey's needed to be in step to achieve resolution of their common domestic problem. Stacey needed to recognize "There is nowhere to go but here"; Margaret, "what I have here is not ideal but it is real." She wrote Adele, "I am not able to believe in rebirth and everything suddenly being okay, but only in trying to do the best we can with what we have."[1] She felt justified in the reconciliation: the novel flowed freely and the guilt was assuaged.

That letter to Adele, written less than three months after taking the decision, nevertheless reveals Margaret's oscillation over her situation. She and Jack were scheduled to leave on the thirteenth of January for two weeks in Spain, alone, leaving Jocelyn and David with the Charletts. Margaret was urgently hopeful that the trip would be a success, especially for Jack. Not only did she feel persistent guilt for failing to be the wife he needed, but she regretted that the reconciliation had not awakened in her a fuller commitment to Jack. She confessed to Adele that she was keeping something back, "an enormous reserve,"

> like saying, "I'm yours, but I keep my own bank account and intend to go on being responsible for my own livelihood, and I own this house, not you. . . ." Maybe my mistake was in making too much of a total commitment, 20 years ago, and then slowly edging away from it. . . . yet I can't bear to part with him. . . .[2]

She decided not to take the children to Canada that year: she and Jack are part of a family and with the children will go to Europe together, all four, "and share expenses." That statement begins conditionally: "If Jack and I are going to. . . ." Margaret seemed to be forcing herself into the dutiful role: the letter ends with a postscript, "it is a very good thing to have Jack back again in England."

She still found self-effacing excuses for Jack's dubious behaviour. In mid-October 1967, when Dalhousie University beckoned, she asked Jack's permission to take the children to Canada and suggested he stop their allowance, but took care not to imply he was not needed. His response was that if he died tomorrow it would be good to feel he wasn't essential to anyone. "I *know* it's emotional blackmail," she acknowledged; "—God, Adele, I know, but he doesn't know he's doing that."[3] Jack's next letter said he realized that "if I had to give up anything, it certainly wouldn't be him. I cannot bear this any longer," she wailed to Adele. "I have hurt him more than any human being ought ever to hurt any other." *That* ploy led to the reconciliation and her report of Jack's generosity: "he's willing to accept me as a separate and real person if I'm willing to accept myself as that."[4] How could she refuse such an offer!

Margaret and Jack spent the latter half of January 1968 in Spain. She wrote Adele that it was "very good,"[5] and felt no need to live in Canada. The tone was of a dutiful Margaret (all is okay). Two quiet items seemed to contradict that tone: "there is some chance I may be in Canada in 69," and Margaret's hopes to do three more Vanessa MacLeod stories. *Fire-Dwellers* was near completion.

On the day Margaret completed *The Fire Dwellers* (10 March 1968),

Jack left for British Honduras for some three months. She reported that "miraculously we seem closer than in many years, which is like a kind of unexpected gift,"[6] and turned immediately to revision and typing Stacey's novel. The University of Toronto invited Margaret to come as writer-in-residence for 1969-70. Jack not only agreed that she should accept the invitation but assured her he would be in England, at his base in Surbiton, during her absence and would spend as many weekends as possible in Penn. She sent her acceptance to Jack Sword, acting president during the absence of President Claude Bissell. Constance Sword, wife of the acting president, had been a teacher at Neepawa Collegiate Institute when Margaret was a student there; they had curled together during those winters.[7] That relationship facilitated arrangements in Toronto.

Delighted, Margaret wrote to Adele, "Five years ago I would have been scared stiff to contemplate such a job, and if I had, Jack would certainly never have agreed to put himself out in any way to make it possible, as he then believed a woman's place was etc etc."[8] The Toronto invitation, furthermore, was a useful compromise: Margaret could return to Canada on a temporary basis and be back "in her place" after the visit. She was not evading her duty, and Jack was being generous. Margaret's desire to return to Canada was part of a growing need to feel secure about who she really was and where she truly belonged. She knew the roles of wife and mother, but her position as a writer was an inescapable commitment and not just a role; was it enough of an identity?

At Easter vacation she took Jocelyn and David on the promised trip to Scotland. They had first been into the Highlands almost exactly three years earlier. This time they went initially to the Scottish Lowlands, to Burntisland on the Firth of Forth, "the village in Fifeshire where my people came from."[9] This was not the quest of 1965, "In Pursuit of My Past," but perhaps a sequel—"In Pursuit of *My People's* Past." She had wanted to complete the series of semi-autobiographical short stories featuring Vanessa MacLeod. The trip to Burntisland might move her to write the three stories needed to finish the job.[10]

They went through Dundee into the Highlands, stopping at Kincraig in Inverness-shire to see Balavil, the abandoned house of James Macpherson. Margaret felt a distinct affinity with this translator of old Gaelic poetry from "the still-surviving oral literature of the Highlands," and was eager to defend him against Samuel Johnson's claim that he had perpetrated a hoax. She assured Adele that "Dr. Johnson just did not know bugger all about oral literature," and asserted her own authority: "I know quite a bit about African oral literature, but nothing yet about Scots, and that literature came out of the same conditions, roughly, as the African—i.e. a tribal situation in a non-mechanized but culturally highly developed area."[11] James Macpherson had been engaged, Margaret felt, in exactly the sort of activity she had undertaken in translating, and giving more permanent form to, works of the Somali oral tradition. A two-volume edition of *The Works of Ossian*, ordered from an Edinburgh bookseller, was in her hands before the middle of May, and it confirmed her belief that Macpherson had "got a raw deal from Dr. Johnson." She added a teasing comment that hints at some future development. She affirmed to Adele that she is not "getting hooked on Gaelic epics. . . . I'm really interested in it for another reason—nothing specific, but just a general feeling that it will come into something, sometime."[12]

Margaret spent a weekend in Brighton with Alex and Delores Baron after finishing the typescript of *The Fire-Dwellers*. The murder of Robert Kennedy hit Margaret hard as it drew together several signs of grief that had grabbed her attention. Purdy's collection *The New Romans* came out with her poignant tale about the death of Joe Bass in Detroit. She was still full of sympathy with Stacey MacAindra's life as a woman entering middle age and worrying about her children. At the end of June, Jocelyn was smitten with acute appendicitis; hurriedly summoned, the doctor announced the appendix was about to burst and prepared her for immediate surgery in High Wycombe

Hospital. Margaret cabled Jack, who phoned Jocelyn at once; Margaret comfortably wrote Adele to say that she "knew all over again that he really is the only human being upon whom I can really call in crises affecting my children."[13]

The appendectomy was a success and Jocelyn healed quickly. Margaret sent jovial greetings to Adele on Canada Day: "HAPPY JULY FIRST!" and announced she was on the way to High Wycombe to see the patient. But the wound reopened and Jocelyn was faced with almost a week of new recovery. Margaret's letter of 8 July to Adele notes that Jack was not home yet from British Honduras, but she could use his presence to help with Jocelyn, and also for his own sake as "I guess I do love him, eh?" Finally, she "just realized that in 10 days time" she will be forty-two and thus "married to Jack for exactly half my life." That mix of emotions rallied Margaret and the children to rise early on the 25th and hustle off to the airport to meet Jack, due to arrive at 7:00 a.m.

The reunited family planned a trip for late August. Jack wanted to go to Ireland; the other three voted for sunny northern Italy, a more expensive venture but Margaret would pay the difference. She had just sold a severely abridged version of *The Fire-Dwellers* to the *Ladies Home Journal*. The Laurences spent twelve days based at a posh hotel on Lake Como, 17-29 August.[14] A success, except for Margaret's intestinal discomfort, which she attributed to tension. "Tension over what?" the family wanted to know.[15] It was partly due to her usual postpartum response to finishing a novel, but also to the month of adjustment that followed Jack's return. The adjustment included a good deal of talk about Margaret's temporary return to Canada as well as a certain amount of Jack's reminiscing about his childhood, of which he had heretofore disclosed little more than the broad outlines. The two topics inevitably went together: Margaret's attitude to Canada was regularly mixed with, and vexed by, her attitude to Jack, and both attitudes were complicated by her writing. To understand those depended on Margaret's discovering who she really was and where she properly belonged.

What she required grew increasingly clear to her during the latter part of 1967 at the approach of her return to Canada. Many of her letters to Al Purdy in those months pondered that eventuality. "What has been bugging me . . . for months now, is that I really do not belong in this country, Al."[16] She listed reasons why life would be better for her and the children: educational opportunities, reduced isolation and improved social contacts, reimmersion in the Canadian idiom and even in Canadian culture! But the voice of duty was strong, and she determined to do what her conscience dictated. Her analysis of the impulse to deny duty's call is interesting: she had been distracted by the seductive appeal of the money Dalhousie University was offering; her desire to return to Canada was a camouflaged desire to return to Jack; finally, "All this nonsense" was a subtle attempt to evade working on the novel! The suppressed Laurentian tendency that so resembled the attitudes of William Blake and Henry James would have led her to some such declaration as, "What I want to do defines who I am, and where I want to be will help me to realize who I am."

A year later, in the autumn of 1968, Margaret moved, almost unwittingly, toward such a declaration as she became aware that this period of her life was one of profound change. At the beginning of the year she had declared to Adele realistically, as she glanced at her fortunate reconciliation with Jack, that she did not believe in rebirth and everything suddenly changed for the better. In October she had slightly different words to send to Al Purdy as she reaffirmed the reconciliation, a bit left-handedly: "I'm not really ready to make any kind of leap again, as I did in 1962 when I came here, but I'm not any longer trying to accept the fact that nothing can change—it will, and when the right time comes, I guess I'll know." She closed the letter with a apparent non sequitur: she had seen the film of *A Jest of God* ("My characters and my town") and was very favourably impressed by it and by Joanne Woodward, with whom she had lunched a few days earlier in London.[17]

Plans for Toronto were being firmed up, but her vacillation

continued. She summed up her frustration succinctly for Purdy: "I love the damn country, that's the trouble."[18] Jack was in Malawi for the month of November and Margaret completed the rewriting of *Jason's Quest* and awaited reviews of *Long Drums and Cannons*. She told Adele she had planted ten new rosebushes, and added that she had planted herself there in Penn as well. The oscillation resumed; "I realized all over again how much I love this goddam ramshackle house," but "I'm never likely to be entirely at home anywhere, . . . but I do love this place more than I can remember any other place except the house I was born in." Yet, she dismisses her notions about a return to Canada as, once again, a fantasy, an escape: all four Laurences cosy in "a lovely little A-frame on the edge of a lake . . . happily ever after, in the garden of Eden, when we were all young again." Her self-mockery is an echo of Stacey's in *The Fire-Dwellers*; "Come on, Stacey. Home" (155-56). Margaret braces up and bravely declares that what she has here, at Elm Cottage, "isn't ideal but it is real."[19]

Adele's report that she had seen and in general approved of the film *Rachel, Rachel*[20] nudged Margaret to take another look at the stories about Vanessa MacLeod, though she told Adele that she "dreaded" starting work on them.[21] Certainly they were very personal and quite relevant to her current dilemma about the return to Canada. Then Al Purdy sent his favourable report on the film.[22] Margaret's response is revealing, maybe as revealing to her as it is to us. She told Purdy that she liked the film, too, and was especially struck by signs in the movie like "Manawaka Theatre" and by the cemetery and the Cameron family stone in black granite: "that goddam stone could have been my family's burial stone."[23] She was reminded of her last visit to Neepawa, in the late summer of 1966, and of her thoughts at the family gravestone, of "my father and mother being skeletons somewhere there, quite meaninglessly, for if they exist at all (and they do—all the ancestors do) it is not in crumbling calcium bone but in my head." That was a strong nudge toward *home*, in the representative form of Manawaka, and Margaret was ready to give her attention to completing the series of Vanessa MacLeod stories at the end of 1968. Al and Eurithe Purdy were about to bring Canada a bit closer as they pursued their European tour and promised to visit Margaret in Penn; accounts of their walking the streets of Athens raised her envy, and with it memories that touched on Canadian matters as well.

The new year began with news that sharpened Margaret's sense that she had indeed arrived at a moment of change: Adele, on the brink of forty, was pregnant; Margaret was filled with excitement and yearning sympathy with her old friend and Adele's partner, Dmitry Stone. Oddly, her New Year's letter to Adele announced confidently that she had only one more book left to write and that she had always had that kind of clairvoyance about her work. Three years earlier, while at work on *A Jest of God*, she had told Adele she planned on doing two or three more books: i.e., *The Fire-Dwellers*, the series of Vanessa stories, and another (she did not specify them, however).[24] Two years after that, with *A Jest* behind her, she wrote Purdy that she wanted to try "about three more novels."[25] She had been publishing the Vanessa stories since 1963 and had envisioned a series of ten; she now realized there would be only eight. "I just think I am undergoing some kind of metamorphosis," she confided to Adele, "and I'm not sure what's going to emerge, but I'm curiously optimistic."[26] She exuberantly sent Adele and Dmitry a bagful of advice on the pregnancy and also a check for $1000. Dmitry Stone's divorce was imminent and sure to be costly. Margaret explained that McMaster University was about to purchase the manuscript of *The Fire-Dwellers* and she felt generous. Adele, Dmitry, and his eldest son did not reject Margaret's gift: they each ate a third of it. Adele pronounced the adventure "the most satisfying money I've ever eaten."[27] In January Margaret shared with Adele plans for her academic year at Massey College, University of Toronto, and added quietly, "This is a turning point":

> I am coming to the immediate end of my backlog of writing. . . . for 14 years I have been going like a bomb, trying to catch up on what was there to be written. I have now caught up, or

> nearly. I have only one short story left to write, and then I will have written myself out of my past.[28]

A week later Jack left for a nine-month tour in Swaziland. Margaret told Adele, "we will not see each other until I come home next Christmas."[29] Margaret had begun preparations for the last of the Vanessa MacLeod stories. She called it "Jericho's Brick Battlements." The title seems to promise a sequel to *This Side Jordan*, and perhaps it is. By the first week of March she had a draft done; she wrote to Purdy that the whole collection of eight stories "really add up to a kind of character sketch of an old Irish-Protestant puritanical authoritarian pioneer from Ontario, who happened to be my grandfather. What a terrible man he was."[30]

Constructing this collection spanned most of a decade and actually brackets the creation of the three other books of Manawaka fiction. The first of the Vanessa MacLeod stories, "The Sound of the Singing," was published a year before *The Stone Angel*; the last was published a year after *The Fire-Dwellers*. The collection is strongly autobiographical, a fictionalized depiction of the two immediate strands of Margaret's family: the Connors are based on the Simpsons, and the MacLeods on the Wemysses. Vanessa is thus Margaret's alter ego. During creation of her other heroines, Hagar, Rachel, and Stacey, she frequently recurred to the development of that alter ego as though the two activities were somehow necessarily parallel. Whatever she was doing (for herself) in working with the other three evidently depended on what she was doing in her semi-autobiographical recreation of the young life of Vanessa. That recreation is a series of cumulative rediscoveries, of revaluations, of Vanessa's experience between ages six and forty.

In spite of Margaret's describing *A Bird in the House* as a character sketch of her grandfather, Grandfather Connor in the book, the narrative is as much the story of Vanessa as the series of adventures narrated by Huckleberry Finn is the story of Huck himself. It is a dual narrative, young Vanessa's experiences as she remembers them years later but told as if by the girl at the time they occurred. The retrospective view makes possible the "revaluation" Kent Thompson mentioned in his review of the book in 1970:

> the adult narrator learns from what the child experienced and failed to understand. . . . This throws a great deal of stress upon the narrator, who has been learning throughout the book the very process of re-valuating [the young] Vanessa's judgements.[31]

What Margaret discovered that her Vanessa had learned aids our understanding of all her heroines, and of Margaret herself.

Grandfather Connor plays an important role in Vanessa's life, as the very shape of the book makes clear: it begins and ends with his dominating influence. The role of another important man in her life, her father, is also emphasized by the shape of the book. The most substantial revision of the individual pieces for inclusion in the book (and on the whole she did very little revision) is the addition of some 500 words to "To Set Our House in Order" to strengthen the depiction of Vanessa's father, both in his position as a medical man and in his relation to his daughter.

The first half of the book concludes with the title story, "A Bird in the House," third in order of publication but moved to fourth in the collection. It is largely concerned with the relationship between Vanessa and her father and with the impact on her of his death. The second half of the book departs from the regular chronological development of Vanessa's career.[32] There are hints, from the earliest page (even in the opening sentence), of the retrospective nature of the narrative view, but the clearest adjustment in chronology occurs in the conclusion of "A Bird." Unlike the vague temporal reference in the last paragraph of "Mask of the Bear"—"Many years later . . ."—the last page of "A Bird" specifies "During the Second World War, when

I was seventeen . . ." and leads to Vanessa's coming to terms with the loss of her father when she was twelve: "Now that we might have talked together, it was many years too late," but "I grieved for my father as though he had just died now."[33]

The next two stories are the equivalent of flashbacks. "The Loons" begins with Vanessa at age eleven and ends with her at eighteen; "Horses of the Night" goes further back, to Vanessa at age six, and ends with her vaguely between eighteen and twenty. But both of them add to Vanessa's understanding and love of her father through testimonials given her by Piquette Tonnerre in "The Loons"—"Your dad was the only person in Manawaka that ever done anything good to me" (124)—and by Chris in "Horses"—"I used to talk with Ewen sometimes. He didn't see what I was driving at, mostly, but he'd always listen, you know? You don't find many guys like that" (149). Such comments reinforce Vanessa's observation in "A Bird in the House" that "Everything changed after my father's death" (110), and again in "Horses" that "After my father died, the whole order of my life was torn" (144). The loss of her father is associated, in "A Bird," with the loss of a house, the MacLeod house,

> when it was no longer ours, and when the Virginia creeper had been torn down and the dark walls turned to a light marigold, I went out of my way to avoid walking past, for it seemed to me that the house had lost the stern dignity that was its very heart. (111)

This passage is an artfully placed anticipation of the opening of the final story: "the Brick House . . . was a fine place for visiting. To live there, however, was unthinkable. This would probably never have been necessary, if my father had not died suddenly that winter" (173).

Vanessa's struggle with Grandfather Connor is a major theme in the book. It was to escape his clutches that Vanessa yearned to leave Manawaka and pursue her independence. Yet success in that pursuit depends on coming to terms with him. Not all the major themes are immediately associated with Grandfather Connor. The most prominent is announced by the title both of the book and of the story of Vanessa's father's death. Noreen utters the old wives' saw that "A bird in the house means a death in the house" (102).[34] The book is full of birds and of death. Indeed, death is the focus of each of the seven pieces that follow "The Sound of the Singing"; and we notice its understated role in that initial piece (announced in Vanessa's Sunday school text, "How are the Mighty fallen in the midst of battle") only after we have read the last one—and smile. The theme of the importance of recognizing mortality is ubiquitous in Margaret's fiction.

Another persistent theme is the importance of respecting Nature and the complementary evil of humanity's failure of that respect. Natural creatures figure in each of the five central stories and are identified in each title: Bear, Bird, Loon, Horse, and Husky. There is a distinct echo here of the opposition between Nature and intrusive civilization that begins in the sixth paragraph of *The Stone Angel.* That conflict appears early in "The Sound of the Singing," in Grandfather Connor's domain:

> On the lawn a few wild blue violets dared to grow, despite frequent beheadings from the clanking guillotine lawn mower, and mauve-flowered Creeping Charlie insinuated deceptively weak-looking tendrils up to the very edges of the flower beds where helmeted snapdragon stood in precision. (4)

There are no accompanying Cree in the shadows of the Connor spruce, but up at the MacLeod cottage on Diamond Lake one summer, Piquette Tonnerre, part Cree and part French-Canadian, makes her presence felt in young Vanessa's experience. She is kin to the boys Hagar Currie's brothers knew, as did her adored son John. Piquette, outcast and alien in her own land, is now reluctantly associated (by the naïve Vanessa) with the natural world, specifically and eloquently with the loons, which are driven away by encroaching civilization.

Quite apparent also is the related theme of alienation, with which

Vanessa is closely associated. It is a principal feature of Vanessa's developing self-recognition, her moving from Innocence through Experience of the recognized evil of the world and on to the state of Higher Innocence—a progress prominently portrayed by John Milton, William Blake, and Henry James.[35] Vanessa readily sympathizes with the alien creatures she encounters in Manawaka, from the "untidy old men who sat on the Bank of Montreal steps. . . . I was inexplicably drawn to them, too" (9) and the delightful old fraud, Uncle Dan, onward.[36] That sympathy figures largely in Piquette's story, "The Loons," and in Chris's story, "Horses of the Night," and less obviously in "A Bird in the House," with Ewen MacLeod's yearning to escape, expressed both in his library of travel literature and in the late-discovered liaison he enjoyed during the Great War. That yearning, product of alienation, anticipates Vanessa's.

The other obvious alien figure is Harvey Shinwell of "Half-Husky," who is about as unattractive a character as was Buckle Fennick (*Fire-Dwellers*) or Grandfather Connor. What we know of Harvey is that he is as much a victim of the social organization as Buckle Fennick. The symbolic relationship of Harvey and the dog Nanuk is obvious: both are abused victims, both are made vicious by nefarious treatment, both are turned into creatures not "safe to go free" (172), as Jon Kertzer nicely observes.[37] The last word of the story clarifies Vanessa's puzzled sympathy. She learns that Nanuk has been chloroformed, that Harvey has been released from jail but likely to go right back in, and that, as for Harvey's caretaker, well, here is what the story says: "I used to see his aunt occasionally on the street. She was considered safe to go free. Once she said hello to me. I did not reply, although I knew that this was probably not fair, either" (172). In the next and final story Vanessa recognizes that she does indeed resemble her Grandfather Connor.

Margaret made one very significant change in "Half-Husky" when she prepared it for publication in *A Bird in the House*. Originally, the English title was "Nanuk" and the French translation "Le bâtard" (perhaps best of the three);[38] the change highlighted the resemblance between mixed-breed Nanuk and bastard Harvey Shinwell. It also highlights the similarity between those two and the Métis characters of the Manawaka Saga—and the "surrogate" Aboriginal/Métis in the saga, such as "Iroquois" Buckle.

Vanessa can sympathize readily with the alienated through her strength of imagination and her artist's sensitivity, and because she is possessed of the alien heart, the heart of a stranger, seeing she was herself an alien in the land of Manawaka, as was true of Vanessa's alter ego, Margaret Laurence.

The vigorous criticism of the social organization of Manawaka that Vanessa's view provides is fully compatible with Margaret's critical view of her Canadian home. In his 1970 review of *A Bird in the House*, Kent Thompson observes that "Vanessa was naturally [sic!] angered by the various 'religions' she had to face up to in Manawaka. . . . Vanessa quite rightly kicks at these unjust, unfair strictures."[39] Those "religions" include more than Presbyterians, Methodists, and Baptists: they include the religious devotion to hierarchical social structures, racial discriminations, and narrow moralism quite as fully. The trick, of course, is to avoid becoming a zealot oneself in one's opposition to such misguided "religions." Vanessa is blessed not only in her heart of an alien but in her artistic vision, and, like Margaret Laurence herself, she displays the association Henry James made to conclude his essay "The Art of Fiction": "There is one point at which the moral sense and the artistic sense lie very near together; that is in the light of the very obvious truth that the deepest quality of a work of art will always be the quality of the mind of the producer."[40] Vanessa learns to employ those two senses according to some such principle as "Beware of false representation." Bad moral behaviour and bad artistic performance are alike in being a kind of hypocrisy.[41] In this respect, too, she closely resembles Margaret.

The success of such guidance is affirmed by the comedic ending of the final story, "Jericho's Brick Battlements," and thus of the collection as a whole. The story is built principally on memories, from age twelve and a half to age forty, of her encounters with Grandfather Connor, the main agon of her existence. The earliest is of her driving with the old man in his MacLaughlin-Buick, "gazing with love and glory at my giant grandfather as he drove his valiant chariot through all the streets of this world" (179). A later memory is of the giant grandfather's apparent hatred of all love relationships; for example, of Aunt Edna and her Wes (which turned out happily) and of Vanessa and her already married airman Michael (which didn't); the latter relationship is repeated from "A Bird in the House" and so strengthens the connection between the two halves of the book and associates Vanessa's reconciliation with her father and his death with her need to be reconciled with her grandfather and his. Both resolutions are associated with Vanessa's third loss of an important man in her life.

The collection is structured to focus on Vanessa's increasing opposition to Grandfather Connor and her need finally to come to terms with him to effect the necessary denouement. Vanessa's mother says of her own relation to the stubborn old man, "It's like batting your head against a brick wall" (176); the simile indicates the particular significance of the story's title and echoes the earliest reference to the *Brick* House as an "embattled fortress" and a "massive monument" (3). Vanessa's response to Grandfather's treatment of her young airman augments the brick wall figure: "I shouted at him, as though if I sounded all my trumpets loudly enough, his walls would quake and crumble" (199). The opening of *A Bird* prepares for the conclusion; the preparation is sustained and accumulates as the book develops in the manner of a well-structured novel.[42]

Margaret's editor at Knopf publishing house, Judith Jones, strongly objected to the construction of *A Bird in the House*: she wanted Margaret to make a more unified book out of the collection of stories, "to 'de-story' them and make a continuous and chronological narrative," Margaret complained to Al Purdy. "I just CAN'T do it."[43] She knew very well that the stories hung together quite nicely as they were and she did not want to spend further time fooling with them. She had already reviewed them as she prepared to write the concluding story, during the closing weeks of 1968, and made what revisions in them she deemed necessary. A couple of years after publication of the collection, she admitted the stories were "conceived from the beginning as a related group"; she further acknowledged that while each story is self-contained, "the net effect is not unlike that of a novel"[44] as one might say of Joyce's *Dubliners*, or of Faulkner's *Go Down, Moses*. The comparison is otherwise instructive: both *Moses* and *A Bird* exhibit the essential qualities of a *Bildungsroman*, with the earlier focussing on Isaac McCaslin (where *die Bildung* fails tragically) and the latter on Vanessa MacLeod (where it manifestly succeeds).

For Vanessa *does* succeed; she has learned from her experience. And she does "go home again" (in Thomas Wolfe's famous terms) as though to show that one not only can[45] but sometimes—here, obviously—really must. Her final return is an apt equivalent of what Nathaniel Amegbe demands of his infant son at the end of *This Side Jordan*: "I beg you. Cross Jordan, Joshua." *A Bird in the House* does, then, qualify as something of a sequel to Margaret's African novel. Vanessa has "crossed Jordan" and confronted the walls.[46]

What Grandfather Connor has been is obvious enough, but there is another detail, less apparent: Grandfather Connor is the most imposing alien in Vanessa's life and at least as much in need of sympathy and love as Piquette and Chris and Harvey. The old man is a thorny representative of some of the oppressive "religions" rampant in Manawaka.[47] Yet the final question is not whether Vanessa has defeated the old curmudgeon. The brick battlements have fallen, but other echoes reach Vanessa's ears: she has heard Grandfather's unmourning progeny reluctantly recognize his status as alien. At Grandmother Connor's death, Uncle Terence startles the mourners by focussing on the widower: "it might have been rough for him. . . . Another person's virtues could be an awful weight to tote around. We all loved her. Whoever loved him? Who in hell could? Don't you think he knew that?" (86). Terence adds: "I don't believe Mother ever realised he might have wanted her tenderness. . . . He could never show any of his own" (87). Then, on the old man's death, Vanessa's mother asks her sister: "Edna—were we always unfair to him?" Edna answers, "Yes, we were, . . . And he was to us, as well" (205).

Vanessa triumphs, but not through defeat of Grandfather Connor. She triumphs over herself, and by granting him his victory—as though by reversing the two parts of Edna's reply to Beth's question. Vanessa phrases her epiphany succinctly for herself: "I had feared and fought the old man, yet he proclaimed himself in my veins" (207). Vanessa's triumph comes from her reconciliation with him, or with his spirit, that gives her important self-knowledge and consequent freedom. Among the characteristics proclaimed in her veins one might list the courage and strength and self-reliance of the pioneers, the survivors.

For Vanessa has faced that final confrontation and reconciliation alone. She has married and borne two children,[48] but finally she is self-reliant and independent and has evidently become reconciled to a loss of all her men. Even Vanessa's husband and the father of her children is missing. To what extent, one wonders, did Vanessa MacLeod's alter ego feel similarly alone and on her own as she finished her telling of Vanessa's story—and with how much sense of that self-reliance and independence?

By the time she completed *A Bird in the House*, Margaret, too, had achieved a necessary reconciliation. Clara Thomas has argued that for Margaret Laurence

> the writing of the stories was a journey back in time and memory, to exorcize the intimidating ghost of her grandfather and to sublimate her youthful bitterness toward him by the process of art, until all bitterness burned away and the old man became part of her and Canada's past—Grandfather Connor standing not only for Grandfather Simpson but for all the proud, tough, puritanical pioneers who were Canada's "upright men". . . .[49]

One need only add that while the MacLeod heritage (like the Wemyss) is directly Scottish—and in spite of the phony claims of Grandmother MacLeod on "the lairds of Morven and the constables of the Castle of Kinlochaline" (46, 49)[50]—the heritage of Grandfather Connor (like that of Grandfather Simpson) is Canadian: he was born in Ontario, as *A Bird in the House* frequently reminds us. Vanessa's reconciliation with the old masked bear represents Margaret's reconciliation with Canada. She was ready for a repatriation.

Al Purdy's first two letters from Athens to Margaret at the end of 1968 quickened her friendly envy, and a poem he included in the first of them wakened a significant memory of her own visit to Greece in 1964. "The Shout" tells of a stroll among Greek pedestrians while "thinking of Pericles in Kerameikos graveyard . . . with human millions under the ground." The speaker is abruptly interrupted: "The kid came from nowhere / behind me shouting loudly in my ear. . . ."[51] Margaret thanked Purdy for the letters and said the poem reminded her of her experience in Mycenae: "I did not want to listen to the guide reeling off the facts . . . so I left the party. . . ."[52] She gives her account of the kid who intruded on her reveries; it differs slightly from the version she sent to Adele on 25 June 1964. The differences are instructive as they indicate changes that occurred in the five-year interval. The account to Purdy continues,

> Walked to the top of the hill where—at least mythically—Agamemnon, King of Men, fell by his wife's hand. . . . And when I reached the place . . . where Agamemnon fell . . . , suddenly a small high-pitched voice said in American to me, "Hi." And there was this kid, both less and more real than Agamemnon. . . . I said "Hi." Agamemnon was the ancestors, in a sense the romanticized ancestors. The kid was now, here, real, and possibly mine. One couldn't cast off either one.

The salient items in the account to Adele were the ancient Greek Past, reverently respected yet almost alive and real as embodied (imaginatively in Margaret's mind) in Agamemnon and Clytemnestra, and the modern and familiar Present in the kid's friendly salutation, "Hi." The apparent contrast was sharpened by Margaret's pondering "which had the most meaning for me personally." The young compatriot was explicitly associated with Margaret by his idiom—"my own speech and accent . . . [used] in a way I could understand"; but the ancient pair, Agamemnon and Clytemnestra, were also contemporary, associated with Jack and Margaret in terms of the conjugal arrangement. The association was urged by the emphatic use of "compelled": "I was compelled to break away" and "the compelled queen." "I" was likened to "queen"; and Jack newly returned home was likened to Agamemnon newly returned home and "expecting with a calm and giant egotism to find all well . . . , heroic but blinder than Oedipus." Further, the kid and Agamemnon were evidently equally meaningful to Margaret and equally present there in Mycenae. Nine months later Margaret and Jack separated, as one might have expected.

In the interval separating that letter to Adele and the letter to Purdy, the figure of Agamemnon reappeared publicly twice. The travel essay "Sayonara, Agamemnon," based on her Greek holiday with Jack (and thus on her letter of 25 June 1964 to Adele) and published in *Holiday* magazine for January 1966, developed the theme of the presentness of the Past quite extensively to prepare for its appearance in the confrontation scene between the kid who says "Hi" and the imagined figure of Agamemnon.[53] Since that theme needs no extra emphasis in the intrusion scene, the focus there is given to justification of Clytemnestra's killing of her husband. He has returned, "expecting a pleased pride from his queen," and she is "burning" with the memory of his sacrifice of Iphigenia, their youngest, "to the gods for luck in war," and the memory is "*compelling* her towards the revenge that would have no ending . . ." (my italics).[54]

Second, in *The Fire-Dwellers*, Stacey herself likened her husband to

Agamemnon when they married: "hopeful, confident, lean, Agamemnon king of men, or the equivalent" (2). She tells Luke Venturi, sixteen years later, that she "thought he [Mac] was like Agamemnon, King of Men" but does so no longer (176); Mac's humanness and increasing taciturnity have removed all the romantic features from Mac's appearance. Furthermore, Stacey's memory of her night course in Ancient Greek Drama provides a justification of Clytemnestra that complements that in "Sayonara, Agamemnon." Her pity for Clytemnestra exasperated the young instructor:

> *Mrs. MacAindra, I don't think you've got quite the right slant on Clytemnestra.* Why not? The King sacrificed their youngest daughter for success in war—what's the queen supposed to do, shout for joy? *That's not quite the point we're discussing, is it? She murdered her husband.* (Oh God, don't you think I know that? The poor bitch.) (27)

The "compelled queen" has become a "poor bitch" as Stacey's sympathy embraces the unromanticized view of her ancient double.

These two intervening appearances catalogue the development that culminated in the letter of 9 December 1968 to Al Purdy. The focus on Agamemnon was modified to question his value as a heroic representative of the Past. The emphasis shifted from Agamemnon's vain and blind egotism to justification of Clytemnestra's slaying of her King. Margaret managed the confrontation in a way that is superficially as balanced and noncommittal as it seemed in the letter to Adele ("which had the most meaning") but that is at bottom significantly different. The attraction of the kid had been his speaking her idiom and of the King of Men being blind but heroic. Two features underline the difference (in spite of "both less and more real"): Agamemnon is not only "the ancestors" but "in a sense, the romanticized ancestors"; the kid, on the other hand, is "now, here, real, and possibly mine." This passage ends with an apparently balanced view of the obligation not to "cast off either," but the "privileged" presentation of the kid indicates where "the most meaning" really lies for Margaret, or did at that moment in December of 1968. A reordering of her attitude to ancestors, to the necessary connection of Past and Present, indeed to the Agamemnon figure in her actual life, that was always a possibility.

In spite of Margaret's projections of her own conjugal situation into that of Agamemnon-Clytemnestra and what that might indicate, she continued to sustain at least the façade of a relatively happy, reconciled wife as 1969 began. There is perhaps just sufficient evidence to influence the odds.

During the first few weeks of 1969 Margaret wrote frequently to Al Purdy in Greece, and he responded generously with a number of manuscript poems. Then on 13 February he wrote to say that Eurithe had fallen ill and they had rushed to London; she was booked to enter Chelsea Women's Hospital on the 24th. Margaret at once invited them to Elm Cottage. She had agreed to give a lecture at the University of Leeds on 17 February—"Tribalism in Nigerian Contemporary Literature"—and to repeat it at the Institute of Commonwealth Studies, University of London, but was back in Penn at the end of the week and got Purdy's announcement that he and Eurithe were installed "in one very large room for 12 pounds, plus approximately 7 more for gas and electric."[55] She urged them to come down to Penn immediately, explaining that her friend Clare Slater stood ready to drive them down whenever.

Eurithe's surgery took place on 5 March; she was out of the hospital a week later, and on Sunday the 16th Clare Slater drove the Purdys to Elm Cottage. They stayed with Margaret for a couple of weeks, and then Eurithe was well enough to tour modestly. Meanwhile, Margaret prepared for the trip to the Highlands she had promised David for the Easter vacation. He was to bring along a pal; Jocelyn would be with her classmates in Italy. The Purdys were expected to return to Elm Cottage just when the Laurence group was to head north, at the beginning of the second week of April. She wrote them at the last moment, "all packed and ready to go," leaving an address in

Scotland where she could be reached and instructions for closing up Elm Cottage when they left to go back to Greece, at the beginning of the third week of April, and the request "Have one very small sedate glass of retzina for me in Greece." Al and Eurithe were gone, of course, when Margaret got back from Scotland. Their sojourn in Greece (including Crete and Rhodes) and Turkey lasted until 12 May. On regaining England, the Purdys came out to Penn; they had a crock of retzina for Margaret. They partied together but the Purdys had a plane to catch next morning for their flight to New York and Margaret had one to meet that was to bring her niece Robin Laurence.

The party was variously justified. Certainly the Purdys' visit to Greece was cause for celebration. Yet Margaret had also a more personal reason for welcoming the company of dear friends: just before the Purdys' arrival, she had received Jack's request for a divorce. She wrote to them later that day, 13 May, to explain "last night . . . I was feeling lower than a snake's belly for several reasons. Mixture of relief re: J[ack], plus terrible and reprehensible sense of envy." After the initial shock of Jack's request, Margaret recognized that it afforded her an important liberation. She had two quick responses to the request, significant and intimately related, and was eager to share them with her closest friends: now I can be my real self ("another psychic change . . . to self-image of professional writer . . . that being, as they say, the REAL ME. Which I always knew"); and now I can go home ("I shall be so much more free to return to Canada").[56]

The sense of liberation in Margaret's reaction to Jack's request for a divorce is not surprising. She could now lay aside the charade aspect of their relationship and accept a more accurate view of her real self. To both Adele and Purdy she insisted, late in May of 1969, "whether or not he decides to go through with it, as far as I'm concerned, I will have to go through with it now. This decision fills me with panic and alarm, but it is 100% necessary, as I guess I have long known although not admitted."[57]

The clearing vision of herself and of the conjugal arrangement she would be leaving appeared in her review of the past few years:

> Now have realized why the whole bit flung me into emotional disturbance—it took me years after getting to Eng [fall 1962] to see myself as myself, and someone who could cope on her own and also be a professional writer. Then, when J and I decided to try to make a go of it again [in March 1965 and October 1967], I reverted abruptly to trying to see myself as the compleat housewife once more, although I knew I wasn't—and decided the only way to make the situation work was to never discuss or reveal how I really thought or felt about anything, at least not within the confines of the family. Well, none of this was his fault in the very slightest—only the fact that we *were* really at that point too different and not likely again to relate except in terms of what we had meant to one another in the past. . . . I really wish him only well, . . . I also do really want to be freed at last from this enormous guilt for not having been his kind of wife.[58]

She recognized that the best times in recent years had been when they were separated and "considered that we were friends rather than married."[59]

During the early months of 1969, Margaret began plans for the year in Toronto. Moles again became a problem in the lawns of Elm Cottage in March, and Margaret suffered the guilt of having them exterminated: she felt a particular affinity for the moles then as she revised her mole-fable, *Jason's Quest*. The Easter trip to the Highlands was not a blessing. David had a severe attack of constipation and had to be driven the sixty kilometres to Inverness through a snowstorm. He spent two days there, sharing a ward with "a half-insane Pole . . . an alcoholic" who suffered with delirium tremens. Margaret concluded, "I think it made David think of things he'd never considered before."[60] All this in the midst of their brief recess from Purdy's visit.

In May Margaret was interviewed by Marjory Whitelaw for the CBC—just after Jack's request for divorce. She reported to Al Purdy: "[I] somehow found myself telling her . . . that I was a religious atheist and writing was my way of praying. God knows what they will make of that in Halifax!"[61] The confession was serious enough and of a piece with the whole pattern of conversation between Margaret and Purdy during his visit at Elm Cottage. "Al and I talk writing a lot" (she told Adele at that time), "I find him easier to talk to on this subject than anyone except you."[62] The focus was evidently a writer's creative control of his or her material and the familiar experience of being guided or dictated to by someone or something "other"—not automatic writing, to be sure, but perhaps "muse-inspired." Purdy's letter of 6 April 1969 to George Woodcock clarifies the matter somewhat: "I've been yakking away with Margaret Laurence. . . . Her idea is that one is visited in the best moments, with a condition of non-religious grace. . . . My own thoughts are . . . that while writing the mind will inexplicably take sideways darts and tangents . . . that will oddly be relevant to the main theme. . . . This and Margaret's 'grace' seem closely related."[63]

Such intercourse continued that of the preceding summer, which had culminated then in her *apologia* echoing Rachel Cameron and illuminating Purdy's reference to her "grace":

> It's odd—I talk of God as though He were there, but don't really believe at all, and yet there is some kind of residual belief somewhere. . . . Always feel when I'm writing that I have a kind of personal god—I think of it in terms of African religions, sort of like a patron saint, a kind of lesser deity, not one of the Olympians—the Ibo call it the "chi," the god within, that part of a person's spirit which directs their destiny. I . . . just feel when doing a novel that some kind of faith is absolutely essential, just so I shouldn't manipulate the characters but . . . accept the fact that they *are* free, free to be themselves and speak in their voices, not mine.[64]

Margaret's "personal god" is in the tradition of the artist's muse, but entails more than the "non-religious grace" Purdy mentioned to Woodcock.

Plans for Canada included a trip with Jocelyn and David to the coast and Alberta, and then back east to Montreal for a week with Adele. Seeing the Canadian metropolis was to be a special gift for Jocelyn's seventeenth birthday. Then Jocelyn and David would fly back to England and blessed Elm Cottage, where they would find Ian and Sandy Cameron awaiting them.

In the middle of October 1968, Margaret had enlisted the help of Dave Godfrey to find a young Canadian couple to stay with Jocelyn and David during her year in Toronto. Godfrey was a writer and co-founder (with Dennis Lee) of the House of Anansi Press and then on the faculty of Trinity College, University of Toronto. Margaret preferred a Canadian writer and his wife to take on Elm Cottage, "rent and food free, in return for making my kids' dinner at night and generally looking after the place," she told Purdy—the flat in Elm Cottage would do for such a couple.[65] Ian Cameron, a graduate student of Clara Thomas's at York, and his wife Sandy were already in England. Ian was ostensibly finishing his dissertation on D.H. Lawrence but actually working on his own fiction. They visited Elm Cottage in June for mutual scrutiny. Margaret found them "very likeable," although Jocelyn and David remained "slightly withdrawn."[66]

June was full of final preparations for Canada. The Camerons were installed as the on-site caretakers, the Charletts as standby auxiliaries, Jack as occasional weekend visitor. Departure date was 14 July, destination West Vancouver, hostess Mona née Spratt (at the moment Mrs. Hickman but about to be divorced); 31 July would take them to Victoria to see mother-in-law, Aunt Ruby Simpson, and cousins; more friends and family in Edmonton and at Lac La Biche for the first weeks of August; finally, on August 23, they would fly to Montreal.

On 20 June Margaret told Al Purdy that she had won her battle over *A Bird in the House*: it would not be de-storied but would retain its original format. On the 28th of the month she received a cable announcing the birth of Adele's daughter, Tamara. Revision of *Jason's Quest* was completed at the end of the month. During the first week of July she told Jocelyn and David about the divorce. Jocelyn was not surprised; she grinned; she had read the signs. David would be "more tricky," his mother knew,[67] but he felt somewhat compensated by the assurance that the domestic situation would not be otherwise disturbed until he finished his secondary schooling, another three years away. Jack wrote a "very good" letter to each of the kids and Margaret received from Esther, Jack's wife-to be, "a very touching letter."[68] "Our domestic crisis is working out quite nicely," she assured Purdy on 12 July.

Three days earlier she had told him that the University of Manitoba journal *Mosaic* had accepted an article of hers, "subject: The influence of the prairies on the writing of guess-who." She added that she had quoted lines from his "Roblin Mills"—"hope you don't mind." She planned to use the article, "Sources,"[69] for public lectures. She was in good and familiar company. This was the Manitoba Centennial Issue of the magazine (Spring 1970) and the roster a collection of literary celebrities with firm connections to Manitoba. It included her dear friends W.L. Morton, Gabrielle Roy, Sinclair Ross, Rudy Wiebe, and Adele Wiseman; close members of her tribe Pat Blondal, Paul Hiebert, Jack Ludwig, and James Reaney; the revered Roy Daniells, Watson Kirkconnell, Dorothy Livesay, Martha Ostenso, John Peter, Louis Riel, Laura Goodman Salverson; and others. A brief selection from *The Stone Angel* appeared along with "Sources." The thesis of "Sources" is that a writer must know herself, and therefore must know where she comes from; and her fiction must be set in that known locale to permit authentic presentation. Margaret touches briefly on the fundamental tenet, already mentioned in her Preface to *Long Drums and Cannons*—"Literature . . . must be planted firmly in some soil"—

with a slight modification: "Writing, for me, has to be set firmly in some soil, some place, some outer and inner territory which might be described in anthropological terms as cultural background" (83).

Characters are slightly more important and must similarly ring true. She should know from whom she came as well as whence, to know her ancestors as well as the soil on which they had their being: the two items are mutually sustaining. Margaret insists on the fusion of the typical and the particular. She offers Hagar, of *Stone Angel*, as an example—not only of that fusion but also of the reciprocal influence of place and people. Hagar is "an old woman anywhere" but also "very much a person who belongs in the same kind of prairie Scots-Presbyterian background as I do, and it was, of course, people like Hagar who created that background, with all its flaws and its strengths" (84). Hagar's self-discovery is a realization of her past—her people and her place. Margaret sums up her case with the conclusion of Purdy's "Roblin Mills, Circa 1842":

> They had their being once
> And left a place to stand on.
>
> They did indeed, and this is the place we are standing on, for better and for worse.[70]

A Bird in the House is dominated by "my maternal grandfather, who came of Irish Protestant stock" (82); she later adjusts the ancestry to "a Scots Irish background" (83). The Irish background seems reluctant acknowledgement, as though she would like to confer Highland Scottish identity upon all her ancestors, wherever they were actually born. If her true roots were not in the Highlands, perhaps her heart inescapably was.[71]

"In Pursuit of My Past" had prepared for *A Bird in the House*, especially its conclusion, "Jericho's Brick Battlements." That fiction dramatizes a coming to terms with her immediate, Canadian past as represented in the figure of Grandfather Connor, otherwise her Irish-Canadian Grandfather Simpson, and, in Ewen MacLeod, with her father. There remains yet another progenitive figure with whom reconciliation is needed: the paternal grandfather, whose ghost flickers across the bookshelves in Ewen MacLeod's den (in "To Set Our House in Order"). That is Grandfather MacLeod, based on Margaret's Grandfather Wemyss, born, raised, and trained in the law in Glasgow. She needed, still, to come to terms with him as well, and between the lines of "Sources" lurks perceptible evidence of her unrealized attempt to do so.

Coming to terms with her Scottish past, with those "generations of my father's family," would require a rethinking of the "true roots" she claimed were firmly planted in Canada. Those Canadian roots came from somewhere—and, in the case of her Canadian-born father, came rather recently—just as did the names of Manitoba towns and Winnipeg streets that Margaret recognized in the Highlands. Uprooted Scots emigrants brought with them roots to be planted in the new soil, along the banks of the Red and Assiniboine rivers. They knew their roots and whence they came. Achieving such recognition was a much more complicated affair for the Canadian-born, as complicated as for the colonized African, as "Sources" indicates in its third paragraph. Margaret's research into contemporary Nigerian writing (for *Long Drums and Cannons*) showed her she had followed the same path to self-understanding as those writers had. There is, then, something of an irony in the paragraph that follows, a passage much quoted and, I believe, misunderstood: it claims that her sojourn in Africa fortunately prevented her writing an autobiographical first novel. *This Side Jordan* nevertheless is quite sufficiently autobiographical, and precisely because the African situation she confronted was similar to her own.

It is easy, however, to overestimate the similarity Margaret claims between herself and the Nigerian writer. The Nigerians seeking their roots were already standing on the place where their ancestors had long had their being. Their original roots were still in their place of origin and had withstood—just barely, if you like—the vigorous attempts of colonizers and missionaries to kill those roots. The same was not true for Margaret despite her brave, explicit claim: there were still no Canadians when Margaret first saw the light of day—none, indeed, until she reached the age of five (when the British Statute of Westminster gave autonomy to the Dominion of Canada). The place she had to stand on was not originally the place of "her people," for her ancestors had no traditional claim there, no established connection, unless they had fused with aborigines, people of the First Nations there. This aspect of the dilemma is one Margaret deliberately blinks, although it peers out from between the lines. One understands her bold assertion that her true roots are here, but hears simultaneously a kind of descant, grace notes, that expresses something more.

"Sources" may prepare for another piece of fiction, as "In Pursuit" did *A Bird*. If so, it may be a return to Manawaka, in spite of her categorical statement to Al Purdy that "Jericho's Brick Battlements" (of *A Bird*) marked the end of her Manawaka fiction.[72] Perhaps the subsequent fiction will be a return to the African material. In either case she might decide to go back beyond the period already covered by her published fiction—to "a more distant past which one has not personally experienced" (80). The new fiction might then be predominately mythic rather than realistic, according to the explicit thesis of both "Sources" and "In Pursuit of My Past." In the earlier essay Margaret anticipated that possibility and modified her claim that "no one past my great-grandparents has any personal reality for me": "I care about the ancestral past very much but in a kind of mythical way."[73] She had said, a year earlier, her work after *The Fire-Dwellers* might involve her in myth.[74] As she was composing "Sources," she wrote to her old friend Jack Borland:

> I'm glad you liked Scotland—I love it . . . Scotland has a fascination for me, because it is the ancestral roots, but I am

> coming to the conclusion that what really matters for people like myself is not the real Scotland but the fact that we were brought up with myths of a country which wasn't real, the fantasy Scotland, the paradise .. *and we in dreams behold the Hebrides* .. in dreams is right.[75]

It looks as though in subsequent work the myths might be her reality.

Preparing "Sources" served as appropriate preface to her going to live—temporarily, but for many months—in her home and native land. On their final Saturday, 12 July 1969, Elm Cottage was the scene of the farewell party before departure on the Monday. Niece Robin Laurence was there for the weekend; the Camerons had two folksinger friends—now "strumming away with Ian"—and Clare Slater was due to arrive with five opera singers; pals of Jocelyn and David were also due for the afternoon and maybe dinner; Sandy Cameron was nobly "cooking a 9-lb roast of beef." Margaret's running account to Adele accompanied the festivities: "(Good God, someone has a trombone in the old livingroom—what next?)"; and a postscript gives the hour, "it is 3 p.m."

She turned immediately to write Purdy of the fun, giving the crucial information and the hour: "just poured myself a massive gin and tonic—3 p.m."[76] (The last touch of her letter to Adele was a laconic announcement in ink, "I am going to have a huge gin & tonic.") *Gainsay Who Dare!* But a more serious note entered when Margaret commented on the interesting young Ian Cameron. She worried that in spite of his championing of *doing your own thing*, Ian hadn't quite the courage of his convictions: "Let's face it—talk of liberation is cheap; liberation isn't. Price of writing always more than one is prepared to pay; never more than one can actually pay, when chips are down."

And then it was Monday. In a wink they found themselves on the rim of the Pacific, enjoying the hospitality of the faithful Mona. Nearly seven years had passed since Margaret and Jocelyn and David had left that scene. It was Margaret who reacted to the changes most sensitively. Culture shock: she was struck by the "mountains and acres and jungles of food . . . 15000 diff kinds of ice cream"—and thought of the fall of Rome.[77] But the kids went off with old friends to Cultus Lake and left her to talk and sip Scotch with Mona, her oldest and dearest friend. By the end of the two weeks she was easing back into things; she was seeing as many people as duty demanded, giving some necessary and some unnecessary interviews, and reading a lot of American reviews of *The Fire-Dwellers*, mostly favourable, and feeling rather better about the whole venture.

They left Mona's on 31 July and went across to Victoria to see Margaret's Aunt Ruby and cousin Catherine, Laurence cousins of Jocelyn and David, and especially mother-in-law Elsie Fry Laurence. A particularly dramatic moment came when Margaret and David were hurrying from their interesting morning at the Undersea Gardens, Victoria's aquarium, to keep an engagement for lunch with Gran Laurence and a number of people she had invited to meet her famous daughter-in-law. There was additional urgency in the air—and tension—for Elsie Fry had just received from her son a letter explaining the coming divorce. Margaret's account of the drama to Al Purdy begins: "It was high noon in Victoria when I ran into a lamp post." They were hurrying because they had to catch the coming bus or be twenty minutes late for the luncheon. Her eye fixed unwaveringly on the nearing conveyance, Margaret zoomed across the street, David keeping pace. "There was a metal box which housed the controls of the traffic lights, and it was attached to the lamp post." A police car conveyed mother and son to St. Joseph Emergency Ward where several stitches were taken in her right eyebrow. Sister-in-law Muriel picked them up at St. Joseph's and drove them frantically to Gran's, "running every yellow light." Margaret recalled that the lunch went off as though nothing had happened.[78]

From Victoria eastward, stopping off in Alberta, first in Edmonton to see Henry Kreisel, critic, writer, and English professor, who had reviewed Margaret's books with intelligence and sensitivity, and publisher Mel Hurtig, who informed her that Purdy's edition of *The New Romans* (including Margaret's "Open Letter to the Mother of Joe Bass") had been reviewed all over the United States and was enjoying very good sales. Her remaining days were spent with the Wemyss family in Lac La Biche (about 160 kilometres northeast of Edmonton). They were back in Edmonton on Saturday.

By that time Margaret's attitude to Canada had become decidedly favourable. Her letter to Al Purdy from her brother's in Lac La Biche ended on a pretty positive note: she had about concluded that she wanted to come back to Canada to live, as soon as David has finished secondary school in Bucks. The question was "Where?" She asked the Purdys "if there are any small towns on a lake somewhere in S[outhern] Ont[atio], undesirable places in most people's eyes, old shack which would not cost the earth?" Now, just a couple of days before Margaret had decided to try reconciliation with Jack (late in October of 1967) and was still contemplating a return to Canada (preferably for the academic year 1968-69, but with the possibility of returning permanently soon after that), she had written a similar letter to Adele. Something in or near Toronto would be the necessary location: "Best would be to buy house in Rosedale, . . . then if I can arrange it, and need to, move out to some old shack somewhere to write from time to time."[79] That idea seemed a step closer to realization.

Montreal proved to be a bittersweet celebration. Margaret was delighted to see Adele, and especially maternal Adele with her new baby daughter. Jocelyn's seventeenth birthday fell on the day little Tamara turned two months old. All too soon, however, Margaret had to put Jocelyn and David on a plane to England for the beginning of the school year. In her memoir, *Dance on the Earth*, Margaret remarks, "I can't remember, either before or afterwards, when it had been so difficult to say goodby to anyone" (191). She pulled herself together and boarded her own flight to Toronto. The farewells to Adele and Dmitry had been softened by the knowledge that they would soon be together again, as the new parents were about to move to Toronto also. In fact, their move began just as Margaret was leaving.

Margaret spent the last couple of days of August and the first week of September as a guest of Clara and Morley Thomas at their home on Lewes Crescent. She visited the house she had arranged to rent at 9 Westgrove Crescent and was pleased but intimidated by the lovely cinquecento furniture the Glickmans, the owners, had (Mrs. Glickman was Italian). On Monday, 8 September, Margaret took possession of the house and learned her way around the neighbourhood in a surprisingly short time; she also learned, less surprisingly, to order groceries to be delivered and even a means of ordering booze as well. The Purdys were a more important resource. Al phoned her before she actually moved out of the Thomases' and they agreed that she would go out to Ameliasburgh for the weekend of the 19th. It was a godsend. Her thank-you note said she was "restored . . . somewhat": it was "partly the talk and partly the sitting beside the lake and listening to the quiet."[80] Some of the talk certainly had to do with a place for Margaret to stay after the year as writer-in-residence. She would not plan a permanent return to Canada before 1973, but certainly entertained the notion of a *pied-à-terre* she could flee to—having properly arranged for Jocelyn and David—to write, undisturbed, for a few months in intervening summers—"some old shack somewhere."

The Purdys proposed their farm at Beaver Pond, some 140 kilometres from Belleville, Ontario. Eurithe Purdy offered to drive Margaret up to see the place but they couldn't then find a day suitable to both. Three weeks after her first weekend at Ameliasburgh, however, she repeated the visit and got to see Beaver Pond. She fell in love with the place and agreed to take it. A cooler head prompted her to rescind the agreement in her Tuesday letter of thanks for the weekend. Beaver Pond, alas, was simply too far from Toronto and in its beautiful isolation was just too lone: "even the presence of intruding neighbours may be necessary from time to time."[81]

That marked the end of the therapeutic visits. Purdy had accepted an appointment at Simon Fraser University in British Columbia, and he and Eurithe left at the beginning of November. Their friendship was very important for Margaret, especially during those first weeks at the University of Toronto, and she was grateful for it. The mutual respect and affection are apparent in their correspondence at that time and obvious in the ending of their letters, from October on: Margaret's of 1 October—"Love/Margaret"; Purdy's of 4 October—"Love/Al." She felt very needy that autumn, depressed, tense, intimidated. She missed Jocelyn and David and worried constantly about how they were managing without her. The divorce awaiting her at the end of 1969 was another obvious cause of depression. Her position as writer-in-residence lacked the support of a definite program, or clear guidelines, except that she was required to give two public lectures at the university each term and expected to accept invitations to speak at other venues—university women's societies, literary clubs, post-prandial gatherings of medical students and young engineers. Furthermore, the self-effacing graduate of little old United College couldn't help but question her right to a position, however temporary, among the exalted faculty of the University of Toronto. (In Winnipeg in the 1940s we students at United College had looked with awe-filled respect toward the University in the East as to a New World Mecca.) At the beginning of October she made an appointment with a doctor; she claimed she felt as if she had a fractured skull and her brains were seeping out through the cracks—or so she told Purdy. The doctor asked her if she had been under any strain. "'HAVE I BEEN UNDER ANY STRAIN?' I bellowed. 'WELL, I SHOULD SAY SO!' So I gave him a very strictly edited and expurgated version of same."[82] He gave her a prescription for tranquilizers. By the time the Purdys left for the coast, the pills had done her much good.

Margaret's lecture program began when she accepted an invitation from the wife of W.L. Morton, the pre-eminent Canadian historian, to speak to a group in Peterborough. The topic, "My Prairie Background," which was the article "Sources" that *Mosaic* had accepted.

She had agreed to write half a dozen articles for the *Vancouver Sun*, and had sent off the first before the end of September. Then, at the beginning of October, she accompanied the impressive Robertson Davies, then Master of Massey, to meet with a group of grade thirteen students from Newmarket, Ontario—coincidentally, the home of her Aunt Norma, Mrs. Morden Carter. She was in her office three days a week to accept all comers, but soon reduced the consequent flood of the curious by instructing her secretary to restrict applicants for her counsel to legitimate students and members of the university. Margaret was the first woman to be given an office in Massey College, and with that came her own secretary!

At the beginning of November she signed a film option contract for *The Fire-Dwellers*. "Say a prayer," she urged Purdy.[83] In the same letter, she reported that, encouraged by that event (*Stacey, Stacey* shining on a marquee), she invested in real estate.

> I have bought a cedar shack and lot on the Otonabee River! . . . 76 feet of river front . . . three small bedrooms (room for my friends and kids); huge front window going up to roof, with view of the river—trees etc. . . . only 5 miles from Peterborough. . . . At least now I own a piece of Canada. . . .

She paid cash. That investment helps account for Margaret's agreeing to write articles for the *Vancouver Sun* and the *Toronto Star*; and to read manuscripts for the Canada Council: "all this casual money really counts for me, this year."

Margaret's social life with members of her "tribe" and associated academics flourished as she met a number of writers and editors. In the last week of October she slipped off to New York to spend a few days with her agent and his wife and to visit the publishing crew at Knopf, where she learned that *A Bird in the House* would come out in February of the new year and *Jason's Quest* in April. She got back to Toronto on 3 November and next day had to face an interview for CBC television. All this while suffering from the severe ankle sprain she incurred earlier in October.[84] She met the poet Dennis Lee, co-founder (with Dave Godfrey) of the House of Anansi Press; and the poet and fiction writer Don Bailey, who had a shack next to hers on the Otonabee River and whose *Memories of Margaret* rehearses with honest frankness the story of their meeting and friendship.[85] Mid-November was very busy: she gave her second (required) public lecture at the university and a couple of days later went to the McClelland and Stewart "bash," where she renewed her association with Farley Mowat, whose wisdom and taste appear in his estimate of Margaret as "the greatest writer we've ever had";[86] she also met Jim Bacque, with whom she arranged to work on Duke Redbird's material, and the admirable novelist and critic Robert Kroetsch.[87] The week ended with Margaret escaping to Peterborough to pick up the keys to her new acquisition on the Otonabee and check it out, and then send a list of domestic questions to the Purdys. It was in Peterborough that Margaret met Budge Wilson, who had not yet begun to publish but soon became a good friend. To the list must be added the names of the generous and variously talented Timothy Findley and William Whitehead, who were closer to Margaret than most of the others. At the University of Toronto there were two other young writers in whom she was interested, Gary Geddes and Scott Symons. Some of the friendships ripened and endured.

With Jim Bacque, Margaret undertook to tape the life story of Duke Redbird, "Indian [Chippawa]—brought up in foster homes; worked the carnivals, etc."[88] The recording sessions went on almost to Margaret's departure for England in December; she found them exhausting but her heart was committed and she hoped the project would "ultimately turn into a good book."[89] Her involvement signals a resurgence of Margaret's interest in the First Nations Canadians, including the Métis, an interest that grew in all the Manawaka fiction from *The Stone Angel* through *A Bird in the House*. Parallel to that development was her interest in the great Métis figure Louis Riel, with whom she was involved as early as the spring of 1965 when preparing "The Poem and the Spear."[90] Her involvement with the Duke Redbird project seems to suggest that Margaret really had more to say about the family of Piquette Tonnerre.

With the chill of December and her acute awareness of the miserable confrontation in the divorce court that awaited her in England, a cruel blast struck just three days before her departure. Both the substance and the manner of its communication jarred Margaret as she readied to leave for Elm Cottage: she heard, not from her solicitor or from Jack but from Sandy Cameron, that Sandy herself, along with Jack and his wife-to-be, Esther, might all be obliged to appear in court. The news shook her as it threatened the introduction of flagrant publicity—a show. The sense of grisly comedy was augmented by the Christmas celebration traditionally held at Massey College, "Gaudy Night." She was, of course, expected to attend and participate, but was suffering from nausea. Her account for Purdy: the kindly wife of the Master phoned to urge, "you must come, it will take yr mind off yr troubles"; brief response, "Can't come, am retching."[91] This prologue assured a miserable departure and flight across for Margaret. She arrived on 16 December 1969, the day before the divorce hearing, absolutely beat, but relieved to see Jocelyn and David at Elm Cottage.

A bright touch to the wretched business of the hearing, which was at the court in Guildford, down in Surrey, rather than in London, was that on the day of her arrival she received a phone call from old friend Alan Maclean to say that her publisher (Macmillan) did not want her negotiating buses and trains on Wednesday morning and would therefore send an automobile and chauffeur to convey her and Sandy Cameron (lest her testimony be required) to the court and back. The rest of 17 December was not quite so nifty. Only she and Jack testified, but she suffered: her own nervous shaking was not so much for herself as in her full empathy with Jack's discomfort—as she conceived it. Her point was, as she told Purdy, that she at least was somewhat used to speaking in public and Jack was not. Her typically generous and self-effacing concern is painfully evident, the irony excruciating: "I shook . . . yet it was tougher for him, even though he had his woman to go to, to hold his hand, to marry. . . ."[92]

Back at Elm Cottage, Margaret took a handful of tranquilizers and went to bed for two days, waking up every five hours or so to swallow two more pills and go back to a deep sleep. Then on Saturday, 20 December, she was up and doing, writing her report to the deeply sympathetic Purdy. Al Purdy's response was pithy: "In some way, I don't know why exactly, J. strikes me as a bit of a child."[93]

The end was not yet, however. Christmas had to be faced. Jack came to Elm Cottage on the 25th to open gifts; a strain for both him and Margaret, but he left as quickly as he could. Margaret had fourteen guests for Christmas dinner.[94] Her final letter of the year to Purdy (30 December) makes no mention of Christmas but does reveal that Jocelyn and four of her girlfriends invited 100 people for a New Year's Eve party. Jocelyn's boyfriend "has lined up 4 husky footballers as bouncers."[95] As for herself, there was a half-bottle of Scotch to take up to her room; she intended lock herself in, maybe write an article for the *Vancouver Sun*, and try not to think too much about the lost love of her life.

fifteen

Mixing Memory and Desire

THE FESTIVE CONCLUSION TO 1969 AT ELM COTTAGE WAS LESS hectic and overwhelming than it had promised. The number of guests at the New Year's Eve party was a mere seventy rather than the threatened 100, and a few of them quietly came up to Margaret's bedroom at the magic hour to offer good wishes. She was also struck by the fact that her seventeen-year-old daughter was on the very threshold of adulthood and independence, and had already "mentally left the nest," as Margaret's New Year letter to Al Purdy put it, a situation, Margaret added, which was "surprisingly heartening for me."[1] By this time she had put aside the tranquilizers she had relied on after the trauma of the divorce proceedings, and promised to drink only "modestly" and to feel "no more guilt."

Jack was still a force to be reckoned with, however. Although he was no longer simply "away" but now officially "gone," he remained a presence—as a conspicuous and demanding absence. As she reviewed "the many differences of personality" that had plagued the marriage, Margaret focussed again on the cause of her flight to England with Jocelyn and David in the autumn of 1962: "he said he didn't think I was a novelist and nothing much happened in THE STONE ANGEL—so I packed my manuscript and left."[2] A month later, she reported to Al Purdy, she still had to deal with demands from her ex-husband.

Jack had written to complain about the domestic situation at Elm Cottage during Margaret's absence. Ian and Sandy Cameron were entertaining a couple of guests who were unmarried but living together under the same roof as Jocelyn and David. Jack was "shaking with rage" that he was thus prevented from visiting his own children at their home, for to do so would seem to condone the immoral arrangement there.[3]

Fortunately, Margaret's responsibilities as writer-in-residence helped draw her attention away from that sort of grief. She had returned to Toronto in mid-January and soon set a full schedule of activities to supplement her regular intramural duties. That schedule included much more than the required "talks" to organizations like the University Women's Club and guest attendance at her colleagues' classes; for example, Gordon Roper's Canadian literature class. In early February she went to a women's residence for dinner followed by an informal chat with the girls; later in the month she entertained a similar invitation to a men's residence. She asked the young man from the residence if they wanted her to talk about Canadian literature in general or about her own work in particular. He replied, "Talk about women." She accepted.[4] There were calls from further afield. She went to McGill University to give a lecture, a repeat of "Form and Voice in the Novel," which she had given at the University of Toronto. Then, on the sixth of March she went to the Maritimes for a busy week of two lectures, two seminars, five interviews, and three parties. Returning to Massey College was a relief.

She singled out two writers in her final term at Toronto for special mention as promising prospects—one was Dave Kennedy, and the other, "just out of Kingston Pen," Don Bailey. Margaret's connection with the latter blossomed into lasting friendship. She sketched briefly her pedagogical technique for managing the young writers: "I am tactful with the really unpromising ones, . . . they may develop. With the really promising ones, I'm hard as nails and really tear their work apart, because they can take it, and whatever I say, they're going to be okay anyway."[5] Another young prose writer in her classes who merited mention was Paul Mutton. He was already publishing poetry in the *Canadian Forum*, and he visited Margaret at Elm Cottage at Christmas, bringing his friend Bonita Clark with him.[6] Other young writers pursued their association with her all the way to her corner of Penn, Bucks, to benefit from her stern pedagogy. Gary Geddes, another young colleague of hers at Toronto during 1970, recalled her rigour at Elm Cottage a year later: "you cornered me in the kitchen at Elm Cottage and said with finality, *Don't waste my time if you're not serious.* I marvel at the words. We were writers, not lovers, yet you demanded a pledge."[7]

There were some scary moments that spring. Margaret attended a Conference of Ontario English Teachers in Toronto during the third week of March (she was part of a panel discussing African literature), and at a cocktail party in the Royal York Hotel she was surrounded by a number of the participants, virtually cornered: "A whole lot of them decided they wanted to see—and (this was subtly terrifying) touch—a real writer. I kept backing into a corner—they were like bacchantes; I felt I would be torn to pieces. There was something really appalling about it."[8]

Near the end of term, Margaret spent the second week of April in Peterborough with friends from Trent University, and during that time sought means for repair and refurbishing of the Otonabee cottage, and scouted the area as a possible future location.[9] She also spent a long weekend with the Purdys in early May. A week later she was at her cottage again to supervise the work of plumber, carpenter, and electrician. On the Sunday, 17 May 1970, Mary and journalist Ken Adachi, whom she had met in England, came down from Toronto to help her with non-professional preparations of the cottage, her "shack." The domain had boasted a well since the middle of January: she had discovered a diviner and well-digger who performed his duties mystifyingly and expertly. He phoned Margaret in Toronto to report success at fifty feet; the shallowness of the well startled her and she said so.

"Lord, woman," he replied confidently, "you got enough water there for haffa Toronto."[10] And so she had. Before leaving Toronto she had arranged with David and Helen Billington to take over the shack during her absence in England. A Canadian journalist, Billington had been with Reuters in London, and was to return to Canada that fall and join the Toronto *Telegram*.

With her responsibilities at Massey College ended, Margaret retired to her Otonabee cottage and her own responsibilities for the month of June, "doing nothing but looking at the river and the birds," she wrote to Timothy Findley.[11] Such recreation was necessary after her months as writer-in-residence and the continuing trauma of the divorce. Necessity and "creative laziness," perhaps. For there was evidently a novel demanding her attention, and her patience, until it was ready to discover itself; and she was making notes and outlines to aid in its arrival. She was also fatigued by the strain produced by a sort of duality in her existence, a double commitment to Canada and to England—to, say, her "shack" on the Otonabee River and to good old Elm Cottage in Buckinghamshire.

That duality reasserted itself when she regained Elm Cottage at the beginning of July. She began her letter to Al Purdy, "Safely 'home' at last," perfectly intentional and carefully planned, as the rest of the paragraph shows.

> That word "home," I have now decided, has to mean both England (ie Elmcot) and Canada (in general and shack in particular). Why not be able to have 2 homes? It merely represents my split personality. Strange now to think how much this bugged me a couple of years ago, when I felt I had to decide permanently between the two. Now . . . I think I can live happily in either place.[12]

She concludes, "Gives me a good feeling to know the shack is there" and "guess it means all sorts of complicated things to me." Some of those "things" have to do with the complex relationship between

Margaret's separating from Jack and her separating from Canada, between her repulsion from "Jack's house" in Canada and her attraction to Elm Cottage, and so on, during the preceding decade. Intermingled with them was the need to recognize and accept her true identity and discover just where that required her to live. Both questions, "Who am I?" and "Where do I belong?" (or perhaps "Where is here?"), continued to confront her and vex her most important decisions.

Back in Elm Cottage were more mundane matters. The house was suffering from dry rot and rising damp. Dry rot had attacked the old living room floor—perhaps as much as half of it—and rising damp was in many of the walls, into which damp courses would be put to dry them out and prevent them from getting damp in future. But, as she explained to Adele Wiseman, "The really old part (200 yrs) of the house, I need hardly say, is sound as anything, with no rising damp and no rot."[13] A procession of visitors continued: one of Jack's sisters, to whom she had always related well, and her husband's sister came in early August; they were followed by Clara and Morley Thomas in mid-August, and by Jack McClelland's eldest daughter at the end of the month.[14]

Margaret observed that life was markedly better since (and obviously because of) her divorce. She wrote to Adele that "the relation with Jack was pretty much of a strain for quite a few years and isn't now."[15] Yet she admitted to both Adele and Purdy that the loss of Jack left "a vacuum." She saw the contradiction: "odd that; one gets used to having something there even if it is painful, so when it isn't, one is both relieved and at a loss, temporarily."[16] In the autumn she received a "gloomy letter" from Jack, in Kathmandu, regretting the terrible younger generation,"including (he believes) his own son. . . . I will always passionately regret, tho, that his total life view and mine can't correspond."[17]

Meanwhile, son David discovered a fault in the Elm Cottage electrical system, and Margaret consequently learned that when the house had been rewired at about the time they had moved in, a main switchbox had not been replaced. Jocelyn had left for the University of Birmingham to study sociology, and Margaret was delighted to discover that her old friend Harry Ferns was at the university, had been since 1950, and would be teaching Jocelyn political science. Ferns had been in the history department at United College while Margaret was there and was also the founder of the *Winnipeg Citizen*, on which she had worked during its brief career.[18] Soon it was Christmas, bringing snow, four house guests, twelve for Christmas dinner, and fifteen for Boxing Day. Margaret announced that "compared to last Christmas . . . this year was like paradise."[19]

The work, however, was not coming along. Margaret couldn't find the right voice for the narration, feared the story was too blatantly autobiographical. She put her finger on the problem in a letter to Al Purdy at the end of the year: "one problem with this novel—part takes place in Africa somewhere."[20] When she had completed *The Fire-Dwellers*, she had told Adele that her next would be set in Canada or in Africa.

In the last week of February 1971, she recognized she had been working at the "wrong novel." Writing to Al Purdy, she referred to the wrongness, with this explanation: the novel "stemmed from an idea I had many yrs ago, and I have *outgrown the necessity to do it*. . . . So I'm back in my own territory, in a sense, both geographically and spiritually . . ." (my italics).[21] In her memoirs Margaret would recognize that "What I was avoiding was the necessity of coming closer to home, closer to myself."[22] Perhaps she now felt that a new definition of "real" was in order and would attempt to provide that in the newly recognized *right* novel.

Margaret wrote to Al Purdy that she was "kind of upset" at having to confront Jack again over Jocelyn's decision to drop out of the University of Birmingham, but, "heavenly days, he is in Nepal—what can he do?" Then she comments on the right novel:

> Am beginning to feel oddly lighthearted about this novel. . . . I feel a kind of relief in following what I obviously

> wanted to do all along—chuck out an 8-yr-old idea which no longer compels me, and get to the things which do compel me.[23]

At the end of the month she joyfully announced that the novel had begun, and indicated the good omen: "tomorrow is May 1st."[24]

The courage to make the decision derived in great part from visits paid to Elm Cottage by two young couples. Margaret saw that individuals need not be simply absorbed into a "couple" but can retain their discrete identity and strength in such an arrangement—the "star equilibrium" envisioned by D.H. Lawrence. Two of her four house guests over Christmas 1970 were Phyllis and Gary Geddes, whom she had met at the University of Toronto. In a long letter to Al Purdy, Margaret comments on the Geddes couple as individuals:

> p.s. I really like Gary, and find him good to talk with. Also, as often happens, when one talks with Phyllis alone, you find how intelligent and great she is. Guess that was my problem as a wife .. wouldn't restrain my verbal expression in the presence of my husband![25]

Margaret (Peggy) Atwood and her husband, James Polk, were at Elm Cottage for the weekend of 9 January 1971. Atwood's writing career was still in early stages. To this point, she had published four books of poetry and one novel, *Edible Woman.* Margaret Laurence's observations on that couple recall her comment on the Geddes couple and on her own situation:

> Jim is a great guy; strong enough in himself . . . to be married to someone like Peggy. Christ, I am so glad to see that, at least occasionally! No man of my generation could possibly be married to me. . . . I really like Peggy very much indeed. . . .[26]

Margaret obviously identified with the potentially overshadowed individual in each couple, remembering her own marriage and realizing that she could be as strong as Phyllis and Polk—even though "I really like Gary" and "I really like Peggy."

Relief at discovering she had been flogging the wrong novel, combined with her recognition about couples and individuals, encouraged Margaret to unburden herself on the topic of Women's Liberation, claiming that the whole year had been for her (in great part) "The Year Of The Women's Lib,"

> as I spent a long time, in connection with the outthrown novel, realizing (a) how damn much I am in basic sympathy with that movement and how much of their creed I discovered for myself years ago, and (b) all useless re: novel writing, as NO WAY I CAN OR WILL WRITE PROPAGANDA EVEN IF IT MIGHT BE WORTHY PROPAGANDA.

Then comes the crucial association—

> This was, of course, the false lure of that discarded novel—the temptation to do the theme of "Wow, how terrible it is to be a woman, poor me, etc." No. It's terrible in many ways (& also great) to be human, that's all that matters. I don't now feel that all that time and thought was wasted—I found out a lot that I needed to know, & that is the truth.[27]

Encouraged, Margaret also opened herself to whatever muse or grace she knew was responsible for her literary creativity. As she had in the past, she stopped trying to plan out and force the novel and surrendered herself to the direction of her "chi," her private divinity. On May Day 1971, she carolled to Al Purdy, "it has begun."

> Not anything like what I thought it was going to be. I don't even know where the hell it's going, except in a general sort of way. . . . For the first damn time since I finished The Fire-Dwellers . . . I don't mind getting up in the mornings. . . . I really don't know what's going to happen next, and can hardly wait to find out.[28]

She couldn't give the novel her full attention until she got back to the Otonabee, for she had to attend to another encouraging matter. Just prior to identifying the "wrong novel," she had lunch with Will Ready, librarian at McMaster University in Hamilton, to discuss purchase of her manuscripts. The luncheon went well and in mid-April she informed Adele that he had "bought all my manuscripts" and that McMaster would confer upon her an honourary degree, Doctor of Literature, at their spring convocation.[29] She flew to Toronto on 20 May 1971, spent a week with Clara Thomas, then travelled around the end of the lake to Hamilton in time for the convocation on the 28th. She then joined Adele for a couple of days at the beginning of June before she finally rushed to the shack. There she worked diligently for the rest of the summer—a fertile stretch of almost four months. By the beginning of September she had a first draft of sections I and II—some 200 pages and roughly a quarter of the novel as she conceived of it, and in five sections. She expected section III to be difficult. Once into III she can hardly sleep because of its demands, which she cannot turn off. She stumbles out of bed to make brief notes on the scenes, "composing themselves in full technicolour in my head—even if only a few words."[30] She described her quotidian regime for Al Purdy:

> I began Section III. . . . Worked for five hours, went for a long walk to unwind my head, have now just come back from a swim, and I feel Great! . . . Like some kind of phoenix, I keep rising (staggering up, rather) from my own ashes.[31]

It had not been a constant grind, of course. The Purdys dropped in at the shack in the latter half of August. At the beginning of September Jack McClelland came by for dinner after doing a TV show in Peterborough, indulged in post-prandial libations for the sake of their Scottish ancestry, and spent the night. And there was a string of visitors more or less just passing through, perhaps the newest of whom was the young Neepawa writer Dale Zieroth and his friend Marge.

Margaret remembered gratefully the generosity of the shack: "Those 4 months in Can last summer were a lifesaver."[32] She was booked to fly back to England on 27 September, and she spent her last week of the summer in Toronto with Adele Wiseman.[33]

Returning to genial Elm Cottage was, as usual, a great comfort, yet it was also its usual hectic self: "Well, back to the looney bin . . . the same old six-ring circus," she greeted Al Purdy; and by the morrow, "Back to the sixteen-ring circus!" she exclaimed to Adele. The children were all right, though at ages nineteen and sixteen not really children any longer. Jocelyn was enrolled in a secretarial course in London. She commuted from Penn for the first week, then she and her current partner, Canadian-born Peter, found a flat in town. Peter's mother was currently a guest at Elm Cottage. Margaret's niece Robin, daughter of Jack's brother and wife—Rob and Peg Laurence—had also just arrived. Robin had phoned Elm Cottage immediately after Margaret got back from Canada to ask if she could visit. She had dropped out of the University of Calgary and wanted to write and paint. When she told a classmate of her plans, the friend (having just read *The Stone Angel* in a Canadian literature class) exclaimed, "Gee, *she* lives in a castle in England." Robin delighted Margaret with her reply, "Yeh, Elm Castle." Percy Janes, a novelist from Newfoundland, was about to begin his term as boarder at Elm Cottage, to finish his second novel, and remained until spring of 1972. A former student of Margaret's at the University of Toronto was due to show up with a female friend the following week and spend a couple of days. Margaret had not yet found a new cleaning lady. She told Adele of her predicament—"so I am cleaning this enormous dump"—and observed wryly, "it bloody well feels like castle-size when you clean it."[34]

The novel was on hold, but Margaret was writing. She had promised Peter Newman, new editor of *Maclean's* magazine, to do an article for him in the "My Canada" series, and she owed another half-dozen pieces to the *Vancouver Sun*. She promised to have them all done within a month, which was necessary to pay the bills and fund the freedom to pursue her more serious creative work. An added supplement, suggested to her by Clara Thomas, was to sell all the reviews of her fiction to York University in Toronto; she expected $800 from that venture.[35] The *Maclean's* article went off at the end of October and the pieces for the *Sun* on the third Saturday of November. She announced to Purdy (15 November) that in the past week she had done "five articles, 1500 words each," and then (21 November) that the last, "Put Out One or Two More Flags," was finished "yesterday." Two of the items she wrote for the *Sun*, "Salute to the Swallows" (from an earlier batch of three) and "The River Flows Both Ways," were directly relevant to the novel in progress—or in suspended progress.[36]

As the holiday season of 1971 closed in, various weaknesses in Elm Cottage appeared, beginning with the two main water pipes, which seemed on the point of bursting. Margaret's newly revived courage and confidence were tested. And her Celtic gloom. Her letter to Purdy from Canada at the beginning of September was full of that. His response agreed that her "bit about being forlorn and bereaved because a woman writer etc is true" (2 November). That pierced any lingering Celtic gloom:

> my bit about being forlorn and bereaved . . . is probably true. . . . Yeh, I guess it matters to me. It would, of course, matter much more had I never related to a man deeply, and to other men peripherally, and had I never had my kids. . . . I had to do what I had to do, and have to live alone in some way now forevermore but honestly that does not any longer bug the hell out of me. Like, it would bug me more if I'd *not* decided to go my own way, if I'd let the writing go.[37]

The grit of her rejoinder was timely with the ailing water pipes of Elm Cottage, a huge leak in the washing machine, two tiles blown off the roof, and plaster falling down in the hall. "One day," she told Adele, "we had 3 builders and 2 plumbers here all day, and I spent about four hours making tea for them at least half a dozen times."[38] During the Christmas season the house was full of guests coming and going but many staying on: for two weeks she had ten boarders and eight living in. Among the group was Paul Mutton and his girlfriend, former student at the University of Toronto. With that came my wife and me and our family of three; I was on leave from the University of Michigan and beginning a book on William Faulkner (whose Yoknapatawpha Saga so nearly resembles the Manawaka Cycle).[39] Best of all, the novel was now flowing richly, and section III was nearing completion. As the new year 1972 dawned, Margaret looked forward to a long and fruitful sojourn at the shack, eager to discover how the story would end.

The character and quality of the new novel had been defining themselves in her unconscious mind since the daft old lady of *The Stone Angel* began demanding Margaret's attention, and were furthered by features of her experience during the 1960s, which Margaret recognized partially—or not at all—as they occurred. Prominent among them were Scotland and Margaret's continuing search for the truth about herself, who she was, where she came from, where she belonged.

Margaret's visits to Scotland sadly revealed to her nothing of her past or even of her grandparents' past (her one true Scots grandparent died within days of her birth). She conceded Canada held her "true roots." Yet something kept drawing her back, the sense that some connection lingered, like echoes of a lost language, and that there was something recoverable beyond one's personal and visitable past. Clarification came to her with Purdy's poem "The Horseman of Agawa." She wrote to him, "The poem . . . gets across that quality which is in all your best poems, I think—i.e. the sense of the present being part of the past and also of the future; the sense of everything being connected, somehow, so that the ancestors are everybody's ancestors, and we ourselves are ancestors-in-the-making."[40] The first paragraph of her "Sources" had vaguely anticipated that in noting that a writer's self-knowledge must involve not just personal past but "sometimes a more distant past . . . not personally experienced."

Margaret's "Time and the Narrative Voice"[41] shows further progress in her attitude to the past. By "time" she means not clock time but "historical time, variable and fluctuating." By "narrative voice" she means something very like Henry James's "point of view"—the voice of the principal character who controls the focus or dominating angle of vision and the narrative idiom. That character also manipulates the chronology, departing from the linear tradition of "and then, and then, and then" (as E.M. Forster puts it in his *Aspects of the Novel*) to achieve authentic a-chronological narrative, the tactic of "chronological looping" that Joseph Conrad and Ford Madox Ford insisted was the more faithful means of representing actual experience.

It soon becomes clear in Margaret's essay that narrative technique is not the main concern here. The second paragraph insists that the focussing character's management of the *content* of time, "everything acquired and passed on as a kind of memory-heritage," must include "the inherited time of two or even three generations, . . . parents' and grandparents' recollections, and the much longer past which has become legend, the past of a collective cultural memory." More specifically (in paragraph four), that character "chooses which parts of the personal past, the family past and the ancestral past have to be revealed in order for the present to be realized and the future to happen." (That clause is repeated verbatim to conclude the final sentence of the essay.) To illustrate this important responsibility, Margaret refers to Vanessa MacLeod's function in *A Bird in the House* as she narrates her memories of childhood: "The narrative voice, therefore, had to speak as though from two points in time, simultaneously" (paragraph eight); indeed, her story "is actually perhaps . . . more than anything else, about the strangeness and mystery of the very concept of *past, present and future*" (paragraph eight; Margaret's italics)—that is, subject.

Resolution of the conflicts among those temporal items is accompanied by reconciliation of the competing claims of family roots and ancestral roots, which might be identified as spatial items, Canadian roots *here*, say, versus Scottish roots *there*. These accompanying items become a thread that provides a spatial complement running perpendicular to the temporal thread—a warp to that woof—and thus links Here and There, Us and Them, with Now and Then to create a social and historical cultural fabric.[42]

How to image that achievement? Margaret found a way in the essay she wrote in late October 1971, "Where the World Began."[43] It looks like a companion to her earlier Scottish essays but proves to be a sequel to "Time and the Narrative Voice." The retrospective view announced in her title leads to her cottage on the Otonabee and discovery of a very important image, the view from the cottage window:

> The wind most often blew from the south, and the river flowed toward the south, so when the water was wind-riffled and the current was strong, the river seemed to be flowing both ways. I liked this, and interpreted it as an omen, a natural symbol.[44]

That paragraph begins, "I used to look out at the river and at the tall trees beyond. . . . The river was bronze; the sun caught it strangely, reflecting upon its surface the near-shore sand ripples underneath"; that is certainly part of the scene but not yet a contributing element in the "natural symbol."

A more integrated image appears in an article she wrote at almost the same time, "The River Flows Both Ways."[45] The title indicates its importance. The fifth paragraph completes the image left unintegrated:

> Mid-days, the river would often lie still, and then you could see in its mirror the trees beyond, the great maples and oaks, the silvergreen willows. Sometimes you could even see the double flight of swallows—the birds flying in air and on the waterscreen.

There is the vertical complement to the horizontal river-that-flows-both-ways. The shoreline is the *warp* now interwoven with the river *woof* to create a fabric, an expressive image, in which oppositions are reconciled, fused to become a natural symbol of wholeness and simultaneity. The seventh paragraph notes, "this seemed like a message which one might one day be able to interpret." She has received the message, completed the natural symbol, and sketched out the image. But could one develop that into a novel? She was trying her best to do just that.

As she pushed ahead, typically discovering her story as she went, Margaret was even more exercized than usual about the autobiographical aspect of the novel. This time it was not just similarities between fictional and real-life characters and life's situations; it was the way those similarities occurred. They came unbidden, and they surprised and startled her. In mid-October 1970, still on the "wrong" novel, Margaret described the autobiographical dilemma even there:

> The irony is that the basic fictional situation has been in my head for some 7 years, and in that time, the life situations of several people (not only myself) have followed a somewhat parallel line. What do you say to anyone who knows you and who thinks you've based it all on actual happenings? "I had that line of events in my head since 1962, long before it happened sort of that way in real life"? Because that's what it amounts to, which seems kind of spooky and also unconvincing, although true.[46]

The first specific reference to such a connection between Margaret's actual experience and the "right" novel came at the beginning of September 1971, when she was approaching the crucial third section. The deluge of creative assistance gave her two sleepless nights, while "portions of the opening part . . . were composing themselves in technicolour in my head. . . . Got up and scrawled down key words, and in morning would look at them and think 'what did I mean by

Jerusalem?'"[47] As "Halls of Sion," section III of *The Diviners*, opens, Morag is at her table, looking at the river and puzzling over her notes:

> Last night . . . long and stupendously vivid scenes unfolded. . . . couldn't shut the projector off for the night. Got up and jotted down key words. . . . Staring at these words now, she wondered what in heaven's name they had been meant to unlock.
>
> *Jerusalem*. Jerusalem? Why? Gone. What had she meant by it?[48]

Fortunately, Margaret and Morag recovered the meaning, actually the key to the climactic epiphany of *The Diviners*. Morag discovers the meaning at Prin's funeral as she listens to the singing of Prin's favourite hymn; it develops the elaborate image of Jerusalem the golden—"those halls of Sion, / All jubilant with song, / . . . The Prince is ever in them. . . ." And Morag asks herself if that vision represents what she had anticipated in marrying Brooke Skelton. For grace has already descended upon Morag and she has begun to write her first novel, "almost unexpectedly," which she reluctantly shows to Brooke. He has just rebuffed her final request that they try to have a baby; now, quite as gently, he offers no encouragement to her artistic creativity. She sends out *Spear of Innocence*, Lilac Stonehouse's story, significantly under her own name, Morag Gunn—not Skelton. Shortly after, Jules Tonnerre re-enters her life, has a glimpse into it, and tries to understand her tension and grief. "It sounds crazy," he says; and by way of explanation Morag responds, "Ever hear that hymn, 'Jerusalem the Golden'?"[49]

Margaret had added, in a letter to Purdy, that with "Jerusalem" the novel "began to come together"—understandably. A further observation there returns us to the question at issue, the autobiographical problem.

> You mention the people talking inside my head. Yeh. . . . —
> the people are both the writer and not the writer. You could

> make some shrewd guesses about the main character in this novel . . . and you would be both right and not right. . . . The division between fiction and so-called reality in my life seems an awfully uncertain one.[50]

She followed that hint about autobiographical traits in a letter to Adele that contained her aching confession: "the main character's best friend, coming into this last chapter for the first time, talks awfully like you. . . . any fool who knows both of us would never believe I didn't base the character on you. ADELE, I'M SORRY!!! I NEVER MEANT TO!" And the floodgates have been opened:

> Also, . . . the guy Morag marries—I swear to God he is not Jack . . . but of course some of the underneath emotional things are the same. . . . Also, the main character, Morag, is not me, but alas is a writer about my age and certainly talks in one of my voices.[51]

It might seem she doth protest too much.

At the outset of section III, Margaret deflected her concern about the "division between fiction and so-called reality" onto young Morag Gunn. Now in college and with her new friend Ella Gerson, Morag contemplates her first adult story. It concerns a suicidal prairie farmer and his young daughter who keeps him in this life. From personal experience? Ella wonders. Oh no: "the child isn't her," Morag asserts. "She realizes almost with surprise that this is true. The child *isn't* her. Can the story child really exist separately? Can it be both her and not her?"[52] The answer, within the novel, is evidently "Yes." Perhaps the same is true outside it.

At the climax in section III, with Morag's writing Lilac Stonehouse's story, Margaret created a meaningful parallel that one might think was calculated to encourage such an answer outside the novel. Morag is reminded of Christie's words to her as she leaves Manawaka after her premarital visit: it's a good thing she has got away from this dump, he tells her, but "It'll all go along with you, too. That goes without saying" (168). Then, as she and Brooke discuss the scenes of their early past and the impossibility of returning to them, Morag thinks, "She wouldn't go back to Manawaka for all the tea in China or Assam. And yet the town inhabits her, as she once inhabited it" (185). A moment later Morag ponders her heroine: "How much of Lilac's heritage remained with her? *All.* It always does" (187). That goes without saying.

More gripping, perhaps, is the scene early in Six of section III where Morag and Ella are discussing Pique, Morag's daughter: she's coming home, but "she's split up with Gordon," her boyfriend. "So?" asks Ella. "So, did I pass *that* on? I mean—what if she can't have any kind of lasting relationship?" (173). Not so terrifically gripping, except for Morag—but also for Margaret a few weeks after she wrote the scene. Section III was completed in March 1972; she wrote shakily to Adele:

> Real problem—Joc and Peter seem to be splitting up. . . . And I am wondering what kind of inability to establish stable relationships I have passed on to her. . . .
>
> p.s. a month before this happened, in the novel, I was writing about Morag's daughter just having broken up with her boyfriend, and M worrying that she had passed on the inability to form a stable relationship. This scares the bejesus out of me. Of course life *is* full of spookiness, but need it get this close?[53]

Margaret was sufficiently spooked to write virtually the same account, on the same day, to Al Purdy and to conclude, "This novel is very autobiog and yet not at all in many ways. . . . But the interaction of life and fiction (or poetry) seems to spook me quite a bit, all the same." Yet the most spooky evidence came early in September 1972, when she had just finished the first draft of *The Diviners*—most spooky because least personal. She was talking with her friend Jean Cole, who was doing research on her great-great-grandfather, Archibald McDonald. He had led the first wave of Selkirk settlers from Churchill to York Factory and on to Red River. The story of McDonald was, of course, reminiscent of the tales Christie Logan told of Piper Gunn, and Margaret mentioned that to Jean Cole, who replied that in McDonald's case also there was a piper—"of course you'd know that"; then she added, "His name . . . was Gunn."[54]

With *The Diviners* safely off her hands early in 1973 and into her publisher's, Margaret pondered again her experience of the spookiness of creativity, and she shared her thoughts with Al Purdy:

> Yeh, being a product of one's own writing. I *know* I am, partly. Reciprocating current is exactly right. I create the novels and the novels also create me. Spooky? Yes. Sometimes seem prophetic, too, the novels—in various ways as tho I partly drew from my own experience in order to write them, and on the other hand, partly acted out in my own life what I'd already written about. . . .[55]

The last two examples of spooky connections need a further word. The "prophetic" or anticipatory scene of mother worrying about what she has passed on to daughter had, of course, been in Margaret's mind for some time as part of her unconscious worry about Jocelyn and her several boyfriends. What grabbed Margaret's attention was that she had "realized" that worry in her fiction before she consciously realized it in her actual life. Similarly, Margaret knew something of Clan Gunn of the Parish of Kildonan in Sutherland—that they were the first to be evicted as a result of the Highland Clearances—from her reading in Scottish history and fiction as preparation in 1965 for her visit to the Highlands.[56] She created the piper of that name, and his wife, Morag, namesake of the protagonist, out of her imagination before historian Jean Cole gave her the fact of Robert Gunn, piper. These examples tell us something about how the writer's mind works and about such terms as "creativity" and "realization," and about how James Joyce, for example, understood the mystery of the word made flesh. The examples also help indicate answers to Morag's questions about the child in her story at college: could she really exist separately? Could she be "both her and not her?"

Furthermore, the examples address not only the connection between fact and fiction but also the interpenetration of past and present, of what was and what now is. That leads to the question of Margaret's development in *The Diviners* of the "natural symbol" of the Otonabee River. Margaret's river becomes Morag's river: both exhibit the "apparently impossible contradiction, made apparent and possible," of flowing both ways, The River of Now and Then, as the title of section I proposes. To encourage the sense of closer proximity, to emphasize the impression of simultaneity, the novel uses the past tense to narrate the present moment of the novel (Morag's forty-seventh year), and the present tense to narrate the past moments.[57]

Reconciliation of the evident separation of past and present also involves resolution of the evident opposition between the personal, visitable past (one's own and one's immediate progenitors') and the distant past of one's ancestors. In *The Diviners*, this resolution is accomplished by the tales Christie Logan tells Morag of his own Highland ancestors and of her Gunn ancestors. The tales thus become part of her own past, and of her future. With that resolution another conflict arises, and here Margaret again deflected her own conflict—between the competing perceptions of rootedness, either in Scotland or in Canada—onto Morag. (That conflict was later accompanied by the competing attractiveness of the places of undetermined rootedness and of the characters who peopled them.) But at the very outset of uttering his ancestral tales and rehearsing with Morag the catechism of Highland traditions (as Jason Currie did with his daughter, Hagar, and her two brothers), Christie stops to add a severe word of caution:

> Then the spirits start to get gloomy in him.
>
> "Och, what the hell does it matter? It's here we live, not

> there, and the glory has passed away, and likely never was in the first place." (39)

The gloomy observation threatens to undercut the glory of the tales, or maybe it is just a leaven to question the facts of his tales.

Young Morag questions the authority of the tales and raises the problem of their validity. Christie agrees there may be more than the one view of matters. His "Tale of Piper Gunn and the Rebels" is interrupted by the fifteen-year-old Morag: "Louis Riel, Christie. We took it in school. He was hanged." Christie responds typically, "Well, some say that. Others say different" (106). But confronted by the authority of Morag, student of history, Christie is about to capitulate: "Well, well, hm. Maybe the story didn't go quite like I said. Let's see" (107). Later, Christie gloomily rehearses the Highland catechism—clan crest, motto, war cry. It is Morag's turn to be conciliatory and accommodating, and she echoes his own words: "What does it matter, Christie? It was all so long ago." To no avail. His gloomy denial begins, "It matters to me . . ." (131).

Successful reconciliation is achieved with the parallel but apparently conflicting tales of the Tonnerre family—the account of Chevalier Tonnerre and Old Jules, of Louis Riel and Gabriel Dumont—as Skinner rehearses them. They have been handed down to him as the tales of Piper Gunn have been to Morag. And she interrupts Skinner's rehearsal as she did Christie's, with a somewhat similar result:

> It was some place around Red River, there, and they [the Métis] see all these Englishmen and their hired guns the Arkanys [Scots].
>
> (Hired guns? I bet they weren't!)
>
> Sure, they were. Anyway it's just a story. (118)

The obvious conflict in the tales is that Christie's favour the Scots while the Tonnerre version favours their opponents, the Métis. With that, however, Morag's rather similar responses to the two (based on her knowledge of history) finally differ in that her interruptions of the

Tonnerre tales are often corroborative amplifications: "Hey—I know. That would be 'Falcon's Song,' and the battle would be Seven Oaks" (118), or "You're talking about Riel" (119).

Morag's sharing in the Tonnerre tales has been made possible by the physical coming together of Morag and Skinner at his shack in the valley. But they have already mutually acknowledged their association as "mavericks," and in the classroom when Morag is embarrassed—

> she takes a quick glance around. . . . She catches the eye of Skinner Tonnerre. . . .
>
> He grins at her. Well, think of that. The grin means *Screw all of them, eh*? Astounded, Morag grins back. (56)

There is a kind of visual echo following their primary coupling: "They smile, then, at each other. Like strangers who have now met. Like conspirators" (112). Morag and Jules are significant reflections of each other in spite of differences (like the two sets of ancestral tales); and united, to the extent they are, they resolve or reconcile many of the conflicting or opposed features of *The Diviners*.

That initial lovemaking introduces another theme of reconciliation. Jules has joined the army and is about to leave on active service overseas with the Cameron Highlanders. He invites Morag to watch the farewell dress parade on the morrow: "Wait'll you see me in a kilt, kid. A Tonnerre in a kilt is some sight, I can tell you" (113).[58] He sketches a glaring anomaly, the reverse of the fomenting anomaly of Morag Gunn. Jules's Scottish-ness is the visible exterior beneath which his *native* self is hidden; Morag's *native* self is the visible exterior beneath which her Scottish-ness is hidden.

Reconciliation of those evidently anomalous elements leads to a related problem for Morag. In pursuit of self-discovery and self-knowledge, she wants to identify the place where her true roots are, not to chase the wraith of spurious belonging-ness. Certainly the "glory" captured in Christie's tales appealed to the romantic side of

Morag's nature, just as the Highlanders suffering from the Clearances touched her sympathy and pity. When her Scots friend Dan McRaith—a temporary love—invites her up to Crombruach and then offers to drive her into Sutherland "where your people came from," Morag is granted another epiphany, one equal to her recognition of herself as writer rather than wife to Brooke Skelton. Here, two points are illuminated. First, she doesn't need to go over to Sutherland to see the real thing—because Christie's "myths are my reality," she declares. Second, "It's a deep land here," she admits, but "it's not mine, except a long way back." Her land is "Christie's real country," where she was born (319). The recognition enables her to fuse past and present and the deep Scots past recorded in Christie's mythic account. Consequently, she can accept as hers the distant Scots ancestors and those immediate progenitors retained in her snapshots. Those progenitors are almost as "mythic" as the original Morag Gunn, wife of that "giant of a man" Piper Gunn; and perhaps not more so, finally, than Christie Logan, the only father she has known. It is all there, inside her head, along with all of Manawaka. She has it both ways, simultaneously.

Immediately following that recognition, *The Diviners* offers two events that combine to conclude Morag's experience. Both salient points in her epiphany are associated with Christie Logan: the importance of his myths and the importance of his representing her native land. Christie has contributed much to her discovery of who she is and where she belongs; he has done his job well and can now be released from further responsibility. Returned to London, Morag receives the cable announcing Christie's severe decline. A very meaningful exchange with her daughter ensues:

> "Pique, we're going back home."
> "Home?" (What means *Home?)*
> "Yes. Home." (319)[59]

They do that, and they arrive in Manawaka in time for Morag to affirm the realization of the second salient point in this epiphany. At the hospital she tells the dying Christie, "you've been my father to me"; he manages to respond, "Well—I'm blessed" (323). Then Christie is gone to his ancestors. Morag arranges to have a piper play the lament "The Flowers of the Forest" at Christie's funeral. That goes without saying.

The apparent anomaly in Morag's situation has thus been satisfactorily resolved: the terms—her innate, ancestral Scots element and her native Canadian element—are reconciled. The symbolic anomaly in Jules's situation—a Tonnerre in a kilt—is resolved in his very appearance and most appropriate behaviour. A soldier, he goes to fight (notably at Dieppe) in defense of his native land, clad in a kilt of the Cameron tartan but as a member of the regiment The Queen's Own Cameron Highlanders *of Canada*.

Pique's unuttered question "(What means *Home?*)" further clarifies the novel's amplification of Morag's discovered "natural symbol." "Home" is where the distant past and the personal, visitable past join with the present to achieve a kind of simultaneity, and where ancestors and progenitors—wherever they are—cohabit in the present with one's parents and friends. Those apparently impossible contradictions are made possible via the tales or legends or myths that keep the distant past and its inhabitants alive and with us, not as mere statistics but as true individuals enlivened, vivified, and displaying still the "glory" of their actuality.

Pique's very existence, of course, is the equivalent of the river that is the source of Morag's, as of Margaret's, natural symbol. Pique is at once the resolution of the conflict between Christie's tales of Piper Gunn and the long march, and the Tonnerre tales of Rider, Jules, Riel, and Dumont—between the Selkirk settlers and the Métis—and likewise of the different racial strains involved in the problem of settling Manawaka, Manitoba, and indeed Canada itself. Simultaneously. Pique *is* all that and *will be* (if God is good) more as well.

"More" because she will, in her turn, leave her own mythic accounts in her songs, as her father did in his songs, and her mother has done in a slightly different medium. Morag has taught her to distinguish fact and truth with the tale of Christie Logan and his legends and her own progress in understanding them: "I used to believe every word. Then later I didn't believe a word of them, and I thought he'd made them up out of whole cloth." To which Pique poses another of her wonderful questions that produce wonderful answers—

> (What means *Whole cloth?*)
>
> Out of his head—invented them. But later still, I realized they'd been taken from things that happened, and who's to know what really happened? So I started believing in them again, in a different way. (300)

Pique has thus provided for the appropriate reconciliation of another pair of opposites, a pair that flows both ways.

In the opening chapter of "The Nuisance Grounds," Morag began that undertaking. Looking at the river, she tries to describe it, unsatisfactorily: "A daft profession. Wordsmith. Liar, more likely. Weaving fabrications. Yet, with typical ambiguity, convinced that fiction was more true than fact. Or that fact was in fact fiction" (21). Finally, the answers to those questions appear in Morag's letter to Ella in which she discusses her novel—about Piper Gunn and the Sutherlanders, about Christie's version and the facts—most revealingly. "Christie always said they walked about a thousand miles—it was about a hundred and fifty, in fact, but you know, he was right; it must've felt like a thousand" (341). She makes a similar distinction between the factual piper, Robert Gunn, and Christie's mystic piper: "in my mind the piper who played them on will always be that giant of a man, Piper Gunn, who probably never lived in so-called real life but who lives forever." Morag then appends a significant recognition: "Christie knew things about inner truths that I am only just beginning to understand" (341).

Morag's letter to Ella completes the reconciliation: "I like the thought of history and fiction interweaving" (341). This may indeed be the most important reconciliation in the novel.

An aid to understanding the issue is provided by Margaret's anger and near despair over readers who insisted on reading the Cameron sisters' novels (*A Jest of God* and *The Fire-Dwellers*) as if they were autobiographical *romans à clef*. Such reading derives from a misunderstanding of what a novel is. Not a gathering of pieces of information, of facts, from which you may select what interests you, a novel is a created, "made-up" (dangerous admission!), whole structure whose meaning depends on how it is put together, how its pieces are interrelated, how its facts are used. A novel is very much more than a sum of its parts. Failure to read a novel for what it is can lead to a confusion of pornography and literature; some would insist that it leads to serious misunderstanding of sacred texts such as the Bible. The enthusiastic censor who comes upon, for example, the first lovemaking scene between Morag and Jules will cry "Filth!" He fails to recognize how the scene is part of the novel's pattern that develops the theme of creativity and dramatizes the theme of personal relations. That scene is eloquently connected to the personal relation of Morag and Brooke and to her creativity (beginning, of course, with the first lovemaking scene between them, which closely reflects that between her and Jules). Unfortunately, those responsible for planning and directing the much-acclaimed TV movies "based on" *The Diviners* were guilty of just such misreading.[60]

Evidently the image of the "contradictory river" could be developed into a novel, and one that could, if attentively read, communicate something of the message Margaret felt was there to be interpreted. Most of my discussion of the image has focussed on the temporal conflicts, the horizontal aspect of the river. The passage in Morag's letter to Ella (341), more particular and artistic, uses the metaphor of interweaving history and fiction—the metaphor I used to express the connection between the temporal/horizontal feature of the river and the spatial/vertical aspect, the woof and warp of the fabric imaged. The reflecting aspect of the river needs another word.

Our introduction to the novel is, of course, the river in its temporal mode of "now and then," flowing both ways. Almost immediately, however, the theme of reflectiveness appears as we learn the ages of Morag and her friend Royland, forty-seven and seventy-four. (I once asked Margaret if she had done that intentionally, created that reflection. "No," she said quickly, "but I did notice it.") Literal reflection is imaged a bit later in the novel, in the third paragraph of Four, as Morag typically ponders her river.

> The river was still. No breeze. The trees across the river were reflected in the water so sharply you could imagine it was another world there, a treeworld in the water, willows and oaks and maples, all growing there, climbed upon by river-children, and slithered finnily through by muskie and yellow perch. (77)

It is an adaptation of the passage in "The River Flows Both Ways" that completed the integrated image and seemed to promise a message. Furthermore, a reflection shows the opposite of what it reflects: this vertical feature, complement to the temporal aspect of the river flowing both ways, also contains both dimensions in the reflection: the river-children climb the trees and the fish slither through them.

Royland and Christie Logan are a reflecting pair. Their relation to Morag is tutelary. Christie tells the girl Morag (virtually his stepdaughter) much of importance as he attends to her learning as to her welfare. The same is true of Royland's protective and instructive attention to the mature Morag; this point is gently introduced (with others sharply discernible in retrospect) on his first appearance in the novel: "Royland . . . out fishing for muskie. Seventy-four years old. . . . Eyesight terrible. . . . a water diviner. Morag always felt she was about to learn something of great significance from him, something which would explain everything. But things remained mysterious, his work, her own, the generations, the river" (4).

Their tutelary role is reinforced by their reflected paternal quality. Morag's triumphant confession to Christie when he is about to go to his ancestors, "you've been my father to me," and his response are prepared for by Pique's observation (earlier in the novel but a generation later, appropriately, in Morag's life)—

> "You should've had grandchildren. You'd make a fine granddad. You know that?" . . .
>
> "Well, Pique," Royland said, "I always thought I was kind of like that to you."
>
> "You are," Pique said. (198)

Their reflected role (not to mention the obvious reflection of Morag in her daughter) is in turn enhanced by the subtle attribution of mythic royalty to the two men. The name Royland (as Margaret frequently admitted) is obvious enough—king of the land; although a sort of irony clings to that. Christie, in his turn, is appropriately associated with legendary royalty. As he drives his garbage wagon, little Morag seated beside him, he provokes the taunts of the Manawaka youngsters; the most memorable is, "there goes Old Man Logan on his Chariot!" (31). The trumpeting echo of that is sounded twenty pages later when Christie reads from Ossian's poetry (as translated by Macpherson) to Morag about "A chariot! the chariot of war, . . . The shapely swift car of Cuchulain . . ." (51). Almost an equation.

Beyond that, Royland is not only the water diviner but also (the little irony) a great fisherman (perhaps not the "compleat angler" that Walton was interested in—not the Walton of the publishing firm that produced Morag's fictions, Walton and Pierce—but equally important to Morag). The symbolic value of fish is familiar enough, and we can imagine Christie exclaiming at this juncture, regrettably, "A fisherman, for Christ's sake!" Christie himself, thanks to such utterances, to his name, and to his function in Manawaka, is a reflection of this aspect of Royland. Writer and critic Michel Fabre notes that the Christ-like Christie "takes upon himself the physical and moral muck of the Manawaka community."[61]

The Gunn and Tonnerre legends are reflections of each other. Apparently reciprocally negating, they become complementary—reminding us that reflections show the opposite of what they reflect—and, in fact, converge to help complete the novel's expressive image, its "natural symbol." The characters Morag and Jules, who participate in those legends as beneficiaries, are in the same way reflections. They are mavericks (one male, one female); they suffer similarly from the prejudice and insensitivity of Manawaka; they are aliens. They are diviners as well—Morag in her fictions, Jules in his songs. Their loving convergence produces the living image of their reflection, Pique. Their daughter's name—Piquette Tonnerre Gunn or Gunn Tonnerre—apparently an opposition simply, actually reproduces that reflection. To an important degree, Pique is the point that the novel has been driving toward. She too is a diviner, as are all the major characters; she helps significantly in sharpening the novel's focus.

sixteen

The Point of Pique

"... we have to look backward to see forward in life."
George Meredith, *Diana of the Crossways*

PERCEPTIVE READERS OF *THE DIVINERS* HAVE RECOGNIZED IT as a fitting conclusion to the Manawaka Saga. It gathers up and presents the whole of the saga—like a successful lyric poem—between its covers; it recalls families and individual characters from Manawaka novels that preceded it. That impression is driven home by the last sentence of the novel. Furthermore, the composite Laurentian heroine, from Hagar through the Cameron sisters to Vanessa, is summed up and contained in Morag Gunn.

The odyssey of Morag Gunn is similar to that of Hagar Currie Shipley, and it is presented in similar fashion by the intermingling of past and present, the quasi-simultaneous narrative of the heroine's childhood and growing up along with her brief, present moment. All five Laurentian heroines participate in the quest for self, the discovery and acceptance of the self and recognition of where it belongs. In Morag's case, that quest is, in large part, punctuated and defined by the men in her life, the guidance, instruction, and education they give her, their representative quality and peculiar influence, even by the significant flavour of their voice and language. Each of the men also contributes an important impetus to her search for her true roots, the place she will recognize as *home*, and they impress on her, variously, that you not only can go home again but indeed have to do so, in one way or another.

Christie Logan, the earliest important man in Morag's life, teaches her much about humanity, hypocrisy, and charity. As he "tells" the garbage, he instructs her in the necessary values of life. Royland, his counterpart in many ways, resumes Christie's role as he imparts further necessary knowledge to the mature Morag (age forty-seven), and becomes, as we have noted, virtually a grandfather to Pique as Christie was virtually father to Morag. Each seems to have a particular lesson to teach Morag. When that lesson has been learned, each is released from involvement in her life. She shows that she has learned the place of distant ancestors in her life and the place she must herself call home. She returns to that home to bid Christie farewell and to prepare his funeral. Her last lesson has to do with the gift of grace that allows Royland and her to do the work of their lives. That grace, like the gift of life itself, will be withdrawn. When Royland tells Morag he has lost the gift of divining, Morag's thoughts suggest the completing of the circle: "Was this, finally and at last, what Morag has always sensed she had to learn from the old man? . . . She had known it all along, but not really known. The gift, or portion of grace, or whatever it was, was finally withdrawn, to be given to someone else" (369). Royland assures Morag it has really happened to him; then he hastens to add, "it's not a matter for mourning." Morag's reply is initially as surprising as her refusal to go over to Sutherland with Dan McRaith, but quite as solidly founded: "'I see that now,' Morag said." They are the last words spoken in the novel. Royland leaves.

Three young men likewise play influential roles in Morag's life. In each of them she discerns a kind of equivalent to her discovery of herself and her roots, and the place of her ancestry in all that. In the voice of each man is the echo of a lost language, as there is also in Christie's the echo of a language he never really spoke, the Gaelic. There is the same echo in the voice of Dan McRaith, although he actually retains just enough to call her Morag Dhu (in honour of the Black Celt in her). Jules Tonnerre has lost two languages, French and Cree, has kept only the odd word. Yet, the echo of both remains in his speech. Morag thinks, "it seemed a bad thing to have lost a language" (200). Brooke Skelton is a slightly different case. He has lost the Hindi he spoke as a boy; no echo remains, for it was never his, just as the India in which he learned it was never his or his parents' as colonizers. The echo of the lost languages of the Scots McRaith and the Métis Jules Tonnerre is the persistence—almost the availability—of the distant, ancestral past, as distinct from the personal, visitable past; Christie's voice carries the echo of a time that spans both of those. Morag's men contribute, thus, to the image realized by the novel, a natural symbol of simultaneity.

Crucial to the development of the novel and of Morag's realization of her own individual identity is the central conflict of Jules and Brooke. Jules is the simple, natural boy from her hometown and the past she wishes to flee. Brooke is evidently the opposite of that—cultured, civilized, couth, and all she aspires to. Jules has always accepted her for herself, as she is; Brooke prompts her to deny her past, to pretend to the innocence he wants to find in her, and to allow him to mould her into the partner he wishes her to be. From the outset, Margaret uses the sexual relationship between Morag and each of these men to underline the difference between them, especially as they influence her creative urges—or try to do so. Jules awakens her femininity and begins her maturing (she is sixteen), and their first physical coming together assumes an almost ritual quality. There is no actual penetration, but the result is meaningfully satisfactory.

> They smile, then, at each other. Like strangers who have now met. Like conspirators.
>
> "That wasn't so bad for you, after all," he says.
>
> "It was—oh Skinner—"
>
> "Hey, could you call me by my real name, eh?"
>
> As though now it were necessary to do this. By right. Does she understand what he means? (112)

Three years later, Morag begins her liaison with Brooke, and their first physical coming together recalls Morag's first lovemaking with Jules. Naked, Brooke reassures the attentive Morag that the first time, a woman always wonders if she has enough room to accommodate him, and she has. Morag ponders, "The first time. . . . Should she tell him? . . . If she tells him about Jules, he will leave her" (161). The parallels are nicely set up: Brooke dons a condom, Morag is embarrassed, Brooke does not manage penetration. They do not smile at each other like conspirators; Brooke, however, congratulates her on her virginity (162). They plan to marry and he urges her to get a diaphragm: "We don't want accidents." Morag translates: "Accidents. He means kids" (164). Her maturing is arrested; she remains his "little one," his "child," and their lovemaking is the equivalent of child-raising. Their foreplay begins with his paternal "Have you been a good girl?" before he rewards her with his donation. Her desire for maternal creativity is repulsed; her desire for artistic creativity is discouraged.

Margaret has expressed the virtual equation of the two kinds of creativity via the artful juxtaposition in Morag's response to the generosity of Ella Gerson's family, which impresses her with all that she has missed. She weeps, wondering why: "Because she wants her own child and doesn't believe she will ever have one? Because she wants to write a masterpiece and doesn't believe she will ever write anything which will even see the light of day?" (150). To fulfill her desire for artistic creativity, she must risk sacrificing the material care Brooke provides. Her first novel proves to be the means of liberating her from Brooke.

Now Brooke needs a special word. As the antagonist figure, the villain who aims to stifle Morag, he needs Margaret's artistic "protection" to prevent the story from sinking into melodrama. Margaret enables us to see that behind Brooke's opposition to and frustrating of Morag's double creative urges there lies a basic insecurity and envy. When Morag tells him that her first novel has been accepted for publication by Walton and Pierce, Brooke is initially full of warm congratulations. Then Morag gently refuses his offer to help her with revisions. He bristles at the rejection—"I see. My reactions aren't any longer welcome to you" (213)—and suggests sarcastically that it might be arranged for her to take over his university course in the contemporary novel. Behind this, again, is his recurring dream of the lost Minoo, associated with his difficult childhood and his martinet father. The first dream follows Morag's request that they try to have a child (179); the second is set up by her request that he not call her "child" (181), and his own depression over his doubts about his effectiveness as a teacher (185). Morag has begun writing *Spear of Innocence* "almost unexpectedly," interrupts it to accept Brooke's invitation to a movie, and then, feeling she would much rather "go back to Chapter Three" (184), recognizes her deception: "How many times has she lied to him before, or is this the first time? No it is not the first time. She never thought of it that way before. It never seemed like lying. Now it does" (185).

Morag then sees the self-doubt in Brooke; "she once imagined him to be totally certain of himself. . . . His vulnerabilities are not on display. He learned his lessons almost too well as a child" (185). She suggests he might get a teaching job in India. His explanation reveals much: he couldn't go back because it's all changed too much, "I wouldn't know it. I wouldn't feel at home there any longer" (185). (As part of the Anglo-Indian establishment, of course, he had no right to be there in the first place.) The dream of Minoo recurs that night. Brooke at last reveals that Minoo, a kind of nursemaid (Ayah), was the only person to treat him with loving care: she would caress him at night when he found it hard going to sleep—"I mean, all over," he specifies. ("Minoo" evidently came up from deep in Margaret's memory: David Wemyss, brother of her great-great-grandfather, went to Mauritius and India and there wedded his Eastern bride, Minshoo.) Poor Brooke indeed. Morag promises to be happy and cheerful, as he needs her to be: "Brooke, I will. . . . I will." And then she wonders "if this act of willing . . . is false to her can it be true to Brooke" (186). Margaret has tried to soften the edges of Brooke's character and enlist our sympathy, even our pity, as she endeavours to share the blame for the break-up of the marriage between Morag and Brooke a bit less unequally.

To summarize briefly, Brooke's response to her first novel, Morag's attending Prin's funeral back in Manawaka, Brooke's demeaning terms of endearment, and Morag's recognition of her betrayal of herself and therefore of Brooke (or vice versa), these cluster and produce the climax. Morag walks out into the sun—it has "the warmth of Indian summer" (215)—and encounters Jules and invites him home. Brooke enters, insults Jules, who leaves. Morag follows, and soon thereafter a second ritual lovemaking takes place:

> she doesn't expect to be aroused, and does not even care if she isn't, as though this joining is being done for other reasons, some debt or answer to the past, some severing of inner chains which have kept her bound and separated from part of herself. She is, however, aroused quickly. . . . (222)

Then she tells Jules she is leaving Brooke. "'So you had to do this first, eh?' He puts a hand between her legs and his fingers explore the triangle of hair there." And he explains, "Magic. You were doing magic, to get away" (223).

Morag gives Brooke her decision and hears again the anguished cry that accompanied his dreams of the lost Minoo, this time augmented with his condemning rhetorical question "Why, Morag? Are you so determined to destroy me?" (227), and finally she is granted the recognition—"she sees for the first time that he has believed he owns her" (227). When she returns to Jules, the last touch is added to the contrast of the two men. The question of "accidents" comes up as Jules tells her he has taken no precautions and "you don't want to get pregnant, do you?" Morag replies, "Would you mind very much if I didn't do anything to try not to?" (228). Thus Pique.

But first Dan McRaith, whose role is distinct from the contrast between Jules and Brooke, but not altogether separate. Dan and Morag have in common their artistic natures and urges, which comprise an extra aspect to their mutual love and respect (and they are thus somewhat similar to the Morag-Jules pair). They also have Scottish blood: Dan is a true Scot and a Highlander at that. Morag's visit to his home in Crombruach brings her a double revelation of especial value. She sees that Dan is tied to his home by his love for Bridie and their children; and there is ample evidence of his paternal creativity. Only at home, furthermore, is he able to function satisfactorily as a painter: home is the nurturing source of his artistic creativity as well. He also serves symbolically to contribute to Morag's crucial decision on the shores of the firth, facing Sutherland. For all his amicable solidity and friendship, he is to Morag's needs just what his name, McRaith, hints at. A common definition of the homonym *wraith* is "an apparition of a living person, or one supposed to be living, reputed to portend death." In a sense, to Morag's eye Dan has represented *The Highlander*—even though, like Christie, he lacks the Gaelic. Dan McRaith is not just a two-dimensional figure of allegory, yet some of his qualities allow him to function symbolically for Morag. Dan now represents something which is not. And it is to Dan, appropriately, that she confesses the reasons for refusing to go over to Sutherland—the strength and quality of Christie's myths, and the fact that Christie's real country is *Home* for her—as she soon tells the almost intentionally conceived Pique.

The point of Pique is that she is the focus of Morag's life and career. Pique represents the reconciliation of the opposed or reflecting elements in *The Diviners*, the elements contained in Christie's tales for Morag Gunn and the Métis tales for Jules Tonnerre. Pique is a fusion of the British "blood" (predominantly Scottish, to be sure) of her mother and the already fused "blood" (French and Cree) of her father; her parents have combined to give her the myths of both sides. Her very name, Tonnerre Gunn or Gunn Tonnerre (depending on who is speaking, Morag or Jules), announces that fusion—the sequence is unimportant, the contiguity is of paramount importance. As the novel draws to its close, Pique is making her own songs about herself, which she has lately been in the process of discovering and realizing.

Pique is also the final item in the emergence into prominence of the Métis family that has been lurking in the shadows and around the periphery of the Manawaka Saga from its inception—the "half-breeds" or "Indians." They have always been there, along with other alien figures who are depicted as surrogate "Indians." Hagar's brothers and later her sons play with the Tonnerre boys; and her husband, Bram, is notoriously (how else?) associated with half-breed men and women. The alien Bram is only the first surrogate "Indian," as we have seen. Then the Tonnerre family play major roles in *The Diviners*, with signal emphasis on Pique, niece of the Piquette killed in the fire, and an eloquent emblem.

Pique is more than a symbol of fusion of the racial strains in her parents. She functions, emblematically, like the river that flows both ways as well, for she is the repository of myths related to the ancestral past and also the promise for the future: as the novel ends Pique is off to Galloping Mountain to visit again the Tonnerre relatives there, who are her personal past.

Pique is the offspring of two mavericks, both rebels against traditional, civilized institutions, they are very nearly pagan or heathen in the eyes of proper society, and are perhaps best seen against the background provided by Margaret's very early poem "Pagan Point." They belong with the forces of the "forgotten gods" Neptune and Thor,[1] and with the "raucous and heathen" cry of the loons (as Piquette is in *A Bird in the House*). Their offspring is a *natural child*, in both senses of that term. Pique is truly a natural symbol, like the river.

That aspect of her role is reflected in two other important images in *The Diviners*: Royland's divining rod and the typical form of the flight of geese. Here is Margaret's first description of the divining rod in the novel: "Royland had a Y-shaped piece of willow, one hand on each branch of the fork. . . . The tail of the Y was held well up" (83); and here is her first description of the geese: "The Canada geese are flying very high up in their wide V-formation, the few leaders out in front" (143). The emblem of the geese is a kind of equivalent to the river that flows both ways: the southward flight of the geese clearly implies the return northward flight—at the same time. As Pique participates in the symbolic significance of the river that flows both ways, so is she also similar to the geese; the flying wedge of geese is itself a natural symbol as well, and it symbolizes continuity, the apparently endless cycle of life. Pique joins distant past, visitable past, present, and future (simultaneously, as does the river). She also expresses Margaret's theme of the necessary acceptance of mutability and mortality.

The geese appear twice more (336, 340); on each appearance they are headed south. The last reference to them opens section V of the novel and underlines the significance of the southward flight: "The Canada geese had been gone for a week now, and the wind was fringed with cold. The leaves were beginning to fall . . ." (357). Margaret knew Shelley's hopeful rhetorical question, "If winter comes, can spring be far behind?" The geese know it too. And so does Morag. Looking at her new daughter, Morag wonders if Pique's life will be better or worse than her own: "*Mine hasn't been so bad. Been? Time running out. Is that what is really going on, with me, now, with her? Pique, harbinger of my death, continuer of life*" (239).

It is not the same geese that fly back and forth constantly, of course; it is the everlasting pattern sustained by successive generations of geese. The novel reinforces that idea by a close juxtaposition late in "Rites of Passage"; Royland introduces himself to Pique and Morag and extends an invitation, "I'm divining a well tomorrow, Pique. . . . Want to come along?" Then—

> "Gee. Well, sure. What's it mean, divining?"
>
> "You'll see."
>
> A hoarse eerie sound from overhead, and they look. . . . the flock is flying in its V-formation, the few leaders out in front. (340)

That juxtaposition recalls another presented at the first description of Royland's divining rod. It is there quite clearly a setting out of two apparent opposites. Royland holds the willow fork properly and begins walking slowly, "Like the slow pace of a piper playing a pibroch [lament]. Only this was for a reverse purpose. Not the walk over the dead. The opposite" (83). The opposites in the flights of the geese; the opposites of the meanings of Pique—both harbinger of death and continuer of life. It is the same force that drives one's green age and also is one's destroyer, as Dylan Thomas has pointed out.

Morag knows that death is not to be denied: her attitude resembles Wallace Stevens's in "Sunday Morning"—"Death is the mother of beauty," a kind of necessary sacrifice (as of course all true sacrifices are). Michel Fabre comments on Christie Logan's "Christlikeness": "he takes upon himself the physical and moral muck of the Manawaka community, making the Nuisance Grounds homologous to a peaceful cemetery. His symbol is a heart pierced by a passion nail, not unlike the image of the Bleeding Heart of Jesus Morag can see on the wall of Lazarus's shack."[2] The image of the Bleeding Heart of Jesus seen in Lazarus's shack occurs again in Morag's room in the Crawley house, where she lives while at college, and in fact the association is insisted on: "It looked familiar . . .—the Tonnerres' place" (142).

The Diviners, however, is full of such imagery associated with sacrifice. In an interview with Margaret, Michel Fabre asked, "Do you know the meaning of *piquette* in French? Do you know it means *cheap wine*—something like 'red biddy' in your book [*The Diviners*]?"

> *Laurence*: Absolutely not. For me the connotation of Piquette was that of *pique*, of mischief, piquancy. But then this adds poignancy to the death of the Métis in the fire after drinking too much. But . . . such things happen . . . : words and elements reverberate and they mean more than you wanted them to.[3]

"Red biddy" is Christie's favourite libation in *The Diviners*, but it has appeared at least twice earlier in the Manawaka Saga. Early in *A Jest of God*, Rachel Cameron ponders "the other side of the tracks, where the shacks are and where the weeds are let grow, . . . and where a few bootleggers drive new Chevrolets on the strength of home-made red biddy" (15). The cheap wine is the instrument of sacrifice applied to the shack-dwellers seeking forgetfulness and for the benefit of the bootleggers, for their "salvation" (health or wholeness) from the life of shack-dwellers. As usual, something of value must be surrendered: here, the lives of the poor. Toward the close of *The Fire-Dwellers*, Stacey runs into Val Tonnerre, who recounts Piquette's death by fire in Lazarus's shack: "They used to make red-biddy down there, she was stoned out of her mind most likely" (240). The Tonnerres have learned to wield the implement of sacrifice against themselves. Michel Fabre's explanation of *piquette* discovers that the Tonnerre girl of that name represents self-sacrifice: she *is* the red biddy, implement of that sacrifice. "The Loons" prepared for the rehearsal of her fate in *The Diviners*. There Vanessa commented on the expelled birds, "never once did I hear that long-drawn call . . . *spearing* through the stillness across the lake," and finally observed that "Piquette might have been the only one, after all, who heard the crying of the loons" (127; my italics).

The principal consumer of red biddy in *The Diviners* is Christie Logan. The wine is the implement of his sacrifice in the sense that as it loosens his tongue and facilitates the flow of his tales—for Morag's benefit, her "salvation"—it also uses him up, contributes to his aging and death. As the novel emphasizes Christie's role in Morag's progress to mental health and wholeness, so is he "freed" from the novel by Morag's recognition that for her, Scotland and her ancestors reside in "Christie's myths" and that home is "Christie's real home." His own Logan ancestry has qualified him for that role; the crest badge of the Logan clan is a memorial to courageous sacrifice by its members for the salvation of the clan as a whole: "a passion nail piercing a human heart, proper" (39). In developing the theme of sacrifice, the verb "pierce" (here as present participle) regularly recurs, and its function is augmented by near synonyms, such as "spearing" was in reference to the remembered cry of the lost loons.

That pattern, with its appropriate vocabulary, involves Morag as a figure of sacrifice. At the beginning of her self-assertion that precipitates the climax, Morag begins her first novel, *Spear of Innocence*. Morag at Sunday school wondered about Jesus's sacrifice: "Who put it into the head of that soldier, then, to pierce His side? (*Pierce?* The blood all over the place, like shot gophers and)" (63). That event is recorded only in the gospel of St. John: "But one of the soldiers with a spear pierced his side, and forthwith came thereout blood and water" (XIX. 34). The publishing of *Spear of Innocence* under her maiden name is the beginning of her "salvation," is the first major step in freeing herself from Brooke, who cherished his young Galatea with no past, because of her innocence: "you have a great quality of innocence that's very moving . . . I don't mean naïveté. I mean genuine innocence . . . it's a quality I love in you" (159). The publishers of the novel are Walton and Pierce. The dust jacket bears a familiar emblem—"a spear, proper, piercing a human heart, valentine" (214), echo of the Logan clan crest badge. They continue to publish Morag's work and to give support and guidance; that continued work is, of course, prolonging the initial sacrifice of the protection and material welfare Brooke would have provided her.

Pique is namesake of Jules's sister Piquette. "Pique" also derives from the French verb *piquer*, meaning to prick or pierce or sting, and the noun means a pointed item—pick, prick, goad, picket—literally or figuratively. It is thus an appropriate name for an implement that belongs beside "spear" (and red biddy) and the various items capable of piercing meaningfully, sacrificially. So we have the rendering of Pique's birth: "The child rips its way into life, tearing its mother's flesh in its hurry, unwilling to wait" (250). And she takes her place beside the sacrificial spear of innocence as a sword beneath her mother's heart. Pique will demand other sacrifices: for example, the simple question, "my dad. Did you love him?" (192), to which Morag answers, "I guess you could say love. . . . I guess I felt—feel—that he was related to me in some way." And then the hurt cry from Pique "which must have been there for years, 'Why did you *have* me?'" (193).

Morag's necessary creative urges, the artistic and the maternal, frustrated and denied by the insecure Brooke, have been satisfied; both have demanded sacrifices by Morag, and the benefit, salvation, realized from both is summed up in the "harbinger of my death, continuer of life." From various angles, Pique is the figure of hope, a gauge for the future. That is the point of Pique.

Just a couple of pages before asking the painful question "Why did you *have* me?" Pique has told Morag about her travels, including a visit to Jules in Toronto: he gave her his broad belt and old brass buckle, like a talisman or family heirloom, and some of his own songs. Pique will come to write the first of her own songs before *The Diviners* is completed, and so help to justify the sacrifice that has been made for her. Thus she will carry the talents and practice of her parents into the future. One might call it the practice of divining.

For they are all diviners, we recognize as we reflect on the fact that the title of the novel is plural. A diviner, most dictionaries reveal, is a soothsayer, a teller of truth, especially about the future; he works mysteriously, evidently by supernatural means. The first real divining in the novel is done by Royland, who used a willow fork as divining rod to work his miracle of finding water, finding where to dig. Strictly speaking, Royland is a simple dowser. At the opening of Two he invites Morag to his divining at the Smiths'; the actual divining occurs two chapters later. Morag envies Royland his kind of divining and disparages her own: "Her area was elsewhere. He was divining for water. What in hell was she divining for? You couldn't doubt the value of water" (83). The questions posed are critically inviting. They arise again at the very end of the novel. By then, one knows the answers, or else the novel—or, rather, the reader—has failed. Morag sits quietly contemplating Royland's disclosure that he has lost the gift:

> At least Royland knew he had been a true diviner. There were the wells, proof positive. Water. . . . There to be felt and tasted. Morag's magic tricks were of a different order. She would never know whether they actually worked or not, or to what extent. That wasn't given to her to know. In a sense it did not matter. The necessary doing of the thing—that mattered. (369)

The value of the dowser is that he provides something necessary for the support of life—something, but not everything: one does not live by water only. Self-knowledge (and acceptance of that self) is quite as necessary to support a life that is not merely vegetal. It requires the contributive knowledge of one's past, including the distant, ancestral past; that helps one recognize where one comes from and where one belongs. We have followed Morag's vexed and valuable quest for that knowledge. Christie Logan is a diviner, a soothsayer who *tells* the garbage, and again as he tells of his Logan forebears, his tales of Piper Gunn, and his and Colin's time in World War I. He does that for his own benefit as well as for Morag's. Obviously that divining contributes to Morag's self-discovery, makes possible her reliance on the sustaining myths and recognition of Home. Morag and Jules travel to aid in their divining to find the truths of their lives, of their identity, of their ancestry—embodied in their respective and related myths—of where they belong. As the novel traces Pique's approach to adulthood, Morag shares the lore of her inherited tales, the Tonnerre and the Gunn, with Pique; and she anxiously focusses attention on Pique's quest, her divining for the truth about her ancestry and her past to know herself.

All of them produce the results of their divining—as Royland provides access to life-sustaining water—both for themselves and for others as well. Jules sings the songs of the Tonnerres and the Métis. Pique has just begun to make her songs;[4] she sings one for Morag and provides the words for Jules. Morag has been producing her own literary creations. Paul Hjartarson observes that "Morag locates her past, locates herself, in the world of stories . . . they structure her life . . . ," and in this connection quotes a friend of Margaret's: "'Hearing the silence of the world, the failure of the world to announce meaning,' Robert Kroetsch writes, 'we tell stories.'"[5] Some stories will be better than others, perhaps because they have captured a bit more of the meaning or perhaps presented it in a more broadly available form, and the best find publication.

As we move into the last few pages of *The Diviners*, it is liable to dawn on us that while Pique has apparently been the focus of much of the narrative, it is Morag who has been the true focus of the book. Even as Pique has been mostly in her eye, she focusses attention on Morag herself. Morag's focussing on Pique is much of the concern of the novel. Section V of the novel, "The Diviners," begins the ending and also sharpens the ultimate focus—Morag. The geese have been gone for a week now; winter is coming, and if winter comes . . . , well, it certainly comes; Pique has sung her first song, appropriately announcing her name (as though it were now necessary to do this. By right), for her mother, who carries it to the dying Jules, who more than ever resembles his father, Lazarus (362-64). Morag gives the ⊣ knife to Pique, it is one of the Tonnerre-Gunn talismans, and promises her the other Gunn-Tonnerre talisman, actually the Currie plaid pin, "When I'm gathered to my ancestors" (367).[6] Morag soon thereafter hears the train whistle as it takes Pique out west, out to her remaining Tonnerre kin, out of the story. The focus sharpens finally on Morag—as it must.

One feels increasingly in these final pages Margaret's intense personal involvement in the matter of Morag's fate, almost as though she were Margaret's surrogate or were in fact telling Margaret's own story. The principal lines of Morag's career trace those of Margaret's career. Morag's struggles to come to terms with the apparent conflict between her Scottish ancestry and her immediate Canadian background is a repetition of Margaret's similar struggle. Indeed, the similarities between the personal qualities of Morag and the depiction of her husband, friends, and even her daughter, and the personal qualities of Margaret, her husband, friends, and even, to some extent, Jocelyn, are certainly compellingly striking—and our perception of those similarities is heightened by the revealing specificity of her correspondence with Adele Wiseman, and in particular her "confessions" letter of 13 January 1972.

The difficulties and sacrifices in Morag's life as she creates her five books of fiction repeat those of Margaret's life as she created the five books of the Manawaka Saga. There is even the near relationship involved in the authors' name change: Morag asserts her selfhood by publishing her fiction under her maiden name (and that is a crucial step in her separating from her husband). And although Morag's last novel is called *Shadow of Eden*, her letter to Ella Gerson so describes the novel as to indicate that its concerns are close to those of *The Diviners* (341). Finally, there is Margaret's frank admission to Michel Fabre, "Morag is a writer and she is deliberately setting out to construct her life and of course the novel she is writing is *The Diviners*."[7]

How explain this phenomenon? Two points are obvious. Margaret had long felt that this would be her final novel; certainly, her last Manawaka novel and probably the end of her career. Indeed, she had even said that *A Bird in the House* was to be her farewell to Manawaka. That mild contradiction brings up the second point, which has to do with the basic difference between *The Diviners* and not only *A Bird in the House* but the other three as well. I suggested strongly, in focussing on the autobiographical features of the first four Manawaka books, that in addition to their value as accomplished works of fiction they served Margaret as necessary means of managing her own personal problems. "Solving" is not quite the word here, but setting out those problems in her fictional terms so as to enable her to confront them, understand them (and of course her self as well), and so get on with her life. Her divorce from Jack effectively, though painfully, removed the most urgent and grievous personal problems she had to deal with. She was at last free, once the "right" novel discovered itself, to review herself, her problems overcome, and her achievements, to write something like an *apologia pro vita sua*. I do not mean, to be sure, that she wanted to say she was sorry, but much rather to offer a justification—this is what I had to do, and this is how I did it.

So Morag wrote her last novel, telling Margaret's story, *The Diviners*.

Citizen Margaret (1974-1987)

seventeen

Where I Belong

THE COMPLETION OF *THE DIVINERS*, AND WITH IT THE Manawaka Saga, stands out in Margaret Laurence's career as the great achievement of 1973. Other events of scarcely less significance surround that event, however, and combine to mark the year as crucial in Margaret's life. Plans were already fixed for her fall term at the University of Western Ontario, and her spring term at Trent University. She intended to return to England in 1974 and arrange to sell Elm Cottage, thus allowing son David ample time to finish his schooling. At the beginning of March 1973, however, her accountant revealed that a year's absence from England (summer 1973 to summer 1974) would make her liable for severe taxation penalties. Since David's school year ended mid-July, she would remain in England until then, hoping to sell Elm Cottage in the interval. She had to be in London, Ontario, by mid-September for the University of Western Ontario's fall term. The new agenda required repatriation at once. She was eager enough: "I can't wait to go back home," she wrote Al Purdy; "*it's where I belong.*"[1]

That left her about five months to manage affairs. She would need a bit of luck to sell Elm Cottage and get ready to return to Canada in August (as she visualized it). The luck came ("this house has always been lucky for me"[2]) from just across the road, Mr. Wilson, "squire" at the Beacon: he offered her exactly the sum she had hoped to get,

£25,000. He wanted to buy Elm Cottage furnished, and he also asked Margaret if she could recommend a couple as suitable tenants for at least a year. Ian and Sandy Cameron were happy to move in to the familiar dwelling, and David could remain there comfortably after his final examinations. All was settled by the end of March; Margaret and Jocelyn took a week's holiday in Rome at the beginning of April.

Margaret was ready to leave for Canada on 22 July 1973, looking ahead to revising the manuscript of *The Diviners* with Judith Jones—"best goddam editor I've had, and we can relate"[3]—and then to the settling in at Western in early September. She had a moment alone with Elmcot to bid a fond adieu on her last night there, saying goodbye to the portrait of The Lady and expressing her thanks to the house: "I went through the rooms and just touched them here and there. My study, the bookshelves, the many fireplaces. . . . I went to bed and slept peacefully. The house, as always, protected me until the very end of our association."[4] She wrote to Al Purdy: "May the luck of this place follow me."[5]

Margaret arrived in London, Ontario, on 7 September as planned. In the English department she found a group of near contemporaries with Winnipeg connections, "the Manitoba Mafia." John Graham and his wife Angela (née Baird) had been with her at United College; Ross Woodman had been in Malcolm Ross's seminar on Seventeenth Century Thought with us at the University of Manitoba; and James Reaney had taught briefly in the English department at Manitoba. She saw students individually for three hours in the afternoon, Tuesday, Wednesday, Thursday, and usually ended the day at 5:00 p.m.—tired! She also visited classes in Canadian literature. High schools in the London area invited her for informal discussion sessions. Invitations came from as far afield as Regina, Moose Jaw, and Edmonton to give readings from *The Diviners*, including the songs she had created with Ian Cameron at Elm Cottage.

In addition to the academic demands, Margaret was deeply involved in the founding of The Writers' Union of Canada. She had agreed before leaving England to serve as its first president. The founding members were ready to pounce when she arrived. Adele wrote, "Ave, old pal, and Welcome Home! . . . the entire complement of the new Canadian Writers' Union awaits you—but entire. You were elected by acclamation. . . ."[6] The union was officially formed in Ottawa early in November. Margaret had accepted the interim presidency since she carried the least political baggage of all the members of the "tribe"; but she had decided well in advance that she would not stand for president at the inaugural meeting. Marian Engel accepted that task with Harold Horwood (Newfoundland) and Rudy Wiebe (Alberta) elected as the two executive assistants. Margaret agreed to serve on two important committees: the Membership Commitee and the Emergency Commitee.

After Christmas in Newmarket, Ontario, with Aunt Norma and Uncle Morden Carter, she wisely worked on the galley proofs of *The Diviners*. Then on to Peterborough, Ontario, as the first writer-in-residence at Trent University.

She had found a house in Lakefield, a few miles north of Peterborough, almost exactly what she had sought. The luck of Elmcot had followed her. On her arrival at the cottage she had told a local realtor that she wanted a house in Lakefield and her specifications were quite definite: "an old, two-storey, brick house," three bedrooms and a study, with a small, self-contained apartment that could be rented to a Trent University student "to keep an eye on the place" when she was away, "and it has to be right in the village," as she didn't drive.[7] One had just come on the market. She looked at it and took it; she rented it at once to a young couple, he a high school teacher, for her term at Western. When she came to take possession of 8 Regent Street herself, they told her—carefully—that it had been a funeral home. This was the kind of discovery that had hovered over her creation of *The Diviners*, a kind of "spookiness" that appealed to the Black Celt in Margaret. This former mortuary in the small town of Lakefield was a yellow brick house and thus distinctly reminiscent of the mortician's residence in the small town of Neepawa, which was the yellow brick house of her Grandfather Simpson. The beginning of a new cycle?

In Peterborough, Margaret was installed in a Don's Suite (#C-6), a small apartment with living quarters and a convenient study in which she could also hold office hours, in Champlain College, on the bank of the Otonabee River, several miles north of "the shack." She was quite familiar with Trent University, having accepted an honourary degree two years earlier, and now enjoyed working with various members of the staff—Robert Chambers, Orm Mitchell (son of W.O.), Michael Peterman, Gordon Roper, Christl Verduyn, and John Wadland in English and Canadian literature, and W.L. Morton in history. She agreed to serve on the editorial board of the *Journal of Canadian Studies/Revue d'études canadiennes*. Again, Margaret not only met with her own writing students individually (six hours a week) but also sat in on classes in Canadian literature, and visited local high schools. Just a few days after term began, Margaret declared to Al Purdy, "I really like this university." Toward the end of term Professor A.O.C. Cole (Jean's husband) asked her for something he could use in a university brochure he was editing. In July she wrote a piece on her impressions of the campus: Professor Cole used it fifteen years later as the Preface to his history of the university. Margaret recalled her arrival in January 1972: "I realized I'd never before seen a campus which looked so beautiful in the winter"; then followed a more recent impression, her delight in the urban colleges of Trent, "apart from the main campus . . . old and lovely houses, places which recognize and respect our past and incorporate it into our present."[8] Her associations with Trent continued and strengthened.

In early May 1974, Margaret took possession of the house at 8 Regent Street. It felt almost like home. Jocelyn and her husband were due on Victoria Day and David at the end of the month. The family was together again. Margaret would turn forty-eight in six weeks, the kids twenty-two and nineteen just a month later. A year earlier, she had written to Adele a brief and rather chilling observation on her new sense of liberation. Elm Cottage safely sold, Margaret freed at last of maternal responsibilities, she was

> sad to leave David and Jocelyn, but they're adults now—one has to leave them; . . . it is also good to be at last leaving them and going to something else which is hopeful and interesting. . . . I *know* it's the right thing to be doing, for me and for them.[9]

But now here was David, still careful of the leg he had broken in a motorcycle accident,[10] and Jocelyn married but still carefully adjusting to the bonds of matrimony. Margaret was not quite the forsaken matriarch. In fact, Jocelyn and Peter were planning to return and settle in Canada at the end of the summer. Jocelyn would join the McClelland and Stewart publishing firm.

The middle seventies found Margaret riding the cresting wave of her popularity. A number of critics had reviewed *The Diviners* favourably (although not all);[11] her terms as writer-in-residence were earning her a reputation as an effective and sympathetic teacher; and her venturing afield as public speaker won her acclaim as a "performer." At the beginning of February 1975, she faced the Women's Art Association of Peterborough as part of a three-person panel to discuss her fiction. Margaret has given an amusing account of the event on several occasions. She had been advised that a majority of the audience would be eager to hear her response to one question in particular: why had she used all those four-letter words in *The Diviners*? She would explain, persuasively, she felt, that they were part of the customary idiom of the characters who used them. To be faithful in her depiction of those characters, she was obliged to retain that idiom and not substitute the polite and decorous language she was herself using as she spoke to the ladies. They nodded appreciatively. There were some 200 of them gathered in the United Church Hall. Her talk ended, Margaret relaxed, fumbled a cigarette unobtrusively out of her bag, and leaned down to light it without a blatant flourish. She sat up again to field remaining questions. In a matter of seconds she perceived that she had also lighted the fringe of the cover of the table. It blazed merrily. Margaret lapsed frantically into the customary idiom of Christie Logan and Skinner Tonnerre: "My God! I've set fire to the bloody tablecloth!" She batted the blaze into submission; about a third of her audience fell into fits of laughter.[12] Two months later she reported that April had ended with "an incredible week": the Canada Council had informed her that she would receive a Molson Prize ("FIFTEEN THOUSAND BUCKS TAX FREE!!!!") and *The Diviners* had won the Governor General's Award for Fiction.[13] She wrote a half-dozen reviews, mainly for the *Globe and Mail* and also one of Ernest Buckler's *The Rebellion of Young David* for the Montreal *Gazette*.[14] By far the most important is her review of George Woodcock's *Gabriel Dumont: The Métis Chief and His Lost World* (1975), published as "Man of Honour." Her letter of 12 August 1975 to Woodcock tells him that she has just finished the review. It appeared in *Canadian Forum* at the end of the year.[15] Another important little publication of December 1975 was her story "The Olden Days Coat."[16]

The unlikely pairing of her review of *Gabriel Dumont* with what is obviously a children's book nevertheless makes perfect sense when seen in a context that extends from Margaret's preparation for writing *The Diviners* to well beyond the actual writing and revision of the novel and on to her attempt to create another major novel. The pairing is the first step in a cumulative development that persisted through the next eleven years. That step began with her response to Al Purdy's poem "Scott Hutcheson's Boat—for Angus Mowat," a copy of which he sent Margaret at the beginning of June 1974.[17] At its core, the poem echoes his "Horseman of Agawa" and the basic concerns of *The Diviners* as well. The poem speaks of "continuity"—

> where we have been
> where are we going
> . . .
> dead but pre-knowing we're there. . . .

It is another version of Morag Gunn's characterization of Pique: "harbinger of my death, continuer of life."

Margaret's response to "Scott Hutcheson's Boat" is predictable, and it says what is important to her; as for the rest, that is implicit and understood between the two communicating artists:[18]

> tremendously moving. . . . it expresses . . . the same kind of thing I tried to express . . . in The Diviners. The sense that the past is always the present is always the future, and that the future, although in one way totally unknown, in another way *is* kind of known to us.

In another way, that is, "pre-knowing we're there."

Margaret extends Purdy's concern here with "continuity," and adds a spatial dimension to the temporal one—a warp to that woof:

> One thing I have always loved in your poetry is the recurring themes of the connectedness of life — . . . in yr poems, deeply out of Canada, you can make reference to the Greeks . . . etc etc etc, with perfect ease and naturalness, because it fits and we are not isolated nor ever have been. . . .

She hopes that "the same ancestral feeling" expressed in *The Diviners* "comes across"—

> in some ways, after a certain time, the ancestors are everyone's ancestors—mine, in some ways, are not only the Scots but also the Métis; I was born in a land which they had inhabited, shaped and invested with their ghosts. . . . And oh Al, we *are* haunted by more than our deaths.

Finally, she comes close to specifying "the rest" I mention, what is understood between them:

> at this point in life . . . we begin to address ourselves not to our own wounded psyches or our un-understanding lovers . . . but to our inheritors. Like Tiresias or Cassandra, maybe—"Listen!"

It is a comment on the artist as soothsayer, diviner, shaman—or, as Margaret might put it, *shawoman*. And the final word of the passage quoted will return and resonate in the utterances of both Margaret and Purdy.

On 26 February 1975, Margaret wrote to fellow novelist Ernest Buckler that she was trying to "clear the decks . . . so I can begin writing a kids' book."[19] The months went by, but on 14 November 1975 she wrote to Hubert Evans in a slightly more optimistic tone, "I want to do a children's book, if I can, and may also try to gather a collection of essays, a few of the articles I've written over the years."[20] The children's book must have been partly written or an idea ready to be realized. "The Olden Days Coat" appeared a month later. The "collection" is a perfectly relevant part of the context: one of the essays was her review of Woodcock's *Gabriel Dumont*.

"The Olden Days Coat" is a fantasy containing a little moral fable. Sal likes things to remain unchanged—we *don't* go to Gran's on Christmas (not so) except this year Gran no longer has Grandad (not the same). She learns indirectly from Gran's comments something about holding on to the past. Sal's dad had always said about the photo album left in the shed, "*Mother, shouldn't all that stuff be in the house?*" Gran replied that she had no room for it "*and anyway, the past is in my mind—I've got no great need for photographs.*" The butterfly box is evidently special, a kind of talisman, a gift of love: "I've kept this to give you when you were ten [Gran tells her]. . . . they gave it to me the year I was ten." Gran adds that she had nearly lost the box the day she got it—"nearly lost it in the snow," just as Sal's strange friend Sarah nearly lost hers in the snow when the frightened horses reared and bolted, but Sal had found it, with help from a jay. "How did you find it?" she eagerly asks Gran. But Gran "never could quite remember, afterwards."

When the story was revised for publication by McClelland and Stewart in 1979, it was accompanied by beautiful and appropriate illustrations by the distinguished artist Muriel Wood. The first two depictions of Sal's grandparents' house are unmistakably based on Margaret's house at 8 Regent Street in Lakefield.[21] Muriel Wood evidently arranged such imaging with Margaret's approval, at least, if not at her prompting. This is the house, of yellow brick and once a mortuary, that Margaret recognized as a kind of reflection of her Simpson grandparents' house in Neepawa. The autobiographical element—expressed in the house visited by Sal (or sometimes "Sally") as the Simpson house was visited by Peg (or sometimes "Peggy")—is also a reiteration of the autobiographical element in the story of Morag Gunn, specifically as her dwelling at McConnell's Landing recalls Margaret's cottage on the Otonabee.

The Olden Days Coat appears to be a kind of coda to *The Diviners* and perhaps to the whole Manawaka Saga. The handsome little fantasy (or myth) is concerned with the presentness of the past and the continuity of both past and present into the future and also with the importance of ancestors. Those are the terms Margaret used to praise "Scott Hutcheson's Boat" and what she herself had attempted in *The Diviners*. The butterfly box, furthermore, functions in *The Olden Days Coat* much as the boat does in the "Scott Hutcheson" poem or as the rock painting does in "Horseman of Agawa"; and all three artistic works use the central item—box, boat, and painting—as a focus for the love that is at the heart of each.

The companion piece "Man of Honour," Margaret's review of Woodcock's *Gabriel Dumont*, is a more obvious example of "continuity" (in Purdy's use—not in the sense of being a coda). It is a further realization of the idea already presented in Morag's association with Jules Tonnerre, and in the other Tonnerre figures and their surrogates in earlier Manawaka fiction. The continuity rises out of Margaret's interest in the side trips Al and Eurithe Purdy took en route to Vancouver in the early fall of 1971. The highlights quickened her interest—"Churchill, the 94-year-old survivor of the N.W. Rebellion, Batoche two days"[22]—and she hoped to visit the territory. Her response to Purdy includes reference to Eurithe's supplementary report: "ps. Eurithe's card from Batoche made me realize I really *have* to go."[23] The Purdy reports touched closely on the Tonnerre legends Margaret was currently developing in *The Diviners*, especially the experience of Old Jules, Skinner's grandfather, at Batoche. Reinforcement came with the poem "The Battlefield at Batoche" that he wrote soon after the "two days" there.[24] It was published along with "Horseman of Agawa" in his *Sex and Death* (1973). "Battlefield" is a familiar enough account of the tragic encounter, but there is an echo that further extends "continuity": not the *word* "Listen" but in the situation that recalls the ending of "Horseman of Agawa" and "Scott Hutcheson's Boat," in the final expression of art and love, in which the word is implicit.

> I ask my wife "Do you hear anything?"
> She smiles "Your imagination again?"

And later he repeats,

> And I say to my wife, "Do you hear nothing?"
> "I hear the poem you're writing" she says
> "I knew you were going to say that" I say

Margaret's praise of Woodcock's biography of Dumont rises from her continued interest in examples of imperialist and colonialist injustice and her commitment to the social gospel. The review also reveals development of her ideas about ancestry. At the outset she expresses her gratitude that Woodcock had undertaken the study of Gabriel, a figure tragically overlooked in school books, for he was "fully as interesting and significant as Louis Riel"—"a truly heroic man." And she needed to know more, for the Métis were part of her *defining* past—necessary knowledge, as little Sal's knowledge of her grandmother was necessary and (lucky for Sal) readily available. The review repeats the association made some years earlier in Margaret's substantial essay on the Somali warrior-poet the Sayyid Mahammed 'Abdille Hasan, that is the similarity among his Somali followers in the early years of the twentieth century, the Highlanders at Culloden in 1876, and the followers of Riel and Dumont at Batoche, when "the Métis nation was born and died in May 1885."[25] For "the ancestors are everyone's ancestors."

In November 1975 she began gathering various essays and articles (most of which had already been published) to form the collection *Heart of a Stranger*, and by the next Valentine's Day had a manuscript of fourteen pieces. The collection was published that September, expanded to nineteen items; five of them address directly topics here under discussion—the presentness of the past and the anticipation of the future (Purdy's "continuity"), ancestry and place as functions of identity, and the problem of political and social inhumanity. Preparation of the *Gabriel Dumont* review for the collection involved the addition of the last page and a half (210-12 of *Heart*), including Gabriel's prayer (210), and a new title, "Man of Our People," with its eloquent and revealing pronoun. The penultimate paragraph begins, "Has the voice of Gabriel anything to tell us here and now, in a world totally different from his? I believe it has," she affirms and notes that other voices are speaking to us along with his, those of Riel, Big Bear, and Poundmaker.[26] And it is urgent that we *Listen!*

> Will we ever reach a point when it is no longer necessary to say Them and Us? I believe we must hear native peoples' voices and ultimately become part of them, for they speak . . . of the things needed to be known.

The brief and pointed conclusion validates "Our" in the title:

> There are many ways in which those of us who are not Indian or Métis have not earned the right to call Gabriel Dumont

> ancestor. But I do so, all the same. His life, his legend, and his times are part of our past which we desperately need to understand and pay heed to.

Margaret's confirming visit to Batoche had to be held off for more than a year.

Early in 1976, complaints were registered with the Board of Education in Lakefield by two local parents. They felt *The Diviners* was an immoral book and would have a bad effect on the grade thirteen students. The book had been approved by the Ministry of Education and appeared on the supplementary book list, yet the local protest was sufficient to oblige Robert J. Buchanan, head of the English department at Lakefield Secondary School, to remove it from the list until the Textbook Review Committee had evaluated it for use in grade thirteen. (Meanwhile, A.B. Sweeney, principal of Kenner Collegiate and Vocational School in Peterborough, faced a similar protest over Alice Munro's *Lives of Girls and Women*.) Immediately, English department heads at all Peterborough County's high schools quickly stepped up to support Robert J. Buchanan's objections. The Writers' Union of Canada quietly stepped up as well to oppose the unjust censorship. Prominent among the book-banners were zealots from some fundamentalist churches. One of them, James Telford, was a Board of Education trustee and a member of the Textbook Review Committee. Telford was a science teacher at the local community college; his broad-mindedness was illustrated by his suggestion that Darwin's theory of evolution be taught together with the Genesis story of Adam and Eve—as two views of Creation.[27] As justification for his opposition to *The Diviners*, he gave this explanation: "Through God's grace I am a Christian. . . . The Holy Spirit allows me to see a broader view of things. Only true Christians, who are a small minority, are capable of a broad perspective." It would follow, then, that "Only true Christians can set education standards."[28] Of course, he had not read *The Diviners*.

At Telford's side was the Reverend R.L. McPhee, minister of a Lakefield church, as innocent of direct experience of *The Diviners* as was Telford. That innocence did not prevent him condemning the novel because of its sexual content: the young people will think sex is approved, he opined, "then it's all right to do it."[29]

The opposition to the book-banners was comparatively quiet, rational, and eloquent. One of the most substantial attacks on the censorious zealots was a letter of some four and a half pages, single-spaced, from Joan Johnston of Peterborough to Secretary Hamley of the Peterborough Board of Education, dated 26 March 1976. The letter quoted Mary Rawlings, head of girls' physical education at Kenner Collegiate, who "hoped students would develop respect and a healthy, mature attitude toward sex"; and also Canadian novelist Sylvia Fraser on the "horrendous and tragic" banning: "you abandon the child with his sexuality . . . I can't think of anything more beautiful than a child learning sexuality by reading sensitive authors such as Alice Munro and Margaret Laurence." Joan Johnston responded directly to fears about sexual content and its influence on grade thirteen students, that if the parents "have exposed them to a healthy home environment . . . and a sense of moral and social values" they need not fear the influence of works like *The Diviners*. Indeed, she pointed out, the opposite is true, and observed that the work of both Laurence and Munro had been crowned by the Governor General's Award for Fiction.

The intervention on Margaret's behalf by Joan Johnston, whom Margaret did not know, led to an acquaintanceship that quickly blossomed into a close friendship destined to last to the end of Margaret's life and career. Not everyone who sympathized deeply with Margaret entered publicly into the fray, however. A good example of tacit supporters is historian Dr. Jean Murray Cole, professor of history, author of a biography of Archie McDonald, and a dear friend of Margaret. She explained to me that she felt there was quite enough public notice of the attack on *The Diviners*; that she knew Margaret was—privately—well aware of her sentiments and sympathy; that the two of them could quite nicely keep a dignified silence together. Both kinds of support were welcome—*chacun à son goût*.[30]

On 22 April 1976, the Textbook Review Committee reported their unanimous approval of *The Diviners* to the Board of Education. Strife persisted, but finally the board voted ten to six in favour of restoring the novel to its place in the grade thirteen curriculum.

The battle was then taken up by "a number of local fundamentalist churches . . . collecting signatures on a petition against" *The Diviners*. Margaret provided a resumé of the struggle to the May newsletter of the Writers' Union, page 9:

> One minister, Rev. Sam Buick of the Dublin Street Pentecostal Church, kept his church open from 8 a.m. to 8 p.m. one day, so that people could sign the petition. . . . Copies of THE DIVINERS were on hand, with so-called obscene words marked, and also sex scenes marked. A handy xerox copy of page reference numbers was available.

At a subsequent meeting of the school board, the petition was presented and a supporter of it rose to affirm (the voice of James Telford): "I speak for a delegation of eight—myself, my wife, our five children, and God." Once again the board voted ten to six in favour of *The Diviners*.

When Margaret rehearsed all this to me a few months later, looking amazed and disappointed, she mused, "I always thought I was a *religious* writer." She moved on to other things, yet the experience continued to rankle, and finally in 1984 she published in *Toronto Life* "The Greater Evil." It addressed directly her experience of early 1976, and also her commitment to the future. It is a condemnation of the blind and zealous censorship that had threatened her literature and that of others. The essay quotes F.R. Scott, poet and lawyer: "The time for defending freedom never goes by. Freedom is a habit that must be kept alive by use." It also quotes words of John Milton's *Areopagitica*, written 300 years earlier: "I cannot praise a fugitive and cloistered virtue, unexercised and unbreathed, that never sallies out and seeks her adversary . . ."; and again, "That which purifies us is trial, and trial is by what is contrary."[31]

Another distraction during the weeks of "the controversy," as the to-do over possible censorship came to be known locally, was the increasing strain in the relations of Margaret and Al Purdy. The result of misunderstanding, failure of sense of humour, touchiness—and of separation—it was finally settled after persevering, off and on, for over two years. Around Valentine's Day 1977, the clouds were finally dispersed. Purdy sent her three poems, including "Handful of Earth," which she praised warmly. Purdy in turn praised *The Diviners*, which he had read at last (one of the sore points)—"the best part of it was . . . the homogeneity of time and . . . how incidents float in time."[32] He suggested they meet at the annual Canada Day seminar in Hamilton, 22-23 April ("maybe can drink some wine"), then "And hey, I think you're a pretty nice person, if I haven't said so lately—much larger than you know about."

The healing of their quarrel was only one of the happy events that marked 1977 as a kind of *annus mirabilis*. Four other events, interrelated and indeed overlapping, occurred that year. At the beginning of February, Margaret agreed to participate in the Prairie Writers' Workshop at Evan Hardy Collegiate in Saskatoon, organized by the poet and publisher Glen Sorestad for mid-March. She would be with fellow-writers such as Robert Kroetsch, Henry Kreisel, Paul Hiebert, and Rudy Wiebe. Sorestad also arranged with David Carpenter of the University of Saskatchewan (also in Saskatoon) for a reading by Margaret, followed by an hour of questions and answers.[33] She enjoyed her visit, but in her eye the highlight was the visit to Batoche—"that really memorable day" she exclaimed to Glen Sorestad in her letter of 25 March 1977: "When I came home, I spent three days rereading a lot of things re: the rebellion of Gabriel—it put it all into a kind of fresh perspective to have actually seen the place."[34] A year before her Batoche visit Sorestad had sent her a volume of his own poetry, *Wind Songs* (including his own poem on Batoche). Her letter of thanks sounds a note that anticipated revision of her review of Woodcock's *Gabriel Dumont*:

> It seems to me that you catch *exactly* the feeling of the prairies, . . . of the people . . . and of the ancestors—and there is a sense, of course, in which Riel and Dumont, Big Bear and Poundmaker, become our ancestors even though we have not yet earned the right to call them that, I know.[35]

Margaret's visit to Batoche provoked an essay, as Purdy's had his "The Battlefield at Batoche." The very title of the essay, "Listen. Just Listen,"[36] recalls a prominent theme in the poem, uttered in the speaker's questioning of his wife and at the conclusion for the poem (which she has already heard): "an extension of anything that ever happened / . . . whispering across the fields of eternity." Margaret's essay was written for the collection edited by Gary Geddes, *Divided We Stand*. The collection was frankly a response to the victory of the separatist Parti Québecois in the November 1976 election (its platform featured the separation of Quebec from the rest of Canada). The book urgently addressed the continuing crisis posed by Canada's "dual culture," English-Canadian ways and *les moeurs canadiennes-francaises*. The contents are bracketed by the essay "For an Independent Quebec" by René Lêvesque (at that time leader of the Parti Québecois and premier of the province of Quebec), and the poem "A Handful of Earth: to René Lévesque," by Al Purdy. The list of contributors between those two reads like a Who's Who of Canada's best writers (although Timothy Findley's name is conspicuously absent).

"Listen. Just Listen" begins with praise for the spirit of the Métis and their leaders, Louis Riel and Gabriel Dumont, who fought to defend the right to live where their ancestors had lived and against those who believed that might allowed them to treat people and land alike as chattels—that alone was their purpose, and not to impose their ways on others or to gain the others' space and land. Her position was in sympathy with a majority of the contributors. Naim Kattan's essay, "In Praise of Imprecision," immediately precedes "Listen" and is representative of that position.

> Groups and peoples may seek unity in order to assert their presence and repel their neighbours' influence. Yet cohesion founded on a power relation leads to confrontation over power sharing and asserting authority. There are other forms of relation: exchange, mental enrichment, an openness to influence.
>
> For me, the noblest race is the Métis race. (18)

Rational. Reasonable.

On the example of the Métis, Margaret bases her argument for retaining the mosaic configuration of Canada, the unity in its diversity, which the loss of Quebec would destroy. The adjuration of her title, "Listen. Just Listen," announces the need for communication that must lead to understanding—not only with our "neighbours" but with our ancestors, which together comprise the warp and the woof of our social fabric, with our history and our place. Listen! At Batoche, she writes, "the old voices are here yet . . . are everywhere in the wind" (20). "We are, all of us, . . . bound up in one another's history . . . the ancestors ultimately become all our ancestors" (22). At Batoche, memory of Gabriel made her think of Gabrielle, the ancestral Dumont and the contemporary Roy (with whom Margaret could claim *tribal* kinship—Canadian writers/*écrivains canadiens*): "We in spirit being linked to the land, are also linked to the ancestral voices which arise out of many voices" (22):

> in the beginning of this country as a "country," the taking away of the land from the native peoples by colonialists who believed men could actually *own* the land, whereas the original inhabitants believed that the land belonged to God, the Great Spirit, and was for mankind's shared use. (24)

Margaret's somewhat later essay, "Quebec's 'freedom' is a vital concern, but freedom itself is that, and more,"[37] offers a more sharply political argument than does "Listen," as it attacks Prime Minister Pierre Trudeau's cavalier gestures: his statement that he doesn't want to know what the RCMP is up to (and that we shouldn't either) and his proud reference to having invoked the War Measures Act in 1970 and willingness to do so again "if something illegal is attempted by the province of Quebec." Margaret worries about the rights of anglophones in Quebec, but recognizes that English-speaking Canada has established a dismal record of neglecting the similar rights of francophones. She urges recognition and guarantees of the rights of all the constituent members of Canada—"and above all, the grievances, needs and rights of the native peoples, who have suffered more injustice than any other people in this land." Returning to the matter most urgently at issue, Margaret notes that "without Quebec this country would be poorer in spirit and culture than it is"; but she asserts that use of violence to keep Quebec within Confederation is as "unthinkable" as it is "to keep in Confederation any part of this country that did not want to remain."

Finally, however, "Listen" is much less a political argument than a poetic expression of the importance of love, of respect for the earth and its creatures. In this poetic essay, as in a lyric poem, the themes accumulate and coalesce so that the conclusion delivers all of them fused, at once, to emphasize its strongly religious basis. Margaret finally acknowledges her reliance on the advice of novelist Rudy Wiebe for her imminent visit to Batoche: "'When you get there,' he said, 'listen. Just listen'" (25).[38] Repetition of Wiebe's admonition has been increasing as the essay reaches its end. And with that, the emphasis on "God, the Great Spirit" has been increasing as well, had begun, indeed, with the opening words of the essay—"On a raw and *windy* day in March 1977 . . ." (20; my italics). For the wind (like the thunder, *le tonnerre*) is a familiar, traditional vehicle of the voice of God, the Great Spirit.[39]

> . . . "*listen*. Just *listen*."
> The voices in the wind at the Métis cemetery that day spoke

of courage and of faith and of injustice. They spoke of our intertwined history, of our ancestors, of our children.

Listen. Just *listen.* (25)

In late April she was in Hamilton, attending the Canada Day festivities at Mohawk College and drinking some wine with Al Purdy (as he had hoped). Something moved her to make another act of coming home. She phoned two former classmates of United College days, Roy and Lois Wilson, now both ordained ministers of the United Church and serving a joint pastorate in Hamilton, Ontario. With that phone call Margaret reconstituted a bond that persisted and strengthened during her remaining years.

Adroit mingling of the active and the contemplative modes of life continued after the meeting at Mohawk College, bringing challenging tasks and merited rewards. Margaret participated in the Prairie Writers' Workshop in Saskatoon and met with students at the University of Saskatchewan, attended meetings at the University of Guelph, and made an unlikely trip to Sudbury in northern Ontario. She flew to the coast to accept an honourary Doctor of Literature at Simon Fraser University in Burnaby, British Columbia, and give the convocation address, and she flew down east to Fredericton to be installed as a Fellow of the Royal Society of Canada, a considerable honour.[40] But most important to Margaret was the Writers' Union conference, in May, held in Toronto, at which she met young David Williams—writer, prairie person, and an academic at the University of Manitoba. She knew and admired his novel *The Burning Wood* (1975), and Purdy had met him while writer-in-residence at the University of Manitoba and pronounced him "a good guy" (high praise from Purdy). He also recounted that talking with David had given him the information that Riel's grave was "quite nearby," as well as the beginning of a poem (most likely "Ritual"—full of Mircea Eliade, Carl Jung, and myth).[41] Purdy wrote Margaret that David Williams has a high opinion of *The Diviners*: "Since he's a Faulkner man the compliment doesn't seem entirely puerile."[42]

Margaret's letter to David Williams refers to her busy weeks since their meeting in Toronto and gives some information about her unlikely trip up to Sudbury. She had promised to visit the United Church minister there, "a guy I went to United College with, and I hadn't seen him in 30 years."[43] The guy in Sudbury was the Reverend Charles Harkness Forsyth, probably the most brilliant of our classmates in the arts program at United College, and a classmate in theology of Lois (née Freeman) Wilson, and well worth a trip from Lakefield or anywhere else. Margaret also got to meet his wife, Myrna, from Sioux Lookout.[44] Of course they talked about "old times" and their memories of "the gang from north of Portage" (Avenue, that is, where United College/University of Winnipeg is located). "The years fell away," Margaret reported. But more immediately relevant was their talk "about some of the biblical references in my work," and most of all,

> my own concept of grace, or how I feel about it as a gift given not because deserved but just given, by life, by some mystery at the core of life which mankind sometimes calls God, in our need to put names to and define unnamed forces and indefinable ones, perhaps.[45]

The coincidence of her meeting with Lois and Roy Wilson and then with Charles Forsyth was more fortunate than fortuitous, and part of Margaret's not altogether haphazard "coming home." Her rediscovery of these ministers of the gospel was an almost intentional program to help satisfy her need for a firmer and more sympathetic basis for her recovered interest in formal Christianity.

Though they had not been close friends in college, she and Lois quickly recognized a shared intellectual curiosity, in religion and literature, respectively; "we were kind of intrigued to see what made each other tick," as Lois put it. They were also intruders into traditional male realms. Lois graduated in theology a year after Roy; they married a year later. Lois was not ordained as minister in the United

Church of Canada, however, until June of 1965 (their fifteenth wedding anniversary as well), by which time she was mother of four children, Mistress of the Manse, and assistant to the Reverend Roy. She and Margaret discussed matters religious and social, to their mutual benefit; they prepared and exchanged bibliographies—Lois's list of theological and philosophical works, Margaret's list of Canadian literary works. The relationship flourished to a kind of climax (there would be another) in the fall of 1979, when Margaret hesitantly accepted Lois's invitation to share in a dialogue-sermon at the Wilsons' Chalmers United Church in Kingston, Ontario. Lois had originally invited her to be a guest preacher. Margaret flatly declined but accepted the idea of a free discussion with Lois. She had participated in a similar arrangement with Charles Forsyth and his congregation in Sudbury.

Margaret had become involved in the controversy over a piece of sculpture by the Canadian artist Almuth Lutkenhaus, *Crucified Woman*. It is a dramatic, symbolic rendering of the victimization of women and thus appealed to the experienced Margaret, who vigorously defended its mounting at Toronto's Bloor Street United Church during Easter Week, 1977. (Bloor Street United became Margaret's church in the metropolis even as she was becoming part of the congregation of Lakefield United.) Her intervention was a defense of the right of an artist to freedom of expression and especially of a female artist to express herself; it was also a defense of her right to free artistic adaptation of Christian terms, symbols, and myths. *Crucified Woman* touched her deeply and permanently and from various angles.

For the dialogue-sermon with Margaret in Chalmers United that autumn, Roy had arranged a small end table, a comfortable chair on either side of it, on a platform at the front of the sanctuary.[46] Lois began by asking if Margaret felt a vocation to writing comparable to the "call" to the ministry felt by the clergy. Margaret said "Yes," firmly: all serious writers know that sense of vocation. And how had her life as a female writer affected her experience of God? Margaret was not quite ready to discuss God per se (as her comments to David Williams seem to indicate). She referred to "the informing spirit of the universe" but affirmed it must include both a male and a female principle. To Lois's invitation to discuss the concept of Justice, Margaret replied she tended to approach it by examining its absence, the fact of Injustice. She demanded we not see injustice as "the Fault of God or Fate. It is our human fault!"[47] (She might have offered this example: "Where was God in the Holocaust? That is not the question. Where was humankind?"[48]) The dialogue led them to consider death and immortality. They agreed that resurrection was not about the resuscitation of a corpse, but about God, whose power transforms death to life and despair to hope.[49]

In June of the following year Margaret gave the convocation address at York University in Toronto. She departed from her usual format, she told Hubert Evans when she sent him a typed copy, to a more confessional mode, "to tell kids how I myself was feeling right now, about the world, about life itself." Evans would understand, she felt, because they were alike "Christian radicals"; and she offered a brief comment on the relation between faith and good works—a comment that further illuminates her attitude to Gabriel Dumont, especially in his relation to Louis Riel:

> it seems that good works without faith isn't enough, as we all stand so much in need of grace. But "faith" without "good works" . . ie a sense of social responsibility and the belief that the world around us *is* our responsibility, seems to me to be . . if not an empty faith, then at least a faith lacking in some kind of human dimension, the recognition of the reality of others' pain.[50]

Her basic attitudes remained but she was considering them philosophically, making careful distinctions, refining her principles. She continued to do so in her increased domestic solitude—not loneliness. She still held to the principle that being alone is not necessarily the equivalent of loneliness. She had reviewed but very little revised the piece in *Heart of a Stranger* called "The Shack." It accurately reflected her attitude, her tribute to the solitude possible on the banks of the Otonabee, now "The most loved place," where she spent her days "writing, bird-watching, river-watching." The weekend will begin on the morrow and bring friends and conversation well into the night, "but for now, I'm content to be alone, because loneliness is something that doesn't exist here, in this best place of mine."[51]

Jocelyn and David were back in Canada, pursuing their studies at Ryerson Polytechnical Institute in Toronto. Jocelyn graduated in the spring of 1978, Bachelor of Applied Arts (major in radio and television). In September she went to Corfu to teach English, and she invited Margaret to visit next spring. David had a year left in his program at Ryerson. Margaret felt lucky, she told Jean Cole at the end of July 1978, "that both my kids have been within shouting distance for some four years," and she then added that she was off to Corfu to take up Jocelyn's invitation.[52]

The writer was still active. The year 1979 saw publication of her littlest book for little people, part of a series on "the real lives of real kids," intended to be read-it-yourself volumes aimed at beginning readers aged five to six years.[53] *Six Darn Cows* is a little item in simple language and with lots of repetition to aid familiarity. Two kids are sent out to bring home the family's cows; the gate to the field was left open, the cows have gone, and the kids feel terrible. But the six darn cows are found and the kids have learned a lesson, for the family, though poor, has been ready to work together. And Margaret wrote a song for the ending.[54]

Although something else seemed to be wanting to be written, Margaret turned to a more substantial book for children, *The Christmas Birthday Story*. It is a retelling of the Nativity, and it has an interesting history that makes it the fourth additional happy event to distinguish 1977. At Christmastime that year at a small dinner party at the home of friends near Lakefield, Margaret was introduced to a woman who had attended the same Unitarian Church in Vancouver that the Laurences attended in those years. She asked Margaret if she remembered retelling the Nativity story for Christmas of 1959, for she and her husband had read it to their children when young every Christmas after. Margaret confessed that while she did remember doing the story, she had lost it during the bustle of moving to England with Jocelyn and David in 1962. An original copy arrived within a few days; Margaret read it, revised it, and sent it off to McClelland and Stewart, who published it in 1980, with illustrations by Helen Lucas.[55]

When Margaret recounted the history of *The Christmas Birthday Story* to Gabrielle Roy, she supplied this poignant conclusion:

> Imagine! . . . it came home to me after so long. I thought this must mean something, so I rewrote the story slightly, and added to it a little, and then I asked the Toronto artist, Helen Lucas (whom I had recently met—another wonderful happenstance) if she would consider doing some pictures for it.[56]

Margaret confirmed the sense she had had about the recovery of the story when she observed in her memoirs, "The return of the story seemed to mean something."[57]

She had written the story in response to the objections of parents at the Unitarian Church in Vancouver about continuing to read the Nativity narrative in the New Testament "because we knew angels weren't actually flitting around the sky."[58] She had been confronted by a sort of moralistic censorship based on a narrow literalistic reading of the scriptures—very like the situation she had met so recently in and around Peterborough and derived from the same naïve censorious approach to narrative that wanted to ban *The Diviners*. Margaret had been horrified in 1959 as in 1976. She did not want her children, Jocelyn at age seven and David at age four, to be "denied that part of their heritage," including that story, "which has some basic truths."[59]

Basing her Birthday Story on the gospels of St. Matthew and St. Luke, but taking some liberties, she created a version she felt was appropriate for small children. Here, Mary and Joseph didn't know and didn't care what sex the baby would be. "I really wanted to emphasize the birth of the beloved child into the loving family," she told Gabrielle Roy in her letter of 25 September 1980. That is the prominent feature of the retelling. It is couched in the modern idiom easily understandable to 1950s children. It relies on suspense (where will the couple spend the night? where will the baby be born? will it be a boy or girl?); and the setting is created with plenty of solid, realistic detail: "It was the olden days, remember, so they didn't have cars or trains or buses or planes. Mary rode on a donkey, a tame gray donkey with long pointy ears, and Joseph walked beside her." Finally the stable, where a cow mooed softly, a lamb cried "in its small voice" and the mother ewe answered "in her deeper voice," and "Soft yellow hay . . . has a faint sweet smell. Mary liked the sweet smell" and it filled the manger. All familiar, thus, and palpable. Helen Lucas's modern illustrations fit exactly, though not quite in the genre of old-fashioned realism. The element of mystery (and more suspense) is added when the three kings find the stable and the baby: they know immediately that the baby is special!

Divinity is unobtrusively implied (for parents) in the mystery and also in the natural setting—the stable, the animals, and Joseph himself. He comes out of Margaret's early writing, a poem she published in *The Manitoban* for 26 January 1945; a sonnet *manqué*, it describes the response of a woman "upon the hill that day . . . kneeling as if in prayer." The woman speaks:

> "Man with worker's hands, I have watched you walk away.
> Strong one, I loved you—will the world so love your life?
> Jesus, son of Joseph, I would have been your wife."
> I think there was a woman upon the hill that day.

The recognizable impulse had evidently been there from early on in

Margaret's life. Lois Wilson has provided the clearest, most sympathetic, and most persuasive recognition of that impulse in Margaret and of the profound religious quality of her work in "Faith and the Vocation of the Author." That essay is essential reading for anyone who would fully understand Margaret Laurence—and for anyone who would like a glimpse into the intelligent heart of Lois Wilson, for that matter.

The Christmas Birthday Story also includes a prophetic note: the first king thinks the baby will grow up to be strong and hard-working, like Joseph; the second, that he will be gentle and kind, like his mother; the third, "that he will be a wise teacher and a friend to all people." And it was so, the narrative voice assures the reader.

A similar voice recalls, in *Dance on the Earth*,

> I retold it in a way that I myself understand it and believe in it. Jesus is . . . a beloved child, born into a loving family, a child who grew up to be a wise teacher, and a friend to all people. This is really how I think of our Lord. (221)

Clearly enough, *The Christmas Birthday Story* derives from the social gospel; is as sturdy and gentle, as physical and spiritual, as Gabriel Dumont appeared to Margaret's eye; and—carefully attended to—is redolent of the concerns of all of Margaret's life and work. Apparently the final book in her creative career, it has a singular appropriateness.

As though in recognition of that fact, Margaret divested herself of one of her cherished possessions—her "shack" on the bank of the Otonabee River. It had served her well for a decade, she felt, as a kind of sanctuary where she could accept the descent of grace that enabled her to complete the Manawaka Saga. Having to look after two establishments now seemed too great a responsibility. Clear and plausible, the explanation may yet have concealed another truth. In a couple of instances at least, Margaret's manner of announcing the sale to friends seems to imply more than it actually says. She wrote to Hubert Evans thus: "Just recently sold my cottage. . . . [It] was so much bound up in my mind with the writing of The Diviners," not the cottage *itself*, however, "but that particular view of the Otonabee."[60] Then, a touch more explicitly to Gabrielle Roy: "I sold my cottage this spring. . . . I could not write there, now, because I think in my mind the river in that place was too much connected with the writing of *The Diviners*."[61] If the view of the river seemed to threaten the creation of another novel, then maybe another novel was vaguely there to be threatened. Just maybe. . . .

It was clear to those closest to Margaret that *The Diviners* indeed marked the end of the Manawaka Saga (excluding, perhaps, the little coda, *The Olden Days Coat*) and very likely the end of her career as a novelist. She kept an active pen, of course, writing several very good non-fiction pieces—book reviews and urgent comments on social issues. A significance in her life now was the absence of the kind of intimately personal problem that—like the oyster's provocative grain of sand—had been responsible for her works of fiction. The urge to create serious major fiction nevertheless remained, not to be denied; and it was accompanied by not quite a "problem," but a sense of incompleteness, of something yet to do or, perhaps, to redo in a slightly different mode. The last "happy event" marking 1977 as a specially significant moment in Margaret's career was the apparent promise of the return of grace. In April of that year she wrote to Walter Swayze that "an idea or series of ideas have begun flooding into mind" since the beginning of the month. "I have such a strong longing to get back to my proper work, and . . . an embryo of a novel seems to be forming in my mind. . . ."[62] Three months later, she sent Walter another encouraging note: "I'm doing all kinds of weird reading right now, as a kind of background for what may be another novel. I don't do 're-search' and never have. I simply think about things, and hope the characters will present themselves and talk to me. . . ."[63] She ends the letter with a word of thanks for the invitation to stay with the Swayzes when she comes to Winnipeg, and observes that she will "have to go back to Winnipeg for a visit, to check on some places, etc."

The suspicion thus aroused, that the embryo novel would have something to do with Winnipeg and environs, is further encouraged by her letter to Jean Cole a year later, announcing her plan to visit Winnipeg in October 1978, "to see the old city again, with thoughts, maybe, about a possible novel."[64] Coincidentally, perhaps, Margaret also mentioned her summer reading, which included *The Canadian Left* (1977) by Norman Penner, son of Winnipeg North End's communist alderman Jacob Penner and older brother of Roland. Surely that was part of the "weird reading" she mentioned to Walter Swayze. In another account, she included Penner's book along with Tim Buck's memoirs, *A Conscience for Canada* (1975), in a list of "v. serious reading . . . in between some thinking . . a lot of things . . and note-taking about what comes next for me."[65] Then, on New Year's Eve she wrote again to Newfoundlander Harold Horwood, "I am writing again . . . but. . . ." And it is apparent that something else was involved, some interference that might threaten the new novel.

Early in 1979, she wrote a long letter to her friend Professor Gordon Roper, formerly a colleague of hers at Trent University, that casts a good deal of light on the situation and on the prospective future novel. She had given it up: she realized "just after Christmas" (i.e., evidently at about the time she was writing to Horwood) that she couldn't do it. She had felt she had to write once again out of her prairie background and relying on the reading she had been doing—"weird" or "v. serious"—about western Left Wing movements, especially Winnipeg's Old Left; and the Ukrainians in the prairies, their sufferings and achievements as early immigrant settlers. (Those two items overlap significantly: a number of important politicians from the Old Left, along with their supporters, were descendants of Ukrainian immigrants.) To Professor Roper she lamented her ignorance of the Ukrainians, that she couldn't really write about them "from *inside*" and their story needed to be told by someone like Saskatchewan poet Andy

Suknaski. It didn't occur to her, apparently, that she could intermarry them with some Scots immigrants and focus on the generations that followed, as she did very briefly with Pique in *The Diviners*. She was by no means sure, furthermore, that she wanted to treat the Old Left fictionally. But the most decisive impediment was something already hinted at: "I decided," she explained to Roper, "if I attempted to say more about the Manawaka background [in fiction], it would not come out right because I don't feel that inner *need* to say more about it."[66] And although in the following year, early and late, she confided to close friends like Adele Wiseman and Al Purdy that she continued to grapple with the novel ("I am trying to write a novel" and "I still have not got into this new novel"),[67] her words to Roper seem sternly final.

Of course one never knows what tomorrow, or the new decade, may bring.

eighteen

Amazed by Love

ON WEDNESDAY, 26 NOVEMBER 1980, THE *TRENT FORTNIGHTLY* announced that on 1 January 1981 Margaret Laurence would become the fourth Chancellor of Trent University, "succeeding a fellow Manitoban," Canadian historian W.L. Morton. The *Fortnightly* quoted university president Donald F. Theall on the appropriateness of the appointment of Margaret Laurence to the position, "a dedicated Canadian and a creative artist who has been a constant friend of Trent"; it also reported the new chancellor's hope that "she will be all that Trent is accustomed to in its chancellor and all that it hopes for." Those bright expectations were, however, not to be fully realized. Margaret had indeed been a friend of this small academic institution committed to the ideals of a liberal education. One of her first official acts was to lead a delegation from the Trent faculty to the offices of Dr. Bette Stephenson, Ontario Minister of Colleges and Universities, to emphasize the importance of Trent's application for a "differentiation grant" to pursue its rather peculiar goals. The Advisory Memorandum to Minister Stephenson explained,

> In the course of its development, Trent has chosen to differentiate itself from other institutions in the Ontario system and has a particular role to play as the only institution in the

> Province engaged almost entirely in undergraduate Arts and Science instruction.[1]

The representation was successful and Trent received the first and only differentiation grant awarded in Ontario—$1,400,000. Dr. Stephenson "was obviously impressed that Canada's leading woman writer of the period would take the time to lead a delegation on Trent's behalf and to speak so warmly and knowledgeably about the needs of her adopted university."[2] (The position of chancellor carried no stipend.)

Later in the year Margaret once again rose in defense of her adopted university. The Executive Committee of the university Board of Governors held what was virtually a secret meeting to discuss changes in budget, the university's academic structuring, reorganization of the editorial board of the prestigious *Journal of Canadian Studies*, and related matters—the Hansen Report. The university Senate was scheduled to deal with the report at two meetings in November 1981; Margaret did not receive a copy of the document (although she was an *ex officio* member of the Board of Governors) until 12 November, some two weeks after the other members of the board had received them. She spent the next two days studying the report closely, then wrote a six-page, single-spaced letter to board chair Erica Cherney, giving a detailed criticism of the proposals in the report. The late Professor Alf Cole observed of Margaret, "What she saw in the report was the end of the university she had come to love."[3] The chancellor explained:

> I was invited to become Chancellor of a university of a certain kind, a small liberal arts and science university whose emphasis has strongly been on caring about students as individuals, on excellence of academic standards, and on the valuable exchange of ideas between students and faculty, both inside the classroom and in the life of the colleges.[4]

When President Theall saw the letter, he confronted Margaret over lunch, at her home in Lakefield. That night, she put her case succinctly to her friends Jean and Alf Cole: "Kid, if they wanted a silent Chancellor, they shouldn't have chosen me."[5]

Letters of support for her position poured in to the offices of President Theall and the chair of the board, from faculty, staff, students, and alumni. There were none in support of the Hansen Report. This flurry set the tone for Margaret's tenure over her remaining two years. During that time she conferred honourary degrees upon her old friend and mentor Malcolm Ross, upon her newer friend Timothy Findley, and upon one of her chief political heroes, Tommy Douglas. On leaving the post, she arranged to confer another doctorate, that upon The Very Reverend Lois M. Wilson, on 1 June 1984.

During her first year as chancellor at Trent, Margaret became involved in the project to bring the Chinese writer and near-martyr Ding Ling (the pen name of Jiang Wei) to Toronto as part of her visit to Canada. Adele Wiseman sent introductory information on the visitor early in September 1981; Margaret found her story fascinating and lent her support.[6] Clara Thomas, professor of English at York University, was immediately involved and added her enthusiasm. Part of the attraction was Ding Ling's dedication to communism, the social revolution in China, and her staunch feminism, for which she had suffered humiliation and imprisonment. She was China's most famous woman writer, with a career that had begun in the twenties. She was brought to Canada under the auspices of the Canada Council and accompanied by her husband and her translator, Richard Liu. Gary Geddes, then of Concordia College, served as her official escort.

A reception was planned in her honour for Saturday, 28 November 1981, in Winters College of York University in North Toronto. A small dinner party to precede the reception was planned for 6:00 p.m., including Ding Ling and her husband, Adele Wiseman, Clara Thomas, Alice Munro, Gary Geddes, and Margaret.[7] The guest list for the reception included the presidents of the three universities of York, Toronto, and Trent, Dr. and Mrs. Sword, Dr. and Mrs. Northrop Frye,

Dr. and Mrs. Robertson Davies, Mary and Ken Adachi, Beth Appeldorn and Susan Sandler, Margaret Atwood and Graeme Gibson, Timothy Findley and William Whitehead, Robert Kroetsch, Mr. and Mrs. Dennis Lee, James and Colleen Reaney, Miriam Waddington, and Earle Birney. Margaret found the celebration "wonderful," and declared that she had "learned from her [Ding Ling], in that short time." A couple of days later she reported that Clara Thomas thought "IT ALL WENT WELL!" and that the puckish Clara had taken to calling the whole event "The Ding Ling Wing Ding" from behind the altar.[8]

The affair in honour of the victimized Chinese artist was closely followed by an acknowledgement of a related kind of victimization—and right at home. A suite of poems by Terrance Cox on a visit to Israel appeared in *Contemporary Verse II* (Summer 1981) and provoked a reply from Adele Wiseman in the form of sharply satiric verse aimed directly at Cox and what she perceived as being his anti-Semitic poems. Adele circulated copies of Cox's verse and her own satire among a number of her friends. Having got wind of that move, Cox instructed his attorney to contact Robert Foster of the editorial staff of *Contemporary Verse II* to enjoin him to suppress publication of Adele's "libel and slander" in the volume. That was in early March. A month later Margaret threw her support to Adele by writing a pithy letter to Foster. She had read, she informs him, Cox's poems on Israel and finds them distasteful.

> They seemed to insult both Jewish Israelis and Muslim Palestinians. . . . Ms. Wiseman's rebuttal takes strong issue with the expressed feelings and opinions of one man. Mr. Cox's poems appeared to be an attack upon an entire people. . . . By seeking to suppress Ms. Wiseman's rebuttal, he would appear to wish to deny her that freedom of expression which he has himself been given. This would . . . endanger the freedom of speech of our literary journals.[9]

At the same time, Margaret's sense of justice, or rather of injustice, was again alerted by an article in *Saturday Night* for January 1982 by Rick Salutin—"The Conversion of the Jews"—that was accompanied by illustrations by Anita Kunz. Margaret wrote to the editor, Robert Fulford, to complain about the "ugly and vicious caricatures" (as they would appear to most of her friends, including me): "they are extremely offensive" and, further, "The horrendous realities of the Holocaust . . . have their beginnings in attitudes which grotesquely stereotype and distort an entire people, thus setting them up as convenient potential scapegoats." The editor promised to run this letter of 2 January 1982 "in an early issue." Then, as though calculated to add insult to injury, those very illustrations were given the National Magazine Gold Medal Award.

A letter of objection was quickly created, signed by Adele and her husband and various others—such as Naomi Diamond, Irving Layton, Seymour Mayne, Joe Rosenblatt, and Helen Weinzweig—and sent to the awards committee, the *Globe and Mail*, and the *Toronto Star*: "We find these illustrations racist. They are offensive to Jews, and indeed to everyone who recognizes with distaste their affinity with the style and spirit of the 1930s Nazi propaganda. We wonder precisely what you chose to reward here."[10] (The *Star* chose not to publish the letter.)

Further evidence of the impulse of the alien heart appears in Margaret's participation in other "good causes."[11] She served with Lois Wilson on the board of Energy Probe, which actively monitored and opposed proliferation of nuclear armaments, and also in Project Ploughshares—an interfaith disarmament organization—as well as in the similarly oriented Operation Dismantle. She also supported the principles and action of women's rights groups, notably the Canadian Abortion Rights League (CARAL), representing a much more sane and moral "right to life" than what that term has come to signify; of course, she was a vigorously active member of the NDP.

Margaret engaged in these pursuits with the hearty sympathy not only of Lois Wilson but usually also of Adele Wiseman. There was one occasion during these months, however, on which she differed rather seriously with Adele. Their devotion to duties as members of the Writers' Union was challenged when the suggestion—largely Adele's responsibility—that a social club would be a happy adjunct to the union led to a meeting in early July 1982. Minutes of that meeting indicate that a group of half a dozen artists (including Margaret) gathered at Adele's Toronto home to discuss formation of "a loosely knit . . . social club for an alliance of artists from various disciplines"—membership by invitation—"for inter-disciplinary cross-pollination." Workshops and seminars were envisaged as useful means to that end. There remained the question of locating a physical gathering point or simply, as Sylvia Fraser suggested, choosing a restaurant where the members could meet informally. The half-dozen inaugurating individuals faced the two most serious problems: (1) what criteria for membership in the social club would guide the selection committee for each genre? and (2) would an initial fee of $1000 and a subsequent annual fee of $300 suffice?[12]

The meeting was adjourned amicably at 11:30 p.m. Margaret spent the night at Adele's and returned to Lakefield on Saturday morning. She stewed for the next few days over the decisions taken, and on the first Tuesday wrote to Adele with deep apologies that she could not participate in the social club and, in particular, she could not function as a member of the selection committee. She wasn't in sympathy with the workshop-seminar aspect of the plan, and she feared that the whole matter of membership by invitation, with its implicit policy of exclusion, would prove to be a divisive force among her "tribe." Further, the initial fee particularly struck Margaret as an immediate obstacle for a number of invités. She concluded, "I implore you, try to understand and forgive me for this stance."[13]

If there was any consequent rift between Adele and Margaret, it was quickly healed and without discernible scar. A few weeks later, a similar group met to inaugurate a slightly different, fondly frolic, and somewhat lunatic social club, without affiliation with the union. The Loons (so-called on the recommendation of Meg Merrilees Laurence) came into being on 24 August 1982. Each of the six pre-loonies was to sound out, in strict confidence, ten participants from each discipline with an eye to offering them membership, and it was hoped that "a pub or restaurant which has a big reasonably quiet place, with a (preferable) big table" could be found for future meetings.[14]

At the next meeting less formality prevailed, and the matter of fees was tabled, along with regular dates for subsequent meetings. They did, however, settle on a place and time for the next flocking together: The Dell, 300 Simcoe (corner of Elsa and Simcoe), 3 November 1982, 12:30 p.m., individual cheques. In November, the covey of nineteen relaxed its rigorous informality sufficiently to agree to meet on the first Monday of each month, to rely on a "no-agenda agenda," and to interpret the criteria for membership in a shockingly unbuttoned manner. Margaret was not able to get to a meeting until that of 7 February 1983—held at an attractive Greek restaurant, Anesty's—at which she served as recording secretary. Her minutes sustain the tone of informal "loonacy" that obviously characterized the meeting, and she embellished them with ink drawings (self-portrait, flowers, and the smiley snail that had been in her repertoire since serving as pattern for her first African window curtains). She also included a treatise on the loon, as part of her vigorous campaign for adoption of that fowl creature as the club's totem.

By that time Margaret had severed relations with the Writers' Union of Canada. She sent a formal letter of resignation to the National Council of the union on 8 October 1982.[15] The union, she explained, seemed to have "departed from its original intentions," and thus she no longer felt "bound to remain in an organization whose ideals and aims I can no longer endorse." The reports of general meetings (in the union newsletter) characterizing them as "love-ins" and "great partying" implied not simply a lack of seriousness on the part of the general membership but also—more grave—a lack of responsibility therein, "that the union is now run far too much by the Executive and by the Toronto office staff." The question of fees seemed vexed; the loss of revenue from membership obliged the union to rely increasingly on financial support from the government. The union's loss of autonomy struck Margaret as inevitable. That failure was accompanied by the union's increasing inability, or unwillingness, to recognize superior quality and to distinguish among the varied abilities of its members.

Margaret chose to emphasize this prime concern in a *Private and Confidential* letter to Naim Kattan (then head of the Writing and Publication section of the Canada Council), which contained the large initial paragraph of her grievances as presented to the Writers' Union. Union and council, she saw, would benefit from mutual support: "If the Canada Council becomes a political branch of whatever government is in power, the arts in this country will be greatly threatened." She believed the union's control of such programs as funded tours needed the reciprocity of the traditional judgement of the council—and that was being neglected. Consequently, the union's practice of sending out to high schools, libraries, and universities any member who was ready and willing threatened the whole idea of the reading tours, Margaret insisted.

> I simply do not believe that the work of every writer in the union is equally suitable. . . . any sense of quality or suitability goes out the window, to the detriment of students and reading public. . . . there are standards in writing, and I do not like to see high school students, etc, being subjected to the readings of mediocre writers.[16]

During the early eighties it became apparent that the discarded novel, the "embryo" she had written Walter Swayze about at the end of April 1977, was not stillborn after all. It persisted, demanded her attention, and bade her prepare for the old familiar descent of grace. She had written Al Purdy on 3 November 1980, "I still have not gotten into this new novel"; but subsequent references make clear that the new one was the same engrossing embryo comprised of Ukrainians and the Old Left. A few months later she wrote almost identical reports to Alice Munro and George Woodcock and on the same day, 26 March 1981: "The novel that maybe I will be able to write has been brewing in my mind for some 4 years, but only this week have I got myself into the New Regime . . . working from 9 a.m. to 2 p.m. . . ." Margaret may have had more reason to inform Ms Munro of the renascence than she herself realized. The next year, letters to Timothy Findley (15 January) and to Hubert Evans (19 March) indicate that she was persevering: "Maybe *this* time I'll progress beyond Chapter One" and "I'm writing—I think—a novel, or, as it may turn out, some stories."[17]

The obvious questions are "Where are the results of those persistent attempts to write the novel—or maybe 'some stories'?" and "What could one make of such results that might enlighten us further about the career and life of Margaret Laurence?"

The result of Margaret's sustained attempt to create another novel is an armful of manuscript pages, including three comparatively substantial narratives of from ten to sixty-six pages in length. Particularly useful are the pages of notes devoted to the *dramatis personae*—their background, dates of birth and death, interrelations, dwelling places, and, in a few cases, their profession or employment, and also a word on neighbours and neighbourhoods. On the basis of these notes and the modest narratives, it is possible to sketch out Margaret's evident intentions. All this material, with one significant exception, was deposited in Mills Library at McMaster University some years after Margaret's death, having been kept privately by Jocelyn and David Laurence. The exception is a manuscript in the archives of the Scott Library of York University, a sustained narrative, which Margaret herself had prepared for the Special Collections.[18] The narrative bears the date "July 1983," which marks it as the latest of the sustained narratives that remain (the two others closest in date are those marked 20 February 1983 and 3 August 1982). Margaret Wigmore, a professor at the

University of Regina and a Laurence scholar, says of this exception,

> there is something special about the fact that the chapter in York University Archives was placed there by Laurence herself, perhaps . . . because she felt that the subject matter of women dancing on the earth and . . . what that dance on the earth had been was too important to be destroyed.[19]

The project, called "Dance on the Earth," focusses on two families, one Ukrainian in origin and the other Scots-English in origin, who emigrated to Canada near the beginning of the twentieth century. The two families are united in 1942 by marriage—or rather, the Scots descendant, Alys "Allie" Lansdowne-Pryce, is absorbed into the Ukrainian family upon her marriage to Steve Chorniuk.[20] And thus the second Ukrainian-Canadian generation is wedded to the first Scottish-Canadian. The family is traced through two more generations: the only surviving child of Steve and Allie Chorniuk, Stefan, marries the Irish-Canadian Jennifer "Jen" O'Brien in 1975. In 1977, their daughter Mairi is born. The genealogy refers to her as the inheritor; she is named after her maternal grandmother, Mary McDuff, whom she never knew, and her aunt, Mary Chorniuk, who died in 1947 at age three. This inheritor is to be the focus of "Dance on the Earth" in the same way Pique is the focus of *The Diviners*.

In late May of 1986, Margaret slipped away for her last professional visit to Winnipeg to accept an honourary degree—at last—from the University of Manitoba. While there, she luckily agreed to an interview with two professors of English in St. John's College, David Arnason and Dennis Cooley.[21] The first question asked for a comment on the Ukrainians in Manawaka. Her reply has particular relevance to the Chorniuks in "Dance on the Earth":

> there were a very large number of Ukrainians and Scottish people in my town, in fact they were the two largest groups. . . . in the class structure of Manawaka the Ukrainians were looked down upon by the Scots . . . [but] the Ukrainians of

> my generation were incredibly determined that their children would have an education. (32)

The most perceptive question—abundantly relevant to the incomplete novel as to *all* of the Manawaka fiction—proposed that

> the orderly passage of property from one generation to another in a patriarchal world is endangered because of female sexuality and because this female sexuality may express itself in relationships with the feared lower class, it seems to me that your novels develop a kind of erotic dimension out of that. (33)

Almost breathlessly she began, "Well, I think this is true," and developed a brief, specific agreement, invoking as illustration Rachel of *A Jest of God* and Morag of *The Diviners*.

The proposed title of "Dance on the Earth" is followed by a dedication—"For Jocelyn and David with faith, hope and love"—to her own inheritors. Next, a quotation from a modern hymn, "Lord of the Dance" by Sydney Carter:

> I danced in the morning when the world was begun
> and I danced in the moon and the stars and the sun
> and I came down from heaven and I danced on the earth—
> at Bethlehem I had my birth.

The narrative surface is strongly reminiscent of *The Diviners* and, in various ways, of most of Margaret's fiction. The importance of ancestors and of sustaining the relation of the ancestral past to the visitable past, the present, and the inheriting future is an important theme in "Dance." This narrative opens with Allie explaining that she must set down "for all the children"—but especially for her granddaughter, young Mairi—what she knows of the ancestors from hearing voices "from times long past": "Sometimes the stories are those they really did tell me and sometimes those they might have told, imagined by me from what I know or guess about their lives." As Morag confessed in her letter to Ella, so Allie could say, that "I like the thought of history and fiction interweaving."[22] And Allie's history, her Scots background, is similar to Morag's and thus very like Margaret's. The grandmother Allie never knew came from the southwest edge of the Highlands, specifically from the notorious slums of Glasgow, The Gorbals: "I sometimes . . . think I may have inherited some qualities from them ["my long ago people"], the Gaelic ones, and especially the ancient Pictish ones, the aboriginals of Scotland." (In a letter to Purdy, Margaret had explained that the Wemyss family, her father's, "descended from the Picts—the aborigines of Scotland! . . . , a dark and magic people."[23] The information arrived too late to be used in *The Diviners*, but it was not meant to be wasted.)

A strong "feminist" impulse moves Allie to set down what she has learned from the voices, the stories of "those women whose histories, whose stories, are lost, disappeared, vanished." The lines of descent are always traced through fathers, Allie observes, so "I am going to set down the line of descent through your mothers on your father's side." Part of that line of descent must include Allie's sister-in-law Stella, her best friend, who is childless.

Allie and Stella discuss the family as they close the cottage for the winter. Stella does a man's job in bringing the boat up from shore to stow it away. Allie meanwhile stands on the long oak table (like the one Margaret brought from Elm Cottage) to be able to wash the huge front window of the cottage (like the huge front window of Margaret's "shack" on the Otonabee River). Stella muses on the terror of their world of threatening cold war and the horrors of nuclear weapons: "so much damn power in the hands of a few. . . . Democracy is a charade here. The power of the workers is a charade over there." The observation moves Allie to muse on the "political Chorniuks . . . no child of Peter Chorniuk's ever grew up without some sense of the raging injustice of this world." Allie's husband, Peter's son, has a special note on the title page of this narrative: "Steve—Communist—why?" The question is less one of puzzlement on Margaret's part than an artistic admonition—*show* why Steve is a communist; Stella's comments, an example of which was just quoted, are part of that showing.

Perhaps most important of all is Allie's profoundly religious basis. That includes the need to recognize death as truly a part of life, of the natural cycle, and as real as birth—delivery; that basis also includes an understanding and appreciation of nature. As night approaches, Allie wanders out to say goodnight and an autumnal farewell to Jordan's Lake. She expresses her recognition of the universal relationship of all creation, of humankind and nature, and of the autumn as an encouraging part of the cycle (if winter comes . . . ?).

On the dock, Allie thinks of the loons, "but tonight their ancient grieving voices are silent." Here is a distinct echo of the early poem "Pagan Point—Approaching Night" by Peggy Wemyss and of the piece "The Crying of the Loons" twenty years later (absorbed into *A Bird in the House*). The echo of the prose piece is much stronger in Allie's stern castigation of the principal cause of the disappearance of the loons—*Homo sapiens* "is driving them away from these lakes, or killing them off." She hears the waves speak "of ages before humankind. That time may come again—after humankind. The thought . . . hurts unbearably."

Despair, however, is arrested. Stella has put on some music—"fiddles and whistles and Irish pipes"—and come down to join Allie and to dance, perhaps for the last time, as this may be the last closing of the cottage these two women will undertake. They dance. "Here each of us can be a shawoman, ancestral foremother, equivalent of and equal to shaman. Sha-womb-an. . . . Two women of the elders, dancing." An appropriate ending to this brief narrative, which began, "tonight Stella and I danced. Two old women, dancing on the earth, dancing our lives, dancing joy, dancing grief." The implication surely is that the need to dance is prompted by the *élan vital* and, one might add, *créateur et artistique*.

An authentication for such quasi-ritual dancing, here and elsewhere in Margaret's writing in the seventies, is hinted at in a comment by

Alice Munro to accompany her letters from Margaret included in *A Very Large Soul*. Ms Munro remembers "a wonderful night spent at the cabin she had on the River. I remember we had dinner . . . and then we put on some records. . . . Scottish music. . . . We got up and danced, we both danced . . . around the cabin for hours to this music. . . . That is the greatest memory I have of her. Yeah, that was a wonderful night." She places the memorable occasion in "the summer of 1972, maybe August. . . . both of us in long bright dresses." Surely Margaret remembered as well.[24]

The names also play an important role in affirming connections between "Dance on the Earth" and the rest of the Laurence oeuvre, and also in asserting the metaphoric character of the narrative surface, of the mere "story." The association of "Dance" with the Manawaka Saga is perhaps most solid in the location of Allie's mother-in-law, Baba Rose Chorniuk: she lives "up at the mountain in Manitoba." Not many mountains in Manitoba, but the genealogical charts make the task even easier with the little list, "Galloping Mtn / South Wachakwa / Manawaka." The original is, of course, Riding Mountain, north of Neepawa, and Manawaka is Manawaka. Second, and more significant, Allie's husband, Steve, has an aunt Teresa who is married to Nestor Kazlik. Nothing more than a name on a list, but we know him from *A Jest of God*. Allie is then a cousin of Rachel Cameron's lover, Nick Kazlik, and his deceased twin brother. We might also note that marriage to Teresa makes Nestor the son-in-law of Wasyl Chorniuk. A distinguished lawyer and prominent member of the Ukrainian community in Winnipeg was Wasyl Swystun; his son Nestor, a successful QC, was a classmate of ours at United College. (Margaret did things like that for her own amusement—and perhaps to anchor, subtly, the fictive in the historic.) Finally, we have also met, in a brief but important walk-on role, the man who delivers wood to the Connor residence and brings to Vanessa the mixed-breed puppy in "The Half-Husky" of *A Bird in the House*. He is Peter Chorniuk of Galloping Mountain—brother-in-law, thus, of Nestor Kazlik and uncle of Nick. The final story of *A Bird* lists the families of boys lost at Dieppe in 1942; "Chorniuk" is there (169)—and the *dramatis personae* of "Dance" indicates that Steve's brother, Stanislaus, was one of the casualties, "Stanislaus (1920-42). Dieppe"—and it is followed by "Kamchuk," Stella's married name until she was divorced. A shortened version of that list, but with brief commentaries added, is repeated in *The Diviners*:

> Chorniuk, S. (That would be Stan Chorniuk, from the BA Garage.)
> Kamchuk, N. (Nick, who quit school after Grade Ten.) (116)

A small and interrelated world.

The cabin on the shores of Jordan's Lake, in "Dance on the Earth," which Allie and Stella close for the winter and where they dance, obviously derives from Morag's dwelling at McConnell's Landing on the bank of the river that flows both ways, or, more accurately, maybe, from Margaret's dwelling on the Otonabee. It is, however, the *name* that catches our attention, and lest it fail to do so Margaret repeats it shamelessly. The cabin on Jordan's Lake is near Jordan's Landing and not far from Jordan's River, where Allie and Stella live. This seems a not too subtle reminder of Margaret's first novel, *This Side Jordan*, in which title the biblical River Jordan is invoked as part of the metaphor to express the struggle of the colonized Gold Coast people to seize control of their future—to prepare (on this side Jordan) to cross over that barrier and enter the "promised land" of self-government and, it is hoped, freedom. Nathaniel Amegbe's supplication to his appropriately named son—the conclusion of the novel—underlines the rich significance that obtains: "Joshua. I beg you. Cross Jordan, Joshua."

The very similarity, however, emphasizes the difference in Margaret's intention. Her early Jordan, like the biblical river, is a barrier to be negotiated: it separates here from there. The late

Jordan of Allie and Stella, on the other hand, lake, landing, and river, is like the river that not only flows both ways but is a source of nourishment, a medium to ride upon, and an element to immerse oneself in—as Margaret and Morag swam in their medium and Allie and Stella swim here "ungraceful in our bathing suits and middle-to-old age, yet given a strange grace here." The element is not a barrier, an impediment, but a sustaining means—very like life; and it is also very like the "destructive element" into which one must immerse oneself (as Stein sagely advises Conrad's Lord Jim). For birth and death are very similar and life is the step between (like Purdy's "tightrope over Niagara Falls say / the beginning middle and end of the rope / are all present simultaneously" in "Gossamer Ending"—or Dylan Thomas's "The force that through the green fuse drives the flower / Drives my green age"; same thing). As in the published Manawaka fiction, Margaret here insists on embracing life, on the vital necessity of accepting the natural reality of death and also the importance of grasping the encouraging metaphor of resurrection as expressed in "the whole earth." Here is hope.

Allied with this means of developing a major theme in "Dance on the Earth" is the name shared by the two men to whom Allie is most closely related—"Steve" her husband and "Stefan" her son. Margaret's use of the name has an impressive history. She maintained that the first piece of writing she submitted to student publications at the University of Manitoba bore the pen name "Steve Lancaster"—"After the Lancaster Bomber, and I had always liked the name Steve."[25] Perhaps the young Ukrainian from the wrong side of the tracks in Neepawa who came to do repairs at Grandfather Wemyss's house and provoked the starry-eyed Mona Spratt and Peggy Wemyss (about nine years old) to attempt to engage his attention by chanting "Hunky, hunky, hunky" with impressive effect,[26] was named Steve. The red-haired circus hand with "friendly eyes," who generously shows the little runway around the fair and buys him lemonade, in "Calliope" (*Vox* 1945), is actually named Steve.

After graduation from United College, Margaret worked on a rather long poem entitled “North Main Car—Winnipeg (‘written in 1948’).” It was never published until its recovery by Margaret Wigmore and publication in the summer of 1999.[27] The streetcar ride southward takes the reader through the east edge of the North End of Winnipeg; the conductor calls out the streets and the poem gives brief portraits of seven passengers as each gets on board. Between the portraits are sketches of North End life. The focus is that of an acute social consciousness such as a member of the CCF or NDP or the Communist Party would have—of workers in poorly paid and otherwise unrewarding jobs. Collectively, the portraits and interspersed scenes convey the ethnic diversity of Winnipeg’s North End (and synecdochically of Canada as a whole), with a perhaps disproportionate emphasis on the Ukrainian element. The first passenger is the young man Steve—“Your last name does not matter . . you are all names / And all races . . .”—the proto-passenger.

> Rise at six on work days die
> Within two years of retiring . . it is your cry, soundless,
> . . “our future is today!”

The last stops are Henry Avenue and, following a Dantesque descent under the CPR subway and ascent (the way down and the way up are the one way), the CPR station, where finally the “people . . . disperse like dust” and “The crowd dissolves to one face . . a young man,” and the representative value of the proto-passenger is emphasized:

> Steve, your face is the face of my city.
> . . .
> let us build . . . a new structure, a fortress
> founded on common creed, our bond as workingmen:
> a base against oppression, our first bastion of tomorrow.

A probable offshoot from this Winnipeg Steven is the Ukrainian-Canadian youth featured in the novel Peggy was working on in 1950 and 1951 as the Laurences moved from England to Somaliland. It is discernibly autobiographical: a young woman of Peg's background falls in love with the attractive young man, and part of the attraction is the opportunity to rebel against the prejudice of her family and home town. This unpublished novel clearly anticipated the situation of Rachel Cameron and Nick Kazlik in *A Jest of God.* In the interval, the unused name of the young alien was salvaged for use in Peg's first Manawaka novel.

Another Steven appears briefly in *The Stone Angel.* He is Hagar's grandson, close to thirty, and she is pleased with his visit to her in the hospital; his cameo role contributes to the depiction of Hagar's reconciliation with life. He asks "Anything you want, Gran?" and, like a generous almoner, gives her his pack of cigarettes. She is pleased: "You're very like your grandfather, Steven. . . . you could almost be Brampton Shipley"; then, "He was a fine-looking man, your grandfather."[28] In the manuscript of the novel this character is named "George." Margaret evidently had a reason for changing the name—perhaps to contribute to the sense that better times were ahead?

In *A Jest of God*, the deceased twin brother of Nick Kazlik (son of Nestor, who is Allie's uncle by marriage) was named Stefan. Dead, Stefan functions in *A Jest* about as Hamlet Sr. does at Elsinor. Rachel learns about Stefan from Nick, and on those occasions when Rachel and Nick are making love (if that's what it is)—necessarily. We learn (at the end of Five) that Nick and Steve are twins. Why? Nick insists, however, that Rachel remember they were "not identical." Why? Margaret evidently wanted to emphasize their similarity and yet to distinguish between them. Simply, during their eighteen shared years, Stefan was the better twin. Nick admits he didn't like having a twin—"How would you like there to be someone exactly the same as yourself?"—but Steve "never seemed to mind. He just laughed it off. But I hated it."[29] Nick and Steve had slingshots when they were boys; "we were both pretty good, Steve especially" (107). Always a plus for Steve, a minus for Nick.

Soon after, just before Nick and Rachel consummate their budding relationship, he tells her about his uncle up at Galloping Mountain, his mother's brother, who "was never actually a Communist, but was pretty far left" and believed Ukraine belonged in the USSR. Nick's father disagreed (Nick "couldn't care less"); Nestor's father "couldn't accept the fact that I never learned to speak Ukrainian" (109). This recalls the early note about Allie's husband: "Steve—Communist—why?" One obvious response, that Margaret would understand, is her gentle observation to David Williams (27 June 1977): "I have known in my life a few Communists who seemed to me to embody some of the Christian virtues more than many Christians did"[30]—and also her fondness for the far Left clergy at United College.

We get a clear glimpse of what is at the bottom of all this at the midpoint of Eight of *Jest*, another love scene, in which Nick is complaining about his father's not so subtle attempts to persuade him to remain on the Kazlik farm and take over the responsibilities. Nestor has been calling him by the name of his deceased twin. Note: "'Three times in the last week,' Nick says, 'he's called me Steve.'" And three times Nick has been called upon to make the denial. (Just a bit like Peter, who denied Christ—as foretold—just before Jesus was crucified and became a dead man: "Peter remembered . . . thou shalt deny me thrice." See the gospel of St. Matthew, Chapter 26, especially verse 75.) Nick goes to gather wild raspberries for Rachel and gets scratched by the thorns. "Bloody hell," he says (maybe a biblical reference?). "My right hand seems to have forgotten its cunning." A biblical reference!—to Psalm 137, an expression of faithful commitment:

> 4. How shall we sing the Lord's song in a strange land?
> 5. If I forget thee, O Jerusalem, let my right hand forget her cunning. (King James version)

We might recall just here the settings in which Nick unburdens himself about his father's demands, and the extent of his similarity to his twin brother. Nick is evidently all right at the lovemaking but incapable of the love. "Darling," he says, memorably, to Rachel, "I am not God. I can't solve anything" (182 and cf. 232). Then, his defense of his refusal to accept his father's appeal to remain on the Kazlik farm. Nick explains that his father thinks

> "that he may be able to shame me into doing what he wants. . . . that role wouldn't suit me. I'm not going to be taken over by a—"
>
> He breaks off. . . .
>
> "—a dead man. That's what he is. . . . Not my brother, not anybody's anything. A dead man." (175)

But why is Nick's brother called "Steve"—this brother we have just seen Nick deny—"A dead man"—as though repeating Cain's rhetorical question, "Am I my brother's keeper?"

The source of these Steve/Stefan characters, the Ur-Stephen, is, of course, the proto-martyr St. Stephen, whose story is told in the book of the Acts of the Apostles. He was one of the deacons of the church at Jerusalem appointed to dispense alms to the widows there. He became an ardent preacher of the gospel of Jesus, announcing the promise of a new order to be anticipated. In consequence, a number of prominent members of the synagogue branded him a blasphemer, and Stephen was stoned to death. He died because of his faith and commitment to his belief—evidently perceiving the importance of the social gospel (as then it was) and obeying the admonition "Feed my sheep." The Saints Day of the first Christian martyr is the day after Christmas, 26 December, the day on which good King Wenceslas looked out upon the snow and spied the needy peasant to whom he then gave flesh and wine and other necessities,[31] and associated thus with the British tradition of Boxing Day, another day of generous behaviour. St. Stephen, another figure of generosity, also represents the inauguration of a new, hopeful dispensation. Steve Lancaster (if he did indeed exist, as Margaret claimed) was to mark the outset of her career of adult publication, of welcome good news. It should now be clear how the subsequent Laurentian Steves participate in that role, and especially how additional promise dwelt in the figures of Steve Chorniuk and his son, Stefan—awaiting only the descent of the grace that would permit their realization.

But still, Allie and Stella continue their meaningful dance on the earth, "Dancing memory, dancing faith, dancing grief and hope, dancing the dance of time, dancing because there are times when we choose to dance." What went wrong?

In the very rich letter to Hubert Evans, when Margaret noted, with a touch of regret, "I'm writing—I think—a novel, or, as it may turn out, some stories,"[32] it is an anticipation of what she wrote almost a year and a half later on the cover page of the York manuscript:

> ⊛July 1983
>
> I'm not going to write this
> novel. Maybe this is a short
> story or maybe not.

Something was going wrong almost from the moment of the inception of the "happy event" she had written Walter Swayze about in April 1977. It is simplest to say that the gift of grace was not vouchsafed for the creation of this last novel; but the truth is somewhat more complex. Margaret recognized during the summer of 1978 that the demands of another project were intruding and becoming an impediment to the progress of "Dance on the Earth." Why, though, did she yield to those demands instead of continuing to pursue the novel, close as it was to her heart? Of course she continued to oscillate; her attention alternated between the novel and the intruder over some five years until a definite decision was evidently taken in July 1983.

Three specific reasons for her abandonment of "Dance" are discernible in Margaret's own words on the topic. The clearest and most enlightening is her account to Harold Horwood: "I realized last summer that I had not one book but two, simmering in my mind. A novel that isn't ready to be written, and . . . a kind of memoir, a kind of discursive story of my life. . . ."[33] (The adjective "discursive" seems rather odd in that context, somehow misplaced; it may indicate the involvement of other, related, thoughts.) The first two reasons are basically artistic. One, she wanted to write about Ukrainian immigrants but felt she did not know enough about Ukrainians "from the inside"[34] to give them a credible presentation. That was a real problem, one she had faced bravely in creating Jules Tonnerre, "the most difficult character I ever undertook," she told Tom Saunders, who misunderstood her. Two, she wanted to write about the Winnipeg Old Left but questioned whether she "*really* want[ed] to write *fictionally* about the Old Left. . . ."[35] These two reasons are based on Margaret's artistic integrity and her Jamesian conception of the art of fiction. The proper focus is provided by her emphatic use of "*fictionally*" in the comment on the Old Left, and surely in her odd employ of "discursive" in her account to Horwood. The business of a fiction writer is to show, not to discuss. Margaret feared she could not convincingly portray the Ukrainians without true knowledge of their inner workings, and that her portrayal of the Old Left could well descend into an explanatory or indeed polemical portrayal—merely discursive instead of "dramatic." (The two books were both together "simmering" in her mind; the adjective was only slightly misplaced.)

The third reason for letting the novel slip away was even more deeply personal. Two comments in her letter of 19 February 1979 to Gordon Roper are particularly instructive. She decided the novel "would not come out right because I don't feel that inner *need*" (her own italics); a paragraph later, she points to the lack of "any genuine urgency to write fiction right now, and may not ever again." The sense of need and urgency may have been the condition required for the descent of grace. That sense, as I have argued above—to justify consideration of the "autobiographical" quality of the Manawaka books—that prompted her writing of those earlier novels was removed by her divorce in 1969: the intimate, personal problems had gone, not all her problems, of course, just the most intimate and crucial. It was the pressure of those problems that made her feel the need, the genuine urgency, to resort to her fiction as a kind of therapy; and we must be grateful for the consequent pearls.

The accepted project, the memoirs, continued to be associated in Margaret's mind with the forsaken novel. She tended to call the nascent memoirs "Four Mothers" (sometimes "Three Mothers"); and the novel's emphasis on women, on the female line of descent, included the four mothers important in Allie's life—Rose (Malanchuk) Chorniuk (her mother-in-law), Mairi (McDuff) Lansdowne-Pryce (her mother), Jen (O'Brien) Chorniuk (her daughter-in-law), and of course Allie herself. Margaret's final choice of title for the memoirs was the novel's, *Dance on the Earth*—and surely with firm recognition of the significance of "dance." Her decision to turn to the "discursive story of my life" gave the chance to talk about her association with all sorts and conditions of men—and women—regardless of how well she knew them "from the inside," and about all kinds of social and political institutions without fearing to indulge in argument and polemic.

Eager to get the memoirs written by her own established deadline in order to take on yet another project, Margaret was doubly disturbed by the interference of recurrent censorship. That recurrence may, however, have confirmed her in the commitment to her choice of memoirs over novel.[36] Just before Christmas of 1984, a Mrs. Helen Trotter of Burleigh Falls, north of Lakefield, circulated a petition to submit to the Peterborough County Board of Education for the removal of Margaret's *The Stone Angel*, *A Jest of God*, and *The Diviners*, and Salinger's *Catcher in the Rye* from all high school courses and libraries as a threat to public morality. The petition was signed by all Mrs. Trotter's co-members of the township council—none of whom had read the novels in question. This time Margaret decided to fight: during the last three weeks of January 1985 she gave numerous TV, radio, and press interviews. She was gratified by the amount of support that rallied to her cause.[37] The *Toronto Star* reported (21 March 1985) that information released on the 20th of the month indicated that the Peterborough County Board of Education had received 218 letters of complaint about and 800 in support of the books named; among the 800 were letters from the leader of the NDP, Ed Broadbent, Canadian film producer Norman Jewison, and Dr. Malcolm Ross. The *Star* quoted from Ross's letter: "In Margaret Laurence's fictional world there are indeed sinners. But grace abounds." (His allusion to Bunyan was doubtless lost on the literary censors.) Margaret's friend and former teacher further affirmed that in her work "the human condition is never prettified or falsified," and that "there is no Canadian writer who can be read and studied with greater moral and spiritual profit than Margaret Laurence."[38]

The result this time was the same as in 1976, with the added benefit that the file of news clippings Joan Johnston had gathered was sold to York University Library for a sum later put to a worthy cause. Sad to say, seven years after this to-do, the topic of immorality in Margaret's fiction was still hot enough to justify public utterance by Dr. Walter Swayze, under the apt heading "The Threat of Margaret Laurence." His essay agrees with the relevance of such censorship "to the psychological, moral, and religious health of our country." He identifies the problem for readers of her fiction:

> They get into a Margaret Laurence novel or story because it is written in the actual words that ordinary people use . . . real characters come to life, often characters that they can identify with neighbours, relatives, or even themselves. But then, to their horror, they find these characters admitting to thoughts and actions that they, the readers, would never admit to having had or done, and they feel naked and vulnerable and disgraced. . . .
>
> . . . Being convinced or compelled to see something beyond what we had accepted as the clear outline of reality is often a very painful, frightening experience. But . . . probably the most liberating experience that human beings can have.
>
> . . . When she told us convincingly that the emperor had

> no clothes on, some of us were shocked. We wanted to shoot the messenger.[39]

Margaret kept at her memoirs, and in her newsletter[40] of 10 January 1986 bravely announced that "selected memoirs dealing mainly with my three mothers had begun"; the 21 March newsletter reported that "work progresses on memoirs." By 11 July she had completed the first draft and was anticipating their publication.[41] On that day she wrote to the Canadian sculptor Almuth Lutkenhaus (whose work she had defended against public outcry) that she "would dearly love" to use a picture of *Crucified Woman* for the dust jacket of the memoirs; "I want to call the book DANCE ON THE EARTH." The letter does not acknowledge any connection there with the novel whose title she claimed for the memoirs; but for us there is acknowledgement enough—

> My sense of myself, and my 3 mothers, is that of women dancing pain, dancing joy, dancing humankind's dilemma, . . . and in a deeply religious sense, your sculpture says all that to me . . religious and humanly moving.

It is important to keep in mind Margaret's comment to Harold Horwood that indicates her recognition of what the memoirs will be—"a kind of" story of her life, "not perhaps as it actually happened but as perceived by me."[42] As it turned out, that is perfectly accurate, for Margaret's perceptions do not always tally factually with what available evidence indicates occurred. She did well to retain the title, for the memoirs affirm Margaret's conception of dance as the *élan vital.* The memoirs retain the "four mothers" structure promised by the provisional title and by the outline for the novel, realized with Margaret's biological mother, Verna; her "Mum," originally Aunt Margaret; her mother-in-law, Elsie Fry Laurence; and herself. The whole concludes with Margaret's utter gratitude and general prayer, "May the dance go on" (222).

By that time it is not just the dance of Margaret and of all those who have contributed to it, but the dance of life entire. The concern with which "Dance on the Earth" (York manuscript) opens thus permeates the memoirs. At the outset Allie announces that she is "Dancing hope. Despite everything in our bleak world. . . . We will it so, and pray it so." A couple of paragraphs later she resumes the concern: "Is it only to witness the final death of all . . . that we've born and raised our children?" She muses, "I think a lot about the death of all . . . a conception culminating not in birth but in the total death. My own death is insignificant. But impending as it always is, significant to me."

This understanding of the relevance of that final prayer, "May the dance go on," is born in on us by the effect of the structure of the book, of the incremental repetition: the discursive story of her life has been elevated to the poetic. Perhaps there really has been a need, a genuine urgency at work here that created the appropriate conditions for the descent of yet another kind of grace.

The workaday world continued outside, as it does in Auden's "Musée des Beaux Arts"—while "something amazing" occurs. Margaret's health was declining markedly in these months devoted to the memoirs and the dancing *élan vital* (*créateur et artistique*). At the beginning of March 1984 she complained to Adele of arthritis in her right hand, and a bent finger, and her worry about "blood sugar."[43] (A decade earlier she had written to Harold Horwood to explain her reluctance to accept the presidency of the Writers' Union because "all the stress situations in the past year apparently added considerably to my developing diabetes.")[44] A couple of weeks later she composed her amusing little "A Tale of a Typewriter"—a history of her machines, culminating now in an electric typewriter, "Pearl Cavewoman" ("Pearl" from "Margaret" and "Cavewoman" from the Pictish word for "Cave"—Weems); this last a necessity because of her failing right wrist and bent finger. Partially blind in her right eye now, Margaret arranged for surgery to remove cataracts and implant a new lens on 2 August 1985.[45] On 27 April she told Timothy Findley she now had carpal tunnel syndrome in the right wrist—also that she was preserving her strength to visit

David and Soña (married in September 1984) in San Francisco. Late in the year she reported the eye surgery a success (19 November 1985 newsletter). It had, however, obliged her to postpone a session with sculptor Connie Gallotti and her helper Peta March for the taking of her "life-mask." In March the deed was done, and Margaret joined the ranks of the famous folk who had been so "done," including Pierre Berton, Peter Gzowski, Jean Little, and David Suzuki. (Gallotti's "Cultural Connections" collection of masks is dedicated to Margaret Laurence.)[46] Jocelyn was now executive editor at *Toronto Life*.

As Margaret's sixtieth birthday loomed, she and Joan Johnston decided to use the money earned from York University for the purchase of the Johnston file on censorship against Margaret: they would stage a gala anniversary celebration and propose such toasts as "To the people who want to ban Margaret's books, without whom this party would not have been possible."[47] Joan Johnston gave Margaret a handsome set of journals (Clara Thomas's suggestion) to accommodate the post-memoirs project. Though the draft of *Dance* was completed, much work was left to get it ready for publication. The equivalent of Auden's Icarus falling out of the sky occurred on 22 August 1986.

Typing up that draft, which of course meant revising as well, was the chore that faced Margaret following the birthday celebration; and she was handicapped by severe shortness of breath exacerbated by the sultry summer weather. Her first entry in the new journals commented on that discomfort; the second (22 July) complained that the air was so humid at her birthday party that she "was gasping and sometimes found it difficult to talk. I suppose if I didn't smoke . . ." it wouldn't be so bad. A month later (22 August) her difficulty in breathing was so severe as to prevent her from keeping an appointment with Joan Johnston to go shopping and in fact led to her hospitalization at St. Joseph's Hospital in Peterborough. On Saturday, 30 August, she wrote in her journal: "A lifetime has happened since last I wrote in this Journal . . . the likelihood is that I have lung cancer . . . actually I am very frightened of dying quite soon." The diagnosis was cancer in the lining of her right lung and also in a kidney, where the cancer had begun. The doctor gave her six months. Margaret's immediate concern was getting the memoirs into acceptable shape.

She soon had in hand the scribblers she had already filled (eight or nine of them) and a typewriter, a table to put it on, and reams of paper, all in her private room at the hospital; she set to work. She averaged some five pages a day, but by the end of the first week of September was convinced that at that rate she would never get the job done, not even a clean second draft. Joan Johnston had been closely attentive from the outset and at this crisis urged Margaret to dictate to a tape from which Joan could type. Margaret reluctantly agreed. Before the end of October, she had edited the first typed draft and Joan had completed typing of the second. The rest would be left to Jocelyn's editorial expertise, and on 2 November Margaret noted in the journal that her daughter had begun reading *Dance*.

The declining health of Margaret's brother, Bob, hung over her urgent work on the memoirs and also over the first weeks of journal entries. A bizarre sort of sympathy had sprung up between them, for Bob's cancer had also begun in a kidney and spread to his lung. He phoned her (as Loretta, my wife, and I and many, many others did) on getting news of Margaret's hospitalization, and was relieved to know that she could return to 8 Regent Street on 9 September. She was relieved as well to be back in familiar surroundings and continue work there, and also to begin to set her house in order and tuck in all the loose ends. Margaret asked us to come up to Lakefield for a brief visit at Thanksgiving and added the urgent request, "Find Borland if you can and bring him, too." Jack Cameron Borland—our classmate at United College, editor of the college magazine, *Vox*, in which Margaret had published her earliest adult writing, and, equally important, the first love of her adult life—had been out of touch with us for years. He had gone to graduate school (in English) at the University of Minnesota in Minneapolis. A bit disillusioned, he joined the Honeywell Company and was soon working in advertising. He formed his own, very successful, company in Philadelphia and lived in a comfortable apartment in Rittenhouse Square. A success story. We got together, two couples and Johnnie Walker, and reminisced as though we hadn't seen each other for a couple of weeks. He called her "Peg"; she called him "Borland" as the intervening years fell away. Tears all 'round, and Margaret insisting there was no cause for tears, that she had had a full life. And she sang, something Borland's mother had used to sing to the two of them, "Will ye no come back again?" (Borland and I did, at the beginning of January.) Sid Perlmutter phoned her that night. Sid was another North-Ender, an old friend of mine at St. John's Technical High School. His path crossed Margaret's when he was on the faculty of Ryerson Polytechnical Institute in Toronto, and he counted Jocelyn and David Laurence among his students. Lois Wilson also phoned on the weekend. Sustaining communications.

Bob's death on 17 October struck hard and marked a turning point for Margaret—physical decline accompanied by a spiritual upsurge that was difficult but determined. She had, as she confided to her journal several times, been familiar with death from the age of four and recognized it (as all her fiction testifies) as a natural part of life; now, however, she had to confront it as distinctly hers, in part, by an informal and spasmodic reconsideration of her religious basis. That review was as greatly aided by her friendship with Lois Wilson, which had its beginning in the conversations that led to their dialogue/sermon of autumn 1979. She phoned Lois (22 October) to raise the question of her own funeral and to suggest three suitable hymns for the service at Bloor Street United—whenever—to be conducted by Lois. Margaret selected "Unto the hills mine eyes do I lift up," "All people that on earth do dwell" (which the Reverend Mr. Troy sings so successfully for Hagar near the close of *The Stone Angel*), and "Guide me, O thou great Jehovah," which Margaret remembered her political hero Tommy Douglas had requested for his funeral. Lois recalled Margaret's explanation for this last choice; "She wrote: 'Partly because it expresses to me some of my life's struggles for peace and justice and partly because it reminds me of the social gospel. The old Welsh coal-miners sang it as they marched up to Whitehall in 1929.'"[48]

Three days later a journal entry indicates her seriously contemplating suicide: she had discussed, with a devoted friend, selection of prescribed medication sufficient for a lethal dose, "the only person in the *world* I would trust" for such a discussion. At once her strengthened religious attitude asserts itself:

> Please, Lord, help me. Could you forgive? Of that I have *no* doubt. . . . But I do *not* want the kids to go through what Bob and I went through with Mum's trying to die. . . . I could not believe in a punitive Holy Spirit, *ever*. A Holy Spirit that informs our lives, as we try to accept it—*Yes*.

The journal notes (29 October) that Lois Wilson drove up from Toronto to spend two very satisfactory hours discussing Margaret's funeral and their shared views on religion—a kind of recap. They agreed again that the resurrection of the body, as Margaret had noted in the 20 August entry that she had heard in the Apostles Creed at an Anglican Church recently, was a misguided idea, and that what occurs after death is "a continuity, a community, and a mystery." Gratefully, Margaret noted after Lois's visit, "What a wonderful woman she is—how *gifted* with laughter, compassion, and grace." (Amen.) Yet she ruefully recognized her own reluctance to "let go," and affirmed again and again that life remains attractive. She had written to Ernest Buckler, years earlier, a rather prophetic letter responding to his remarks on suicide. He had said he couldn't end his own life because he was "too damn curious to see what's coming next"; Margaret said she had twice considered suicide "and rejected it for exactly that reason."[49] She frequently notes in the journal how life is full of "interest and love" (for example, entry of 27 October), and although it is all very well to hold the belief that there is no personal immortality, one is faced with the daunting "concept of ceasing to exist as *me*" (11 November).

Another alteration in the tone of the journal came in November, even as she was conscious of further tidying up her life. David and his wife, Soña, returned to Canada and would live in the apartment attached to 8 Regent Street (1 November). Margaret was aware of her own "deterioration" (2 November), yet she was able by mid-November to write a tribute to her old friend and publisher, Jack McClelland, which ended, "He is a Canadian pioneer. He has risked his life for us, Canadian writers. I think we have proved him right. Thanks, Boss."[50] The tribute was intended for a festschrift in his honour and is available in *The Selected Letters of Jack McClelland*, most appropriately the last item in the book. In that important moment at the centre of November, as she turned over the question of her yearning to continue even as she recognized her general slouching decline, she seized on the importance of the concept of the "informing Holy Spirit"—not unlike Wordsworth's spirit "that rolls through all things" including "the mind of man"[51]—of *continuity*, as both Lois Wilson and Al Purdy used the term. In the 11 November entry she added to her pondering, "no personal immortality" and her regret thereof, her memory of a poem she wrote half a life ago and published in *Vox* (June 1945), and quoted "this land will be my immortality" (always the professional, she has to add, "I meant 'land' as in soil, earth, not as in nation. Now I would say 'people' too, meaning humankind."). The poem begins, "This is a land of living things / Of life within life" that "Sings of death becoming birth . . ." and ends with the line she quoted. The poem both anticipates and echoes Morag Gunn's thought at the birth of her daughter, Pique: "Harbinger of my death, continuer of life." It is also an echo of what Margaret and Lois Wilson decided in their dialogue/sermon and is repeated in the journal entry for 15 November: "Delivery. / I thought about that word a lot. A word used about both death and birth." There is the notion of cyclical continuity. Further prominence was given to that notion as Margaret prepared for the wedding of Jocelyn to Gary Dault.

Margaret made several contributions to the wedding, significant to her and to Jocelyn as well. She gave her daughter Grandma Simpson's Bible to carry at the ceremony—Margaret's grandmother had given it to *her* in 1935 (she noted in the 15 October entry); her journal also records her memory of giving Jocelyn the diamond engagement ring Mum had given her for her marriage in 1947; "So my daughter has the diamond that was her mother's and grandmother's. I am really thrilled to see it now taking on new life, new hope, new meaning" (24 November). Jocelyn has recently corrected that memory: "She gave me that *many* years before; she just didn't remember."[52] Continuity. With Clara Thomas's help, a piper was found—Piper Major Ross Stewart—to pipe the happy couple into St. Anne's Church, Toronto. Margaret's suggestion for a passage of scripture to be read at the ceremony was readily incorporated into the service; she chose Chapter 22, verses 36-40, of St. Matthew's Gospel, which are concerned with the two commandments that serve as the basis of Judaism and Christianity alike—Love God and your neighbour as yourself. Looking back at the service and its inclusion of the passage she recommended, Margaret observed that it "expresses the social gospel, . . . the rock upon which I have based my life" (2 December).[53]

Another feature of the event that added to Margaret's comforting sense of the wheel's having come full circle, of cyclical progress, was the presence of Jocelyn's father and his wife, Esther—again, new life, hope, and meaning, mingling change and permanence.

> It was hard for me, after the service, to see Jack—I hugged him and Esther (bless her), and he was talking so controlled and brusquely, as was always his way, and I knew he was holding back the tears. Of joy. (30 November)

That is a gratifying complement to an earlier response (12 September) to receiving the photos of Jack's seventieth birthday, which Jocelyn and David attended in North Vancouver.

> I really want to cry and celebrate, Jack, my old comrade, my mate—we lived to see our children into adulthood. . . . Jack, we are so lucky. My only real love, father of my children—we are lucky.

And Margaret addresses Jack directly, as though he were actually there.

Joan Johnston reported that writing in this journal, which fills seven of the volumes she gave Margaret, "became a kind of therapy for her. . . . She told me that the Journal had become like a friend and that she could write things in it that she couldn't talk to anyone about."[54] That "friend" proved to be a composite of many to whom she wanted to tell things—and she did, to them in their several persons. Jack was not the only one she addressed via the journal. Much of the time she is simply talking to herself, of course; but she addresses brother Bob directly, a few days after his death, telling him she is playing records for him, pipe music, to be sure, but also African highlife, and "Zorba's Dance" (27 October). She addresses Jocelyn and David and their spouses, "my dear ones," frequently. And increasingly the journal becomes a fairly sustained conversation with God—quite reminiscent of Stacey MacAindra's conversations (in *The Fire-Dwellers*) with the God in whom she professes not to believe. Margaret and God are evidently on pretty good terms, as the colloquial flavour of some of her remarks suggests: "God, please let me not go on very long, eh?" (19 October; and God is apparently used to the Canadian idiom, *eh*?) and "God, you know something? . . . Life is *interesting*" (20 October).

Margaret has gone a step beyond Stacey's attitude of professed doubt; although she has not abandoned her feeling for the Holy Spirit, she has distinctly acknowledged the First Person of the Trinity. The passage in Matthew's gospel, her suggestion for the wedding, clearly includes both basic commandments—Love God and your neighbour—yet it is the second that is most obviously the grounds for the social gospel. In a brief theological argument with herself, and with God, she seems about to reaffirm her customary preference: "I can't even *imagine* how anyone could compare the so-called 'love of God' to the love of people, friends, children. I can't see it in the abstract, Lord." She immediately adds, "I suppose, though, the 'love of God' *does* mean the love of people." Another loose end tucked in: the two great commandments are really one (11 November).

The conversation continues, and as December arrives it becomes more anguished and urgent. The last straw was the catastrophe of a broken leg. On 7 December, wearing her Birkenstocks, carrying the usual cup of coffee and a cigarette, Margaret bustled around the corner of her house to reach the apartment of Soña and David; she slipped on a patch of black ice and "landed hard with my right leg under me . . ." (12 December). Two bones broken, just above her right ankle; the leg was set in a cast—"foot to thigh." She told herself—and God—"I just cannot bear to live on and on, increasingly dependent and enfeebled" (12 December). She got home from the hospital on 13 December.

Enough was enough. She had the store of lethal medication and had learned from reliable sources how to use it effectively. On Christmas Day she was able to share usefully in the festivities: "I actually made my famous (?) stuffing this one last time." Her conviction was firm: "the decision is between me and the Holy Spirit, as it always was for the work" (24 December). The note for Boxing Day—

> Please, Lord, help me to do this one
> last thing. . . .
> I have had an incredible life.
> Amazed by love.

On the last day of 1986: "I want to die. For that I need a) privacy and b) resolve."

Twelve years before, Margaret had completed her response to Ernest Buckler's comments on suicide and death by observing that the end of life "will entail what happened to Hagar in *The Stone Angel*, a helpless and terrible anger. I hope I can meet it with pride—but I'm not sure at all I will be able to" (30 August 1974). There is, of course, pride and pride. At the beginning of December she confided to her journal, "Unlike Hagar, I do not want to 'rage, rage against the dying of the light.' I want to 'go gentle into that good-night.' Of course that's what I meant to convey with Hagar—strength and pride were also an affliction" (5 December).[55] Of course.

There is yet something admirable in the way Hagar retains (pridefully, to be sure) what control she can muster as her story ends. Early in *Dance on the Earth* Margaret quotes from W.E. Henley's once-famous "Invictus"—"My head is bloody but unbowed." One might well adapt that title as appropriate to Hagar—"Invicta," mistress of her fate, as far as can be. When Margaret's good friend and neighbour on the bank of the Otonabee, Jack Villerup (principal source for Royland in *The Diviners*), was in his last illness, she wrote to Al Purdy: "he is 84 and has had a long and (in the real sense) honourable life. I hope to God he dies quickly—he would hate being an invalid."[55] More recent is the case of Jules "Skinner" Tonnerre—not so old as Jack Villerup nor so feisty, perhaps, as Hagar—who is rapidly reaching the end when Morag last visits him in *The Diviners*. Jules's old friend Billy Joe brings the news to Morag—she knows, but asks, "It's not usually that fast. Is it?"

> "He didn't wait for it," Billy Joe said.
> Just that. He didn't wait.
> "I see." Her voice had an unusual calm.
> "Billy—how did he—"
> "It don't matter how he done it," he said with finality. (366)

Margaret was alone during the first weekend of the new year, 3-4 January 1987. The journal entry for 4 January begins, "Clea the cat is racing around. I guess she knows something is going on"; it ends, "I have been so fortunate."

And then—

endnotes

INTRODUCTION

1. Northrop Fry, "Conclusion to a Literary History of Canada," in *The Bush Garden: Essays on the Canadian Imagination* (Toronto: House of Anansi Press, 1971), 219.
2. Margaret Laurence, *The Diviners* (Toronto: McClelland and Stewart, 1974), 319.

CHAPTER ONE

1. Margaret Laurence, *Heart of a Stranger* (Toronto: McClelland and Stewart, 1976), 219.
2. "The Wemyss and Simpson Families: Some Facts, Dates, Legends." The five-page typescript with title page, obviously created by Margaret Laurence from sources, both written and oral, in her family, is part of the Margaret Laurence archive at York University, Toronto, Canada. The title page and first page ("Simpson") of the typescript are unnumbered; the remaining pages ("Wemyss") are numbered 1-4.
3. "Families," 1.
4. Ibid., 2.
5. Fred C. Lucas, ed., *An Historical Souvenir Dairy of the City of Winnipeg, Canada* (Winnipeg: Cartwright and Lucas, 1923), 80.
6. Evelyn A. Vivian, curator of the Beautiful Plains Museum in Neepawa, Manitoba, wrote to me, in her letter of 25 September 1991:

   > Regarding your question about John Wemyss being the first solicitor for the town of Neepawa. Although his obit so states as well as Margaret refers to it in her book [*Dance on the Earth*],

it just is *not* so. I went to the town office and read the minutes for the first year after incorporation. At their first meeting, they discussed hiring a solicitor but it was laid over. It was not until June of 1884 that they engaged Alexander Stewart as their solicitor.

7. "Families," 3.

8. Interview with his granddaughter, Catherine S. Milne, August 1989.

9. *The Amherstburg Echo*, 25 May 1988. Ms Eleanor Gignac, an Amherstburg antiquarian, provided me with the following biographical information about Jane Bailey.

10. Mary Turnbull Mindess, 15 July 1988; Mona Spratt Meredith, 30 October 1988 and 19 April 1989. Tom Saunders talked with me about the article, late August 1988, in Winnipeg.

11. Marguerite Crawford Street, 8 March 1989, responded thus to my enquiry about a Métis girl treated in Neepawa hospital for tuberculosis of the leg (a possible source for Piquette Tonnerre in *A Bird in the House*). I interviewed Wes McAmmond in Winnipeg, 24 August 1988, and the late Mildred Musgrove in Brandon, Manitoba, 26 August 1988. On 2 March 1989, I interviewed Ms Gignac in Windsor, Ontario.

12. I interviewed David Williams in St. John's College, University of Manitoba, 25 August 1988; and the late Professor B.W. Andrzejewski at the London School of African and Asian Studies, September 1991.

13. Interview with Jack Laurence in Vancouver, 21 August 1989.

14. Ms Alice Williams gave me this report at Joan Johnson's home in Peterborough, Ontario, 5 September 1992; and Don Bailey told me of Laurence's comments in Toronto, 16 October 1992.

15. In spring 1995, Jocelyn and David Laurence and Adele Wiseman's daughter Tamara Stone gave me access to the Laurence and Wiseman archives in Scott Library, York University, North York, Ontario. This letter was later published in *Selected Letters of Margaret Laurence and Adele Wiseman*, ed. John Lennox and Ruth Panofsky (Toronto: University of Toronto Press, 1997). None of the persons I interviewed concerning Laurence and her possible Aboriginal ancestry had read this letter at the time.

16. Laurence's review of George Woodstock's *Gabriel Dumont: The Métis Chief and His Lost World* (Edmonton: Hurtig, 1975) first appeared as "Man of Honour" in *Canadian Forum* (December 1975-January 1976); revision published in *Heart of a Stranger*, 204-12. The quotation is from the revised version, 211-12.

17. Relying on accounts in the files of the *Neepawa Press* (1899-1901), Mrs. Evelyn Vivian was able to report, in her letter of 25 September 1991 to

me, the commercial success of John Simpson. The real-estate records of the town of Neepawa enabled Mrs. Vivian to report to me the history of the ownership of the property and house that John Simpson purchased in 1904: the house was evidently erected between 1895 and 1898 by the then owner of the lot, Christine Coulter. When John Simpson had a front walk laid up to the steps of the house, he had "Simpson" imprinted in the cement at the point where the walk began at First Avenue. The house still stands sturdily (although the lot has been reduced by about half); it is currently the Margaret Laurence Home and once again contains a handsome pair of substantial wooden chairs made by John Simpson himself and bequeathed to the home by his first granddaughter, Catherine Simpson Milne.

18. Manitoba antiquarian Mary Musil, *The Simpson Family*.

19. Interview of August 1989. Mrs. Milne also showed me a copy of Margaret Laurence's *A Bird in the House* inscribed to her Aunt Ruby, which points out the autobiographical nature of the book; she told me much Simpson history.

20. Anecdote related to me by Mrs. Vivian.

21. Conclusion of "The Mask of the Bear," in *A Bird in the House: Stories by Margaret Laurence* (Toronto: McClelland and Stewart, 1970).

22. A. Gerald Bedford, *The University of Winnipeg: A History of the Founding Colleges* (Toronto and Buffalo: University of Toronto Press, 1967), 23-37.

23. Harold "Nero" Thompson of Neepawa and Clear Lake, Manitoba, a contemporary and hockey teammate of Pate Chaboyer; interview of summer 1989, Clear Lake.

24. Interview by Helen Hutchinson, *Speaking of Winnipeg*, ed. John Parr (Winnipeg: Queenston House, 1974), 68.

25. Mona (Spratt) Meredith, letter to me, 27 November 1991.

26. In her letter of 25 September 1991 from Neepawa to me, Mrs. Evelyn Vivian clarifies "the time frame she says [Margaret Laurence, in *Dance on the Earth*] she spent in the Wemyss brick house."

27. *Dance on the Earth: A Memoir* (Toronto: McClelland and Stewart, 1989), 29.

28. Ibid., 63-64.

29. Ibid., 294.

CHAPTER TWO

1. *The Diviners*, 58.

2. Conversations with Louise (Alguire) Kubik and Mona (Spratt) Meredith, summer 1989, and subsequent correspondence.

3. Greta M. Coger's interview with Wes McAmmond, in Neepawa, 25 July 1984; he confirmed these memories in my interview with him in Winnipeg, summer 1989.

4. A. Conan Doyle, *The White Company*, The Crowborough Edition VIII (Garden City, New York: Doubleday, Doran, 1930), 96.

5. Margaret Laurence, *A Bird in the House*, Seal Books (Toronto: McClelland and Stewart, 1978), 107. In her essay "Books that Mattered to Me" (1981), Laurence gives prominent mention to *The White Company* and associates it with her reading in grade seven, when she was twelve. See *Margaret Laurence: An Appreciation*, ed. Christl Verduyn (Peterborough, ON: Broadview Press, 1988), 240.

6. "The Mask of the Bear," 67.

7. *Dance*, 67.

8. Much of the information about Peggy's schooling—dress, academic records, the school journal, dramatics program, music program—comes from the late Miss Mildred Musgrove, her high school teacher, especially her letter of 21 September 1988 to me and personal conversations; and also from my own experience of Manitoba schools in those years.

9. Letter to me from Marguerite (Crawford) Street, 27 March 1989, from Portage la Prairie, Manitoba.

10. Conversation with Mildred Musgrove, the first Margaret Laurence Conference, Brandon University, Brandon, Manitoba, 25-28 August 1988.

11. Conversation with Mona (Spratt) Meredith, May 1996.

12. Conversations with Louise (Alguire) Kubik and Mona (Spratt) Meredith, summer 1989; the alliterative characterization is Mona's.

13. Conversation with Nancy (Mrs. Frank) Collier, in Amersham, Bucks., England, September 1991.

14. Ms Musgrove's letter to me, 21 September 1988.

15. Greta M. Coger's interview of 25 July 1984 with McAmmond, confirmed by my interview, summer 1989 in Winnipeg.

16. *The Diviners*, 168, 290.

CHAPTER THREE

1. A. Gerald Bedford, *The University of Winnipeg*. For the character and career of Salem Bland, especially in relation to Wesley College, see pp. 127-39. The classic study of the social gospel is Richard Allen's *The Social Passion: Religion and Social Reform in Canada, 1914-28* (Toronto: University of Toronto Press, 1971).
2. A. Ross McCormack, *Reformers, Rebels, and Revolutionaries: The Western Canadian Radical Movement 1899-1919* (Toronto: University of Toronto Press, 1977). See, for example, p. 87:

   > Methodists were the most important influence upon the movement. While labourites across the West were affected by the social gospel, nowhere was the impact so great as in Winnipeg, because nowhere was there collected such a group of brilliant and energetic radical churchmen. Wesley College became the dynamic centre of the social gospel in Canada when Salem Bland went there in 1903. Because of his . . . commitment to reform, Bland was respected by all radicals and was influential among the labourites. In 1907 J.W. Woodsworth began his mission in the north end; and, although he was not political in his early years at All People's [on Stella Avenue, sometimes called Stella Mission], his work among the immigrants won him the respect of the labourites.

   See also the *University of Winnipeg Alumni Bulletin*, July 1979, pp. 30-35, 58-60, a reprint of Richard Allen's "Children of Prophecy: Wesley College Students in an Age of Reform."
3. Norman Penner, *The Canadian Left: A Critical Analysis* (Scarborough, ON: Prentice-Hall Canada, 1977), 33-34.
4. Doug Smith, *Joe Zuken: Citizen and Socialist* (Toronto: James Lorimer, 1990), 101.
5. A.R.M. Lower, *A History of Canada: Colony to Nation* (Toronto: McClelland & Stewart, 1977) 473; first published in 1946. The *Canadian Tribune*, weekly newspaper of the Communist Party of Canada, had been banned under the War Measures Act, but the ban was rescinded by Spring 1941.
6. Henry Gutkin, *The Worst of Times, The Best of Times* (Markham, ON: Fitzhenry and Whiteside, 1987), 202. According to the respective Student Records Offices, Peggy was at United College 1944-47, Adele was at the University of Manitoba 1945-49 (in the five-year Honours program), and they were both in Malcolm Ross's course in 1947.
7. Published by Coles bookstore, Toronto, vol. 8, no. 5, October/November 1992, 2.
8. *Dance*, 5. Margaret Laurence's reprise of her literary debut, in *Dance on the Earth*, is unclear and tends to cloud the issue—at least so far as I have

been able to discover the facts. She recalls: "I submitted several poems under the pseudonym of Steven Lancaster. I suffered severe suspense each week as I rushed to grab a copy of *The Manitoban*. . . . And yes, one day a poem of mine appeared. . . . [I feared] that I would hear, from the lips of someone whose opinion I valued, the comment, 'Did you see that poem by Steven Lancaster? Piece of garbage.' No such comment came" (p. 96). I have found no poem or other publication by Steve(n) Lancaster; apparently her initial publication in *The Manitoban* was the short fiction "Fallen King" (6 October 1944) and her second was the poem "Thought" (13 October 1944).

9. "Pagan Point: Approaching Night" was published in *The Manitoban*, 3 November 1944. Principal changes from the original version (discussed above) are these: the identifying place name "Wasagaming" is dropped in the 1944 title; 1, 20, "The waves again approach the shore with ease" was "The wavelets once again caress the shore"; 1, 24, "The lake is stilled, the marsh birds cry no more" was "The lake is stilled, the marsh birds call no more."

10. Letter to Gabrielle Roy, 12 February 1979.

CHAPTER FOUR

1. Mona (Spratt) Meredith, who knew both men, told me Jack was "a more robust and less soulful Derek Armstrong" (conversation in Vancouver, May 1996).

2. Jack Laurence gave me this information and much of what the succeeding two paragraphs are based on (concerning Watson Thomson) in an interview in Vancouver, summer 1989; that was supplemented by subsequent conversations with John Marshall in Toronto and Nancy Collier in Amersham, Bucks., England.

3. Quoted in Garson Coon and Blair Witherspoon, "Popular Education for Participatory Democracy," *Briarpatch* 21, no. 7 (September 1992): 7.

4. Interview with Madge (Hetherington) Allen in Toronto, fall 1992.

5. See Gutkin, *The Worst of Times*, 202.

6. Smith, *Joe Zuken*, 7-8, 30, 36, and *passim.*

7. Ibid., 109.

8. Conversation with me in Toronto, spring 1992.

9. See *Dance*, 107, on Peggy's review of a book of poems by Joe Wallace.

10. H.S. Ferns, *Reading from Left to Right: One Man's Political History* (Toronto, Buffalo, London: University of Toronto Press, 1983), 247.

11. Opening paragraph of her "Afterword," Sinclair Ross, *The Lamp at Noon and Other Stories*, New Canadian Library (Toronto: McClelland and Stewart, 1988); reprint of "Introduction" to 1968 edition.

12. Smith drove the last spike in the same year as Riel was hanged, 1885; but Smith was made Baron Strathcona and Mount Royal by Queen Victoria in 1897.

CHAPTER FIVE

1. Conversation with Mrs. Nancy Collier, 16 March 1993.
2. Letter to Wiseman, 16 July 1950.
3. Letter of 28 January 1950 to Wiseman.
4. Margaret Laurence, *The Prophet's Camel Bell* (Toronto: McClelland and Stewart, 1963), 2; see also Fiona Sparrow, *Into Africa with Margaret Laurence* (Toronto: ECW Press, 1992), 19. When completed, however, the "earth dams" proved capable of holding only nine million litres (*Into Africa*, 41).
5. Letter of 15 June 1951 to Wiseman.
6. *Dance*, 53-54.
7. Letter of 17 July 1950 to Wiseman.
8. *Camel Bell*, 3.
9. Letter to Wiseman family, 17 November 1950.
10. Letter to Wiseman, 27-28 December 1950.
11. *Camel Bell*, 6.
12. Letter of 12 February 1951.
13. Ibid.
14. Ibid.
15. As adapted for *Camel Bell*, 27.
16. *Camel Bell*, 125.
17. See I.M. Lewis, *A Modern History of Somalia* (London and New York: Longman's, 1980), 63-85; and Sparrow, *Into Africa*, 70-73.
18. Margaret Laurence, *This Side Jordan*, New Canadian Library (Toronto: McClelland and Stewart, 1989), 274-75.
19. Margaret Laurence to Professor Bogumil W. Andrzejewski, 9 November 1951; copy of the letter given to me by Professor Andrzejewski.
20. *Camel Bell*, 68-70.
21. Ibid, 94-96; see her letter to Wiseman, 21 June 1951.
22. Letter to Wiseman, 4 September 1951.
23. Letter to Wiseman, 19 February 1951.

24. Letter of 2 May 1951.

25. Letter of 4 September 1951.

26. Letter of 9 November 1951 to Wiseman.

27. 9 November 1951. Copy of the letter given to me by Professor Andrzejewski.

28. Peggy reported that the accident—c. 19 October 1951—happened thus: "the apron of the scraper had caught his hand. . . . the bones were sticking out the ends of the three middle fingers of the left hand, and the fingers themselves were completely flattened, like a rag doll's." No amputation was necessary, and Hersi was "patched up." Peggy concluded, "Anyway, we decided to call the new balleh, Balleh Hersi Jama. . . . I think he's quite pleased about it" (letter to Prof. and Mrs. Andrzejewski, 9 November 1951). It was their first and only serious accident.

29. Letter to B.W. Andrzejewski (22 April 1952): "He's [Jack] finished five ballehs now, and hopes they will fill up this rainy season" (copy of letter given to me by Prof. Andrzejewski).

30. Letter to B.W. Andrzejewski, 22 April 1952 (copy of letter given to me by Prof. Andrzejewski).

31. *Camel Bell*, 235.

32. Ibid., 236.

CHAPTER SIX

1. *Story: The Magazine of the Short Story in Book Form*, ed. Whit and Hallie Burnet (New York: A.A. Wyn, Inc., 1953), no. 4, pp. 9-34.

2. Fiona Sparrow explains that the site of the story, Bor Mado, is based closely on Hargeisa, and the club on the Hargeisa Club, which the Laurences avoided as much as possible; see *Into Africa*, 86.

3. Yusuf was modelled on Abdi, who was part of Jack's crew in the construction of reservoirs and who figures prominently in *Camel Bell.* Mrs. Sparrow also notes this association (*Into Africa*, 85-86).

4. Margaret Laurence, *A Tree for Poverty: Somali Poetry and Prose, Collected by Margaret Laurence* (Hamilton: McMaster University Library Press, 1970), iv; B.W. Andrzejewski and I.M. Lewis, eds. (in *Somali Poetry: An Introduction* [Oxford: Clarendon Press, 1964]), translate this passage as, "on the edge of the Awl Plain, poverty has a tree (to sit under)," 42. In an earlier note to Adele (2 May 1951), Peggy had a slightly different translation.

5. Andrzejewski and Lewis begin their Introduction to *Somali Poetry* with this very recognition, "that the Somali are a nation of bards: . . . Poetry occupies a large and important place in Somali culture, interest in it is

universal, and skill in it is something which everyone covets and many possess" (3). Said S. Samatar, early in his Introduction to *Oral Poetry and Somali Nationalism* (Cambridge: Cambridge University Press, 1982), poses the question of what "makes poetry such a pervasive force in Somali society?" and gives this answer: "The pastoral poet . . . exercises a powerful influence in clan affairs. For . . . Somali pastoral verse is a living art affecting almost every aspect of life" (3).

6. Twenty years before that, when Peggy was preparing her Introduction for *A Tree*, the question of orthography was already a sensitive matter—and especially with a scholar like Andrzejewski, to whom she had evidently written about her intentions in the almost finished manuscript. There had been, apparently, a rigorous exchange of letters with Guś, and on 22 April 1952 Peg wrote to apologize for her latest tart response and to thank Guś for his advice. Then follows her informative account to him: "I explained, however, about the orthography to Mr. Shirley, who quite understood how you felt about it, and said that he thought the best thing would be to publish the poems without the Somali versions. . . . In this connection, I went through the script and checked all tribe and place names, and I have spelled them according to the old system, as I found in the Gazeteer and in the Secretariat list of tribal names. I thought it would be better. . . . luckily, I've used very few Somali words in the text, but where these have appeared, I've tried to spell them according to [J.W. C.] Kirk [author of *A Grammar for the Somali Language* (Cambridge: Cambridge University Press, 1905)], in instances where I could check. Where I couldn't, I just had to guess, but I don't think this matters, as it is quite clear that any spellings in the book have nothing to do with the new way of spelling." (Politics and the Somali language!)

7. *Camel Bell*, 100. Illustration of this process is available in the Margaret Laurence archive in the Scott Library, York University (Toronto), which contains evidence of the several stages of development of a "translated" *gabei*: 1. the Somali original of "Anaan Waayeel"—literally "reproof of an elder"—by Abdillaahi Muuse (cf. Andrzejewski and Lewis, eds., *Somali Poetry*, 103, 105); 2. a literal translation of the poem, "Reproof from an Elder" (cf. *Somali Poetry*, 102, 104), with Peggy's marginal and interlinear notations; 3. two versions of a headnote and textual notes; 4. her English "equivalent," evidently unpublished. Similar evidence for the development of "To a Faithless Friend" is available there also.

8. Donez Xiques, in "Margaret Laurence's Somali Translations," *Canadian Literature* 135 (October 1992): 41, quotes this passage from a letter Prof. Andrzejewski wrote to her, 18 March 1989. Samatar quotes the last five lines of Peggy's extract "To a Faithless Friend," though various other translations were available; see *Oral Poetry and Somali Nationalism*, 87.

9. See *A Tree*, ix, 17; *Camel Bell*, 100.

10. See Andrzejewski, "Somali Literature," *Literatures in African Languages* (Cambridge: Cambridge University Press, 1985), 338; and his former student John W. Johnson, *Heellooy, Heelleellooy: The Development of the Genre Heello in Modern Somali Poetry* (Bloomington: Indiana University Press, 1974), 51-57; the *belwo* to Khadiija is quoted in Johnson, 54. Johnson explains that provenance of the *heello* was originally "a 'tacking on' of many *belwo* to make one long poem. Each stanza then, was a separate *belwo*" (72). Peggy makes no mention of *heello* in *A Tree*, but in a letter to Wiseman (4 September 1951) she describes it clearly enough: "When sung, they have a rhythmic, syncopated beat, very similar to American jazz. . . . These belwo are usually not more than 3 or 4 lines long, altho' they are often sung in ballad form, with 10 or 15 put together, and a chorus." Further, chapter Ten of *Camel Bell* begins with the meaningless refrain that often introduced the *belwo*: "'*Helleyoy, helleyoy* —.' Mohamed was always singing *belwo*."

11. *Somali Poetry*, 338.

12. *A Tree*, 40.

13. In "Margaret Laurence's Somali Translations," Donex Xiques refers (in note 18) to "features of Anglo-Saxon poetry which Laurence no doubt studied as an undergraduate: for example 'Beowulf' and perhaps 'The Battle of Maldon,'" 45. Peg's letter to the Andrzejewskis (1 October 1968) indicates her ignorance of Anglo-Saxon poetry in her African years: "a friend of mine, an editor of Macmillan, has just published his translation of Beowulf and I've just read it. I was fascinated to see how many things it has in common with Somali war gabay." See *Beowulf*, translated by Kevin Crossley-Holland, and introduced by Bruce Mitchell (New York: Farrar, Straus and Giroux, 1968).

14. "Somali Literature," 343.

15. R.E. Drake-Brockman, *British Somaliland* (London: Hurst and Blackett, 1912), 169.

16. Sparrow, *Into Africa*, 14.

CHAPTER SEVEN

1. Letter to Wiseman, 7 July 1952.

2. Letter of 6 September 1952; and see *Dance*, 138-39, for an account of Jocelyn's birth.

3. Letter of 1 December 1952 to Wiseman.

4. *Dance*, 142.

5. George Padmore, *The Gold Coast Revolution: The Struggle of an African People from Slavery to Freedom* (London: Dennis Dobson, 1953), 222.
6. Letter to Wiseman of 1 December 1952.
7. Sparrow, *Into Africa*, 91.
8. Padmore, *Gold Coast Revolution*, 248.
9. Robert Beck Fitch and Mary Oppenheimer, *Ghana: End of an Illusion* (New York and London: Monthly Review Press, 1966), 203.
10. Padmore, *Gold Coast Revolution*, 235.
11. Ibid., 235-36.
12. Richard Wright, *Black Power: A Record of Reactions in a Land of Pathos* (New York: Harper and Brothers, 1954), 343.
13. Letter of 1 December 1953 to Wiseman.
14. Letter of 16 February 1953. See also Donez Xiques, "New Light on Margaret Laurence's First African Short Story," *Canadian Notes and Queries*, 42 (1990): 14-21.
15. See Laurence's vivid recall in *Dance*, 143.
16. See, for example, letter of 19 February 1954 to Wiseman.
17. Letter of 20 July 1953 to Wiseman.
18. Letter of 22 December 1952 to Wiseman.
19. Letter of 8 June 1953 to Wiseman.
20. Letter of 7 April 1954 to Wiseman.
21. Letter of 20 July 1953 to Wiseman.
22. Ibid.
23. Letter of 19 September 1953 to Wiseman.
24. Letter of 27 November 1953 to Wiseman.
25. Letter of 14 December 1953 to Wiseman.
26. Ibid.
27. Letter of 7 April 1954 to Wiseman.
28. Letter of 15 November 1954 to Wiseman.
29. *Dance*, 147.
30. Letter of 31 December 1954.
31. Letter of 29 March 1954 to Wiseman.
32. Handwritten letter of 12 August 1955 to Wiseman.
33. *Dance*, 112.
34. Letters of 27 January and 10 February 1956 to Wiseman.
35. Letter of 31 July 1956 to Wiseman.

36. Letter of 3 April 1956 to Wiseman.
37. Letter of 28 May 1956 to Wiseman.
38. Letter of 23 July 1956 to Wiseman.
39. Ibid.
40. Letter of 31 July 1956 to Wiseman.
41. Letter of 23 July 1956 to Wiseman.
42. Letter of 10 July 1956 to Wiseman.
43. Letter of 23 July 1956 to Wiseman.
44. Letter of 26 November 1956 to Wiseman.
45. Letter of 4 December 1956 to Wiseman.
46. Letter of 14 December 1956 to Wiseman.
47. See *Dance*, 154.

CHAPTER EIGHT

1. See *Dance*, 114, and letter of 18 February 1957 to Wiseman: "I can't bear not to have some place to call my own."
2. *Dance*, 116-18.
3. Letter of 12 July 1957 to Wiseman.
4. Handwritten letter of 1 December 1957 to Wiseman.
5. See *Dance*, 119-20.
6. Handwritten letter of 1 December 1957 to Wiseman.
7. Letter of 13 September 1958 to Nancy and Frank Collier.
8. Letter of 27 February 1958.
9. Letter of 14 August 1958.
10. Handwritten letter of 1 December 1959 to Wiseman.
11. Handwritten Christmas card note, 1959, to Wiseman.
12. Handwritten letter of 16 January 1960 to Wiseman.
13. Conversations with Zella Clark, 17-19 August 1988.
14. Zella Clark, "My Personal Tribute," *Minus Tides* no. 1; written "just a few weeks after Margaret died." Letter of 28 January 1989 to me from Zella Clark.
15. Interview with Jan Bhatti, 20 September 1988.
16. Interview with Jocelyn and David Laurence, July 1987.
17. Letter of 22 January 1961.
18. Letter of 3 April 1956 to Wiseman.
19. Letter of 31 July 1956.

20. Margaret Laurence, *This Side Jordan*, New Canadian Library (Toronto: McClelland and Stewart, 1989). 8.

21. See George Lamming, *The Pleasures of Exile* (Ann Arbor: University of Michigan Press, 1992). Margaret Laurence was tremendously impressed by Lamming—"the kind of personality that hits you like the spirit of god between the eyes. Very revolutionary in outlook," she wrote to Wiseman (5 August 1962). He was a Canada Council Fellow, and just a year younger than she. The brief encounter was important at that vexed moment of her life: it helped her recognize the real possibility of making the big change she was secretly contemplating. That congress remained a cherished memory for her until her death. *Pleasures* develops the claim, "Caliban is here to stay" (63): "The world from which our reciprocal ways of seeing have sprung was once Prospero's world. It is no longer his. . . . It is ours. . . ." (203); "Caliban has learnt that democracy is a way of being together. . . . Freedom, in a political sense, is the recognition of the demand to be collectively responsible. . . . Democracy is an atmosphere and a future toward which you work. . . . the very reverse of what Prospero himself demanded of Caliban to understand by democracy" (158-59).

22. Amegbe sees that "Victor has never made use of his advantages. . . . a journalist on a hand-set newspaper. He could have been an assistant professor at the university here, or at least a journalist on a more important newspaper" (51).

23. Dominique O. Mannoni, *Prospero and Caliban: A Study of the Psychology of Colonization* (London: Methuen, 1956).

24. See Lamming, *Pleasures of Exile*, 158.

25. Letter of 31 July 1956.

26. "Sources," *Mosaic* 3, no. 3 (1970): 81; reprinted in *Margaret Laurence: Critical Views on Canadian Writers*, ed. William H. New (Toronto: McGraw-Hill Ryerson, 1977).

27. Letter of 31 July 1956 to Wiseman.

28. The essay was reprinted in *Heart of a Stranger*; "Fetish" was published in *The Tomorrow-Tamer* (Toronto: McClelland and Stewart, 1963).

CHAPTER NINE

1. Margaret Laurence, *The Tomorrow-Tamer and Other Stories*, New Canadian Library 70 (Toronto: McClelland and Stewart, 1986), 208. Cf. Northrop Frye's comment on the Canadian dilemma, in *The Bush Garden*, 219: "It seems to me [he wrote in 1956] that Canadian sensibility . . . is less perplexed by the question 'Who am I?' than by some such riddle as 'Where is here?'"

2. *Queen's Quarterly* 2 (Winter 1956): 498.

3. Revision of the 1956 text takes into account that the Gold Coast became the independent Ghana on 6 March 1957. The original passage reads, "But underneath nothing was the same. What was the change? I don't know exactly. It was so many things. It was an old chieftain . . ." (499). Then follows the catalogue of items retained in *Tomorrow-Tamer.*

4. The second of her Ghanaian stories, published in *Prism International*, September 1959.

5. In the original version Danso assures Lemon that African pantheism was moving toward a monotheism: "And above all others is Nyame the Creator" (*Prism*, 62); that preceded the sentence in the revised version, "If we'd been left alone, our gods would have grown, as yours did, into One" (*Tomorrow-Tamer*, 63).

6. *Hath Not a Jew* (1940), a collection by the Montreal poet Abraham Moses Klein (1909-72), was part of our brief introduction to Canadian poetry at United College. This sentence is omitted from the revised version.

7. *The Manitoban*, 26 January 1945.

8. Tetteh's family—particularly his father, Kobla—has managed compromise similar to Bonsu's: members of Quarshie's Saint Sebastian Mission, they yet participate in Tetteh's mock ritual of python-god worship for Hardacre's instruction, though Kobla hesitates lest the powers they mock—the old gods—be offended. Kobla is an elder in the mission.

9. It was reprinted, again reduced by about one third, in *The Saturday Evening Post*, 3 June 1961; that version was in turn reprinted, verbatim, in *The Saturday Evening Post Stories 1962*, selected from 1961 publications, which included stories by Ray Bradbury, C.S. Forster, Shirley Ann Grau, William Saroyan, and others—twenty stories in all.

10. Archipelago's character is embellished by one feature of his native Genoa that he acknowledges, the Staglieno cemetery, where he would "sit beside the tombs of the rich, a small fat boy with the white marble angels—so compassionate they looked, and so costly—I believed then that each was the likeness of a lady buried beneath" (25-26). The ladies of his dreams in adulthood are their cousins. *Camel Bell* records the source of the image: "At Genoa . . . the Staglieno cemetery, where marble angels loomed like spirits of vengeance among green-black Cyprus trees and where the poor rented graves for seven years . . ." (6).

11. See *Dance*, 155.

12. Laurence echoes here the locution she had used in the original version of "The Drummer of All the World" in reference to Afua, Matthew's early love: "Possessing her, I possessed all Africa, all earth" (*Queen's*

Quarterly, 498; cf. *Tomorrow-Tamer*, 12); and apparently with the same intent. To have retained it in the revision would have heightened (perhaps unnecessarily) Africa's symbolic value in "Godman's Master" and certainly would have sharpened the contrast between the pathos of Matthew's loss and the joy of Godman's achievement.

13. See Isaiah 7:14 and Matthew 1:23.

14. Laurence commented of her hero, a decade after writing the story, that ". . . he does tame tomorrow for his people. . . . Kofi is both scapegoat, unintentionally, and messiah, also unintentionally. He himself is the bridge, not between better and worse cultures, but simply between different cultures, between people who do not understand one another, and who, at some point, must try." In *Sixteen by Twelve*, ed. John Metcalf (Toronto: McGraw-Hill Ryerson, 1970), 71-73; these are the concluding lines of her "Author's Commentary."

15. *Dance*, 155.

16. Revision camouflages that fact, perhaps to avoid limiting the relevance to one location and to discourage easy identification of the Show-Boy political leader with Nkrumah. The third sentence of the opening paragraph of the original read, "You might claim that there were as many honest traders in Ghana as there were elephants"; revision replaces "in Ghana" with "here."

17. "The African Stories of Margaret Laurence," *The Canadian Forum* (April 1961), reprinted in *Margaret Laurence: Critical Views on Canadian Writers*, 105-10, quotation from 108.

18. Ga is a Ghanaian dialect and also refers to those who speak it.

19. See, e.g., Fitch and Oppenheimer, *Ghana: End of an Illusion*, 78-80.

20. Letter of 18 July 1960.

21. Letter of 3 December 1960 to Wiseman.

22. Letter of 22 January 1961.

23. Ibid.

24. Letter of 29 March 1961 to Wiseman.

25. Letter of 28 April 1961 to Wiseman.

26. When she deposited a small collection of her translations at York University (Toronto) in 1982, she wrote on the cover page that these translations "that I did after A TREE FOR POVERTY was completed, were never published." The collection includes a typescript of "A Faithless Friend" corrected in Margaret's hand; the corrections create a text that matches the version published in *The Somaliland Journal*. One looks in vain for public confirmation of that publication, apart from the *Journal* itself.

27. Letter of 26 October 1953.

28. Susan J.Warwick's *Margaret Laurence: An Annotated Bibliography* (Toronto: ECW Press, 1979), makes no reference to "Uncertain Flowering" and when Margaret Laurence penned supplementary items into my copy of the *Bibliography* she omitted "Uncertain Flowering." *Dance on the Earth* clearly identifies "The Drummer of All the World" as her first adult piece of fiction: "If you haven't published a thing except one story in *Queen's Quarterly* and a small book of translations from Somali poetry, you can't really claim to be a professional writer, or so I felt" (152).

29. Letter of 13 January 1962.

30. Letter of 17 March 1962.

31. See Chapter Six, "Somaliland Creations," 115-20.

32. "Uncertain Flowering," in *Story*, 18.

33. *Camel Bell*, 49.

34. See earlier discussion of her poem "Pagan Point," pp. 43-46.

35. Cf. closing lines of Milton's *Paradise Lost* (XII, 645-49), with "Eden" replaced by "*Sheikh* they."

36. See *Canadian Literature* 8 (Spring 1961): 62-63. "African Poem" appeared in the *Tamarack Review*—of which Dobbs was then co-editor—vol. 19 (Spring 1961): 61-66. Laurence's December letter made the now-obvious connection, "This is what the novel I hope to write deals with, more or less. One cannot identify oneself with another culture, because everyone carries his own culture with him, like his blood group." Dobbs saw *Jordan* as "an effort of the will rather than of imagination" (62) and found the novel "condescending" (63)—like his review. Margaret's letter to Wiseman is dated 5 September 1961.

37. See letters of 16 December 1960 and 8 October 1961 to Wiseman.

38. Letter of 1 July 1961 to Wiseman.

39. Letter of 5 September 1961 to Wiseman; she found a reference to Buchholzer in Isak Dinesen's *Shadows on the Grass* and "went to great lengths to obtain the book [*Horn of Africa*]."

40. Letter of 5 September 1961; see "Somaliland Creations," 240-73.

41. Letter of 5 September 1961 to Wiseman.

42. Handwritten letter of 8 October 1962 to Wiseman. The terminal adverb is significant.

43. Letter of 5 September 1961 to Wiseman.

44. Letter of 8 October 1961 to Wiseman.

45. Letter of 13 January 1962 to Wiseman.

46. Letter of 17 March 1962 to Wiseman.

47. Letter of 16 April 1962 to Wiseman.
48. Letter of 13 June 1962 to Wiseman.
49. Letter of 5 August 1962 to Wiseman.
50. Letter of 20 August 1962. Years later Margaret's memory had it that she was very reluctant to let Jack read the novel—"I think I knew his response would be pivotal in our marriage. . . . I allowed him to read it in the end and he didn't like it much . . ." (*Dance*, 158). That is a somewhat gentler version than is recorded in her correspondence with Wiseman.
51. See Laurence's letter of 19 February 1961 to Wiseman: "P.S. Please keep on calling me Peg, as always."
52. Handwritten letter of 28 October 1962 to Wiseman.
53. Letter of 25 November 1962 to Wiseman.
54. Letter of 11 December 1962 to Wiseman.
55. Letter of 13 January 1962 to Wiseman.

CHAPTER TEN

1. Letter of 24 September 1962 to Nancy and Frank Collier.
2. Handwritten letter to Nancy and Frank Collier, 23 September 1962.
3. *Dance*, 160. Mrs. Collier told me she could claim no credit for locating the flat other than finding temporary lodging for them while Margaret hunted, but she accepted responsibility for discovering an appropriate school in the area for Jocelyn and David. Conversation with Nancy Collier in Amersham, Bucks., England, summer 1992.
4. Letters to Wiseman, 28 October and 25 November 1962.
5. *Dance*, 159.
6. Letter to Wiseman, 2 January 1963.
7. Letter to Wiseman, 22 February 1963.
8. Letter to Wiseman, 14 February 1963.
9. Letter of 2 October 1964 to Wiseman.
10. Handwritten letter to Wiseman, 8 April 1963. The line is from "The Sparks Fly" in Layton's 1963 volume. Margaret was living in London's Hampstead district; Layton's line refers to a district of Montreal, as she learned later.
11. The term was evidently Adele's but eagerly adopted by Margaret; see her letter to Wiseman of 4 March 1963.
12. See, e.g., letter to Wiseman, 21 July 1963.

13. *Ethel Wilson: Stories, Essays, and Letters*, ed. David Stouck (Vancouver: University of British Columbia Press, 1987), 229, 8 March 1963.

14. Letter of 11 February 1963.

15. Letter of 29 March 1961.

16. To Wiseman, 12 June 1963; the next sentence reveals, "I gave an enthusiastic account of A. Wiseman's 'The Sacrifice' in this regard, naturally."

17. Letter of 18 February 1963.

18. I am grateful to the late B.W. Andrzejewski for giving me a copy of the text of this series.

19. Letter of 12 June 1963.

20. Letter to Wiseman, 21 July 1963.

21. Ibid.

22. *Dance*, 163.

23. Letter to Wiseman, 20 September 1963.

24. Letter of 17 August 1963; in her letter of 19 February 1961 she had exempted Adele from the request to call her "Margaret."

25. Letter to Wiseman, 20 September 1963.

26. See especially her letter to Wiseman, 15 October 1963; her letter of 23 October 1963 to Wiseman refers to "my 11/2 acres."

27. Letter of 1 October 1963.

28. Letter to Wiseman, 15 October 1963.

29. So she put it to Wiseman, 18 December 1963.

30. Ibid.

31. Letter from Ross, 31 March 1964.

32. Letters from Wilson, 10 November 1963 (on *Tomorrow-Tamer*), 231; and 27 May 1964 (on *Stone Angel*), 239.

33. Letter from Ross, 1 June 1964.

34. Margaret Laurence, *The Stone Angel* (New York: Knopf, 1964), 3. Pagination of this edition is the same as in that published by McClelland and Stewart, Toronto, 1964.

35. Son Marvin arranges for a semi-private ward for Hagar. When Doris adds that it's a new wing, Hagar snaps, "That's all I need. . . . A new wing" (280). As Hagar visualizes rebirth in the hereafter, she guesses, "I'd pass out with amazement. Can angels faint?" (307).

36. Michel Fabre, "From *The Stone Angel* to *The Diviners*: An Interview with Margaret Laurence," in *A Place to Stand On*, ed. George Woodcock (Edmonton: NeWest Press, 1983), 205. Laurence also distinguishes

between Hagar's "strictly chronological" memories and the quite distorted line of Stacey's memories in *The Fire-Dwellers* to observe that the chronological line must be regular to suit its function in *Angel*.

37. *Heart*, 27.

38. Lorraine M. York, *"The Other Side of Dailiness": Photography in the Works of Alice Munro, Timothy Findley, Michael Ondaatje, and Margaret Laurence* (Toronto: ECW Press, 1988), 121-22.

39. *Heart*, 23.

40. Letter of 18 February 1963.

41. Walter E. Swayze, the most useful critic of Laurence's career, has written persuasively on this and related topics in "Knowing through Writing: The Pilgrimage of Margaret Laurence," in *Crossing the River: Essays in Honour of Margaret Laurence*, ed. Kristjana Gunnars (Winnipeg: Turnstone Press, 1988), 3-23.

42. *Rime of the Ancient Mariner*, 11, 141-42.

43. See Constance Rooke, "Hagar's Old Age: *The Stone Angel* as *Vollendungsroman*," in *Crossing the River*, 25-42.

44. "Sources," first published in *Mosaic* 3, 3 (1970): 80-84; reprinted in *Margaret Laurence: Critical Views on Canadian Writers*, 12-16; quotation from 13.

45. See Laurence, "The Wemyss and Simpson Families"; see also *Dance*, 30.

46. Letter of 2 January 1963.

47. Letter of 28 January 1950.

48. Letter of 17 May 1981 to Wiseman.

CHAPTER ELEVEN

1. Margaret's letter, 6 March 1982, to the current owners of Elm Cottage, Marie and Gerald Colwell.

2. *Dance*, 169.

3. See Jocelyn Laurence, "As for Me and My Houses," *Toronto Life*, August 1986, 15-17. "I recognized this ghost immediately. . . . She looked at me and I at her for several seconds. Then she walked into the kitchen and was gone" (15). Gerald Colwell's letter of 21 May 1998 to me adds to the story. Jocelyn's article continues, on Elm Cottage, "We . . . loved the place instantly and totally, with a blind, love-at-first-sight devotion. . . ."

4. Margaret's letters of 10 April 1964, 24 August 1964, and 17 May 1965 to Wiseman.

5. Letter of 26 April 1967 to Wiseman.

6. Letters of 14 November 1965 and 17 May 1967 to Wiseman.

7. Letter of 11 February 1963 to Wiseman.

8. Republication of these stories, in *Journal of Canadian Fiction* 27 (1980), indicates that their order of composition is the reverse of their order of publication—"A Queen in Thebes," *The Tamarack Review* 32 (Summer 1964): 25-37; "Mask of Beaten Gold," *The Tamarack Review* 29 (Autumn 1963): 3-21. See the quotation from her "Letter to Bob Sorfleet (13 November 1978)" in the *Journal of Canadian Fiction* 27, p. 52.

9. "Letter to Bob Sorfleet," 52.

10. This is an echo of the abrupt death of the three-year-old neighbour child in Accra, in November 1953, that so affected Margaret. See her letter of 27 November 1953 to Wiseman.

11. *Tamarack Review* 32 (Summer 1964): 26.

12. Mary Wollstonecraft Shelley, *Frankenstein; or, the Modern Prometheus*, 1818 facsimile text (Berkeley: University of California Press, 1984), 108—vol. II, near the beginning of Chapter Four.

13. "A Queen in Thebes," 36. The scene ends, "She knew that he was afraid of her too. They were afraid of each other."

14. Swayze, "Knowing through Writing," 19.

15. Letter of 25 June 1964.

16. Ibid., my italics. This letter is obviously the basis of the article Margaret published in *Holiday*, January 1966, 21-24, 28-30, and then in *Heart*, 19-32; its title is "Sayonara, Agamemnon" in both publications.

17. Letter of 24 August 1964.

18. Letter of 19 November 1964 to Wiseman.

19. Letter of 17 August 1963.

20. She uses this memory in connection with Nestor Kazlik's sleigh in *A Jest of God.*

21. Letter of 31 December 1964 to Wiseman.

22. Letter of 7 February 1965 to Wiseman.

23. Letter of 24 January 1965 to Wiseman. See Eliot's "Tradition and the Individual Talent," in *Selected Essays*, New Edition (New York: Harcourt, Brace and World, 1960), 10: "Poetry . . . is not the expression of personality, but an escape from personality"; also see Walter E. Swayze, "Margaret Laurence: Novelist as Poet," *New Perspectives on Margaret Laurence* (Westport, CT: Greenwood Press, 1996), 3-16, and especially p. 14: " . . . *all* of Margaret Laurence's fiction is poetry."

24. Letter of 8 March 1965 to Wiseman.

25. See letter of 24 August 1964 to Wiseman.

26. "The Poem and the Spear," in *Heart*, 74. The headnote provided for this, its initial publication, claims she wrote the essay in 1964, "just after the publication of *The Stone Angel*." The essay had doubtless been in her mind then, and the more so as 1964 was the centennial of the Sayyid's birth. First reference to the essay, however, is in the letter of 19 March 1965 to Wiseman: "I've been writing one or two articles, . . . I'm working on a very interesting one which I've wanted to do for a long time, on the Sayyid Mohammed Abdulah Hassan [sic], . . . this seems a good time to do it." This is the version of the Sayyid's name Margaret had used in *A Tree for Poverty* and adhered to until she published this essay. She then relied on the scholarship of her old friend Guś Andrzejewski and adopted his spelling of the name.
27. See letter of 19 March 1965 to Wiseman.
28. Letter of 8 March 1965 to Wiseman.
29. Letter of 5 April 1965.
30. Letter of 17 May 1965 to Wiseman.
31. Letter of 5 April 1965, handwritten, to Wiseman.
32. Letter of 17 May 1965.
33. Letter of 11 May 1965 to Nadine Jones Asante.
34. I remember this phenomenon clearly from our visits to Elm Cottage during Aunt Ruby's tenure there, and our own difficulty in adapting orally to "Margaret."
35. Letter of 27 June 1965 to Wiseman.
36. Letter of 17 August 1965 to Wiseman.
37. See letter of 24 January 1965 to Wiseman.
38. Voice is also an important feature of narrative technique in *A Jest*: use of first-person interior dialogue enables us to be privy to Rachel's thought processes and to feel involved in her seeking solutions to problems. Use of the present tense adds a sense of immediacy to her discussions with herself.
39. Margaret Laurence, *A Jest of God* (Toronto: McClelland and Stewart-Bantam, 1977), 50.
40. See the persuasive ecstatic utterance of Aritha van Herk, "The Eulalias of Spinsters and Undertakers," in *Crossing the River*, 133-45. Professor van Herk calls Rachel's *speaking* at the tabernacle "the orgasm of voice" (138). See also George Bowering's seminal reading "That Fool of a Fear: Notes on *A Jest of God*," *Canadian Literature* 50 (1971): 41-56, reprinted in *A Place to Stand On*, 210-26. Bowering identifies Laurence's "courage" in *A Jest* as the ability "to confront social and deep personal stupidities and fears in the womb of the narrator" (211). Bowering's reading pleased Laurence: she felt it was the most perceptive response to *A Jest of God*.

41. Another such preparation is the scene in which Rachel's frustration over failed communication with her favourite student, James Doherty, leads to her striking him with her ruler and drawing blood.

42. Laurence completes the descriptions of Nick by indicating that these details are part of his Slavic appearance—"Eyes rather Slavic, slightly slanted" (78), "it seems a hidden Caucasian face, one of the hawkish and long-ago riders of the Steppes" (106); but the specific comparison of Nestor to a Cree tends to highlight and "privilege" those features quoted above. In any case, treatment of Nick and Nestor indicates another step in Laurence's developing preoccupation with First Nations Canadians, or "Indians," following the appearance of Bram Shipley and his associations and of the Tonnerre boys in *The Stone Angel*, anticipating development of Luke Venturi and Buckle Fennick in *The Fire-Dwellers*, and Piquette in "Crying of the Loons" ("The Loons" in *A Bird in the House*), and culminating in the Tonnerre family in *The Diviners*.

43. Nick Kazlik participates in the development of another Laurentian motif—deriving perhaps from the biblical Cain and Abel and also Jacob and Esau, as well as from her knowledge of her family history—that of twins or sometimes only *pairs* of siblings, a motif that enjoys some prominence in *A Jest*. Nick and Stefan Kazlik are twins; there are also the outlandish pair of teenagers, Clare and Carol, former students of Rachel's, whose conical Silver Blonde Coiffure makes them "look like twins from outer space. . . . Venusians" (14); and the twin girls born to the unwed Cassie Stewart, of whom May Cameron disapproves—not only the illegitimacy but its doubling by twinfold, and Cassie's awful intention to keep them (72).

44. Calla resumes calling Rachel "child" later, after other changes have occurred that provide a context that alters the quality of the term.

45. See letter of 11 September 1967 to Wiseman; there the term is used in reference to *Jason's Quest*.

46. Margaret frankly described the novel, in a letter of 6 September 1965 to Wiseman, as "a study in ironies."

47. At the beginning of Seven, for example, Rachel's response to her mother's questioning is the mean wish that such occurrences would cease "completely"; yet, "Surely I love her as much as most parents love their children. I mean, of course, as much as most children love their parents" (141). Again, Rachel thinks, "She looked at me with eyes as wide and shadowed with troublement as a child told to fetch something from an unlighted cellar" (170). Leaving to visit Calla, Rachel promises that she won't be away long: "As I leave, she looks at me trustingly, like a child" (213). Furthermore, this motif of the reversal of roles between mother and daughter—a phenomenon, Margaret implies, as urgently to

be recognized as that of mutability and mortality, and in fact as part of it—functions importantly in *The Fire-Dwellers.*

48. This theme begins with Rachel's visit to Calla's tabernacle, her disgust with the congregation's making fools of themselves and her fear that she herself has actually done so in "speaking." See also Calla in Eight, just before she introduces Rachel to her bird, Jacob; and, at the close of Ten, Rachel's seeking help from Calla and thinking, "I was always afraid that I might become a fool. Yet I could almost smile with some grotesque lightheadedness at that fool of a fear, that poor fear of fools, now that I really am one" (222).

49. Letter of 29 April 1963 to Wiseman: "Why I should feel such a sense of terror at beginning anything, I don't know, but I do."

50. Letter of 29 March 1964 to Wiseman.

51. The pertinent language in these two letters is virtually identical. See also Margaret's letter of 20 January 1979 to Wiseman: "I burned 100 pp. of manuscript when I got off to a false start with The Fire-Dwellers. I then realized I had to write A Jest of God first." See also *Dance,* 176.

52. Letter of 17 August 1965.

53. Letters of 8 March, 5 April, 17 May, and 27 June 1965 to Wiseman.

CHAPTER TWELVE

1. Letter of 16 January 1966 to Wiseman.

2. Margaret complained to Wiseman that the director had "visualized a kind of 'impressions of Africa,' through contemporary African writing" aided by a commentary based on her personal experiences. "Africa is kind of a big place—you know," she observed drily, and imagined commenting in blasé fashion, "I recall, in Ghana once, the Asantehene said to me . . . etc."

3. Margaret Laurence, *Long Drums and Cannons* (London: Macmillan, 1968), 9.

4. See *Paradise Lost* III 116ff: "they themselves decreed / Their own revolt, not I. If I foreknew, / Foreknowledge had no influence on their fault, / Which had no less proved certain unforeknown . . . / I formed them free, and free they must remain. . . ." Margaret wrestled with this problem (as several of us eagerly did) in Malcolm Ross's popular course in Seventeenth Century Thought at the University of Manitoba.

5. In a letter of 24 March 1966 to Adele Wiseman, Margaret wrote, "I would almost be prepared to fight to the death for one of the very very few things I now at this time believe in—which is, that humans can

really only be seen, in detail or in depth, one at a time, and that these scrawny individual units, broken reeds as they are, do matter. If they don't matter in any universal sense, or if they don't matter in any eternal way—even if they don't matter to God (which I don't really believe, but with one part of my mind only)—they still matter. . . . the whole thing, really, seems to be that if the individual has value, one has to accept the reality of other individuals, persons outside oneself, as well as the reality of oneself. . . . I think in some way that is what fiction must be—not really any kind of a big deal, after all, but only a kind of setting down of how you look at one or two people, one or two dilemmas, according to your own way of seeing."

6. *Long Drums*, 10. In a letter of 13 May 1959 Margaret had told Wiseman that her ambition was to reach even one reader who understood and sympathized with her work, her point of view. Her modest *hopes*, however, were certainly much larger than that. Her attitude to these writers persisted: see her "Ivory Towers or Grass Roots?: The Novelist as Socio-Political Being," in *A Political Art: Essays and Images in Honour of George Woodcock*, ed. William New (Vancouver: University of British Columbia Press, 1978), 15-25.

7. John Prebble (*The Highland Clearances* [London: Secker and Warburg, 1963]) specifies two periods of major clearances: 1782-1820 (covering clearance of Glengarry's estates of much of Sutherland—including Kildonan—and emigration to the Red River Valley and to Upper Canada); and 1840-1854 (covering clearance of Ross and the Isle of Skye—following, one might say, the road *from* the Isles). This book was part of Margaret's preparatory reading, as she acknowledges in the article.

8. *Maclean's* 79 (2 May 1966): 26a-26h; quotation from 26b.

9. *Maclean's*, 26g. The article refers to Eric Linklater's Introduction to Ian Grimble's novel *The Trial of Patrick Sellar*, one of the books she read in preparation for her Highland sojourn, especially his opening comment on the "most incongruous spectacle" of little girls dressed in Gaelic costume performing Highland dances for tourists—"the tartan dolly trade." Margaret specifies (as Linklater does not) the Highland Fling (26g), but she might more appropriately have chosen the Seann Triubhas, which represents a celebration of the 1782 rescinding of the decree of 1746 that banned the wearing of the kilt; the name of the dance means, literally, shedding trousers—a good dance for little girls!

10. In fact, the peninsula of mountains that juts northeast above Cromarty Firth leads to the Dornoch Firth, and it is across this more northern firth that the county of Sutherland begins, with Dornoch the county town.

11. See *Margaret Laurence—Al Purdy: A Friendship in Letters*, ed. John Lennox (Toronto: McClelland and Stewart, 1993), 34-35, 39-40; the unidentified "American couple with 3 kids" is my family.
12. Letter of 14 March 1967 to Wiseman.
13. Letter of 9 April 1967 to Wiseman.
14. Letter of 27 April 1966 to Wiseman.
15. Letter of 29 May 1966 to Wiseman. Margaret could report a happy ending to the saga of Scottish Ann to Al Purdy a couple of years later: "She now has a new man and has put on about 20 lbs and no longer looks like a medical-school skeleton, so some good things do happen" (2 July 1968).
16. Letter of 31 May 1966.
17. Letter of 27 April 1966 to Wiseman.
18. Letter of 29 May 1966 to Wiseman; cf. letter of 18 June 1966 to Nadine Jones Asante: "Have only been out with him several times, but it was like rain in the desert, believe me. He is intelligent, charming, sexy, and the most accomplished diplomat I've ever met. . . . Nothing serious about it, but it was just marvelous not to have to be serious, for a change."
19. Letter of 18 December 1963 to Wiseman.
20. The completion of that remark is worth a glance in view of what the immediate future held in store for Margaret: she is lonely "even for the puritanical responses which make a Canadian man long for passionate sex while at the same time worrying like mad about what the landlady will think."
21. *Dance*, 172-73, 177-78.
22. Letter of 18 June 1966 to Nadine Jones Asante.
23. Letter of 9 July 1966 to Wiseman.
24. *Dance*, 181.
25. Letter of 12 June 1966 to Bob and Anne Hallstead: "United wants to make me a United College Fellow—gosh! . . . I'm really delighted about it."
26. Letter of 27 November 1999 to me from Walter Swayze.
27. Nadine Jones Asante has contributed to the story of Margaret's unrestrained behaviour and salty talk during this Canadian tour (interview with Nadine Jones Asante, Vancouver, summer 1989).
28. Letter of 23 October 1966. She repeated those statistics in her letter to me, 17 January 1967, except that for "talks" she wrote "lectures (or what was jokingly referred to as lectures)."
29. Letter of 23 October 1966 to Wiseman.

30. "Good Morning to the Grandson of Ramesses the Second," *Heart*, 92; 98. Also on p. 98, Margaret "corrects" Shelley's descriptions in "Ozymandias"—e.g., "'The lone and level sands' don't in fact 'stretch far away' at all." But she allows that he caught the spirit all right.
31. See her account in a letter to Wiseman, 18 January 1967; the two articles were finally published in *Heart of a Stranger*—one as identified in note 30, the other, "Captain Pilot Shawkat and Kipling's Ghost" (109-29).
32. Letter of 26 February 1967 to Bob and Anne Hallstead.
33. Letters of 18 January 1967 and 13 March 1967 to Wiseman.
34. Letter of 23 June 1966 to Wiseman.
35. "Pilot Shawkat," 110-11.
36. "Good Morning," 108.
37. Letter of 16 January 1967 to Purdy.
38. Letter of 7 April 1967.
39. Letter of 17 May 1967 to Wiseman.
40. Letters of 2 May 1967 to Wiseman and to Purdy.
41. Letter of 2 May 1967 to Purdy.
42. Letter of 13 March 1967.
43. See letters of 6-7 May 1967 from Wiseman to Margaret; letters of 15 and 17 May and of 21 July 1967 from Margaret to Wiseman; and Wiseman's report on the panel in letter of 3 November 1967 to Margaret.
44. Letter of 8 May 1967.
45. *The New Romans: Candid Canadian Opinions of the U.S.*, ed. A.W. Purdy (Edmonton: M.G. Hurtig, and New York: St. Martin's Press, 1968), 34-37; and *Heart*, 200-03. Here is a crucial illustrative passage from near the end of the brief essay:

    > I am not even sure who is responsible. . . . The wheels turn, but no one admits to turning them. People with actual names and places of belonging are killed, and there is increasingly little difference between these acts and the fake deaths of the cowboys who never were. The fantasy is taking over, like the strangler vines of the jungle taking over the trees. It is all happening on TV (*New Romans*, 36; *Heart*, 203).

46. Letter of 13 October 1967.
47. Letter of 9 April 1967 to Wiseman. She had referred to him in a letter of 23 October 1966, to Adele, as "my ex-friend the Ambassador." In announcing the April invitation Margaret noted, "what a hell of a charming guy he is, and how much we have in common," but concluded,

"I don't know whether I want to do any more than have dinner with him, and talk, but if it turns out that I do, it would of course happen at the moment when I'm giving up my bed-sitter, wouldn't it? The hell with it all."

48. *Dance*, 186-87.
49. Letter of 6 June 1967 to Wiseman; cf. letter of 23 October 1967 to Purdy.
50. Letter of 6 June 1967 to Wiseman. It might be inferred that Margaret almost missed her plane back to Montreal and therefore the connection with her flight back to England. The change of plans, however, seems clearly indicated by the opening of the third paragraph of the letter: "Ottawa, as I told you on the phone, was much better than I thought it would be"; and a brief rehearsal of the ceremony etc. follows.
51. Letters of 7 April 1967 and 10 July 1967 to Bob and Anne Hallstead.
52. Letter of 17 August 1967 to Purdy; cf. letter of 11 September to Wiseman.
53. Letter of 17 August 1967. David was then almost exactly twelve years old; Chris Powers was a year older, Graham a year younger (sister Victoria, eight, enjoyed Jocelyn's big-sisterly attention).
54. Letter of 11 September 1967 to Wiseman.
55. Letter of 21 June 1967 to Wiseman.
56. Letter of 29 June 1967 to Wiseman. She wrote virtually the same letter to Purdy on that date: "I am a firebug. I have just burned all the hundreds of pages which I wrote on this novel 3 years ago. . . ."
57. Letter of 31 August 1967 to Purdy. The four pages of *Adam* (27-30) are roughly the equivalent of pp. 2-7, chapter One, of *The Fire-Dwellers* (New York: Knopf, 1969); the excerpt is markedly different from the published novel, especially in its use of first-person narrative, whereas the novel uses an effective complex of first, second, and third person. But the essence of the final version—as indicated by the well-chosen title for the excerpt—is here clearly established.
58. *Jason's Quest* (New York: Knopf, 1970), 167.
59. Letter of 11 September 1967 to Wiseman. It is, of course, the pattern of the career of the typical Hero, according to various anthropologists and embedded in numerous familiar texts well known to Margaret, including the New Testament.
60. Letter of 11 September 1967 to Wiseman.
61. Letter of 8 July 1967.
62. Letter of 11 September 1967 to Wiseman.
63. Reported in letter of 22 February 1963 to Wiseman.

64. Letter of 18 December 1963 to Wiseman. In her letter of 13 March 1967 Margaret explained to Adele, "He believes quite honestly that I have no financial worries at all, and made such remarks as 'You can't be worried by money—look at the way you live—big house in the country, and so on' . . . ." She added that Jack "has worked out what he thinks it ought to cost me per week, per kid—and so it might, if I lived in a coldwater flat in Camden Town." And a marginal note to that appeared, in ink, in the left-hand margin: "And yet this assessment is *very* unfair to him, because it is *my* choice to live here, and I *am* extravagant in many ways—we *don't* live on hamburger and potatoes, but damn it, I will NOT, unless absolutely necessary."

65. Letter of 21 October 1967 to Wiseman.

66. Letter of 24 October 1967.

67. Letter of 8 November 1967 to Wiseman: "all this nonsense has been . . . some kind of subtle attempt to evade the novel."

CHAPTER THIRTEEN

1. Margaret Laurence, *The Fire-Dwellers* (Toronto: McClelland and Stewart, 1984), 1.

2. Letter to Wiseman, 8 March 1965.

3. This depiction (42) is enhanced in Eight: "*Buckle Fennick . . . the dark skin of his Indian-like face*" (213).

4. Here is another link between Stacey's story and Rachel's. Stacey's frank disclosures prompt Luke to describe the throbbingly vital atmosphere in the Venturi family when he was a kid: "an accordion, a guitar, and my dad on drums . . . people bawling their eyes out over great classical airs like 'Santa Lucia.' It was murder [etc.]" (177). Stacey's response sounds the echo: "I wish I'd had that kind of family." See Rachel's response to Nick Kazlik. Rachel told Nick, "I envied you . . . [you] always seemed more free," and added, "Not so boxed in, maybe. . . . I remember the great bellowing voice he [your father] had, and how emotional he used to get—cursing at the horses, or else crooning to them" (*A Jest of God*, 108-109).

5. The vexed but steadily improving relationship between Stacey and Katie is an important concern, corollary to the major themes of *The Fire-Dwellers*, and deserves mention, however brief. Stacey gradually recognizes that Katie is inevitably growing into adulthood and (it is to be hoped) maturity, and that she herself has left her youth behind and already reached adulthood and (with perseverance) maturity. In fact, Stacey's ability to accept Katie's maturing is a gauge of her own maturity. This relationship is anticipated by and roughly parallel to that of Rachel

and her mother in *A Jest of God*—although there it is seen from the daughter's view—and in turn anticipates a similar relationship in Margaret's *The Diviners*. This topic has been given persuasive treatment by Professor Helen Buss in her *Mother and Daughter Relationships in the Manawaka Works of Margaret Laurence* (Victoria, BC: University of Victoria Press, 1985).

6. This is a promising repetition of his action in his previous job as encyclopaedia salesman: he had persuaded a customer to buy a set, a "pensioner, old retired logger, who wanted to see the picture of Piccadilly, London, where he'd gone on leave in 1917. . . . Mac suddenly grabbed the contract and tore it up, telling the old guy he needed encyclopedias like he needed a hole in the head and there was a public library only a few blocks away" (18).
7. See Psalm 69, especially verses 2, 15, and 16; and The Book of Jonah, Chapter II (Jonah's Prayer), especially verses 3, 5, 6, and 10.
8. See the sixth paragraph of the opening chapter of *The Stone Angel*.
9. The question "Where is home?" or, better, "What means *Home?*" grows in importance as the Manawaka Saga unfolds. If space allowed, the function of this question in *The Fire-Dwellers* could be fruitfully traced and its contribution recognized. Perhaps this word of alert will encourage readers to give the question special notice on their own.
10. Jennifer Rachel MacAindra will be able to utter words of greeting to her namesake Aunt Rachel and Grandma Cameron on their imminent arrival in Vancouver. Near the beginning of Six in *A Jest of God*, we learn that Stacey "gave the last daughter my name . . . Jennifer Rachel. But they call her Jen" (122).
11. *The Tomorrow-Tamer*, 128.
12. Clara Thomas, *The Manawaka World of Margaret Laurence* (Toronto: McClelland and Stewart, 1975), 123.
13. Purdy's letter of 28 June 1968; Margaret's of 2 July 1968.
14. Letter to Purdy, 11 October 1967.
15. Margaret's letter of 8 November 1967 to Purdy.
16. Letter of 11 October 1967.
17. Letter of 10 December 1965.
18. Ibid.
19. Letter of 21 September 1967 to Wiseman.
20. Letter of 3 September 1968.
21. Letter of 21 October 1967.
22. Letter of 21 September 1967. Even earlier she wrote to Adele: "The snag seems to be Jack. . . . [I] still feel that after these years of fighting

with circumstances, here I am back in Square One. When he is in England . . . I feel myself bull-dozed in the old manner. I still, you know, cannot disagree with him" (letter of 11 September 1967).

23. Letter of 27 November 1967 to Wiseman.
24. Letter of 2 July 1968 to Purdy.
25. Letter of 24 June 1968.
26. Letter of 19 February 1968.
27. Letter of 10 March 1968.
28. Letter of 27 November 1968.
29. Letter of 3 September 1968 to Wiseman.
30. Letter of 27 November 1968.
31. Letter of 4 September 1968 to Purdy.

CHAPTER FOURTEEN

1. Letter of 11 January 1968.
2. Ibid.
3. Letter of 21 October 1967. Her account specified, "I would keep the kids, and would pay our fares over here to England in the summer holidays, and might go halves with him for him to go to Canada at Xmas, because . . . I could afford to do this more than he could. . . . but how do I get around the problem of somehow always for his sake to pretend that all this with my work is some kind of meaningless hobby which doesn't affect him?"
4. Letter of 8 November 1967.
5. Letter of 19 February 1968.
6. Letter of 10 March 1968.
7. Letter of 16 April 1968 to Wiseman, and interview with the Swords in Toronto, June 1989.
8. Letter of 16 April 1968.
9. Letter of 4 May 1968 to Wiseman.
10. The letter of 16 April 1966 to Wiseman specified quite exactly, "3 short stories to complete a series of 10," and the letter of 19 February 1968 to Adele says simply, 'I want to do 3 more short stories."
11. Letter of 4 May 1968.
12. Letter of 13 May 1968.
13. Letter of 30 June 1968.
14. Letter of 3 September 1968 to Wiseman.

15. Letter of 10 September 1968 to Wiseman.
16. Letter of 31 August 1967.
17. Letter of 21 October 1968.
18. Letter of 31 October 1968.
19. Letter of 27 November 1968 to Wiseman.
20. Wiseman's letter to Margaret, 24 November 1968.
21. Letter of 29 November 1968.
22. Purdy's letter to Margaret, 3 December 1968.
23. Letter of 9 December 1968.
24. Letter of 5 April 1965.
25. Letter of 19 February 1967.
26. Letter of 1 January 1969.
27. Letter of 21 January 1969 to Laurence.
28. Letter of 26 January 1969.
29. Ibid.
30. Letter of 19 March 1969.
31. "A Bird in the House," *The Fiddlehead* 84 (1970): 108-11; reprinted in *Margaret Laurence: Critical Views on Canadian Writers*, 152-53.
32. Sherrill Grace offers a similar observation in her helpful essay "Crossing Jordan: Time and Memory in the Fiction of Margaret Laurence," *World Literature Written in English* 16, no. 2 (1977): 333. Robert Gibbs also illuminates the organization of the book by commenting on this "pivot of the title story" and the change of scene from *inside* "the two ancestral houses" in the first half to the world *outside* them in the second; see his "Introduction" to *A Bird in the House*, New Canadian Library 96 (Toronto: McClelland and Stewart, 1974), iv.
33. *A Bird in the House: Stories by Margaret Laurence* (Toronto: McClelland and Stewart, 1970), 112-13. Subsequent references are to this edition.
34. This theme is left untouched by three of the best commentaries on *A Bird*—Kent Thompson's 1970 review of the book, Clara Thomas's 1976 *The Manawaka World of Margaret Laurence*, and Jon Kertzer's 1992 *"That House in Manawaka": Margaret Laurence's A Bird in the House* (Toronto: ECW Press, 1992).
35. See the seminal commentary by Clara Thomas (to whom all critics of Margaret Laurence are indebted) in *The Manawaka World of Margaret Laurence*, 103-104, on the essence of *A Bird in the House*: "The adult world seen through the eyes of a child, the maturing of the child, innocence to experience—this is so populated a branch of literature as to constitute a genre in itself."

36. Catherine Simpson Milne, Margaret Laurence's eldest cousin, told me how she and her younger cousins—Peggy Wemyss included—loved their grandfather's charming ne'er-do-well brother (on whom Uncle Dan was based) when they were children. She also told me of Margaret's admitting the autobiographical quality of *A Bird* in the copy with handwritten dedication to Aunt Ruby: "I simplified these stories . . . for obvious reasons, but they were written with love. I had two mothers, but *I also had two splendid aunts.* M." Visit to Catherine Milne, Sidney, BC, August 1989.

37. Kertzer, "*That House in Manawaka*," 76.

38. See "Nanuk," *Argosy* (November 1967): 52-65; and "Le Bâtard," *Liberté* 11 (mars-avril 1969): 143-61.

39. Reprinted in *Margaret Laurence: Critical Views on Canadian Writers*, 154.

40. This is the initial sentence of the last paragraph of the essay of 1884. See *Henry James: Literary Criticism*, ed. Leon Edel, Library of America (New York: Viking Press, 1984), 63-64.

41. The young Vanessa is, of course, a nascent literary talent and responsibly concerned with the representations she commits to her scribblers, and particularly with their honest verisimilitude. Sherrill Grace has succinctly and accurately summed up that aspect of Margaret's depiction of Vanessa: "Young Vanessa was right to abandon her fantastic stories of pioneers, barbaric queens, and French-Canadian servant girls." See her "Crossing Jordan," 334. The story of the pioneers is a bit more complex but it does properly belong with the other two stories as Grace groups them.

42. Kent Thompson, in his review of *A Bird in the House*, 155; Robert Gibbs, in his 1974 Introduction to *Bird*, iv; and Bruce Stovel, in his essay "Coherence in *A Bird in the House*," in *New Perspectives on Margaret Laurence*, ed. Greta Coger (Westport, CT: Greenwood Press, 1996), 81-96 (and in his original paper on the topic, read at the original Margaret Laurence Conference, Brandon University, Manitoba, August 25-28, 1988) comment usefully on the cumulative effect of the arrangement of materials in the book; for example, "the stories are not only connected with each other, but connected into a single, progressive, cumulative story" (Stovel, "Coherence," 90).

43. Letter of 6 June 1969.

44. "Time and the Narrative Voice," originally in *The Narrative Voice*, ed. John Metcalf (Toronto: McGraw-Hill Ryerson, 1972), 126-30; reprinted in *A Place to Stand On*, 155-59, quotation on p. 157.

45. See letter of 4 September 1968 to Purdy: "Maybe I just haven't yet accepted that you can't go home again. (On the other hand, it is so certain that one can't . . . ?)."

46. That concluding story was originally called "A Time of Waiting," appropriate for Vanessa's career. A draft was finished in March, and publication, still as "A Time of Waiting" but abridged, came in *Chatelaine* for February 1970. In that interval Margaret had various distractions: winning her battle not to de-story *A Bird*, completing revision of *Jason's Quest*, preparing for her year in Toronto (departure 14 July), and, above all, facing Jack's request for a divorce. "A Time" was re-titled for publication of *A Bird* that spring, and to emphasize Vanessa's triumph, and Margaret's as well.

47. Jon Kertzer makes similar observations (in *"That House in Manawaka")* on Grandfather Connor's social views. He also suggests that "the stolen telescope symbolizes the magnified view that she [Vanessa] finally attains" (76). He might have added that it may also symbolize a magnified view that poor Harvey hoped for.

48. Vanessa comments, "my own elder child was already fourteen" (206).

49. Thomas, *The Manawaka World of Margaret Laurence*, 100-101.

50. "To Set Our House in Order," in *A Bird in the House*, 46. That deception is of a piece with her denial of a basic feature of life: mutability and mortality. Her house, especially her bedroom, is a virtual Altar of the Dead (see 42-43), and her devotion to the dead son, Roderick, rather than to the living Ewen, reinforces that impression. Her insistence that the new baby be named after the dead uncle provokes an emphatic rejoinder from Ewen, "Roderick Dhu! . . . That's what you'll call him, isn't it? . . . As though he were a character out of Sir Walter Scott . . ." (55).

51. Letter of 2 December 1968.

52. Letter of 9 December 1968.

53. The tour guide speaks "as though the past and present were one" (*Heart*, 23) and as though the wars between Athens and Sparta had continued to the present time. At the entrance to the Stadium at Olympia, Jack wanted to take a photograph of the ancient gateway but an American boy in denims and with a camera was in the way; Margaret urged him to take it anyway as an arty shot—"Today facing Yesterday" (27). Jack agreed and was about to do it, but the boy turned—"Today was facing Today . . . holding cameras aimed at each other."

54. *Heart*, 31.

55. Letter from London, 18 February 1969.

56. Margaret wrote virtually the same pair of responses to Wiseman and Purdy. The first quotation is from her letter of 24 May 1969 to Purdy, the second from her letter of 10 June 1969 to Wiseman. See also letters of 25 May and 27 May 1969 to Wiseman and of 6 June 1969 to Purdy.

57. Letter of 24 May 1969 to Purdy. To Wiseman she wrote, the very next day, "Even if he does not go through with it . . . I shall have to."

58. Letter of 25 May 1969 to Wiseman.

59. Letter of 27 May 1969 to Wiseman.

60. Letter of 17 April 1969 to Wiseman.

61. Letter of 24 May 1969.

62. Letter of 25 March 1969.

63. *The Purdy-Woodcock Letters: Selected Correspondence 1964-84*, ed. George Galt (Toronto: ECW Press, 1988), 47.

64. Letter of 2 July 1968 to Purdy. See Margaret's explanation of the *chi* in her chapter on Chinua Achebe in *Long Drums and Cannons*, 99.

65. Letter of 21 October 1968 to Purdy. Margaret's recollection (*Dance*, 190) was that "Clara Thomas put me in touch with Ian and Sandy Cameron. Clara had known them both for some time, Ian as a graduate student of hers at York and Sandy as a don there." Margaret wrote to Purdy (21 October 1968), "Saw Dave Godfrey when he was in London about a week ago, and we discussed possibilities of some Canadian writer (he's going to suggest several) and wife taking over house [etc.]"; and again to Purdy (16 January 1969), "it was through him [Dave Godfrey] that I found a young Can writer and his wife who will take over Elm Cottage and be company for my kids while I'm in Toronto."

66. Letter of 20 June 1969 to Purdy.

67. Letter of 9 July 1969 to Purdy.

68. Letter of 12 July 1969 to Wiseman.

69. *Mosaic* 3, 3 (Spring 1970): 80-84; a special issue, "Manitoba in Literature: An Issue on Literary Environment."

70. "Sources," 84. This essay was reprinted, with only minor revisions and with the new title "A Place to Stand On," as the first item in *Heart*, 13-18.

71. Lowlanders and other aliens should see "my heart's in the Highlands, my heart is not her / My heart's in the Highlands, a-chasing the deer"—the refrain (traditional) from Robert Burns's poem, "My Heart's in the Highlands."

72. Letter of 5 March 1969.

73. *Heart*, 157.

74. Letter of 16 April 1968 to Wiseman: "Re: possible new areas . . . something new for me, namely the area of myth."

75. Letter of 11 February 1969. Laurence quotes from "Canadian Boat Song" by John Galt (?) 1779-1839, *Blackwood's Magazine*, 1829: "From the sheiling on the misty island / Mountains divide us, and the waste of

seas, / Yet still the blood is strong, the heart is highland, / And we in dreams behold the Hebrides."

76. At this point in the letter of 12 July 1969 to Purdy, Margaret inserts "(have just writ to Adele)."
77. Letter of 12 July 1969 to Purdy.
78. Letter of 19 August 1969 to Purdy; see also *Dance*, 191.
79. Letter of 21 October 1967.
80. Letter of 23 September 1969.
81. Letter of 14 October 1969.
82. Letter of 1 October 1969.
83. Letter of 5 November 1969.
84. Letter of 5 November 1969 to Purdy.
85. Don Bailey, *Memories of Margaret* (Scarborough: Prentice-Hall of Canada, 1989).
86. J.A. Wainwright, ed., *A Very Large Soul: Selected Letters from Margaret Laurence to Canadian Writers* (Dunvegan, Ontario: Cormorant Books, 1998), 141.
87. Letter of 24 November 1969 to Purdy.
88. Ibid.
89. Letter of 3 December 1969 to Purdy. This became *Red on White* by NeWest Press in Edmonton, 1970-71; a startling and impressive little volume, touching and naïve.
90. See *Heart*, 44-76, esp. 74-75.
91. Letter of 20 December 1969.
92. Ibid.
93. Letter of 24 December 1969.
94. Letter of 30 December 1969 to Wiseman.
95. Letter of 30 December to Purdy.

CHAPTER FIFTEEN

1. Letter of 3 January 1970.
2. Letter of 5 February 1970 to Purdy.
3. Letter of 5 March 1970.
4. Letter of 11 February 1970 to Purdy.
5. Ibid.
6. Letter of 31 December 1971 to Purdy.

7. Gary Geddes, "The Tribe, for Margaret Laurence," in *Flying Blind* (Frederiction: Goose Lane Publications, 1998), 80.

8. Letter of 25 March 1970 to Purdy.

9. Letter of 31 March 1970 to Purdy.

10. Letter of 21 January 1970 to Purdy; and *Dance*, 197. He was obviously a source for Royland in *The Diviners*.

11. Letter of 26 October 1970.

12. Letter of 5 July 1970. The familiar term of endearment, Elmcot, for Elm Cottage had been in use in her letters to Wiseman since 22 September 1967, and to Purdy since 10 March 1968.

13. Letter of 25 July 1970; see also letter of 24 July 1970 to Purdy.

14. Letter of 16 August 1970 to Wiseman, and Clara Thomas, *Chapters in a Lucky Life* (Ottawa: Borealis Press, 1999), 306.

15. Ibid.

16. Ibid. Not so odd, perhaps; and her choice of terms is revealing. Nature, one knows, abhors a vacuum. Early in January 1970, Margaret combined a brief celebration of her new liberty with an attempt to fill that vacuum on a junket into London, where she met an old friend. She wrote Purdy, "Came back today with scarred and bleeding chin. . . . Thought of saying I grazed it on a bearded man, which, being the truth, nobody would've believed. . . . I am vulnerable, sure, at the moment, but not so vulnerable as to go berserk . . ." (3 January 1970).

17. Letter of 23 October 1970 to Purdy.

18. Letter of 6 October 1970 to Wiseman.

19. Letter of 28 December 1970 to Purdy. Her letter to Wiseman, ten days later, says "10 people for Christmas dinner and 14 for Boxing Day" (7 January 1971).

20. Letter of 28 December 1970.

21. Letter of 1 March 1971.

22. *Dance*, 198.

23. Letter of 3 April 1971.

24. Letters of 30 April 1971, one each to Purdy and Wiseman.

25. Letter of 28 December 1970.

26. Letter of 15 January 1971 to Purdy.

27. Letter of 15 April 1971 to Purdy. In his letter of 30 March 1971, Purdy had written to Margaret: "I lament your novel, but hell, it's a good thing you found yourself out. . . . Okay, 8 mos, but I dunno if it's really wasted—how the human mind and guts work is mysterious— One can always say one learned something. . . ."

28. Letter of 30 April 1971. She had written Purdy on 1 March that the "wrong novel" had been concealing the new one that was discovered to her; it "may possibly have been growing under the surface while I was sweating and straining at the other one. . . . Woke up this morning and began to sing *Onward Christian Soldiers, To Be A Pilgrim, Battle Hymn of the Republic, Little Joe the Wrangler*, and others. Must be a good omen."

29. Letter of 14 April 1971.

30. Letter of 3-7 September 1971 to Purdy.

31. Ibid.

32. Letter of 16 September 1971 to Purdy. She explained further that "The last couple of weeks in a place are never good for me for writing, as in my mind I am already packing and leaving."

33. Letter of 10 December 1971 to Wiseman.

34. Letter of 13 October 1971 to Purdy and of 14 October 1971 to Wiseman.

35. The actual sale, the following spring, brought $700; see letter of 18 April 1972 to Purdy.

36. "Salute" in the Vancouver *Sun*, 22 May 1971, and "The River" in the Vancouver *Sun*, 11 December 1971, both on p. 6 of the respective Saturday numbers.

37. Letter of 15 November 1971.

38. Letter of 13 January 1972 to Wiseman; see letter of 31 December 1971 to Purdy.

39. Letter of 13 January 1972 to Wiseman. Margaret listed us among the "various Can friends" who visited over the holiday, and added "I know they are Amer citizens, but I can't think of them as such. . . ."

40. Letter of 5 August 1970.

41. Letter of 23 April 1971 to Purdy: "I've just . . . written an article for . . . John Metcalf . . . re: technique used in 2 of my Can stories . . . TIME AND THE NARRATIVE VOICE."

42. This phenomenon closely resembles E.M. Forster's creation, in *Howards End*, of a social fabric woven of (to simplify a little) Wilcox-ism and Schlegel-ism; the threads of both warp and woof are strengthened (appropriately) with *bast*—Leonard.

43. See letters of 13 October and 15 November 1971 to Purdy, and of 14 October 1971 to Wiseman. The essay was published in *Maclean's* in December 1972 and later in *Heart of a Stranger*.

44. *Maclean's*, 80.

45. See letters of 21 November 1971, one each to Purdy and Wiseman.

46. Letter of 13 October 1970 to Purdy.

47. Letter of 7 September 1971 to Purdy.

48. *The Diviners*, 137.

49. Ibid., 221.

50. Letter of 7 September 1971.

51. Letter of 13 January 1972.

52. *The Diviners*, 146-47.

53. Letter of 7 April 1972.

54. *Dance*, 200-201. See Margaret's letter to David Williams, 14 August 1977, in *A Very Large Soul*, 209-10. Jean Murray Cole, *Exile in the Wilderness: The Biography of Chief Factor Archibald McDonald, 1790-1853* (Don Mills, ON: Burns and MacEachern, 1979), 24ff, identifies "the young piper, Robert Gunn."

55. Letter of 17 October 1973 to Purdy.

56. See Clara Thomas's excellent essay, "Margaret, Morag, and the Scottish Ancestors," *British Journal of Canadian Studies* 7, no. 1 (1992): 95.

57. As planned in Margaret's notes for the novel, quoted in Thomas, "Margaret, Morag, and the Scottish Ancestors," 97.

58. See my essay "Skinner in a Kilt: Flower of the Forest," *Margaret Laurence Review* 8 (1998): 19-22, originally read at the conference "Margaret Laurence: Her Life and Work" held at the University of Brandon, 25-28 August 1988.

59. The cable, "CHRISTIE LOGAN VERY ILL . . . ," arrives "two months after" their return, but in the physical design of the novel (notice that Morag's epiphany appears on the same page and just a few lines below her declaration, "Christie's real country. Where I was born.") the juxtaposition is very close. The dramatic effect of the near contiguity is important and is, furthermore, sustained: at the bottom of the same page begins the Memorybank Movie that shows her final reunion with Christie.

60. The CBC Television adaptation, 3 January 1993, had the benefit of excellent actors to portray Jules, young Morag the girl, adult Morag, and Christie; yet the benefit failed of full realization because—one can only suppose—of serious misreading of *The Diviners*. The movie presented the sexual relations between Morag and each of her men, Jules, Brooke, and McRaith, as mere factual phenomena—for their own, possibly titillating, effect—and with no hint of their contribution as expressive elements in the total arrangement of the novel. The portrayal of Christie Logan escaped the misreading: the concept and the actor (Wayne Robson) were brilliant. See the sane review by John Haslett Cuff, the Arts, *Globe and Mail*, January 1993.

61. Michel Fabre, "Words and the World," in *A Place to Stand On*, 250. Further support for this association comes from the reflective pairing of Christie Logan and Colin Gunn (Morag's biological father), comrades in arms during World War I. Christie tells Morag, "Your dad saved my life" (72). In perhaps the last lucid moment of her life Prin denies that assertion—"He never done that for my Christie"—and as it continues we must pay close attention to the words Margaret provides for Prin: "He never done that for my Christie. *Saved him*, like. Or maybe he done it. I dunno. . . . He was . . . just a boy . . . and that scared. Poor *lamb*. The poor *lamb*. He would cry, and Christie would hold him" (167; my italics). A reflecting pair, Christie and Colin. But who saved whom, and exactly how? Is the one who did the saving the one who is truly Morag's father? Probably.

CHAPTER SIXTEEN

1. Since the Manawaka Saga contains a character called Thor Thorlakson, this coincidence—and perhaps seeming contradiction—needs a comment. The character's real name is Vernon Winkler; he is Eva's little brother; in *The Diviners* he is obviously one of the alien figures. When he escaped Manawaka he attempted to re-create himself, the better to combat the society that so oppressed him, and he flourishes as Thor in *The Fire-Dwellers*. His choice of the Scandinavian persona was wise; the "pagan and heathen" name, ironically, is safe in the civilized society of Manawaka and Manitoba, where there were (are) many Scandinavians—mainly blond and blue-eyed. There is another irony: after Val Tonnerre has identified this Thor, Stacey thinks, "God of thunder. Vernon Winkler" (*Fire-Dwellers*, 244).
2. Fabre,"Words and the World," 250.
3. Michel Fabre, "From *The Stone Angel* to *The Diviners*: An Interview with Margaret Laurence," *A Place to Stand On*, 209.
4. Margaret began composing songs for *The Diviners* at about the end of the first week in December 1972, and by the 18th of the month reported to Wiseman, "I've written 3 songs and am about to write a 4th and maybe a 5th." The songs are Jules's: first for his grandfather, old Jules, then one for his father, Lazarus, and a few days later one for his sister Piquette. "I made up a tune for the first one," she says, then adds that Ian Cameron composed the music for the others. In her letter of 30 December 1972 to Purdy, Margaret gives Ian Cameron credit for all the music. Furthermore, she explains, defensively, that the songs "seemed to come of their own accord," as though to assure the unsympathetic Purdy they weren't really her fault; she knew he disapproved. (These two letters are included, respectively, in *Selected Letters of Margaret Laurence and Adele Wiseman*, 329; and *A Friendship in Letters*, 262.)

The songs have received very little attention from critics of *The Diviners*, apart from the observation that they add touches of characterization and comment helpfully on the history of the Tonnerre family. There are, however, two quite excellent commentaries on the songs. First, Walter E. Swayze's brief but sharply perceptive and revealing "Margaret Laurence: Novelist-as-Poet," in *New Perspectives on Margaret Laurence*, especially 9-15; and the longer essay—with biographical and other contributing details—by Wes Mantooth, "Laurence's 'Album' Songs: Divining for Missing Links and Deeper Meanings," *Great Plains Quarterly* XIX, 3 (Summer 1999): 167-79.

5. "'Christie's Real Country. Where I Was Born': Story-telling, Loss and Subjectivity in *The Diviners*," in *Crossing the River: Essays in Honour of Margaret Laurence*, 56, 49.

6. After his tale of the battle of Bourlon Wood, Christie gave Morag the knife marked ⊣ (he will not part with the 60th Canadian Field Artillery Battery Book, but Morag gets it after he is gathered to his ancestors), which he got from a kid, John Shipley, in a trade for a pack of cigarettes. This Shipley, Hagar's younger son, had in an earlier trade exchanged the plaid pin with his friend Lazarus Tonnerre for a knife. That is the plaid pin of the Curries, sept of the Clanranald Macdonalds, and a wonderfully appropriate strand by which to connect the Curries of *The Stone Angel* with the remaining Gunn of *The Diviners*. Jules produces the plaid pin after having sung his songs—about his grandfather, old Jules, at Batoche in 1885, about his own father, Lazarus ("oh man, you didn't die"), and about his sister Piquette, and he and Morag exchange the family talismans (347-52) as "Rites of Passage" ends.

7. Fabre, "From *The Stone Angel* to *The Diviners*," 205.

CHAPTER SEVENTEEN

1. Her letter of 9 March 1973 to Purdy explains in some detail what penalties she would incur from the British government.

2. Letter of 21 April 1973 to Purdy.

3. Letter of 4 July 1973 to Purdy.

4. *Dance*, 204.

5. Letter of 13 April 1973.

6. Letter of 9 June [i.e., July] 1973.

7. *Dance*, 205.

8. A.O.C. Cole, *Trent: The Making of a University, 1957-1987* (Peterborough, ON: Trent University Communications Department, 1990), Preface, xi.

9. Letter of 23 April 1973 to Wiseman.

10. Letter of 22 March 1974 to Purdy.

11. Always sensitive to criticism, Margaret was sometimes overly touchy with reviews. She bridled at her encounter with Valerie Miner, who interviewed her for *Saturday Night* early in January 1974 (published May 1974, 17-20). Ms Miner seemed to be insisting, densely, that *The Diviners* was thinly concealed autobiography, and the description of her *person*, in the review, Margaret felt was the reverse of flattering. Yet the review is, on the whole, a rather sensible and perceptive treatment of the novel. See Margaret's letter of 25 January 1974 to Wiseman.

12. *Dance*, 215. Her account to Ernest Buckler was more subdued, her letter of 15 February 1975 shows; see *Very Large Soul*, 33-34.

13. Letter of 30 April 1975 to Ernest Buckler, *Very Large Soul*, 36.

14. She wrote reviews of Doris Lessing's *Memoirs of a Survivor* (7 June), Jane Rule's *Themes for Diverse Instruments* (25 June), Lovat Dickson's *Radclyffe Hall at the Well of Loneliness* (30 August), and Robert Chambers's *Sinclair Ross and Ernest Buckler* (8 November).

15. *Canadian Forum* (December 1975/January 1976): 28-29; then published revised and with a new title, "Man of Our People," in *Heart of a Stranger.*

16. *Toronto Globe and Mail Weekend Magazine* 25, no. 51(20 December 1975): 2-4.

17. Margaret acknowledges receipt of the poem in her letter of 12 June 1974 to Purdy. The poem was published in 1973 in a limited edition of 223 copies in the Canadian Writing Series, Prince George, BC, and was inscribed "For Margaret—for being Margaret—and much more than much, or little multiplied by marvelous, love Al—" (see *Friendship in Letters*, 322, note 1; 323, note 8). It was republished in Purdy's *The Woman on the Shore* (Toronto: McClelland and Stewart, 1990), 95-97.

18. The following quotations are from Margaret's letter to Purdy, 12 June 1974.

19. *Very Large Soul*, 35.

20. Ibid., 67.

21. The illustration facing p. [1] in the first edition is clearly the veranda of 8 Regent St. and the white frame house next door is similarly 10 Regent St. That on p. [2] shows 8 Regent St. but the neighbourhood has been rearranged. The Anglican church that appears to be two doors away is really (*pace*, Margaret) across the street from Margaret's Lakefield home. That on p. [11] is also quite accurate, but an "olden days" depiction of the scene—no neighbours. Furthermore, the illustrations depicting Sal's father, p. [34], and her mother, p. [35], are reminiscent of photos one has

seen of Margaret's father and of her Mum. It is worth mentioning that Margaret, even when still "Peg" (or "Peggy"), was Mum's namesake. Muriel Wood's illustrations for the 1998 edition are also handsome, and that across pp. [1-2] is similar to that on pp. [2-3] of the 1979 edition.

22. Purdy's letter of 10 September 1971 to Margaret.

23. Letter of 16 September 1971 to Purdy.

24. Letter of 2 November 1971 to Margaret.

25. The headnote to the revised version of the review in *Heart of a Stranger* points out the similarity in question, and other connections as well: "this article has a great deal of relevance to my own life-view, . . . found in much of my work, best perhaps seen in its broadest sense in my novel, *The Diviners*, and more narrowly and politically (as a study of another nomadic tribal society in conflict with imperial power) in 'The Poem and the Spear' in this collection" (204).

26. *Heart*, 211. She also dropped the last seven lines of the *Forum* essay—one sentence of tribute to Woodcock's sustained intelligent industry and then a brilliant conclusion: "In this book . . . he is giving us back a part of our mythology and our past which we desperately need" (29).

27. Margaret's letter of 13 March 1976 to Wiseman.

28. Quoted in Joan Johnston's letter of 26 March 1976 to M.L. Hamley, Secretary of the Peterborough Board of Education. This letter was included in the March newsletter of the Writers' Union.

29. Joan Johnston's letter to Hamley.

30. Conversation with Dr. Jean Cole, Peterborough, 19 April 2000.

31. The essay is republished in *Dance*, 265-74; quotation from Scott on 267 and those from Milton on 269 and 273.

32. Letter of 18 February 1977.

33. *Very Large Soul*, 262, note 3; cf. Margaret to Will Ready, 17 March 1977, *Very Large Soul*, 164.

34. *Very Large Soul*, 197.

35. Letter of 15 February 1976 to Sorestad, *Very Large Soul*, 194; cf. the concluding paragraph of "Man of Our People," *Heart*, 212. The first two poems in Sorestad's collection present the figures of Big Bear and Louis Riel, respectively, and their people, and also the wind; in both poems, the heroes *listen* to it, attentively, for guidance (*Wind Songs* [Saskatoon: Thistledown Press, 1975]).

36. In *Divided We Stand*, ed. Gary Geddes (Toronto: Peter Martin, 1977), 20-25.

37. *Maclean's*, 17 April 1978, p. 18.

38. See Wiebe's "Batoche, May 12, 1885," an excerpt from his novel *The Scorched-Wood People* (1979); also in *Divided*, 26-30, immediately following Margaret's piece.

39. The religious implications in the wind and spirit motifs may be resisted by some readers, but at least Margaret's intentions seem clear enough. Just as she repeats, from her review "Man of Our People," "will we ever reach a point when it is no longer necessary to say Them and Us?" (*Heart*, 211) in her affirmation "someday we will not have to say 'Us' and 'Them'" (*Divided*, 21), so also does she repeat Gabriel Dumont's prayer—"Lord, strengthen my courage, my faith, and my honour, that I may profit all my life from the blessings I have received in Thy Holy Name" (*Heart*, 210; *Divided*, 21). Gabriel's prayer is obviously echoed in the concluding lines of "Listen."

40. Letter of 27 June 1977 to E. Buckler, *Very Large Soul*, 41; see also letter of 28 June to Purdy—she neglected to mention the FRSC in this one.

41. Letter of 28 June 1977. See Purdy's *Collected Poems* (1986) 217-18. Another result is his "Shall we gather at the river: for Dave Williams," 230-31—an agnostic's humorous (but deadly serious) struggle with belief: "to think of that unprovable God / meeting me at the river."

42. Letter to Margaret, 11 August 1976.

43. Letter of 27 June 1977.

44. Lois Wilson's letter of 28 June 2000 to me.

45. *Very Large Soul*, 204-205. This is very like what she would say in their dialogue-sermon in the fall of 1979.

46. Lois Wilson, *Turning the World Upside Down: a Memoir* (Toronto: Doubleday Canada, 1989), 234.

47. The account of the dialogue-sermon, *United Church Observer*, February 1980, 10-12.

48. She did just that in a letter of 27 March 1985 to Wiseman.

49. Lois Wilson's summary in *Turning the World Upside Down*, 234. Wilson's "Faith and the Vocation of the Author," in *Margaret Laurence: Critical Reflections*, ed. David Staines (Ottawa: University of Ottawa Press, 2001), 151-62, provides a brilliantly focussed and succinct digest of the dialogue-sermon and includes excerpts under specific headings—"Laurence on vocation . . . Laurence on morals and values . . . Laurence on how her experience has informed her knowledge of God . . . Laurence on justice . . . on hope . . . on grace" (153-55).

50. Letter of 4 July 1980 to Hubert Evans, *Very Large Soul*, 71. The convocation address is reprinted in *Dance*, 278-83.

51. *Heart*, 187-91; originally entitled "Loneliness Is Something That Doesn't Exist Here," in *Weekend Magazine*, *Globe and Mail* (11 May 1974): 7.

52. See also note of 2 May 1979 to Purdy.

53. *Dance*, 217; letter of 19 August 1979 to Will Ready, *Very Large Soul*, 165.

54. *Dance*, 217-18. Margaret Laurence, *Six Darn Cows* (Toronto: James Lorimer, 1979).

55. "The Christmas Birthday Story: Retelling the gospels of St. Matthew and St. Luke for the very young—and the young at heart" was published in the *Globe and Mail*, 25 December 1980, p. 7.

56. Letter of 25 September 1980, *Very Large Soul*, 188. See letter of 3 November 1980 to Purdy: "a re-telling of the Nativity; . . . I first wrote it 21 years ago, when my kids were 4 and 7. . . ."

57. *Dance*, 220.

58. Ibid., 219.

59. Ibid.

60. Letter of 4 July 1980.

61. Letter of 25 September 1980.

62. Letter of 28 April 1977.

63. Letter of 14 July 1977.

64. Letter of 23 July 1978.

65. Letter of 5 September 1978 to Harold Horwood.

66. Letter of 19 February 1979; italics are Margaret's.

67. Letters of 14 February 1980 to Wiseman; of 3 November 1980 to Purdy.

CHAPTER EIGHTEEN

1. Cole, *Trent*, 154.

2. Ibid., 53-54.

3. Ibid., 169.

4. Quoted in Cole, *Trent*, 170; other parts of her letter are quoted in the *Trent Fortnightly* for 3 December 1981.

5. Cole, *Trent*, 170.

6. Wiseman's letter of 9 September 1981 to Margaret, and Margaret's reply of 14 September 1981.

7. Letter of 5 October to Clara Thomas.

8. Letters of 30 November 1981 and 4 December 1981 to Wiseman.

9. Letter of 10 April 1982.

10. A copy of this brief letter (in York University Archives) is enclosed with Margaret's letter of 2 January 1982 to the editor of *Saturday Night*.

11. Margaret listed most of these in the first entry of the journal she began keeping on 18 July 1986.

12. "Minutes of a Meeting Held at the Home of Adele Wiseman"—Friday, 9 July 1982.

13. Letter of 13 July 1982 to Wiseman.

14. "Informal Minutes of meeting Aug. 24, 1982, at Harry Freedman's."

15. June Callwood was chair of the Writers' Union at the time. Her recollection is that Margaret did not resign from the union, but chose not to attend meetings.

16. "Letter to the National Council of the Writers' Union"; cf. Margaret's letter to Naim Kattan, 16 November 1982, included in the Laurence-Wiseman correspondence in the Scott Library, York University.

17. *Very Large Soul*, 83, 74.

18. In the summer of 1988 I was given access to the Laurence archive at York University and permitted to make a copy of this document (and other related material) through the kindness of Jocelyn and David Laurence.

19. *Prairie Fire: A Canadian Magazine of New Writing* 20, 2 (Summer 1999): 113, note 9.

20. Allie (McDuff) Lansdowne-Pryce observes that she doesn't have the same feeling about her father's family as about her mother's: "He was English . . . a remittance man. . . ." And Margaret's unpublished typescript "The Wemyss and Simpson Families" notes that the Wemysses were "a Lowland Scots family from Fifeshire, a sept of the clan MacDuff" (3).

21. The interview was published as "Outcasting: A Conversation with Margaret Laurence about the World of Manawaka," *Border Crossings: A Quarterly Magazine of the Arts* 5, 4 (September 1986): 32-35.

22. *The Diviners*, 341.

23. Letter of 17 February 1973.

24. See *Very Large Soul*, 145. Ms Alice Munro kindly sent me this information, 6 July 2000.

25. See Margaret's "Forewords," *Dance*, 5. I have been unable, even with the aid of diligent harrowing of Winnipeg libraries by Danielle Pilon, to find a piece attributed to "Steve Lancaster" either in *Vox* or in *The Manitoban*.

26. *Dance*, 53-54.

27. *Prairie Fire*, 20, 2: 100-109. Professor Wigmore notes that "The words 'written in 1948' appear in Laurence's hand on the manuscript beside the title" (109).

28. *Stone Angel*, 264.

29. *Jest of God*, 104.

30. *Very Large Soul*, 207.

31. I am indebted for this insight to my friend and colleague Dr. Ralph Williams.

32. Letter of 19 March 1982, in *Very Large Soul*, 74.

33. Letter of 31 December 1978, in *Very Large Soul*, 101. She said much the same thing in her letter of 20 January 1979 to Wiseman.

34. Letter of 19 February 1979 to Gordon Roper; she added that honest depiction of the Ukrainians ought to be left to someone knowledgeable like Andy Suknaski.

35. Letter of 20 January 1979 to Wiseman.

36. In her newsletter of 30 January 1985, Margaret said, "I also want to get to my own writing . . I know what I want to do, and I must do it, and it will not, I think, be another novel . . . that is up to my inheritors. But I have some memoirs I want to write." The ellipsis mark— . . —is Margaret's.

37. Margaret's newsletter of 30 January 1985.

38. Malcolm Ross to the Text Book Committee, Peterborough Board of Education, 28 February 1985.

39. Delivered on Wednesday, 24 June 1992, at the Margaret Laurence Home, Neepawa, Manitoba, as part of the Mortgage Burning Ceremony.

40. Margaret's newsletters seem to have begun as a result of her developing carpal tunnel syndrome in April 1985; her right wrist and hand would swell up and pain her severely. She had maintained a voluminous correspondence for many years and of course had committed the first draft of her works by longhand to her scribblers. Her first newsletter, dated 1 May 1985, begins, "Dear Friends: Please excuse this xeroxed letter. I will write you all, personally, with this Newsletter"; and recounts the carpal tunnel problem. That grief was compounded, six months later, by cataracts and consequent surgery. Under the date 19 November 1985, she explained, "Dear Friends: Here is another Newsletter from Yours Truly. The eye surgery has been a success." Newsletters were dispatched at irregular intervals thereafter during the rest of her life.

41. Joan Johnston recounts that Margaret had set her sixtieth birthday (18 July 1986) as the deadline for finishing the first draft of her memoirs, and that she was able to finish it a week before that.
42. Letter of 31 December, *Very Large Soul*, 101.
43. Letter of 6 March 1984.
44. Letter of 22 July 1974, *Very Large Soul*, 99.
45. Newsletter of 30 January 1985.
46. Letter of 21 March 1986.
47. *Dance*, 217; cf. Joan Johnston's "Remarks for the Mortgage Burning Ceremony," 24 June 1992.
48. Wilson, *Turning the World Upside Down*, 236-37.
49. Letter of 30 August 1974, *Very Large Soul*, 28.
50. Journal entry 14 November. Also see Margaret Laurence, "My Story of Jack McClelland," in *Imagining Canadian Literature: The Selected Letters of Jack McClelland*, ed. Sam Solecki (Toronto: Key Porter Books, 1995), 289-90.
51. "Lines, Composed a few miles above Tintern Abbey . . . ," 11, 96-102.
52. Letter to me 10 March 2003.
53. Some time before the wedding, Margaret was pondering her place in the Christian community of faith and the Second Great Commandment, "thou shalt love thy neighbour," and confessed explicitly what is everywhere implicit in her writing, "it seems to me to sum up the social gospel in which I have believed all my life" (18 November).

    Margaret made her fourth contribution to the wedding when she confessed to Jocelyn that she had had a brief but meaningful love affair that began "shortly after I knew that Jack and I were going to have to separate": "one reason I embarked with my kids to England [fall of 1962]. . . . I did see him in London a few times. . . . he was a crucial, if brief, part of my life." Margaret gratefully recounts, "Joc very spontaneously put her arms around me, and said 'Mum, I can't tell you how glad I am that you told me.'" Even in the privacy of her own journal (27 October) Margaret refused to name the Barbadian George Lamming, as Jocelyn did when she told me of the confession—almost the first piece of personal information she gave me about her mother: the confession was still very important to Jocelyn almost a year after it was made. I met George Lamming some years later when he came to speak at the University of Michigan in Ann Arbor (1992 and again in 2002), and I was able to talk with him about Margaret Laurence.
54. "Remarks at the Ceremony," 24 June 1992.

55. Lois conducted both funeral services, the first in Lakefield on 8 January 1987, for family and close friends, and the larger, public service next day at Bloor Street United Church, which Jocelyn and David were understandably reluctant to allow because it seemed an intrusion on a very private and personal occasion—for their Mum. With some difficulty they were persuaded that the service on 9 January 1987 in Toronto was to respect and celebrate the very public achievements of Margaret Laurence, not simply their mother. The services were quite similar: in Toronto Lois was assisted by the Reverend David Allen of Bloor Street United; the Reverend Doris Dyke, who had stood with Margaret in defense of *Crucified Woman*, read scripture; a piper played the lament "Flowers of the Forest"; and the hymns Margaret had chosen were sung. She was buried in the cemetery in Neepawa. (See Lois Wilson, *Turning the World Upside Down*, 237).

55. Letter of 30 May 1973.

bibliography

WORKS BY MARGARET LAURENCE

Abbreviations: * indicates poetry; *TT - The Tomorrow-Tamer; BH - A Bird in the House; HS - Heart of a Stranger; DE - Dance on the Earth*

"The Case of the Blond Butcher." Winnipeg *Free Press*, Young Authors Page, 16 and 25 January 1941.

"Fallen King." *The Manitoban*, 6 October 1944, p. 3.

"Thought."* *The Manitoban*, 13 October 1944, p. 3.

"The Imperishable."* *The Manitoban*, 17 October 1944, p. 3.

"Bus Ride at Night."* *The Manitoban*, 30 October 1944, p. 3.

"Pagan Point—Approaching Night."* *The Manitoban*, 3 November 1944, p. 3.

"The Departure."* *The Manitoban*, 26 January 1945, p. 3.

"Song"* and "Cabbages."* *Vox*, April 1945.

"This is a land of living things."* *Vox*, June 1945.

"In these a thousand thousand years."* *Vox* 1945.

"Calliope." *Vox*, June 1945.

"Some day, I shall make me a song."* *The Manitoban*, 13 October 1945, p. 3.

"When songs are sung and voices have died."* *The Manitoban*, 13 October 1945, p. 3.

"Clay-fettered Doors."* *The Manitoban*, 9 November 1945, p. 3.

"Tal des Walde." *Vox*, graduate no., 1946.

"Classical Framework."* *Vox*, December 1946.

"Song of the Race of Ulysses."* *Vox* 1947.

"Bread Hath He."* *Vox*, March 1947.

"The Earlier Fountain: A Study of Robertson Jeffers, his early poems and philosophy." *Vox*, March 1947.

"North Main Car—Winnipeg."* Written in 1948. *Prairie Fire: A Canadian Magazine of New Writing* 20, no. 2 (Summer 1998): 100-109.

"Uncertain Flowering." In *Story: The Magazine of the Short Story in Book Form*, ed. Whit and Hallie Burnett, 80-84. New York: Wyn, 1953.

A Tree for Poverty: Somali Poetry and Prose. Published for the British Protectorate of Somaliland. Nairobi: Eagle Press, 1954. Reprint, Dublin: Irish University Press and Hamilton: McMaster University Library Press, 1970.

"The Drummer of All the World." *(TT) Queen's Quarterly* 2 (Winter 1956).

"To a Faithless Friend."* A gabei by Salaan Arrabey, trans. Margaret Laurence. *The Somaliland Journal* 1, no. 3 (December 1956): 138-43.

"The Merchant of Heaven." *(TT) Prism* (Spring 1959).

"Godman's Master." *(TT) Prism* (Spring 1960).

"A Gourdful of Glory." *(TT) The Tamarack Review* (Autumn 1960).

"The Perfume Sea." *(TT) Winter's Tales* (1960). Abridged, *Saturday Evening Post*, 3 June 1961; *Saturday Evening Post Stories*, 1962.

This Side Jordan. Toronto: McClelland and Stewart; London: Macmillan; New York: St. Martin's Press, 1960.

"The Tomorrow-Tamer." *(TT) Prism* (Fall 1961).

"The Rain Child." *(TT) Winter's Tales* (1962).

"The Spell of the Distant Drum." (*TT* as "The Voices of Adamo") *Saturday Evening Post*, 5 May 1962.

"Mask of Beaten Gold." *The Tamarack Review* (Autumn 1963).

"The Sound of the Singing." *(BH) Winter's Tales* (1963).

The Tomorrow-Tamer and Other Stories. Toronto: McClelland and Stewart; London: Macmillan, 1963.

The Prophet's Camel Bell. Toronto: McClelland and Stewart, 1963. Retitled *New Wind in a Dry Land*, New York: Knopf, 1964.

"A Queen in Thebes." *The Tamarack Review* (Summer 1964).

"To Set Our House in Order." *(BH) Ladies Home Journal* (March 1964). Reprinted in *Modern Canadian Short Stories*, ed. Giose Romanelli and Roberto Ruberto, 247-61. Toronto: Ryerson Press, 1966.

"The Very Best Intentions." *(HS) Holiday* (November 1964).

The Stone Angel. Toronto: McClelland and Stewart; London: Macmillan; New York: Knopf, 1964.

"A Bird in the House." *(BH) Atlantic* (November 1964). Reprinted in *Canadian Winter's Tales*, ed. Norman Levine, 79-102. Toronto and London: Macmillan, 1968.

"The Mask of the Bear." *(BH) Chatelaine* (February 1965) and *Winter's Tales* (1965).

"The Epic Love of Elmii Bonderii." *(HS) Holiday* (November 1965).

"Sayonara, Agamemnon." *(HS) Holiday* (January 1966).

"The Crying of the Loons." (*BH* as "The Loons") *Atlantic Advocate* (March 1966).

A Jest of God. Toronto: McClelland and Stewart; London: Macmillan; New York: Knopf, 1966. Also published as *Rachel, Rachel*, New York: Knopf, 1966.

"Horses of the Night." *(BH) Chatelaine* (July 1967).

"Nanuk." (*BH* as "The Half-Husky) *Argosy* (November 1967). Published as "Le bâtard" in *Liberté* (mars-avril 1969).

"Everything is all right." Four-page excerpt from chapter One of unrevised manuscript of *The Fire-Dwellers*. *Adam International Review* 313-15 (1967).

"Afterword." From Sinclair Ross, *The Lamp at Noon and Other Stories*. Toronto: McClelland and Stewart, 1968.

Long Drums and Cannons: Nigerian Dramatists and Novelists 1952-1966. London: Macmillan, 1968.

"An Open Letter to the Mother of Joe Bass." *(HS)* In *The New Romans: Candid Canadian Opinions of the U.S.*, ed. Al Purdy. Edmonton: Hurtig; New York: St. Martin's Press, 1968. Reprinted in *Maclean's* (October 1968).

"Ten Years' Sentences." *Canadian Literature* 41 (1969).

The Fire-Dwellers. Toronto: McClelland and Stewart; London: Macmillan; New York: Knopf, 1969.

"I am a Taxi." *(HS) Vancouver Sun*, 7 February 1970.

"A Time of Waiting." (*BH* as "Jericho's Brick Battlements") *Chatelaine* (February 1970).

A Bird in the House. Toronto: McClelland and Stewart; London: Macmillan; New York: Knopf, 1970.

"Sources." (*HS* as "A Place to Stand On") *Mosaic* 3, no. 3, Manitoba Centennial Issue (1970).

"Author's Commentary." In *Sixteen by Twelve*, ed. John Metcalf. Toronto: McGraw-Hill Ryerson, 1970.

"The Natives Are Restless Tonight." *Vancouver Sun*, 26 December 1970.

Jason's Quest, illus. Steffan Torell. Toronto: McClelland and Stewart; London: Macmillan; New York: Knopf, 1970.

"Down East." *Vancouver Sun*, 20 March 1971.

"Salute of the Swallows." *Vancouver Sun*, 22 May 1971.

"The River Flows Both Ways." *Vancouver Sun*, 11 December 1971.

"Time and the Narrative Voice." In *The Narrative Voice*, ed. John Metcalf. Toronto: McGraw-Hill Ryerson, 1972.

"Put Out One or Two More Flags." *(HS) Vancouver Sun*, 25 February 1972.

"Voices from Future Places." *Vancouver Sun*, 23 April 1972.

"Hello Aunt Nellie, I'm on the Telly." (*HS* as "Inside the Idiot Box") *Vancouver Sun*, 17 June 1972.

"Commentary." *Journal of Canadian Fiction* 1, no. 3 (Summer 1972).

"Living Dangerously … By Mail." *(HS) Vancouver Sun*, 23 September 1972.

"Where the World Began: A Small Prairie Town as an Aspect of Myself." (*HS* as "Where the World Began") *Maclean's* (December 1972).

"I Saw a Lot of Good Canadian Books: That's What Counts." *Toronto Star*, 31 December 1972, D5.

"The Wild Blue Yonder." *(HS) Vancouver Sun*, 1 September 1973.

"Introduction." In Jack Ludwig, *Above Ground*. NCL. Toronto: McClelland and Stewart, 1973.

"Loneliness Is Something that Doesn't Exist Here." (*HS* as "The Shack") *Globe and Mail, Weekend Magazine*, 11 May 1974.

The Diviners. Toronto: McClelland and Stewart; London: Macmillan; New York: Knopf, 1974.

"The Greatest Gift of All." (*HS* as "Upon a Midnight Clear") *Globe and Mail, Weekend Magazine*, 21 December 1974.

"A Flowering Art." *Journal of Canadian Studies* 10, no. 2 (May 1975)

"The Olden-Days Coat." *Globe and Mail, Weekend Magazine*, 10 December 1975.

"Man of Honour." (Review of G. Woodcock's *Gabriel Dumont*. *HS* revised and titled "Man of Our People") *Canadian Forum* (December 1975/January 1976).

"Introduction." In Percy Janes, *House of Hate*. NCL. Toronto: McClelland and Stewart, 1976.

Heart of a Stranger. Toronto: McClelland and Stewart, 1976.

"Listen, Just Listen." In *Divided We Stand*, ed. Gary Geddes. Toronto: Peter Martin, 1977.

"Introduction." In Adele Wiseman, *Crackpot*. NCL. Toronto: McClelland and Stewart, 1978.

"Quebec's 'freedom' is a valid concern." *Maclean's*, 17 April 1978.

"Ivory Towers or Grass Roots? The Novelist as Socio-Political Being." In *A Political Art: Essays and Images in Honour of George Woodcock*, ed. William New. Vancouver: University of British Columbia Press, 1978.

Cook's Tour: A Sprightly Amble through the Simple Country Paths of Rough and Ready Canadian Cooking. By Margaret Laurence and Clara Thomas. North York: Slink Services, 1978.

Six Darn Cows, illus. Ann Blades. Toronto: James Lorimer, 1979.

The Olden Days Coat, illus. Muriel Wood. Toronto: McClelland and Stewart, 1979.

"Gadgetry or Growing: Form and Voice in the Novel." *Journal of Canadian Fiction* 27 (1980).

"Open Letter to the Inheritors." Convocation Address, York University, June 1980.

"The Christmas Birthday Story: Retelling the gospels of St Matthew and St Luke for the young—and the young at heart." *Globe and Mail*, 25 December 1980.

"A Constant Hope." Convocation Address, Emmanuel College, Victoria University, Toronto, 6 May 1982. Reprinted as "A Statement of Faith" in *A Place to Stand On: Essays by and about Margaret Laurence*, ed. George Woodcock. Edmonton: NeWest Press, 1983.

A Christmas Birthday Story, illus. Helen Lucas. Toronto: McClelland and Stewart, 1982.

"My Final Hour." *Canadian Literature*, 25th Anniversary Issue (Spring 1984). Address delivered to Trent University Philosophy Society, 29 March 1983.

"Fable—For the Whaling Fleet." (*DE*) In *Whales—A Celebration*, ed. Greg Gatenby. Toronto: Prentice-Hall and Lester & Orpen Dennys, 1983.

"The Greater Evil." (*DE*) *Toronto Life*, September 1984.

"Margaret Laurence's Cauliflower Soup [and reminiscence of church suppers.]" In *Those Marvellous Church Suppers: Celebrating a Canadian Heritage*, ed. Elaine Towgood and Anne Nightingale, 36-37. Winfield, BC: Wood Lake Books, 1985.

"Foreword." (*DE*) In *Canada and the Nuclear Arms Race*, ed. Ernie Regehr. Toronto: James Lorimer, 1985.

"When you were five and I was fourteen." *Quill and Quire*, 50th Anniversary Issue (April 1985).

"Prayer for Passover and Easter."* (*DE*) 1985.

"A Constant Hope: Women in the Now and Future High Tech Age." *Canadian Women's Studies/Les cahiers de la femme* (1985).

"My Story of Jack McClelland." Written September 1986. In *The Selected Letters of Jack McClelland*, ed. Sam Solecki. Toronto: Key Porter Books, 1995.

Dance on the Earth: A Memoir. Toronto: McClelland and Stewart, 1989.

PUBLISHED INTERVIEWS WITH MARGARET LAURENCE

Arnason, David and Dennis Cooley. "Outcasting: A Conversation with Margaret Laurence about the World of Manawaka." *Border Crossings: A Quarterly Magazine of the Arts* 5, no. 4 (September 1986).

Bowland, Viga. "Interview: Margaret Laurence—First Lady of Canadian Literature." *Canadian Author and Bookman* (Spring 1977).

Cameron, Donald. "The Black Celt Speaks of Freedom." In *Conversations with Canadian Novelists*. Toronto: McClelland and Stewart, 1973.

Fabre, Michael. "From *The Stone Angel* to *The Diviners*: An Interview with Margaret Laurence." Developed from *Études canadiennes* (1981) for *A Place to Stand On*, ed. George Woodcock. Edmonton: NeWest Press, 1983.

Gibson, Graeme. "Margaret Laurence." In *Eleven Canadian Novelists*. Toronto: House of Anansi Press, 1973.

"June Sheppard talks with Margaret Laurence." *Branching Out* (Preview Issue, December 1973).

Kroetsch, Robert. "A Conversation with Margaret Laurence." In *Creation*, ed. Robert Kroetsch. Toronto and Chicago: new press, 1970.

Law, Harriet. "Our Myths, Our Selves." *Indirections* 2, no. 2 (Winter 1977).

Lever, Bernice. "Literature and Canadian Culture: An Interview with Margaret Laurence. *Alive* 41 (1975).

Sullivan, Rosemary. "An Interview with Margaret Laurence." Lakefield, 1983. In *A Place to Stand On*, ed. George Woodcock. Edmonton: NeWest Press, 1983.

Thomas, Clara. "A Conversation about Literature: An Interview with Margaret Laurence and Irving Layton." *Journal of Canadian Literature* 1, no. 1 (Winter 1972).

PUBLISHED CORRESPONDENCE

Margaret Laurence—Al Purdy: A Friendship in Letters, ed. John Lennox. Toronto: McClelland and Stewart, 1993.

The Selected Letters of Jack McClelland, ed. Sam Solecki. Toronto: Key Porter Books, 1995.

A Very Large Soul: Selected Letters from Margaret Laurence to Canadian Writers, ed. J.A. Wainwright. Dunvegan: Cormorant Books, 1995.

Selected Letters of Margaret Laurence and Adele Wiseman, ed. John Lennox and Ruth Panofsky. Toronto: University of Toronto Press, 1997.

PUBLISHED SECONDARY SOURCES CITED

Allen, Richard. *The Social Passion: Religion and Social Reform in Canada, 1914-28*. Toronto: University of Toronto Press, 1971.

Andrzejewski, B.W. "Somali Literature." In *Literatures in African Languages*. Cambridge: Cambridge University Press, 1985.

Andrzejewski, B.W. and I.M. Lewis, eds. *Somali Poetry: An Introduction*. Oxford: Clarendon Press, 1964.

Bailey, Don. *Memories of Margaret*. Scarborough: Prentice-Hall of Canada, 1989.

Bedford, A. Gerald. *The University of Winnipeg: A History of the Founding Colleges*. Toronto and Buffalo: University of Toronto Press, 1967.

Bowering, George. "That Fool of a Fear: Notes on *A Jest of God*." *Canadian Literature* 50 (1971).

Buss, Helen. *Mother and Daughter Relationships in the Manawaka Works of Margaret Laurence*. Victoria: University of Victoria Press, 1985.

Clark, Zella. "My Personal Tribute." *Minus Tides*, 1, no. 1.

Coger, Greta, ed. *New Perspectives on Margaret Laurence*. Westport: Greenwood Press, 1996.

Cole, A.O.C. *Trent: The Making of a University 1957-1987*. Peterborough, ON: Trent University Communications Department, 1990.

Cole, Jean Murray. *Exile in the Wilderness: The Biography of Chief Factor Archibald McDonald, 1790-1853*. Don Mills, ON: Burns and MacEachern, 1979.

Coon, Garson and Blair Witherspoon. "Popular Education for Participatory Democracy," *Briarpatch* 21, no. 7 (September 1992).

Drake-Brockman, R.E. *British Somaliland*. London: Hurst and Blackett, 1912.

Dunn, Marty. *Red on White: The Biography of Duke Redbird*. Toronto: new press, 1971. (The acknowledgement reads in part: "The book ... could never have been created without the loving help of Margaret Laurence and her hours of taped interviews with Duke....")

Edel, Leon, ed. *Henry James: Literary Criticism*. Library of America. New York: Viking Press, 1984.

Eliot, T.S. "Tradition and the Individual Talent." In *Selected Essays*. New edition. New York: Harcourt, Brace and World, 1960.

Ferns, H.S. *Reading from Left to Right: One Man's Political History*. Toronto, Buffalo, London: University of Toronto Press, 1983.

Fabre, Michel. "Words and the World." In *A Place to Stand On*, ed. George Woodcock. Edmonton: NeWest Press, 1983.

Fitch, Robert Beck, and Mary Oppenheimer. *Ghana, End of an Illusion*. New York and London: Monthly Review Press, 1966.

Fry, Northrop. *The Bush Garden: Essays on the Canadian Imagination*. Toronto: House of Anansi Press, 1971.

Galt, George, ed. *The Purdy-Woodcock Letters: Selected Correspondence* 1964-84. Toronto: ECW Press, 1988.

Geddes, Gary. "The Tribe, for Margaret Laurence." In *Flying Blind*. Fredericton: Goose Lane Publications, 1998.

______, ed. *Divided We Stand*. Toronto: Peter Martin, 1977.

Gibbs, Robert. "Introduction." In *A Bird in the House*, by Margaret Laurence. NCL 96. Toronto: McClelland and Stewart, 1974.

Grace, Sherrill. "Crossing Jordan: Time and Memory in the Fiction of Margaret Laurence." *World Literature Written in English* 16, no. 2 (1977).

Gunnars, Kristjana, ed. *Crossing the River: Essays in Honour of Margaret Laurence*. Winnipeg: Turnstone Press, 1988.

Gutkin, Henry. *The Worst of Times, The Best of Times*. Markham: Fitzhenry and Whiteside, 1987.

Hjartarson, Paul. "'Christie's Real Country. Where I was Born.' Story-telling, Loss and Subjectivity in *The Diviners*." In *Crossing the River: Essays in Honour of Margaret Laurence*, ed. Kristjana Gunnars. Winnipeg: Turnstone Press, 1988.

Johnson, John W. *Heellooy, Heelleellooy: The Development of the Genre Heello in Modern Somali Poetry*. Bloomington: Indiana University Press, 1974.

Kertzer, Jon. *"That House in Manawaka": Margaret Laurence's A Bird in the House*. Toronto: ECW Press, 1992.

Lamming, George. *The Pleasures of Exile*. Ann Arbor: University of Michigan Press, 1992.

Laurence, Jocelyn. "As for Me and My Houses." *Toronto Life*, August 1986.

Lever, Bernice. "Margaret Laurence. November 20, 1974." *Waves* 3, no. 2 (Winter 1975).

Lewis, I.M. *A Modern History of Somalia*. London and New York: Longman's, 1980.

Lucas, Fred C., ed. *An Historical Souvenir Diary of the City of Winnipeg, Canada.* Winnipeg: Cartwright and Lucas, 1923.

Mannoni, Dominique O. *Prospero and Caliban: A Study of the Psychology of Colonization*. London: Methuen, 1956.

Mantooth, Wes. "Laurence's 'Album' Songs: Divining for Missing Links and Deeper Meanings." *Great Plains Quarterly* 3 (Summer 1999).

McCormack, A. Ross. *Reformers, Rebels, and Revolutionaries: The Western Canadian Radical Movement 1899-1919*. Toronto: University of Toronto Press, 1977.

Metcalf, John, ed. *The Narrative Voice*. Toronto: McGraw-Hill Ryerson, 1972.

New, William H., ed. *Margaret Laurence: Critical Views on Canadian Writers*. Toronto: McGraw-Hill Ryerson, 1977.

Padmore, George. *The Gold Coast Revolution: The Struggle of an African People from Slavery to Freedom*. London: Dennis Dobson, 1953.

Parr, John, ed. *Speaking of Winnipeg*. Winnipeg: Queenston House, 1974.

Penner, Norman. *The Canadian Left: A Critical Analysis*. Scarborough: Prentice-Hall, 1977.

Powers, Lyall. "Skinner in a Kilt: Flower of the Forest." *Margaret Laurence Review* 8 (1998).

Prebble, John. *The Highland Clearances*. London: Secker and Warburg, 1963.

Purdy, A.W., ed. *The New Romans: Candid Canadian Opinions of the U.S.* Edmonton: M.G. Hurtig, and New York: St. Martin's Press, 1968.

Rooke, Constance. "Hagar's Old Age: *The Stone Angel* as *Vollendungsroman*." In *Crossing the River: Essays in Honour of Margaret Laurence*, ed. Kristjana Gunnars. Winnipeg: Turnstone Press, 1988.

Samatar, S. *Oral Poetry and Somali Nationalism*. Cambridge: Cambridge University Press, 1982.

Smith, Doug. *Joe Zuken: Citizen and Socialist*. Toronto: James Lorimer, 1990.

Sorestad, Glen. *Wind Songs*. Saskatoon: Thistledown Press, 1975.

Sparrow, Fiona. *Into Africa with Margaret Laurence*. Toronto: ECW Press, 1992.

Staines, David, ed. *Margaret Laurence: Critical Reflections*. Ottawa: University of Ottawa Press, 2001.

Stouck, David, ed. *Ethel Wilson: Stories, Essays, and Letters*. Vancouver: University of British Columbia Press, 1987.

Stovel, Bruce. "Coherence in *A Bird in the House*." In *New Perspectives on Margaret Laurence*, ed. Greta Coger. Westport: Greenwood Press, 1996.

Swayze, Walter E. "Knowing through Writing: The Pilgrimage of Margaret Laurence." In *Crossing the River: Essays in Honour of Margaret Laurence*, ed. Kristjana Gunnars. Winnipeg: Turnstone Press, 1988.

______. "Margaret Laurence: Novelist-as-Poet." In *New Perspectives on Margaret Laurence*, ed. Greta Coger. Westport: Greenwood Press, 1996.

Thomas, Clara. *Chapters in a Lucky Life*. Ottawa: Borealis Press, 1999.

______. *The Manawaka World of Margaret Laurence*. Toronto: McClelland and Stewart, 1975.

______. "Margaret, Morag and the Scottish Ancestors." *British Journal of Canadian Studies* 7, no. 1 (1992).

van Herk, Aritha. "The Eulalias of Spinsters and Undertakers." In *Crossing the River: Essays in Honour of Margaret Laurence*, ed. Kristjana Gunnars. Winnipeg: Turnstone Press, 1988.

Verduyn, Christl, ed. *Margaret Laurence: An Appreciation*. Peterborough, ON: Broadview Press, 1988.

Warwick, Susan J. *Margaret Laurence: An Annotated Bibliography*. Toronto: ECW Press, 1979.

Wilson, Lois. *Turning the World Upside Down: A Memoir.* Toronto: Doubleday Canada, 1989.

______. "Faith and the Vocation of the Author." In *Margaret Laurence: Critical Reflections*, ed. David Staines. Ottawa: University of Ottawa Press, 2001.

Woodcock, George, ed. *A Place to Stand On*. Edmonton: NeWest Press, 1983.

Wright, Richard. *Black Power: A Record of Reactions in a Land of Pathos*. New York: Harper and Brothers, 1954.

Xiques, Donez. "Margaret Laurence's Somali Translations." *Canadian Literature* 135 (October 1992).

______. "New Light on Margaret Laurence's First African Short Story." *Canadian Notes and Queries* 42 (1990).

York, Lorraine M. "*The Other Side of Dailiness*": *Photography in the Works of Alice Munro, Timothy Findley, Michael Ondaatje, and Margaret Laurence*. Toronto: ECW Press, 1988.

index

JL refers to Jack Laurence. ML refers to Margaret Laurence.

C

L